•Locating United States Government Information

A Guide to Sources
Second Edition

by

Edward Herman

William S. Hein & Co., Inc.
Buffalo, New York
1997

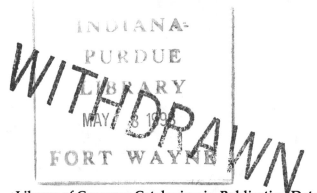
Library of Congress Cataloging-in-Publication Data

Herman, Edward, 1949-
    Locating United States government information : a guide to sources
/ by Edward Herman. -- 2nd ed.
        p.   cm.
    Includes bibliographical references and index.
    ISBN 1-57588-203-5
    1. Government Information--United States.   I. Title.
ZA5055.U6H47 1997
025.17'34--dc21   96-51490
                                                                        CIP

Copyright 1997 by William S. Hein & Co., Inc.

Printed in the United States of America.

This volume is printed on acid-free paper by
William S. Hein & Co., Inc.

•Table of Contents

•Preface

Like the first edition, the purpose of this book is to provide a practical how-to guide for locating United States government publications. Its workbook format incorporates illustrations from appropriate indexes and abstracts, plus questions and answers. Emphasis is upon locating and using government information, rather than policy issues. Practicing librarians and library school students can use the book to review basic indexes and abstracts to government information. College and university students--especially those studying social sciences and law; faculty; businessmen; market researchers; attorneys; and others who need to consult government information should also find the book valuable.

Many changes in government information occurred since the first edition appeared in 1983. The proliferation of electronic information on floppy disks, CD-ROMs, and the Internet is the most prominent change. Excluding the Dialog and BRS online systems, researchers used few electronic sources in the early 1980's. Today, policy makers consider a future where almost all government information available to the public will be in electronic format.

Throughout the text, I emphasize the integration of traditional library resources with electronic ones, providing the researcher with a balanced view of government information in multiple formats. The introduction defines government information and depository libraries; explains how government information differs from other library resources; and describes selected problems of using government data. Chapter 1 deals with basic numbers associated with U.S. government information. These include Superintendent of Documents numbers; item numbers; technical report numbers; contract numbers; and stock numbers. Chapter 2 describes current comprehensive indexes that cover a wide spectrum of resources published by multiple agencies. Three important ones are the *Monthly Catalog of United States Government Publications;* the *Publications Reference File;* and the Government Information Locator Service (GILS). Chapter 3 examines selected comprehensive indexes to historical documents.

The next group of chapters deal with Congressional information. Chapter 4 describes and illustrates different kinds of Congressional publications. Chapters 5 and 6 cover the *Congressional Information Service Index* and describe sources of legislative histories. Chapter 7 looks at three electronic resources available on the Internet: the Library of Congress Information System (LOCIS), the GPO ACCESS System, and the THOMAS database. Chapter 8 summarizes historical indexes to Congressional publications.

Congressional activities lead to legislation and policy making. Chapters 9 and 10 consider sources that index, abstract, and reprint laws and regulations.

Chapters 11 through 15 evaluate statistical sources. The U.S. government is the largest producer of statistics in the world. Chapter 11 introduces statistics by summarizing problems associated with their use and by suggesting solutions to these problems. Chapter 12 describes selected ready-reference statistical compendiums dealing with a variety of topics, and Chapter 13 examines the *Statistical Abstract* on CD-ROM. The following two chapters consider the *American Statistics Index*-- the most comprehensive index and abstract to U.S. government statistics, and census publications.

The results of research and development funded by the government are often published as technical reports. Chapter 16 describes technical reports and the National Technical Information Service (NTIS)--a division of the Department of Commerce that publishes report literature. It also examines the FEDWORLD database developed by NTIS, and selected other sources of technical reports.

Chapters 17 and 18 cover government data outside the usual purview of libraries. Topics include:

-The Freedom of Information Act that gives researchers the right to request information from executive and independent agencies.

-The Privacy Act that protects personal information held by the government from inappropriate disclosure.

-The acquisition of personal copies of government documents through the GPO sales program, the Consumer Information Center, the General Accounting Office, and private booksellers.

People who work for the government are sometimes leading experts in their respective fields. When having difficulty locating and/or understanding government information, contacting the appropriate agency official is often the most effective way of solving these problems. Chapter 19 describes directories to offices and personnel in all three branches of government.

The book includes sample searches and illustrations from selected significant Internet resources. Hopefully, readers will attempt to replicate the searches to get a better handle on this data. These illustrations reflect Internet resources as of Spring and early Summer, 1996. Be aware that data retrieved later may be different from that shown in the book. Limited descriptions of Internet sources appear in the main text because the Internet is such a fluid medium. Most information about the Internet is in the

"Internet Supplement" to the book. Its arrangement follows that of the chapters. I expect to prepare pamphlets that update the "Internet Supplement" regularly.

A project of this magnitude requires the assistance of many people. I am grateful to colleagues and administrators who supported my sabbatical leave. (Karen Smith-- Coordinator, Business and Government Documents Center; Judy Adams--Director of Lockwood Library; Stephen Roberts--Associate Director of University Libraries; and Barbara Von Wahlde--Director of the University Libraries) Two grants provided by the New York State/UUP Professional Development and Quality of Working Life Committee were invaluable. Donna Rubens, a Graduate Assistant in the Business and Government Documents Center, spent countless hours editing the text and offering many suggestions that improved the book. I am also grateful to Charlotte Hedgebeth who edited selected parts of the text. Donna Serafin, the University Libraries Preservation Officer, provided immeasurable assistance preparing the many illustrations.

I thank the many publishers who allowed me to reproduce illustrations from their books. The *Congressional Information Service, Inc.* deserves special mention. I am grateful to Brian Jablonski and the wonderful staff at the William S. Hein Company for their patience and assistance.

Despite the help provided by those mentioned above, this book still could not have been written without the support of my family. I thank my wife Linda for editing the manuscript and for creating an atmosphere at home that allowed me to complete the project. I also thank my children, Michelle and Andy, for their support and understanding. They sometimes allowed me to work in a quiet house.

Edward Herman
Business and Government Documents Center
Lockwood Library
University at Buffalo
April 1997

• Introduction

Answer the following questions while reading the Introduction:

1. What kinds of information are available from governments?

2. What are depository libraries?

3. What are depository documents, as opposed to non-depository publications?

4. What obstacles do citizens face when attempting to use government information?

WHAT IS GOVERNMENT INFORMATION?

Government information is information prepared by governments at all levels. These include, but are not limited to, national, state, and local governments; and international governing bodies, such as the United Nations. Government publications or government documents are available in print formats, such as paper, microfilm, or microfiche; in electronic formats, such as computer tapes, CD-ROMs, and floppy disks; and in audiovisual formats, such as videos and slides. Former Ohio Senator Frank Lausche notes the importance of government documents in our society:

> ...an intelligent, informed populace has been, is, and will continue to be the fundamental element in the strength of our nation. Contributing greatly to that intellectual strength is the so-called government document, designed to disseminate to the American public important information relative to the activities and purposes of its Government[1]

Most people have misconceptions about the kinds of materials published by the United States government. They believe documents are limited to laws, regulations, court decisions, and loads of statistics. In reality, federal publications cover all subjects from A through Z. The National Aeronautic and Space Administration's volumes include beautifully illustrated color plates of photographs taken from spacecrafts. The Air Force issues color posters of its airplanes, and the Department of Justice publishes public opinion surveys about crime. The Consumer Products Safety Commission published comic books designed to teach children electrical safety and poison prevention, and the House Government Operations Committee published hearings on the safety of intrauterine contraception devices. These, plus, thousands more just as diverse, interesting, and informative, are government documents. Much of the information published by the United States government is often the most recent available. Hopefully, this book will be a key that helps researchers unlock the mysteries of these very valuable sources.

LOCATING UNITED STATES GOVERNMENT INFORMATION IN DEPOSITORY LIBRARIES

WHAT ARE DEPOSITORY LIBRARIES?

Depository libraries are libraries that acquire government information from the Government Printing Office without charge. The depositories in turn must provide the public free access to these materials. In 1995, there were approximately 1,400 depository libraries throughout the nation. The sources described in this book are available in many such libraries.

Three principles govern the depository library system:

1. It is a mean for keeping citizens informed. A knowledge-able public that is aware of activities of its representatives is essential for proper functioning of democracy.

2. The government has an obligation to guarantee the public the availability of and access to documents at no cost.

3. A centralized distribution system relieves the burdens on agencies and legislators to respond to many individual requests for information.

There are two kinds of depositories, regional libraries and selective libraries. Regional depositories collect all materials distributed through the depository library system. Federal law limits the designation of regional libraries to two in each state and Puerto Rico. Fifty-three of the 1,400 depository institutions are regionals. Selective depository libraries have the option of electing to receive only those materials that fall within their needs, while bypassing publications that are irrelevant to them. *A Directory of U.S. Government Depository Libraries, July 1994*[2] lists all such collections.

Our nation has a long history of providing public access to government information. An 1813 Congressional resolution authorized the distribution of Congressional publications to state governments and legislatures. The American Antiquarian Society became the first depository library in 1814. Congressional resolutions enacted in 1857 and 1858 designated local depository libraries, and the printing law of 1895 specified that publications of executive agencies should be distributed to depository libraries.

A pamphlet published by GPO, *Designation Handbook for Federal Depository Libraries*[3], describes procedures for becoming a depository library. The library must express an interest to its state library. After consulting with regional library associations and other libraries, the state library will evaluate the request, and if the determination is positive, issue a recommendation to the appropriate Senator or Representative.

Federal law allows for designation of depository libraries on the following criteria:[4]

-Each Congressional district can have 2 depository libraries.

-Senators can designate 2 depositories in their states.

-The Commissioner of the District of Columbia, the Resident Commissioner of Puerto Rico, and the Governor of the Virgin Islands can designate 2 depositories each in their respective areas.

-State libraries, the District of Columbia Public Library, and the Library of the American Antiquarian Society are eligible for depository status.

-Libraries of the highest state appellate courts; land grant colleges; independent agencies; major bureaus and divisions of departments and agencies; military academies; and accredited law schools are eligible for depository status.

-The Governors of American Samoa, Guam, and the Northern Mariana Islands can each designate 1 library.

CHARACTERISTICS OF DEPOSITORY LIBRARIES AND THEIR USERS

As of 1995, 50% of all depositories were academic libraries, 20% were public libraries, and 11% were law schools.[5] Libraries of federal agencies, courts, state agencies, historical societies, private membership organizations, and other types of institutions comprised the remaining depositories. A 1989 survey by Charles McClure and Peter Hernon estimated that 167,000 people used depository libraries during the sample week.[6] On a per library basis, 143-243 people used academic depository libraries, and 68-161 people used public library depositories. Large majorities of users were college educated. These people included students, professionals, those working in technical occupations, managers, homemakers, and retired people.

WHAT ARE DEPOSITORY DOCUMENTS?

The Government Printing Office distributes depository documents to depository libraries. According to Government Printing Office guidelines, depository libraries are eligible to receive the following types of materials:[7]

-Press releases, public notices, bulletins, newsletters, journals, periodicals, and newspapers published on a recurring basis.

-Handbooks, manuals, and guides, such as the *Social Security Handbook*.

-Circulars--advisory statements warning about dangers and citing proper conditions for safety.

-Directories that cite locations of agencies, list agency personnel, and describe agency services.

-Proceedings of symposia, public meetings, conferences, and hearings.

-Survey forms and applications for services, grants, jobs, or admission into programs.

-Maps, atlases, charts, and posters.

-Catalogs that include bibliographies and descriptions of educational courses, events, and other activities.

-Reports that describe research results, investigations and other studies. Depository libraries receive preliminary versions unless they are intended for internal agency review.

-Monographs.

-Draft, as well as final, environmental impact statements.

-Legal materials, such as laws, decisions, opinions, regulations, and treaties.

-Brochures, booklets, and pamphlets.

-Statistical publications.

ACQUIRING GOVERNMENT INFORMATION
OUTSIDE THE DEPOSITORY LIBRARY SYSTEM

Although this book is primarily aimed toward library users, the Government Printing Office also sells documents to the public. The GPO sales inventory includes approximately 12,000 titles and net income from document sales was $6.2 million in fiscal year 1994.[8] Also, government agencies will sometimes supply individuals with copies of their documents upon request. A subsequent chapter describes the Government Printing Office sales program, and directories that provide names, addresses and telephone numbers of agencies. Furthermore, the National Technical Information Service (NTIS), a division of the Department of Commerce, maintains a sales inventory of 2.5 million titles.[9]

OBSTACLES TO USING GOVERNMENT DOCUMENTS

WHY DO LIBRARIES TREAT DOCUMENTS
DIFFERENTLY THAN OTHER MATERIALS?

Government documents present many unique difficulties for library users. Library catalogs in many large depositories fail to include documents. Since GPO is the largest publisher in the world, libraries simply cannot afford to catalog all or even some of its documents as they do other information. In just the first quarter of fiscal year 1995, GPO distributed to depositories 3,444 titles on paper, 8,745 titles on microfiche, and 84 electronic products.[10] Fortunately, this situation is beginning to change as more libraries automate their catalogs. It is quite economically feasible to catalog government documents in an online environment.

Also, the arrangement of documents is often different from other library materials. Depending upon the library, shelving is usually by Library of Congress or Dewey Decimal classification numbers. However, most depository libraries arrange their collections by Superintendent of Document (SuDoc) classification numbers. Differences among the systems are sometimes confusing to the public.

WHAT ARE NON-DEPOSITORY DOCUMENTS AND WHAT PROBLEMS DO THEY CREATE?

Non-depository documents are not distributed to depository libraries. They include items that are either printed and distributed by the issuing agencies, or if printed by the GPO, are made available only through the agency for which it was printed. Title 44 of the *United States Code,* section 1902, exempts three kinds of documents from depository distribution:

1. Those intended for administrative purposes that have little or no educational value.

2. Those required for official use only.

3. Those classified for national security purposes.

Section 1903 exempts a fourth type of document, "cooperative" publications that must be self sustaining. Agencies must recoup their costs by selling these documents. The law requires that agencies prepare for GPO a monthly list of non-depository documents that are not classified for national security purposes.

Examples of documents GPO guidelines do not consider for receipt by depository libraries include:[11]

-Job vacancy notices.

-Rules, notices, and handbooks concerning recreational and welfare activities and services for federal employees. (e.g.: picnic notices)

-Memos, directives, notices, and manuals that implement personnel policies and training in specific agencies; and other types of materials that deal with internal agency operations. Depository libraries receive training materials published by the Office of Personnel Management that cover government wide training.

-Computer input data forms; forms used for correspondence, data collection, or routing information; personnel evaluation forms; and control forms used to manage property and inventory.

-Access passes for automobiles, people, or buildings.

-Signs and bumper stickers.

-Working drafts of documents intended for internal review and revision.

-Data covered by the Privacy Act, and user manuals to computer programs in areas covered by the Privacy Act,

-Information classified for national security purposes.

The distinctions between depository and non-depository publications are problematic. Agencies make subjective decisions that certain titles have little or no educational value, or must be classified to preserve national security. What has little educational value to a consumer might be very significant to an historian, a policy maker, or a medical researcher. Likewise, what has limited value to John Q. Public can be very important to Jane Q. Public. The Nixon Administration argued that release of the Pentagon Papers would violate our national well being; the Supreme Court disagreed.

It is difficult for libraries to maintain control over non-depository documents. No one knows how many exist because there is no central source for their publication and distribution. Agencies rarely provide the Government Printing Office with lists of non-depository documents despite the law requiring them to do so.

Most libraries lack staff needed to request publications from individual agencies and their subordinate offices. Even large, well-endowed institutions cannot afford to do so. Several private publishers sell microform copies of non-depository documents to libraries. However, these very expensive collections are usually beyond the financial means of many depositories.

WHAT ARE FUGITIVE DOCUMENTS AND WHAT PROBLEMS DO THEY CREATE?

"Fugitive documents," titles that ought to be distributed to depository libraries, but are not, create further problems. John McGeachy of North Carolina State University discovered that between May 1982 and December 1986, 799 depository items were never distributed to depository libraries.[12] A second study by Jeanne Isacco of the Readex Corporation found that between 16% and 20% of a small collection of 1,600 popular titles were never distributed to depositories.[13] Frequent types of fugitive documents include scientific and technical reports; contracted reports prepared for agencies by private consultants; and reports prepared and distributed by district and field offices.

Desktop publishing systems create additional complications, since agencies can now prepare decent looking in-house publications inexpensively. When distributing the information, the agencies think only about their primary clientele, not GPO depository operations and the general public.

SHORTCOMINGS OF THE DEPOSITORY LAW

Shortcomings of the depository law are a factor in the fugitive documents problem. Agencies lack incentives to make their publications available to depository libraries and officials often fail to recognize the responsibility of making information accessible to the public. Connie Tasker, the Environmental Protection Agency's Deputy Director for Information Management and Service, stated that her agency considers itself a regulatory enforcement body, not an information dissemination one.[14] She further admitted that EPA offices throughout the nation are unaware of publishing activities elsewhere in the agency.

Hopefully, this book will enable library users to overcome these problems and use documents effectively.

Endnotes

1.   U.S. Office of Technology Assessment, *Informing the Nation: Federal Information Dissemination in an Electronic Age* (OTA-CIT-396)(Washington, D.C.: GPO, 1988), 10. SuDoc #: Y3.T22/2:2IN3/9.

2.   United States. Congress. Joint Committee on Printing (S.Prt. 103-81) 103 Cong., 2nd sess. (Washington, D.C.: GPO, 1990). SuDoc # Y4.P93/1-10:994.

3.   U.S. Government Printing Office (Washington, D.C.: GPO, 1995). SuDoc number: GP3.29:D44/3.

4.   *Ibid*, 5.

5.   "1995 Biennial Survey: Preliminary Results," *Administrative Notes* 16:15 (November 15, 1995), 25.

6.   U.S. Government Printing Office, *Use of Academic and Public GPO Depository Libraries* by Charles R. McClure and Peter Hernon (Washington, D.C.:GPO, 1989), 44. SuDoc #: GP3.2:US2.

7.   "Types of Publications Included in the Depository Library Program," *Administrative Notes* 11:16 (July 31, 1990), 11-16.

8.   Michael F. DiMario, "Prepared Statement Before the House Oversight Committee on Government Printing Reform," *Administrative Notes* 16:11 (September 1, 1995), 8.

9.   U.S. Department of Commerce. National Technical Information Service, *1995-1996 NTIS Catalog of Products and Services* (PR-827) (Springfield, VA.: NTIS, 1995), 2.

10.   Sheila M. McGarr, "Library Programs Services Operations Update," *Administrative Notes* 16:3 (February 15, 1995), 18.

11.   "Types of Publications Excluded From the Depository Library Program," *Administrative Notes* 11:16 (July 31, 1990), 17-18.

12.   U.S. Congress. Joint Committee on Printing, *Government Information as a Public Asset* Hearings, April 25, 1991, 101 Cong., 1st sess. (Washington, D.C.: GPO, 1991), 21. SuDoc #: Y4.P93/1:G74/12.

13.   *Ibid*, 106.

14.   *Ibid*, 23.

•Chapter 1

Basic Numbers

Answer the following questions when reading this chapter:

1. What is the significance of each type of number and how are they distinguished from each other?

2. What are similarities and differences between the *List of Classes* and the *Guide to U.S. Government Publications*?

It is important to understand the purpose and significance of the following types of document numbers: item numbers, Superintendent of Documents numbers, series/report and technical report numbers, stock numbers, and contract numbers. All are described in the Basics section of this chapter. The more detailed information in the following section describes two reference sources, the *List of Classes* and the *Guide to U.S. Government Publications*. Both are guides to Superintendent of Documents numbers.

BASICS

ITEM NUMBERS

Remember, selective depositories have the option to acquire certain materials and bypass others. The Government Printing Office uses item numbers as a recordkeeping system to identify which depository documents selective depository libraries choose.

Depository documents have item numbers; non-depository documents do not. Different series of documents have different item numbers. In most indexes and abstracts, heavy black dots or bullets (•) precede item numbers. Figure 1-1 shows that item number 133 pertains to the *Census of Retail Trade* series. GPO forwards documents with that item number to depositories electing to receive them.

Figure 1-1
Depository Document

91-17736

C 3.255/3:RC 87-SP-1
Census of retail trade (1987). Special report series.
1987 census of retail trade. Special report series. Selected statistics. — Washington, DC : U.S. Dept. of Commerce, Bureau of the Census : For sale by Supt. of Docs., U.S. G.P.O., [1991]
1 v. (various pagings) ; 28 cm. Shipping list no.: 91-255-P. "Issued January 1991." Includes bibliographical references. "RC87-SP-1." ●Item 133 S/N 003-024-06912-1 @ GPO ISBN 0-1603-2208-1 : $6.00
1. Retail trade — United States — Statistics. I. United States. Bureau of the Census. II. Title. III. Title: Special report series, selected statistics. IV. Title: Selected statistics. HF5429.3.C4 1990a 88-600228 381/.1/0973021 /19 OCLC 18192407

Source: *Monthly Catalog*, **1991.**

SUPERINTENDENT OF DOCUMENTS NUMBERS

In most depository libraries, documents are shelved according to Superintendent of Documents (SuDoc) classification numbers. Library users need only follow the alphanumeric sequence of SuDoc numbers to retrieve information from the shelves. Many of the indexes described in this book cite SuDoc numbers. The Superintendent of Documents number of the title in Figure 1-1 is C3.255/3:RC87-SP-1. Remember, item numbers, not SuDoc numbers, determine depository status. The publication in Figure 1-2 is non-depository because it does not have an item number, yet it still has a SuDoc number. Although it is not distributed by GPO to depository institutions, the Government Printing Office still indexes and classifies this title to make the public aware of possible availability from the issuing agency.

Figure 1-2
Non-Depository Document

91-1008

I 28.152:(nos.)

Technology news (United States. Bureau of Mines)
    Technology news : from the Bureau of Mines, United States
Department of the Interior. [Washington, D.C.?] : The Bureau,
Technology Transfer Group, Bureau of Mines, 2401 E St.,
N.W., Washington, DC 20241
    v. : ill. ; 27 cm.
    Irregular Not distributed to depository libraries. Descrip-
tion based on: No. 58 (Nov. 1978); title from caption. Indexed
by: Coal abstracts ISSN 0309-4979 Indexed by: Energy research abstracts ISSN 0160-3604 April, 1977- Numbering
began with No. 3 (Apr. 1974) "Provides information on the
results of the Bureau of Mines Mining Research program."
ISSN 0196-0792
    1. Mineral industries — United States — Equipment and sup-
plies — Periodicals. 2. Mineral industries — United States —
Safety measures — Periodicals. I. United States. Bureau of
Mines. sc-79004716 OCLC 03457103

Source: *Monthly Catalog Periodical Supplement*, **1991.**

Test your ability to identify SuDoc numbers:

What is the Superintendent of Documents number of the title in
Figure 1-2?

(I28.152:)

   HH1.2:Eq2/4/v.1, the SuDoc number for *The Barriers To Equal Opportu-*
nity In Rural Housing Markets, is a typical one. Chart 1-1 below explains
different parts of the number.

Chart 1-1
Superintendent of Documents Number
HH1.2:EQ2/4/V.1

SuDoc Notation	Explanation of Notation	Discussion of Notation
HH	Department of Housing and Urban Development	SuDoc numbers begin with upper case letters or groups of letters which represent the publishing agencies. For instance, Department of Agriculture documents are identified by A, Department of Commerce documents by C, and Department of Housing and Urban Development by HH.
HH1	Document was published by the Secretary's Office	The numbers following the initial letter(s) indicate the division or bureau within the parent agency which published the document. The number 1 tells you that the publication was issued by the Secretary's Office of the Department rather than a subdivision. For example, documents whose SuDoc numbers begin with A1 are those issued by the Secretary of Agriculture, but others whose classification numbers begin with A68 are published by the Department's Rural Electrification Administration.
HH1.2	Monographic or general publication	The number(s) that follow the period indicate kinds of documents. For instance, .1 usually represents annual reports and .2 stands for monographs. A1.1 is the classification for the Department of Agriculture's annual report, while A68.1 is the classification for the annual report of that Department's Rural Electrification Administration.
HH1.2:	All succeeding information in the SuDoc number, in this case EQ 2/4/v.1, identifies the title of the document.	The colon separates the more general information about the publishing agency and its various series of documents from the more specific information that relates to individual titles.
HH 1.2: EQ2	Keyword in title	EQ2 represents a keyword in the title. In other cases, numbers identify titles. For example, the SuDoc number for Dairy Market Statistics, the 601st publication in the Department of Agriculture's Statistical Bulletin Series, is A1.34:601.
HH1.2: EQ2/4	Fourth title in series	This is the fourth time EQ2 has been used for a monograph published by the Secretary's Office of HUD.
HH1.2: EQ2/4/ v.1	Volume 1 of this title	Implies a multivolume set of which this is volume 1.

When attempting to locate documents in depository libraries, remember differences between Superintendent of Documents numbers and Library of Congress classification numbers. In the Library of Congress system, HE1.2 comes after HE1.12 because the period (.) is read as a decimal point. However, in the Superintendent of Documents system, HE1.2 comes before HE1.12. The SuDoc system considers the number after the period a whole number, not a decimal.

GPO published a detailed description of the Superintendent of Documents classification system, *GPO Classification Manual: A Practical Guide To the Superintendent of Documents Classification System*[1]

Test your ability to arrange SuDoc numbers:

Arrange the following SuDoc numbers in alphanumeric order.

ED1.302:C68/3   ED1.118/2:AW1   ED1.118:10-MU-01
ED1.2:W89   ED1.124:983   ED1.2:T22/6

(ED1.2:T22/6, ED1.2:W89
ED1.118:10-MU-01, ED1.118/2:AW1
ED1.124:983, ED1.302:C68/3)

In the examples immediately above, ED1.118:10-MU-01 is filed before ED1.118/2:AW1 because the colon separates the two parts of the number. ED1.118: comes before ED1.118/2:.

TECHNICAL REPORT NUMBERS/SERIES REPORT NUMBERS

Technical report numbers/series report numbers are codes agencies apply to their documents for internal convenience. Among all the numbers described here, these are the most difficult to deal with because they have no set pattern. In some cases, the report numbers are more obvious than others. For instance, selected agencies will preface their report numbers with abbreviations, such as:

DHHS   Department of Health and Human Services
EPA   Environmental Protection Agency
DOE   Department of Energy
EIA   Energy Information Administration

Report numbers can include either alphanumeric or numeric codes that are recognizable only to those familiar with that agency. Two useful references that help identify report numbers are *Report Series Codes Dictionary*[2] and the *Directory of Engineering Document Sources*.[3]

Do not assume that all materials with technical report numbers are scientific. Many titles dealing with the social sciences and humanities have report numbers. A report by the National Center for Education Statistics, *Postsecondary Student Outcomes: A Feasibility Study*, whose report number is NCES 92-013, is just one example.[4]

It is important to understand report numbers because professionals working in various fields use them when referring to their literature. For instance, a health specialist may refer to his title as PHS... (Public Health Service publication number...) or an engineer may refer to his Environmental Protection Agency document as EPA...

Report numbers may or may not be part of Superintendent of Documents numbers. The SuDoc number of the title in Figure 1-1 is C3.255/3:RC 87-SP-1 and its report number is RC87-SP-1. The report number of the document in Figure 1-3 is EPA/540/A5-89/012 and its SuDoc number is EP1.2:Ul8/2.

Figure 1-3
Technical Report Number Not-Reflected in SuDoc Number

91-14537

EP 1.2:Ul 8/2

Ultrox International ultraviolet radiation/oxidation technology : applications analysis report. — Cincinnati, OH : Risk Reduction Engineering Laboratory, Office of Research and Development, U.S. Environmental Protection Agency, [1990]

    viii, 69 p. : ill., map ; 28 cm. "Funded by the U.S. Environmental Protection Agency under the auspices of the Superfund Innovative Technology Evaluation (SITE) Program (contract no. 68-03-3484)"—P. ii. Shipping list no.: 90-754-P. "September 1990." Includes bibliographical references. "EPA/540/ A5-89/012." ●Item 431-I-1

    1. Organic compounds — Oxidation — Evaluation. 2. Ultraviolet radiation. 3. Water, Underground — Pollution — United States. I. Risk Reduction Engineering Laboratory (U.S.) II. Superfund Innovative Technology Evaluation Program (U.S.) OCLC 23158202

Source: *Monthly Catalog,* **1991**

STOCK NUMBERS

Stock numbers are warehouse identification numbers used by GPO to identify titles in the sales program. They have an S/N indication followed by a series of twelve numbers. (e.g.: S/N xxx-xxx-xxxxx-x) The stock number of the document in Figure 1-1 is S/N 003-024-06912-1. The Government Printing Office requires individuals who buy documents to indicate titles and stock numbers on order forms.

GPO recently began assigning International Standard Book Numbers (ISBN) to its publications. ISBN numbers are international controls that facilitate ordering, distribution, inventory control, and accounting in the book trade. All titles have unique numbers. The ISBN number of the document in Figure 1-1 is 0-1603-2208-1. Despite some documents having ISBN numbers, remember to use stock numbers when ordering publications from GPO.

CONTRACT NUMBERS

Government agencies will sometimes enter into contracts with other parties to study a subject and prepare a report. The resulting report has a contract number. That for the title in Figure 1-3 is 68-03-3484.

SUPERINTENDENT OF DOCUMENTS NUMBERS: A MORE IN DEPTH DISCUSSION

Two reference tools are useful in locating SuDoc numbers of government publications: *List of Classes of United States Government Publications Available For Selection By Depository Libraries*[5] and *Guide to U.S. Government Publications.*[6]

LIST OF CLASSES

The *List of Classes* is a guide that cites materials selective depositories can elect to receive. References are alphanumeric according to SuDoc class numbers. The class number is the part of the SuDoc number through the colon (:). For example, the class number of the document in Figure 1-3 is EP1.2:. The *List of Classes* provides titles of document series, item numbers, and availability in paper (P), microfiche (MF), or CD-ROM formats (Figure 1-4).

Figure 1-4
List of Classes

Youth Development Office

HE 1.309:	Bibliographies and List of Publications (P) 0532-C-04
HE 1.310:	Grants, Preventive Services, Training Technical Assistance and Information Services (P) 0532-D-03
HE 1.312:	Source Catalog on Youth Participation (numbered pamphlets) 0532-D-05

Child Development Office

HE 1.402:	General Publications 0454-C-01
HE 1.411:	Bibliographies and Lists of Publications (P) 0454-C-06

Child Development Services Bureau

HE 1.462:	General Publications 0445-N-02
HE 1.468:	Handbooks, Manuals, Guides 0445-N-01

Consumer Affairs Office

HE 1.502:	General Publications 0857-I-05
HE 1.508:	Handbooks, Manuals, Guides 0857-I-02
HE 1.508/2:	Consumer's Resource Handbook (P) 0857-I-02

Social Security Administration

HE 3.1:	Annual Report (MF) 0513-A
HE 3.2:	General Publications 0516
HE 3.3:	Social Security Bulletin (monthly) (P) 0523
HE 3.3/a:	Social Security Bulletin (separates) 0523-A-03
HE 3.3/3:	Social Security Bulletin, Statistical Supplements (annual) (P) 0523-A-01
HE 3.3/5:	Author, Title, and Subject Index (P) 0523

Children, Youth and Families Administration

HE 23.1002:	General Publications 0530-B-01
HE 23.1005:	Laws (P) 0530-B-06
HE 23.1008:	Handbooks, Manuals, Guides 0530-B-03
HE 23.1010:	Research Demonstration and Evaluation Studies (annual) (P) 0530-B-04
HE 23.1011:	Bibliographies and Lists of Publications (MF) 0499-M
HE 23.1012:	Annual Report of Department of Health, Education, and Welfare to Congress and Services provided to Handicapped Children in Project Head Start (MF) 0454-C-05
HE 23.1013/2:	Toward Interagency Coordination: FY Federal Research and Development on Early Childhood (annual) (MF) 0499-M-02
HE 23.1015:	Domestic Violence Information Series: (MF) 0530-B-07
HE 23.1015/2:	Domestic Violence Monograph Series (MF) 0530-B-07
HE 23.1016:	Forms (P) 0530-B-08

Children's Bureau

HE 23.1202:	General Publications 0452
HE 23.1208:	Handbooks, Manuals, Guides 0452-C
HE 23.1210:	National Center on Child Abuse and Neglect: Publications (MF) 0445-L-01
HE 23.1210/2:	Child Abuse and Neglect Research: Projects and Publications (semiannual) (MF) 0445-L-05
HE 23.1210/3:	Annual Review of Child Abuse and Neglect Research (P) 0445-L-03
HE 23.1210/4:	National Center on Child Abuse Neglect: User manuals (series) (P) 0445-L-04
HE 23.1211:	Child Abuse and Neglect Programs (semiannual) (P) 0445-L-01
HE 23.1215:	Directories (P) 0445-L-06

Source: *List of Classes*, **1991 edition, 2nd quarter, 86 and 106.**

Test your knowledge of the *List of Classes*: Answer the following using Figure 1-4:

1. Explain why the SuDoc number of the 1990 *Annual Report* of the Social Security Administration is HE3.1:990.

> (Annual reports published by the Social Security Administration are HE3.1:. 990 refers to that for 1990.)

2. Is the *Annual Report* available to depository libraries in paper or microfiche?

> (microfiche)

3. How often is the *Social Security Bulletin* published?

> (monthly)

4. What are the item and Superintendent of Documents numbers of the *Social Security Bulletin*?

> (0523; HE3.3:)

Appendix 1 to the *List of Classes* is an "Alphabetic Listing of Government Authors." It lists agency names and the SuDoc class numbers of publications (Figure 1-5). Note, this index is alphabetic according to exact agency names. Each agency appears only once according to the first word in its name. The National Institute of Justice is under "National Institute..., not Justice.

Figure 1-5
List of Classes
Alphabetic Listing of Government Authors

Central Intelligence Agency PrEx 3.
Chemical Corps D 116.
Child Development Office HE 1.400:
Child Development Services Bureau HE 1.460:
Child Support Enforcement Office HE 24.
Children, Youth and Families Administration HE 23.1000:
Children's Bureau HE 23.1200:
Civil Aeronautics Board C 31.
Civil Aviation Security Service TD 4.800:
Civil Rights Commission CR
Civil Service Commission CS
Civilian Manpower Management Office (Navy) D 204.
Coast Guard TD 5.
Commerce Department C
Commission on Fair Market Value Policy for Federal Coal
    Leasing Y 3.C 63/3:
Commission on Security and Cooperation in Europe Y 4.Se
    2:

Source: *List of Classes*, **1991 edition, second quarter, 249.**

Test your knowledge of the *List of Classes*--"Alphabetic Listing of Government Authors:"

1. List the agencies in Figure 1-5 that are most likely to publish information about children.

> (Child Development Office; Child Development Services Bureau; Child Support Enforcement Office; Children, Youth and Families Administration; and Children's Bureau)

2. In Figure 1-4, why are the class numbers listed under the Youth Development Office and the Children's Bureau different?

> (SuDoc numbers are based upon agencies, divisions within agencies, and types of publications, not subjects. Each agency and subdivision has a unique number.)

3. Are agencies other than those listed in Figure 1-5 likely to publish information about children?

> (Yes. The agencies in Figure 1-5 are those that begin with the words "Child" or "Children." Any number of other agencies beginning with other words also publish information about children.)

GUIDE TO U.S. GOVERNMENT PUBLICATIONS

Donna Andriot's *Guide to U.S. Government Publications* is an annotated guide to the Superintendent of Documents system. Like the *List of Classes*, it is arranged by SuDoc class numbers, but unlike its counterpart, Andriot includes references to both depository and non-depository series. Class numbers of Children's Bureau publications are reproduced in Figure 1-6.

Figure 1-6
Guide to U.S. Government Publications
List of Classes Section

HE 1.402:CT • Item 454-C-1
GENERAL PUBLICATIONS.

Earlier HE 21.2

HE 1.402:C 43/9 • Item 454-C-1
200 YEARS OF CHILDREN. 1977. 486 p.

PURPOSE:–To provide a look into the lives and lifestyles of children over the last 200 years, documenting the remarkable changes that have occurred and identifying some current issues that have implications for the future. Written about children but not for them, 200 Years of Children is concerned with the condition of, and changes in, children's lives, their needs in health, education, and welfare, the growing interest in children's recreation and literature, and the more recent focus on the rights of children to develop to their full potential.

HE 1.402:R 31 • Item 454-C-1
RESEARCH, DEMONSTRATION, AND EVALUATION STUDIES. [Annual] (Research and Evaluation Division)

Report covers fiscal year.

CHILDREN'S BUREAU
(1975—1977)

CREATION AND AUTHORITY

The Children's Bureau (HE 21.100) was placed directly under the Secretary of Health, Education, and Welfare in 1975. In 1977, the Bureau was transferred to the newly established Children, Youth and Families Administration (HE 23.1200).

HE 1.451:date
ANNUAL REPORT.

Earlier HE 21.101
Later HE 23.1201

HE 1.452:CT • Item 425
GENERAL PUBLICATIONS.

Earlier HE 21.102
Later HE 23.1202

HE 1.452:F 81/4 • Item 425
FOSTER FAMILY SERVICES SELECTED READING LIST. 1976. 78 p.

Suggests books dealing with foster parents and children.

HE 1.458:CT • Item 452-C
HANDBOOKS, MANUALS, GUIDES. [Irregular]

Earlier HE 21.108
Later HE 23.1208

CHILDREN'S BUREAU
(1977—   )

CREATION AND AUTHORITY

The Children's Bureau (HE 1.450) was placed within the Office of Human Development Services by Secretary's reorganization order of July 26, 1977.

INFORMATION

Children's Bureau
Office of Human Development Services
Department of Health and Human Services
P.O. Box 1182
Washington, D.C. 20013
(202) 755-7418

HE 23.1201:date
ANNUAL REPORT.

Earlier HE 1.451

HE 23.1202:CT • Item 452
GENERAL PUBLICATIONS. [Irregular]

Earlier HE 1.452

HE 23.1208:CT • Item 452-C
HANDBOOKS, MANUALS, GUIDES. [Irregular]

Earlier HE 1.458

Source: Andriot, *Guide to U.S. Government Publications,* 1991 edition, 489 and 588.
Reprinted with permission. Copyright 1991 by Documents Index (McLean, VA.).
All rights reserved.

Andriot summarizes information about the creation, authority, and history of agencies. The *List of Classes* does not do this. Figure 1-6 illustrates that between 1975 and 1977 the Children's Bureau was part of the Secretary's Office in the Department of Health, Education, and Welfare. Its SuDoc number was in the HE1.450.. series. The Bureau became part of the Children, Youth and Families Administration in 1977, and its SuDoc class number became HE23.1200. Remember, SuDoc numbers often reflect changes in agencies names because the classification system is based upon agencies, not subjects. Figure 1-6 also shows that Andriot annotates significant documents. A summary of *200 Years of Children* (SuDoc number: HE1.402:C43/9) is given.

> **Test your knowledge of the *Guide To U.S. Government Publications*:** Answer the following questions using Figure 1-6.

1. What is the SuDoc number of the 1976 *Annual Report* of the Children's Bureau?

(HE1.451:976)

2. What is the SuDoc class number of *Annual Reports* published by the Children's Bureau since 1977?

(HE23.1201:)

3. What is the Sudoc class number for handbooks, manuals, and guides published by the Children's Bureau since 1977? Are these documents depository titles?

(HE23.1208:; yes--the item number is 452-C)

4. True or false: The *Annual Reports* of the Children's Bureau are depository documents.

(False--neither HE1.451: nor HE23.1201: have item numbers.)

The *Guide to U.S. Government Publications* also describes title changes. Figure 1-7 shows that *Region V Public Report* (SuDoc number: EP1.28/5:) was superseded by *Environmental Midwest* (SuDoc number: EP1.28/7:). It also indicates that *Environmental Midwest* was discontinued with the December 14, 1981 issue. This history of the title is very important to researchers who are attempting to determine what happened to a particular document. The *List of Classes* covers only those materials currently available to depositories.

Figure 1-7
Guide to U.S. Government Publications
Title Changes

EP 1.23/8:nos. • Item 431-I-62 (MF)
INTERAGENCY ENERGY-ENVIRONMENT
RESEARCH AND DEVELOPMENT PRO-
GRAM REPORTS. 600/7-(series) [Irregular]

EP 1.23/9:nos. • Item 431-K-12
EPA SPECIAL REPORTS. 1– [Irregular]
(EPA 600/8-[nos.])

EP 1.24:v.nos.&nos.
EPA LOG, WEEKLY LOG OF SIGNIFICANT
EVENTS.

EP 1.25:date
OIL POLLUTION RESEARCH NEWSLET-
TER. –March 1972. [Irregular] (Edison Water
Quality Research Laboratory, National Envi-
ronmental Research Center, Edison, New Jersey
08817)

EP 1.25/2:v.nos.&nos. • Item 431-I-62
OIL POLLUTION ABSTRACTS. 1–7. –1980.
[Quarterly]

　　Formerly entitled Oil Pollution Report, and
issued as part of EP 1.23/8.

EP 1.26:CT
POLICIES AND TRENDS IN MUNICIPAL
WASTE TREATMENT (series). 1972–
[Irregular]

EP 1.27:v.nos.&nos.
YOUTH ADVISORY BOARD NEWSLETTER.
[Irregular]

EP 1.28/5:date
REGION V PUBLIC REPORT. [Monthly]
(Office of Public Affairs, Region V, Environ-
mental Protection Agency, Chicago, Illinois)

　　Superseded by Environment Midwest
(EP 1.28/7).

EP 1.28/6:date • Item 431-I-36
ENVIRONMENT MIDWEST, TOGETHER.
[Annual]

EP 1.28/7:date • Item 431-I-43
ENVIRONMENTAL MIDWEST. [Monthly]
(EPA, Public Affairs Office–Region V, 230 S.
Dearborn, Chicago, Illinois 60604)

　　Supersedes Region V Public Report
(EP 1.28/5).
Discontinued with Dec. 14, 1981 issue.
ISSN 0364-2151

The Guide to U.S. Government Publications has a comprehensive Title Index. Figure 1-8 illustrates *Environmental Midwest*.

Figure 1-8
Guide To U.S. Government Publications
Title Index

Environmental Hotline, EP 1.95
Environmental Impact Statements—
  Bureau of Mines, I 28.150
  Coast Guard, TD 5.32
  Consumer Product Safety Commission, Y
    3.C 76/3:15
  Corps of Engineers, D 103.62
  Defense Logistics Agency, D 7.35
  Department of Commerce, C 1.68
  Department of Interior, I 1.98
  Department of State, S 1.133
  Department of Transportation, TD 1.41
  Economic Development Administration, C
    46.30
  Energy Research and Development
    Administration, ER 1.25
  Environmental of Energy, E 1.20
  Federal Aviation Administration, TD 4.48
  Federal Power Commission, FP 1.33
  Federal Railroad Administration, TD 3.17
  Foreign-Trade Zones Board, FTZ 1.10
  General Services Administration, GS 1.25
  Interstate Commerce Commission, IC 1.32
  Maritime Administration, C 39.239
  National Institutes of Health, HE 20.3026
  National Marine Fisheries Service, C 55.328
  Pesticides Office, EP 5.14

Environmental Impact Statements (Continued)
  Public Buildings Service, GS 6.9
  Rural Electrification Administration, A
    68.22
  Urban Mass Transportation Administration,
    TD 7.15
  Veterans Administration, VA 1.59
Environmental Inventories, C 55.232
Environmental Law Series, EP 1.5/2
Environmental Midwest, EP 1.28/7
Environmental Monitoring, 600/4- (series), EP
  1.23/5
Environmental News, EP 1.7/2, EP 1.7/9
Environmental News Summary, EP 1.7/7
Environmental Outlook, EP 1.93
Environmental Overview and Analysis of
  Mining Effects, I 29.101
Environmental Planning Papers, HH 1.39

Test your knowledge of the *Guide To U.S. Government Publications*--"Title Index": Answer the following using Figure 1-8.

1. What is the class number of the *Environmental Planning Papers*?

    (HH1.39:)

2. What are the SuDoc numbers of environmental impact statements published by the Coast Guard?

    (TD5.32:)

Unlike the *List of Classes*, Andriot cites report numbers. Figure 1-7 indicates that report series 600/7-... and EPA/600/8-... are classified under EP1.23/8: and EP1.23/9. The Title Index shows that *Environmental Monitoring* is part of the "600/4-" series (Figure 1-8).

Andriot's "Agency Class Chronology" section traces changes in SuDoc numbers. Figure 1-6 indicates that the Children's Bureau was once classified in the "HE1.450" series. Checking that class number in the Agency Class Chronology provides a history of Children Bureau class numbers since 1912 (Figure 1-9).

Figure 1-9
Guide to U.S. Government Publications
Agency Class Chronology

HE 1.400

HE 21	1970–1975	Child Development Office
HE 1.400	1975–1977	Child Development Office
HE 23.1000	1977–	Children, Youth and Families Administration

HE 1.450

C 19	1912–1913	Children's Bureau
L 5	1913–1946	Children's Bureau
FS 3.200	1947–1963	Children's Bureau
FS 14.100	1963–1967	Children's Bureau
FS 17.200	1967–1969	Children's Bureau
HE 21.100	1970–1975	Children's Bureau
HE 1.450	1975–1977	Children's Bureau
HE 23.1200	1977–	Children's Bureau

Source: *Guide to U.S. Government Publications*,
1991 edition, 1204. Reprinted with permission.
Copyright 1991 by Documents Index (McLean, VA.).
All rights reserved.

Test your knowledge of the *Guide to U.S. Government Publications*--"Agency Class Chronology": Answer the following using Figure 1-9.

Test your knowledge of the *Guide to U.S. Government Publications-* *-"Agency Class Chronology":* Answer the following using Figure 1-9.

1. What is the SuDoc class number for publications issued by the Children's Bureau in 1914?

(L5...)

2. What is the SuDoc class number for publications issued by the Children's Bureau during the 1950's?

(FS3.200:)

SUMMARY

Chart 1-2 summarizes differences among the basic numbers, and Chart 1-3 summarizes differences between the *List of Classes* and the *Guide to U.S. Government Publications*.

Chart 1-2
Summary of Basic Numbers

Item number	Indicates depository status. Non-depository documents do not have item numbers.
Superintendent of Documents number	Classification number used for shelving documents in most depository libraries.
Technical report/series number	Alphanumeric or numeric codes applied to documents by publishing agencies.
Contract number	Identifies documents prepared for agencies on contract.
Stock number	Used in GPO sales operations to maintain control over inventories. Use stock numbers to identify documents when buying them.

Chart 1-3
List of Classes **Compared to** *Guide to U.S. Government Publications*

	List of Classes	Guide to U.S. Government Publications
Arrangement	Alphanumeric by SuDoc numbers.	Alphanumeric by SuDoc numbers.
What SuDoc numbers are included?	SuDoc numbers of current depository documents.	SuDoc numbers of current and superseded depository and non- depository documents.
Index by agencies	Yes	Yes
Title index	No	Yes
Cites report numbers	No	Yes
Traces histories of SuDoc numbers	No	Yes

Endnotes

1. U.S. Government Printing Office, edited by Marian W. MacGilvray. rev.ed. (Washington, D.C.: GPO, 1993). SuDoc number: GP3.29:P88/993.

2. Eleanor J. Aronson, 3rd ed. (Detroit, MI.: Gale Research Company, 1986).

3. Vasantha Nathan, ed., 4th edition (Clayton, MO.: Global Engineering Documents, 1989).

4. U.S. National Center for Education Statistics, by Roslyn Korb (Washington, D.C.: GPO, 1992). SuDoc #: ED1.302:ST9/5.

5. U.S. Government Printing Office (Washington, D.C.: GPO, quarterly). SuDoc number: GP3.24:.

6. Donna Andriot, ed. (McLean, VA: Documents Index, annual).

Exercises

1. The document in Figure 1-10 is a (depository/non-depository) title.

Figure 1-10

91-1362

TD 4.10/4:(nos.)

FAA airworthiness directive : biweekly listing / U.S. Department of Transportation, Federal Aviation Administration, Mike Monroney Aeronautical Center. Oklahoma City, Okla. : The Center, U.S. Dept. of Transportation, Federal Aviation Administration, Mike Monroney Aeronautical Center, P.O. Box 26460, Oklahoma City, OK 73125-0460

   v. ; 28 cm.

   Biweekly Other title: Airworthiness directive biweekly listing Not distributed to depository libraries. Description based on: No. 82-23; title from caption.

   1. Airplanes — Airworthiness — Periodicals. I. Mike Monroney Aeronautical Center. sn-87042621 OCLC 09272381

Source: *Monthly Catalog*, **1991.**

2. The following questions refer to Figure 1-11.

Figure 1-11

91-22154

NAS 1.21:4306

Dawson, Virginia P. (Virginia Parker)

   Engines and innovation : Lewis Laboratory and American Propulsion Technology / Virginia P. Dawson. — Washington, DC : National Aeronautics and Space Administration, Office of Management, Scientific and Technical Information Division : For sale by the Supt. of Docs., U.S. G.P.O., 1991.

   x, 276 p. : ill., map ; 26 cm. — (NASA SP ; 4306) (The NASA history series) Shipping list no.: 91-449-P. Includes bibliographical references and index. ●Item 830-I S/N 033-000-01095-8 @ GPO ISBN 0-1603-0742-2 : $16.00

   1. Propulsion Laboratory (U.S.) — History. 2. Engines — Technological innovations. I. United States. National Aeronautics and Space Administration. Scientific and Technical Information Division. II. Title. III. Series. IV. Series. TL568.P76D38 1991 90-020747 629.4/06/079493 /20 OCLC 22665627

Source: *Monthly Catalog*, **1991.**

A. This title is a (depository/non-depository) document.

B. The item number of the document is_____. Why is the item number important?

C. The SuDoc number is_____. What does the SuDoc number represent? Why is it important?

D. The stock number is _____. When does the stock number become important?

E. The report number of this publication is_____.

3.   The following questions are based upon the *Guide to U.S. Government Publications*, 1991 edition.

A. The SuDoc class number(s) of the Community Relations Service are_____ and_____.

B. Why does that agency have more than one number?

C. The SuDoc class number of publications issued by the Community Relations Service during the 1980's was_____.

D. Handbooks, manuals, and guides issued by the Community Relations Service prior to 1966 had the SuDoc class number_____.

E. The SuDoc class number of the *Monthly Labor Review* is _____. Has this number varied?

F. The *Monthly Labor Review* first published in _____.

G. What kind(s) of information does the *Monthly Labor Review* contain?

H. The current SuDoc class number for the Immigration and Naturalization Service is J21. That number was first used in_____. The class number between 1913 and 1933 was _____.

Answers

1. This document is non-depository because it does not have an item number.

2. A. Depository.

   B. 830-I. Presence of item numbers indicate titles are depository documents that are distributed to depository libraries.

   C. NAS1.21:4306. The Superintendent of Documents (SuDoc) number is used by many depository libraries to organize documents on shelves.

   D. S/N 033-000-01095-8. Titles of documents and their stock numbers are needed when purchasing publications from GPO.

   E. NASA SP 4306.

3. A. The Agency Index indicates that the class numbers are C50 and J23.

   B. Superintendent of Document numbers are based upon agencies. When agencies reorganize, different SuDoc numbers often reflect these changes.

   C. J23.8:.

   D. C50.8:.

   E. L2.6: (Use the Title Index). This number never varied.

   F. 1915.

   G. Articles about labor economics, industrial relations, and summaries of studies and reports appear in the *Monthly Labor Review*.

   H. The Agency Class Chronology section indicates that "J21" has been used since 1940, and that "L3" was used between 1913 and 1933.

•Chapter 2

Comprehensive Indexes

Answer the following questions when reading this chapter:

1. What are the similarities and differences between the *Monthly Catalog* and the *Publications Reference File?*

2. Does use of the online and CD-ROM versions of these indexes offer advantages over that of the paper and microfiche formats?

3. How can you effectively incorporate use of the Government Information Locator Service (GILS) into your work?

4. Explain which comprehensive index(es) are most useful to your needs.

This chapter covers comprehensive indexes that provide access to wide varieties of documents. These include the *Monthly Catalog*, plus related cumulative indexes and supplements. The *Monthly Catalog* covers materials published by all three branches of government. The *Publications Reference File (PRF)*, which cites documents available for sale from the Government Printing Office, is then discussed. Descriptions of three Congressional Information Service sources follow that discussion: the *U.S. Government Periodicals Index*, the *American Foreign Policy Index*, and *Reports Required by Congress*. The text then considers the Government Information Locator Service (GILS), an electronic network that attempts to describe all information prepared by the executive branch. The final section of the chapter lists and describes comprehensive bibliographies of government publications. Related electronic sources are noted within the chapter and in an internet supplement to the chapter. The text mentions various kinds of numbers. When necessary, consult the "Basic Numbers" chart in the summary section of Chapter 1 for a quick review.

MONTHLY CATALOG

The *Monthly Catalog of United States Government Publications*[1] is the basic bibliography or catalog for United States documents available to the public. GPO publishes it monthly since 1895 under various titles. The *Monthly Catalog* includes depository and non-depository documents. Remember, GPO distributes depository documents to depository libraries and does not distribute non-depository titles. Most titles are predominately depository items because these are usually materials printed or filmed by GPO. Consequently, they are usually readily available for cataloging and distribution to depositories.

MONTHLY CATALOG, JANUARY 1996-PRESENT

The current version of the *Monthly Catalog* includes two parts. The first section lists bibliographic references and Superintendent of Documents (SuDoc) numbers that are necessary for locating information in most depository libraries. The second section is an index based upon keywords from titles.[2] To locate information in the *Monthly Catalog*:

1. Consult the index and note the *Monthly Catalog* entry number.

2. Locate the entry number in the bibliographic section and note the Superintendent of Documents (SuDoc) number.

3. Use the SuDoc number to retrieve the item from the shelf.

Suppose you are interested in information about the Americans with Disabilities Act, check the index under the appropriate terms (Figure 2-1).

Figure 2-1
Monthly Catalog
Title Keyword Index

Directory	of automated criminal justice informatio	**96-2184**
"	of drug abuse and alcoholism treatment a	**96-1724**
"	of organizational technical report acron	**96-1443**
"	., California ZIP4 state	**96-3076**
"	., California ZIP4 state	**96-3077**
"	., California ZIP4 state	**96-3078**
"	., California ZIP4 state	**96-3079**
"	., EOS	**96-2363**
"	., FAA certificated maintenance agencies	**96-3196**
"	., FDA narcotic treatment programs	**96-1704**
"	., National drug code	**96-1703**
"	., Regional adult dental care resource	**96-3216**
disabilities	under Section 504 of the Rehabilitati	**96-1524**
Disabilities Act	and criminal justice., The Americ	**96-2162**
disability	benefits., When you get Social Security	**96-3154**
disc	brake lathes and components thereof., In the	**96-2142**
discharges	associated with offshore production ope	**96-2134**
disciplinary	action., Resolution for	**96-3229**
"	action., Resolution for	**96-3230**
disclosure	., HMDA. MSA 380, Anchorage, AK. Individ	**96-1640**
"	., HMDA. MSA 450, Anniston, AL. Individu	**96-1611**
"	., HMDA. MSA 1000, Birmingham, AL. Indiv	**96-1614**
"	., HMDA. MSA 2030, Decatur, AL. Individu	**96-1617**
"	., HMDA. MSA 2180, Dothan, AL. Individua	**96-1620**

Source: *Monthly Catalog*, **January 1996, 141.**

Test your understanding of the *Monthly Catalog* Title Keyword Index: The following questions refer to Figure 2-1.

What is the *Monthly Catalog* entry number of a document dealing with disabilities and law enforcement?

(96-2162)

The entry number, 96-2162, in Figure 2-1 is the 2,162nd reference in 1996 *Monthly Catalog*. Figure 2-2 illustrates the bibliographic reference for this title.

Figure 2-2
Monthly Catalog
Bibliographic Citation

NATIONAL INSTITUTE OF JUSTICE
Justice Dept.
Washington, DC 20531

96-2161 J 28.15/2:100-95

Preliminary investigation of Oleoresin Capsicum. — [1995]
    vi, 11 p. : — (NIJ report ; 100-95) Shipping list no.: 96-0002-P. ●Item 0717-J
    OCLC 33265258

96-2162 J 28.15/2-2:D 63/3

The Americans with Disabilities Act and criminal justice. — [1995]
    7 p. ; — (Research in action) ●Item 0717-J-01
    OCLC 33270618

96-2163 J 28.15/2-2:M 32

The use of computerized mapping in crime control and prevention programs. — [1995]
    11 p. : — (Research in action) Shipping list no.: 95-0319-P. ●Item 0717-J-01
    OCLC 33286077

96-2164 J 28.15/2-2:T 41

Threat assessment. — [1995]
    7 p. ; — (Research in Action) Shipping list no.: 96-0006-P. ●Item 0717-J-01
    OCLC 33322329

Source: *Monthly Catalog*, **January 1996, 54.**

In Figure 2-2, the *Monthly Catalog* entry number appears in the upper left corner of the citation and the Superintendent of Documents number appears in the center of the citation. Remember, the bullets (●) followed by item numbers indicate that GPO distributes these materials to depository libraries. The OCLC and shipping list numbers are irrelevant to most library users.[3]

Test your understanding of *Monthly Catalog* **entries:** Refer to Figure 2-2 when answering the following questions.

1. What is the title of the document represented by entry number is 96-2162?

    (The Americans with Disabilities
    Act and Criminal Justice)

2. What is its SuDoc number?

    (J28.15/2-2:D63/3)

3. What is the difference between the Monthly Catalog entry and the SuDoc number?

    (Use the entry number to refer from the index
    to the bibliographic section. The SuDoc num-
    ber is the call number of the document used
    by most depository libraries.)

4. True or false: You might be able to locate this document in your local depository library?

    (True. The bullet (●) followed by the item num-
    ber indicates that this is a depository docu-
    ment--one distributed to depository libraries.
    Note, before visiting your local depository li-
    brary, call to confirm that this item number
    was selected. Remember, all depository librar-
    ies do not acquire every item.)

MONTHLY CATALOG, JULY 1976-DECEMBER 1995

During this time, the bibliographic section of the *Monthly Catalog* provided more complete information than that shown in Figure 2-2. Also, this version of the *Monthly Catalog* had six indexes for authors; titles; subjects; series report numbers; stock numbers; and title keywords. GPO published cumulative indexes annually. The discussion below considers selected multiyear cumulative indexes.

LOCATING INFORMATION BY SUBJECTS

Suppose you are interested in locating information about food allergies. Use the Subject Index or the Title Keyword Index to locate relevant references. Figure 2-3 reproduces selected information from the Subject Index. It displays authors, titles, Superintendent of Documents numbers, and *Monthly Catalog* entry numbers. Use the Superintendent of Documents number to locate titles on the shelves. Use the *Monthly Catalog* entry number to locate more information about the documents in the *Monthly Catalog*'s bibliographic section. The Title Keyword Index is similar to that seen above in Figure 2-1 and below in Figure 2-7.

Figure 2-3
Monthly Catalog
Subject Index

**Food — Labeling — Law and legislation —
United States.**
An Act to Make Technical Amendments
to the Nutrition Information and Labeling Act, and for Other Purposes.
United States. (AE 2.110:102-108), 92-
1257

Food — Labeling — United States.
Food allergies : separating fact from
"hype." Thompson, Richard C. (Richard Church), 1922- (HE 20.4010/a:F
739/16), 92-2313

Review of dietary guidance and the role
of nutrition labeling : hearing before
the Subcommittee on Domestic Marketing, Consumer Relations, and Nutrition of the Committee on Agriculture,
House of Representatives, One Hundred Second Congress, first session,
November 21, 1991. United States.
Congress. House. Committee on Agriculture. Subcommittee on Domestic
Marketing, Consumer Relations, and
Nutrition. (Y 4.Ag 8/1:102-44), 92-
14676

Source: *Monthly Catalog*, **1992 Index, I-1836.**

Test your understanding of the Subject Index: All questions refer to Figure 2-3.

1. What is the title of the document dealing with food allergies?

   (Food Allergies: Separating Fact From "Hype")

2. Who is the author?

   (Richard C. Thompson)

3. What is the SuDoc number?

   (HE20.4010/a:F739/16)

4. What is the *Monthly Catalog* entry number for *Data For Food
   Analysis?*

   (92-2313)

BIBLIOGRAPHIC SECTION

As with the current version of the *Monthly Catalog*, the bibliographic section lists documents numerically according to their entry numbers (Figure 2-4).

Figure 2-4
Monthly Catalog
Bibliographic Section

92-2313

HE 20.4010/a:F 739/16

Thompson, Richard C. (Richard Church), 1922-
      Food allergies : separating fact from "hype." — [Rockville,
Md. : Dept. of Health and Human Services, Public Health
Service, Food and Drug Administration, Office of Public Af-
fairs, 1986]
      [4] p. : ill. ; 28 cm. — (HHS publication ; no. (FDA) 86-2213)
Caption title. "Reprinted from June 1986 FDA consumer"—P.
[4].   Shipping list no.: 91-206-P.   ●Item 475-H-1
      1. Food allergy.   2. Food — Labeling — United States.   3.
United States. Food and Drug Administration.   I. United
States. Food and Drug Administration. Office of Public Affairs.
II. Title.   III. Series.   OCLC 24483433

Source:*Monthly Catalog*, **January 1992, 155.**

**Test your understanding of the *Monthly Catalog's* bibliographic
section:** Refer to Figure 2-4 when identifying the following parts of the
citation.

1.   Monthly Catalog entry number.

(92-2313)

2.   Superintendent of Documents number.

(HE20.4010/a:F739/16)

3.   Title

(*Food Allergies: Separating Fact From "Hype"*)

4.   Personal author.

(Richard C. Thompson)

5.   Issuing agency or publishing agency.

(Department of Health and Human Services.
Public Health Service. Food and Drug
Administration. Office of Public Affairs)

6.   Date of publication.

(1986)

7.   Report number.

(HHS publication no ; (FDA) 86-2213.
Remember, report numbers are codes used
by agencies to identify their publications.
Consult Chapter 1 for more information.)

AUTHOR INDEX

Government publications can have two types of authors, the individuals who write the documents (personal authors) and the agencies that

publish them (corporate authors). *Food Allergies: Separating Fact From "Hype"* appears in the Author Index twice, once under the personal author and once under the agency author (Figure 2-5) .

Figure 2-5
Monthly Catalog
Author Index

Personal Authors   **Agency Authors**

Thompson, Richard C. (Richard Church), 1922-
  Food allergies : separating fact from "hype.", 92-2313

Thompson, T. H. (Terry H.), 1937-
  Hydrology of the Citrus Park quadrangle, Hillsborough County, Florida /, 92-20072

  Summary of hydrogeologic, water-quality, and biologic data from two small basins, southeast Hillsborough County, Florida [microform] /, 92-23684

Thompson, W. Scott (Willard Scott), 1942-
  Approaches to peace : an intellectual map /, 92-18926

United States. Food and Drug Administration. Office of Public Affairs.
  Acne, taming that age-old adolescent affliction /, 92-15766

  Arthritis, modern treatment for that old pain in the joints /, 92-19988

  Childhood asthma : more than snuffles /, 92-15767

  Fiber, something healthy to chew on /, 92-15771

  Food allergies : separating fact from "hype.", 92-2313

  Getting information from FDA /, 92-2315

  Getting the lead out— of just about everything /, 92-17730

  Good nutrition for the highchair set /, 92-15774

Source: *Monthly Catalog*, 1992 Index, I-359, I-627.

Indexing of agency names are sometimes under the divisions of the agency responsible for the report, instead of the full agency name. For example, in Figure 2-5, *Food Allergies: Separating Fact From "Hype"* appears under "United States. Food and Drug Administration. Office of Public Affairs." The bibliographic section of the *Monthly Catalog* (Figure 2-4) illustrates the full agency name, United States. Department of Health and Human Services. Public Health Service. Food and Drug Administration. Office of Public Affairs.

TITLE INDEX

Information in the Title index is alphabetical. Citations show authors, SuDoc numbers, and *Monthly Catalog* entry numbers (Figure 2-6).

Figure 2-6
Monthly Catalog
Title Index

Followup fieldwork : AIDS outreach and IV drug abuse. Nurco, David. (HE 20.8202:Ac 7/6), 92-2357

Fontenelle Reservoir SE quadrangle, Wyoming, 1968 : 7.5 minute series (topographic) / Geological Survey (U.S.) (I 19.81:42110-A 1-TF-024/978), 92-8058

Food, Agriculture, Conservation, and Trade Act Amendments of 1991. United States. (AE 2.110:102-237), 92-10774

Food aid : AID's activities under the 1990 farm bill : hearing before the International Task Force of the Select Committee on Hunger, House of Representatives, One Hundred Second Congress, first session, hearing held in Washington, DC, July 24, 1991. United States. Congress. House. Select Committee on Hunger. International Task Force. (Y 4.H 89:102-8), 92-14798

Food allergies : separating fact from "hype." Thompson, Richard C. (Richard Church), 1922- (HE 20.4010/a:F 739/16), 92-2313

Food and agricultural export directory. Food and agricultural export directory (Washington, D.C. : 1981) (A 1.38:1481), 92-19209

Food and agricultural export directory (Washington, D.C. : 1981) Food and agricultural export directory (Washington, D.C. : 1981) (A 1.38:1481), 92-19209

Source: *Monthly Catalog*, **1992 Index, I-961.**

Test your ability to interpret the Title Index: Refer to Figure 2-6 when answering the following:

1. Who wrote the document entitled *Followup Fieldwork: AIDS Outreach and IV Drug Abuse*?

    (David Nurco)

2. Its SuDoc number is____and its *Monthly Catalog* entry number is____.

    (HE20.8202:Ac7/6; 92-2357)

KEYWORD INDEX: TITLE APPROACH

The Keyword Index is a useful source when the exact title is unknown. Titles with many keywords have multiple index entries. For instance, suppose the title of the document in Figure 2-4 is incorrectly thought to be *Separating Hype From Fact: Food Allergies,* the Keyword Index still enables you to locate it (Figure 2-7).

Figure 2-7
Monthly Catalog
Keyword Index, Title Approach

hydroxy fatty acids for industrial projects /, Les	**92-15037**
hygiene samplers for soil-gas measurement /, The u	**92-11320**
" survey field, NSN 6545-00-935-5881, LIN M2	**92-9146**
hygrothermal environment, Progressive fracture in	**92-22176**
Hymenoptera:Eumenidae, Vespidae, Pompilidae, and C	**92-5563**
Hyong Cha Kim Kay : report (to accompany S. 391).	**92-10360**
hype.", Food allergies : separating fact from "	**92-2313**
hyperbolic equations, Absorbing boundary condition	**92-3049**
hypercube computers, Performance of a parallel cod	**92-8322**
" multiprocessor, Ordered fast Fourier tra	**92-20499**
" , Multiphase complete exchange on a circu	**92-5451**
Hypermedia and visual technology	**92-5483**
" technology to support a new pedagogy of	**92-1930**
hypermixing nozzle, Experimental investigation of	**92-3124**
" nozzles, Progress toward synergistic	**92-14396**
hypersonic aircraft. Part 1, Body weight of	**92-10156**
" cruise-turn maneuvers, Control integrat	**92-22209**
" engine applications high temperature le	**92-22182**
" engine ceramic wafer seal, High tempera	**92-8357**

Source: *Monthly Catalog*, **1992 Index, I-3854.**

REPORT NUMBER INDEX

Figure 2-8 displays the Report Number Index. HHS publication ; no. (FDA) 86-2213 refers to the Thompson report on food allergies seen in Figure 2-4.

Figure 2-8
Monthly Catalog
Report Number

HHI-22/3-92 (15 M) E,   92-16440

HHS publication ; no. (CDC),   92-638, 92-639,   92-640

HHS publication ; no. (CDC) 87-8391,   92-9477

HHS publication ; no. (CDC) 88-8395,   92-23565

HHS publication ; no. (FDA) 86-2213,   92-2313

HHS publication ; no. (FDA) 87-4217.,   92-6438

HHS publication ; no. (FDA) 91-4179.,   92-4606

HHS publication ; no. (FDA) 91-4244.,   92-4605

HHS publication ; no. (FDA) 91-4246.,   92-4604

Source: *Monthly Catalog*, **1992 Index, I-3085.**

STOCK NUMBER INDEX

Remember, GPO uses stock numbers to maintain control over sales inventory. When buying documents, customers must supply GPO with titles and stock numbers. Figure 2-9 displays typical stock numbers.

Figure 2-9
Monthly Catalog
Stock Numbers

003-003-02706-5 GPO ,	92-6071
003-003-02789-8 GPO ,	92-19436
003-003-02828-2 GPO ,	92-15123
003-003-02874-6 GPO ,	92-17144
003-003-02882-7 GPO ,	92-19438
003-003-02900-9 GPO ,	92-15124
003-003-02905-0 GPO ,	92-13042
003-003-02909-2 GPO ,	92-10822
003-003-02929-7 GPO ,	92-13044
003-003-02967-0 GPO ,	92-10827
003-003-02972-6 GPO ,	92-9024
003-003-02977-7 GPO ,	92-1366
003-003-02980-7 GPO ,	92-19439
003-003-03002-3 GPO ,	92-10824
003-003-03017-1 : GPO ,	92-1368
003-003-03060-1 GPO ,	92-15122
003-003-03065-1 GPO ,	92-9022
003-003-03075-9 GPO ,	92-9021
003-003-03085-6 GPO ,	92-10823
003-003-03097-0 GPO ,	92-1362

Source: *Monthly Catalog*, **1992 Index, I-3216.**

The Stock Number Index also displays other types of order numbers for titles sold outside GPO (Chart 2-1).

Chart 2-1
Monthly Catalog
Stock Number Index Order Numbers Other Than Stock Numbers

ED	Available from the Educational Reproduction Information Center (ERIC), a division of the Department of Education.
ISBN and ISSN	International Standard Book Number and International Standard Serial Number.
N..-..........	Available from the National Aeronautic and Space Administration (NASA).

MONTHLY CATALOG PRIOR TO JULY 1976

The Government Printing Office changed the format of the *Monthly Catalog* in July 1976. Before then, the main bibliographic section resembled Figure 2-10. The *Monthly Catalog* entry number is in the left column, and the Superintendent of Documents number is in the lower right part of the citation.

Figure 2-10
Monthly Catalog, **Old Format**
Bibliographic Section

31159 Presidential campaign activities of 1972, Senate Res. 60, hearings, 93d
Congress, 1st session, Watergate and related activities. ● Item 1009–A
L.C. card 73–602551   Y 4.P 92/4 : P 92/phase 1/bk. (nos.) –
Phase 1, bk. 1. Watergate investigation, May 17–24, 1973. 1973. v+456 p. il.
* Paper, $3.00 (S/N 5270–01843).
Phase 1, bk. 2. Watergate investigation, June 5–14, 1973. 1973. v+457–910 p.
il. * Paper, $3.00 (S/N 5270–01962).

Source: *Monthly Catalog*, **November 1973, 30.**

Test your ability to interpret the *Monthly Catalog's* old format. Answer the following using Figure 2-10:

1. What is the *Monthly Catalog* entry number?

    (31,159)

2. What are the titles of these documents?

    (Both titles are *Watergate Investigation.*
    Their dates differentiate them.)

3. Phase 1, bk. 1 is a Congressional hearing held (dates) and
    its SuDoc number is_____.

    (May 17-24, 1973) (Y4.P92/4: P92/Phase1/bk1)

4. Were these documents available for sale in 1973? If yes,
    how much did they cost and what information is needed
    to buy them?

    (Each cost $3.00. To order documents supply
    GPO with titles and stock numbers, in this case
    S/N 5720-01843 and S/N 5270-01962.)

GPO first used three separate author, title, and subject indexes in 1974. Before that date, the *Catalog* had one alphabetic index that was primarily subject oriented (Figure 2-11).

Figure 2-11
Monthly Catalog, **Old Format**
Subject Index

```
Waterborne exports and general imports,
    19012
Watercraft, see Boats.
Waterfowl, see Water birds.
Waterfronts :
    security of vessels and waterfront facil-
        ities, 16825
    urban river, staff proposal for waterfront
        development in District of Columbia,
        23719, 25562
Watergate hearings, see Presidential Cam-
    paign Activities, Select Committee on.
Watergate investigation, 31159
Waterloo, Iowa :
    area wage survey, 26618
    housing and education, civil rights aspects,
        walk together children, 24257
Watersheds :
    annual streamflow summaries from 4 sub-
        alpine watersheds in Colorado, 23276
    computer simulation of snowmelt within
        Colorado subalpine watershed, 28966
    cost analysis of clearing ponderosa pine
        watershed, 28946
```

Source: *Monthly Catalog* **Index, 1973, 660.**

CUMULATIVE SUBJECT INDEX TO THE MONTHLY CATALOG OF UNITED STATES GOVERNMENT PUBLICATION: 1900-1971

The *Cumulative Subject Index to the Monthly Catalog of United States Government Publication: 1900-1971*[4] simplifies the retrieval of older documents. When seeking information about the relocation of the Seneca Indians and the dates of publication are unknown, search the *Cumulative Subject Index* (Figure 2-12).

Figure 2-12
Cumulative Subject Index to the *Monthly Catalog*

Seneca Indians (01) 10, 109, 132, 198, 507; (02)
421; (04) 180, 219; (05) 121: (07) 480, 540;
(11) 342, 415, 441, 508
constitution and by-laws (37) 1072
fiction, legends, and myths (19) 572, 626
fish and game (27) 438
Allegany, etc., reservations (33) 618; (34)
807, 922; (35) 249, 271, 717
money from leased lands -
laws (50) 18296; (61) 18622
reports (49) 19340; (50) 16450; (61) 14627,
16718
morphology and dictionary (67) 13001
New York commute annuities (48) 10714; (49)
9411
Niagara River, hearing (15) 31
ratification of certain leases (30) 1078; (32)
1085
ratification of certain leases - continued
hearing (31) 680
report (31) 500
receipts, from leasing lands, rp. (32) 1123
relocation -
hearings (64) 6359, 8448
law (64) 17392
reports (64) 6275, 8418, 17596

Source: *Cumulative Subject Index to the Monthly Catalog*, **Volume 13, 211, 212.**
Reprinted with permission from *Cumulative Subject Index to the Monthly Catalog*
of United States Government Publication:1900-1971. **Copyright 1973 by Carrollton**
Press. Owned by Research Publications, International (Woodbridge, CT).
All rights reserved.

The last 2 digits of the year (64) are in parentheses following the index
terms, relocation - hearings. Figure 2-13 displays the reference to this title
from the 1964 *Monthly Catalog*, entry number 6359.

Figure 2-13
Monthly Catalog

[Committee hearings], serial, 88th Congress. † ● Item 1023
Y 4.In 8/14 : 88/ (nos.)

6359   6. Kinzua Dam (Seneca Indian relocation), hearings before Subcommittee on
           Indian Affairs, 88th Congress, 1st session, on H.R. 1794, H.R. 3343 and
           H.R. 7354, May 18-Dec. 10, 1963. 1964. v+515 p. il. 3 pl. [These
           hearings were held in Salamanca, N.Y. and Washington, D.C. Includes
           list of selected references on Kinzua Dam controversy.]
           L.C. card 64-60610

Source: *Monthly Catalog*, **April 1964, 36.**

Y4.In8/14:88(nos), located in the top right hand corner of Figure 2-13
indicates that all SuDoc numbers for hearings issued by the House Interior and
Insular Affairs Committee during the 88th Congress begins with that notation.
Entry number 6,359 was the sixth document published in that series. Thus, the
complete SuDoc number for this title is Y4.In8/14:88/6.

Citations to documents listed in the *Monthly Catalog* before September 1947 refer to page numbers rather than catalog entry numbers. The Government Printing Office did not adopt the consecutive entry number approach until then. For instance, citations to publications about fiction, legends and myths of the Seneca Indians appeared on pages 572 and 626 of the 1919 *Monthly Catalog* (Figure 2-12).

GPO published seven cumulative multi-year indexes to the *Monthly Catalog*.[5] They cover 1941-1950, 1951-1960, 1961-1965, 1966-1970, 1971-1976, 1976-1980 and 1981-1985. As in Figure 2-12, references provide *Monthly Catalog* years and page or entry numbers.

CUMULATIVE PERSONAL AUTHOR INDEXES, 1941-1975:

A set of cumulative personal author indexes provides access by personal authors to documents listed in the *Monthly Catalog* between 1941 and 1975.[6] *Monthly Catalog* year and entry numbers, or when appropriate, page numbers, display following the authors' names. For instance, Peter Hirs' *Discussion of the Slovak Theater*, part of the Political Translations on Eastern Europe series, was entry number 784 in the January 1963 Catalog (Figure 2-14).

Figure 2-14
Personal Author Index, 1961-1965

```
Hiner, R.L. and Marsden, S.J.. REF.62-06541
Hiner, Richard L. ................ 65-15189
Hines, Bob ...................... 63-17451
    ILLS.65-00619
Hinnov, E. et al. ........... REF.65-10173
    REF.65-17103
Hinshaw, L.B. et al. ........ BIB.64-13728
Hinshaw, Lerner B. et al. .... REF.63-04503
    REF.64-05994 REF.64-05997
    REF.64-13734
Hinson, William C. and Strickler, Paul E.
    62-12929
Hinson, William F. and Falanga, Ralph A.
    REF.62-20137
Hinson, William F. and Foffman, Sherwood
    REF.64-03016
Hinson, William F. et al. .... REF.62-06280
Hintenberger, Heinrich and Ewald, Heinz
    LIT.63-01817
Hinteregger, H.E. ........... REF.64-20960
Hinteregger, H.E. and Hall, L.A.
    REF.61-08337
Hinteregger, H.E. et al. ..... REF.64-20965
    REF.65-10112
Hipp, Grace R. and Ateca, Harriet G.
    ASSI.63-03406
Hippollitus, Vincent P. ....... REM.61-04787
    REM.62-01572
Hipsley, Elmer et al. ........ TEST.62-23421
Hiraklis, Emanuel C. ......... BIB.61-03752
Hirs, Peter ................... 63-00784
Hirsch, Stanley N. ........... REF.62-17559
Hirschberg, Marvin H. et al. . REF.63-09152
Hirschfeld, A.B. ................ 61-09908
Hirschtritt, Moses and Lowe, Louise F.
    PREP.61-09037
Hirsh, N.B. ................... REF.65-20114
```

Source: *Personal Author Index, 1961-1965,* **page 110. Reprinted with permission from *Author Indexes To The Monthly Catalog, 1940-1975.* Copyright 1971-1979 by Pierian Press (Ann Arbor, MI). All rights reserved.**

SUPPLEMENTS TO THE *MONTHLY CATALOG*

SERIAL SUPPLEMENT AND *PERIODICAL SUPPLEMENT*

GPO incorporated a *Serial Supplement* into the *Monthly Catalog* between 1945 and 1984. In 1985, it became the *Periodical Supplement.*[7] The *Periodical Supplement* includes titles published at least quarterly. References to materials that appear semiannually, annually, and less frequently are in the *Monthly Catalog.* The *Title Index to U.S. Government Serials As Published by Readex Microprint Corp.*, a five volume set compiled by Margaret Rich, lists titles in the *Serial Supplement* between 1953 and 1980.[8] Consult the section below for information about Readex microprints of the *Monthly Catalog.*

Chapter 8 describes another *Monthly Catalog* supplement, the *United States Congressional Serial Set Catalog: Numerical Lists and Schedule of Volumes.*[9] The *Serial Set* is a compilation of reports and documents published by Congress.

READEX CORPORATION FILMS OF THE *MONTHLY CATALOG*

Filmed copies of documents listed in the *Monthly Catalog* are sold by the Readex Corporation. The two parts of this collection are *United States Government Publications (Depository)*[10], which covers 1956 to date, and *United States Government Publications (Non-Depository)*[11], which covers 1953 to date. Before 1981, Readex distributed the films on microprints, six by nine inch opaque cardboards, which are organized by *Monthly Catalog* entry numbers. Since then, distribution is on microfiche. Depending upon the library, locate the fiche by either SuDoc numbers or *Catalog* entry numbers.

ELECTRONIC VERSIONS OF THE *MONTHLY CATALOG*

The Government Printing Office put the *Monthly Catalog* on its world wide web server. (http://www.access.gpo.gov/su_docs/dpos/adpos 400.html). It includes documents cataloged since January 1994. Search for keywords that appear anywhere in the records, or limit keywords and numbers to specific fields. (e.g.: titles, years of publication, Superintendent of Documents numbers, item numbers, and stock numbers) Figure 2-15 displays a typical entry.

Figure 2-15
Monthly Catalog
GPO Web Server

WAIS Document Retrieval (p1 of 2)

Food allergies : rare but risky. 1994. United States. Food
and Drug Administration. HE 20.4010/A:AL 5/3. [[0475-H-01]].

****

<001> ocm30707607
<005> 19940705105054.0
<040a> GPO
<040c> GPO
<043a> n-us---
<074a> 0475-H-01
<086a> HE 20.4010/A:AL 5/3
<099a> HE 20.4010/A:AL 5/3
<049a> GPOO
<245a> Food allergies :
<245b> rare but risky.
<260a> Rockville, Md. :
<260b> Dept. of Health and Human Services, Public Health Service,
Food and Drug Administration,
<260c> 1994!

Titles, agencies, SuDoc numbers and item numbers appear across the top of the entry. The data below that reflect more detailed information that is associated with different fields in the database. Library users do not need to understand these fields to locate information on the shelves.

The CARL Corporation also makes the *Monthly Catalog* available to the public without charge. (telnet://database.carl.org) This version covers July 1976 to date. Screen displays are neater than that on the GPO web site (Figure 2-16).

Figure 2-16
Monthly Catalog
CARL

--Government Publication-----
TITLE(s):   Food allergies : rare but risky.

[Rockville, Md. : Dept. of Health and Human Services,
  Public Health Service, Food and Drug Administration, 1994]

1 folded sheet (6) : ill. ; 28 cm.
Publication ; no. (FDA) 94-2279
Caption title.
Shipping list no.: 94-0205-P.
A reprint from FDA consumer magazine, reprinted from
  December 1993--P. [4].

OTHER ENTRIES: Food allergy United States.
  United States. Food and Drug Administration.
  HHS publication ; no. (FDA) 94-2279.
DEP ITEM #   0475-H-01

LOCN: SEE OWNERS   STATUS: Current call number
CALL #: HE 20.4010/A:AL 5/3

more follows -- press <RETURN> (Q to quit)

**Reprinted with permission from the Colorado Alliance of Research Libraries
(Denver, CO). All rights reserved.**

Several commercial database vendors also provide online[12] and CD-ROM[13] access to the *Monthly Catalog*. GPO hopes to publish the *Monthly Catalog* on CD-ROM beginning in 1996.

PUBLICATIONS REFERENCE FILE

The *GPO Sales Publications Reference File*[14] is the Government Printing Office's sales catalog. It lists documents available for purchase from GPO on approximately 150 microfiche. A supplement to the *PRF*, *GPO New Sales Publications Microfiche* appears monthly on one or two microfiche. The *PRF* often indexes new documents more rapidly than the *Monthly Catalog*.

The *Publications Reference File*'s three sections include a numerical one by GPO stock numbers; an alphanumerical one by Superintendent of Documents numbers; and an alphabetical one by subjects, keywords, titles, authors, and series. The supplement only has an alphabetic section.

HEADERS, INDEX FRAMES, AND GRIDS

All fiche, regardless of the sections to which they belong, have headers and index frames. Headers located at the tops of the fiche include the *PRF* title, dates, fiche numbers, and ranges of information covered on specific fiche (Figure 2-17).

Figure 2-17
PRF **Headers**
Stock Number Section

FR: 001-000-00622-3 GPO SALES	·	1 OF 140
TO: 003-024007113-4 PUBLICATIONS REFERENCE FILE		APRIL 16, 1992

SuDoc Number Section

FR: A 1.10:984 GPO SALES	33 OF 140
TO: AE 2.110:101-246 PUBLICATIONS REFERENCE FILE	APRIL 16, 1992

Alphabetical Section

FR: A GPO SALES	45 OF 140
TO: AERONAUTICS AND SP PUBLICATIONS REFERENCE FILE	APRIL 16, 1992

Test your knowledge of *PRF* headers: Answer the following questions using Figure 2-17.

1. When was this edition of *PRF* made available?

(April 16, 1992)

2. The upper right hand corner of the Alphabetic Section header indicates 45 of 140. What does this mean?

    (This microfiche is the 45th in a set consisting of 140.)

3. True or false: SuDoc numbers beginning with AE2.2: are located on fiche 33 of 140.

    (True. Fiche 33 of 140 includes SuDoc numbers A1.10:984 through AE2.110:101-246.)

Index frames enable researchers to determine on which grids information is located. Grids are alphanumeric rows and columns that pinpoint specific microfiche frames. Horizontal rows are A-O and vertical columns are 1-18. For instance, the first frame on the fiche is A1. (Row A, column 1) (Figure 2-18)

Figure 2-18
PRF **Microfiche Grid Arrangement**

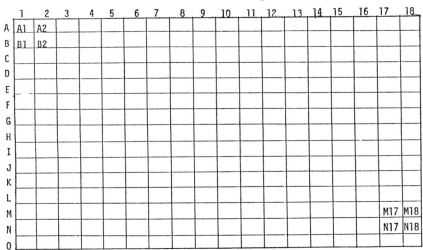

The following illustrates typical entries from index frames (Figure 2-19).

Figure 2-19
PRF **Index Frames**

GRID		KEY PH
J	3	ALIENS
K	3	ALIMONY
L	3	ALL HANDS MAGAZINE
M	3	ALL WORLD IMPORTS
N	3	ALLEN E J
O	3	ALLEN M D
A	4	ALLEN ROBERT V
B	4	ALLEN SHERIDA
C	4	ALLENSPACH F
D	4	ALLERGIES
E	4	ALLIANCE FOR EXCEL
F	4	ALLISON C M
G	4	ALLISON C M
H	4	ALLOWANCES FOR TRA
I	4	ALLOYS
J	4	ALMANAC FOR COMPUT

Test your knowledge using the index frames: Answer the following using Figure 2-19:

Which frame includes information about allergies?

(D4)

Researchers can also determine which columns have their information by scanning horizontally across row A. Suppose grid A1 begins with the keyword car and A2 with census, entries about cats appear in column 1.

Figure 2-20
PRF: **Scanning Subjects Across Top Line of Grid**

Cars	Census			
Cats				

ALPHABETIC SECTION

Figure 2-21 illustrates how the *PRF* displays information by subjects.

Figure 2-21
PRF **Citation**
Subject Entry

```
KEY PHRASE                 ALLERGIES
                                                    STOCK NUMBER:  001-000-04512-1
  STOCK STATUS:  IN STOCK - WAREHOUSE & RETAIL (PRICED)          LOCATION: U3
  STATUS CODE  04     STATUS DATE:  09/11/89    ISBN:  0-16-000073-4
                                                  CLASS NO. A1.77:246
        TITLE:          Cooking for People With Food Allergies.
        DOCUMENT SOURCE: Agriculture Dept., Human Nutrition Information Service
        IMPRINT:         1988: 40 P.
        DESCRIPTION:     Home and Gargen Bulletin 246.  Provides information to help in selecting
                         and preparing foods that do not contain milk, eggs, corn, or wheat; tips
                         to help recognize these ingredients in prepared foods; and recipes
                         designed to help avoid them.  Item 011.
        NOTE:            Supersedes: Baking for People with Food Allergies, A1.77:147/2, S/N
                         001-000-03362-0.  BIP.  DSL 88-182-P 03/25/88.  NB1205.  GB1104  GB1105 GB1106
                         GB1107
        SB NOS:          276EC 291DC                                     PUB DATE:  88/03/21
        BINDING:         Paper cover, stitch; Paper.
        PRICE:           02/25/88                    Discount              Weight: 4 oz.
                         Each           $1.50 domestic     $1.88 foreign
```

Key parts of Figure 2-21 most useful to library users include:

-**Stock no:** Cite the stock number when ordering documents from GPO.

-**Key Phrase:** The Key phrase determines the type of entry cited. (i.e. stock number, SuDoc number, subject heading, author, title, or series)

-**Class no:** SuDoc number.

-**Title**.

-**Document source:** Publishing agency.

-**Imprint:** Date of publication and pagination.

-**Description:** A brief abstract; a report and/or contract number; a series title; an alternate title; the Library of Congress card number; and/or the item number are sometimes included.

-**Note:** Information describes the weight of the document and supersession data.

-**SB NOS:** The Subject Bibliography numbers on which this title appears. Subject Bibliographies are discussed below in the "Selected Bibliographies of Government Publications" section of this chapter, and in Chapter 18 that describes the GPO sales program.

-**Price:** Discount notations in the price section indicate that one hundred or more copies are available at a twenty-five percent reduction.

Figure 2-22 is an example of a *PRF* title entry.

Figure 2-22
PRF Citation
Title Entry

```
KEY PHRASE              COOKING FOR PEOPLE WITH FOOD ALLERGIES
                                                   STOCK NUMBER:  001-000-04512-1
STOCK STATUS:  IN STOCK - WAREHOUSE & RETAIL (PRICED)        LOCATION: U3
STATUS CODE  04    STATUS DATE:  09/11/89    ISBN:  0-16-000073-4
                                             CLASS NO. A1.77:246

        TITLE:          Cooking for People With Food Allergies.
        DOCUMENT SOURCE: Agriculture Dept., Human Nutrition Information Service
        IMPRINT:        1988: 40 P.
        DESCRIPTION:    Home and Gargen Bulletin 246.  Provides information to help in selecting
                        and preparing foods that do not contain milk, eggs, corn, or wheat; tips
                        to help recognize these ingredients in prepared foods; and recipes
                        designed to help avoid them.  Item 011.
        NOTE:           Supersedes: Baking for People with Food Allergies, A1.77:147/2, S/N
                        001-000-03362-0.  BIP.  DSL 88-182-P 03/25/88.  NB1205.  GB1104  GB1105 GB1106
                        GB1107
        SB NOS:         276EC 291DC                                   PUB DATE:   88/03/21
        BINDING:        Paper cover, stitch; Paper.
        PRICE:          02/25/88                  Discount              Weight: 4 oz.
                        Each            $1.50 domestic        $1.88 foreign
```

Test your knowledge of *PRF* **citations**: The following questions relate to Figures 2-21 and 2-22.

1. What is the title of this document?

   (Cooking For People With Food Allergies)

2. What is its SuDoc number?

   (A1.77:246)

3. Which agency published this title?

   (Agriculture Department, Human
   Nutrition Information Service)

4. The stock number is_____.

   (001-000-04512-1)

5. Its domestic price is_____ and its foreign price is_____.

   (domestic--$1.50; foreign--$1.88)

PUBLICATIONS REFERENCE FILE: STOCK AND SUDOC NUMBER SECTIONS

Information in the stock number and Superintendent of Documents Number sections of the *PRF* appear similar to that in Figures 2-21 and 2-22. Instead of a keyword or title as the key phrase, substitute the relevant number.

OUT OF PRINT DOCUMENTS

The *Out-of-Print GPO Sales Publications Reference File*[15] indexes documents that are no longer available for sale. Cumulative editions cover 1980, 1985-1989, and 1990-1993.

FURTHER INFORMATION ABOUT THE *PRF*

Consult *PRF User's Manual: A Guide to Using the GPO Sales Publications Reference File*[16] for more information.

ELECTRONIC VERSIONS OF THE *PRF*

Several commercial database vendors provide online access to the *PRF*.[17] *Popular Government Publications*[18] is a CD-ROM version of the database. The Readex Corporation sells microfiche copies of documents indexed in *Popular Government Publications*.[19]

COMPREHENSIVE INDEXES

PUBLISHED BY THE CONGRESSIONAL INFORMATION SERVICE

The Congressional Information Service (CIS) is a leading publisher that indexes, abstracts, and films government publications. Three CIS products are important comprehensive indexes.

American Foreign Policy Index: A Guide To Foreign Policy and Foreign Relations Publications of the U.S. Government. Bethesda, MD.: Congressional Information Service, Inc., 1993-quarterly.

Indexes information about all aspects of U.S. foreign policy. It includes executive agency publications, Congressional reports, and reports of quasi governmental agencies. The subject matter covers the analysis of foreign policy; official statements; data about political and socioeconomic conditions in foreign countries; and treaties and executive agreements. Use the following five indexes to locate information: the Index by Subjects and Names, the Index by Titles, the Index by Agency Report Numbers, the Index by Congressional Bill Numbers, and the Index by Superintendent of Documents Classification Numbers. CIS also publishes a comparable microfiche collection that includes the texts of the documents.[20] The fiche include publications downloaded from federal electronic sources.

Reports Required by Congress: CIS Guide to Executive Communications. Bethesda, MD.: Congressional Information Service, Inc., 1994-quarterly.

Indexes documents that executive agencies must submit to Congress. These materials are usually difficult to locate because GPO distributes few to depository libraries. Locate information in the Index by Subjects under subject headings, names of agencies, and personal names. Two additional indexes include the Index by Executive Communication Numbers, the numbers assigned to the documents by Congress, and the Index by Statutory Authorities, which is arranged by *U.S. Code (U.S.C.)* citations. The *U.S.C.* is a compilation of federal laws that is described in a subsequent chapter. CIS films copies of documents indexed in *Reports Required by Congress*, providing the same have not already been filmed for another CIS collection.[21]

U.S. Government Periodicals Index. Bethesda, MD.: Congressional Information Service, Inc., 1993-quarterly.

Indexes articles in nearly 200 periodicals published by the U.S. government. Coverage includes items that review research results; discuss government programs and policies; and provide general interest information. Bibliographies, calendars, in-house news designed to boost agency morale, and documentary materials, such as texts of regulations or the *Weekly Compilation of Presidential Documents*[22], are excluded. CIS also publishes this product in CD-ROM format.[23] It is available online from the Research Libraries Group.[24] An earlier index, the *Index to U.S. Government Periodicals*[25], covers 1970-1987.

GOVERNMENT INFORMATION LOCATOR SERVICE (GILS)

INTRODUCTION

The Government Information Locator Service (GILS) is an electronic network that describes all information prepared by the executive branch. A locator is an information resource that describes other resources and explains how to acquire that data. Library users depend upon card or online catalogs to describe a library's holdings and to locate the relevant sources through call numbers. The federal government expects GILS to become a "virtual card catalog" of government information.[26] The Clinton Administration argues that:

> Every year, the federal government spends billions, of dollars collecting and processing information (e.g. economic data, environmental data, and technical information). Unfortunately, while much of this information is very valuable, many potential users either do not know that it exists or do not know how to access it. We are committed to using new computer and networking technology to make this information more accessible to the taxpayers who paid for it.[27]

The Office of Management and Budget required agencies to have their GILS systems available to the public by December 31, 1995 and required agencies to update their systems regularly.[28]

GILS is a powerful and flexible information resource. Its user friendly design appeal to lay people, yet it also has sufficient power to accommodate complex research queries. Besides being an information access tool, GILS also has the potential of assisting agencies in fulfilling their recordkeeping, document retention, and document appraisal functions.

KINDS OF INFORMATION INCLUDED AND EXCLUDED FROM GILS

GILS deals with all information formats, including print, audio visual, and electronic sources. Agencies must include three kinds of data.

-Information access tools, such as catalogs and related materials that describe books, cd-roms, studies, and patents.

-Automated information systems that process, maintain, transmit or disseminate information.

-Privacy act record systems.

GILS excludes four types of data.

-E-mail messages.

-Word processing systems.

-Information that could compromise national security.

-Information that could interfere with law enforcement.

HOW DOES GILS WORK?

Although each agency develops and maintains its locator service in a decentralized fashion. The requirement to base the systems upon Federal Information Processing Standard 192[29] guarantees consistency and inter-connectivity. Agencies have options to create the systems themselves; contract with information processing services operated by other agencies or the private sector; or develop interagency cooperative efforts. GPO has the responsibility of integrating all the GILS into one umbrella system.

The public use GILS directly or through intermediaries, such as depository libraries and private vendors. Office of Management and Budget Bulletin No. 95-1 requires that availability be without charge "...particularly to depository libraries, other libraries, and members of the public with Internet access."[30]

GILS RECORDS

Compare the similarities and differences between an online catalog record and a GILS record to better understand the GILS concept. Figure 2-23 displays typical online catalog data for *Americans with Disabilities, 1991-92* and Figure 2-24 displays a GILS record for the identical title.

Figure 2-23
Online Catalog Record

TITLE: Americans with disabilities, 1991-92 : data from the Survey of
            income and program participation / by John M. McNeil.

AUTHOR: McNeil, John M.

CONTRIBUTORS: United States. Bureau of the Census.

PUBLISHED: Washington, DC : U.S. Dept. of Commerce, Economics and
              Statistics Administration, Bureau of the Census : For sale
              by the Supt. of Docs., U.S. G.P.O., [1993]

DESCRIPTION: 1 v. (various pagings) : ill. ; 28 cm.

SUBJECTS (SL=): Handicapped--United States--Statistics.
            Handicapped--Employment--United States--Statistics.
            Handicapped--United States--Economic conditions--Statistics.

SERIES: Current population reports. Series P-70, Household economic
            studies ; no. 33.

NOTES: Shipping list no.: 94-0057-P.
            "Issued December 1993."
            Includes bibliographical references (p. 14-15).

CALL NUMBER: C3.186:P-70/2/no.33

Figure 2-24
GILS Record

Title: Americans With Disabilities: 1991-92 (P-70 No. 33)
Originator:
   Department/Agency Name: U.S. Department of Commerce, Bureau of
        the Census
Controlled Vocabulary:
   Index Terms - Controlled:
        Controlled Term: Earnings
        Controlled Term: Employment (USE for Employment Services)
        Controlled Term: Household Economic Studies (USE for P-70
    Local Subject Term:
Abstract: Presents data on the disability status of the
        noninstitutional population of the United States.
        Tables show number and percent distribution of persons
        with disabilities; low-income status; employment status;
        number and percent of employed persons; mean earnings;
        distribution of workers; conditions reported as cause of
        physical limitations on Activities of Daily Living (ADL)
        or Instrumental Activities of Daily Living (IADL); and
        disability status of children. Tables cross-classify
        data by age, sex, type of disability, race and Hispanic
        origin, family relationship, years of school completed,
        ratio of income to low-income threshold, health
        insurance coverage status, means-tested assistance, and
        whether in an owner-occupied or renter-occupied unit.
Purpose: To be entered.
Agency Program:
Availability:
Distributor:
    Name: Ordering Desk
    Organization: Government Printing Office
    Mail Stop: Ordering & Inquiry
    Street Address: North Capitol & G Streets, NW
    City: Washington
    State: DC   Zip Code: 20401
    Telephone: (202) 783-3238
    Additional Information: Retail Sales Outlet: (301)
                953-7974
                Bookstores:
                    Central Office (202) 512-0132
                    Farragut West (202) 653-6075
  Resource Description: S/N 803-044-0021-0.
  Order Process: This is a printed report. Price: $6.50
   Available Linkage:
   Available Linkage Type:
Sources Of Data:
Access Constraints: None.
Use Constraints: None.
Point of Contact:
    Name: Customer Services
    Organization: Bureau of the Census
    Mail Stop:

            Telephone: (301) 457-4100
    FAX: (301) 457-4714
    TDD: (301) 457-4611
    Additional Information:
  Control Identifier: DOC   CENSUS   00003
  Record Source:
    Department/Agency Name: U.S. Department of Commerce
    Name of Unit: Bureau of the Census
  Date Of Last Modification: 12/16/95

Chart 2-2 describes selected significant parts of the GILS record. Figure 2-24 illustrates that agencies do not always complete every part of the record. In many cases, particular sections are irrelevant. Consult the National Archives document, "Information for Archivists and Records Managers/GILS Guidance," for detailed explanations of all parts of GILS records.[31]

Chart 2-2
Significant Parts of GILS Record

Title	Name assigned by the originating agency.
Originator	Agency that created the data.
Controlled Vocabulary	The subject terms from a thesaurus that guarantees consistency among subject headings. All related records prepared by the same agency use identical or similar subject headings.
Local Subject Term	Subject headings not based upon a thesaurus.
Abstract	A summary that should enable readers to determine if the information is useful to their needs. Abstracts are generally within 500 words.
Purpose	Explains why the information was produced. The abstract describes content of the information, not its reason for being.
Agency program	Describes the agency program or mission the data supports and often includes citations to legislative authority.
Availability	Explains how to acquire the data. In figure 2-28, the data in question is a printed report available for sale from GPO for $6.50.
Resource description	Identifies the item as referred to by the distributor. Figure 2-24 cites the stock number (S/N), the code used by GPO sales staff for this title.
Access constraints	Describes limitations to access and instructions for acquiring manuals/documentation. Privacy concerns or disclosure of trade secrets are two examples that inhibit access.
Use constraints	Covers any constraints or legal prerequisites for accessing the information. Copyrights and other trade restrictions are limiting factors. Use constraints also cover disclaimers that the information may be inappropriate for some purposes. For instance, statistical limitations sometimes inhibit usefulness of data.
Point of contact	Informs the researcher who to contact in the originating agency for more information.

Test your understanding of GILS records: Refer to Figures 2-23 and 2-24 when answering the following.

1. Which type of record is more useful to your needs: an online catalog record or a GILS record?

2. Can you think of situations where you would prefer one over the other?

SEARCHING GILS

The Government Printing Office ACCESS system includes a comprehensive collection of GILS databases. (http://www.access.gpo.gov/su_docs/gils/gils.html) Search the system using a three step process.

1. Select databases for one or more agencies or select "All Records on GPO ACCESS GILS Site" by pressing enter. Selected databases have asterisks (*) (Figure 2-25).

Figure 2-25
Selecting GILS Databases on GPO ACCESS

(*) All Records on GPO Access GILS Site
( ) Pathway GILS Records created by GPO
( ) Pointer Records to other GILS sites
( ) Individual Agency GILS databases on GPO Access
( ) ....Consumer Product Safety Commission
( ) ....Department of Commerce
( ) ....Department of State
( ) ....Department of Treasury
( ) ....Equal Employment Opportunity Commission
( ) ....Farm Credit Administration
( ) ....Federal Communications Commission
( ) ....Federal Emergency Management Agency
( ) ....Federal Labor Relations Authority
( ) ....Federal Maritime Commission
( ) ....Federal Reserve Board

2. Enter search terms and click on submit. The example in Figure 2-26 searches all databases for information about children with disabilities. Figure 2-26 also summarizes search protocol.

Figure 2-26
Searching GILS Databases on GPO ACCESS

(*) All Records on GPO Access GILS Site
( ) Pathway GILS Records created by GPO
( ) Pointer Records to other GILS sites
( ) Individual Agency GILS databases on GPO Access
( ) ....Consumer Product Safety Commission
( ) ....Department of Commerce
( ) ....Department of State

Enter search term(s):
children AND disabilities_____ SUBMIT CLEAR

Maximum Records Returned: 40_ Default is 40. Maximum is 200.

Phrases must be in quotation marks (" "). The operators ADJ
(adjacent), AND, OR and NOT can be used, but must be capital letters.
For example: "foreign affairs" AND "cd-rom". Word roots can be
searched using an astersik (*) following the word stem. For example:
legislat* will retrieve both legislation and legislative.

3.   Highlight the appropriate reference and press enter (Figure 2-27).

Figure 2-27
Viewing Search Results

For: "children AND disabilities"

Total Hits: 3

[1]
GILS: Medical Discrimination Against Children with Disabilities.
    Size: 3498 , Score: 1000 , TEXT
[2]
GILS: Americans With Disabilities: 1991-92 (P-70 No. 33)
    Size: 3672 , Score: 983 , TEXT
[3]
Query Report for this Search
    Size: 1571 , Score: 1 , TEXT

Additional features allow people to search specific fields of GILS records (Figure 2-28). Asterisks (*) highlight fields that are selected.

Figure 2-28
Searching Specific Fields Within GILS Records

Select one or more of the following fields (mandatory GILS core
elements) to search:

(*) Abstract	( ) Originator
( ) Access Constraints	( ) Point of Contact for Further Information
( ) Agency Program	(*) Purpose
( ) Availability	( ) Record Source
( ) Control Identifier	( ) Sources of Data
(*) Controlled Vocabulary	( ) Spatial Reference
( ) Cross Reference	( ) Schedule Number
( ) Date of Last Modification	( ) Supplemental Information
(*) Local Subject Index	( ) Time Period of Contact
( ) Methodology	(*) Title
( ) Original Control Identifier	( ) Use Constraints

SUBMIT CLEAR

SELECTED BIBLIOGRAPHIES OF GOVERNMENT PUBLICATIONS

Bailey, William G., comp. *Guide to Popular U.S. Government Publications.*
3rd ed. Englewood, CO: Libraries Unlimited, 1993.

Lists popular interest government documents that are appropriate for
school and public libraries. Entries include authors, titles, dates, stock
numbers, Superintendent of Document numbers, and prices. Although the
annotations are brief, they are still informative. Indexing is by titles and
subjects.

Government Reference Books. Englewood, CO: Libraries Unlimited,
1968/69-biennial. Latest editions compiled by LeRoy Schwarzkopf.

Covers atlases; bibliographies; catalogs; compendia; dictionaries; directories; guides; handbooks; indexes; and other reference works published
by the federal government during the most recent two years. Most publications are depository documents. Documents published in microfiche
format are included with the tenth edition. Indexing is by authors, titles,
and subjects.

Robinson, Judith. *Subject Guide to U.S. Government Reference Sources.*
Englewood, CO: Libraries Unlimited, 1985. (Revised edition forthcoming
in 1996).

Four sections deal with general; social science; science and technology;
and humanities reference sources. The compilers include print and electronic sources published by GPO, the National Technical Information
Service, and other federal agencies. They also cite references to commercial
database vendors.

U.S. Government Printing Office. *New Books: Publications For Sale by the Government Printing Office.* Washington, D.C.: GPO, 1982-bimonthly. SuDoc #: GP3.17/6:.

Covers publications made available for sale by GPO during the preceding two months. Purchase information, order forms, and a list of GPO bookstores and their telephone/fax numbers are given. *New Books* is available gratis.

U.S. Government Printing Office. *Subject Bibliographies.* Washington, D.C.: GPO. Most bibliographies are updated regularly. SuDoc #'s: GP3.22/2:.

Subject bibliographies are brief lists of popular items available for sale from GPO. They deal with approximately 300 broad topics. See Chapter 18 that describes the GPO sales program for more information.

U.S. Government Printing Office. *United States Government Information.* Washington, D.C.: GPO, quarterly. SuDoc number: GP3.17/5:. Previous title: *U.S. Government Books: Publications For Sale by the Government Printing Office.*

This colorful, attractive, quarterly sales catalog is comparable to those of commercial publishers. Two sections describe "New Selections" and "Popular Favorites." Helpful annotations describe each title. Most items deal with current issues that appeal to general audiences. Purchase information, order forms, and a list of GPO bookstores and their phone and fax numbers are provided. *U.S. Government Information* is available free upon request.

Zink, Steven D. *United States Government Publications Catalogs.* 2nd ed. Washington, D.C.: Special Libraries Association, 1988.

Describes over 370 catalogs, bibliographies, and publication lists prepared by federal agencies. This important research tool will sometimes be the only way to become aware of non-depository materials that are not widely available. Coverage includes print, audiovisual, and electronic formats. Note, during the 1990's many agencies discontinued publications of the sources Zink mentions due to financial restrictions.

CONCLUSION

Unfortunately, there is no one source that lists all United States government publications. Problems associated with locating government documents are described in the "Introduction" to this book. Chart 2-3 summarizes major features of three comprehensive sources: the *Monthly Catalog*, the *Publications Reference File*, and the Government Information Locator Service.

Chart 2-3
Monthly Catalog, Publications Reference File, **and**
Government Information Locator Service: **A Comparison**

	Monthly Catalog	PRF	GILS
Main Focus	Comprehensive catalog of publications issued by executive and independent agencies, Congress and congressional agencies, and the judiciary.	Catalog of materials available for sale from the Government Printing Office.	All federal government information sources in all formats. Includes both published and unpublished data.
Author Index	Yes	Included in alphabetical section.	Yes
Title Index	Yes	Included in alphabetical section.	Yes
Subject Index	Yes	Included in alphabetical section.	Yes
Key Word Index	Yes	Included in alphabetical section.	Yes
SuDoc Index	Yes	Yes	No
Report Number Index	Yes	Yes	Yes
Stock Number Index	Yes	Yes	Resource description field.
Online Access	Dialog/Knight Rider file 66. OCLC EPIC file 10.	Dialog/Knight Rider file 166.	(http://www.gpo.access.gov/su_docs/gils/gils.html)
CD-ROM Access	Government Documents Catalog Service. Government Publications Index on InfoTrac. GPO on SilverPlatter. LePac: Government Documents Option. Marcive GPO CAT/PAC.	Popular Government Publications Index on CD-ROM.	None

Endnotes

1. U.S. Government Printing Office (Washington, D.C.: GPO, 1951-monthly). SuDoc number: GP3.8:. Earlier editions were published under other titles: *Catalog of Publications Issued by the Government of the United States* (January-March, 1895); *Catalog of United States Public Documents* (April, 1895-June, 1907); *Monthly Catalog, United States Public Documents* (July, 1907-December, 1939); and *United States Government Publications: A Monthly Catalog* (1940-1950).

2. Preparation of annual cumulative indexes is still under consideration by GPO. GPO recognizes the importance of cumulative indexes and is approaching this with an open mind. Cost consideration is a significant issue. Improved access to the GPO WWW site is an alternative to cumulative indexes. (Telephone conversation with Thomas A. Downing, Chief of the Cataloging Branch, Library Programs Service, GPO, May 30, 1996).

3. Librarians use OCLC numbers to identify cataloging records in the OCLC database. Shipping lists are inventories that identify documents sent to depository libraries by GPO.

4. William W. Buchannan and Edna M. Kanely (Washington, D.C.: Carrollton Press, 1973-1975). 15 vols.

5. U.S. Government Printing Office, *United States Government Publications, Monthly Catalog: Decennial Cumulative Index 1941-1950* (Washington, D.C.: GPO, 1953); U.S. Government Printing Office, *Monthly Catalog of United States Government Publications: Decennial Cumulative Index 1951-1960* (Washington, D.C.: GPO, 1968). 2 vols.; U.S. Government Printing Office, *Monthly Catalog of United States Government Publications: Cumulated Index. . .* (Washington, D.C.: GPO). Five editions cover 1961-1965, 1966-1970, 1971-June 1976, July 1976-1980 (microfiche), and 1981-1985 (microfiche). SuDoc numbers: GP3.8/3:. Reprints of the microfiche indexes covering 1976-1980 and 1981-1985 are available. (*Monthly Catalog of United States Government Publications Cumulative Index 1976-1980* (Phoenix, AZ.: Oryx Press, 1987), 6 vols. and *Monthly Catalog of United States Government Publications Cumulative Index 1981-1985* (Phoenix, AZ.: Oryx Press, 1988), 7 vols.)

6. Edward Przebienda, ed., *United States Government Publications Monthly Catalog: Decennial Cumulative Personal Author Index* (Ann Arbor: Pierian Press, 1971). 2 vols. cover 1941-1960. Przebienda deals with 1961-1975 in three additional volumes, *United States Government Publications Monthly Catalog: Quinquinnial Cumulative Personal Author Index* (Ann Arbor: Pierian Press, 1971-1979).

7.   U.S. Government Printing Office, *Monthly Catalog of United States Government Publications. Periodical Supplement* (Washington, D.C.: GPO, 1985-annual). SuDoc number: GP3.8/5:.

8.   (New York: Readex Corp., 1978-1987). 5 vols. cover 1953-1955, 1956-1960, 1961-1970, 1971-1975, 1976-1980.

9.   U.S. Government Printing Office (Washington, D.C.: GPO, 1983/1984-biennial). SuDoc number: GP3.34:. Title and SuDoc number for the 1981/1982 edition varies: U.S. Government Printing Office. *Monthly Catalog of United States Government Publications. United States Congressional Serial Set Supplement* (Washington, D.C.: GPO, 1985). SuDoc number: GP3.8/6:981-982.

10.   (New York: Readex Microprint Corporation, 1956-monthly).

11.   (New York: Readex Microprint Corporation, 1953-monthly).

12.   *GPO Monthly Catalog* (File 66) (Online database). Available on: Dialog/Knight Ridder, Mountain View, CA.; *GPO Monthly Catalog* (File 10) (Online database). Available on: OCLC EPIC, Dublin, OH.; and *GPO Monthly Catalog* (File 8) (Online database). Available on: OCLC First Search, Dublin, OH.

13.   All CD-ROMs cover July 1976 to date. *Government Documents Catalog Service* (CD-ROM) (Pomona, CA.: Auto-Graphics, Inc., monthly, bimonthly, or quarterly, depending upon the subscription); *Government Publications Index* (CD-ROM) (Forest City, CA.: Information Access Company, monthly); *GPO CAT/PAC* (CD-ROM) (San Antonio, TX.: MARCIVE, Inc., monthly); and *GPO on SilverPlatter* (CD-ROM) (Norwood, MA.: SilverPlatter Information, Inc., monthly).

Both the Auto-Graphics and Information Access versions are menu driven and easy to use. However, Auto-Graphics provides more search options than Information Access. Users can search by authors, titles, subjects and keywords, and can combine more than one phrase. SilverPlatter is not menu driven, but experienced searchers will find this package more powerful than the others.

A study by a group of library school students evaluated the MAR-CIVE, SilverPlatter and OCLC versions (OCLC is no longer produced). It concluded that "Marcive was...the easiest to use for a beginner, with clear menus and an intuitive user interface." (Charles Seavey, "Three CD-ROM Versions of the GPO Database: A Comparison with an Editorial Observation," *Documents To The People* 19:2 (June 1991), 117.)

14.   (Washington, D.C.: GPO, 1977-bimonthly). SuDoc number: GP3.22/3:.

15. U.S. Government Printing Office (Washington, D.C.: GPO, 1980-annual). SuDoc number: GP3.22/3-3:. The 1980 edition was published as U.S. Government Printing Office. *Exhausted GPO Sales Publications Reference File* (Washington, D.C.: GPO, 1980). SuDoc number: GP3-22/3-3:.

16. (Washington, D.C.: GPO, 1981). SuDoc number: GP3.29:P96.

17. *GPO Publications Reference File* (File 166) (Online database) Dialog/Knight-Ridder, Mountain View, CA.; and *GPO Publications Reference File* (File GOVE1) (Online database) Compuserve Knowledge Index, Columbus, OH. Bernan and Claitors, two book dealers that sell government documents, provide free Internet access to the *Publications Reference File*. Contact Bernan at gopher://kraus.com; telnet kraus.com; or telnet bernan.com. Type gpn at the login prompt. Contact Claitors at http://www.claitors.com.

18. *Popular Government Publications* (CD-ROM) (New Canaan, CT: Readex Microprint Corporation, quarterly).

19. *Popular Government Publications.* (New Canaan, CT: Readex Microprint Corporation, 199(?)-quarterly) (Microfiche).

20. *American Foreign Policy Index* (Bethesda, MD.: Congressional Information Service, Inc., 1993-quarterly). Microfiche.

21. *Reports Required by Congress: CIS Guide to Executive Communications* (Bethesda, MD.: Congressional Information Service, Inc., 1994-quarterly). Microfiche.

22. *Weekly Compilation of Presidential Documents* (Washington, D.C.: GPO, 1965-weekly). SuDoc number: AE2.109:.

23. *U.S. Government Periodicals Index* (CD-ROM) (Bethesda, MD.: Congressional Information Service, Inc., 1993-quarterly). Consult the following for more information: *U.S. Government Periodicals Index on CD-ROM: Reference Manual* (Bethesda, MD.: Congressional Information Service, Inc., 1994).

24. *U.S. Government Periodicals Index* (Online database) Available on: Research Libraries Group CitaDel Service, Palo Alto, CA.

25. (Chicago: Infordata International, 1970-1987).

26. U.S. Office of Management and Budget. *Establishment of Government Information Locator Service* (OMB Bulletin No. 95-01) December 7, 1994. (http://www.whitehouse.gov/WH/EOP/OMB/html/bulletins/95-01.html)

27. William J. Clinton and Vice President Albert Gore, Jr. *Technology for America's Economic Growth: a New Direction to Build Economic*

Strength (Washington, D.C.: GPO, 1993), 29. SuDoc number: PR42.2:AM3/4. Cited in Eliot J. Christian, "Helping the Public Find Information: The U.S. Government Information Locator Service (GILS)," *Journal of Government Information.* 21:4 (1994), 305.

28. *Establishment of Government Information Locator Service* (OMB Bulletin No. 95-01), December 7, 1994. Referenced: June 3, 1996. Internet address: http://www.whitehouse.gov/WH/EOP/OMB/html/ bulletins/95-01.html

29. *Application Profile For the Government Information Locator Service (GILS)* (FIPS Pub 192) (Springfield, VA.: NTIS, 1994). NTIS accession code: FIPS PUB 192/XAB. Also available on Internet. Referenced: May 22, 1996. Internet address: http://www.dtic.dla.mil /gils/documents/naradoc/fip192.html.

30. *Establishment of Government Information Locator Service* (OMB Bulletin No. 95-01).

31. March 1995. Referenced May 22, 1996. Internet address: http://www.nara.gov:70/1/managers/gils/guidance.

Exercises

1. Use the *Publications Reference File* to locate a list of maps that are currently available for sale from the Government Printing Office. Note the titles and costs of three maps.

2. Locate a document published by the Office of Technology Assessment that deals with greenhouse gases.

    A. What is the title?

    B. When was this item published?

    C. What is the SuDoc number?

    D. Is this title available for sale from the Government Printing Office? If yes, how much does it cost?

    E. Locate three additional documents that deal with global warming.

3. The federal government recently published a document about technologies used for treating hazardous wastes. I think the title might be *Technologies: A Compendium of Strategies Used in the Treatment of Hazardous Wastes*, but I am uncertain.

    A. If the given title is incorrect, what is the correct one?

    B. Who published it?

    C. What is the Superintendent of Documents number?

    D. What is the report number of this document?

    E. Locate three additional documents about technologies used for treating hazardous wastes. Note the publishing agencies, titles, dates of publication, and SuDoc numbers. Use one of the following Internet sites that covers the *Monthly Catalog*.
    http://www.access.gpo.gov/su_docs/dpos/adpos400.html
    telnet database.carl.org
    telnet pucc.princeton.edu

4. Search the Government Information Locator Service to find information about programs that track expenditures for pollution control.

Answers

1.   Search the *PRF* under the term "Maps."

2. A. *Changing by Degrees: Steps to Reduce Greenhouse Gases.*

   B. 1991.

   C. Y3.T22/2:2D36/3.

   D. Consult the *PRF*.

3. A. *A Compendium of Technologies Used in the Treatment of Hazardous Wastes.*

   B. Center for Environmental Research Information, Office of Research and Development, Environmental Protection Agency.

   C. EP1.2:T22/8.

   D. EPA 625/8-87/014.

4.   As of July 1996, the search, pollution AND expenditures, resulted in three items:

   GILS: BEA Reports: Pollution Abatement and Control Expenditures
   GILS: Stocks and Underlying Data for Air and Water Pollution
   GILS: Environmental Estimates - General Information

•Chapter 3

General Indexes to Historical Documents

Answer the following questions when reading this chapter:

1. What problems do researchers face when using historical government publications?

2. What are the similarities/differences and advantages/disadvantages of using the *Checklist of United States Public Documents, 1789-1909* and the *CIS Index to U.S. Executive Branch Documents, 1789-1909*?

3. Explain which source cited in the "Additional Guides and Indexes to Historical Documents" section of the chapter is most useful to your needs.

The previous chapter discussed general indexes to current government publications. This one covers guides and indexes to historical documents. The nature of historical documents and problems associated with their use are examined first. Detailed descriptions of the *Checklist of United States Public Documents, 1789-1909* and the *CIS Index to U.S. Executive Branch Documents, 1789-1909* follow. The discussion also summarizes selected additional indexes, catalogs, and handbooks.

HISTORICAL GOVERNMENT PUBLICATIONS AND PROBLEMS ASSOCIATED WITH THEIR USE

Executive agencies in the 19th century, such as the Immigration Bureau, the Treasury Department, and the Surgeon General, faced restrictions on their printing. The definition of public documents was "Such publications or books as have been or may be published procured, or purchased by order of either House of Congress, or a joint resolution..."[1] Consequently, most printing was done by Congressional mandate. The *Congressional Serial Set*, a compilation of reports and documents published by Congress since 1817, included many executive agency documents. Each volume has been numbered consecutively since then. A subsequent chapter includes a detailed description of the *Serial Set*. Furthermore, newspapers, rather than the government, published a great deal of information. Donald Ritchie explains how details of Senate executive or closed sessions were leaked to the press.[2] The Senators who provided the information in turn received favorable newspaper coverage.

Until recently, access to 19th century documents was poor. F.A. Crandall, the first Superintendent of Documents, stated in 1896 that:

> "There is probably not a man living who could tell off hand
> what is the subject matter of Part 2 of Part 2 of Volume 4
> of part 5 of no. 1 of part 2, volume 14 of the House
> Executive documents of the Fifty-First Congress, second
> session. One might as well try to commit to memory
> lettering on a Chinese tea chest as charge one's mind with
> such a rigmarole."[3]

Historians today still believe that documents are indexed very poorly. Even when they are identified, the Superintendent of Documents classification scheme is too cumbersome to use without assistance.[4] Historians also believe that the amount of time spent attempting to locate government publications is not worth the effort expended.[5]

CHECKLIST OF UNITED STATES PUBLIC DOCUMENTS, 1789-1909

The *Checklist of United States Public Documents, 1789-1909* was the first attempt to list all documents published during that time. In 1985 it was still "the indispensable tool for nineteenth century documents research."[6] The *Checklist* is based upon GPO's Public Documents Library. Despite its usefulness, a weakness of the *Checklist* is its failure to cite many pre-1895 documents. GPO began its library in 1895 and was sometimes unable to acquire copies of older items.

Organization of the *Checklist* is alphanumeric according to Superintendent of Documents classification numbers. The top of Figure 3-1 shows that the part of the classification number before the colon (:) is in bold face type and serves as a header. The part of the SuDoc number following the colon appears within that header. For example, the SuDoc number for *Yellow Fever, Its Nature, Diagnosis, Treatment, and Prophylaxis, and Quarantine Regulations Relating Thereto* is T27.2:Y3/2. Note, the citation references other printings of the identical and related titles.

Figure 3-1
Checklist of United States Public Documents, 1789-1909
Citations to Monographs

T27.2:	General publications
As7 [1]	Assistant surgeon. [Circular concerning examination of candidates for position of assistant surgeon in Public Health and Marine-Hospital Service, to be held Apr. 15, 1907.] Feb. 12, 1907. 4°
As7 [2]	Same [to be held Jan. 7, 1909]. Nov. 5, 1908. 4°
F76 [1]	Formaldehyde. Rapid disinfection with high percentages of formaldehyd, researches conducted at Hygienic Laboratory of Marine Hospital Service; by Ezra Kimball Sprague. 1897. 12°
F76 [2]	Formaldehyde. Report on formaldehyd disinfection in vacuum chamber; by E. K. Sprague. 1899.
N72	Nomenclature of diseases, being classification and English-Latin terminology of provisional nomenclature of Royal College of Physicians, London; [prepared for use of medical officers of United States Marine-Hospital Service by John M. Woodworth]. 1874.
P83	Portable laboratories of Marine Hospital Service; by H. D. Geddings. [1901.] [Reprinted from International clinics, v. 4, 10th series. Distributed at Pan-American Exposition, Buffalo, N. Y., 1901.]
Se1	Seamen. [Circular letter] to collectors of customs, medical officers [etc., concerning Treasury Department circular 42, June 19, 1908, on Contracts for care of seamen, etc.]. June 22, 1908. 4°
Su7	Supply table for Marine-Hospital Service. 1901.
Y3 [1]	Yellow fever. Preliminary report on yellow-fever epidemic of 1882 in Texas. [1882.] (Treas. Dept. doc. 341.)
Y3 [2]	Yellow fever, its nature, diagnosis, treatment, and prophylaxis, and quarantine regulations relating thereto. 1898. [The articles in this pamphlet, with the Value of autopsic findings (T27.2:Y3 [3]) and another paper on Train inspection were reprinted in the annual report for 1889 (T27.1:898). The combined articles were again issued in pamphlet form in 1899, with certain additional matter; *see* T27.12:4. Another article belonging to this group is entered under T27.12:5.]

Source: *Checklist of United States Public Documents, 1789-1909*, **1128**.

Test your knowledge of the *Checklist:* The following questions relate to Figure 3-1.

1. When was *Yellow Fever, Its Nature, Diagnosis...* published?

(1898)

2. Was this title and/or related ones reprinted in other editions? If yes, list the SuDoc numbers.

(T27.2:Y3/3; T27.1:898;
T27.12:4; T27.12:5)

3. What is the report number of *Yellow Fever. Preliminary Report on Yellow-Fever Epidemic of 1882 in Texas?* SuDoc number?

(Treas. Dept. doc. 341;
T27.2:Y3/1)

4. From what source was document T27.2:P83 reprinted?

(*International Clinics,* volume 4, 10th series)

The *Checklist* indicates when Superintendent of Document numbers change. According to Figure 3-2, Immigration Bureau *Circulars* (T21.4:) were issued under T1.4: before July 1, 1903 and under C7.4: after that date.

Figure 3-2
Checklist of United States Public Documents, 1789-1909
Tracing Changes in SuDoc Numbers

Classification no.	**T21. IMMIGRATION BUREAU**—Continued
T21.2:	**General publications**
C16	Canadian border inspection. Report of immigrant inspector in charge of Canadian border inspection for fiscal year 1902, with report of special immigrant inspector Robert Watchorn, concerning immigration to United States via Canada. Aug. 1902.
T21.3:	**Bulletins**
(nos.)	[None issued.]
T21.4:	**Circulars**
(nos.)	[Circulars relating to the work of this bureau prior to July 1, 1903 were issued in the series of Treasury Department circulars; *see* certain issues under T1.4: *See*, for Circulars since July 1, 1903, C7.4:]

Source: *Checklist of United States Public Documents, 1789-1909*, **1083**.

Circulars classified under T1.4: are listed in Figure 3-3.

Figure 3-3
Checklist of United States Public Documents, 1789-1909
Citations to Numbered Series

T1.4:	**Circulars** 4°
(date)	[Department circulars have been issued ever since the Treasury Department was established, the first printed issue bearing date May 12, 1791, but those issued in early years are not now obtainable. Much information concerning circulars, instructions, decisions, etc., up to 1850, may be found in Mayo's Synopsis of commercial and revenue system (T1.2:C73 1-3). The present method of numbering serially by calendar years was begun in 1872. The Public Documents Library has no circulars in the original form of earlier date than 1874. Beginning 1875, the set in the Public Documents Library is believed to be complete.]

1874, nos. 1–54	*	1875, nos. 126–170	
no. 55 †		1876, nos. 1–154	
nos. 56–70	*	1877, nos. 1–146	
no. 71 †		1878, nos. 1–145	
no. 72	*	1879, nos. 1–180	
no. 73 †		1880, nos. 1–100	
nos. 74–81	*	1881, nos. 1–122	
no. 82 8°		1882, nos. 1–142	
nos. 83–107	*	1883, nos. 1–144	
no. 108 †		1884, nos. 1–183	
nos. 109–111	*	1885, nos. 1–183	
no. 112 †		1886, nos. 1–175	
1875, nos. 1–124		1887, nos. 1–146	
no. 125 8°		1888, nos. 1–131	

Source: *Checklist of United States Public Documents, 1789-1909*, **1008**.

Test your knowledge of the *Checklist of United States Public Documents:* Answer the following questions using Figure 3-3.

1. When was the first Treasury Circular issued?

(May 12, 1791)

2. What source includes information about Treasury Circulars issued through 1850? What are the SuDoc numbers?

(Synopsis of Commercial and Revenue System;
T1.2:C73/1, T1.2:C73/2, and T1.2:C73/3)

3. Which Treasury Circulars published in 1876 are included in the Public Documents Library?

(1-154)

Besides providing publication histories, the *Checklist* also summarizes agency histories and authorities, and indicates if documents are in the *Serial Set* (Figure 3-4).

Figure 3-4
Checklist of United States Public Documents, 1789-1909
Documents Reproduced in the *Serial Set*

T22. INTERNAL REVENUE COMMISSIONER

[Office created by act of July 1, 1862 (Stat. L. v. 12, p. 432).]

T22.1: | **Annual reports**
(date) | [1863-1909, the report without accompanying tables is included in annual reports of Treasury Department (Finance reports, T1.1:).]

See, for special report of commissioner, Jan. 13, 1863, concerning organization of office, etc., [1149–20].

See, for Preliminary reports on collection of internal revenue and condition of service, T22.7:

1863		1868	[1371–5]
1864 } [Not in Congressional set.]		1869	[1416–4]
1865		1870	[1452–4]
1866	[1291–55]	1871	[1508–4]
1867	[1329–5]	1872	[1563–4]

Source: *Checklist of United States Public Documents, 1789-1909,* **1083.**

Figure 3-4 illustrates three points.

1. The Internal Revenue Commissioner was established on July 1, 1862.

2. Legislation that created the office is in the *Stat. L.* (*Statutes at Large*), volume 12, page 432. The *Statutes at Large*[7] is a compilation of laws enacted by Congress. The chapter covering federal law has a detailed description of the *Statutes at Large*.

3. IRS *Annual Reports* published between 1866 and 1872 are in the *Serial Set* or the *Congressional Set.* That for 1866 is document number 55 in *Serial Set* volume 1291. Each

Congress numbers its reports and documents in sequential order and each *Serial Set* volume generally contains a range of report or document numbers.

The Congressional Tables section of the *Checklist* provides additional information about the *Serial Set* (Figure 3-5). The table has six columns, but only columns 1, 4, and 5 contain information necessary to locate a document in the *Serial Set*. Descriptions of each appear below.[8]

Figure 3-5
Checklist of United States Public Documents, 1789-1909
Congressional Tables

Serial no.	Vol.	Part	Series	Document no.	Notes

39th CONGRESS, 2d SESSION

Dec. 3, 1866—Mar. 2, 1867

Serial no.	Vol.	Part	Series	Document no.	Notes
1275			S. journal		
1276	1		S. ex. docs	1–6	2 is a special Revenue rp.; 6 is Freedmen's affairs.
1277	2		......do	7–38	26 is Sand Creek massacre.
1278			S. misc. docs	1–54	53 is Arkansas loyal troops.
1279			S. reports	141–178	156 is Condition of Indian tribes.
1280			H. journal		
1281	1	1	H. ex. docs	1	Message and Foreign relations, 1866, pt. 1.
1282	1	2	......do	1	Same, pt. 2.
1283	1	3	......do	1	Same, pt. 3.
1284	2		......do	1	Interior, 1866.
1285	3		......do	1	War, 1866.
1286	4		......do	1, 2	Navy and Post-Office, 1866.
1287	5		......do	3–8	3 is Comptroller of Currency, 1866; 4 is Treasury (Finances) 1866.
1288	6		......do	9–24	12 is Receipts and expenses, 1865; 17 is Mexican affairs.
1289	7		......do	25–49	29 is Mineral resources west of Rockies (Browne), 1866.
1290	8		......do	50–54	Case of Geo. St. Leger Grenfel in Chicago conspiracy; etc.
1291	9		......do	55, 56	Internal Revenue Comr., 1866; Rivers and harbors.
1292	10		......do	57–70	68 is New Orleans riots.
1293	11		......do	71–116	Except **76**, in serial no. 1294; **81**, in serial no. 1295; **87**, in serial no. 1296; **107**, in serial no. 1297, and **109**, in serial nos. 1298–1300. 72 is Norfolk riot.
1294	12		......do	76	Mexican affairs, 1865–66.
1295	13		......do	81	Commercial relations, 1866.
1296	14		......do	87	Coast Survey, 1866.
1297	15		......do	107	Agriculture, 1866.
1298	16	1	......do	109	Patent Office, 1866, v. 1.
1299	16	2	......do	109	Same, v. 2.
1300	16	3	......do	109	Same, v. 3, illustrations.
1301	17		......do	Unnumbered	Commerce and navigation, 1866.

Source: *Checklist of United States Public Documents, 1789-1909*, **44.**

Column 1: Serial no.: Each bound volume in the *Serial Set* has a serial number.

Column 4: Series: This data describes the kinds of documents reproduced in each volume. For example, *Serial Set* volumes 1281-1301 include House executive documents.

Column 5: Column 5 gives document numbers. Serial volume 1279 includes Senate Reports 141-178.

Test your knowledge of the *Checklist of United States Public Documents*: The following questions relate to Figure 3-5.

1.   In what *Serial Set* volume is House Executive Document 58 printed?

(1292)

2.   What is the *Serial Set* volume number and document number of a publication about mineral resources west of the Rocky Mountains.

(*Serial Set* volume 1289;
House Executive Document 29)

3.   In which *Serial Set* volume is House Executive Document 76 printed?

(Serial 1294)

Since the *Checklist* is organized by SuDoc numbers and has neither subject nor title access, researchers must know the names of agencies likely to publish information. This creates problems when agencies change names and when parts of one agency are reorganized into another. Remember, arrangement of the SuDoc scheme is by agencies, not subjects. Andriot's *Guide to U.S. Government Publications*,[9] described in Chapter 1, and Mary Elizabeth Poole's *Documents Office Classification*[10] are useful when tracing histories of agencies and their Superintendent of Documents numbers. Like Andriot, Poole organizes information by SuDoc numbers, but her indexing is poor.

CIS INDEX TO EXECUTIVE BRANCH DOCUMENTS, 1789-1909

INTRODUCTION

Unlike the *Checklist*, the *CIS Index to Executive Branch Documents, 1789-1909*[11] has name, title, subject, and report number indexes. It is the most comprehensive source of its type. Like the *Checklist*, it is based upon GPO's Public Documents Library. However, CIS also includes additional titles found in other major libraries. Despite its title, the *Index to Executive Branch Documents* also cites publications issued by the Library of Congress and the Government Printing Office. The documents were microfiched by CIS, making access to them more widely available for the first time. Four types of materials are excluded:

1. Those covered in *CIS Index to Presidential Executive Orders and Proclamations*[12] and the *Statutes at Large*. Subsequent chapters describe both.

2. Those that agencies reprinted in other formats.

3. Judiciary publications.

4. Maps and charts published by the Coast and Geodetic Survey were too numerous to include and could not be microfiched in a quality fashion. However, the subject heading Maps indexes other maps.

Six parts of the *CIS Index to Executive Branch Documents* cover different agencies.

Part 1 Treasury Department, and Commerce and Labor Department. (Labor Department publications issued before July 1903 are in Part 3.)

Part 2 War Department.

Part 3 Interior, Justice, and Labor Departments, Interstate Commerce Commission, and Library of Congress. (Labor Department publications include those issued before July 1903. Items published since are in Part 1.)

Part 4 Agriculture Department, American Republics Bureau, Civil Service Commission, District of Columbia Commission, Fish Commission, Freedman's Savings and Trust Company, Geographic Board, Government Printing Office, and General Supply Committee.

Part 5 Navy Department.

Part 6 State Department, National Academy of Sciences, National Home for Disabled Volunteer Soldiers, Post Office Department, the President, and the Smithsonian Institute.

REFERENCE BIBLIOGRAPHY

Each part of the *Index to Executive Branch Documents* has two sections, the Reference Bibliography and the indexes. The Reference Bibliography lists all documents in the collection. Figure 3-6 displays the identical title shown in Figure 3-1, *Yellow Fever: Its Nature, Diagnosis...* Citations give three types of information.

Figure 3-6
CIS Index to Executive Branch Documents, 1789-1909
Reference Bibliography

T2702-16

Preliminary report on yellow-fever epidemic of 1882 in State of Texas [with data on incidence and deaths]
11/6/1882. 63 p. Treas. Dept. Doc. No. 341. °T27.2:Y3/1.
Descriptors: Public Health and Marine-Hospital Service; Yellow fever; Texas; Deaths; Quarantine regulations

T2702-17

Yellow fever: Its nature, diagnosis, treatment, and prophylaxis, and quarantine regulations relating thereto, by officers of U.S. Marine Hospital Service
1898. 174 p. °T27.2:Y3/2.
Descriptors: Public Health and Marine-Hospital Service; Yellow fever; Pests and pest control; Drugs; Quarantine regulations

T2702-18

Value of autopsic findings in cases that have died of suspected yellow fever [supplement report on yellow fever and its nature, diagnosis, etc.]
1898. 11 p. °T27.2:Y3/3.
Descriptors: Public Health and Marine-Hospital Service; Autopsies; Yellow fever; Wasdin, Eugene

Source: *CIS Index to Executive Branch Documents, 1789-1909*, Vol. 2, 485.
Reprinted with permission from *CIS Index*
To Executive Branch Documents, Part 1.
Copyright 1990 by Congressional Information
Service, Inc. (Bethesda, MD). All rights reserved.

1. **Accession number:** Alphanumeric code used to arrange entries in the bibliography and to file microfiche. An "x" in the accession number indicates that the document was not available for review or filming, but will be included in a *Supplement.* An "a" in the accession number identifies documents excluded from the *Checklist of United States Public Documents.*

2. **Bibliographic data:** Information includes titles, dates, illustrations, indexes, oversize materials, report numbers, frequency of publication (monthly, annually), and SuDoc numbers.

3. **Descriptors:** Subject headings and personal names are listed.

Reference Bibliography citations sometimes include abstracts and notes as well. When appropriate, titles are expanded to provide more descriptive data. Notes cross reference titles to related series, and cite items that have not yet been located for review or filming. They also refer users to the Index by Superintendent of Documents Numbers for information about titles in the *Serial Set*.

Test your knowledge of the Reference Bibliography: The following questions relate to Figure 3-6.

1. What is the accession number of the document entitled *Preliminary Report on Yellow-Fever Epidemic of 1882...?*

    (T2702-16)

2. Why is part of the title in brackets?

    (Editors added the bracketed information to provide a more useful description of the document.)

3. What is its SuDoc number?

    (T27.2:Y3/1)

4. What is its series report number?

    (Treas. Dept Doc. No. 341)

5. Compare information provided in Figures 3-1 and 3-6 relating to *Yellow Fever: Its Nature, Diagnosis, Treatment....* Does the 1909 *Checklist* provide information not seen in the newer *Index to Executive Branch Documents*?

    (The 1909 *Checklist* provides a brief history of other versions of the title.)

The *CIS Index to U.S. Executive Branch Documents* analyzes individual titles that are published in a series. Figure 3-7 reproduces Treasury Department *Circular 1874/2, Customs Collectors Requirements For Monthly Statements and Deposit of Funds*, from the Reference Bibliography.

Figure 3-7
CIS Index to U.S. Executive Branch Documents, 1789-1909
Documents published in a series

T104
Secretary
Circulars

Circulars have been filmed in the order in which they are bound in volumes; occasional Circulars are out of chronological order or are separated from transmittal documents. In some cases, non-Circular documents have been included in Circular volumes. Where these anomalies occur, the separated or non-Circular documents are fully indexed under the same accession number as the documents with which they have been filmed in the microfiche for that Circular volume year.

All available bibliographic information for the separated or non-Circular documents is provided in a special note in the Reference Bibliography under the accession number of the document under which it has been filmed.

1874

T104-1.1 to T104a-1.116
Treasury Department circulars, 1874
*Annual cumulation, with index. Treas. Dept. Circ. No. 1874/1 to 1874/116. *T1.4:874/(nos.).*
Descriptors: Secretary, Treasury Department

T104-1.1: Admeasurement of Italian vessels
*1/2/1874. 1 p. Treas. Dept. Circ. No. 1874/1. *T1.4:874/1.*
Descriptors: Tonnage taxes and measurements; Italy

T104-1.2: [Customs collectors requirements for monthly statements and deposit of funds]
*1/5/1874. 1 p. Customs Commissioner Circ. No. 42. Treas. Dept. Circ. No. 1874/2. *T1.4:874/2.*
Descriptors: Office of the Commissioner of Customs; Customs forms and paperwork

T104-1.3: [Customs officers reporting requirements for shipwrecks and other vessel casualties occurring within their collection districts]
*1/7/1874. 1 p. Revenue-Marine Circ. No. 8. Treas. Dept. Circ. No. 1874/3. *T1.4:874/3.*
Descriptors: Revenue-Cutter Service; Customs forms and paperwork; Marine accidents and safety; Shipwrecks

Source: *CIS Index to U.S. Executive Branch Documents, 1789-1909,* Vol. 2, 9.
Reprinted with permission from CIS Index
To Executive Branch Documents, Part 1.
Copyright 1990 by Congressional Information
Service, Inc. (Bethesda, MD). All rights reserved.

Figure 3-3 above shows that the *Checklist* only cites report numbers without describing specific titles.

INDEX BY SUBJECTS AND NAMES

The Index by Subjects and Names lists subject headings, and names of organizations, agencies, authors, and people referred to as subjects. It has numerous see and see also references. Spelling of geographic places is standardized. For example, all references appear under "Puerto Rico," not "Porto Rico." Asterisks (*) precede titles indicate that have statistics. Citations include titles, dates of publication, and accession numbers.

Yellow Fever: Its Nature, Diagnosis, Treatment, . . ., the document illustrated above in Figures 3-1 and 3-6, is in the Index by Subjects and Names under the subject heading, Yellow fever (Figure 3-8).

Figure 3-8
CIS Index to U.S. Executive Branch Documents, 1789-1909
Index by Subjects and Names

Yellow fever
    Addition to quarantine regulations to be observed at foreign ports
    and at sea
        (4/5/1899) T104-26.54
    Amending U.S. Treasury quarantine regulations: Cuba
        (4/26/1902) T104-29.43
    Amendment to quarantine regulations
        (2/28/1906) T104-33.24; (3/4/1908) T104-35.14
    Amendment to quarantine regulations [on entry of ships from ports
    suspected of being infected with yellow fever]
        (3/10/1893) T104-20.37
    Amendment to quarantine regulations: Period of detention on
    Mexican frontier after exposure to yellow fever
    Value of autopsic findings in cases that have died of suspected
    yellow fever [supplement report on yellow fever and its nature,
    diagnosis, etc.]
        (1898) T2702-18
    Yellow Fever Institute, bulletins [results of research on yellow fever]
        T2710-1 to T2710-11
    Yellow fever: Its nature, diagnosis, treatment, and prophylaxis, and
    quarantine regulations relating thereto, by officers of U.S. Marine
    Hospital Service
        (1898) T2702-17

Source: *CIS Index to U.S. Executive Branch Documents, 1789-1909,* **Vol. 4, 1026-7.**
Reprinted with permission from *CIS Index To Executive Branch Documents, Part 1.*
**Copyright 1990 by Congressional Information
Service, Inc. (Bethesda, MD). All rights reserved.**

Remember, the 1909 *Checklist* has neither a subject nor a name index.

INDEX BY TITLES

The Index by Titles is alphabetical. A range of accession numbers identify documents in a series. For example, the *Yellow Fever Institute, Bulletins* have accession numbers T2710-1 through T2710-11 (Figure 3-9).

Figure 3-9
CIS Index to U.S. Executive Branch Documents, 1789-1909
Index by Titles

Yacht licenses for yachts and pleasure-vessels
  under 5 tons burden [withdrawing
  restrictions on licenses]
    (8/29/1883) T104-10.112
Yellow fever in France, Italy, Great Britain,
  and Austria, and bibliography of yellow
  fever in Europe
    (5/1902) T2710-2
Yellow Fever Institute, bulletins [results of
  research on yellow fever]
    T2710-1 to T2710-11
Yellow fever: Its nature, diagnosis, treatment,
  and prophylaxis, and quarantine regulations
  relating thereto, by officers of U.S. Marine
  Hospital Service
    (1898) T2702-17
Yellow fever, its nature, diagnosis, treatment,
  and prophylaxis, and quarantine regulations
  relating thereto, from annual report,
  Marine-Hospital Service, 1898; with abstract
  of report of medical officers detailed as
  commission to investigate cause of yellow
  fever
    (1899) T2712x-4

Source: *CIS Index to U.S. Executive Branch Documents, 1789-1909*, **Vol. 5, 445.**
Reprinted with permission from *CIS Index*
To Executive Branch Documents, Part 1.
**Copyright 1990 by Congressional Information
Service, Inc. (Bethesda, MD). All rights reserved.**

INDEX BY AGENCY REPORT NUMBERS

The Treasury *Circulars* displayed above in Figures 3-3 and 3-7 are in the Index by Agency Report Numbers (Figure 3-10).

Figure 3-10
CIS Index to U.S. Executive Branch Documents, 1789-1909
Index by Agency Report Numbers

Treas. Dept. Circ. No.
1872/136 .... T111-5
Treas. Dept. Circ. No.
1872/139 .... T111-5
Treas. Dept. Circ. No.
1873/1 to 1873/147 .... T104a-41.1
to T104a-41.147
Treas. Dept. Circ. No.
1874/1 to 1874/116 .... T104-1.1
to T104a-1.116
Treas. Dept. Circ. No.
1875/1 to 1875/170 .... T104-2.1
to T104-2.170
Treas. Dept. Circ. No.
1876/1 to 1876/154 .... T104-3.1
to T104-3.154
Treas. Dept. Circ. No.
1877/1 to 1877/146 .... T104-4.1
to T104-4.146
Treas. Dept. Circ. No.
1878/1 to 1878/145 .... T104-5.1
to T104-5.145
Treas. Dept. Circ. No.
1879/1 to 1879/180 .... T104-6.1
to T104-6.180

Source: *CIS Index to U.S. Executive Branch Documents, 1789-1909,* **Vol. 5, 465.**
Reprinted with permission from *CIS Index*
To Executive Branch Documents, Part 1.
Copyright 1990 by Congressional Information
Service, Inc. (Bethesda, MD). All rights reserved.

INDEX BY SUPERINTENDENT OF DOCUMENTS NUMBERS

The Index by Superintendent of Documents Numbers is alphanumeric by SuDoc numbers (Figure 3-11).

Figure 3-11
CIS Index to U.S. Executive Branch Documents, 1789-1909
Index by Superintendent of Documents Numbers

T27.2:Su7
Supply table for Marine-Hospital Service of U.S.
(1901) T2702-15

T27.2:Y3/1
Preliminary report on yellow-fever epidemic of 1882 in State of Texas [with data on incidence and deaths]
(11/6/1882) T2702-16

T27.2:Y3/2
Yellow fever: Its nature, diagnosis, treatment, and prophylaxis, and quarantine regulations relating thereto, by officers of U.S. Marine Hospital Service
(1898) T2702-17

T27.2:Y3/3
Value of autopsic findings in cases that have died of suspected yellow fever [supplement report on yellow fever and its nature, diagnosis, etc.]
(1898) T2702-18

T27.3:[1]
Preliminary note on viability of bacillus pestis
(1900) T2703-1

Source: *CIS Index to U.S. Executive Branch Documents, 1789-1909,* **Vol. 5, 236.**
Reprinted with permission from
CIS Index To Executive Branch Documents, Part 1.
Copyright 1990 by Congressional Information Service, Inc. (Bethesda, MD).
All rights reserved.

This index also lists volume and document numbers for materials reproduced in the *Serial Set*. Figure 3-12 illustrates the 1866 *Annual Report* of the Commissioner of Internal Revenue, the same item considered in figures 3-4 and 3-5. (document number 55, serial volume number 1291)

Figure 3-12
CIS Index to U.S. Executive Branch Documents, 1789-1909
Index by Superintendent of Document Numbers--
References to the *Serial Set*

T22.1:866
Annual report of Commissioner of Internal
Revenue, 1866
[Serial 1291-55]

T22.1:867
Annual report of Commissioner of Internal
Revenue, 1867
[Serial 1329-5]

T22.1:868
Annual report of Commissioner of Internal
Revenue, 1868
[Serial 1371-5]

T22.1:869
Annual report of Commissioner of Internal
Revenue, 1869
[Serial 1416-4]

T22.1:870
Annual report of Commissioner of Internal
Revenue, 1870
[Serial 1452-4]

Source: *CIS Index to U.S. Executive Branch Documents, 1789-1909,* **Vol. 5, 200.**
Reprinted with permission from *CIS Index To Executive Branch Documents, Part 1.*
Copyright 1990 by Congressional Information Service, Inc. (Bethesda, MD).
All rights reserved.

CIS INDEX TO U.S. EXECUTIVE BRANCH DOCUMENTS, 1910-1932

CIS intends to pubish the *Index to U.S. Executive Branch Documents, 1910-1932* beginning in 1996. It will be comparable to the index covering 1789-1909. Printed indexes and the related microfiche collections will appear in the following parts during a seven-year period.

Part 1 Treasury Department; Smithsonian Institution; Tariff Commission; Veterans Bureau; Veterans Administration; and Vocational Education Board.

Part 2 Commerce Department.

Part 3 War Department, plus other agencies.

Part 4 Interior Department; Justice Department; and other agencies.

Part 5 Agriculture Department, plus other agencies.

Part 6 Navy Department, plus other agencies.

Part 7 State Department, plus other agencies.

ADDITIONAL GUIDES AND INDEXES TO HISTORICAL DOCUMENTS

HANDBOOKS/GUIDES

Schmeckebier, Laurence F. and Roy B. Eastin. *Government Publications and Their Use.* 2nd rev. ed. Washington, D.C.: The Brookings Institution, 1969.

Government Publications and Their Use, which was first published by Schmickebier in 1936, is a classic U.S. documents text. It is the best one available on Federal historic documents. Eastin revised this latest edition. Separate chapters cover catalogs and indexes; bibliographies; Congressional publications; federal and state constitutions; laws and regulations; Presidential papers; foreign affairs; reports of executive agencies; maps; technical information; periodicals; and microforms. Eastin provides detailed descriptions of most indexes published before 1969 that are considered in this chapter.

GENERAL INDEXES (Listed in chronological order)

Poore, Benjamin Perley. *A Descriptive Catalogue of the Government Publications of the United States, September 5, 1774 - March 4, 1881.* 48th Cong., 2nd session, S. Misc. Doc. 67. Washington, D.C.: G.P.O., 1885. *Serial Set* volume 2268.

Poore's work is the result of a Congressional mandate to compile a "Descriptive catalogue of all publications made by the authority of the Government of the United States and the preceding government of the colonies, and all departments, bureaus, and offices thereof..." (iii) The editors located 63,600 items in major libraries throughout the nation, including the Library of Congress, the Senate and House Libraries, the Department of Agriculture Library, the Smithsonian Institute Library, and the Boston Public Library. Duplicate copies are cited occasionally because compilers working in different locations sometimes indexed the identical materials. Organization is chronological. References give titles, authors, dates, Congresses, and Congressional document numbers. Indexing is by subjects and personal names. Emphasis is upon Congressional publications, since executive agencies published little before the 1880's. The index in Figure 3-13 illustrates information about the arrests of slave traders in New York. The corresponding bibliographic section in Figure 3-14 displays that citation.

Figure 3-13

*A Descriptive Catalogue of the Government Publications of the United States,
September 5, 1774 - March 4, 1881*

Index

sale into slavery of colored freemen captured by
    rebels 809.
Seminole Indians, holding of slaves by 316, **383**, 446.
slave trade, the—
    arrests of persons and vessels in New York, south-
      ern district (1852–1862) 805.
    capture of slaves 299, 780, 782, 798, 810.
    case of—
      bark Augusta 802.
      Mickle & Frias 299.
      ship Louisa 183.
      ship Marino 183.
    correspondence with—
      Brazil concerning 505.
      Great Britain concerning 460.
    disbursements for the suppression of, by Secretary
      J. P. Usher 462.

Source: *A Descriptive Catalogue of the Government Publications of the United States,
September 5, 1774 - March 4, 1881,* **1367**

Figure 3-14

*A Descriptive Catalogue of the Government Publications of the United States,
September 5, 1774 - March 4, 1881*

Bibliographic Section

A Certified Copy of the Constitution of the State of West Virginia.   May 29, 1862
  Senate Mis. Docs., No. 98, 37th Cong., 2d sess.   28 pp.
    Proposed by the convention assembled at Wheeling on the 26th November.
    1861, and ratified by a vote of the people.

Report on Vessels in the Slave Trade. Secretary C. B. Smith.   May 30, 1862
  Senate Ex. Docs., No. 53, 37th Cong., 2d sess., Vol. V.   4 pp.
    Statement of the names and number of vessels arrested and bonded, from May
    1, 1852, to May 1, 1862, in the southern district of New York, charged with
    being engaged in the slave trade. Names of persons arrested.

Report on Case of Jane McAllister. Senator L. F. S. Foster.   May 30, 1862
  Senate Reports, No. 50, 37th Cong., 2d sess.   1 p.
    On petition of Jane McAllister, praying a pension. Committee report ad-
    versely.

Source: *A Descriptive Catalogue of the Government Publications of the United States,
September 5, 1774 - March 4, 1881,* **805**.

Ames, John. *Comprehensive Index to the Publications of the United States Government, 1881-1893.* 58th Cong., 2nd session, H. Doc. 754. Washington, D.C.: GPO, 1905. *Serial Set* volumes 4745 and 4746.

Continuing where Benjamin Poore's work left off, this index deals with 1881-1893. Coverage includes publications of Congress and the executive branch. Arrangement is alphabetical by subjects. Each page has three columns (Figure 3-15).

Figure 3-15

Comprehensive Index to the Publications
of the United States Government, 1891-1893

ATKINSON, L. E., District of Columbia.	National Metropolitan Fire Insurance Co. of D. C., extension of charter of, recommended. Aug. 8, 90. H. B. 11538.	H. R. 51-1, v. 9. No. 2941, 1 p.
	National military and naval museum. (*See* Military and Naval Museum.)	
	National Museum, U. S., annual reports of Assistant Director and curators of . . . . In annual reports of Smithsonian Institution, 1881-1883. Issued separately as Part 2, from 1884.	
	—— bibliography of, 1892 . . . . Report of National Museum, 1892, p. 495-526.	H. M. 52-2, v. 23. No. 114, pt. 2.
MORRILL, J. S., Public Buildings and Grounds.	—— building for, erection of additional, recommended . . . . June 12, 88. S. B. 3134.	S. R. 50-1, v. 6. No. 1539, 4 p.
MILLIKEN, S. L., Public Buildings and Grounds.	—— *Same* . . . . Jan. 9, 91. S. B. 2740.	H. R. 51-2, v. 1. No. 3399, 2 p.
LANGLEY, S. P., Secretary	—— *Same*, letter relative to . . . . Mar. 21, 90.	S. M. 51-1, v. 2. No. 116, 5 p.
Do	—— employees of, schedule of classified service of, with letter . . . . Mar. 2, 89.	S. M. 50-2, v. 2. No. 92, 4 p.
Architect of the Capitol	—— estimate of cost of basement story under . . . . Feb. 28, 90.	H. M. 51-1, v. 9. No. 126, 2 p.

Source: *Comprehensive Index to the Publications*
of the United States Government, 1891-1893 **Vol. 2, 937.**

The first column lists issuing agencies, Congressional committees, and names of Congressmen and Senators responsible for the reports. The second one is alphabetic by subjects and cites bibliographic information, and when appropriate, bill numbers that relate to Congressional reports. The third column lists Congressional document numbers needed to locate the publications. Documents have only one subject heading.

U.S. Government Printing Office. *Catalogue of the Public Documents of Congress and of Other Departments of the Government of the U.S.* Washington, D.C.: GPO, 1893-1940.

The *Documents Catalogue* is a popular name for this title. Information is alphabetic under personal names, agencies, selected titles, and subject headings. Each edition covers an entire Congress. When items are reproduced in the *Serial Set, Serial Set* volume numbers are in bold type. For instance, the title in Figure 3-16, *Campaign Funds in Presidential Elections,* appears in serial volume 6897.

Figure 3-16
Catalogue of the Public Documents of Congress and Other Departments of the Government of the U.S.
Reference to the *Serial Set*

PRESIDENT OF UNITED STATES—Continued.
Election. Foreign and Domestic Commerce
Bureau. Army, Navy, civil service, pen-
sions [Congressional apportionment, and
Presidential elections of United States].
(In Foreign and Domestic Commerce Bu-
reau. Statistical abstract, 1916. 1917. p.
657–675.)

—— Privileges and Elections Committee.
Campaign funds in Presidential elections,
report to accompany S. 669 [to limit use of
campaign funds in Presidential and national elections]; submitted by Mr. Lea of
Tennessee. Jan. 27, 1916. 1 p. (S. rp. **75,**
64th Cong. 1st sess. In v. 1; **6897.**)

Source: *Catalogue of the Public Documents of Congress and Other Departments of the Government of the U.S.,* **Vol. 13, Part 2, 1811.**

Note, the *Documents Catalogue* also describes parts of larger documents. Figure 3-17 references the article by Aristides Agramonte, "Review of Present Yellow-Fever Situation." It was published on pages 100-105 in the 1915-16 *Proceedings* of the Pan American Scientific Congress.

Figure 3-17
Catalogue of the Public Documents of Congressand Other Departments of the Government of the U.S.
Parts of Larger Documents

YELLOW FEVER.
Agramonte, Arístides. Review of present
yellow-fever situation [with list of refer-
ences]. (In Pan American Scientific Congress. Proceedings, 1915–16. 1917. v. 9,
p. 100–105.)

Carter, H. R. Immunity to yellow fever
[with bibliography]. (In Pan American
Scientific Congress. Proceedings, 1915–16.
1917. v. 9, p. 41–47.)

Source: *Catalogue of the Public Documents of Congressand Other Departments of the Government of the U.S.,* **Vol. 13, Part 2, 2398.**

Monthly Catalog of United States Government Publications. Washington, D.C.: GPO, 1895-monthly.

See Chapter 2 for a discussion of the *Monthly Catalog* and its cumulative subject and author indexes.[13] Although GPO's *Monthly Catalog* began publication in 1895, an earlier one was published privately between 1885 and 1894.[14]

TITLE INDEX: 1789-1976

Lester, Daniel W. et al, comp. *Cumulative Title Index to United States Public Documents, 1789-1976.* Arlington, Va.: United States Historical Documents Institute, Inc., 1979. 15 vols.

Titles published between 1789 and June 1976 that are in GPO's Public Documents Library are indexed. Entries are alphabetical by titles. References provide dates and Superintendent of Documents numbers. It is sometimes unclear if dates refer to the year of publication or to when the GPO library acquired the materials. Titles in the *Serial Set* are excluded. This source is the most comprehensive title index to U.S. federal documents.

LIBRARY CATALOGS

New York Public Library. *Catalog of Government Publications in the Research Libraries: The New York Public Library.* Boston: G.K. Hall, 1972. 40 vols.

This printed copy of the card catalog of the New York Public Library's Economics and Public Affairs Division cites over 1 million volumes published by governments throughout the world. Information is alphabetic by jurisdiction. Entries for American colonies appear before those for states. U.S. documents in the *Catalog* cover colonial times through the late 1960's. The Catalog offers neither subject entries nor added entries for personal names. Annual supplements update the information.[15]

The *Dictionary Catalog of the Research Libraries*[16], a general catalog providing access to many New York Public Library collections through 1971, has subject and title access.

INDEXES TO HISTORICAL CONGRESSIONAL PUBLICATIONS

The above sources index and describe publications issued by all three branches of government. Consult the descriptions of the following Congressional indexes in the chapter below that deal exclusively with historical publications of Congress:

-*CIS US Serial Set Index*[17]

-*CIS US Congressional Committee Hearings Index*[18]

-*CIS indexes to unpublished hearings*[19]

-*CIS US Congressional Committee Prints Index*[20]

-*CIS Index to US Senate Executive Documents and Reports*[21]

CONCLUSION

Chart 3-1 summarizes guides, indexes, and catalogs to historical U.S. government publications in chronological order.

Chart 3-1
Guides, Indexes, and Catalogs to
Historical U.S. Government Publications

Time Period	Author/Title	Key Points/ Arrangement
- 1969	Schmeckebier, Laurence F., Government Publications and Their Use	A handbook that is organized in topical chapters. This volume is the most comprehensive of its type.
- late 1960's	New York Public Library, Catalog of Government Publications in the Research Libraries: The New York Public Library	Documents published by governments throughout the world are included. Arrangement is by issuing agencies.
1774 - 1881	Poore, Benjamin Perley, A Descriptive Catalogue of the Government Publications of the United States, September 5, 1774 - March 4, 1881	The first attempt to compile a comprehensive catalog of government publications.
1789-1976	Lester, Daniel W. et al., Cumulative Title Index to United States Public Documents, 1789-1976	Information is based upon titles in GPO's Public Documents Library.
1789-1909	U.S. Government Printing Office, Checklist of United States Public Documents, 1789-1909	Until recently, this title was the most comprehensive of its type. It is based upon GPO's Public Documents Library.
1789-1909	Congressional Information Service, CIS Index to Executive Branch Documents	The most comprehensive index of its type. Most items indexed are available in a corresponding microfiche collection.
1881-1893	Ames, John, Comprehensive Index to the Publications of the United States Government, 1881-1893	Arrangement is by subject.
1885-1894	Hickcox, J.H., United States Government Publications	A version of the Monthly Catalog which predates that prepared by GPO.
1893-1940	U.S. Government Printing Office, Catalogue of the Public Documents of Congress and of Other Departments of the Government of the U.S. (Popular name: Documents Catalog)	The Documents Catalog provides good subject and author access.
1895 - present	U.S. Government Printing Office, Monthly Catalog of United States Government Publications	The official bibliography published by GPO that includes documents issued by all three branches of government.
1895 - 1971	Kanely, Edna A., Cumulative Subject Index to the Monthly Catalog: 1895-1899 and Cumulative Subject Index to the Monthly Catalog: 1900-1971	References refer to page or entry numbers in the Monthly Catalog.
1941 - 1975	Przebienda, Edward, United States Government Publications Monthly Catalog: Decennial Cumulative Personal Author Index (1941-1960) and United States Government Publications Monthly Catalog: Quinquinnial Cumulative Personal Author Index (1961-1975)	The most comprehensive personal author index to the Monthly Catalog between 1941 and 1975.

Endnotes

1. United States. Government Printing Office, *Checklist of United States Public Documents, 1789-1909* (Washington, D.C.: GPO, 1911), vii.

2. "No Secrecy Possible: One Aspect of the Relationship Between the U.S. Senate and the Press in the Nineteenth Century," *Government Publications Review* 18:3 (1991), 239-244.

3. Robert E. Kling, Jr., *The Government Printing Office* (New York: Praeger Publishers, 1970), 112.

4. Margaret F. Steig, "The Information Needs of Historians," *College and Research Libraries* 42:6 (November 1981), 553. Cited in James A. Stewart, "Government Documents as Historical Source Material: An Illumination," *Illinois Libraries* 69:7 (September 1987), 452.

5. *Use of Government Publications by Social Scientists* (Norwood, NJ: Ablex Publishing, 1979), 43. Cited in Stewart, "Government Documents as Historical Source Material: An Illumination," 452.

6. Elizabeth A. McBride, "The 1909 Checklist Revisited," *Government Publications Review* 12:5 (1985), 421.

7. *United States Statutes at Large* (Washington, D.C.: GPO, 1789-annual). SuDoc number: AE2.11:. Publisher and SuDoc number varies.

8. Column 2 in Figure 3-5 itemizes the number of *Serial Set* volumes in a group. For example, Congress published seventeen volumes of House executive documents during the 39th Congress, 2nd session. Column 3 illustrates the parts of multivolume sets. That is, volume 1 is a three volume set dealing the President's message and foreign relations. It appeared as *Serial Set* volumes 1281-1283. Column 6 describes the titles of the documents. Likewise, volume 16, *Serial Set* issues 1298-1300, includes the 1866 *Annual Report of the Patent Office*, which is a 3 part set.

9. Donna Andriot (McLean, Virginia: Documents Index, annual).

10. 5th ed. (Arlington, Virginia: The United States Historical Documents Institute, Inc., 1977). 3 vols.

11. Congressional Information Service, *CIS Index to U.S. Executive Branch Documents, 1789-1909: Guide to Documents Listed in Checklist of U.S. Public Documents, 1789-1909, Not Printed in the Serial Set* (Bethesda, MD: Congressional Information Service, Inc., 1990-1996). CIS intendes to publish a supplement in 1997.

12. *CIS Index to Presidential Executive Orders and Proclamations* (Bethesda, MD.: Congressional Information Service, Inc., 1986-87). 21 vols. issued in 2 parts. Documents are available in a corresponding

microfiche collection. *CIS Presidential Orders and Proclamations* (Bethesda, MD.: Congressional Information Service, Inc., 1987). Approximately 9,000 microfiche.

13.   Edna A. Kanely, *Cumulative Subject Index to the Monthly Catalog of United States Government Publications, 1895-1899* (Washington, D.C.: Carrollton Press, 1977). 2 vols.; William W. Buchanan and Edna M. Kanely, *Cumulative Subject Index to the Monthly Catalog of United States Government Publication: 1900-1971* (Washington, D.C.: Carrollton Press, 1973-1975). 15 vols.; Edward Przebienda, ed., *United States Government Publications Monthly Catalog: Decennial Cumulative Personal Author Index* (Ann Arbor: Pierian Press, 1971). 2 vols. cover 1941-1960. Przebienda covers 1961-1975 in three additional volumes, *United States Government Publications Monthly Catalog: Quinquinnial Cumulative Personal Author Index* (Ann Arbor: Pierian Press, 1971-1979).

14.   *United States Government Publications* (Washington, D.C.: J.H. Hickcox, 1885-1894). A related item was compiled by Edna A. Kanely. *Cumulative Index to Hickcox's Monthly Catalog of the United States Government Publications, 1885-1894* (Arlington, Virginia: Carrollton Press, 1981). 3 vols.

15.   New York Public Library, *Bibliographic Guide to Government Publications--Foreign* (Boston: G.K. Hall, 1975-annual); New York Public Library, *Bibliographic Guide to Government Publications--U.S.* (Boston: G.K. Hall, 1975-annual). 1974 edition published as *Government Publications Guide: 1974* (Boston: G.K. Hall, 1974). 2 vols.

16.   New York Public Library, *Dictionary Catalog of the Research Libraries of the New York Public Library, 1911-1971* (Boston: G.K. Hall, 1979). 800 vols.

17.   (Washington, D.C.: Congressional Information Service, Inc., 1975-1979). 12 parts published in 36 vols.

18.   (Bethesda, MD: Congressional Information Service, Inc., 1981-1985). 8 parts in 42 vols.

19.   *CIS Index to Unpublished US House of Representatives Committee Hearings, 1833-1936* (Bethesda, MD: Congressional Information Service, Inc., 1988). 2 vols.; *CIS Index to Unpublished US House of Representatives Committee Hearings, 1937-1946* (Bethesda, MD: Congressional Information Service, Inc., 1990). 2 vols.; *CIS Index to Unpublished US Senate Committee Hearings: 18th Congress-88th Congress, 1823-1964* (Bethesda, MD: Congressional Information Service, Inc., 1986). 5 vols.; *CIS Index to Unpublished US Senate Committee Hearings: 89th Congress-90th Congress, 1965-1968* (Bethesda, MD: Congressional Information Service, Inc., 1989).

20.   *CIS US Congressional Committee Prints Index from the Earliest Publications Through 1969* (Washington, D.C.: Congressional Information Service, Inc., 1980). 5 vols.

21.   *CIS Index to US Senate Executive Documents and Reports Covering Documents and Reports Not Printed in the Serial Set, 1817-1969* (Washington, D.C.: Congressional Information Service, Inc., 1987). 2 vols.

Exercises

1. Like today, in the 1880's, people thought about the significance of education as a deterrence to crime. Use the *CIS Index to U.S. Executive Branch Documents, 1789-1909*, Part 3, to locate a document on this topic by J.P. Wickersham.

   A. What is the title?

   B. What is the accession number?

   C. In what context does this deal with the topic?

   D. What is the year of publication?

   E. What is the Superintendent of Documents classification number?

2. Use the *Comprehensive Index To The Publications of the United States Government, 1881-1893* to locate a document by A. MacDonald about criminology and criminal sociology.

   A. What agency published this item?

   B. When was it published?

   C. In what series was it published and what is the issue number?

3. Use the *CIS Index to U.S. Executive Branch Documents, 1789-1909*, Part 3, to locate additional information about the document in question 2.

   A. What is the complete title?

   B. What is the author's full name?

   C. What is the Superintendent of Documents classification number?

Answers

1. A. *Education and Crime.*

   B. I1602-29.

   C. It examines high school education as a safeguard against criminal tendencies.

   D. 1881.

   E. I16.2:ED8/2.

2. A. Bureau of Education.

   B. 1893.

   C. Circular of Information Series, 1893, number 4.

3. A. *Education and Crime and Related Subjects, With Digests of Literature and Bibliography.*

   B. Arthur MacDonald.

   C. I16.5:893/no.4

•Chapter 4

Congressional Publications —Part I: Types of Publications

Answer the following questions when reading this chapter:

1. How do the various types of Congressional publications relate to the legislative process?

2. What types of Congressional publications are most useful to your needs? Why?

Congressional publications have valuable information. Congress debates and studies the advantages and disadvantages of all policies and issues affecting the nation and the world. Documentation generated from Congress offers insightful analysis of agencies activities, and successes and/or failures of government programs.

The initial part of this chapter summarizes how a bill becomes a law and cites the kinds of Congressional publications available at each step of the legislative process. Detailed definitions and explanations of kinds of Congressional publications follow that discussion. Consult Chapter 6, which deals with legislative histories, for information about related electronic databases and Internet sites.

I use rept as a standard abbreviation for Congressional reports despite different references sources referring to them as rept, rpt, and rp.

HOW A BILL BECOMES A LAW

To understand the various kinds of Congressional publications, it is necessary to review very briefly the legislative process. Chart 4-1 summarizes how a bill becomes a law and the various types of publications issued by Congress during each step of the process.

Chart 4-1
The Legislative Process and Types of Publications

	The Legislative Process	Publications
1.	Senators and Representatives introduce bills and resolutions into their respective chambers.	Bills and resolutions
2.	Bills are referred to appropriate committees for hearings.	Hearings
3.	Committees report recommendations to their respective houses.	Reports
4.	House bills are debated by the entire House, and if approved, are forwarded to the Senate for consideration. The process is reversed for Senate bills.	Congressional Record
5.	Differences between House and Senate versions of bills are settled by Conference Committees that include legislators from both Chambers.	Conference report
6.	Compromises are forwarded to the respective houses and the bill is again debated.	Congressional Record
7.	Bills are forwarded to the President for his approval. A. President signs bill into law, or B. President vetoes bill and sends it back to Congress.	Slip law* Veto messages are published in the Congressional document series.
8.	A two-thirds vote of each house overrides the veto.	Congressional Record and Journals. Slip law is published if veto is over-turned.

* Despite slip laws being National Archive publications, rather than Congressional publications, this discussion includes them to illustrate continuity within the legislative process.

DEFINITIONS AND EXPLANATIONS
OF CONGRESSIONAL PUBLICATIONS

BILLS

(SuDoc numbers: House--Y1.4/6:Congress-fiche number;

Senate--Y1.4/1:Congress-session-fiche number)

INTRODUCTION AND DEFINITION

Bills are proposals for the enactment of new legislation or the amendment of existing laws. Those introduced during each Congress are numbered in sequential order. S. 1500 represents the 1,500th Senate bill introduced, whereas H.R. 7000 represents the 7,000th House bill introduced. Different sessions of the same Congress maintain continuous numerical schemes. Suppose the last Senate bill introduced during the 102nd Congress, 1st session, was S. 1479, then the initial bill the following session is S. 1480. However, the first bill introduced into the Senate during the 103rd Congress is S. 1. Two types of bills deal with different kinds of information. Public bills affect the entire nation, whereas private ones apply only to specific individuals, such as John Doe or Jane Smith. Although House bills are most often identified by H.R., some citations refer to them by a mere H.

IDENTIFYING DIFFERENT KINDS OF BILLS

Figures 4-1 through 4-3 illustrate different versions of the identical bill, H.R. 828, introduced during the 101st Congress, 1st session. Figure 4-1 depicts the bill as it was first introduced on February 2, 1989.

Figure 4-1
H.R. 828 as Introduced

101st CONGRESS
1st Session

H. R. 828

To authorize appropriations for programs, functions, and activities of the Bureau of Land Management for fiscal years 1990, 1991, 1992, and 1993.

IN THE HOUSE OF REPRESENTATIVES

February 2, 1989

Mr. Vento introduced the following bill; which was referred to the Committee on Interior and Insular Affairs

---

A BILL

To authorize appropriations for programs, functions, and activities of the Bureau of Land Management for fiscal years 1990, 1991, 1992, and 1993.

1 *Be it enacted by the Senate and House of Representa-*

2 *tives of the United States of America in Congress assembled,*

3 That there are hereby authorized to be appropriated such

4 sums as may be necessary for programs, functions, and ac-

5 tivities of the Bureau of Land Management, Department of

6 the Interior (including amounts necessary for increases in

7 salary, pay, retirements, and other employee benefits author-

8 ized by law, and for other nondiscretionary costs) during

9 fiscal years beginning on October 1, 1989, and ending Sep-

10 tember 30, 1993.

O

After its introduction, Congress considered the bill in committee and then reported it back to the House. Figure 4-2 displays the reported bill.

Figure 4-2
H.R. 828 Reported from Committee

Union Calendar No. 89

101ST CONGRESS
1ST SESSION

H. R. 828

[Report No. 101–132]

To authorize appropriations for programs, functions, and activities of the Bureau
of Land Management for fiscal years 1990, 1991, 1992, and 1993.

IN THE HOUSE OF REPRESENTATIVES

FEBRUARY 2, 1989

Mr. VENTO introduced the following bill; which was referred to the Committee on
Interior and Insular Affairs

JULY 11, 1989

Reported with amendments, committed to the Committee of the Whole House on
the State of the Union, and ordered to be printed

[Insert the part printed in italic]

A BILL

To authorize appropriations for programs, functions, and activities of the Bureau of Land Management for fiscal years
1990, 1991, 1992, and 1993.

1   *Be it enacted by the Senate and House of Representa-*

2 *tives of the United States of America in Congress assembled,*

3 That there are hereby authorized to be appropriated such

4 sums as may be necessary for programs, functions, and ac-

5 tivities of the Bureau of Land Management, Department of

Figure 4-2 indicates that the bill was placed on Union Calendar No. 89
and that House Report 101-132 deals with H.R. 828. Congressional *Calendars* and reports are described in detail below.

Bills become acts following passage by one chamber of Congress. Figure 4-3 illustrates the version of H.R. 828 that was approved by the House and sent to the Senate for its consideration.

Figure 4-3
H.R. 828--An Act

101st CONGRESS
1st SESSION

H. R. 828

IN THE SENATE OF THE UNITED STATES

July 19 (legislative day, JANUARY 3), 1989

Received; read twice and referred to the Committee on Energy and Natural Resources

AN ACT

To authorize appropriations for programs, functions, and activities of the Bureau of Land Management for fiscal years 1990, 1991, 1992, and 1993, and for other purposes.

1   *Be it enacted by the Senate and House of Representa-*

2 *tives of the United States of America in Congress assembled,*

3 That there are hereby authorized to be appropriated such

4 sums as may be necessary for programs, functions, and ac-

5 tivities of the Bureau of Land Management, Department of

6 the Interior (including amounts necessary for increases in

7 salary, pay, retirements, and other employee benefits author-

8 ized by law, and for other nondiscretionary costs) during

9 fiscal years beginning on October 1, 1989, and ending

10 September 30, 1993.

Figure 4-4 is an example of a private bill whose purpose is to benefit Cathy-Anne Hughes, not the public at large.

Figure 4-4
H.R. 1177--Private Bill

101ST CONGRESS
1ST SESSION

H. R. 1177

For the relief of Cathy-Anne Hughes.

IN THE HOUSE OF REPRESENTATIVES

FEBRUARY 28, 1989

Mr. MARTIN of New York introduced the following bill; which was referred to the Committee on the Judiciary

JULY 28, 1989

Reported with amendments, committed to the Committee of the Whole House, and ordered to be printed

[Strike out all after the enacting clause and insert the part printed in italic]

NOVEMBER 7, 1989

Recommitted to the Committee on the Judiciary

A BILL

For the relief of Cathy-Anne Hughes.

1   *Be it enacted by the Senate and House of Representa-*

2 *tives of the United States of America in Congress assembled,*

3 ~~*That (a) subject to subsection (b), for the purposes of the*~~

4 ~~*Immigration and Nationality Act, Cathy-Anne Hughes shall*~~

15 *That "(a) subject to subsection (b), for the purposes of the*

16 *Immigration and Nationality Act, Cathy-Anne Morrison*

17 *shall be considered to have been lawfully admitted to the*

Note that lines 3 and 4 in H.R. 1177 (Figure 4-4) are crossed out. Congressional committees often vote to amend bills. When reporting amended bills, committees cross out sections of the bills that are to be either deleted or changed. Information that is to be inserted appears in italic type.

Line 16 indicates that Cathy-Anne Morrison is to be inserted into the bill in place of Cathy-Anne Hughes who appeared on line 4.

Star prints are corrected versions of bills that have already been printed. Note that a star appears at the bottom of Figure 4-5.

Figure 4-5
Star Print

101ST CONGRESS
1ST SESSION

H. R. 712

To amend title XVIII of the Social Security Act with respect to payment for capital-related costs for inpatient hospital services under the medicare program.

IN THE HOUSE OF REPRESENTATIVES

JANUARY 27, 1989

Mr. STARK introduced the following bill; which was referred to the Committee on Ways and Means

---

A BILL

To amend title XVIII of the Social Security Act with respect to payment for capital-related costs for inpatient hospital services under the medicare program.

1   *Be it enacted by the Senate and House of Representa-*

2   *tives of the United States of America in Congress assembled,*

3   SECTION 1. SHORT TITLE.

4   This Act may be cited as the "Medicare Inpatient

5   Hospital Capital Expenditures Amendments of 1989".

✱

RESOLUTIONS

Three types of resolutions are joint, concurrent and simple resolutions.

JOINT RESOLUTIONS

(SuDoc numbers: House--Y1.4/8:Congress-fiche number; Senate--Y1.4/3:Congress-fiche number)

Like bills, joint resolutions become law after approved by both houses and the President. There is no practical difference between bills and joint resolutions, except that the latter usually deals with more limited matters. For instance, joint resolutions sometimes correct errors in existing legislation, provide for special appropriations, or express Congressional foreign policy initiatives. Two identical measures, House Joint Resolution 1145 and Senate Joint Resolution 189 are among the most significant ones. President Johnson used these Gulf of Tonkin Resolutions to justify America's involvement in the Vietnamese War. Continuing resolutions on the budget are also joint resolutions. If a new budget is not in place by October 1, the beginning of the new federal fiscal year, Congress usually enacts continuing resolutions. This enables agencies to continue spending at the previous year's level or at levels agreed upon in the resolution.

Joint resolutions have consecutive numbers within each Congress and use H.J.Res. (House Joint Resolution) and S.J.Res. (Senate Joint Resolution) identifiers. H.J.Res. 32 (102nd Congress, 1st session), which deals with the enforcement of U.N. sanctions against Iraq, is illustrated in Figure 4-6.

Figure 4-6
Joint Resolution

102D CONGRESS
1ST SESSION
H. J. RES. 32

To support continued efforts to enforce United Nations sanctions against Iraq, and to prohibit offensive United States military action against Iraq in the absence of authorization from Congress.

IN THE HOUSE OF REPRESENTATIVES

JANUARY 3, 1991

Mr. STUDDS (for himself and Mr. MOAKLEY) introduced the following joint resolution; which was referred to the Committee on Foreign Affairs

---

JOINT RESOLUTION

To support continued efforts to enforce United Nations sanctions against Iraq, and to prohibit offensive United States military action against Iraq in the absence of authorization from Congress.

CONCURRENT RESOLUTIONS

(SuDoc numbers: House--Y1.4/9:Congress-fiche number; Senate--Y1.4/4:Congress-fiche number)

Concurrent resolutions, identified by either H.Con.Res. or S.Con.Res., deal with matters that affect the operations of both chambers. Concurrent resolutions must have House and Senate approval, but do not require Presidential support. Each house numbers them consecutively. The term concurrent does not reflect simultaneous introduction and consideration in the Senate and House. The annual Concurrent Resolution on the Budget is among the most important resolutions Congress considers. Figure 4-7 reproduces that for fiscal years 1992 through 1996. It sets guidelines for appropriations and revenues.

Figure 4-7
Concurrent Resolution on the Budget

Calendar No. 66

102D CONGRESS
1ST SESSION
S. CON. RES. 29

[Report No. 102–40]

Setting forth the congressional budget for the United States Government
for fiscal years 1992, 1993, 1994, 1995, and 1996.

IN THE SENATE OF THE UNITED STATES

APRIL 18 (legislative day, APRIL 9), 1991
Mr. SASSER, from the Committee on the Budget, reported the following
concurrent resolution; which was placed on the calendar

CONCURRENT RESOLUTION

Setting forth the congressional budget for the United States
Government for fiscal years 1992, 1993, 1994, 1995,
and 1996.

Congress sometimes realizes that parts of bills sent to the Whitehouse for Presidential approval are incorrect. Concurrent resolutions recall these bills. Such concurrent resolutions rescinds Congressional approval and specifies what the proposed legislation should say. The Secretary of the Senate and the Clerk of the House amend the original bill accordingly and then resubmit it to the President.

SIMPLE RESOLUTIONS

(SuDoc numbers: House--Y1.4/7:Congress-fiche number; Senate-- Y1.4/2:Congress-fiche number)

Simple resolutions reflect issues of concern to only one house and require neither ratification of the other chamber nor Presidential approval to become effective. They have consecutive numbers within each house and use H.Res. and S.Res. identifiers. Figure 4-8 shows a Senate resolution that proclaims the courage of the American hostages held in Lebanon.

Figure 4-8
Simple Resolution

102D CONGRESS
2D SESSION

S. RES. 244

Relating to the Americans held hostage in Lebanon.

IN THE SENATE OF THE UNITED STATES

JANUARY 21 (legislative day, JANUARY 3), 1992

Mr. DeConcini submitted the following resolution; which was referred to the Committee on Foreign Relations

---

RESOLUTION

Relating to the Americans held hostage in Lebanon.

Whereas the last of the Americans held hostage in Lebanon,
some for more than six years, have been released;

LOCATING BILLS AND RESOLUTIONS

The Government Printing Office distributed bills and resolutions to depository libraries in microfiche since 1979. Superintendent of Documents numbers for each type of measure are cited above. The same were distributed in paper between 1939 and 1978. To facilitate more timely distribution, GPO films the bills as they are received, rather holding them until all are gathered in numerical order. Thus, S. 1 could appear on fiche

10 of the Senate bill series, while S. 5 could be reproduced on fiche 1 if it had been available for filming before S. 1.

FINDING AID FOR CONGRESSIONAL BILLS AND RESOLUTIONS

The *Finding Aid For Congressional Bills and Resolutions*[1] is a guide to the microfiche collection. Organization of both the *Finding Aid* and the micro-fiche are by types of bills and resolutions and by chambers. For example, the SuDoc number of the first fiche of Senate bills for the 102 Congress, 1st session is Y1.4/1:102-1-1.

Note, the *Finding Aid* is useful only if researchers know bill or resolution numbers, and the appropriate Congress and session. This source does not offer subject access. The chapter on legislative histories examines selected tools that provide data by subjects. These include the *Congressional Information Service Index (CIS Index)*,[2] the *Congressional Index*,[3] the *Congressional Quarterly Weekly Report*,[4] the *Congressional Quarterly Almanac*[5], the indexes to the *Congressional Record*, related databases, and Internet sources.

Figure 4-9 displays references to H.R. 828, the bill seen above in Figures 4-1 through 4-3.

Figure 4-9
Finding Aid For Congressional Bills and Resolutions

H.R. NO.	FICHE NO.	X-Y COORD
811.	59	G8
812.	59	G10+
813.	64	F3
814.	64	F5
815.	64	F10
816.	64	G1
817.	64	G6
818.	60	A5
819.	60	A12
820.	64	G9+
821.	65	A7
822.	65	B4
823.	65	B9
824.	60	A13
825.	65	B13
826.	65	C7
827.	65	D4
828.	60	B11
RPT.132		
7-11-89	310	E5
ACT		
7-19-89	346	A9

The bill as introduced into the House (Figure 4-1) is on fiche number 60, coordinate B11. (SuDoc number: Y1.4/6:101-60) Coordinates indicate the microfiche frame on which the information appears. Numbers represent horizontal rows going across the microfiche and letters represent vertical columns going down the fiche. H.R. 828, as reported to the House from committee, appears on fiche 310, coordinates E5 (5th row, 5th column) and the Act that was forwarded to the Senate is reproduced on fiche 346, coordinates A9 (1st row, 9th column).

COMMITTEE PRINTS

(SuDoc numbers vary depending upon the committee)

Committee prints are studies prepared by either the Congressional Research Service of the Library of Congress, or committee and/or subcommittee staffs. These factual analyses are sometimes the most objective materials published by Congress. Representatives and Senators use them to study background information.

Until the mid-1970's when they became depository publications, committee prints were difficult to locate. They were intended for internal use within committees and consequently, were produced in limited quantities. Older committee prints became more widely accessible in 1980 when the Congressional Information Service published the *CIS US Congressional Committee Prints Index*.[6] This index and its corresponding microfiche collection provide access to the earliest prints the publisher could locate through those issued in 1969. Other indexes to prints include the *Monthly Catalog*,[7] the *Publications Reference File*,[8] and the *CIS Index*.

HEARINGS

(SuDoc numbers vary depending upon the committee)

Hearings are the debates and proceedings before committees and subcommittees. The committees invite experts from academia, trade and professional associations, industry, government, and the general public to provide testimony. These statements are included in hearings, along with journal articles, statistics, letters, and other types of documentation submitted by the witnesses as evidence.[9]

Hearings are extremely valuable because committees play a significant role in policy making. Congressional committees have been called the "nerve ends of Congress--the gatherers of information, the sifters of alternatives, the refiners of legislation..."[10] Woodrow Wilson argued that Committees are where Congress does its real work. He believed "...it is not far from the truth to say that Congress in session is Congress on Public exhibition, while Congress in its committee rooms is Congress at work."[11]

Moreover, hearings often contain information unavailable in other sources. Information published in documents issued by the Executive

Branch include ideas and data that support the Administration's viewpoint. However, an informed public needs to be aware of all viewpoints, the Administration's, as well as the opposition's. This type of information often surfaces in hearings when Representatives and Senators question witnesses who reflect all opinions, some who are for and others who oppose Presidential policy. Hearings are a rich source of public opinion, bias, and partisanship that are part of American political life.

Hearings are generally open to the public, unless a majority of the committee votes to hold closed executive sessions. That occurs when:

-Confidentiality is in the interests of national security and/or foreign relations.

-Open hearings could violate the privacy or unfairly tarnish the reputation of an individual or a group.

-Open hearings could disclose trade secrets.

-The information to be discussed was acquired through confidential means.

-Federal law requires that the information discussed remain confidential.

Three types of hearings are legislative, oversight, and investigative. Legislative hearings consider bills and resolutions. Few bills pass without hearings. During oversight hearings, committees review laws that fall within their jurisdictions to judge how well they have been implemented and executed, and to evaluate the effectiveness of related agency activities. Oversight hearings also judge the effectiveness of existing law and evaluate the desirability for change. The impacts of revenues and tax policies upon programs are significant aspects of oversight hearings. The purpose of investigative hearings is to inform Congress and the nation about events. Examples include the Iran-Contra Hearings, the Watergate Hearings, and the McCarthy Unamerican Activities Hearings.

The *Congressional Information Service Index (CIS Index)*, the *Monthly Catalog*, and the *Publications Reference File (PRF)*, index current hearings. A subsequent chapter on historical congressional publications examines other Congressional Information Service indexes to retrospective hearings that deal with the mid-1800's through 1969.

REPORTS

(SuDoc numbers: House--Y1.1/8:Congress-report number; Senate--Y1.1/5:Congress-report number)

Reports are statements describing committee findings and recommendations submitted by committees to their respective chambers following the conclusion of hearings. Reports introduced during each Congress are numbered sequentially according to their House or Senate series. S. Rept. 102-3 represents the third Senate report submitted during the 102nd Congress, whereas H. Rept. 102-3 is the third one submitted to that chamber during the same Congress. The subject matter of S. Rept. 102-3 is unlikely to be related to that of H. Rept. 102-3. They will probably have only one common characteristic--both were the third reports submitted to their respective bodies during the 102nd Congress. Figure 4-10 illustrates an example of a report.

Figure 4-10
House Report

100TH CONGRESS 2d Session	HOUSE OF REPRESENTATIVES	REPT. 100-511 Part 1

FAMILY AND MEDICAL LEAVE ACT

———————

MARCH 8, 1988.—Ordered to be printed

———————

Mrs. SCHROEDER, from the Committee on Post Office and Civil Service, submitted the following

REPORT

[To accompany H.R. 925 which on February 3, 1987, was referred jointly to the Committee on Education and Labor and the Committee on Post Office and Civil Service]

[Including cost estimate of the Congressional Budget Office]

The Committee on Post Office and Civil Service, to whom was referred the bill (H.R. 925) to entitle employees to family leave in certain cases involving a birth, an adoption, or a serious health condition and to temporary medical leave in certain cases involving a serious health condition, with adequate protection of the employees' employment and benefit rights, and to establish a commission to study ways of providing salary replacement for employees who take any such leave, having considered the same, reports favorably thereon with an amendment and recommends that the bill as amended do pass.

The amendment is as follows:

Strike title II and insert in lieu thereof the following:

Test your understanding of reports: All questions relate to Figure 4-10.

   1.   What report number is illustrated in Figure 4-10? During which Congress and session was this report issued?

> (H. Rept. 100-511, part 1, the 511th report is-
> sued by the House during the 100th Congress,
> 2nd session.)

   2.   Which committee issued the report and when did it do so?

> (House Committee on Post Office
> and Civil Service; March 8, 1988)

   3.   What bill did the report deal with?

> (H.R. 925)

Reports often include section by section analysis of bills. The courts consider this information the most authoritative statement of legislative intent. Figure 4-11 shows an analysis of Title II of the Family and Medical Leave Act.

Figure 4-11
Section by Section Analysis in a Report

Section Analysis of Title II

Section 201. Family and temporary medical leave

Section 201 amends chapter 63 of title 5, United States Code, by adding a new subchapter III—Family and Temporary Medical Leave—containing the following sections.

Section 6331. Definitions

Paragraph (1) of section 6331 defines "employee" to mean an "employee" as defined by section 6301(2) of title 5, United States Code, excluding an individual employed by the District of Columbia government. Physicians, dentists, or nurses in the Department of Medicine and Surgery, Veterans' Administration, and teachers or

Source: H. Rept. 100-511, 19.

Reports also include factual analysis of situations as seen by the committees and opinions of minority members of the committees. In an attempt to streamline consideration of fiscal issues, reports on bills providing for new spending must include:

   1.   Assessments of inflationary impacts.

   2.   Congressional Budget Office cost estimates for the current fiscal year, plus each of the next five years of the program.

   3.   Analysis of Congressional Budget Office assessments compared to those submitted to the committees by executive agencies.

Moreover, reports on bills that deal with revenue must include information about the effects of the proposed changes upon receipts. Reports issued by the Committees on Appropriations, on Rules, and on Standards of Official Conduct are exempt from these requirements.

When bills are reported, the committees indicate in different typeface the text that is to be added and/or deleted from the law. In Figure 4-12, Congress deletes the 53 that appears in bold brackets and inserts "53, subchapter III of Chapter 63," which is in italic print.

Figure 4-12
Changes in the Law Seen in Different Typefaces

*　　　*　　　*　　　*　　　*　　　*　　　*

PART III—EMPLOYEES

*　　　*　　　*　　　*　　　*　　　*　　　*

Subpart A—General Provisions

CHAPTER 21—DEFINITIONS

*　　　*　　　*　　　*　　　*　　　*　　　*

§ 2105. Employee

(a) * * *

*　　　*　　　*　　　*　　　*　　　*

(c) An employee paid from nonappropriated funds of the Army and Air Force Exchange Service, Army and Air Force Motion Picture Service, Navy Ship's Stores Ashore, Navy exchanges, Marine Corps exchanges, Coast Guard exchanges, and other instrumentalities of the United States under the jurisdiction of the armed forces conducted for the comfort, pleasure, contentment, and mental and physical improvement of personnel of the armed forces is deemed not an employee for the purpose of—

(1) laws (other than subchapter IV of chapter [53] *53, subchapter III of chapter 63,* of this title, subchapter III of chapter 83 of this title to the extent provided in section 8332(b)(16) of this title, and sections 5550 and 7204 of this title) administered by the Office of Personnel Management; or

*　　　*　　　*　　　*　　　*　　　*

Source: House Rept. 100-511, 55.

House and Senate versions of the same bill often differ because each chamber amends the bill before enacting it. In such cases, the House and Senate leadership appoint representatives to serve on a conference committee. This committee attempts to resolve the differences. The resulting conference report suggests compromise language. H. Rept. 1090, a conference report that deals with the *Ocean Dumping Ban Act*, appears in Figure 4-13.

Figure 4-13
Conference Report

100TH CONGRESS 2d Session	HOUSE OF REPRESENTATIVES	REPORT 100–1090

OCEAN DUMPING BAN ACT

OCTOBER 18, 1988.—Ordered to be printed

Mr. JONES of North Carolina, from the committee of conference, submitted the following

CONFERENCE REPORT

[To accompany S. 2030]

The committee of conference on the disagreeing votes of the two Houses on the amendments of the House to the bill (S. 2030) to amend the Marine Protection, Research, and Sanctuaries Act, having met, after full and free conference, have agreed to recommend and do recommend to their respective Houses as follows:

That the Senate recede from its disagreement to the amendment of the House to the text of the bill and agree to the same with an amendment as follows:

In lieu of the matter proposed to be inserted by the House amendment insert the following:

TITLE I—OCEAN DUMPING OF SEWAGE SLUDGE AND INDUSTRIAL WASTE

SEC. 1001. SHORT TITLE.

This title may be cited as the "Ocean Dumping Ban Act of 1988".

SEC. 1002. ESTABLISHMENT OF FEES AND PENALTIES FOR OCEAN DUMPING OF SEWAGE SLUDGE AND INDUSTRIAL WASTE.

The Marine Protection, Research, and Sanctuaries Act of 1972 (33 U.S.C. 1401 et seq.) is amended by striking the second section 104A and inserting in lieu thereof the following:

Test your understanding of reports by answering the following:

In Figure 4-13, why do sections 1001 and 1002 appear in italics?

> (As with bills that have been amended, re-
> ports also cite in italic print information that is
> to be inserted into the proposed legislation.)

The *Congressional Information Service Index* (*CIS Index*) and the *Monthly Catalog* index reports. See a subsequent chapter on legislative histories for a discussion of the *Congressional Index*, the *Congressional Record*, and the *House Calendar*. These sources provide subject access to reports through their indexes to bills and resolutions.

For more information about reports, consult the discussion of the *Congressional Serial Set* and the *CIS US Serial Set Index*[12] in the chapter that deals with historical Congressional information. The *Serial Set* consists of reports and Congressional documents published by Congress. Congressional documents are described below in this chapter.

CONGRESSIONAL RECORD

(SuDoc number: X Congress/Session/volume/issue)

INTRODUCTION AND BACKGROUND

The debates and proceedings before Congress are in the *Congressional Record*[13] since 1873. It is published daily while Congress is in session. At the end of the session, the daily issues are cumulated into the permanent bound edition.[14] The 1985 *Congressional Record* was the first to be distributed by GPO to depository libraries in CD-ROM format.[15] People sometimes have difficulty distinguishing the *Congressional Record* from hearings. The *Record* reflects debates and proceedings on the floors of the House and the Senate, while hearings are committee deliberations.

The *Congressional Record* can sometimes be very entertaining. *Will the Gentleman Yield? The Congressional Record Humor Book,*[16] reproduces what the compilers believe are the most amusing pieces. These include April Fools Day humor, recognition of the fifteenth anniversary of the Hee-Haw television show, and economic theory. Representative Trent Lott (Republican--Mississippi) commenting upon the nation's economic condition asked the Speaker of the House:

> ...when you go to the grocery store, do you drop your false teeth over the outrageous prices you must pay? Perhaps you drop your teeth because you cannot afford the denture adhesive to hold them in anymore. At $2.89 a tube, denture adhesive is beginning to look like a luxury.
>
> What is most disheartening is remembering 25 years ago when prices were about a third what they are now. That same tube of denture adhesive sold for 98 cents then, and a person could afford to keep his choppers in his mouth...[17]

Will Rogers stated:

...the biggest praise that a humorist can have, is to get your stuff into the *Congressional Record*. Just think, my name will be right alongside all those other big humorists.[18]

Before 1873, debates and proceedings were not recorded systematically due to a lack of both American and British precedent. Between 1789 and mid-1873 several private sources[19] printed them and newspaper accounts summarized them. Current reporting, which is close to verbatim acounts, began only after Isaac Pitman developed his shorthand system.

CALENDAR DATES VS. LEGISLATIVE DATES

Dates of the *Congressional Record* are sometimes confusing. The front page of each issue notes calendar dates. This is sometimes different from the Senate legislative day. The rules of the Senate require that the Chamber go through a regimentized process that lasts approximately two hours at the beginning of each legislative session. To avoid this process, at the end of each day's business, the Senate sometimes votes to recess, rather than adjourn. Business then resumes on the following day at the same point. The legislative day is the first day of proceedings that follows the last formal adjournment. Legislative days can last days, weeks, or months.

Test your understanding of calendar vs. legislative days:

What are the calendar and legislative days of the *Congressional Record* illustrated in Figure 4-14?

Calendar day (October 1, 1992)
Legislative day (September 30, 1992)

Figure 4-14
Congressional Record
Calendar vs. Legislative Days

Congressional Record

United States of America

PROCEEDINGS AND DEBATES OF THE 102^d CONGRESS, SECOND SESSION

| *Vol. 138* | WASHINGTON, THURSDAY, OCTOBER 1, 1992 | *No. 138—PART II* |

Senate

(Legislative day of Wednesday, September 30, 1992)

DEPARTMENTS OF COMMERCE, JUSTICE, AND STATE, THE JUDICIARY AND RELATED AGENCIES APPROPRIATIONS ACT, FISCAL YEAR 1993—CONFERENCE REPORT

Mr. HOLLINGS. Mr. President. I sub-

$860.6 million in outlays below the President's budget proposal for this bill. So, the conference report spends a lot less than the administration requested.

The conference agreement before the

Fourth, within our defense allocation, we have been able to accommodate a significant increase for the Ready Reserve Force of the Maritime Administration. Operation Desert Storm underscored sealift as the weak

CONTENTS OF THE CONGRESSIONAL RECORD

The *Congressional Record* has four sections: the debates of the House, the debates of the Senate, the Extension of Remarks, and the Daily Digest. Each section uses different pagination that runs consecutively day to day. Page numbers of Senate and House proceedings have an S and an H; the Extension of Remarks has an E; and the Daily Digest has a D. Suppose the final page of Senate debates on day 1 is S250, the first page on day 2 will be S251. Pagination in the permanent bound edition is continuous throughout the session. The discussion below describes each section of the *Congressional Record*.

Debates and Proceedings in the House and the Senate

The debates and proceedings include the speeches of Senators and Representatives, plus additional information relevant to the topics at hand which legislators insert into the record. Contrary to popular opinion, the *Congressional Record* is not an actual reflection of the debates. Federal law only requires it to be a substantially verbatim account.[20]

Members of Congress can make grammatical changes to their remarks before its publication, providing the content of the information is not affected. In the House, Representatives can still alter the content of their remarks if they are given unanimous consent to do so. Congressional rules recognize that unfortunate remarks are sometimes made in the heat of debate and the speakers immediately regret making them. That is, Congress fails to hold our Representatives and Senators fully responsible for what they say, providing the legislators or their staffs catch the blunders before they are printed.

Besides editing their remarks, members of Congress can also insert information into the *Congressional Record* that was never spoken in either chamber. Congress reasons that the practice saves time and allows all opinions to be heard.[21]

This practice has proven embarrassing. The staff of Congressman Hale Boggs (Democrat--Louisiana) followed his instructions to insert the following into the October 18, 1972 *Congressional Record*: "In the next few minutes, I would like to note for members the great amount of significant legislation enacted during the session..."[22] However, someone forgot to recall the speech from the printer after Boggs died in an Alaskan plane crash two days earlier on October 16. Congressman Kenneth Hechler (Democrat--West Virginia) drew attention to the practice when he remarked:

> I would like to indicate that I am not really speaking these words. I do not want to kid anyone into thinking that I am now on my feet delivering a stirring oration. As a matter of fact, I am back in my office typing this out on my own hot little typewriter, far from the maddening crowd and somewhat removed from the House chamber.[23]

Congress adopted the bullet system in 1978 to limit the insertion of unspoken speeches into the *Congressional Record*. Remarks not made in either chamber were preceded and then followed with bullets (•) (Figure 4-15).

Figure 4-15
Congressional Record
Speech Inserted with a Bullet

**PROFESSIONAL AND AMATEUR
SPORTS PROTECTION ACT**

• Mr. DeCONCINI. Mr. President, I am pleased to report that the President signed S. 474, the Professional and Amateur Sports Protection Act, which Congress passed prior to adjournment. During final consideration of the bill, I entered into colloquies with several of my colleagues who were concerned about the applicability of S. 474's prohibition to Wyoming's calcutta pools, and to parimutuel bicycle racing in New Mexico. At that time, we discussed whether it was the intent of the bill to cover such types of gambling operations. After having had a chance to further review these States' laws, it seems clear that New Mexico's parimutuel bicycle racing and Wyoming's calcutta wagering are exempt because they fall within S. 474's grandfather provision, section 3704. This clarification should resolve any questions regarding the applicability of the bill to the gambling activities in Wyoming and New Mexico described above.•

Source: *Congressional Record*, **October 29, 1992, S18332.**

However, speakers avoided the bullets when any part of the speech was read on the floor, even if it was just the initial sentence. Congressman William Steiger (Republican--Wisconsin), a leading advocate of the change, still believed it was a worthwhile reform despite the limitation. He exclaimed that:

> "...it is an historic thing we are doing ... The reputation of one of the most dishonest and mistrusted publications in the world may yet be saved. The world will little note what we say, but after today, it will have a better idea of what we did not say on the floor of the House and Senate..."[24]

The House modified the bullet system effective September 1985. Since then, speeches not made on the floor appear in a different typeface (Figure 4-16).

Figure 4-16
Congressional Record
House Speech Inserted with Smaller Typeface

Mr. SCHUMER. Mr. Speaker, I once again want to thank the gentleman from Wisconsin [Mr. SENSENBRENNER] for his help on this, and the gentleman from Michigan, [Mr. DINGELL] for his generosity and ability to sit down and compromise, as well as the gentlewoman from Illinois [Mrs. COLLINS], as well as the gentleman from New York and the gentleman from Michigan. I think this is a bill that will be a notable accomplishment of this Congress.

Mr. HOYER. Mr. Speaker, I rise today in strong support of H.R. 4542, the Anti-Car Theft Act of 1992. I would like to thank and commend the chairman of the Judiciary Subcommittee on Crime, Mr. SCHUMER, and chairman BROOKS and DINGELL, for working so diligently to bring this timely legislation to the floor.

Source: *Congressional Record*, **October 15, 1992, H11821.**

Although he never delivered his speech in the House, Congressman Steny Hoyer (Democrat--Maryland) still states "...I rise today in strong support of H.R. 4542, the Anti-Car Theft Act of 1992." In the Senate section of the *Congressional Record*, bullets still precede undelivered remarks.

EXTENSION OF REMARKS

Although the Extension of Remarks was intended to provide more detailed explanations and comments on Congressional activities, it seldom serves that purpose. The Extension of Remarks includes information separate from the day's proceedings, such as speeches, reprints of newspaper articles, telegrams, and excerpts from periodicals, among other sources. Some believe this section of the *Congressional Record* is "bloated with trivia on every conceivable subject," including recipes, jokes, and poetry.[25]

Some legislators have used the Extension of Remarks for political gain. Congresswoman Ileana Ros-Lentinen (Republican--Florida) has been accused of using it as a "billboard for her district."[26] A Bar Mitzvah announcement for Todd Rosen--a resident of her district, a tribute to Kristina Tew--an eleven year old resident of her district who invented a page turner for a piano, and a reference to a Girl Scout cookie sale are among the items she placed in the Extension of Remarks.

A well-known controversy involving the *Congressional Record* occurred during the 1970's. The Joint Committee on Printing refused to allow excerpts from writings by Kurt Vonnegut, Bernard Malamud, Langston Hughes and others to be printed in the Extension of Remarks. The Committee Chairman, Wayne Hayes who was associated with the Elizabeth Ray sex scandal, defended his Committee's decision by arguing that Congress cannot let its *Record* be a "pornographic document." He added, "You preserve the dignity of the Congress if you don't put all the four letter words in it (*Congressional Record*)."[27]

Before 1968, the Extension of Remarks was called the Appendix. It appeared in both the daily and bound *Record* between 1937 and 1954. However, from 1955 through 1967, the Appendix was deleted from the bound editions, unless the information related to legislation under consideration. Since 1968, the Extension of Remarks has appeared in both the daily and bound issues.

DAILY DIGEST

The Daily Digest section of the *Congressional Record* summarizes activities in the House and Senate during the previous day, and lists schedules of committee and subcommittee hearings. The Daily Digest in the first *Congressional Record* published each month includes a statistical Resume of Congressional Activity. The number of days and hours Congress was in session; the number of pages of proceedings in the *Congressional Record*; and the number of bills introduced, reported, and enacted are cited. Statistics are year to date. The Daily Digest has been published in the daily *Congressional Record* since 1947 and it is reproduced in the last bound volume of the permanent *Congressional Record*.

The chapter on legislative histories describes indexes to the *Congressional Record*, plus related databases and Internet sites.

JOURNALS OF THE HOUSE AND SENATE

(SuDoc numbers: *House Journal*--XJH:Congress-session;
Senate Journal--XJS:Congress-session; *Journal of
Executive Proceedings...Senate*--Y1.3/4:Vol.)

Following the termination of a Congressional session, Journals publish the official proceedings of Congress in three editions. The *House Journal* and the *Senate Journal* each cover business conducted in public. A third title, the *Journal of the Executive Proceedings of the Senate of the United States of America*, deals with treaties and nominations discussed in executive or closed sessions. *Journals* are the only publications required by the Constitution. Article I, Section 5 states: "Each House shall keep a Journal of its Proceedings, and from time to time publish the same . . ." Journals include legislative histories, voting records, summaries of petitions and papers, and presidential messages. Unlike the *Congressional Record, Journals* contain neither debates nor Extension of Remarks.

The *Senate Journal* includes a Subject Index and a History of Bills and Resolutions section. The latter lists bills and resolutions in numerical order and cites actions Congress took on the measures. The more elaborate indexes to the *House Journal* also include a History of Bills and Resolutions section, plus indexes to votes, committee actions, messages from the President, and petitions and memorials. Petitions are statements by citizens that reflect opinions on various topics and memorials are resolutions enacted by state legislatures that express feelings on key issues.

HOUSE AND *SENATE CALENDARS*

(SuDoc numbers: *House Calendar*--Y1.2/2:Date-issue number;

Senate Calendar--Y1.3/3:Date-issue number)

House and Senate agendas are in each chamber's respective *Calendar*. Issues come out every day Congress is in session. This chapter only discusses the *House Calendar* because it is cumulated weekly in the first published issue each week, and at the termination of each Congressional session. The *Senate Calendar* has little practical value outside that Chamber, since data are not cumulated.

The *House Calendar* has four sections.

-Union Calendar: Bills and resolutions dealing with appropriations and revenues appear on the Union Calendar.

-House Calendar: Public bills that do not deal with revenues or appropriations are on the House Calendar.

-Private Calendar: Private bills are on the Private Calendar.

-Consent Calendar: Non-controversial bills that are passed with little or no debate are on the Consent Calendar.

The most useful reference value of the *House Calendar* is its History of Bills and Resolutions section. Excluding Senate resolutions that are of no interest to the House, bills and resolutions of both chambers are listed in numerical order. Citations show actions taken by Congress on the bills and the relevant dates. Reference to H.R. 828, the bill seen above in Figure 4-1, appears in Figure 4-17.

Figure 4-17
House Calendar
History of Bills and Resolutions

H.R. 801.—Commemorations and Memorials, "Tuttle Court of Appeals Building, Elbert P.", United States Court of Appeals Building at 56 Forsyth Street in Atlanta, Georgia as, designate. Referred to Public Works and Transportation Feb. 2, 1989. Reported amended June 22, 1989; Rept. 101-102. House Calendar. Passed House amended June 28, 1989. Received in Senate and referred to Environment and Public Works July 11 (Legislative day of Jan. 3), 1989. Committee discharged. Passed Senate Oct. 17 (Legislative day of Sept. 18), 1989. **Approved Oct. 30, 1989. Public Law 101–132.**

H.R. 828 (H. Res. 200).—Bureau of Land Management, Fiscal Years 1990, 1991, 1992, and 1993 authorizations. Referred to Interior and Insular Affairs Feb. 2, 1989. Reported amended July 11, 1989; Rept. 101-132. Union Calendar. Passed House amended July 17, 1989. Received in Senate and referred to Energy and Natural Resources July 19 (Legislative day of Jan. 3), 1989.

Source: *House Calendar, Final Edition*, **101st Congress, 8-5.**

H.R. 828 and H.Res. 200, which is in parenthesis following H.R. 828, are either identical or very similar. In Figure 4-17, H.R. 801 immediately precedes H.R. 828 because the *House Calendar*'s History of Bills and Resolutions section only covers bills that have been acted upon. H.R. 802 through 827 were neither reported from Committee nor debated.

The first *House Calendar* published each week cumulates the History of Bills and Resolutions section from the beginning of a Congress. It also has an index arranged by names of agencies and programs, and by selected subjects. It cites bill numbers, as well as names of legislators who introduced the legislation. Figure 4-18 shows H.R. 828.

Figure 4-18
House Calendar
Index

Budget Reconciliation Act of 1990, Omnibus. H.R. 5835; Mr. Panetta. S. 3209.
    Consideration of. H. Res. 509; Mr. Derrick.
    Correct enrollment. S. Con. Res. 159.
    Waiving certain points of order against consideration of conference report. H. Res. 537; Mr. Derrick.

Budget sequestration for a fiscal year, require. S. 1850.

Bureau of Land Management, fiscal years 1990, 1991, 1992, and 1993 authorizations. H.R. 828; Mr. Vento.
    Consideration of. H. Res. 200; Mr. Beilenson.

Source: *House Calendar, Final Edition*, **101st Congress, 19-6.**

Figure 4-18 illustrates that Congressman Vento introduced H.R. 828 and Congressman Beilenson introduced H.Res. 200. The Final Edition of the *House Calendar*, which covers both sessions of a Congress, provides a comprehensive summary of legislative activity for that Congress.

Other sections of the *House Calendar* cite public laws and corresponding bill numbers; bills that are currently in conference and those that have been reported from their conference committees; and bills that were vetoed.

CONGRESSIONAL DOCUMENTS

(SuDoc numbers: House--Y1.1/7:Congress-document number; Senate--Y1.1/3:Congress-document number)

Congressional Documents refers to this particular group of publications. They should not be confused with government documents, or documents as used in a more general sense. The latter includes all types of government publications--federal, state, local, and international. On the other hand, Congressional documents include:

-Reprints of Presidential messages to Congress (speeches, veto statements).

-Statements to Congress by executive agencies.

-Annual reports to Congress by patriotic organizations (Girl Scouts, Veterans of Foreign Wars).

-Materials that committees believe will be of public interest and value.

Like reports, documents numbers are sequentially by Congress. S. Doc. 102-3 represents the third document issued by the Senate during the 102nd Congress, whereas H. Doc. 102-3 represents the third document issued by the House during the same Congress. Again, as with reports, the subject matter will more than likely, be dissimilar.

Identification of Congressional documents becomes difficult when the term report appears as part of the title. Figure 4-19, indicates that *A Senate View: Latin America and the United States In A Time of Change, A Report to the United States Senate*, is Senate document 97-13. It is a report to Congress, but it is not a Congressional report in the formal sense of being reported from a committee to its respective chamber.

Figure 4-19
Congressional Documents

97TH CONGRESS } 1st Session }	SENATE	{ DOCUMENT No. 97-13

A SENATE VIEW: LATIN AMERICA AND
THE UNITED STATES IN A TIME OF CHANGE

———

A REPORT

TO THE

UNITED STATES SENATE

JUNE 1981

The *Congressional Information Service Index* (*CIS Index*) and the *Monthly Catalog* index documents. The *Publications Reference File* (*PRF*) also indexes them selectively. Like Congressional reports, Congressional documents are also part of the *Serial Set*. Consult a subsequent chapter for detailed information about that collection and its prime index, the *CIS Serial Set Index*.

SENATE EXECUTIVE DOCUMENTS AND TREATY DOCUMENTS

(SuDoc number: Y1.1/4:Congress-document number)

Senate executive documents are Presidential messages to the Senate that contain texts of proposed treaties and supplementary information supporting their ratification. These documents are not to be confused with the *Journal of the Executive Proceedings of the Senate*, which was discussed above. Since 1981, messages relating to treaties have been called treaty documents and have been numbered sequentially within each Congress (Figure 4-20).

Figure 4-20
Treaty Document

100TH CONGRESS *2d Session*	SENATE	TREATY DOC. 100-11

TREATY BETWEEN THE UNITED STATES OF AMER-
ICA AND THE UNION OF SOVIET SOCIALIST REPUB-
LICS ON THE ELIMINATION OF THEIR INTERMEDI-
ATE-RANGE AND SHORTER-RANGE MISSILES

MESSAGE

FROM

THE PRESIDENT OF THE UNITED STATES

TRANSMITTING

THE TREATY BETWEEN THE UNITED STATES OF AMERICA AND
THE UNION OF SOVIET SOCIALIST REPUBLICS ON THE ELIMINA-
TION OF THEIR INTERMEDIATE-RANGE AND SHORTER-RANGE
MISSILES, TOGETHER WITH THE MEMORANDUM OF UNDER-
STANDING AND TWO PROTOCOLS, SIGNED AT WASHINGTON ON
DECEMBER 8, 1987

JANUARY 25, 1988.—Treaty was read the first time, and together with the
accompanying papers, referred to the Committee on Foreign Relations
and ordered to be printed for the use of the Senate.

U.S. GOVERNMENT PRINTING OFFICE
81-428   WASHINGTON : 1988

For sale by the Superintendent of Documents, U.S. Government Printing Office
Washington, DC 20402

Before 1981, Senate executive documents were lettered from A - Z in
an annual series. If more than 26 titles were issued in a year, the 27th
became document AA.

The *Congressional Information Service Index* and the *Monthly Catalog* index executive documents. The *Congressional Index* does not index them, but still cites them. The *CIS Index to US Senate Executive Documents and Reports: Covering Documents and Reports Not Printed in the US Serial Set, 1817-1969*[28] and its corresponding microfiche collection are examined in a subsequent chapter on historical Congressional publications.

Executive documents discussed in this context are different from the House and Senate executive documents issued in the 19th century. Treaty materials are executive documents because the Senate has traditionally discussed these items in executive session. Other materials published in the 1800's were also referred to as House or Senate executive documents because they included all types of communications from the President and Executive branch agencies.

SENATE EXECUTIVE REPORTS

(SuDoc number: Y1.1/6:Congress-report number)

Two types of items are in the Senate executive reports series:

-Committee recommendations to the Senate on proposed treaties, and

-Committee recommendations regarding nominations.

Like other Congressional reports and documents, numbering is consecutive within each Congress. These publications sometimes suggest amendments to treaties or indicate reservations that limit or modify the effect of selected parts of treaties. They also include interpretations or understandings that explain Congressional intent when approving treaties. Reference to S. Exec. Rept. 100-15, which deals with the INF Treaty, appears in Figure 4-21.

Figure 4-21
Senate Executive Report

100TH CONGRESS 2d Session	SENATE	EXEC. REPT. 100–15

THE INF TREATY

———

REPORT

OF THE

COMMITTEE ON FOREIGN RELATIONS
UNITED STATES SENATE

APRIL 14, 1988

U.S. GOVERNMENT PRINTING OFFICE
WASHINGTON : 1988

83-960

The *Congressional Information Service Index* and the *Monthly Catalog* index Senate executive reports.

RADIO AND TELEVISION BROADCASTS OF CONGRESSIONAL ACTIVITIES

INTRODUCTION AND BACKGROUND

Until now, the discussion considered Congressional information in print format. The appearance of radio and television broadcasting offers additional means for acquiring information about Congress. Unfortunately, Congress was not quick to jump on the bandwagon. Radio broadcasters did not get their own press gallery until 1939. Moreover, journalists could bring neither microphones nor television cameras into the House gallery until 1970.

S.J.Res. 144, introduced by Claude Pepper (Democrat--Florida) in 1944, was the first attempt to establish radio broadcasting of Senate proceedings. A second bill introduced by Pepper three years later called for television coverage of Senate proceedings. Both bills failed to pass. Vice-President Nelson Rockefeller's inauguration ceremony in 1975 was the first live television broadcast from the Senate floor.

After the experimental broadcasting of floor activities to selected Capitol offices in 1977 was proven successful, the House began regular broadcasts of its proceedings on April 3, 1979. The Speaker of the House oversees television broadcasting, distribution of broadcasts to the media, and storage of the recordings. The Cable Satellite Public Affairs Network (C-SPAN) televises broadcasts. The Senate voted to broadcast its proceedings regularly in July 1986.

Broadcasting of Congressional proceedings provides the public with benefits the *Congressional Record* does not offer--verbatim coverage of speeches. Representative Robert Smith Walker (Republican--Pennsylvania) stated that TV made proceedings an "accurate presentation of what goes on in the House of Representatives" because the *Congressional Record* is only "a record of what we wish we had said, if only we had said it right."[29]

However, as with the *Congressional Record*, legislators have also used television broadcasting for partisan political ends. Representatives sometimes appear to be making speeches on controversial and timely topics to their peers. As long as the cameras remain focused on the speaker, the public cannot detect that occasionally the day's business had been completed and that the chamber is nearly empty.

ACCESSIBILITY OF VIDEOTAPES:

Videotapes of Congress are available from the following sources. Contact each for the appropriate fees.

House Recording Studio, Records and Registration Office: (202-225-1300) Tapes of the most recent 60 days are available from the Records and Registration Office. Contact the Office for an order form. When submitting the form include a photocopy from the *Congressional Record* that cites the

119

section of the debates you would like to acquire. Older tapes are available from the Library of Congress.

Senate Recording Studio: (202-707-5705) The Senate Recording Studio maintains tapes for the 30 most recent legislative days. Earlier ones are in the Library of Congress. Contact your Senator to make borrowing or purchasing arrangements

Library of Congress, Motion Picture Broadcasting and Recorded Sound Division: (202-707-1120) Tapes of House proceedings are available from 1983 to date and those for Senate proceedings from 1986 to date. The Library of Congress requires people who buy videos to sign statements indicating that the tapes will not be used for political or commercial purposes. Delivery usually takes 4 - 6 weeks. Costs for rush orders, which are processed within 5 - 7 working days, are double the regular fees.

National Archives and Records Service, Motion Pictures Division: (202-501-5449) Researchers must complete a Subject Search Request Form to determine if the National Archives owns the tape. Response times can be 10 days or longer. Costs are determined once tapes are located.

C-SPAN: (202-737-3220) Committee hearings are available from C-SPAN.

Purdue University, Public Affairs Video Archives: (800-423-9630; E-Mail address: Bitnet--PAVA@PURCCVM; Internet--PAVA@VM.CC.PURDUE.EDU) The Public Affairs Video Archives maintains a collection of all C-SPAN broadcasts from 1987 to date. The Archives has a license with C-SPAN that limits distribution of tapes to educators. Indexing is by subjects, places, dates, names, titles, and affiliations of persons and programs.[30] Indexing for 1991 will be on CD-ROM, and efforts to put the entire database on the Internet is in progress. Compiled tapes, which deal with special topics such as the legislative history of the Clean Air Act, are also available.

Tapes are also available from commercial sources, such as Video Monitoring (202-393-7110) and Video Files (703-524-8334). Contact them for price information.

CONCLUSION

This chapter emphasizes the kinds of information available from Congress, setting the stage for the following two chapters.

Chart 4-2 summarizes this information.

Chart 4-2
Summary of Types of Congressional Publications

Kinds of Publication	Descriptions
Bills	Proposed legislation introduced into the House and the Senate. The initial bills introduced into each chamber during a Congress are H.R. 1 and S. 1. Bills require approval by both chambers and Presidential signature to become law.
Joint Resolutions	No practical differences exist between bills and joint resolutions. Both require House and Senate approval chambers and Presidential signature to become law. Joint resolutions often pertain to foreign policy issues and often correct technical inconsistencies in the law. The initial joint resolutions introduced into each chamber during a Congress are H.J.Res. 1 and S.J.Res. 1.
Concurrent Resolutions	Concurrent resolutions require approval of both chambers of Congress to become effective. Presidential approval is unnecessary. These resolutions reflect the consensus of the entire Congress. The initial concurrent resolutions introduced into each chamber during a Congress are H.Con.Res. 1 and S.Con.Res. 1.
Simple Resolutions (often referred to as resolutions)	Simple resolutions reflect the consensus of one chamber of Congress. Approval by the opposite chamber and the President is unnecessary. Simple resolutions often deal with rules and other types of housekeeping matters. The initial resolutions introduced into each chamber during a Congress are H.Res. 1 and S.Res. 1.
Committee Prints	Committee prints are usually factual studies that provide legislators with background to issues and policies.
Hearings	Forums held by Congressional committees where witnesses are invited to testify on the issues. Hearings include this testimony, plus the dialog among the witnesses and the committee members.
Reports	Statements issued by committees to the entire chamber usually following hearings. Reports describe the intent of the committee and often provide section by section analysis of bills.
Congressional Record	Debates and proceedings in Congress. The Congressional Record is often confused with hearings. Hearings are transactions and proceedings in committees, while the Congressional Record are debates and proceedings before the full chambers.
Journals	Proceedings before Congress that summarizes activities in the House and Senate. Unlike the Congressional Record, Journals do not include the debates.
Calendars	House and Senate agendas appear in each chambers respective Calendar. The House Calendar includes significant information about the status of bills, but the Senate Calendar has little practical information useful outside the Senate.
Congressional Documents	Includes reprints of Presidential messages to Congress; statements to Congress by executive agencies; annual reports to Congress by selected patriotic organizations; and other miscellaneous materials that Congress believes would be of public interest and value.
Senate Executive Documents/ Treaty Documents	Presidential messages to Congress that include texts of proposed treaties and supplementary information supporting their ratification. Since 1981, this information has been called treaty documents.
Senate Executive Reports	Includes committee recommendations to the Senate about proposed treaties and Presidential nominations.

Chapter 5 examines the *Congressional Information Service Index*, the most comprehensive index to publications of Congressional committees, and Chapter 6 evaluates sources of comprehensive legislative histories. Legislative histories describe what happens to a bill during the lawmaking process. Coverage includes both print and electronic sources. Again, emphasis is upon the kinds of documentation available at each step of the legislative process.

Endnotes

1. *Final Cumulative Finding Aid for Congressional Bills and Resolutions* (Washington, D.C.: GPO, 1979-annual). SuDoc number: GP3.28:. The *Finding Aid for Congressional Bills and Resolutions* is published periodically throughout the year. The *Final Cumulative* edition is issued at the end of a Congressional session.

2. *CIS Index to Publications of the United States Congress* (Bethesda, MD.: Congressional Information Service, Inc., 1970-monthly).

3. *(Chicago: Commerce Clearing House, 1946-weekly).*

4. (Washington, D.C.: Congressional Quarterly, Inc., 1945-weekly).

5. (Washington, D.C.: Congressional Quarterly, Inc., 1948-annual).

6. Congressional Information Service, *CIS US Congressional Committee Prints Index: From the Earliest Publications Through 1969* (Washington, D.C.: Congressional Information Service, Inc., 1980). 5 vols.; Congressional Information Service, *CIS U.S. Congressional Committee Prints* (Washington, D.C.: Congressional Information Service, Inc., 1976-1980). Approximately 18,000 microfiche.

7. *Monthly Catalog of United States Government Publications* (Washington, D.C.: GPO, 1895-monthly). SuDoc number: GP3.8:. Title varies.

8. *GPO Sales Publications Reference File* (Washington, D.C.: GPO, 1977-bimonthly). SuDoc number: GP3.22/3:.

9. See the article by Judy Manion, "Congressional Conundrums, Dogs and Ponies: Congressional Hearings," *Law Library Lights* 35:2 (November/December 1991), 24-5 for a description of how hearings are edited. Manion argues that the printing of hearings are not among GPO's highest priorities.

10. Judy Schneider, *An Introductory Guide to the Congressional Standing Committee System* (83-165 GOV) (Washington, D.C.: Congressional Research Service, 1983), 1. Reproduced in *Major Studies and Issue Briefs of the Congressional Research Service, 1983-84 Supplement.* (Frederick, MD: University Publications of America, 1984). Reel 3, frame 395.

11. *Ibid.*

12. Congressional Information Service (Washington, D.C.: Congressional Information Service, Inc., 1975-1979). 12 parts published in 36 vols.

13.   *Congressional Record: Proceedings and Debates of the Congress* (Washington, D.C.: GPO, March 1973-daily while Congress is in session). SuDoc number: X Cong./session:Vol./issue.

14.   Beginning with the 1985 edition, GPO distributes the permanent bound edition of the *Congressional Record* to only 65 depository libraries--regional depositories and selected major depositories in states that lack regionals. To acquire it, other depository libraries will have to purchase it through the GPO sales program.

15.   *The Congressional Record: Proceedings and Debates of the 99th Congress, First Session* (CD-ROM) Volume 131 (Washington, D.C.: GPO, 1990). 2 disks. SuDoc number: X99/1:131/CD1,2. Documentation to the CD-ROMs were published as U.S. Congress, *The Congressional Record on CD-ROM Tutorial and Reference Manual: Proceedings and Debates of the 99th Congress, First Session, January 3, 1985-December 20, 1985* (Washington, D.C.: GPO, 1990). SuDoc number: X99/1:131/DOC.

16.   Bill Hogan and Mike Hill (Berkeley, CA.: Ten Speed Press, 1987).

17.   *Ibid*, 57.

18.   *Ibid*, 7.

19.   The debates and proceedings of Congress between 1789 and 1824 were published as *The Debates and Proceedings in the Congress of the United States; With an Appendix Containing Important State Papers and Public Documents,...* (Washington, D.C.: Gales and Seaton, 1834-1856). Alternative title: the *Annals of Congress*. It was based upon press accounts and other published sources. The *Register of Debates* (Washington, D.C.: Gales and Seaton), which covered December 1824-October 1837, was published in a timely manner, but is still only a summary of activities. The *Congressional Globe* (Washington, D.C.: Blair and Rives) covered December 1833- March 1873; See also John C. Rives, *Abridgement of the Debates of Congress from 1789 to 1856* (New York: D. Appleton, 1857-1861). 16 vols.

20.   44 *U.S.C.* 901.

21.   Mildred Amer, *The Congressional Record* (86-152 GOV) (Washington, D.C.: Congressional Research Service, 1986), 20. Reproduced in *Major Studies and Issue Briefs of the Congressional Research Service, 1986-87 Supplement* (Frederick, MD: University Publications of America, 1982). Reel 5, frame 350.

22.   Joe Morehead, "The Forlorn Passion of William Steiger," *Technical Services Quarterly* 3:3/4 (Spring/Summer, 1986), 120.

23.   *Ibid*, 121.

24.   U.S. House. Committee on House Administration, *Accuracy in House Proceedings Resolution* (H. Rept. 99-228) 99th Cong., 1st sess. (Washington, D.C.: GPO, 1985), 12. SuDoc number: Y1.1/8:99-228.

25.   Morehead, "The Forlorn Passion...," 119.

26.   Milton Gwirtzman, "Congress's Daily Advertisement for Itself," *Wall Street Journal*, October 8, 1992, A-14.

27.   Martin Tolchin, "7 Writers' Words Barred by *Congressional Record*," *New York Times*, May 11, 1976, 20.

28.   Congressional Information Service (Washington, D.C.: Congressional Information Service, Inc., 1987). 2 vols.; Congressional Information Service, *Senate Executive Documents and Reports* (Washington, D.C.: Congressional Information Service, Inc., 1987). 1153 microfiche.

29.   U.S. Congress. House. Committee on House Administration, *Task Force on the Congressional Record* (Washington, D.C.: GPO, 1990), 2. SuDoc number: Y4.H81/3:C76/3.

30.   Activities and services of the Archives are described by its Director, Robert X. Browning, in an article: "Archiving the Video Record of Legislatures," *Canadian Parliamentary Review* 12:2 (Summer, 1989), 9-11.

Exercises

1. Describe how each of the following types of measures must be approved to become effective.
    Bills
    Joint resolutions
    Concurrent resolutions
    Simple resolutions

2. Briefly describe the kinds of information contained in each type of Congressional publication and note how this information could be useful in your work.
    Committee prints
    Hearings
    Reports
    Congressional Record
    Congressional documents
    Treaty documents
    Senate executive reports

Answers

1.   Bills: Bills must be approved by both houses of Congress and signed by the President.

     Joint resolutions: Like bills, joint resolutions must be approved by both houses of Congress and signed by the President.

     Concurrent resolutions: Concurrent resolutions must be approved by both chambers of Congress.

     Simple resolutions: Simple resolutions must be approved by only one chamber of Congress.

2.   Committee prints: Committee prints are studies prepared by either committee staffs or the Congressional Research Service. Senators and Congressmen consult them for background information.

     Hearings: Hearings are the proceedings before Congressional committees where government officials and experts from the private sector and academia present their views on the issues.

     Reports: Congressional committees issue reports to their respective chambers. Reports cite and explain the committees' recommendations.

     Congressional Record: The *Congressional Record* reproduces the debates and proceedings before the House and Senate.

     Congressional documents: Congressional documents include executive branch messages to Congress; annual reports to Congress by patriotic organizations; and other information that Congress believes will be of public interest.

     Treaty documents: Treaty documents are Presidential messages to the Senate that include texts of proposed treaties and supporting documentation.

     Senate executive reports: Senate executive reports include two types of items: committee recommendations to the Senate on proposed treaties and recommendations on Presidential nominations.

•Chapter 5

Congressional Publications —Part II: *CIS Index*

Answer the following questions when reading this chapter:

1. What types of publications are included/excluded from the *CIS Index*?

2. How does the *CIS Index* compare to the *Monthly Catalog* and the *Publications Reference File*?

3. When would it be advantageous to use the *CIS Index*?

Chapter 4 considered various kinds of Congressional publications and their characteristics. This chapter describes the *CIS Index to Publications of the United States Congress (CIS Index)*[1], the most comprehensive index to materials published by Congressional committees. The nearly 300 committees, subcommittees, and special offices of Congress produce 800,000 pages of documentation annually.[2] These publications include hearings, reports, Congressional documents, and committee prints. CIS views special publications that do not fall within other categories as committee prints. The *CIS Index* excludes the following materials:

1. Reports that deal with private bills, and ceremonial and housekeeping matters.

2. Congressional documents also published by other agencies.

Microfiche copies of all items indexed in the *CIS Index* are sold by CIS.[3]

I use rept as a standard abbreviation for Congressional reports despite different references sources referring to them as rept, rpt, and rp.

Since its inception in 1970, the monthly *CIS Index* has two parts, an *Index* volume and an *Abstracts* volume. The indexes are cumulated quarterly and annually. To date, the six multiyear cumulative indexes cover 1970-1974, 1975-1978, 1979-1982, 1983-1986, 1987-1990, and 1991-1994.[4] The *Abstracts* volume is cumulated annually. It provides bibliographic information, Superintendent of Documents numbers needed to retrieve the documents from the shelves/microfiche files, and summaries of contents.

Since 1984, CIS publishes an annual legislative histories volume that cites bills and Congressional publications relating to enacted legislation.[5] *Abstracts* volumes published through 1983 included more abbreviated legislative histories. The next chapter deals with legislative histories.

Follow three steps when using the *CIS Index*.

1. Consult the appropriate index in the *Index* volume and note the CIS accession number.

2. Consult the CIS accession number in the *Abstracts* volume for titles, SuDoc numbers, and pages on which information is found.

3. Use Superintendent of Documents numbers to retrieve materials distributed in either paper or microfiche formats by GPO. Use CIS accession numbers to retrieve microfiche purchased from CIS.

This chapter covers steps one and two. The organization and arrangement of the Index of Subjects and Names is examined first. The discussion then considers the *Abstracts* volume and its relationship to the *Index* volume. After that, the text describes the other eight indexes. These include the:

-Index of Titles

-Index of Bill Numbers

-Index of Report Numbers

-Index of Document Numbers

-Index of Senate Hearing Numbers

-Index of Senate Print Numbers

-Index of Superintendent of Documents Numbers

-Index of Committee and Subcommittee Chairmen

The chapter concludes with a discussion of the online and CD-ROM versions of the *CIS Index*.

USING THE *CIS INDEX*

Index of Subjects and Names: An Introduction

The largest part of the Index of Subjects and Names covers:

-Subjects of publications.

-Subjects of testimonies presented by witnesses at hearings.

-Subjects of materials inserted into hearings as evidence.

Information appears under the most specific term or phrase. Cross references refer users from broader to narrower terms. For example, when searching the Index of Subjects and Names under the term Pollution, cross references tell you to consult other headings. These include Air Pollution, Environmental Pollution and Control, and Noise.

The following special subject headings in the *CIS Index* are sometimes useful:

-Bibliographies--includes items that contain bibliographies or themselves are bibliographies.

-Congressional committee activity reports and Congressional Committee Calendars--both subject headings refer to publications that summarize committee activities.

-Court documents

-Directories

-Glossaries

-Statistical data: agriculture

-Statistical data: banking, finance, and insurance

-Statistical data: communications and transportation

-Statistical data: education

-Statistical data: energy

-Statistical data: environmental pollution and control

-Statistical data: government

-Statistical data: health and vital statistics

-Statistical data: industry and commerce

-Statistical data: international trade

-Statistical data: labor and employment

-Statistical data: law enforcement

-Statistical data: natural resources and conservation

-Statistical data: population

-Statistical data: prices and cost of living

-Statistical data: public welfare and social security

-Statistical data: recreation and leisure

-Statistical data: science and technology

-Statistical data: veterans affairs

Indexing follows four conventions:

1. Arrangement is alphabetical word by word. That is, New York is filed before Newark.

2. Numbers appear after the alphabetical section in a digit by digit arrangement. That is, F-14 precedes F-4.

3. Agency names use keywords, not "Department of ..." nor "Bureau of..." Information pertaining to the Bureau of the Census is under Census Bureau and information relating to the Department of Agriculture is under Agriculture Department.

4. Whenever possible, CIS omits the prefix U.S.; for example, search Navy, not U.S. Navy, for information about that topic.

Index of Subjects and Names: Locating Information by Subjects

To locate information about discrimination against the disabled, search the appropriate subject heading in the Index of Subject and Names. Index entries can have either three or four parts. Figure 5-1 shows index entries from the 1987-1990 cumulative index.

Figure 5-1
CIS Four-Year Cumulative Index,
Index of Subjects and Names--Using Cross References

Handicapped

Veterans life insurance programs revision,
90 H761–2

Veterans medical costs for
nonservice-connected disabilities,
reimbursement by third parties,
90 S761–3

Veterans rehabilitation programs review,
88 H761–29

Vietnam-era and disabled veterans
noncompetitive civil service employment
authority, extension and revision,
89 H761–26, **89** H763–9, **90** H763–2,
90 S761–7

Vietnamese amputees prosthetic devices
needs assessment, State Dept rpt,
˙**88** H381–18.1

Vocational educ programs, extension and
revision, **89** H341–51.1, **89** H341–51.3,
89 H343–5, **90** PL101–392

Vocational educ programs, FY90-FY95
authorization, **90** S541–4.9

Voter registration procedures revision,
89 H421–1.2

Voting place access by elderly and
handicapped, Fed requirements
implementation, **88** H421–2

Women's retirement income issues and
problems, **90** H141–19.2

see also Adult day care
see also Architectural barriers
see also Blind
see also Deaf
see also Disability insurance
see also Discrimination against the
handicapped
see also Housing for the handicapped
see also Mental retardation

Source: *CIS Four-Year Cumulative Index, 1987-1990,* **1366.**
Reprinted with permission from the
CIS Four-Year Cumulative Index, 1987-1990.
Copyright 1991 by Congressional Information Service, Inc. (Bethesda, MD).
All rights reserved.

Significant parts of Figure 5-1 include the following:

-Subject heading. (Handicapped)

-Cross references. (Adult day care; Architectural barriers;. . .)

-Brief phrases that describe the documents.

-CIS accession numbers. Bold face numbers indicate which abstract issue to consult because Figure 5-1 is from a cumulative index that covers four years. For instance, *87* refers to the 1987 *Abstracts* volume; **88** refers to the 1988 *Abstracts* volume; **89** refers to the 1989 *Abstracts* volume; and **90** refers to the 1990 *Abstracts* volume.[6]

Annual or monthly indexes do not use bold face notations because of their one-on-one relationship. The 1991 annual *Index* volume refers to the 1991 *Abstracts* volume and the January 1993 index refers to the January 1993 abstracts.

-Cross references. (Adult day care; Architectural barriers;...)

After consulting entries under Handicapped, you decide that Discrimination against the handicapped, a cross reference in Figure 5-1, is more appropriate to your needs. (Figure 5-2) Remember, cross references generally refer to narrower topics because information is usually indexed under the most specific subject term.

Figure 5-2
CIS Four-Year Cumulative Index,
Index of Subjects and Names--Locating More Specific Information

Discrimination against the handicapped
  Acquired immune deficiency syndrome, civil
    rights issues, **87** H401–33.4
  Airline seating restrictions for blind
    passengers, prohibition, **89** S261–34,
    89 S263–10
  Blind workers job placement at sheltered
    workshops, **87** H721–13.3
  "Judge Bork and the Rights of Disabled
    People", **89** S521–26
  "Out of the Job Market: A National Crisis",
    87 S541–43.2
  Prohibition, **89** H341–36, **89** H341–81,
    89 S541–17, **89** S541–37, **89** S543–11,
    90 H341–2, **90** H341–3, **90** H341–4,
    90 H343–6, **90** H343–12, **90** H343–20,
    90 H361–19, **90** H363–9, **90** H521–37,
    90 H523–8, **90** H641–25, **90** H643–1,
    90 H721–24, **90** PL101–336
  Sheltered workshops salary and promotion
    policies, **87** H401–65
  Telephone relay services for the deaf,
    requirement estab, **90** H361–20
  "Toward Equality: Education of the Deaf",
    89 H341–60.2

Using the information in Figure 5-2, locate references in the appropriate *Abstracts* volume with the alphanumeric CIS accession number. The letters (H, S, or J) refer to House, Senate, and joint committee publications. "PL" notations refer to the legislative histories of public laws. PL101-392 represents the 392nd public law enacted during the 101st Congress.

Test your understanding of the Index of Subjects and Names: Answer the following questions that relate to Figure 5-2.

1. Under the phrase Prohibition, how many references to publications are cited in the 1989 abstracts?

    (5)

2. Describe each part of the following citation listed under Prohibition: **90** H341-4.

    (H341-4 is the CIS accession number used to locate this document in the 1990 *Abstracts* volume.)

3. What does the last reference under Prohibition, PL101-336, represent?

    (The 336th public law enacted during the 101st Congress.)

Abstracts Volume:

Figure 5-3 shows the abstract entry for citation 90 H341-4.

Figure 5-3

Abstracts Volume

Volume: Hearings

H341–4   HEARING ON H.R. 2273, THE AMERICANS WITH DISABILITIES ACT OF 1989.

Sept. 13, 1989.   101-1.

iii+168 p.   GPO $5.00

S/N 552-070-07368-0.

CIS/MF/4

•Item 1015-A; 1015-B.

*Y4.Ed8/1:101-51.

MC 90-8975. LC 90-600205.

Committee Serial No. 101-51. Hearing before the *Subcom on Employment Opportunities* and the *Subcom on Select Education* to consider H.R. 2273 (text, p. 132-168) and companion S. 933, both the Americans with Disabilities Act (ADA) of 1989, to prohibit discrimination against the handicapped in various areas, including employment.

Supplementary material (p. 125-168) includes submitted statements.

H341–4.1: Sept. 13, 1989. p. 2-25.

Witness: **KEMP, Evan J., Jr.,** Commissioner, Equal Employment Opportunity Commission.

Statement and Discussion: Barriers to the employment of disabled individuals, focusing on attitudinal aspects; preference for Senate-passed version of the ADA.

H341–4.2: Sept. 13, 1989. p. 26-124.

Witnesses: **ROCHLIN, Jay,** Executive Director, President's Committee on Employment of People with Disabilities.

DONOVAN, Mark R., Manager, Community Employment and Training Programs, Marriott Corp.

RASMUSSEN, Duane A., President and Chief Executive Officer, Sell Publishing Co.; representing National Federation of Independent Business, Minnesota Newspaper Association, and Independent Business Association of Minnesota.

WHAREN, Paul D., Project Manager, Thomas P. Harkins, Inc.; representing Associated Builders and Contractors.

MAYERSON, Arlene B., Directing Attorney, Disability Rights Education and Defense Fund.

Statements and Discussion: Experiences in the development and implementation of programs to facilitate employment of disabled individuals; differing perspectives on H.R. 2273 and companion S. 933, including business concerns regarding employment-related provisions.

Aspects of prejudice against disabled persons; review of studies on nature and extent of disability-based employment discrimination; analysis of employment-related provisions of the ADA; review of case law stemming from employment discrimination prohibitions under the Rehabilitation Act of 1973; need for the ADA.

Key parts of Figure 5-3 include the:

-CIS accession number. (H341-4)

-Title. (*Hearing on H.R. 2273, The Americans With Disabilities Act of 1989*)

-Date. (September 13, 1989)

-Congress and session. (101st Congress, 1st session)

-Pagination. (3 introductory pages followed by 168 pages)

-Price if purchased from GPO. ($5.00)

-Stock number used when purchasing materials from GPO. (552-070-07368-0)

-Price code used when purchasing individual documents on microfiche from CIS. Remember, all items cited in the *CIS Index* are available on microfiche. Contact CIS for current prices, since the dollar values of the codes are not constant. (CIS/MF/4)

-The item number indicates this title is a depository document. (• Item 1015-A covers print format and 1015-B covers microfiche)

-Superintendent of Documents number. (Y4.ED8/1:101-51)

-*Monthly Catalog* entry number. (90-8975)

-Library of Congress catalog card number.[7] (90-600205)

-Main abstract. Data include summaries of topics covered; names of subcommittees that sponsored the hearings; relevant bill numbers; page numbers for texts of bills; and references to supplementary materials appended to the hearings.

-Testimony abstracts. Citations give the names of witnesses who provide testimony before committees; the names of their affiliations; dates of their statements; and relevant pages.

Figure 5-3 shows that witnesses or groups of witnesses who discuss related issues are grouped together under decimal points. For example, Evan J. Kemp, Jr., Commissioner of the Equal Employment Opportunity Commission, provided testimony on September 13, 1989. His statement appears on pages 2-25. He addressed questions relating to employment barriers the disabled face.

Test your understanding of the *Abstracts* volume: The following questions relate to Figure 5-3.

1.	What is the title of this document?

(Hearings on H.R. 2273, The Americans
With Disabilities Act of 1989)

2.   When was the hearing held?

(September 13, 1989)

3.   During which Congress and session was the hearing held?

(101st Congress, 1st session)

4.   What is the Superintendent of Documents number?

(Y4.Ed8/1:101-51)

5.   Who is Mark Donovan and what issues did he address at the hearing?

(Manager, Community Employment and Training Programs for the Marriot Corporation;
Donovan, along with Rochlin, Rasmussen,
Wharen, and Mayerson, spoke about developing and implementing employment programs for the disabled.)

Index of Subjects and Names: Name Approach

Besides subject headings, the Index of Subjects and Names also includes personal names and names of organizations. Thus, it is possible to
locate the names of witnesses who provided testimonies before committees
and subcommittees, such as Mark R. Donovan (Figure 5-4).

Figure 5-4
CIS Four-Year Cumulative Index,
Index of Subjects and Names: Witnesses

Donovan, J. Patrick
Airline operating rights at high-density
airports, allocation and transfer policies
revision, **87** H641–6.4
Donovan, Leisure, Newton, and Irvine
Corporate stockholder proxy voting system
problems, **89** H361–186.1
Donovan, Mark R.
Discrimination against the handicapped,
prohibition, **90** H341–4.2
Donovan, Mary P.
Drug control strategy review, **90** H961–16.3
Donovan, Paul M.
Hazardous materials transportation safety
programs, revision, **89** H641–11.5
RR antitrust immunity repeal, **88** S521–3.4,
89 H521–83.3
RR tracks and facilities access by captive
shippers, **89** H521–65.6
Donoway, Gail
Student loan default reduction measures,
89 H341–12.5
Doo, Leigh-Wai
Fort DeRussy, Hawaii, status and future use,
87 H201–28.7

Source: *CIS Four-Year Cumulative Index, 1987-1990*, **821.**

Note, the index refers to H341-4.2, the section of the abstract in Figure 5-3 where Donovan's testimony is cited. Refer from 4.2 back to the whole number, H341-4, to locate the title and SuDoc number needed to retrieve the hearing.

Suppose you knew that the Marriott Corporation was represented at a hearing, but you did not know who provided the testimony. Consult the Index of Subjects and Names searching under the name of the company (Figure 5-5).

Figure 5-5
CIS Four-Year Cumulative Index,
Index of Subjects and Names: Witness Affiliation

Marrinson, Ralph
Fed hwy programs, oversight and extension,
90 S321–25.2

Marriott Corp.
Discrimination against the handicapped,
prohibition, **90** H341–4.2
Employer tax credits for hiring handicapped
or economically disadvantaged workers,
program review, **90** H781–11.5
Hotel fire safety issues, **87** H701–64.3
Job training and employment programs
implementation in Calif, private sector
role, **87** H341–16.3
Labor mkt long-term trends and business
response, **90** S541–55.1

Marriott, Dean C.
Coastal pollution research and control
programs, expansion and revision,
90 S321–18.8
Groundwater contamination problems and
protection programs in Maine,
88 S321–5.1

Test your knowledge of the Index of Subjects and Names:

1. Consult Figure 5-5 to determine if a representative of the Marriott Corporation provided testimony to a Congressional committee on hotel fire safety. If yes, what is the entry number in the *Abstracts* volume?

(Yes; 1987 *Abstracts* volume,
entry number H701-64.3.)

2.   How could you determine the American Medical Association's position on abortion?

(Consult the Index of Subject and Names
under American Medical Association
for relevant citations.)

Index of Subjects and Names:
Popular Names of Bills and Legislation

The Index of Subjects and Names includes popular names of bills and legislation.   Figure 5-6 shows the hearing seen in Figure 5-3 listed under the Americans with Disabilities Act.

Figure 5-6
CIS Four-Year Cumulative Index,
Index of Subjects and Names:
Popular Names of Bills and Legislation

Americans with Disabilities Act
Discrimination against the handicapped,
   prohibition, **89** H341–36, **89** H341–81,
   89 S541–17, **89** S541–37, **89** S543–11,
   90 H341–2, **90** H341–3, **90** H341–4,
   90 H343–6, **90** H343–12, **90** H343–20,
   90 H361–19, **90** H363–9, **90** H521–37,
   90 H523–8, **90** H641–25, **90** H643–1,
   90 H721–24, **90** PL101–336
Telephone relay services for the deaf,
   requirement estab, **90** H361–20

AmericanTours International
Tourism industry status and promotion
   efforts, **90** S261–1.3

America's Living Standard Act
Trade competitiveness and technology
   enhancement programs, reorganization,
   88 S401–12.7

Source: *CIS Four-Year Cumulative Index, 1987-1990,* **147.**
Reprinted with permission from the *CIS Four-Year Cumulative Index, 1987-1990.*
Copyright 1991 by Congressional Information Service, Inc. (Bethesda, MD).
All rights reserved.

Index of Titles

The Index of Titles lists titles of documents abstracted by CIS.   Remember, index entries appear alphabetical word by word.   Thus, a publication entitled *The Situation in New York...* will be cited before one entitled *The Situation in Newark...*   Figure 5-7 displays the *Hearing on H.R. 2273, The Americans with Disabilities Act of 1989,* the title seen in Figure 5-3.

Figure 5-7
CIS Four-Year Cumulative Index,
Index of Titles

Hearing on H.R. 2235, Workforce 2000
Employment Readiness Act of 1989.,
90 H341–17

Hearing on H.R. 2246, Jobs for Employable
Dependent Individuals "JEDI"., **89** H341–5

Hearing on H.R. 2273, Americans with
Disabilities Act of 1989., **90** H341–3

Hearing on H.R. 2273, the Americans with
Disabilities Act of 1989., **90** H341–4

Hearing on H.R. 2372, To Exempt Natural
Gas Liquids from the Minimum Price
Requirement for Petroleum Produced from
the Naval Petroleum Reserves., **88** H201–6

Hearing on H.R. 2504, To Withdraw Certain
Public Lands in Eddy County, New
Mexico., **89** H201–22

Hearing on H.R. 3, Early Childhood
Education and Development Act.,
90 H341–29

Source: *CIS Four-Year Cumulative Index, 1987-1990*, **3321.**
Reprinted with permission from the *CIS Four-Year Cumulative Index, 1987-1990*.
Copyright 1991 by Congressional Information Service, Inc. (Bethesda, MD).
All rights reserved.

Titles beginning with numbers have two entries, numerically following the Z's and alphabetically within the A-Z arrangement. Recalling the index conventions, *The F14 Airplane...* appears before *The F4 Airplane* because numbers are listed digit by digit. In the alphabetic section, the numbers are inverted and titles are listed according to their initial keywords. Figures 5-8 and 5-9 illustrate the identical title listed both ways, *1985 Farm Bill Revisited: Competing Views.*

Figure 5-8
CIS Four-Year Cumulative Index,
Index of Titles: Titles Beginning With Numbers

Zuni Claims Settlement Act of 1990.,
90 S413–5

Zuni Land Claims; and 1937 Housing Act.,
90 S411–25

100th Congress Legislative Record of the
Committee on Ways and Means, Along with
Brief Historical and Other Pertinent
Information Concerning the Committee.,
89 H782–51

1985 Farm Bill Revisited: Competing Views.,
87 S161–20

1985 Recommended Renewable Resources
Program and the President's Statement of
Policy., **88** H161–19

1986 Drought in the Southeast U.S.,
87 H701–39

Source: *CIS Four-Year Cumulative Index, 1987-1990*, **3391**
Reprinted with permission from the *CIS Four-Year Cumulative Index, 1987-1990*.
Copyright 1991 by Congressional Information Service, Inc. (Bethesda, MD).
All rights reserved.

Figure 5-9
CIS Four-Year Cumulative Index,
Index of Titles: Inverted Titles Cited Under Initial Keywords

Famine in Ethiopia., **90** H381–108,
   90 H961–36
Farm Animal and Research Facilities
   Protection Act of 1990., **90** H163–15
Farm Bill, 1985, Revisited: Competing Views.,
   87 S161–20
Farm Bill, 1990 and Underground Storage
   Tanks., **90** H721–10
Farm Credit Act., **88** H361–68
Farm Credit Act Amendments of 1987.,
   87 S163–6
Farm Credit Administration's Selection of the
   Jackson Land Bank Receiver., **89** H401–13
Farm Credit Capital Corporation Testimony of
   the Board of Directors and Chief Executive
   Officer., **88** S161–4

Source: *CIS Four-Year Cumulative Index, 1987-1990,* **3310.**

Index of Bill Numbers

Committee publications that deal with specific bills, regardless of whether they become law, are referenced in the Index of Bill Numbers. In Figure 5-10, the Congress displays in parenthesis immediately preceding the bill numbers. Note, once legislation passes, the Index of Bill Numbers also cites public law numbers.

Figure 5-10
CIS Four-Year Cumulative Index,
Index of Bill Numbers

(101) H.R. 2257	90 H161–15	(101) S. 931	89 PL101–175
(101) H.R. 2257	90 H163–6	(101) S. 931	89 H443–45
(101) H.R. 2259	90 H261–10.7	(101) S. 931	89 S313–26
(101) H.R. 2264	90 H523–19	(101) S. 931	90 S311–22
(101) H.R. 2267	89 PL101–194	(101) S. 932	90 H701–55
(101) H.R. 2267	90 H521–13	(101) S. 933	89 S541–37
(101) H.R. 2269	90 H781–32.12	(101) S. 933	89 S543–11
(101) H.R. 2273	89 H341–81	(101) S. 933	90 PL101–336
(101) H.R. 2273	90 PL101–336	(101) S. 933	90 H341–4
(101) H.R. 2273	90 H341–2	(101) S. 933	90 H343–6
(101) H.R. 2273	90 H341–3	(101) S. 933	90 H343–12
(101) H.R. 2273	90 H341–4	(101) S. 933	90 H343–20
(101) H.R. 2273	90 H343–6	(101) S. 933	90 H361–19
(101) H.R. 2273	90 H361–19	(101) S. 933	90 H363–9
(101) H.R. 2273	90 H361–20	(101) S. 933	90 H523–8
(101) H.R. 2273	90 H363–9	(101) S. 933	90 H641–25
(101) H.R. 2273	90 H521–37	(101) S. 933	90 H643–1
(101) H.R. 2273	90 H523–8	(101) S. 940	89 S311–62
(101) H.R. 2273	90 H641–25	(101) S. 940	89 S313–27
(101) H.R. 2273	90 H643–1	(101) S. 940	90 PL101–306

Source: *CIS Four-Year Cumulative Index, 1987-1990,* **3445 and 3459.**

Test your knowledge of the Index of Bill Numbers: The following questions relate to Figures 5-3 and 5-10.

1. Which bills were discussed in the hearing illustrated in Figure 5-3?

(H.R. 2273 and S. 933)

2. Identify the two references to that hearing in Figure 5-10.

3. During which Congress were these bills introduced?

(101st Congress)

4. Were H.R. 2273 and S. 933 enacted into law?

(Yes; PL101-336)

5. Did Congressional committees publish many other items pertaining to H.R. 2273 and S. 933 besides the hearing illustrated in Figure 5-3?

(Yes)

6. Why are some bill numbers omitted from Figure 5-10?

(The Index of Bill Numbers only cites bills for which committees published information. Figure 5-10 shows that CIS did not index a title dealing with H.R. 2260. References go from H.R. 2259 to H.R. 2264.)

Other CIS Indexes

-**Index of Report Numbers:** All reports appear regardless of whether they are abstracted. Remember, CIS does not abstract publications about ceremonial/housekeeping matters or private bills. Also, CIS indexes them neither in the Index of Subjects and Names, nor the Index of Titles. In Figure 5-11, H. Rept. 100-442, which deals with a private bill, and H. Rept. 100-447, which deals with a housekeeping matter, are two examples.

Figure 5-11
CIS Four-Year Cumulative Index,
Index of Report Numbers

H. Rpt. 100-442	(Private)
H. Rpt. 100-443	(Private)
H. Rpt. 100-444	(Private)
H. Rpt. 100-445, pt. 1	**87** H363–36
H. Rpt. 100-445, pt. 2	**88** H643–1
H. Rpt. 100-446	**87** H203–9
H. Rpt. 100-447	(Housekeeping)
H. Rpt. 100-448	(Housekeeping)
H. Rpt. 100-449	(Housekeeping)
H. Rpt. 100-450	**87** H433–4
H. Rpt. 100-451	(Housekeeping)
H. Rpt. 100-452	**87** H523–20
H. Rpt. 100-453	**87** H443–74
H. Rpt. 100-454	**87** H403–30
H. Rpt. 100-455	**87** H403–31
H. Rpt. 100-456	**87** H403–32

Source: *CIS Four-Year Cumulative Index, 1987-1990*, **3469**.
Reprinted with permission from the *CIS Four-Year Cumulative Index, 1987-1990.*
Copyright 1991 by Congressional Information Service, Inc. (Bethesda, MD).
All rights reserved.

-Index of Document Numbers: House, Senate, and treaty documents display numerically by document numbers. The index lists Congressional documents that are also published by executive or other Congressional agencies. However, they are neither abstracted, nor indexed subjects or titles. S. Doc. 100-3 in Figure 5-12 is an example.

Figure 5-12
CIS Four-Year Cumulative Index,
Index of Document Numbers
100th CONGRESS
Senate Documents

S. Doc. 100-1	**88** S680–3
S. Doc. 100-2	**87** S920–3
S. Doc. 100-3 (Architect of Capitol, Semi-Ann Rpt, Oct 1986-Mar 1987)	
S. Doc. 100-4	**87** S680–1
S. Doc. 100-5, pts. 1 & 2 (Sec of Senate, Semi-Ann Rpt, Oct 1986-Mar 1987)	
S. Doc. 100-6	**87** S180–2
S. Doc. 100-7	**87** S920–5
S. Doc. 100-8, vol. 1	**87** S140–1
S. Doc. 100-8, vol. 2	**87** S140–2
S. Doc. 100-9	**88** S920–7

Source: *CIS Four-Year Cumulative Index, 1987-1990*, **3486**.
Reprinted with permission from the *CIS Four-Year Cumulative Index, 1987-1990.*
Copyright 1991 by Congressional Information Service, Inc. (Bethesda, MD).
All rights reserved.

-Index of Senate Hearing Numbers and Index of Senate Print Numbers: Senate hearings and committee prints appear according to their respective series numbers as established by the Senate. House hearings and prints do not have comparable numbers.

-Index of Superintendent of Document Numbers: SuDoc numbers of titles cited in the *Abstracts* volume are listed in alphanumeric order (Figure 5-13).

Figure 5-13
CIS Four-Year Cumulative Index,
Index of Superintendent Numbers

Y4.Ed8/1:101-48	**90** H341–9
Y4.Ed8/1:101-49	**90** H341–11
Y4.Ed8/1:101-50	**90** H341–5
Y4.Ed8/1:101-51	**90** H341–4
Y4.Ed8/1:101-52	**90** H341–6
Y4.Ed8/1:101-53	**90** H341–7
Y4.Ed8/1:101-54	**90** H341–10
Y4.Ed8/1:101-55	**90** H341–12
Y4.Ed8/1:101-56	**90** H341–2
Y4.Ed8/1:101-57	**90** H341–3
Y4.Ed8/1:101-58	**90** H341–13
Y4.Ed8/1:101-59	**90** H341–14
Y4.Ed8/1:101-61	**90** H341–15
Y4.Ed8/1:101-62	**90** H341–17
Y4.Ed8/1:101-63	**90** H341–18
Y4.Ed8/1:101-64	**90** H341–19
Y4.Ed8/1:101-65	**90** H341–22
Y4.Ed8/1:101-66	**90** H341–23
Y4.Ed8/1:101-67	**90** H341–20
Y4.Ed8/1:101-68	**90** H341–24
Y4.Ed8/1:101-69	**90** H341–21
Y4.Ed8/1:101-70	**90** H341–25
Y4.Ed8/1:101-71	**90** H341–27
Y4.Ed8/1:101-72	**90** H341–29

Source: *CIS Four-Year Cumulative Index, 1987-1990*, **3533.**
Reprinted with permission from the *CIS Four-Year Cumulative Index, 1987-1990*.
Copyright 1991 by Congressional Information Service, Inc. (Bethesda, MD).
All rights reserved.

Test your knowledge of the Index of Superintendent of Document Numbers:

Identify the SuDoc number in Figure 5-13 that relates to the item seen above in Figure 5-3.

-Index of Committee and Subcommittee Chairs: The two sections of this index list Senators and Representatives in alphabetical order. Bold face type indicates committees and regular type indicates subcommittees chaired by that person (Figure 5-14).

Figure 5-14
CIS Four-Year Cumulative Index
Index of Committee and Subcommittee Chairs

OWENS, Major R. (D-NY)
Select Education, H340 (1987-90)

PANETTA, Leon E. (D-Calif)
Budget, H260 (1989-90)
Domestic Marketing, Consumer Relations,
and Nutrition, H160 (1987-88)
Personnel and Police, H420 (1987-88)

PENNY, Timothy J. (D-Minn)
Education, Training and Employment, H760
(1989-90)

Source: *CIS Four-Year Cumulative Index, 1987-1990,* **3567.**
Reprinted with permission from the *CIS Four-Year Cumulative Index, 1987-1990.*
Copyright 1991 by Congressional Information Service, Inc. (Bethesda, MD).
All rights reserved.

Test your understanding of the Index of Committee and Subcommittee Chairs: All questions relate to Figure 5-14.

1. What committee did Leon Panetta chair?

(House Budget Committee)

2. When did he chair this committee?

(1989-1990)

3. Which subcommittees did Panetta chair?

(House Subcommittee on Domestic
Marketing, Consumer Relations,
and Nutrition; House Subcommittee on
Personnel and Police.)

ELECTRONIC VERSIONS OF THE *CONGRESSIONAL INFORMATION SERVICE INDEX*

ONLINE:

The *CIS Index* is available online through the DIALOG service.[8] Figure 5-15 shows the DIALOG record for the hearing seen in Figure 5-3.

Figure 5-15
CIS Index **Citation on Dialog**
File 101

3/5/1
485140 CIS ACCESSION NUMBER: 90-H341-4 NUMBER OF ANALYTICS: 2
 TITLE: Hearing on H.R. 2273, the Americans with Disabilities Act of 1989.
 SOURCE: Sept. 13, 1989 CONGRESSIONAL SESSION: 101-1 iii+168 p GPO
$5.00
 FICHE: 4 ITEM NO: 1015-A; 1015-B GPO STOCK NUMBER: 552-070-07368-0
 SUPERINTENDENT OF DOCUMENTS CLASS NUMBER: Y4.Ed8/1:101-51
 LC CARD NUMBER: 90-600205
 DOCUMENT TYPE: HEARING
 JOURNAL ANNOUNCEMENT: 9001
 ABSTRACT: Committee Serial No. 101-51. Hearing before the Subcom on Employment Opportunities
and the Subcom on Select Education to consider
H.R. 2273 (text, p. 132-168) and companion S. 933, both the Americans with Disabilities Act (ADA) of
1989, to prohibit discrimination against the handicapped in various areas, including employment.
 Supplementary material (p. 125-168) includes submitted statements.

 DESCRIPTORS: Subcom on Select Education. House; Subcom on Employment Opportunities. House;
Discrimination against the handicapped; Discrimination in employment; Americans with Disabilities Act;
 DESCRIPTORS (Bill Number(s)): (01) H.R. 2273; (01) S. 933;

ANALYTIC RECORD ACCESSION NUMBER: 0485140 CIS ACCESSION NUMBER:
90-H341-4.2
 DATE: Sept. 13, 1989. PAGE(S):p. 26-124.
 WITNESSES: Rochlin, Jay Executive Director, President's Committee on
Employment of People with Disabilities.; Donovan, Mark R. Manager,
Community Employment and Training Programs, Marriott Corp.; Rasmussen,
Duane A. President and Chief Executive Officer, Sell Publishing Co.;
representing National Federation of Independent Business, Minnesota
Newspaper Association, and Independent Business Association of Minnesota.;
Wharen, Paul D. Project Manager, Thomas P. Harkins, Inc.; representing
Associated Builders and Contractors.; Mayerson, Arlene B. Directing
Attorney, Disability Rights Education and Defense Fund.;
 ABSTRACT: Experiences in the development and implementation of programs
to facilitate employment of disabled individuals; differing perspectives on
H.R. 2273 and companion S. 933, including business concerns regarding
employment-related provisions.
 Aspects of prejudice against disabled persons; review of studies on
nature and extent of disability-based employment discrimination; analysis
of employment-related provisions of the ADA; review of case law stemming
from employment discrimination prohibitions under the Rehabilitation Act of
1973; need for the ADA.

 DESCRIPTORS: Social science research; President's Committee on
Employment of People with Disabilities; Marriott Corp.; National Federation
of Independent Business; Minnesota Newspaper Association; Independent
Business Association of Minnesota; Associated Builders and Contractors;
Disability Rights Education and Defense Fund; business; case law;
Rehabilitation Act; ;

Test your understanding of *CIS Index* citations on the Dialog database: All questions relate to Figure 5-15.

1. Identify each of the following parts of the citation:

A. CIS accession number.

B. Superintendent of Documents number.

C. Title.

D. Reference to the Marriott Corporation and its representative, Mark R. Donovan.

E. Item number.

F. Stock number.

2. Is H.R. 2273 reprinted in the hearing?

(Yes, on pages 132-168)

CD-ROM:

The CD-ROM version of the *CIS Index*[9] is a user-friendly system that is much easier for the novice to master than the Dialog database. The well written printed manual[10] and the following four tutorial software packages that come with the CD-ROM are informative.

1. The *Basic Guided Tour* deals with the basics of entering terms, using the index, and restricting searches to specific time periods or types of publications.

2. The *Advanced Guided Tour* explains how to edit searches, display search results, and find specific terms in the records.

3. The *Print/Save Guided Tour* describes how records are printed and saved on floppy disks.

4. The fourth tutorial deals with *Researching Legislative Histories*.

The CD-ROM version of the document seen above in Figures 5-3 and 5-15, *Hearing on H.R. 2273, The Americans with Disabilities Act of 1989*, displays below (Figure 5-16).

Figure 5-16
Congressional Masterfile®2.

CIS NO: 90-H341-4
TITLE: Hearing on H.R. 2273, the Americans with Disabilities Act of 1989.
SOURCE: Committee on Education and Labor. House
DOC TYPE: Hearing   COLLATION: iii+168 p.
DATE: Sept. 13, 1989
CONGRESS-SESSION: 101-1   SUDOC: Y4.Ed8/1:101-51
ITEM NO: 1015-A; 1015-B
LC CARD NO: 90-600205   MC ENTRY NO: 90-8975

Committee Serial No. 101-51. Hearing before the Subcom on Employment
Opportunities and the Subcom on Select Education to consider H.R. 2273
(text, p. 132-168) and companion S. 933, both the Americans with
Disabilities Act (ADA) of 1989, to prohibit discrimination against the
handicapped in various areas, including employment.
  Supplementary material (p. 125-168) includes submitted statements.
CONTENT NOTATION: Discrimination against the handicapped, prohibition
DESCRIPTORS (and special content notations): SUBCOM ON SELECT EDUCATION.
  HOUSE; SUBCOM ON EMPLOYMENT OPPORTUNITIES. HOUSE; DISCRIMINATION
  AGAINST THE HANDICAPPED (Prohibition); DISCRIMINATION IN EMPLOYMENT;
  AMERICANS WITH DISABILITIES ACT
BILLS: 101 H.R.2273; 101 S.933
LEGISLATIVE HISTORY OF: P.L.101-336

90-H341-4 TESTIMONY NO: 1   Sept. 13, 1989 p. 2-25
WITNESSES (and witness notations):
  KEMP, EVAN J., JR. (Commissioner, Equal Employment Opportunity
    Commission)
STATEMENT AND DISCUSSION: Barriers to the employment of disabled
  individuals, focusing on attitudinal aspects; preference for
  Senate-passed version of the ADA.
CONTENT NOTATION: Discrimination against the handicapped, prohibition
DESCRIPTORS: PUBLIC.OPINION; EQUAL EMPLOYMENT OPPORTUNITY COMMISSION

90-H341-4 TESTIMONY NO: 2   Sept. 13, 1989 p. 26-124
WITNESSES (and witness notations):
  ROCHLIN, JAY F. (Executive Director, President's Committee on
    Employment of People with Disabilities)
  DONOVAN, MARK R. (Manager, Community Employment and Training Programs,
    Marriott Corp)
  RASMUSSEN, DUANE A. (President and Chief Executive Officer, Sell
    Publishing Co.; representing National Federation of Independent
    Business, Minnesota Newspaper Association, and Independent Business
    Association of Minnesota)

Reprinted with permission from the Congressional Masterfile®2.
Copyright 1993 by Congressional Information Service, Inc. (Bethesda, MD).
All rights reserved.

Test your understanding of *Congressional Masterfile 2*: Identify each of the following parts of Figure 5-17:

1.   CIS accession number.

2.   Superintendent of Documents number.

3.   Title.

4.   Reference to the Marriott Corporation and its representative, Mark R. Donovan.

FURTHER INFORMATION

Consult the introduction to the most recent annual cumulative *Abstracts* or *Index* volumes for more detailed information about indexing and abstracting practices in the *Congressional Information Service Index*.

CONCLUSION

Congress and its committees consider all topics and issues that affect the nation and the world. Since its inception in 1970, the *CIS Index* has become the most important index to publications of Congressional committees. These publications are the backbone of our national policies and laws. More general sources index many of the same government documents. These include the *Monthly Catalog* and the *Publications Reference File*, but the level of indexing in the *CIS Index* is far more detailed.

The following list summarizes the kinds of information available in the Index of Subjects and Names, the largest part of the *CIS* indexing scheme.

-Subjects of publications.

-Subjects discussed by witnesses.

-Subjects inserted and appended into hearings.

-Names of states, localities, countries, and other types of areas.

-Sites of hearings if they were held outside Washington, D.C.

-Names of witnesses who provide testimony at hearings.

-Names of the organizations the witnesses represent.

-Names of personal authors.

-Affiliations of personal authors.

-Names of corporate authors--reports whose authors are government agencies, companies, research institutes, or other sorts of groups, rather than individuals.

-Names of government agencies.

-Names of subcommittees that published information.

-Popular names of bills and laws.

Endnotes

1. (Bethesda, MD.: Congressional Information Service, Inc., 1970-monthly with annual cumulations.)

2. "Users Guide: Introduction to CIS Indexes and Related Services," in *CIS Annual* (Washington, D.C.: Congressional Information Service, Inc., 1990), xi.

3. All titles indexed and abstracted in the *CIS Index* are filmed in the *CIS Microfiche Library of United States Congressional Publications* (Washington, D.C.: Congressional Information Service, Inc., 1970-monthly). The fiche are sold either on a subscription or on a demand basis through the Documents on Demand service.

4. 1970-1974 is covered in Congressional Information Service, *CIS Five-Year Cumulative Index* (Washington, D.C.: Congressional Information Service, Inc., 1975); Congressional Information Service, *CIS Four-Year Cumulative Index* (Washington, D.C.: Congressional Information Service, Inc. Separate issues cover 1975-1978, 1979-1982, 1983-1986, 1987-1990, and 1991-1994).

5. *CIS Annual: Legislative Histories of U.S. Public Laws* (Bethesda, MD.: Congressional Information Service, Inc., 1984-annual).

6. Quarterly cumulative indexes cite numbers 1-12 in bold print to indicate the appropriate monthly abstract volumes. That is, **1** in the first quarterly index refers to the January *Abstracts* volume and **11** in the fourth quarterly index represents the November *Abstracts* volume.

7. This information is irrelevant to library users. It is used by librarians who purchase catalog cards from the Library of Congress.

8. CIS (Congressional Information Service) (File 101) (Online database) Available on: DIALOG/Knight-Ridder, Mountain View, CA.

9. *Congressional Masterfile 2: CIS Index to Congressional Publications and Legislative Histories* (CD-ROM)(Bethesda, MD.: Congressional Information Service, Inc., quarterly. Covers 1970-present on 2 CD-ROM disks).

10. Congressional Information Service, *Congressional Masterfile 2: CIS/Index Congressional Database on CD-ROM Reference Manual* Version 2.1 (Bethesda, MD.: Congressional Information Service, Inc., 1993).

Exercises

Use the 1991 *CIS Index* or *Congressional Masterfile 2* to answer the following questions:

1. Locate Congressional hearings held in the House in January 1991 that deals with Iraqi human rights violations in Kuwait.

    A. What is the CIS entry number?

    B. What is the title of the hearing?

    C. What is the SuDoc number?

    D. What committee held the hearings?

2. Hearings were held in May 1990 on labeling of consumer products. Did a representative from Proctor & Gamble provide testimony? If yes:

    A. What is his/her name?

    B. What position does he/she hold in the company?

    C. On what pages is the testimony reproduced?

    D. What is the SuDoc number of this title?

3. Locate Congressional hearings on H.R. 7 (102nd Congress).

    A. What is the subject of H.R. 7?

    B. Is the text of the bill reproduced in the hearings? If yes, on what pages?

    C. What is the title of the hearing?

    D. What is its SuDoc number?

    E. What subject heading would you consult to locate additional information on the subject?

4. Student Aid and the Cost of Postsecondary Education is the title of a document.

    A. Which agency prepared this document?

    B. Who is the personal author?

    C. What is its SuDoc number?

Answers

1. A. H381-44.

    B. Human Rights Abuses in Kuwait and Iraq.

    C. Y4.F76/1:K96.

    D. House Foreign Affairs Committee.

2. A. Robert M. Viney.

    B. Associate Advertising Manager.

    C. Pages 71-105.

    D. Y4.C73/7:S.HRG.101-1095.

3. A. Gun control.

    B. Yes; pages 3-11.

    C. Brady Handgun Violence Prevention Act.

    D. Y4.J89/1:102-4.

    E. Firearms and firearms control.

4. A. The Congressional Budget Office prepared this title for the Senate Budget Committee.

    B. Jay Noell.

    C. B.Y10.2:Ai6.

•Chapter 6

Congressional Publications — Part III: Legislative Histories

Answer the following questions when reading this chapter:

1. What are legislative histories?

2. Why are legislative histories important when interpreting laws and policy issues?

3. Can you think of as least two occasions in the recent past when researching the history of a law or a policy issue would have been helpful in your work?

4. Identify the three legislative history sources you find most useful. Explain why?

Chapter 4 defined different kinds of Congressional publications and Chapter 5 examined the most comprehensive index to Congressional committee publications, the *CIS Index*. This chapter and the next one cover legislative histories that describe what happens to bills as they go through the legislative process. Significant parts of legislative histories include:

-Dates of approval or disapproval of bills and laws.

-Intentions of Congress in enacting or rejecting legislation.

-Congressional publications that deal with the bills and related issues.

The initial section of the chapter discusses the importance of legislative histories. A description of the *CIS Legislative Annual*--the most comprehensive guide to legislative histories, follows that. The discussion then considers six additional reference tools:

-The *Congressional Quarterly Almanac*.

-The *House Calendar.*

-The *Senate Journal.*

-The *Congressional Record* and the *Congressional Record Index.*

-The *Congressional Index.*

Summaries describe features of three database services: the Electronic Legislative Search System (ELSS), LEXIS/NEXIS, and Washington Alert. The text then evaluates handbooks and guides to legislative histories. The final section of the chapter provides directory information to Capitol Hill offices that offer information about bills and gratis copies of Congressional publications. See Chapter 7 for a discussion of three additional Internet sources: the Library of Congress Legislative System (LOCIS); GPO Access; and THOMAS.

I use rept as a standard abbreviation for Congressional reports despite different references sources referring to them as rept, rpt, and rp.

WHY ARE LEGISLATIVE HISTORIES IMPORTANT?

Legislative histories are significant to both professionals and laymen. They offer students, social scientists, educators, and the general public insight into the formulation of our national policies. This facilitates consideration of the advantages and disadvantages of alternative policies, and the ideas and beliefs of particular Representatives and Senators. Legislative histories are especially valuable to attorneys because, when interpreting vague and ambiguous legislation, the courts study the intentions of lawmakers. Abner Mikva, a legal scholar, explains why the law is sometimes vague and ambiguous.

> ..we start out with 435 prima donnas in the House and 100 prima donnas in the Senate, and the name of the game is to get them to agree on a single set of words. We are not talking about trying to get Congress to agree on something unimportant or noncontroversial, like whether to declare Grandmother's Day. Instead, we are talking about the hard issues, like the environment, economic decisions and civil rights.[1]

A recent case, *Bray v. Alaxandria Women's Health Clinic* illustrates the importance of legislative histories to the courts and to social policy. A group of women who were blocked from entering an abortion clinic sued under an 1871 law that was intended to provide protection against Ku Klux Klan activities. Although the law was enacted to eliminate violence against former slaves and their supporters, the National Organization of Women argued that the statute is not limited to protecting blacks and their advocates. It also covered the right of those seeking abortions to enter clinics without being harassed.

The opposition took a more limited view of the law arguing that "Nothing in the text of (the statute) indicates an affirmative intention to reach conspiracies based on gender, and it would be fanciful to ascribe such an intent to the 1871 Congress."[2] The only intent of the law was to prevent attacks on blacks and their supporters. The Supreme Court ruled that tactics used by abortion protesters do not violate the rights of those seeking abortions under the Ku Klux Klan Act.[3]

CIS LEGISLATIVE HISTORIES

The *CIS Index*[4], the reference tool described in Chapter 5, is the most comprehensive guide to legislative histories. Beginning with 1984, legislative histories in the *CIS Index* are in a separate volume[5]. Before then, less detailed histories appeared in the *Abstracts* volume. Remember, the CIS *Index* volume provides information by subjects, by popular names of legislation, and by bill numbers (Figures 5-1, 5-2, 5-6, and 5-10). The organization of the *CIS Annual Legislative Histories* volume is numerical by public law numbers.

Figure 6-1 reproduces excerpts from the legislative history of the Americans with Disabilities Act. The *CIS Index* includes in its legislative histories committee hearings[6] and committee prints, information the other sources in this chapter do not to cite. CIS legislative histories cover issues considered in multiple Congresses. Although the Americans with Disabilities Act became law during the 101st Congress, Figure 6-1 cites publications issued during the 100th, as well as the 101st, Congresses.

104 Stat. 327, in the upper right hand corner of Figure 6-1 indicates that the legislation begins on page 327 of the *Statutes at Large*, volume 104. The *Statutes at Large* is an annual publication that reproduces laws enacted by Congress. The chapter on legislation describes it in greater detail.

Figure 6-1
CIS Legislative History **Volume**

Public Law 101-336   104 Stat. 327

Americans with Disabilities Act of 1990

July 26, 1990

Public Law

1.1 Public Law 101-336, approved July 26, 1990. (S. 933)

(CIS90:PL101-336   52 p.)

"To establish a clear and comprehensive prohibition of discrimination on the basis of disability."

Prohibits discrimination against disabled individuals in employment and public transportation, accommodations, and services.

Establishes a general definition of disability.

TITLE I, EMPLOYMENT.

Includes a provision to restrict use of pre-employment medical examinations and inquiries by employers, labor organizations, and employment agencies. Requires employers to make reasonable accommodations to the limitations of otherwise qualified job applicants or employees with disabilities.

P.L. 101-336 Reports

101st Congress

2.1 S. Rpt. 101-116 on S. 933, "Americans with Disabilities Act of 1989," Aug. 30, 1989.

(CIS89:S543-11   107 p.)
(Y1.1/5:101-116.)

Recommends passage, with an amendment in the nature of a substitute, of S. 933, the Americans with Disabilities Act (ADA) of 1989, to prohibit discrimination against disabled individuals in employment, housing, public accommodations, transportation, or telephone services. Includes provisions to:

a. Establish a comprehensive definition of disability.

P.L. 101-336 Bills

100th Congress

HOUSE BILLS

3.1 H.R. 192 as introduced.

3.2 H.R. 1546 as introduced.

P.L. 101-336 Debate

135 Congressional Record
101st Congress, 1st Session - 1989

4.1   Sept. 7, Senate consideration and passage of S. 933, p. S10701.

136 Congressional Record
101st Congress, 2nd Session - 1990

4.2   May 17, House consideration of H.R. 2273, p. H2410.

4.9   July 13, Senate agreement to the conference report on S. 933, p. S9684.

P.L. 101-336 Hearings

100th Congress

5.1   "Hearing on Discrimination Against Cancer Victims and the Handicapped," hearings before the Subcommittee on Employment Opportunities, House Education and Labor Committee, June 17, 1987.

(CIS88:H341-4   iii+115 p.)
(Y4.Ed8/1:100-31.)

Committee Serial No. 100-31. Hearing before the *Subcom on Employment Opportunities* to consider the following bills:
    H.R. 192, to amend the Civil Rights Act of 1964 to prohibit employment discrimination against handicapped persons.
    H.R. 1546, the Cancer Patients' Employment Rights Act, to prohibit employment discrimination against cancer survivors.
Full Committee Member Mario Biaggi (D-NY) presents a statement *(see H341-4.1)* and participates in questioning witnesses.
    Includes correspondence (p. 113-115).

5.8   **"Hearing on H.R. 2273, the Americans with Disabilities Act of 1989," hearings before the Subcommittee on Employment Opportunities and the Subcommittee on Select Education, House Education and Labor Committee, Sept. 13, 1989.**

(CIS90:H341-4   iii + 168 p.)
(Y4.Ed8/1:101-51.)

Committee Serial No. 101-51. Hearing before the *Subcom on Employment Opportunities* and the *Subcom on Select Education* to consider H.R. 2273 (text, p. 132-168) and companion S. 933, both the Americans with Disabilities Act (ADA) of 1989, to prohibit discrimination against the handicapped in various areas, including employment.
Supplementary material (p. 125-168) includes submitted statements.

Sept. 13, 1989. p. 2-25.
Witness: **Kemp, Evan J., Jr.**, Commissioner, Equal Employment Opportunity Commission.
Statement and Discussion: Barriers to the employment of disabled individuals, focusing on attitudinal aspects; preference for Senate-passed version of the ADA.

P.L. 101-336 Committee Prints

101st Congress

6.1   **"Legislative History of Public Law 101-336, the Americans with Disabilities Act, Vol. 1," committee print issued by the House Education and Labor Committee, Dec. 1990. (Not available at time of publication.)**

P.L. 101-336 Miscellaneous

8.1   **Weekly Compilation of Presidential Documents, Vol. 26 (1990): July 26, Presidential remarks and statement.**

The DIALOG service provides online access to the *CIS Index*[7] and the Congressional Information Service publishes a CD-ROM version.[8]

Test your understanding of the *CIS Annual: Legislative Histories of U.S. Public Laws*: The following questions relate to Figure 6-1.

1. What is the SuDoc number of Senate Report 101-116?

    (Y1.1/5:101-116)

2. Were bills dealing with this subject introduced into the House during the 100th Congress? If yes, what were they?

    (H.R. 192 and H.R. 1546)

3. When did the Senate pass S. 933 and on which page of the *Congressional Record* is this documented?

    (September 7, 1989; page S10701)

4. What is the SuDoc number of a hearing about discrimination against the handicapped that took place on June 17, 1987 and what is its CIS accession number?

    (Y4.ED8/1:100-31; 88H341-4 -- entry number H341-4 in the 1988 *Abstracts* volume.)

CONGRESSIONAL QUARTERLY ALMANAC

Suppose you are interested in locating information about the Americans with Disabilities Act of 1990 but were aware of neither appropriate bill nor public law numbers. The *Congressional Quarterly Almanac*[9] is a good starting point that provides essential background information about significant bills and the issues affecting them. The index to the 1990 issue indicates that data appears on pages 447-61. The initial section of the article provides a Box score or summary of key legislative activities (Figure 6-2).

Figure 6-2
Congressional Quarterly Almanac
Box Score of Americans with Disabilities Act

BOXSCORE

Legislation: Americans with Disabilities Act, PL 101-336 (S 933, HR 2273).

Major action: Signed, July 26. Conference report adopted by Senate, 91-6, July 13; by House, 377-28, July 12. Passed by House, 403-20, May 22; by Senate, 76-8, Sept. 7, 1989.

Reports: Conference reports (H Rept 101-596, H Rept 101-558). Public Works and Transportation (H Rept 101-485, Part I); Education and Labor (Part II); Judiciary (Part III); Energy and Commerce (Part IV). Labor and Human Resources (S Rept 101-116).

Source: *Congressional Quarterly Almanac*, **1990 edition, 447.**
Reprinted with permission from *Congressional Quarterly Almanac.*
Copyright 1991 by Congressional Quarterly Inc. (Washington, D.C.).
All rights reserved.

Test your knowledge of the *Congressional Quarterly Almanac* **Box score:** The following questions refer to Figure 6-2:

1. What is the public law number?

> (P.L. 101-336; the 336th public law enacted by the 101st Congress)

2. What were the relevant bill numbers?

> (S. 933 and H.R. 2273)

3. When did the President sign the measure?

> (July 26, 1990)

4. How many Conference reports did the House pass?

> (2; H. Rept. 101-596 and H. Rept. 101-558)

Subsequent parts of the same article describe provisions of the law, Congressional intentions, committee activities, actions before the full chambers, and attitudes of interest groups. References cite bill numbers, report numbers, and other Congressional Quarterly publications when appropriate.

Additional features of the *Almanac* include:

-An analysis of Federal elections.

-Evaluations of Supreme Court decisions.

-A list and index of lobbyists.

-Presidential messages to Congress and Presidential vetoes.

-Results of Congressional roll call votes.

Figure 6-3 illustrates the results of the Senate vote on the Americans with Disabilities Act conference report (vote 152). The Senate adopted the measure 91-6. Republicans supported it by a 37-6 margin and Democrats did so by a 54-0 margin.

Figure 6-3
Congressional Quarterly Almanac
Senate Roll Call Votes

SENATE VOTES 150, 151, 152

	150 151 152		150 151 152		150 151 152	KEY
ALABAMA		**IOWA**		**NEW HAMPSHIRE**		Y Voted for (yea).
Heflin	Y Y Y	Harkin	Y Y Y	Humphrey	Y Y N	# Paired for.
Shelby	Y Y Y	*Grassley*	N N Y	Rudman	Y Y Y	+ Announced for.
ALASKA		**KANSAS**		**NEW JERSEY**		N Voted against (nay).
Murkowski	N N Y	*Dole*	N Y Y	Bradley	N N Y	X Paired against.
Stevens	N Y Y	*Kassebaum*	N N Y	Lautenberg	Y Y Y	- Announced against.
ARIZONA		**KENTUCKY**		**NEW MEXICO**		P Voted "present."
DeConcini	Y Y Y	Ford	Y Y Y	Bingaman	Y N Y	C Voted "present" to avoid pos-
McCain	N N Y	*McConnell*	Y Y Y	*Domenici*	Y Y Y	sible conflict of interest.
ARKANSAS		**LOUISIANA**		**NEW YORK**		? Did not vote or otherwise make
Bumpers	Y Y Y	Breaux	Y Y Y	Moynihan	Y Y Y	a position known.
Pryor	Y Y Y	Johnston	Y Y Y	*D'Amato*	Y Y Y	
CALIFORNIA		**MAINE**		**NORTH CAROLINA**		Democrats *Republicans*
Cranston	Y N Y	Mitchell	Y Y Y	Sanford	Y Y Y	
Wilson	N N Y	*Cohen*	Y Y Y	*Helms*	Y Y N	
COLORADO		**MARYLAND**		**NORTH DAKOTA**		
Wirth	Y N Y	Mikulski	Y Y Y	Burdick	Y Y Y	150 151 152
Armstrong	N N Y	Sarbanes	Y Y Y	Conrad	Y Y Y	

152. S 933. Americans with Disabilities Act/Conference Report. Adoption of the conference report (thus clearing the measure for the president) on the bill to prohibit discrimination against the disabled in public facilities and employment and to guarantee them access to mass transit and telecommunications services. Adopted 91-6: R 37-6; D 54-0 (ND 37-0, SD 17-0), July 13, 1990. A "yea" was a vote supporting the president's position.

The *Congressional Quarterly Almanac* also includes a list of public laws arranged in numerical order (Figure 6-4).

Figure 6-4
Congressional Quarterly Almanac
Public Laws

PL 101-336 (S 933) Establish a clear and comprehensive prohibition against discrimination on the basis of disability. Introduced by HARKIN, D-Iowa, May 9, 1990. Senate Labor and Human Resources reported, amended, Aug. 30 (S Rept 101-116). Senate passed, amended, Sept. 7. House passed, amended, May 22. Conference report filed in the House on June 26 (H Rept 101-558). Senate recommitted conference report July 11. House agreed to conference report July 12 (H Rept 101-596). Senate agreed to conference report July 13. President signed July 26, 1990.

Source: *Congressional Quarterly Almanac*, **1990, 7-A.**
Reprinted with permission from *Congressional Quarterly Almanac.*
Copyright 1991 by Congressional Quarterly Inc. (Washington, D.C.).
All rights reserved.

Researchers should be aware of two related sources. The *Congressional Quarterly Weekly Report*[10] offers information similar to that in the *Congressional Quarterly Almanac*, but in a more timely fashion. The *Weekly Report* is available online through the Washington Alert database service. Also, *Congress and The Nation*[11] is an excellent multiyear summary of legislative activities. See the discussion below about the Washington Alert databases for information about the online version of the *Congressional Quarterly Weekly Report*.

HOUSE CALENDAR

Chapter 4 included a detailed description of the *House* and *Senate Calendars*[12]. Remember, the *House Calendar*, which provides histories of bills and cumulates data for both sessions of Congress, is far more valuable for reference purposes than the *Senate Calendar*. The latter merely represents its Chamber's agenda on a particular day. Moreover, the Senate Calendar is neither cumulated nor indexed. Updates to the *House Calendar* index appear weekly.

The *House Calendar*'s most significant value is its History of Bills and Resolutions section. It lists in numerical order bills and resolutions that have passed either or both houses. Senate resolutions that the editors believe would be of no interest to the House are excluded. Each citation has a legislative history. Figure 6-5 illustrates S. 933.

Figure 6-5
House Calendar
History of Bills and Resolutions

S. 933 (H.R. 2273) (H. Res. 427).—Health, Americans
With Disabilities Act of 1989. Referred to Labor and
Human Resources May 9 (Legislative day of Jan. 3),
1989. Reported amended Aug. 30, 1989; Rept. 101–116.
Passed Senate amended Sept. 7 (Legislative day of
Sept. 6), 1989; Roll No. 173: 76–8. Received in House
and held at desk Sept. 12, 1989. Passed House with
amendment May 22, 1990. House insisted on its
amendment and asked for a conference May 24, 1990.
Senate disagreed to House amendment and agreed to a
conference June 6 (Legislative day of Apr. 18), 1990.
Conference report filed in the House June 26, 1990;
Rept. 101–558. Senate recommitted conference report
July 11 (Legislative day of July 10), 1990. Conference
report filed in the House July 12, 1990; Rept. 101–596.
House agreed to conference report July 12, 1990; Roll
No. 228: 377–28. Senate agreed to conference report
July 13 (Legislative day of July 10), 1990; Roll No. 152:
91–6. **Approved July 26, 1990. Public Law 101–336.**

Source: *House Calendar*, **101st Congress, 12-11.**

Figure 6-6 shows the relevant citation from the *House Calendar*'s Index.

Figure 6-6
House Calendar
Index

Developmental Disabilities Assistance and Bill of Rights
Act of 1990. H.R. 5679; Mr. Madigan et al. S. 2753.

Disabilities Act of 1989, Americans with. H.R. 2273; Mr.
Coelho et al. S. 933.
    Consideration of. H. Res. 394; Mr. Gordon.
    Waiving certain points of order against conference
report. H. Res. 427; Mr. Gordon.

Disabilities Act of 1989, Education of Individuals with.
H.R. 1013; Mr. Owens of New York. S. 1824.
    Correct enrollment. S. Con. Res. 150.

Disabilities Prevention Act of 1990. H.R. 4039; Mr. Conte
et al.

Source: *House Calendar*, **101st Congress, 19-13.**

Figures 6-5 and 6-6 refer to the Americans with Disabilities Act of 1989
because S. 933 was introduced in 1989 during the 101st Congress, 1st
session. However, the law is referred to as the Americans with Disabilities
Act of 1990, since the legislation was not enacted until that year.

Test your knowledge of the *House Calendar* by answering the following question:

Why is information relating to 1989 included in Figures 6-10 and 6-11, even though both illustrations are reproduced from the 1990 *House Calendar*?

(The 101st Congress covered the two year period, 1989 and 1990. The *House Calendar* cumulates data from both sessions of a Congress.)

SENATE JOURNAL

See Chapter 4 for background information about the *House* and *Senate Journals*[13]. Unlike the *House Calendar*, organization of *Journals* are by annual Congressional sessions, not biennial Congresses. To locate complete information about S. 933, consult the History of Bills and Resolutions section in both the 1989 (101st Congress, 1st session) and the 1990 (101st Congress, 2nd session) *Senate Journals*. (Figures 6-7 and 6-8)

Figure 6-7
Senate Journal
History of Bills and Resolutions

933. A bill to establish a clear and comprehensive prohibition of discrimination on the basis of disability.
　　SPONSOR: Harkin

Number, title, and action
COSPONSOR(S): Kennedy; Durenberger; Simon; Jeffords; Cranston; McCain; Mitchell; Chafee; Leahy; Stevens; Inouye; Cohen; Gore; Packwood; Riegle; Graham; Pell; Dodd; Adams; Mikulski; Metzenbaum; Matsunaga; Wirth; Bingaman; Conrad; Burdick; Levin; Lieberman; Moynihan; Kerry; Sarbanes; Boschwitz; Heinz; Glenn (A-05/17/89);
Shelby (A-05/18/89);
Pressler (A-05/31/89);
Hollings (A-06/06/89);
Sanford (A-06/13/89);
Wilson (A-06/13/89);
Sasser (A-06/16/89);
Dixon (A-06/20/89);
Kerrey (A-06/21/89);

May 9, 89	Read twice and referred to the Committee on Labor and Human Resources.
Aug 30, 89	Committee on Labor and Human Resources. Reported to Senate by Senator Kennedy under the authority of the order of August 2, 1989 with an amendment in the nature of a substitute. With written report No. 101-116. Additional views filed.
Aug 30, 89	Placed on Senate Legislative Calendar under General Orders. Calendar No. 216.
Sep 7, 89	Measure laid before Senate by unanimous consent.
Sep 7, 89	Passed Senate with an amendment by Yea-Nay Vote. 76-8. Record Vote No. 173.
Oct 16, 89	Senate ordered measure printed as passed with amendments of the Senate numbered.

Source: *Senate Journal*, **101-1, 1989, H-76.**

Figure 6-8
Senate Journal
History of Bills and Resolutions

933. A bill to establish a clear and comprehensive prohibition of discrimination on the basis of disability.

SPONSOR: Harkin

May 22, 90	Passed House (Amended) by Voice Vote.
May 24, 90	House insisted on its amendments by unanimous consent.
May 24, 90	House requested a conference.
May 24, 90	Speaker Appointed Conferees: Hawkins, Bartlett, Owens (NY), Fawell, Martinez, Dingell, Markey, Thomas Luken, Lent, Whittaker.
May 24, 90	House Conferees Instructed by unanimous consent.
May 24, 90	Message on House action received in Senate.
Jun 6, 90	Measure laid before Senate by unanimous consent.
Jun 6, 90	Senate disagreed to the House amendments by Voice Vote.
Jun 6, 90	Senate agreed to request for conference by unanimous consent.
Jun 6, 90	Senate appointed conferees Kennedy; Harkin; Metzenbaum; Simon; Hatch; Durenberger; Jeffords.
Jun 6, 90	Senate appointed conferees Hollings; Inouye; Danforth from the Committee on Commerce, Science and Transportation, solely for consideration of issues within that Committee's jurisdiction (telecommunications, commuter transit, and drug testing transportation employees).
Jun 6, 90	Senate Conferees instructed.
Jul 11, 90	Conference report considered in Senate. By unanimous consent.
Jul 11, 90	Motion to recommit conference report with instructions entered in Senate.
Jul 11, 90	Conference report recommitted by Senate. Voice Vote.
Jul 12, 90	House Agreed to Conference Report by Yea-Nay Vote: 377-28 (Record Vote No. 228).
Jul 13, 90	Conference report considered in Senate.
Jul 13, 90	Senate agreed to conference report by Yea-Nay Vote: 91-6. Record Vote No. 152.
Jul 17, 90	Measure Signed in Senate.
Jul 17, 90	Presented to President.
Jul 26, 90	Signed by President.
Jul 26, 90	Became Public Law No. 101-336.

Source: *Senate Journal*, **101-2, H-15 - H-16.**

In Figure 6-7, names of cosponsors who supported S. 933 when the bill was introduced are in the paragraph. Those who agreed to cosponsor the measure following its introduction appear separately.

Test your knowledge of the History of Bills and Resolutions section: The following questions relate to Figures 6-7 and 6-8.

1. Who sponsored S. 933?

(Senator Harkin)

2. When did Senator Sanford add his name as a cosponsor?

(June 13, 1989)

3. When did the bill pass the Senate and what was the vote?

(September 7, 1989; 76-8)

4. When did the House first pass S. 933?

(May 22, 1990)

5. When did the House agree to the conference report and by what vote?

(July 12, 1990; 377-28)

When comparing information in Figure 6-5 to that in Figures 6-7 and 6-8, note that the *House Calendar* provides report numbers while the *Senate Journal* fails to do so. However, the chronological sequence of activities pertaining to the bill is easier to follow in the *Senate Journal*.

The *Senate Journal* is comparable to a record of parliamentary proceedings (Figure 6-9). The proceedings took place on Wednesday, June 6, 1990, the 65th meeting of the Senate that year. Number 65.14, the 14th piece of business conducted on the 65th day, dealt with S. 933.

Figure 6-9
Senate Journal

WEDNESDAY, JUNE 6, 1990 (65)

(Legislative day of Wednesday, April 18, 1990)

The PRESIDENT pro tempore called the Senate to order at 11:30 a.m., and the Chaplain offered a prayer.

¶ 65.1 THE JOURNAL

On motion by Mr. MITCHELL, and by unanimous consent,
Ordered, That the Journal of the proceedings of the Senate be approved to date.

¶ 65.14 HOUSE MESSAGE ON BILL S. 933

Under the authority of the order of yesterday,
The PRESIDING OFFICER (Mr. SHELBY in the chair) laid before the Senate the message received from the House of Representatives insisting upon its amendment to the bill (S. 933) to establish a clear and comprehensive prohibition of discrimination on the basis of disability, and asking a conference with the Senate thereon.
On motion by Mr. HARKIN, and by unanimous consent,
Ordered, That the Senate disagree to the amendment of the House to the bill, and agree to the conference asked by the House of Representatives on the disagreeing votes of the two Houses thereon.

Source: Senate Journal, 101-2, 1990, 370, 376.

CONGRESSIONAL RECORD

As with the *House Calendar* and the *Senate Journal*, Chapter 4 also covered the informational content of the *Congressional Record*[14]. This discussion considers the index to the *Record*[15]. It appears biweekly when Congress is in session and is cumulated annually. Consult the indexes for each session to locate full information about a topic or a bill covering an entire Congress.

The *Congressional Record Index* includes two access tools, an alphabetic index and the History of Bills and Resolutions. Use the alphabetic index to locate information by subjects and by names of Senators and Representatives. Data pertinent to the *Americans with Disabilities Act* are under the subject heading Handicapped (Figure 6-10).

Figure 6-10
Congressional Record Index
Alphabetic Index--Subject Entry

HANDICAPPED *see also* HEALTH.

Amendments

Americans With Disabilities Act: enact (S. 933), conference report, S9532, S9543, S9593 [11JY]

Articles and editorials

Necessary AIDS Precaution, S9538 [11JY]

Bills and resolutions

Developmental Disabilities Assistance and Bill of Rights Act: extend and amend (see H.R. 5337)

Intelligence Agency Retirement and Disability System: authorizing appropriations (see S. 2834)

Public buildings: small business leasing to socially and economically disadvantaged individuals (see H.R. 5272)

Letters

Acquired immune deficiency syndrome employment discrimination: Aids Advisory Committee of the Health Resources and Services Administration, S9546 [11JY]

————Association of State and Territorial Health Officials, S9546 [11JY]

————Bob Juliano, Hotel Employees and Restaurant Employees International Union, S9549 [11JY]

————Consortium for Citizens With Disabilities, S9550 [11JY]

Lists

Organizations opposing the Americans With Disabilities Act amendment on diseases transmitted through food handling, S9544 [11JY]

Memorandums

Americans With Disabilities Act: Kenneth P. Moritsugu, S9537 [11JY]

Motions

Americans With Disabilities Act: enact (S. 933), conference report, recommit, S9529 [11JY], H4629 [12JY]

Remarks in House

Americans With Disabilities Act: enact (S. 933), conference report, H4614–H4629 [12JY]

————enact (S. 933), waiving certain points of order against conference report (H. Res. 427), H4611–H4614 [12JY]

States: establish grant programs for comprehensive mental health services for children (H.R. 5306), E2375 [18JY]

Remarks in Senate

Americans With Disabilities Act: enact (S. 933), conference report, S9527–S9556 [11JY], S9680, S9684–S9699 [13JY]

Reports by conference committees

Americans With Disabilities Act (S. 933), H4582–H4606 [12JY]

Reports filed

Americans With Disabilities Act: committee of conference (S. 933) (H. Rept. 101–596), H4607 [12JY]

Developmental Disabilities Assistance and Bill of Rights Act: Authorization: Committee on Labor and Human Resources (S. 2753) (S. Rept. 101–376), S9971 [18JY]

Source: *Congressional Record Index*, Vol. 136, Nos. 86-94, 88.

Figure 6-10 indicates that data are subdivided by different kinds of information, such as amendments; bills and resolutions; letters; lists; memorandums; and remarks in the House and Senate. Citations give dates; page numbers in either the House (H), Senate (S), or Extension of Remarks (E) sections of the *Record*; and bill and resolution numbers.

Test your understanding of the *Congressional Record Index:* All questions relate to Figure 6-10.

1. Where in the *Congressional Record* can one find a list of groups that opposed passage of the Americans with Disabilities Act amendment on diseases transmitted through food handling?

    (Page S9544, July 11, 1990)

2. Cite the relevant date, page number, and bill number for remarks made in the House about a program establishing grants for mental health services to children.

    (July 18, 1990; page E2375; H.R. 5306)

3. A letter about the handicapped was in the *Congressional Record* on July 11, 1990, page S9550. Who submitted this letter?

    (Consortium for Citizens With Disabilities)

Figure 6-11 is an example of an index entry about a legislator, rather than a subject. Note that information is again categorized under various subheadings, such as amendments offered by, appointments, bills and resolutions introduced by, and remarks by.

Figure 6-11
Congressional Record Index
Alphabetic Index--Reference to a Legislator

HARKIN, TOM *(a Senator from Iowa)*
Amendments offered by, to
  Capital punishment: constitutional procedures (S.
    1970), S9477, S9580 [11JY]
  Employment: restore and strengthen laws that ban
    discrimination (S. 2104), S9372, S9454 [10JY]
Appointments
  Acting President pro tempore, S9801 [17JY]
Bills and resolutions introduced by, as cosponsor
  Agriculture: equal opportunity for minority farmers
    (see S. 2881), S10093 [19JY]
  Federal Facility Compliance Act: enact (see S.
    1140), S10259 [20JY]
  Federal Financial Management Improvement Act:
    enact (see S. 2840), S9565 [11JY]
  National Commission To Support Law Enforce-
    ment: establish (see S. 2872), S9971 [18JY]
  Rural Health Care Provider Recruitment and Edu-
    cation Act: enact (see S. 2844), S9645 [12JY]
  Veterans: outpatient medical services for any dis-
    ability of a former POW (see S. 1860), S9449
    [10JY]
  Violence Against Women Act: enact (see S. 2754),
    S9450 [10JY]
  White House Conference on Aging: convene (see S.
    Con. Res. 134), S9451 [10JY]
Cloture motions
  Employment: restore and strengthen laws that ban
    discrimination (S. 2104), S9726 [13JY], S9767
    [16JY]
Remarks by, on
  Agriculture: extend and revise Federal programs (S.
    2830), S10065 [19JY]
  Americans With Disabilities Act: enact (S. 933),
    conference report, S9529, S9531 [11JY], S9684,
    S9685, S9689, S9692, S9697 [13JY]

  Capital punishment: constitutional procedures (S.
    1970), S9511 [11JY]
  Employment: restore and strengthen laws that ban
    discrimination (S. 2104), S9346, S9370, S9371
    [10JY]
  National Commission to Support Law Enforce-
    ment: establish (S. 2872), S9983• [18JY]
  National Council on Disability Policy: duties, S9692
    [13JY]
  Senate: application of Civil Rights Act employment
    laws, S9346, S9370, S9371 [10JY]

Source: *Congressional Record Index*, Vol. 136,
Nos. 86-94, 89.

Test your understanding of the *Congressional Record Index*: All questions relate to Figure 6-11.

1.   Did Senator Harkin either introduce or cosponsor a bill
designed to establish a National Commission To Support
Law Enforcement? If yes, what is the bill number?

(S. 2872)

2. On what pages of the *Congressional Record* are Senator Harkin's statements about the Americans with Disabilities Act printed?

(S9529, S9531, S9684, S9685,
S9689, S9692, and S9697)

The History of Bills and Resolutions section of the *Congressional Record Index* provides more detailed information about bills than the alphabetic index. Figures 6-10 and 6-11, which were reproduced from the alphabetic section, display only sporadic information about S. 933. However, Figure 6-12 shows how the History of Bills and Resolutions section gathers in one spot all reference to S. 933. Arrangement is numerical by bill/resolution numbers.

Figure 6-12
Congressional Record Index
History of Bills and Resolutions

S. 933—A bill to establish a clear and comprehensive prohibition of discrimination on the basis of disability; to the Committee on Labor and Human Resources.
Debated, H2639
Amended and passed House (in lieu of H.R. 2273), H2653
House insisted on its amendments and asked for a conference Conferees appointed, H3070
Senate disagreed to House amendments and agreed to a conference., S7422
Conferees appointed, S7450
Conference report (H. Rept. 101-558); submitted in House, H4170
Explanatory statement, H4184, H4596
Conference report considered in Senate, S9527
Amendments, S9532, S9543, S9593
Conference report (H. Rept. 101-596) submitted in House, H4582
Conference report submitted in the House and agreed to, H4614
Conference report submitted in the Senate and agreed to, S9684
Examined and signed in the Senate, S9855
Presented to the President, S9855
Examined and signed in the House, H4890

Source: *Congressional Record Index*, Vol. 136,
Nos. 86-94, H.B. 1.

Test your understanding of the History of Bills and Resolutions Section of the *Congressional Record Index:* Both questions relate to Figure 6-12.

1. On what pages of the *Congressional Record* can explanatory remarks about S. 933 be found?

(H4184 and H4596)

2. On what pages of the *Congressional Record* can one find House debates on S. 933?

(H2639)

The *Congressional Record Abstracts*[16] database covers the *Congressional Record* from 1981 to date. Information is updated weekly. See the discussions below of the LEXIS/NEXIS databases and the Washington Alert system for other electronic versions of the *Congressional Record*.

CONGRESSIONAL INDEX

The *Congressional Index*[17] is an excellent source that indexes bills and provides concise legislative histories. It has two volumes, the first covering Senate activities and the second covering those of the House. Each edition cumulates information for both sessions of a Congress. The weekly loose-leaf update pages keep information current.

SUBJECT INDEX

The Subject Index lists public bills and resolutions under subject headings, keywords, and popular names. Note, the Subject Index in volume 1 deals with both House and Senate bills and resolutions. The index has three parts:

-The basic Subject Index covers the first session of a Congress.

-The Current Subject Index covers the second session.

-Headline Legislation indexes selected bills that get significant media publicity.

Use all three parts for comprehensive searches. Figure 6-13 shows S. 933 in the Subject Index under its popular name and its subject heading.

Figure 6-13
Congressional Index
Subject Index

Popular Name	Subject Heading
American Indian Religious Freedom Act Amendments. . .S 1124	**Handicapped persons**
American Printing House of the Blind. . .H 1627	. blind or deaf persons
	. . House fellowships. . .H Res 81
	. blind persons
American Trade, Growth, and Employment Promotion Act. . .S 356	. . American Printing House. . .H 1627
	. . dyslexia. . .H 2126
American Victims of Terrorism Day. . .HJR 143	. . social security agency selections. . .H 855
	. children
Americans With Disabilities Act. . .S 933	. . dyslexia, education. . .H 1614
Amtrak	. . program extension. . .S 1454; H 2088
. authorizations. . .H 2364	. counseling services
. funding. . .S 462; S Res 24	. . disabled and ill. . .H 334
An End to Hunger Education Month. . .HJR 341	. discrimination
	. . blind, aircraft seating. . .S 341; H 563
Anabolic Steroid Restriction Act. . .H 995	. . employment. . .S 933; H 291; 2273
Anderson, Sen. Clinton P., commemoration study. . .S 818	. education
	. . state accountability. . .S 1431

Source: *Congressional Index*, 3005, 3047
Reproduced with permission from the *Congressional Index (1989-1990 Edition)*,
published and copyrighted by Commerce Clearing House, Inc.
4025 West Peterson, Chicago, Illinois 60646

AUTHOR INDEX

The Author Index is alphabetical by names of Senators and Representatives who introduced the bills. As with the Subject Index, information is limited to public bills. S. 933 displays under its sponsor's name, Senator Harkin (Figure 6-14).

Figure 6-14
Congressional Index
Author Index

Harkin
. agriculture
. . disasters and emergencies . . . S 1282
. . livestock . . . S 723
. . research . . . S 1387
. . rural development . . . S 862; 1027
. Alternative Agricultural Products Research
    Act . . . S 1387
. Americans With Disabilities Act . . . S 933
. arms control and disarmament
. . space . . . S 752
. Child Nutrition and WIC Reauthorization Act
    . . . S 1484
. Congress
. . members pay levels . . . SJR 49
. Disaster Assistance Extension Act . . . S 1282
. education
. . handicapped children . . . S 1431
. Education of the Handicapped Act
    Amendments . . . S 1431
. Emergency Water Assistance Act . . . S 862
. foods
. . labeling . . . S 623
. foreign affairs and assistance
. . Nicaragua . . . S 1574
. Foreign Ownership Disclosure Act . . . S 289
. foreign trade
. . foreign investors . . . S 289
. labor and employment
. . discrimination . . . S 933
. . fair labor standards . . . S 167
. Low Cholesterol Consumer Education Act
    . . . S 623

Source: *Congressional Index*, **5030.**
**Reproduced with permission from the *Congressional Index (1989-1990 Edition)*,
published and copyrighted by Commerce Clearing House, Inc. 4025 West
Peterson, Chicago, Illinois 60646**

BILLS AND RESOLUTIONS SECTION

The Senate Bills in volume 1 and the House Bills section in volume 2 are comparable. Public bills are in numerical order. Private bills are listed to maintain numeric sequence, but information about them is not provided (Figure 6-15).

Figure 6-15
Congressional Index
Senate Bills

**S 933—Labor and employment—discrimina-
tion—handicapped persons**

By Harkin, Kennedy (E.-MA), Durenberger,
Simon, Jeffords, Cranston, McCain, Mitchell,
Chafee, Leahy, Stevens, Inouye, Cohen, Gore,
Packwood, Riegle, Graham, Pell, Dodd, Adams,

MAY 9, 1989—continued

Mikulski, Metzenbaum, Matsunaga, Wirth, Bingaman, Conrad, Burdick, Levin (C.-MI), Lieberman, Moynihan, Kerry, Sarbanes, Boschwitz
and Heinz.

To establish a clear and comprehensive prohibition of discrimination on the basis of disability. (To Labor and Human Resources.)

**S 934—Foreign trade—duty suspensions—
chemicals**

By Thurmond.

To suspend temporarily the duty on K-Acid.
(To Finance.)

Source: *Congressional Index*, **14201, 14202. Reproduced with permission from the**
Congressional Index (1989-1990 Edition), **published and copyrighted by**
Commerce Clearing House, Inc. 4025 West Peterson, Chicago, Illinois 60646

Data in Figure 6-15 include sponsors names, the names of original
co-sponsors--those who agreed to cosponsor bills when they are introduced, and short abstracts.

STATUS OF BILLS SECTION

Bills and resolutions that have been acted upon are in numerical order
in the Status of Bills sections. Dates of introduction, relevant committees,
report numbers, date of votes and results of votes, and public law numbers
are given. Stars precede bills enacted into law. Measures that have not been
acted upon are excluded (Figure 6-16).

Figure 6-16
Congressional Index
Status of Senate Bills

★ 933

```
Introduced ........................5/9/89
Ref to S Labor Com ................5/9/89
Hrgs begun by Com .................5/9/89
Hrgs begun by Handicapped Subcom ...5/10/89
Ordered reptd w/amdts by Com ........8/2/89
Reptd w/amdts, S Rept 101-116, by Com ......
...............................8/30/89
Amdts adopted (Voice) ...............9/7/89
Passed by S (76 to 8; S Leg 173) ........9/7/89
Passed by H amended to contain H 2273 as fur-
   ther amended (Voice) .............5/22/90
H insisted on its amdts and requested conf (Voice)
...............................5/24/90
H instructed its conferees (Voice)......5/24/90
S agreed to conf (Voice)...............6/6/90
Conferees reached agreement ..........6/25/90
Conf rept filed, H Rept 101-558 ........6/26/90
Rule granted allowing no amdts (H Res 427) ....
...............................6/27/90
Recommitted to Conference Com with instruc-
   tions ..........................7/11/90
Amdts rejected (39 to 61; S Leg 148) ....7/11/90
Amdts adopted (99 to 1; S Leg 149) .....7/11/90
Conf rept filed, H Rept 101-596 ........7/12/90
H agreed to conf rept (377 to 28; H Leg 228) ....
...............................7/12/90
S agreed to conf rept (91 to 6; S Leg 152) ......
...............................7/13/90
Sent to President ...................7/17/90
Signed by President.................7/26/90
Public Law 101-336 (104 Stat 327) .....7/26/90
```

Source: *Congressional Index*, **21, 021. Reproduced with permission from the**
Congressional Index (1989-1990 Edition),
published and copyrighted by Commerce Clearing House, Inc.
4025 West Peterson, Chicago, Illinois 60646

Test your understanding of the *Congressional Index*: The following
questions relate to Figures 6-13 - 6-16.

1. Using Figure 6-13 determine which bills other than S. 933
    dealt with discrimination against the handicapped?

    > (S. 341; H.R. 563; H.R. 291; and H.R. 2273.
    > Note, the *Congressional Index* refers to House
    > bills
    > as H. rather than H.R.)

2. Did Senator Harkin introduce a bill that deals with educa-
    tion of the handicapped?

    > (Yes, S. 1431)

3.   Which Senate committee was the first to hold hearings on S. 933?

(Senate Labor Committee)

4.   According to Figure 6-16, did a House committee hold hearings on S. 933?

(No)

5.   What bill did the House incorporate into S. 933?

(H.R. 2273)

Chart 6-1 describes other sections of the *Congressional Index* not covered above.

Chart 6-1
Additional Parts of the *Congressional Index*

Parts of the Congressional Index	Description
Treaties Nominations-- relates only to Senate activities. Comparable information does not appear in the House Volume.	Treaties submitted to Congress for ratification from 1948 to date are listed, briefly abstracted, and indexed by subjects and countries. Most nominations relate to key positions in the Executive branch. Arrangement is alphabetical by names. Data include appropriate offices and dates of confirmation.
Enactments-Vetoes--cites bills that have been either enacted or vetoed.	Organization is by (1) public law numbers; (2) bill/resolution numbers; (3) popular names; (4) subjects; and (5) authors. Vetoes are listed by bill numbers. Data include short descriptions of the bills and dates of vetoes.
Senate Members (Vol. 1) and House Members (Vol. 2)	Members of the respective chambers appear alphabetically. Data include political affiliations, addresses, and biographies. A separate list gives Committee assignments. The House Members section includes maps of Congressional districts.
Senate Committee Hearings (Vol. 1) and House Committee Hearings (Vol. 2)	Provides subjects and dates of hearings under committee and subcommittee names. Separate lists cover standing committees, joint committees, and select committees that investigate specific activities.
Voting Records on Senate Bills (Vol. 1) and Voting Records on House Bills (Vol. 2)	Organization is chronological. Brief summaries describe the bills, reference the Congressional Record, and list votes for and against by political party.

ELECTRONIC LEGISLATIVE SEARCH SYSTEM (ELSS)

The publisher of the *Congressional Index* produces the Electronic Legislative Search System (ELSS)[18]. Bills introduced in Congress, as well as those introduced in the fifty state legislatures, are indexed by subject, bill numbers, sponsors, dates, and types of actions. Entries are very similar to those in the *Congressional Index*. The database is available twenty-four hours a day, seven days a week and is updated daily. For an additional fee, ELSS subscribers can request automatic monitoring of bills by subjects or jurisdictions, and automatic receipt of the relevant bills. Contact Commerce Clearing House to receive a free pamphlet, *ELSS: Electronic Legislative Search System, ELSS Sampler.*[19] It includes a guide to planning searches and sample search strategies.

LEXIS/NEXIS DATABASES

The LEGIS Library on the LEXIS/NEXIS[20] database system includes many files pertaining to legislative histories. Most are searchable by bill number; public law number; subjects; dates; titles of bills and laws; names of Congressman and Senators; and keywords. Chart 6-2 deals with files pertaining to bills and Chart 6-3 deals with those pertaining to the *Congressional Record*.

Chart 6-2
Selected LEXIS/NEXIS Files
Relating to Bills: LEGIS Library

Types of Information	File Names and Descriptions (File names are in upper case)
Actions taken on bills.	BLTRCK. Describes actions taken on bills introduced during the current Congress. Updates are twice daily--at 1:00 pm and at Midnight. Related files cover earlier Congresses. (File names: BLT101, BLT102, and BLT103)
Texts of bills.	BLTEXT. Reproduces full texts of bills introduced during the current Congress. Updates are twice daily at 1 pm and at midnight. Related files cover earlier Congresses. (File names: BTX101, BTX102, and BTX103)
Floor votes. (Votes in the full House and Senate)	VOTES. Covers the current Congress. The VOTARC file covers the 100th Congress through the most recent completed one.
Odds on passage of a bill.	BLCAST. Statistical odds on passage of bills in committees and on the respective floors are provided for the current Congress. Updates are bi-weekly. The BLARCH file offers historical data covering the 99th Congress through the most recent completed Congress. Both BLCAST and BLARCH exclude private bills, budget bills, and appropriation bills.

Chart 6-3
Selected LEXIS/NEXIS Relating to the *Congressional Record*: LEGIS Library

Types of Information	File Names and Descriptions (File names are in upper case)
Complete Congress-ional Record.	RECORD. Provides full text of the Congressional Record from the 99th Congress to date. Smaller files cover different Congresses. (File names: 99th, 100th, 101st, 102nd, 103rd, and 104th)
House pro-ceedings.	HOUSE. Gives complete House proceedings for the 99th Congress through the present.
Senate pro-ceedings.	SENATE. Provides complete Senate proceedings for the 99th Congress through the present.
Extension of Remarks	REMARK. Gives the full text of the "Extension of Remarks" section from the 99th Congress to date. Smaller files cover individual Congresses. (File names: 102RMK, 103RMK)
Daily Digest	DIGEST. Covers the "Daily Digest" section from the 99th Congress to date.

WASHINGTON ALERT DATABASE

Washington Alert[21] is a system of over twenty individual databases maintained by Congressional Quarterly, Inc. All databases relate to either Congressional activities, public policy, or current affairs. The sources in Chart 6-4 deal with bills, committee reports, the *Congressional Record*, and floor votes. Most databases are searchable by bill, report and public law numbers; dates; committees; bill status; words/phrases; and subjects.

Chart 6-4
Washington Alert Databases Covering Bills, Reports, the *Congressional Record*, and Floor Votes

Database	Description
BILLTEXT	Texts of bills and resolutions are added to the database each day.
BILLTRACK	Provides the current status of bills and resolutions. BILLTRACK has cross references to articles in Congressional Quarterly Weekly Reports, the Congressional Record, related bills, votes, and committee reports.
COMREPORTS	Provides texts of committee reports. Updates are daily.
CRBRIEFS	Abstracts of the Congressional Record summarize floor actions, new legislation, speeches, inserts, and executive communications.
CRTEXT	Provides the full text of the Congressional Record with daily updates.
VOTE	Gives results of floor votes in the House and Senate.

The next group of Washington Alert databases do not directly relate to bills, reports, and the *Congressional Record*, but they are still very helpful when studying legislative histories. (Chart 6-5)

Chart 6-5
Additional Washington Alert Databases

Database	Description
COMMITTEES	Covers committee actions, including committee and subcommittee votes. This information is unavailable from GPO.
NEWS	Summarizes current news that affects legislative activities. This includes analysis by Congressional Quarterly staff, summaries of anticipated floor and committee actions, and predictions of how members will vote.
SCHEDULE	Provides committee schedules up to three months in advance.
TRANSCRIPTS[1]	Provides speeches, press conferences, and press briefings of Executive Branch officials and Congressional leaders. TRANSCRIPTS also offers testimonies of witnesses before Congressional committees. The Congressional testimonies are particularly valuable because months sometimes pass before hearings are published. The Federal News Service on the Lexis/Nexis system provides comparable information.
USPRESS	Includes nearly 100 stories about current Congressional activities from sixteen major national newspapers. Updates are daily.
WR	Covers the full text of the <u>CQ Weekly Report</u>. Information in the <u>Weekly Report</u> is very similar to that in the <u>Congressional Almanac,</u> which was examined above.

HANDBOOKS AND GUIDES TO LEGISLATIVE HISTORIES

Davis, Carol D. *How to Follow Current Federal Legislation and Regulations* (91-66 C) Washington, D.C.: Congressional Research Service, 1991. Reproduced in *Major Studies and Issue Briefs of the Congressional Research Service, 1991 Supplement*. Frederick, MD.: University Publications of America, 1992. Reel 1, frame 1034.

Examines significant primary and secondary sources, and provides telephone numbers of Congressional and White House offices.

Goehlert, Robert U. and Fenton S. Martin, *Congress and Law-Making: Researching the Legislative Process* 2nd ed. Santa Barbara, CA.: ABC-Clio, 1989.

A guide to the legislative process that describes both government and non-government sources. Special features include appended tables that provide a sample legislative history of the Privacy Act of 1974; a checklist of items to include in legislative histories; and a form for tracing legislative histories.

Johnson, Nancy P., comp., *Sources of Compiled Legislative Histories: A Bibliography of Government Documents, Periodical Article and Books 1st Congress-99th Congress* (AALL Publ. Series No. 14) Littleton, CO.: Fred B. Rothman & Co., 1979-irregular. Rothman published three loose-leaf supplements in 1981, 1988, and 1993.

A bibliography that lists legislative histories reproduced in Congressional documents, law journals, law texts, and loose-leaf services. It covers all major legislation enacted between the 1st and the 99th Congresses. References are by Congress and law numbers. Four types of information are excluded: appropriations; ceremonial issues; legislation that relates to limited numbers of people; and laws that cover only specific regions of the nation.

TELEPHONE REFERENCES

The telephone is often one of the most underutilized reference tools. It is sometimes much easier and quicker to contact an expert instead of a print or electronic source. References below are for selected Congressional offices.

HOUSE DOCUMENTS ROOM (202-225-3456)

The House Documents Room provides free copies of bills, reports, House documents, and public and private laws.

HOUSE OFFICE OF LEGISLATIVE INFORMATION (202-225-1772)

Provides status and legislative histories of House and Senate bills. Updates are daily.

SENATE DOCUMENTS ROOM (202-224-7860)

The Senate Documents Room provides free copies of bills, reports, Senate documents, treaty documents, and laws. It offers a maximum of six items per day per individual. Send written requests to the Senate Documents Room, Hart Senate Office Building, Washington, D.C. 20510-7106. Fax requests to 202-228-2815.

CONTACTING OTHER CONGRESSIONAL OFFICES AND CONGRESSIONAL COMMITTEES

The following sources give names, addresses, phone numbers, and descriptions of Congressional offices and committees. Committees provide free copies of hearings, committee prints, and reports upon request.

Official Congressional Directory Washington, D.C.: GPO, 1809-biennial. Title varies: SuDoc number: Y4.P93/1:1/Congress.

Congressional Staff Directory. Mount Vernon, VA.: Staff Directories, LTD., 1959-semiannual.

CONCLUSION

The charts below outline how the sources discussed in this chapter relate to bills, hearings, reports, floor activities and debates, public laws, and policy issues. The following list identifies source numbers.

PRINTED SOURCES

1. *CIS Index*

2. *Congressional Index*

3. *Congressional Quarterly Almanac*

4. *Congressional Record*

5. *CQ Weekly Report*

6. *House* and *Senate Journals*

7. *House Calendar*

8. *Major Legislation of the Congress*

ELECTRONIC SOURCES

9. *Congressional Record Abstracts* (Dialog File # 135)

10. *Electronic Legislative Search System (ELSS)*

LEXIS/NEXIS DATABASE SERVICE--EACH FILE IS IN THE LEGIS LIBRARY.

11. BLCAST

12. BLTEXT

13. BLTRCK

14. COMVTE

15. DIGEST

16. HOUSE

17. RECORD

18. REMARK

19. SENATE

20. VOTES

Washington Alert Database Service

21. BILLTEXT

22. BILLTRACK

23. COMREPORTS

24. CRBRIEFS

25. CRTEXT

26. NEWS

27. TRANSCRIPTS

28. VOTE

29. USPRESS

Chart 6-6
Bills

Bills listed in numerical order	1, 2, 4, 6, 7, 8
Index by subjects	2, 4, 6, 7, 8, 9, 10
Index by Popular names	1, 2
Current status of bills	2, 4, 5, 7, 9, 10, 13, 22
Summaries of bills	2, 3, 4, 5, 6, 7, 10
Sponsors	2, 4, 9, 10
Predictions on passage of bills	11, 26
Committee votes on bills	14
Debates on bills	4, 9, 16, 17, 19, 25
Electronic full texts of bills	12, 21
Summaries of debates	3, 5, 24
Floor votes on bills	2, 3, 4, 5, 6, 7, 9, 10, 20, 28

Chart 6-7
Hearings

Index by subjects	1
Index by titles	1
Index by bill numbers	1, 2
Index by public law numbers	1
Testimonies of witnesses	1, 27
Summaries of hearings	3, 5

Chart 6-8

Index by subjects	1
Index by titles	1
Index by report numbers	1, 7
Index by bill numbers	1, 2, 4, 7
Electronic full texts of reports	23
Summaries of reports	3, 5

Chart 6-9
Floor Activities and Debates

Index by subjects	4, 9
Index by bill numbers	4, 9
Speeches	4,9
Debates	1--<u>Legislative History</u> volume cites page numbers of debates, 4, 9
Votes on bills and amendments	2, 3, 4, 5, 6, 9
Summaries of debates	3, 5, 6, 15, 24, 26
Electronic full texts of debates	16, 17, 18, 19, 25

Chart 6-10
Public Laws

Index by law number	1, 2, 3, 8
Index by bill number	1, 2, 4, 6, 7
Index by subjects	1, 2, 8

Chart 6-11
Analysis of Policy Issues

1, 3, 4, 5, 8, 9, 26, 27, 29

1. The Federal News Service on the Lexis/Nexis system provides comparable information.

Endnotes

1. Abner Mikva, "A Reply to Judge Starr's Observations," *Duke Law Review* 1987:3 (June 1987), 380.

2. "Congress Keeps Eye on Justices as Court Watches Hill's Words, Case Interpretations Can Turn on What Jurists Analyze: The Letter of the Law or the Meaning Behind It," *CQ Weekly Report* 49:40 (October 5, 1991), 2865.

3. "Jayne Bray et al, Petitioners v. Alexandria Women's Health Clinic, et al," 113 *Supreme Court Reporter* 753-805 (1993).

4. *CIS Index to Publications of the United States Congress* (Bethesda, MD.: Congressional Information Service, Inc., 1970-monthly).

5. *CIS Annual: Legislative Histories of U.S. Public Laws* (Bethesda, MD.: Congressional Information Service, Inc., 1984-annual).

6. Selected sources, such as the *Congressional Index* and the *Congressional Quarterly Almanac*, reference hearings, but they fail to provide full bibliographic citations.

7. *CIS (Congressional Information Service)* (File 101) (Online database) Available on: DIALOG/Knight-Ridder, Mountain View, CA.

8. *Congressional Masterfile 2: CIS Index to Congressional Publications and Legislative Histories* (CD-ROM)(Bethesda, MD.: Congressional Information Service, Inc., quarterly. Covers 1970-present on 2 CD-ROM disks). The software includes excellent tutorials. For additional data see Congressional Information Service, *Congressional Masterfile 2: CIS/Index Congressional Database on CD-ROM Reference Manual* Version 2.1 (Bethesda, MD.: Congressional Information Service, Inc., 1993).

9. (Washington, D.C.: Congressional Quarterly, Inc., 1948-annual).

10. (Washington, D.C.: Congressional Quarterly, Inc., 1945-weekly). Title varies: *CQ Weekly Report*; *CQ Congressional Quarterly Weekly Report*.

11. (Washington, D.C.: Congressional Quarterly Service, 1965-irregular). Separate volumes cover 1945-1964; 1965-1968; 1969-1972; 1973-1976; 1977-1980; 1981-1984; 1985-1988; and 1989-1992.

12. *Calendars of the United States House of Representatives and History of Legislation* (Washington, D.C.: GPO, 1880(?)-daily while Congress is in session). SuDoc number: Y1.2/2:Congress-session/#.

13. *Journal of the House of Representatives of the United States* (Washington, D.C.: GPO, 1789-annual). SuDoc number: XJH:Congress-ses-

sion; *Journal of the Senate of the United States of America* (Washington, D.C.: GPO, 1789-annual). SuDoc number: XJS:Congress-session.

14. *Congressional Record: Proceedings and Debates of the Congress* (Washington, D.C.: GPO, March 1873-daily while Congress is in session). SuDoc number: X Cong./session:Vol./issue.

15. *Congressional Record Index.* (Washington, D.C.: GPO, 1878-biweekly). To date (1/96), the 1989 annual cumulative index covering the 101st Congress, 1st session, is the most recent distributed. SuDoc number: X/A: Volume/Index.

16. (File 135) (Online database). Available on: DIALOG/Knight-Ridder, Mountain View, CA.

17. (Washington, D.C.: Commerce Clearing House, 1946-weekly while Congress is in session). Information for each Congress is cumulative.

18. (Online database). Available from Commerce Clearing House, Chicago, IL.

19. (EL 801) (Chicago: Commerce Clearing House, no date).

20. (Online database). Available on: Lexis/Nexis, Mead Data Central, Dayton, OH.

21. (Online database). Available from Congressional Quarterly Service, Inc., Washington, D.C.

Exercises

1. Compile a legislative history of the "Cable Television Consumer Protection and Competition Act of 1992."

    A. What is the Senate bill number?

    B. When was the bill introduced into the Senate?

    C. When did it pass the Senate?

    D. When did it pass the House?

    E. What is the relationship between H.R. 4850 and the Senate bill?

    F. When was the bill first reported from the Senate? What is the report number?

    G. Did this bill go to conference? If yes, what is the report number?

    H. What is a conference report?

    I. The Senate held a hearing on the bill on March 14, 1991. Which committee held the hearing? What are the title and SuDoc number of the hearing?

    J. Did the National Association of Broadcasters provide testimony at the hearing? If yes, who represented the group?

    K. When was the bill enacted into law?

    L. What is the public law number?

Answers

1. A. S. 12.

   B. January 14, 1991.

   C. January 31, 1992.

   D. July 23, 1992.

   E. The House passed S. 12 in lieu of H.R. 4850.

   F. June 28, 1991; S. Rept. 102-92.

   G. Yes; S. Rept. 102-862.

   H. A conference committee irons out differences when each Chamber approves dissimilar versions of the same bill. The conference report cites the compromises that have been reached and the rationale behind them.

   I. Senate Commerce, Science, and Transportation Committee. Subcommittee on Communications; *Cable TV Consumer Protection Act of 1991*; Y4.C73/7:S.HRG.102-132.

   J. Yes; Edward O. Fritts.

   K. October 5, 1992.

   L. Public Law (P.L.) 102-385.

•Chapter 7

Congressional Publications —Part IV: LOCIS, GPO ACCESS and THOMAS

Answer the following questions when reading this chapter:

1. Which features of LOCIS are most useful to your needs?

2. Which features of GPO ACCESS are most useful to your needs?

3. Which features of THOMAS are most useful to your needs?

4. Which database do you prefer using: LOCIS, GPO ACCESS, or THOMAS?

Three Internet sites that pertain to legislative histories deserve special mention in this chapter: the Library of Congress Information System (LOCIS), GPO ACCESS, and THOMAS. LOCIS is especially important because it is the only database available to the public without charge that summarizes bills and resolutions introduced into Congress since 1973. GPO ACCESS includes sources unavailable at other sites, such as Congressional reports and *Calendars*. Also, GPO ACCESS search protocol is different from many other world wide web sites. Media coverage of THOMAS has contributed to its popularity. This source is far easier to use than either LOCIS or GPO ACCESS.

Those who have never used online sources or who have never accessed a database using Telnet or a web server, should read this chapter at a terminal. Try the examples and experiment with other related searches. Unless otherwise indicated, commands to be entered are in uppercase bold type. On most computers, correct typing errors using either the delete or backspace keys, or ^H (the control key and the h key pressed simultaneously).

The discussion about LOCIS first deals with signing on, searching by bill numbers, and differences between the brief and full displays. Following that, the chapter considers searching by subjects, by names of Senators and Representatives, and by public law numbers. The section on GPO ACCESS deals with basic search techniques applicable to all databases in the system. The discussion then examines selected databases that deal with legislative histories. These include full texts of bills, the *House Calendar*, the history of bills, the *Congressional Record*, the *Congressional Record Index*, and Congressional reports. The final part of the chapter covers THOMAS. Information describes how to search for bills, and how to search the *Congressional Record* and the *Congressional Record Index*.

All figures in this chapter were copied using Lynx software. Lynx does not display graphics. The identical illustrations reproduced with software that accepts graphics, such as Netscape, will look different. Also, commands used with other software might differ from those used with Lynx.

I use rept. as a standard abbreviation for Congressional reports despite different reference sources referring to them as rept, rpt, and rp.

LOCIS--LIBRARY OF CONGRESS INFORMATION SYSTEM: BASIC SEARCHING

INTRODUCTION

LOCIS includes six types of information:

-The Library of Congress online catalog.

-Federal legislation.

-Copyright information.

-The Library's holdings of braille and audio materials.

-A directory of organizations that deal with all aspects of American society.

-References to foreign law.

This discussion only deals with the federal legislation section. Entries include detailed abstracts of the bills, not the full texts. The Library updates information within 48 hours. If you are unable to access LOCIS from your Internet account, contact knowledgeable people at your home institution or contact your service provider. Once logged on, the instructions in this chapter are identical. All illustrations pertain to the 101st Congress. If you make typing errors in LOCIS, use the ^H key to backspace.

SIGNING ON TO LOCIS

After logging on to your computer:

1. Type **TELNET LOCIS.LOC.GOV** or if using a WWW browser type **telnet://locis.loc.gov** (in lowercase) and press enter. (Figure 7-1) The ready prompt in Figure 7-1 is for an IBM mainframe using the CMS operating system.

Figure 7-1
Signing On To LOCIS

Ready; T=0.28/0.36 09:25:58

TELNET LOCIS.LOC.GOV

2. Select option **2**, Federal Legislation, at the opening menu. (Figure 7-2)

Figure 7-2
LOCIS Database
Opening Menu

L O C I S : LIBRARY OF CONGRESS INFORMATION SYSTEM

To make a choice: type a number, then press ENTER

1 Library of Congress Catalog	4 Braille and Audio
2 Federal Legislation	5 Organizations
3 Copyright Information	6 Foreign Law

* * * * * * * * * * * *

7 Searching Hours and Basics
8 Documentation and Classes
9 Library of Congress General Information

12 Comments and Logoff

Choice: **2**

3. Select option **5** for the 101st Congress at the Federal Legislation menu. (Figure 7-3)

Figure 7-3
LOCIS Database
Federal Legislation Menu

These files track and describe legislation (bills and resolutions) introduced
in the US Congress, from 1973 (93rd Congress) to the current Congress (the
current Congress is the 103rd). Each file covers a separate Congress.

CHOICE   FILE

1	Congress, 1981-82	(97th)	CG97
2	Congress, 1983-84	(98th)	CG98
3	Congress, 1985-86	(99th)	CG99
4	Congress, 1987-88	(100th)	C100
5	Congress, 1989-90	(101st)	C101
6	Congress, 1991-92	(102nd)	C102
7	Current Congress, 1993-	(103rd)	C103

8   Search all Congresses from 1981-->current
9   Search all Congresses on LOCIS 1973-->current

    Earlier Congresses: press ENTER
12 Return to LOCIS MENU screen.

    Choice: **5**

SEARCHING LOCIS BY BILL NUMBERS: RETRIEVE COMMAND

Search LOCIS two ways, using the retrieve command or using the
browse command. Each has their advantages and disadvantages. Type
RETRIEVE S. 933 or **R S. 933** and press enter to search the legislative history
of that bill (Figure 7-4).

LOCIS Figure 7-4
LOCIS Database, 101st Congress
Search with Retrieve Command

WEDNESDAY, 07/07/93 04:11 P.M.
***C101- THE LEGISLATIVE INFORMATION FILE FOR THE 101ST CONGRESS,
    which was updated on 06/23/93 and contains 16,030 records,
    is now available for your search.

TO START RETRIEVE to find: EXAMPLES:
  SEARCH: member name --------------> retrieve rep wolf
                     retrieve sen kennedy
         bill number --------------> retrieve h.r. 1
         subject keywords ---------> retrieve day care

FOR HELP: Type the word HELP and press the ENTER key.
READY FOR NEW COMMAND: **RETRIEVE S. 933**

Figure 7-4 also instructs searchers to type **HELP** and press enter to receive online assistance.

Twenty-four items in the database relate to S. 933 (Figure 7-5). Set 1 indicates that this search was the first done in the series.

Figure 7-5
LOCIS Database, 101st Congress
Results of a Retrieval

```
LAST COMMAND:  RETR S. 933

SEARCH RESULTS:

SET#   ITEMS   WITH THE WORDS OR TERMS
----   -----   ------------------------
 1      24     S. 933



---EXAMPLES: display     (DISPLAYs the set created by RETRIEVE)
             help display   (gives more info about DISPLAY command)
       OTHER
       COMMANDS: help browse retrieve select combine limit history end

READY: DISPLAY
```

Later sections of the chapter describe the commands listed at the bottom of Figure 7-5.

VIEWING BRIEF DISPLAYS

Type **DISPLAY** or **D** at the ready prompt shown at the bottom of Figure 7-5 and press enter to view the results. Figure 7-6 illustrates the first four bills. Descriptions of different parts of Figure 7-6 appear below.

Figure 7-6
LOCIS Database, 101st Congress
Brief Display

```
ITEMS 1-4 OF 24          SET 1: BRIEF DISPLAY          FILE: C101
                         (ASCENDING ORDER)
```

1. H.R.2273: SPON=Rep Coelho, (Cosp=250); OTLI=A bill to establish a clear and
   comprehensive prohibition of discrimination on the basis of
   disability. LATEST STEP=May 22, 90 House Incorporated this Measure
   in S.933 as an Amendment.
2. S.933: SPON=Sen Harkin, (Cosp=63); Public Law: 101-336(07/26/90); OTLI=A
   bill to establish a clear and comprehensive prohibition of
   discrimination on the basis of disability. LATEST STEP=Jul 26, 90
   Became Public Law No: 101-336.
3. S.AMDT.541: ASPON=Sen McCain, (Acosp=2); ADGST: From House or Senate=To
   amend the Communications Act of 1934 to require telecommunications
   services for hearing-impaired and speech-impaired individuals.
4. S.AMDT.705: ASPON=Sen Hatch; ADGST: From House or Senate=To provide for a
   small entity exemption for public accommodations.

```
NEXT PAGE:      press transmit or enter key
SKIP AHEAD/BACK:  type any item# in set          Example--> 25
FULL DISPLAY:    type DISPLAY ITEM plus an item#   Example--> display item 2
READY:
```

-SET 1: BRIEF DISPLAY (ASCENDING ORDER): The contents of set 1 are in brief, rather full, format. The full format is described below.

-ITEMS 1-4 OF 24: The search retrieved 24 items.   Figure 7-6 shows items 1 - 4.

-FILE: C101: The 101st Congress.

Data include bill numbers, sponsors, number of cosponsors, public law numbers, dates of passage, a brief abstract, and last action taken on the measure.

Test your knowledge of the LOCIS brief display: All questions relate to Figure 7-6.

1. Although S. 933 was searched, why are other measures shown along with S. 933?

   (The other items in some way
relate to S. 933.)

2. Who sponsored H.R. 2273?

   (Representative Coelho)

3. How many Representatives cosponsored H.R. 2273?

   (250)

4. What is the relationship between H.R. 2273 and S. 933?

   (H.R. 2273 was incorporated
into S.933 as an amendment.)

5.   Who sponsored Senate Amendment 541 and how many Senators cosponsored it?

(Senator McCain; 2 cosponsors)

SEARCHING LOCIS BY BILL NUMBERS: BROWSE COMMAND

Type **BROWSE S. 933** or **B S. 933** and press enter to search the bill using the browse command (Figure 7-7).

Figure 7-7
LOCIS Database, 101st Congress
Browse Command

```
FRIDAY, 07/09/93  03:20 P.M.
***C101- THE LEGISLATIVE INFORMATION FILE FOR THE 101ST CONGRESS,
     which was updated on 06/23/93 and contains 16,030 records,
     is now available for your search.



TO START  RETRIEVE to find:          EXAMPLES:
   SEARCH:   member name -------------->  retrieve rep wolf
                               retrieve sen kennedy
          bill number -------------->   retrieve h.r. 1
          subject keywords --------->   retrieve day care


FOR HELP:  Type the word HELP and press the ENTER key.
READY FOR NEW COMMAND: B S. 933
```

Figure 7-8 illustrates results. Twelve bills from S. 928 through S. 939 are in alphanumeric order, each labeled B1 through B12. Line B6 always represents the search word or phrase.

Figure 7-8
Results of Browse Search--Part I
LOCIS Database, 101st Congress

```
B01 S. 928//(BLNO=1)
B02 S. 929//(BLNO=1; XREF=2)
B03 S. 930//(BLNO=1; XREF=2)
B04 S. 931//(BLNO=1; XREF=2; AMDT=1)
B05 S. 932//(BLNO=1)
B06+S. 933//(BLNO=1; XREF=2; AMDT=22)
B07 S. 934//(BLNO=1)
B08 S. 935//(BLNO=1)
B09 S. 936//(BLNO=1)
B10 S. 937//(BLNO=1)
B11 S. 938//(BLNO=1)
B12 S. 939//(BLNO=1)

---EXAMPLES: s b6      (SELECTs line b6; creates a SET for each term type)
        f b6-b8/b10  (FINDs b6-b8 and b10; combines sets, displays result)
        r b6      (RETRIEVEs term on b6; searches text in some files)
        r subj=b6   (RETRIEVEs term type specified; e.g., SUBJ, TITL)

Next page of BROWSE list, press ENTER key.  More info, type HELP BROWSE.
READY: S B6
```

Note, Figure 7-8 displays information about S. 933 not seen above in Figure 7-5.   Figure 7-5 merely indicates that there are 24 references to S. 933, but Figure 7-8 differentiates the following kinds of data:

-A direct reference to S. 933 (BLNO=1),

-Two identical or companion bills (XREF=2), and

-Twenty-two amendments to the bill (AMDT=22).

The sum of the references under B6 is twenty-five, rather than twenty-four, because one item was duplicated in both XREF and AMDT. Type **SELECT B#** or **S B#** at the ready prompt to display each type of data in a separate set. For example, entering **SELECT B6** or **S B6** displays the information in line B06 as three separate sets (Figure 7-9).

Figure 7-9
Results of Browse Search--Part II
LOCIS Database, 101st Congress

```
SET 1      1: SLCT BLNO/S. 933
SET 2      2: SLCT XREF/S. 933
SET 3     22: SLCT AMDT/S. 933
READY FOR NEW COMMAND:
```

To retrieve the brief display of an item in Figure 7-9, type **DISPLAY SET# BRIEF ITEM#** or **D SET# BRIEF ITEM#**. For example, to retrieve the second item in set 3, type either **DISPLAY 3 BRIEF 2** or **D 3 BRIEF 2** and press enter.

Test your understanding of set numbers:

What command was used at the ready prompt in Figure 7-9 to retrieve the information illustrated in Figure 7-10?

(**D 1 BRIEF**; it is unnecessary to type an item number following BRIEF because this set has only one reference)

Figure 7-10
Brief Display of A Single Record
LOCIS Database, 101st Congress

```
ITEM 1 OF 1            SET 1: BRIEF DISPLAY        FILE: C101
                       (ASCENDING ORDER)
1. S.933: SPON=Sen Harkin, (Cosp=63); Public Law: 101-336(07/26/90); OTLI=A
   bill to establish a clear and comprehensive prohibition of
   discrimination on the basis of disability. LATEST STEP=Jul 26, 90
   Became Public Law No: 101-336.


NEXT PAGE:      press transmit or enter key
SKIP AHEAD/BACK:  type any item# in set       Example--> 25
FULL DISPLAY:    type DISPLAY ITEM plus an item#  Example--> display item 2
READY:
```

FULL DISPLAY FORMAT

The full display provides more information about bills than the brief one. In this context, full display refers to the complete array of options the database offers, not full texts of bills. Chart 7-1 illustrates how to retrieve full displays when beginning with information seen in Figures 7-5, 7-6, 7-9, and 7-10. The command format is **DISPLAY SET# FULL ITEM#** or **D SET# FULL ITEM#** and press enter. (e.g.: d 5 full 1--displays the initial record of set 5 in full format)

Chart 7-1
Retrieving Full Displays

Figure #	Retrieve a full display by typing...
7-5	**DISPLAY 1 FULL 1** or **D 1 FULL 1** (retrieves the initial record in set 1)
7-6	**DISPLAY FULL 2** or **D FULL 2** (retrieves the second item)
7-9	**DISPLAY 3 FULL 20** or **D 3 FULL 20** (retrieves the twentieth item in set 3)
7-10	**FULL** (retrieves the full version of the only item in set 1)

Figure 7-11 illustrates the full display of S. 933.

Figure 7-11
LOCIS Database, 101st Congress
Options Available From Full Display

```
S.933          4 REVISED DIGESTS AS OF 07/12/90      (C101) 05/09/89
Sen Harkin, (Cosp=63)              Senate Labor and Human Resources
(CROSS REFERENCE BILLS EXIST)
Public Law 101-336(07/26/90)
OPTIONS FOR THIS BILL:            ITEM 1 OF 1 IN SET 1
ABST    ALL     AMDT    CHRN    COMM    COSP    DGST
INDX    KWIC    OTTL    RDGS    REVD    REVC    REVB
REVA    RSTEP   STEP    STTL    SUMM    XREF
PAGE 1 OF 1. READY FOR NEW COMMAND OR NEW OPTION:
```

Type the appropriate abbreviation at the ready prompt and press enter to view the indicated information. Figures 7-12 through 7-15 describe four options: ABST, RDGS, STEP, and SUMM.

ABST is a brief statement that summarizes the purpose of the bill. RABS retrieves a revised abstract if one is available (Figure 7-12).

Figure 7-12
LOCIS Database, 101st Congress Full Display--Abstract (ABST)

S.933   4 REVISED DIGESTS AS OF 07/12/90   (C101) 05/09/89
Sen Harkin, (Cosp=63)   Senate Labor and Human Resources
(CROSS REFERENCE BILLS EXIST)
Public Law 101-336(07/26/90)
                    ITEM 1 OF 1 IN SET 1
ABSTRACT AS INTRODUCED:
   Prohibits discrimination on the basis of disability, including in the
areas of employment, public services, public accommodations, and
telecommunications relay services.

DGST provides a lengthy summary or digest of the bill. RDGS retrieves the most recent revised digest if one is available. The Library of Congress revises digests regularly as bills go through the legislative process. Each successive digest becomes REVA, REVB, REVC... Note that the revised digest in Figure 7-13 is much more comprehensive than the abstract in Figure 7-12.

Figure 7-13
LOCIS Database, 101st Congress
Full Display--RDGS

S.933   4 REVISED DIGESTS AS OF 07/12/90   (C101) 05/09/89
Sen Harkin, (Cosp=63)   Senate Labor and Human Resources
Public Law 101-336(07/26/90)

REVISED DIGEST: (AS OF 07/12/90)

Conference report filed in House, H. Rept. 101-596
   Americans with Disabilities Act of 1990 - Title I: Employment -
Prohibits discrimination by a covered entity (any employer, employment agency,
labor organization, or joint labor-management committee) against any qualified
individual with a disability in job application procedures, hiring or
discharge, compensation, advancement, training, and other terms, conditions,
and privileges of employment.
   Lists actions construed to be discrimination.
   Allows: (1) actions that are job related and consistent with business
necessity, if performance cannot be accomplished by reasonable accommodation;
(2) a requirement that an individual not pose a direct threat to the health or
safety of other individuals in the workplace; and (3) requirements that an
individual be a member of and conform to the tenets of a religious entity
employer.

STEP lists committee and floor actions taken on the bill and their dates. Organization is chronological with each chamber. RSTEP lists revised steps (Figure 7-14).

Figure 7-14
LOCIS Database, 101st Congress
Full Display--STEP

S.933   4 REVISED DIGESTS AS OF 07/12/90   (C101) 05/09/89
Sen Harkin, (Cosp=63)   Senate Labor and Human Resources
(CROSS REFERENCE BILLS EXIST)
Public Law 101-336(07/26/90)
                        ITEM 1 OF 1 IN SET 1
DETAILED STATUS STEPS:

                 SENATE ACTIONS
  May 9, 89 Read twice and referred to the Committee on Labor and Human
      Resources.
  May 9, 89 Committee on Labor and Human Resources. Hearings held.
  May 10, 89 Subcommittee on Handicapped (Labor and Human Res.).
      Hearings held. (May 16, 89).
  Jun 22, 89 Committee on Labor and Human Resources. Hearings held.
  Aug 2, 89 Committee on Labor and Human Resources. Ordered to be
      reported with an amendment in the nature of a substitute
      favorably.
  Aug 30, 89 Committee on Labor and Human Resources. Reported to Senate by
      Senator Kennedy under the authority of the order of Aug 2, 89
      with an amendment in the nature of a substitute. With written
      report No. 101-116. Additional views filed.

SUMM presents an abstract of the bill and lists actions taken in reverse chronological order (Figure 7-15). The computer codes in the second column under chronology of actions represent different stages of the legislative process.

Figure 7-15
LOCIS Database, 101st Congress
Full Display--SUMM

summ

S.933   4 REVISED DIGESTS AS OF 07/12/90   (C101) 05/09/89
Sen Harkin, (Cosp=63)   Senate Labor and Human Resources
(CROSS REFERENCE BILLS EXIST)
Public Law 101-336(07/26/90)
                        ITEM 1 OF 1 IN SET 1
SUMMARY:
(Abstract as introduced):
    Prohibits discrimination on the basis of disability, including in the
areas of employment, public services, public accommodations, and
telecommunications relay services.

CHRONOLOGY OF ACTIONS:
07/26/90 fact050 Public Law 101-336
07/17/90 fact006 Measure presented to President
07/17/90 fact004 Measure enrolled in Senate
07/17/90 fact002 Measure enrolled in House
07/13/90 conf080 Senate agreed to conference report, roll call #152 (91-6)
07/12/90 conf051 Motion to recommit conference report with instructions-28)
  rejected in House, roll call #227 (180-224)
07/12/90 conf030 Conference report filed in House, H. Rept. 101-596

Chart 7-2 describes the other options shown in Figure 7-11.

Chart 7-2
LOCIS Full Display Options

Command	Description
ALL	Retrieves all the options.
AMDT	Lists amendments to the bill.
CHRN	Displays major floor actions on the bill in reverse chronological order.
COMM	Lists committees to which the bill was referred.
COSP	Lists cosponsors.
INDX	Displays subject headings.
KWIC	Lists keywords in context. The KWIC option works only when searching by a term or phrase. The discussion below considers keywords in context detail.
OTTL	Gives the official title of the bill.
STTL	Displays a short title of the bill.
XREF	Lists cross references to companion or identical bills.

Test your understanding of the full display:

Retrieve the full display of S. 933, and display the various types of information. Try experimenting with other bills as well. If searching for bills from a different Congress, type **END**, and press enter to view the list of Congresses shown in Figure 7-3.

SEARCHING LOCIS BY SUBJECTS

Use the browse or the retrieve commands to search for information by subjects and keywords/phrases. Type **R HANDICAPPED** and press enter to locate references to that term. (Figure 7-16)

Figure 7-16
LOCIS Database, 101st Congress
Keyword Search Using Retrieve

```
TO START  RETRIEVE to find:            EXAMPLES:
  SEARCH:  member name -------------->  retrieve rep wolf
                                        retrieve sen kennedy
           bill number -------------->  retrieve h.r. 1
           subject keywords --------->  retrieve day care

FOR HELP: Type the word HELP and press the ENTER key.
  READY FOR NEW COMMAND: R HANDICAPPED

SEARCH RESULTS:

SET#  ITEMS   WITH THE WORDS OR TERMS
----  -----   -----------------------
 1     446    HANDICAPPED
```

The 446 references to handicapped in Figure 7-16 represent occurrences of the word in either the title, abstract, digest, or index fields.

Limiting the search to bills that are indexed under the subject heading handicapped will yield more precise results. Instead of using "r handicapped," type **R INDX=HANDICAPPED**. (Figure 7-17)

Figure 7-17
LOCIS Database, 101st Congress
Search by Index Term

```
TO START  RETRIEVE to find:             EXAMPLES:
    SEARCH:   member name --------------> retrieve rep wolf
                                   retrieve sen kennedy
              bill number --------------> retrieve h.r. 1
              subject keywords ---------> retrieve day care


FOR HELP:  Type the word HELP and press the ENTER key.
READY FOR NEW COMMAND: R INDX=HANDICAPPED



SEARCH RESULTS:

SET#   ITEMS   WITH THE WORDS OR TERMS
----   -----   -----------------------
 2     146     INDX/HANDICAPPED
```

SEARCHING LOCIS BY NAMES OF SENATORS AND REPRESENTATIVES

Search names of Senators and Representatives using either the **RETRIEVE** or the **BROWSE** commands. Figure 7-18 indicates that 416 items relate to Senator Harkin. The phrase R SEN HARKIN retrieved this information.

Figure 7-18
LOCIS Database, 101st Congress
Searching Names of Senators/Representatives
Retrieve Command

```
TO START  RETRIEVE to find:              EXAMPLES:
    SEARCH:   member name --------------> retrieve rep wolf
                                   retrieve sen kennedy
              bill number --------------> retrieve h.r. 1
              subject keywords ---------> retrieve day care

FOR HELP:  Type the word HELP and press the ENTER key.
READY FOR NEW COMMAND: R SEN HARKIN

SEARCH RESULTS:

SET#   ITEMS   WITH THE WORDS OR TERMS
----   -----   -----------------------
 1     416     SEN HARKIN
```

Test your understanding of the browse command:

How is the browse command used to retrieve information about Senator Harkin?

(Type **B SEN HARKIN** at the ready
prompt and press enter.)

The outcome of searching **B SEN HARKIN** is illustrated in Figure 7-19.

Figure 7-19
LOCIS Database, 101st Congress
Searching Names of Senators/Representatives Results of Browse Search

To choose from list, see examples at bottom.   FILE: C101
Terms alphabetically close to:SEN HARKIN

B01 SEN GORE--//(SPON=52; COSP=426; CWDR=1; ASPON=27; ACOSP=41)
B02 SEN GORTON--//(SPON=22; COSP=373; CWDR=1; ASPON=24; ACOSP=69)
B03 SEN GRAHAM--//(SPON=51; COSP=319; CWDR=2; ASPON=57; ACOSP=69)
B04 SEN GRAMM--//(SPON=11; COSP=153; ASPON=44; ACOSP=47)
B05 SEN GRASSLEY--//(SPON=39; COSP=383; CWDR=2; ASPON=17; ACOSP=63)
B06+SEN HARKIN--//(SPON=49; COSP=265; CWDR=1; ASPON=48; ACOSP=53)
B07 SEN HATCH--//(SPON=55; COSP=420; CWDR=3; ASPON=176; ACOSP=81)
B08 SEN HATFIELD--//(SPON=32; COSP=234; CWDR=1; ASPON=21; ACOSP=51)
B09 SEN HEFLIN--//(SPON=40; COSP=403; CWDR=1; ASPON=11; ACOSP=35)
B10 SEN HEINZ--//(SPON=100; COSP=365; ASPON=60; ACOSP=57)
B11 SEN HELMS--//(SPON=51; COSP=313; ASPON=134; ACOSP=117)
B12 SEN HOLLINGS--//(SPON=39; COSP=400; CWDR=1; ASPON=30; ACOSP=31)

---EXAMPLES: s b6   (SELECTs line b6; creates a SET for each term type)
      f b6-b8/b10 (FINDs b6-b8 and b10; combines sets, displays result)
      r b6   (RETRIEVEs term on b6; searches text in some files)
      r subj=b6 (RETRIEVEs term type specified; e.g., SUBJ, TITL)

Next page of BROWSE list, press ENTER key. More info, type HELP BROWSE.

READY: **S B6**

Like the results seen above in Figure 7-8, the search phrase, sen harkin, which appears on line b6, displays the various kinds of measures he sponsored. Typing **SELECT B6** or **S B6** at the ready prompt at the bottom is Figure 7-19 and then pressing enter will display the different kinds of information in separate sets. (Figure 7-20)

Figure 7-20
LOCIS Database, 101st Congress
Measures Sponsored/Cosponsored by Senator Harkin

SET 1	49: SLCT SPON/SEN HARKIN
SET 2	265: SLCT COSP/SEN HARKIN
SET 3	1: SLCT CWDR/SEN HARKIN
SET 4	48: SLCT ASPON/SEN HARKIN
SET 5	53: SLCT ACOSP/SEN HARKIN

Figure 7-20 shows how many bills the Senator sponsored (SPON), cosponsored (COSP), and withdrew cosponsorship from (CWDR). It also illustrates how many amendments he sponsored (ASPON) and co-sponsored (ACOSP).

Test your understanding of measures sponsored and cosponsored by Senators/Representatives: The following questions refer to Figure 7-20.

1. How many measures did Senator Harkin sponsor?

(49)

2. How many measures did he cosponsor?

(265)

3. How many amendments to bills did Senator Harkin sponsor and cosponsor?

(Sponsored 48 amendments and cosponsored 53 amendments)

4. Practice retrieving brief and full displays.

What command retrieves the brief display of the 3rd item in set 4?

(d 4 brief 3)

What command retrieves the full display of the 10th item in set 1?

(d 1 full 10)

Suppose you were only interested in measures sponsored by Senator Harkin, entering the phrase **R SPON=SEN HARKIN** retrieves the 49 bills and resolutions he sponsored.

Test your understanding of searching by kinds of bills and resolutions: Use the abbreviations in Figure 7-20 as a guide.

1. How would one retrieve references to the 265 measures Senator Harkin cosponsored?

(R COSP=SEN HARKIN)

2. How would one retrieve references to amendments sponsored by Senator Harkin?

(R ASPON=SEN HARKIN)

3. What information does the following statement retrieve: **R ACOSP=SEN HARKIN**?

(The 53 amendments cosponsored
by Senator Harkin.)

4. Attempt to retrieve bills sponsored by Senator Harkin by typing **B SPON=SEN HARKIN**. Describe what happens.

(The browse command retrieves information in
alphabetic or numeric sequence. The phrase B
SPON=SEN HARKIN attempts to locate the word
spon in its alphabetic order, not bills sponsored
by Senator Harkin. Use the phrase B SEN
HARKIN to retrieve relevant information.)

When searching names of representatives, use rep in place of sen. (e.g.: **R REP. GINGRICH; B REP. GINGRICH;** or **R SPON=REP. GINGRICH**)

SEARCHING BY PUBLIC LAW NUMBERS

To retrieve information by public law numbers, type **RETRIEVE** or **R** followed by the law number without spaces. (**PLLAW#**) For example, **R PL101-336** will retrieve reference to Public Law 101-336 (Figure 7-21). Be certain to enter the phrase without spaces because "pl 101-336" will yield different results.

Figure 7-21
LOCIS Database, 101st Congress
Retrieving Public Laws

```
TO START  RETRIEVE to find:              EXAMPLES:
  SEARCH:   member name -------------->   retrieve rep wolf
                              retrieve sen kennedy
            bill number -------------->   retrieve h.r. 1
            subject keywords --------->   retrieve day care


FOR HELP:  Type the word HELP and press the ENTER key.
READY FOR NEW COMMAND: R PL101-336



SEARCH RESULTS:

SET#   ITEMS    WITH THE WORDS OR TERMS
----   -----    -----------------------
1       1       PL101-336
```

Retrieve the same information with the browse command.(**B PL101-336**)

LOCIS ONLINE HELP

LOCIS offers detailed online help screens. Type **HELP** to view a series of menus. This information, which covers more advanced search techniques, is especially useful for those who use legislative histories frequently. Selected techniques cover combining search terms and search statements; limiting information retrieved by specified criteria, such as bills enacted into law, and bills that have received action in either chamber on particular dates. Type help followed by the command name to get help using that command. For example, **HELP RETRIEVE** provides assistance using the retrieve command.

DISCONNECTING FROM LOCIS

To disconnect from LOCIS:

1. Type **END** and press enter. The Opening Menu illustrated in Figure 7-2 appears.

2. Type **12** and press enter.

GPO ACCESS

INTRODUCTION AND BASIC SEARCHING

The Government Printing Office's ACCESS system includes a wide variety of databases pertaining to bills and legislative histories, economic statistics, directory information, and laws and regulations. Many databases are in both ASCII text and PDF formats. Most people will find the ASCII version easier to use. However, it eliminates all graphics and special markings, such as bold face type that PDF format displays. PDF documents resemble typeset pages. Use Adobe Acrobat Portable Document Format software with PDF files.

Login by typing **http://www.access.gpo.gov/su_docs/aces/aaces002.html.**[1] Be certain to use lowercase letters. Once connected, a list of databases appears (Figure 7-22).

Figure 7-22
GPO ACCESS Databases

For simple searches select one OR MORE databases from the list below:

( ) Congressional Bills, 103d Congress (1993-1994)
( ) Congressional Bills, 104th Congress (1995-1996)
( ) Congressional Directory 1995-1996
( ) Congressional Documents, 104th Congress
( ) Congressional Record, Volume 140 (1994)
( ) Congressional Record, Volume 141 (1995)
( ) Congressional Record Index (1992)
( ) Congressional Record Index (1993)
( ) Congressional Record Index (1994)
( ) Congressional Record Index (1995)
( ) Congressional Reports, 104th Congress
( ) Economic Indicators, 104th Congress
( ) Federal Register, Volume 59 (1994)
(*) Federal Register, Volume 60 (1995)
( ) GAO Reports
( ) GILS Records
( ) Government Manual
( ) History of Bills, Volume 140 (1994)
( ) History of Bills, Volume 141 (1995)
( ) House Calendar, 104th Congress
( ) Public Laws, 104th Congress
( ) Senate Calendar, 104th Congress
( ) Unified Agenda (1994)
( ) Unified Agenda (1995)
( ) United States Code

Enter search terms in the space below. Phrases must be in quotation marks (" "). The operators ADJ (adjacent), AND, OR and NOT can be used, but must be capital letters. For example: "environmental protection agency" AND superfund. Word roots can be searched using an asterisk (*) following the word stem. For example: legislat* will retrieve both legislation and legislative. Additional instructions and

Move the cursor to a set of parenthesis and press enter to select a database. Select multiple databases to search them simultaneously. Asterisks indicate databases are selected. Deselect a database by highlighting the asterisk and pressing enter. When signing on, the system defaults to the *Federal Register* database. Be sure to deselect it if you want to search something different. The bottom part of Figure 7-22 describes basic search protocol. To search, enter terms on the bold face line shown in Figure 7-23, highlight SUBMIT, and press enter.

Figure 7-23
GPO ACCESS Search Form

Maximum Records Returned: 0__ Default is 40. Maximum is 200.

Search Terms:

_____

SUBMIT CLEAR

[BACK] [DOCS HOME] [GPO HOME]

(Text entry field) Enter text. Use UP or DOWN arrows or tab to move off.
Enter text into the field by typing on the keyboard
Ctrl-U to delete all text in field, [Backspace] to delete a character

The system can retrieve a maximum of 200 records. It defaults to a maximum of 40 records unless users give instructions to retrieve a different number.

Chart 7-3 describes basic search techniques using the four "operators," OR, AND, ADJ, and NOT. Always enter them in uppercase letters. Chart 7-3 also describes the use of quotation marks ("...") and asterisks (*), and explains how to search by bill numbers.

Chart 7-3
GPO ACCESS Basic Search Techniques

Operator(s)	Example of its use	Explanation
no operator	vocational education	Retrieves all references to either vocational or education. In most documents, the terms are not adjacent.
OR	Same as no operator.	The phrase vocational education is equivalent to 'vocational OR education.'
AND	voacational AND education	Retrieves all references to vocational and education that occur in the same documents. **NOTE:** "AND" may not always be the best operator because documents in full text databases can be thousands of words apart. The first search term might appear in the initial paragraph and the second in a different context 10,000 words latter.
ADJ	vocational ADJ education	Retrieves references to the terms when they are either adjacent to each other or within 20 characters.
Quotation marks ("...")	"vocational education"	Retrieves the phrase.
NOT	vocational not education	Locates references to vocational only when the term education is not present anywhere in the same document.
Astericks (*)	disab*	Astericks (*) truncate stems. That is, the phrase disab* retrieves all references that follow the given stem. (e.g.: disable, disabled, disability, disabilities,...) **NOTE:** Truncate cautiously or run the risk of retrieving irrelevant information. For instance, cat* retrieves cat and cats, but it also might retrieve catch, catalog, catapult, and category, plus many other words.
Bills and resolutions	"h.r. 2491" or "h r 2491" Senate bills "s. 1000" or "s 1000" "h.res. 1" or "h res 1" "s.res. 1" or "s res 1" "h.con.res. 1" or "h con r 1" "s.con.res. 1" or "s con res 1" "h.j.res. 1" or "h j res 1" "s.con.res. 1" or "s con res 1"	Retrieves H.R. 2491. NOTE: leave spaces if you do not type the periods. The phrase "HR 2491" will not work. House and Senate resolutions House and Senate concurrent resolutions House and Senate joint resolutions
Combining 2 ideas.	(vocational ADJ education) AND (disabled ADJ persons)	Parenthesis separate two phrases, each representing different ideas. The terms in each phrase are either adjacent or with 20 characters. All documents that combine both ideas are retrieved.

Figure 7-24 illustrates a subject search in the 1995 Congressional Bills database.

Figure 7-24
GPO ACCESS Subject Search

Maximum Records Returned: 40_ Default is 40. Maximum is 200.

Search Terms:
disabled AND "vocational education"_____

SUBMIT CLEAR

Test your understanding of GPO ACCESS Basic Search Techniques: Refer to Chart 7-3 and Figure 7-24 when answering the following:

1. Describe what the phrase 'disabled people' retrieves.

> (References to either term)

2. How would results of the search 'disabled people' differ from 'disabled OR people'?

> (The phrase 'disabled people' is equivalent to that of 'disabled OR people.' Both retrieve all references to either terms.)

3. Describe differences among the following searches:

   A. disabled ADJ people

   B. "disabled people"

   C. disabled adj people

> (Statement A retrieves the terms adjacent to each other or within 20 characters of each other. Statement B retrieves the phrase disabled people. Statement C will not work because operators must be in upper case.)

4. Describe what the keyword educat* retrieves.

> (Asterisks (*) are truncation symbols that retrieve the stem, plus any letters in the same word that follow it. Educat* retrieves education, educating, educator...)

5. Describe how to search for information about grants or loans for educating the disabled.

> (Option A: (grants OR loans) AND disabled AND educat*; or Option B: (grants loans) AND disabled AND educat*)

6. Describe the search in Figure 7-24.

> (The searcher hopes to find references to vocational education as it pertains to the disabled.)

CONGRESSIONAL BILLS DATABASE

GPO ACCESS provides the full texts of bills beginning with the 103rd Congress. Updates are daily. Figure 7-25 displays the results of the search shown in Figure 7-24.

Figure 7-25
GPO ACCESS Result Screen
Congressional Bills Database, 104th Congress

For: "disabled AND "vocational education""

Total Hits: 29

[1]

H.R. 2491 (enr) To provide for reconciliation pursuant to section 105
of the concurrent
Size: 2967699 , Score: 1000 , TEXT , PDF

[2]

H.R. 2491 (eas)
Size: 2558104 , Score: 740 , TEXT , PDF

[3]

H.R. 2491 (pp)
Size: 2558768 , Score: 740 , TEXT , PDF

In Figure 7-25, the abbreviations immediately following the bill numbers represent different stages of the legislative process. Chart 7-4 defines selected abbreviations. Entry 1 is the bill sent to the White House for Presidential approval (enr); entry 2 represents H.R. 2491 as it passed the Senate with amendments (eas); and entry 3 represents the public print version (pp). Figure 7-25 also gives the size of the files and the relevance ranking. Entry 1 is 2,967,699 bytes and its relevance score is 1000. Relevance ranking depends upon the occurrence of terms in the document, the frequency of the terms as part of the total document size, and conformance with the exact searching phrase. One thousand is the highest ranking. To view the enrolled version of H.R. 2491, highlight entry one in Figure 7-25 and press enter.

Chart 7-4
GPO ACCESS, Congressional Bills Database, 1995
Different Versions of the Same Bill

Abbreviation and Action	Description
(ath) Agreed to House (ats) Agreed to Senate	Concurrent or simple resolutions are not passed like bills, but are agreed to.
(cph) Considered and passed House (cps) Considered and passed Senate	After debate or consideration, bills are voted on and passed.
(eah) Engrossed amendment House (eas) Engrossed amendment Senate (eh) Engrossed bill--House (es) Engrossed bill--Senate	Engrossed bills are passed by a chamber and certified by either the Clerk of the House or the Secretary of the Senate. Bills that have been amended before passage have engrossed amendments.
(enr) Enrolled bill	Bills sent to the White House for Presidential approval.
(ih) Bills introduced--House (is) Bills introduced--Senate	Bills as introduced in either chamber.
(pp) Public print	Versions of bills reported from one chamber after having passed the opposite chamber. For example, the House passed H.R. 2491. The public print of H.R. 2491 is the version reported by the Senate.
(rdh) Received in House (rds) Received in Senate	Engrossed bills accepted for consideration by the opposite chamber.
(rh) Reported bill--House (rs) Reported bill--Senate	Versions of bills as reported from committees to the respective chambers.

HOUSE CALENDAR DATABASE

Remember, *Calendars* reference House and Senate agendas on a given date. The *House Calendar* has special importance because of its legislative histories. Figure 7-26 shows the results of a search of H.R. 2491.

Figure 7-26
GPO ACCESS *House Calendar*, **104th Congress**
Database Results Screen

GPO Access Database Search Results (p2 of 4)

Total Hits: 6

[1]

3/19/96 [[New Databases Online via GPO Access]]
　　Size: 5093 , Score: 1000 , TEXT

[2]

H.Cal. (March 29) HOUSE RESOLUTIONS
　　Size: 79832 , Score: 1000 , TEXT , PDF

[3]

H.Cal. (March 29) SENATE BILLS
　　Size: 104109 , Score: 324 , TEXT , PDF

[4]

H.Cal. (March 29) 1
　　Size: 6918 , Score: 218 , TEXT , PDF

[5]

H.Cal. (March 29) HOUSE BILLS
　　Size: 183192 , Score: 152 , TEXT , PDF

[6]

Query Report for this Search
　　Size: 781 , Score: 1 , TEXT

Select option 5 that gives the history of House bills in the most recent *Calendar*. The following screen lists all House bills that have been acted upon during the 104th Congress beginning with H.R. 1 (Figure 7-27).

Figure 7-27
GPO ACCESS *House Calendar,*
104th Congress, H.R. 1

Numerical order of bills and resolutions which have been reported to
or considered by either or both Houses.

Note. ^GT1Similar or identical bills, and bills having reference to each
other, are indicated by number in parentheses.

No.   Index Key and History of Bill

HOUSE BILLS

H.R. 1 (H. Res. 6) (S. 2).--To make certain laws applicable to the
legislative branch of the Federal Government. Referred to
Economic and Educational Opportunities and in addition to
House Oversight, Government Reform and Oversight, Rules, and
the Judiciary Jan. 4, 1995. Passed House Jan. 5 (Legislative
....

H.R. 2 (H. Res. 55) (S. 4).--To give the President item veto
authority over appropriation Acts and targeted tax benefits in
revenue Acts. Referred to Government Reform and Oversight and
in addition to Rules Jan. 4, 1995. Reported amended from Rules
Jan. 27, 1995; Rept. 104-11, Pt. I. Reported amended from
Government Reform and Oversight Jan. 30, 1995; Pt. II. Union
....

H.R. 4 (H. Res. 117) (H. Res. 119) (H.R. 1214) (H.R. 1135) (H.
Res. 319).--To restore the American family, reduce
illegitimacy, control welfare spending and reduce welfare
dependence. Referred severally to Ways and Means, Banking and
Financial Services, Economic and Educational Opportunities,
the Budget, Rules, Commerce, the Judiciary, and Agriculture
Jan. 4, 19950 Considered Mar. 21, 22, 23, 1995. Passed House
....

Enter a search string: 2491
Arrow keys: Up and Down to move. Right to follow a link; Left to go back.
H)elp O)ptions P)rint G)o M)ain screen Q)uit /=search [delete]=history list

At this point, search the file for H.R. 2491 by typing a / to display the
phrase Enter a search string. Afterwards, type **2491** as shown in the bottom
of Figure 7-27. The system then displays the legislative history[2] (Figure
7-28).

Figure 7-28
GPO ACCESS *House Calendar,*
104th Congress, H.R. 2491

H.R. 2491 (H. Res. 245) (H. Res. 272) (H. Res. 279) (S. 1357).--To provide for reconciliation pursuant to section 105 of the concurrent resolution on the budget for fiscal year 1996. Reported from the Budget Oct. 17, 1995; Rept. 104-280. Union Calendar. Considered Oct. 25, 1995. Passed House amended Oct. 26, 1995; Roll No. 743: 227-203. Received in Senate Oct. 27 (Legislative day of Oct. 26), 1995. Passed Senate with amendment Oct. 28 (Legislative day of Oct. 26), 1995; Roll No. 556: 52-47. House disagreed to Senate amendment and asked for a conference Oct. 30, 1995. Senate insisted on its amendment and agreed to a conference Nov. 13, 1995. Conference report filed in the House Nov. 16 (Legislative day of Nov. 15), 1995; Rept. 104-347. Proceedings on Conference Rept. 104-347 vacated pursuant to H. Res. 272 Nov. 17, 1995. Conference report filed in the House Nov. 17, 1995; Rept. 104-350. House agreed to conference report Nov. 17, 1995; Roll No. 812: 237-189. Senate sustained point of order against conference report Nov. 17 (Legislative day of Nov. 16), 1995. Senate receded from its amendment Nov. 17 (Legislative day of Nov. 16), 1995. Senate concurred with an amendment Nov. 17 (Legislative day of Nov. 16), 1995. House agreed to Senate amendment Nov. 20, 1995; Roll No. 820: 235-192. Presented to the President Nov. 30, 1995. Vetoed Dec. 6, 1995. In House, veto referred to the Budget Dec. 6, 1995.

Test your understanding of the *House Calendar*: The following questions pertain to Figure 7-28.

1. Was an identical or related bill introduced in the Senate?

(Yes; S. 1357)

2. When was H.R. 2491 reported from the Budget Committee? What is the report number?

(October 17,1995; H. Rept. 104-280)

3. An amended version of H.R. 2491 passed the House on October 26. _____ Representatives voted aye and _____ voted nay.

(227 ayes and 203 nays)

CONGRESSIONAL RECORD DATABASE

GPO ACCESS covers the *Congressional Record* from the 103rd Congress, 2nd session (1994) to date Updates are daily. Once again, the *Congressional Record* reproduces the debates and proceedings in Congress. Chart 7-5 describes the field identifiers included in the 1995 edition for the first time.

Chart 7-5
Congressional Record
Field Identifiers, 1995+

Field	Description
Date	"Welfare reform" AND date=2/1/95 retrieves data for February 1, 1995. "Welfare reform" AND date=2/1/95 TO 2/28/95 retrieves data between the indicated dates. "Welfare reform" AND date>2/1/95 retrieves data after February 1, 1995. "Welfare reform" AND date<2/1/95 retrieves before February 1, 1995.
House	House="welfare reform" retrieves information from the House section of the <u>Congressional Record</u>.
Senate	Senate="welfare reform" retrieves information from the Senate section of the <u>Congressional Record</u>.
Extensions	Extensions="welfare reform" retrieves information from the Extension of Remarks section of the <u>Congressional Record</u>.
Digest	Digest="welfare reform" retrieves information from the Daily Digest section of the <u>Congressional Record</u>.

If looking for information published in the *Congressional Record* since 1995, consult a special version of the database that includes forms for limiting searches to particular sections of the *Record* and to a range of dates. (http://www.access.gpo.gov/su_docs/aces/aces150.html)

CONGRESSIONAL RECORD INDEX DATABASE

The *Congressional Record Index* on GPO ACCESS covers the 102nd Congress, 2nd session (1992) to date. Updates are bi-weekly. Figure 7-29 reproduces selected entries from the 1995 *Congressional Record Index* pertaining to the disabled.

Figure 7-29
GPO ACCESS *Congressional Record Index,* **1995**

DISABLED related term(s) Americans With Disabilities Act; Social
  Security
Addresses
  From Disability to Capability: Senator Kennedy, S10742-S10744
    [26JY]
  Vocational Rehabilitation Program: Richard W. Riley, Sec. of
    Education, E1639 [4AU]
Amendments
  Veterans: increase service-connected disability benefits (H.R.
    2394), S16927, S16937 [9NO], H12124 [10NO]
Analyses
  Veterans' Compensation Cost-of-Living Adjustment Act (S. 992),
    S9439 [29JN]

      ....

      ....
Bills and resolutions
  American Samoa: SSI benefits (see H.R. 1060), H2306 [27FE]
  Benefits: study providing services and benefits to individuals
    who served with voluntary organizations assisting the Armed
    Forces during the Vietnamese Conflict (see H.R. 179), H168
    [9JA]
  Capitol Building and Grounds: authorizing use of grounds for
    Special Olympics torch relay (see H. Con. Res. 64), H4441
    [1MY]

      ....

      ....
Lists
  National organizations endorsing the Birth Defects Prevention
    Act, E395 [22FE]
Proclamations
  National Mercy, Love, and Compassion for the Handicapped Month:
    Houston, TX, City Council, E1413 [12JY]
Remarks in House
  American Printing House for the Blind: funding, H7470 [24JY],
    H8342 [3AU]
  American Samoa: SSI benefits (H.R. 1060), E452 [27FE]
  Americans With Disabilities Act: improve, E338 [14FE]
  Amtrak: extend American with Disabilities Act exemption to
    commuter authority facilities, H13822 [30NO]
  Baldwin, Bryan: National Industries for the Blind's Peter J.
    Salmon National Blind Employee of the Year Award recipient,
    E1916 [11OC]

Like the printed copy, this version of the *Congressional Record Index*
separates different types of information.   Figure 7-29 displays addresses,
amendments, analysis, bills and resolutions, lists, proclamations, and remarks in the House.

It is sometimes easier to locate more precise information in the *Congressional Record* by consulting the *Congressional Record Index* first. For example,
Figure 7-29 references Senator Kennedy's statement on July 26 (26jy), pages

S10742-S10744. Using this information, select the 1995 *Congressional Record* and search the phrase **DISABILITIES AND KENNEDY AND DATE=7/26/95** or **DISABILITIES AND KENNEDY AND S10742.**

HISTORY OF BILLS DATABASE

The History of Bills Database provides legislative histories of bills as they pertain to the *Congressional Record*. It corresponds to the History of Bills and Resolutions section of the printed *Congressional Record Index*. It covers the 103rd Congress, 2nd session (1994) to date. Information extends to bills introduced during the 103rd Congress, 1st session, but acted upon during the 2nd session. Entries provide bill numbers, titles, summaries, sponsors, a chronological list of actions, and relevant pages and dates in the *Congressional Record*. Search by bill numbers using the format described in Chart 7-3. Other important search strategies are by subjects, by names of legislators, and by report numbers ("h rept 103-500").

Figure 7-30 illustrates the history of H.R. 2491. The top part of the shows that its introduction by Representative Kasich was on October 17 (17OC). This information appears on page H10145 of the *Congressional Record*.

Figure 7-30
GPO ACCESS History of Bills Database, 1995

H.R. 2491--A bill, the 7-year balanced budget reconciliation act of 1995.

Mr. KASICH, H10145 [17OC]

Reported (H. Rept. 104-280), H10145 [17OC]
Amendments, H10307 [18OC], H10520 [20OC], H10726 [24OC], H10995 [26OC], H11221 [26OC], H13379 [20NO]
Debated, H10781 [25OC], H10872 [26OC], H11409 [30OC], H13379 [20NO]
Made special order (H. Res. 245), H10847 [25OC]
Amended and passed House, H11365 [26OC]
Amended and passed Senate (in lieu of S. 1357), S16095 [27OC]
Text, S16159 [30OC]
House disagreed to Senate amendment and asked for a conference, H11421 [30OC]
Conferees appointed, H11422 [30OC]

....

....
Made special order (H. Res. 279), H13340 [18NO]
House concurred in Senate amendment, H13629 [20NO]
Examined and signed in the Senate, S17665 [28NO]
Examined and signed in the House, H13730 [28NO]
Presented to the President, H13868 [30NO]
Presidential veto message, H14136 [6DE]
Referred to the Committee on the Budget, H14137 [6DE]

Test your understanding of the History of Bills and Resolutions:
Refer to Figure 7-30 when answering the following.

1.   When was this bill first debated in the House and where
      in the *Congressional Record* do the debates occur?

(October 25, page H10781)

2.   An amended version of H.R. 2491 passed the passed the
      Senate in lieu of a related Senate bill. That is, the Senate
      passed H.R. 2491 instead of its own bill. What was the
      Senate bill?

(S. 1357)

3.   When was the bill amended and passed by the Senate and
      where in the *Congressional Record* is this recorded.

(October 27; page S16095)

4.   The House asked for a conference committee to iron out
      differences between versions of the bill passed by each
      chamber. When was this request made and where in the
      Congressional Record is it documented?

(October 30; H11421)

5.   Did the President approve H.R. 2491? If not, what hap-
      pened to it and where is this documented in the *Congres-
      sional Record*?

(The President vetoed the bill; reference
is on December 6, page H14136.)

CONGRESSIONAL REPORTS

Full texts of Congressional reports in GPO ACCESS cover 1995 to date.
Remember, reports are recommendations made by committees to their
respective chambers on bills and other matters that had been considered.
Search by report numbers using only the report numbers. For example,
enter the phrase "104-280" to search for House Rept. 104-280. Be certain to
include the quotation marks. Figure 7-31 displays results.

Figure 7-31
GPO ACCESS Results of Congressional Reports Search

[1]

CATALOG OF AVAILABLE REPORTS
  Size: 95537 , Score: 1000 , TEXT

[2]

H.Rpt.104-280,Vol.1 SEVEN-YEAR BALANCED BUDGET RECONCILIATION ACT OF
  1995 -- VOLUME I
  Size: 3575444 , Score: 1000 , TEXT , PDF

[3]

H.Rpt.104-280,Vol.2 SEVEN-YEAR BALANCED BUDGET RECONCILIATION ACT OF
  1995 -- VOLUME II
  Size: 3903335 , Score: 995 , TEXT , PDF

Test your understanding of GPO ACCESS:

Refer to Figure 7-31 to describe why you would use the statement "104-280*" to search for House Rept. 104-280? Remember the asterisk (*) is a truncation symbol.

(Figure 7-31 shows that ',Vol.1' immediately follows 280 without any spaces. Therefore, the GPO ACCESS interprets '280,Vol.1' as one word. The truncation symbol (*) becomes necessary to retrieve all characters following 280.)

THOMAS

The THOMAS system is one of the easiest ways to obtain the full text of bills and resolutions; the full text of the *Congressional Record*: and the *Congressional Record Index* on the Internet. The Library of Congress updates these sources regularly. Type **http://thomas.loc.gov** and press enter. As with GPO ACCESS, search results are ranked in descending order of importance.

SEARCHING FOR BILLS

THOMAS includes bills and resolutions introduced beginning with the 103rd Congress (1993). At the opening menu, select Bills and then select Bill Text for the relevant Congress. Two options permit searching by bill numbers and by keywords. The keyword selection includes a third alternative, searching by sponsors.

SEARCHING BY NUMBERS

Figure 7-32 displays a search for H.R. 2491. Directions appear in the illustration. Note, the Clear Query option in Figure 7-32 is very important. Users must be certain to clear the previous search prior to starting a new one.

Figure 7-32
THOMAS, 104th Congress
Searching by Bill Numbers

To search by bill number, type the bill number in the space below
(e.g., hr 2408).
Press the RUN QUERY button to start the search.

Enter bill number: **HR 2491**_____
RUN QUERY Clear Query

Figure 7-33 displays the results that include six versions of the bill.

Figure 7-33
THOMAS, 104th Congress
Results of a Search by Bill Numbers

THIS SEARCH	THIS DOCUMENT	GO TO
Next Hit	Forward	New Search
Prev Hit	Back	HomePage
Hit List	Best Sections	Help
	Doc Contents	

Versions of Bill Number H.R.2491

1 . Seven-Year Balanced Budget Reconciliation Act of 1995 (Reported in the House) [H.R.2491]
2 . Seven-Year Balanced Budget Reconciliation Act of 1995 (Received in the Senate) [H.R.2491]
3 . Seven-Year Balanced Budget Reconciliation Act of 1995 (Passed by the House) [H.R.2491]
4 . Balanced Budget Reconciliation Act of 1995 (House Appropriation Bill as Passed by Senate) [H.R.2491]
5 . Balanced Budget Act of 1995 (Engrossed Senate Amendment) [H.R.2491]
6 . Balanced Budget Act of 1995 (Enrolled Bill (Sent to President)) [H.R.2491]

Highlight entry 6 in Figure 7-33 to view the bill sent to the President for approval. (Figure 7-34)

Figure 7-34
THOMAS, 104th Congress
Viewing Sections of a Bill

Item 6 of 6

_____

There are 5 other versions of this bill.

Download this bill. (3,346,513 bytes).
Be sure to set your browser to Save to Disk

_____

H.R.2491

Balanced Budget Act of 1995 (Enrolled Bill (Sent to President))
_____

Table of Contents:

Beginning

Section 1. SHORT TITLE.

Sec. 2. TABLE OF TITLES.

TITLE I--AGRICULTURE AND RELATED PROVISIONS

Sec. 1001. Short title; table of contents.

Subtitle A--Agricultural Market Transition Program

SEC. 1101. SHORT TITLE.

SEC. 1102. DEFINITIONS.

SEC. 1103. PRODUCTION FLEXIBILITY CONTRACTS.

Figure 7-34 lists sections of H.R. 2491 in numerical order. Highlight the appropriate one to view the data. These subdivisions are helpful when studying bills that are especially long. To download the entire bill, highlight the relevant part of Figure 7-34 and press enter.

SEARCHING BY KEYWORDS

THOMAS encourages people to use natural language phrases when searching by keywords.[3] Figure 7-35 displays a search about vocational education for the disabled. THOMAS is not particular about how the keywords are entered. The search form includes directions. Two related searches produced almost the identical results shown in Figure 7-35. ("disabilities and vocational education" and "disabilities vocational education")

In Figure 7-35, the system searches all bills in both chambers. Highlight the relevant set of parenthesis and press enter to limit searches by measures that received floor action; measures forwarded to the President for approval; and measures introduced in either chamber. As in Figure 7-32, be certain to use the Clear Query option if previous searches were performed earlier.

Figure 7-35
THOMAS, 104th Congress
Keyword Search

SEARCH BY KEY WORDS IN BILLS

To search by key words, type your key word(s) or phrase in the space below. You can also limit your search by bill sponsor. Press the RUN QUERY button to start the search.
Enter query:
VOCATIONAL EDUCATION FOR THE DISABLED_____
RUN QUERY Clear Query
Search:
(*)All Bills
( )Only bills for which Floor action has occurred
( )Only enrolled bills sent to the President

Search:
(*)Bills from both Houses of Congress
( )Senate Bills only
( )House Bills only

SEARCHING BY SPONSORS

Figure 7-36 describes how to search for bill sponsors and illustrates a search for bills introduced by Senator Harkin.

Figure 7-36
THOMAS, 104th Congress
Search by Bill Sponsor

Search Full Text of Legislation - 104th Congress (p2 of 6)
To limit your search to bills sponsored by certain members, type the member name(s) in the space below (last names only). If more than one member shares the last name, type in the member's state also, e.g. smith texas. Press the RUN QUERY button to start the search. Member last name(s):
HARKIN_____
RUN QUERY Clear Query

CONGRESSIONAL RECORD ON THOMAS

Search the *Congressional Record* by keywords, by names of Representatives and Senators, by sections of the *Congressional Record* and by dates (Figure 7-37).

Figure 7-37
THOMAS, 104th Congress
Congressional Record **Search Form**

To search by key word(s), type as many significant words as you wish in the space below. You can restrict your search by section of the Record (House, Senate, Extension of Remarks), by speaker (for debates/speeches), and/or by date range.

Press the RUN QUERY button to start the search.
Enter query:

_____

RUN QUERY Clear Query

Search:
(*)All Sections of the Record
( )The Senate Section only
( )The House Section only
( )Extensions of Remarks only

Only those debates/speeches where the following member spoke or submitted remarks for insertion in the Record:
_____ (Enter last name only)

　　Search Full Text of the Congressional Record - 104th Congress (p3 of 5)
Only those debates which occurred between _____ and
_____
RUN QUERY Clear Query

Maximum number of items to be returned: 100_
Larger values may slow response time. Smaller values may miss relevant documents.

CONGRESSIONAL RECORD INDEX ON THOMAS

The *Congressional Record Index* on THOMAS is a very structured database. The initial menus include a range of alphabetic choices. Information about the disabled appears within the option for **DeVINE - DOGGETT** (Figure 7-38). Figure 7-39 displays information within that sequence.

Figure 7-38
THOMAS, 104th Congress *Congressional Record Index,*
Range of Subjects

DANEK - DAYTON
DAYTON - DeMARCO
DeMARCO - DEVINE
DeVINE - DOGGETT
DOGGETT - DRUYUN
DUBEL - EAGLE
EAGLE - EFFECTIVE
EFFECTIVE - EMISON
EMMANUEL - ETHICS
ETHIOPIA - FAMILY
FAMILY - FEDERAL
FEDERAL - FIFTY
FIGUEROA - FLEISCHMAN
FLEISHMAN - FORD
FORD - FRANCIS
FRANCKE - FRIEDMAN
FRIEDMAN - GALLUCCI
GALONSKA - GAY
GAYLE - GI
GIAIMO - GLOUCESTER
-- press space for next page --

Figure 7-39
THOMAS, 104th Congress *Congressional Record Index*
Selecting a Specific Subject

DIRKSEN CONGRESSIONAL RESEARCH CENTER
DIRREN, FRANK M., JR. (SKIP)
DiRUSSO, JOHN
DISABLED
DISABLED AMERICAN VETERANS
DISASTERS
DISCOVER CARD SERVICES, INC.
DISEASES
DISHNER, JIMMY
DISHNER, JIMMY G.
DISMAN, BEATRICE
DISNEY, DIANE M.
DISTRICT OF COLUMBIA
DISTRICT OF COLUMBIA EMERGENCY HIGHWAY RELIEF ACT
DISTRICT OF COLUMBIA SPORTS ARENA FINANCING ACT
DITTMAR, HANK
DIVORCE
DIX, JOHN
DIX, JULIUS C.
DIXON, JULIAN C. (a Representative from California)
-- press space for next page --
Arrow keys: Up and Down to move. Right to follow a link; Left to go back.
H)elp O)ptions P)rint G)o M)ain screen Q)uit /=search [delete]=history list

After selecting **DISABLED** in Figure 7-39, relevant information displays (Figure 7-40). As with the printed *Congressional Record Index* and GPO ACCESS, separate sections differentiate kinds of data about the topic.

Figure 7-40
THOMAS, 104th Congress *Congressional Record Index*
Data About the Disabled

IN CR INDEX	GO TO
Forward	New Search
Back	HomePage
Previous Level	Help

DISABLED

related term(s) Americans With Disabilities Act; Social Security

Addresses

From Disability to Capability: Senator Kennedy, S10742-S10744 [26JY]

Vocational Rehabilitation Program: Richard W. Riley, Sec. of Education, E1639 [4AU]

Amendments

Veterans: increase service-connected disability benefits (H.R. 2394), S16927, S16937 [9NO], H12124 [10NO]

Analyses

Veterans' Compensation Cost-of-Living Adjustment Act (S. 992), S9439 [29JN]

United Voices, E1231 [13JN]

Why the ADA Could Ruin the Superbowl, E338 [14FE]

Bills and resolutions

American Samoa: SSI benefits (see H.R. 1060), H2306 [27FE]

Benefits: study providing services and benefits to individuals who served with voluntary organizations assisting the Armed Forces during the Vietnamese Conflict (see H.R. 179), H168 [9JA]

Capitol Building and Grounds: authorizing use of grounds for Special Olympics torch relay (see H. Con. Res. 64), H4441 [1MY]

National Mercy, Love, and Compassion for the Handicapped Month: Houston, TX, City Council, E1413 [12JY]

Remarks in House

American Printing House for the Blind: funding, H7470 [24JY], H8342 [3AU]

American Samoa: SSI benefits (H.R. 1060), E452 [27FE]

Americans With Disabilities Act: improve, E338 [14FE]

Amtrak: extend American with Disabilities Act exemption to commuter authority facilities, H13822 [30NO]

ADDITIONAL FEATURES OF THOMAS

Additional features of THOMAS include:

-List of major topics in the *Congressional Record Index.* Information links to the *Congressional Record.*

-Bill summaries and status, 1995+.

-Lists of hot bills arranged by topics; by popular and short titles; by numbers; by those enacted into law; and by those under consideration during the current week.

These features provide good summaries of the major domestic issues before Congress and the nation.

ADDITIONAL INFORMATION ABOUT THOMAS

Consult the following files for additional information:

How To Search by Keywords in Bills. (http://thomas.loc.gov/home/words.html)

How To Search the Congressional Record Index. (http://thomas.loc.gov/i104/ i104help.html)

Legislative Research with Thomas by Larry Schankman is an excellent online aid. (http://www.clark.net/pub/lschank/web/mythomas.html)

Searching by Keywords in the Congressional Record. (http://thomas.loc.gov/home/words.cr.html)

CONCLUSION

Chart 7-6 summarizes major features of LOCIS, GPO ACCESS, and THOMAS.

Chart 7-6
Major Features of LOCIS, GPO
ACCESS and THOMAS

	LOCIS, 1973+	GPO ACCESS (Dates differ)	THOMAS, 1993+ (unless otherwise noted)
Bills	Provides legislative histories, status, and very detailed summaries. Does not include full texts of bills.	Provides full texts of bills (103rd Congress+). Two databases give legislative histories and status of bills-- History of Bills (1994+); and House Calendar (104th Congress+).	Provides full texts of bills (103rd Congress+). The Bill Summary and Status section begins with the 104th Congress.
Congressional Reports	Cites report numbers in legislative histories.	Gives full texts of reports (1995+). Four databases cite report numbers-- Congressional Record (1994+); Congressional Record Index (1992+); History of Bills (1994+); and House Calendar (104th Congress+).	Cites report numbers in the Congressional Record (103rd Congress+); Congressional Record Index; and the Bills Summary and Status section (104th Congress+).
Congressional Record	Legislative histories cite dates of debates.	Provides full texts of the Congressional Record (1994+); the Congressional Record Index (1992+); and the History of Bills section of the Congressional Record Index (1994+).	Provides full texts of the Congressional Record (1993+); and the Congressional Record Index (1993+). THOMAS excludes the History of Bills section of the Congressional Record Index.
Public Laws	Brief citations to bills and the more detailed legislative histories cite law numbers.	Provides full text of public laws (1995+). Two databases cite law numbers-- History of Bills (1994+) and House Calendar (104th Congress+).	The Summary and Current Status section cites law numbers (1995+); and the Hot Bills section includes bills enacted into law.

A significant purpose of this chapter is to guide laypeople through the Internet. Hopefully, practicing the examples and sample searches would provide familiarity with the Internet and confidence to use it.

Endnotes

1. The address in the text is for a direct connection to GPO. It is sometimes easier to connect to GPO gateways. Gateways are depository libraries that have agreed to make the GPO ACCESS databases available through their facilities. The Purdue University gateway works especially well. Links to all the gateways are at http://www.access.gpo.gov/su_docs/aces/aaces004.html.

2. Remember, these examples use Lynx software. If you are using other software, the "/" command may not work. For example, Netscape users must click on the find button to locate a keyword or phrase within the item currently displayed.

3. THOMAS documentation also states that natural language searching is not the most precise method to retrieve information. Consult *The Complete Guide to Searching THOMAS Under INQUERY* at http://thomas.loc.gov/home/all.about.inquery.html.

Exercises

1. Use the LOCIS database to answer the following questions about the Brady Gun Bill which was enacted during the 103rd Congress:

    A. What is the bill number?

    B. Who sponsored the legislation?

    C. What is the popular name of the law?

    D. When did the bill pass the House of Representatives?

    E. What is the relationship between S. 414 and the Brady Gun Bill?

    F. Did the Brady Bill go to conference? If yes, cite the conference report number.

    G. When was the bill signed by the President?

    H. What is the public law number?

    I. What command is used to display a detailed summary of the final version of the bill?

    J. Is there a way of comparing the detailed summary of the final version of the bill to one that describes the measure when it was introduced?

2. Use GPO ACCESS to answer the following questions:

    A. Locate a copy of the enrolled version of the Brady Handgun Control Act in the Congressional bills database for the 103rd Congress.

    B. What does enrolled version mean?

    C. Use the *Congressional Record Index* database for 1993 to locate the date and page number of a statement by Sarah Brady on semiautomatic assault weapons.

3. In 1995, Congress paid a tribute to Jim Brady and the gun control legislation enacted in his name. Locate this tribute using the THOMAS system.

    A. Which Representative paid this tribute?

    B. On what day was the tribute made?

    C. On what page of the *Congressional Record* did the tribute appear?

D. Compare use of the *Congressional Record* on the THOMAS system as opposed to GPO ACCESS. Which system do you prefer?

Answers

1. A. H.R. 1025.

   B. Representative Schumer.

   C. Brady Handgun Bill.

   D. November 10, 1993.

   E. The Senate passed the Brady Gun Bill in lieu of S. 414 on November 20, 1993.

   F. Yes. H. Rept. 103-412.

   G. November 30, 1993.

   H. Public Law (P.L.) 103-159.

   I. Type RDGS (revised digest) when viewing the bill in the full display.

   J. Compare information displayed under RDGS to that displayed under DGST. DGST presents a digest of the bill as it was introduced.

2. A. Search by subject or bill number ("h.r. 1025") and select the item marked H.R. 1025 (enr).

   B. Enrolled versions of bills have been passed by both chambers and forwarded to the President for approval.

   C. March 25, 1993, page S3770.

3. A. Anna G. Eshoo.

   B. March 30, 1995.

   C. E748.

•Chapter 8

Congressional Publications —Part V: Guides to Historical Congressional Documents

Answer the following questions when reading this chapter:

1. Describe three similarities and differences between accessing current and historical Congressional publications.

2. How can the indexes described in this chapter be used when compiling legislative histories?

3. Which index to historical Congressional publications is most useful to your needs? Why?

This chapter describes historical Congressional publications not discussed in earlier ones. The text considers the *Serial Set* first. The *Serial Set* is probably the single most important collection of United States government publications. Following that, the discussion then deals with the *CIS US Serial Set Index*-- the most comprehensive guide to *Serial Set* volumes published through 1969. The chapter also describes two other indexes to the *Serial Set*, the *Numerical Lists and Schedule of Volumes* and the *United States Congressional Serial Set Catalog*. Other sources examined include:

-The *CIS Index to US Senate Executive Documents and Reports*.

-The *CIS US Congressional Committee Hearings Index*, the CIS indexes to unpublished hearings, and selected other guides to hearings.

-The *CIS US Congressional Committee Prints Index*.

-*Congressional Masterfile 1*.

CONGRESSIONAL SERIAL SET

INTRODUCTION

The *Serial Set* is a compilation of House and Senate reports and documents. Representative Pickering's motion in 1813 called for the regular printing of Congressional documents. It stated:

> ...henceforward, all Messages and communications from the President of the United States; all letters and reports from the several departments of the Government; all motions and resolutions offered for the consideration of the House; all reports of committees of the House; and all other papers which, in the usual course of proceeding, or by special order of the House, shall be printed in octavo fold, and separately from the Journals--shall have their pages numbered in one continued series of numbers, commencing and terminating with each session.[1]

The 15th Congress in 1817 published the first *Serial Set* volume. Volume numbers of all subsequent issues, which currently amounts to over 14,000, are consecutive.

Serial Set volumes distributed to depository libraries since 1913 have gaps in their numbering. At that time, Congress discontinued distribution of *Serial Set* volumes that reprint executive agency publications, except to five Washington libraries--the House and Senate Libraries, the Library of Congress, the Public Documents Library, and the National Archives Library. Volumes distributed to these special libraries maintained the consecutive number scheme. Thus, materials forwarded to depositories reflect these gaps.

Further changes in *Serial Set* distribution are likely to be implemented in the near future due to financial concerns. Consult the *Report of the Serial Set Study Group*[2] for background information and for descriptions of options under consideration.

The *Serial Set* is related to a second collection of documents, the *American State Papers*[3.] Congress contracted with Gales and Seaton in 1831 to compile and publish a retrospective collection of Congressional publications of the first fourteen Congresses. This thirty-eight volume set has ten categories of publications.

1. Foreign Relations

2. Indian Affairs

3. Finance

4. Commerce and Navigation

5. Military Affairs

6. Naval Affairs

7. Post Office

8. Public Lands

9. Claims

10. Miscellaneous Documents

Selected items published before 1838 appear in both the *American State Papers* and in the *Serial Set*. Volume numbers 01 through 038 distinguish the *American State Papers* from the first thirty-eight volumes of the *Serial Set*.

WHAT DOES THE *SERIAL SET* INCLUDE AND EXCLUDE?

Although selection policies have never been consistent, materials are generally in the *Serial Set* when they:

-Assist legislators and their staffs in fulfilling responsibilities.

-Meet the political needs of Congress by creating permanent records of activities.

-Help Congress influence public opinion.

Chart 8-1 outlines the specifics of what is included and excluded from the *Serial Set*.

Chart 8-1
Information Included and Excluded From the *Serial Set*

Type of Information	Description
Journals	The proceedings of the House and Senate. <u>Journals</u> were included between 1817 and 1952. Note, between 1895 and 1938, only three libraries in each state or territory chosen by the Superintendent of Documents received <u>Journals</u>.
Reports	Statements issued by Congressional committees to Congress. Reports recommend legislative action and describe the intent of legislation by analyzing bills section by section. Reports of House committees have been in the <u>Serial Set</u> since 1819 and those of the Senate since 1847.
Documents	Three types of documents are: - Executive communications to Congress, such as Presidential messages or reports of executive departments. A large part of the <u>Serial Set</u>'s historical significance rests on the fact that publications of executive agencies, such as annual reports and selected investigative research, was included through 1912. These materials would have otherwise been very difficult to locate. - Annual reports issued by patriotic organizations, such as the Veterans of Foreign Wars, the Daughters of The American Revolution, and the Girl Scouts. - Other publications considered by Congress to be in the public interest, such as histories of Congress and its committees, and House and Senate rule manuals. "Executive" documents differed from "miscellaneous" documents between 1847 and 1894. The former are publications prepared by the Executive Branch, such as annual reports and investigative studies. Miscellaneous documents are titles that originated from other sources.
Information excluded from the <u>Serial Set</u>	- Titles originating in executive agencies since 1913. Since then, this information has been excluded because the Government Printing Office provided the same to depository libraries in departmental editions. The documents series still includes Presidential messages. - Bills and resolutions. - Committee publications, such as hearings and prints. With few exceptions, the <u>Serial Set</u> only includes materials issued by the full chambers. Although they are closely associated with committees, reports are included because their intent is to communicate information to the House and Senate. - Many Senate executive documents and Senate executive reports published before 1981. The discussion of the <u>CIS Index to US Senate Executive Documents and Reports</u> defines both kinds of publications. That discussion differentiates executive documents that are included in the <u>Serial Set</u> from those that are not. - Reports on private bills between 1905 and 1938.

CIS US SERIAL SET INDEX TO PRE-1970 VOLUMES

The *CIS US Serial Set Index*[4] is the most comprehensive index to the *Serial Set*. It originally appeared in twelve parts that cover different periods. The discussion considers two supplements separately, Part XIII--an index by bill numbers, and part XIV--an index to maps.

-Part I 1st - 34th Congresses (1789-1857)

-Part II 35th - 45th Congresses (1857-1879)

-Part III 46th - 50th Congresses (1879-1889)

-Part IV 51st - 54th Congresses (1889-1897)

-Part V 55th - 57th Congresses (1897-1903)

-Part VI 58th - 60th Congresses (1903-1909)

-Part VII 61st - 63rd Congresses (1909-1915)

-Part VIII 64th - 68th Congresses (1915-1925)

-Part IX 69th - 73rd Congresses (1925-1934)

-Part X 74th - 79th Congresses (1935-1946)

-Part XI 80th - 85th Congresses (1947-1958)

-Part XII 86th Congress - 91st Congress, 1st Session (1959-1969)

Each part of the *Serial Set Index* consists of three volumes, the two volume Index of Subjects and Keywords, and the one volume supplementary finding aids.

INDEX OF SUBJECTS AND KEYWORDS:

Use the Index of Subjects and Keywords to locate information by topics. It includes ample cross-references. Suppose you are looking for documentation about labor standards during the 1930's, search under the appropriate subject heading (Figure 8-1).

Figure 8-1
CIS US Serial Set Index
Index of Subjects and Keywords

LABOR STANDARDS
see also Fair Employment Practice Committee
Amending fair labor standards act rel. to switchboard operators in
   telephone exchanges of less than 500 stations
      S.rp. 980 (76-1) 10295; H.rp. 1448 (76-1) 10301
Amendments to fair labor standards act of 1938
      H.rp. 522 (76-1) 10298; H.rp. 1376 (76-1) 10301
Amendments to fair labor standards act of 1938. 2 pts.
      S.rp. 1012 (79-2) 11014
Conference report on fair labor standards act of 1938
      H.rp. 2738 (75-3) 10235
Consideration of bill to amend fair labor standards act of 1938
      H.rp. 1444 (76-1) 10301
Estimate for Labor Department for administration of fair labor
   standards act
      S.doc. 207 (75-3) 10248
Fair labor standards act of 1938
      H.rp. 2182 (75-3) 10234
Increasing minimum wage rate under fair labor standards act to 65
   cents an hour
      H.rp. 2300 (79-2) 11025
Investigation of employment of redcaps under fair labor standards
   act of 1938
      S.rp. 260 (77-1) 10544
Printing additional copies of pt. 2 of fair labor standards hearings
      H.rp. 1644 (75-2) 10236
Provision to make funds of Labor Standards Division available to
   pay for preparation of handbook on labor laws
      H.doc. 767 (76-3) 10502

Source: *CIS US Serial Set Index*, **Part X, 711.**
Reprinted with permission from the *CIS US Serial Set Index*. **Copyright 1991 by
Congressional Information Service, Inc. (Bethesda, MD).
All rights reserved.**

In Figure 8-1, the first document deals with amending the Fair Labor
Standards Act. Two related publications are S. Rept. 76-980 published in
Serial Set volume 10295 and H. Rept. 76-1448 published in *Serial Set* volume
10301. Congress issued both during the 76th Congress, 1st session.

Test your understanding of the Index of Subjects and Names: The
following questions relate to Figure 8-1.

1.   Which item deals with raising the minimum wage?

> *(Increasing minimum wage rate under
> the fair labor standards act to 65 cents an
> hour)*

2.   What is the report or document number of this item?

> (H. Rept. 79-2300; the 2,300th report issued by
> the House during the 79th Congress.)

3.   In which *Serial Set* volume is this item reproduced?

(11,025)

SUPPLEMENTARY FINDING AIDS:

The Supplementary Finding Aids have three parts:

1.   Private Relief and Related Actions lists names of individuals and groups that are the subjects of private legislation. Search for Peter Cuccio in the index to locate a report about a bill designed to assist him (Figure 8-2).

Figure 8-2
CIS US Serial Set Index
Private Relief and Related Actions

Crump, Donald
    S.rp. 725 (77-1) 10546
    H.rp. 668 (77-1) 10554
Cuba Memorial Hospital
    S.rp. 301 (77-1) 10544
    H.rp. 195 (77-1) 10552
    H.doc. 253 (77-1) 10599
Cuban-American Sugar Co.
    H.rp. 1781 (77-2) 10661
    H.rp. 85 (78-1) 10760
    H.rp. 88 (79-1) 10931
Cubero, Frank
    S.rp. 631 (75-1) 10080
    H.rp. 649 (75-1) 10087
Cuccio, Peter
    S.rp. 306 (78-1) 10756
    H.rp. 71 (78-1) 10760
Cuccio, Violet
    S.rp. 306 (78-1) 10756
    H.rp. 71 (78-1) 10760

Source: *CIS US Serial Set Index*, **Part X, 1485.**

2.   Numerical List of Reports and Documents cite in numerical order all reports and documents issued during a session of Congress. Within each session, four separate subdivisions cover Senate and House reports, and Senate and House documents. Figure 8-3 reproduces the reference to House Report 79-2300 seen in Figure 8-1.

Figure 8-3
CIS US Serial Set Index
Numerical List of Reports and Documents

House Reports

No.	Vol.	Serial
152. Revision of title 18 of United States Code, entitled Crimes and criminal procedure, pt. 2	1	11019
932. Requiring recording of agreements relating to patents, pt. 2	4	11022
1349. Counting military service of House and Senate employees rel. to civil service status, pt. 2	4	11022
1471. Payment to Henrietta Eigler for funeral expenses, etc., of Joseph R. Eigler	4	11022
2299. Consideration of bill relating to railroad reorganizations	7	11025
2300. Increasing minimum wage rate under fair labor standards act to 65 cents an hour	7	11025
2301. Veteran's pension, compensation, or retirement pay during hospitalization, institutional, or domiciliary care	7	11025
2302. Relief of Margaret M. Utinsky	7	11025
2303. Merchant seamen's wartime service act	7	11025
2304. Protecting and facilitating use of national-forest lands in Ohio in vicinity of Lake Vesuvius	7	11025

Source: *CIS US Serial Set Index*, **Part X, 1971, 1981.**

The notations printed to the left of the *Serial Set* volume numbers in Figure 8-3 are irrelevant to library users. This indicates that *Serial Set* volume 11,025 was the seventh issued in the House report series during that session of Congress. When the report and document numbers are known, use the Numerical List of Reports and Documents to locate *Serial Set* volume numbers.

3. Schedule of Serial Volumes lists *Serial Set* volumes in numerical order and notes the reports and documents included in each volume. When a volume consists of five or fewer titles, CIS cites each one. Otherwise, the publisher lists the relevant numerical sequences. Figure 8-4 displays the entry for volume 11025 which includes House reports 2180 through 2459.

Figure 8-4
CIS US Serial Set Index
Schedule of Serial Volumes
79th Congress, 2nd Session
Jan. 14, 1946-Aug. 2, 1946

Serial	Vol.	JOURNALS
11012	-	Senate Journal, 79th Congress, 2d session
11013	-	House Journal, 79th Congress, 2d session

SENATE REPORTS

11014	1	**Miscellaneous Senate Reports:** 47, 179, 808, 889-1129

Serial	Vol.	**74th - 79th Congresses (1935-46)**
11015	2	**Miscellaneous Senate Reports:** 1130-1344
11016	3	**Miscellaneous Senate Reports:** 1345-1609
11017	4	**Miscellaneous Senate Reports:** 1610-1929
11018	5	110. Investigation of national defense program, pts. 5-8.

HOUSE REPORTS

11019	1	152. Revision of title 18 of United States Code, entitled Crimes and criminal procedure, pt. 2
11020	2	1705. Investigation of Alaska Highway
11021	3	2646. Revision and enactment into law of title 28 of United States Code, entitled Judicial code and judiciary
11022	4	**Miscellaneous House Reports:** 932, 1349, 1471-1699
11023	5	**Miscellaneous House Reports:** 1700-1704, 1706-1939
11024	6	**Miscellaneous House Reports:** 1940-2179
11025	7	**Miscellaneous House Reports:** 2180-2459
11026	8	**Miscellaneous House Reports:** 2460-2615, 2617-2645, 2647-2728

Source: CIS US Serial Set Index, Part X, 2016-17. Reprinted with permission from the *CIS US Serial Set Index.* Copyright 1991 by Congressional Information Service, Inc. (Bethesda, MD).
All rights reserved.

Test your understanding of the Serial Sets' supplementary finding aids: The following questions relate to Figures 8-2 through 8-4:

1. Which reports relate to Peter Cuccio and what are their *Serial Set* volume numbers?

    (S. Rept. 78-306, *Serial Set* volume 10,756;
    H. Rept. 78-71; *Serial Set* volume 10,760)

2. In which *Serial Set* volumes are reports dealing with the Cuban-American Sugar Company printed?

    (10,661; 10,760; and 10,931)

3. What subject does H. Rept. 79-152 deal with?

    (*Revision of title 18 of United States Code enti-
    tled Crimes and criminal procedure, pt. 2*)

4.   In which *Serial Set* volume is H. Rept. 79-152 reproduced?

(11019)

CIS US *SERIAL SET* ON MICROFICHE:

The *US Serial Set on Microfiche*[5] reproduces on film titles in the *Serial Set Index*. Fiche are in numerical order by *Serial Set* volume numbers and are subdivided by report and document numbers. This collection includes the executive agency documents unavailable for general distribution in the *Serial Set* since 1913.

ADDITIONAL INDEXES TO PRE-1970 *SERIAL SET* VOLUMES

Congressional Information Service. *CIS US Serial Set Index, Part XIII: Index by Reported Bill Numbers, 1819-1969*. Bethesda, MD.: Congressional Information Service, Inc., 1994.

Indexes over 100,000 Congressional reports published through 1969 that deal with bills. Organization is numerical by Congress and by bill number. Entries give titles, report numbers, and *Serial Set* volume numbers. The editors do not include a subject index.

Koepp, Donna P., comp. *CIS US Serial Set Index, Part XIV: Index and Carto-Bibliography of Maps, 1789-1969*. Bethesda, MD.: Congressional Information Service, Inc., forthcoming. Will be published in 3 segments covering 1789-1897, 1897-1925, and 1925- 1969.

Provides access to over 50,000 maps printed in the *Serial Set*. Selected topics include natural resources and shorelines; Native American lands; descriptions of explorations; population migration; and battlegrounds. Four indexes deal with subjects and geographic areas; map titles; personal names; and corporate names.

Earlier chapters described three other indexes to the *Serial Set*.

Congressional Information Service. *CIS Index to U.S. Executive Branch Documents, 1789-1909: Guide to Documents Listed in Checklist of U.S. Public Documents, 1789-1909, Not Printed in the Serial Set*. Bethesda, MD: Congressional Information Service, Inc., 1990-.

U.S. Government Printing Office. *Catalogue of the Public Documents of Congress and of Other Departments of the Government of the U.S.* Washington, D.C.: GPO, 1893-1940.

U. S. Government Printing Office. *Checklist of United States Public Documents, 1789-1909*. Washington, D.C.: GPO, 1911.

INDEXES TO *SERIAL SET* VOLUMES PUBLISHED SINCE 1970

Two sources give *Serial Set* volume numbers of items published since 1970: the *Numerical Lists and Schedule of Volumes*[6] and the *United States Congressional Serial Set Catalog: Numerical Lists and Schedule of Volumes*[7].

NUMERICAL LISTS AND SCHEDULE OF VOLUMES

GPO published the *Numerical Lists and Schedule of Volumes* between 1933/34 and 1979/80 (73rd through 96th Congresses). Its two parts are the Numerical Lists and the Schedule of Volumes. The Numerical Lists has four sections that cite Senate Reports, House Reports, Senate Documents, and House Documents. Figure 8-5 illustrates the *Fair Labor Standards Amendments of 1973*, S. Rept. 93-300 and S. Rept. 93-301. Both are in *Serial Set* volume 13017-4.

Figure 8-5
Numerical Lists and Schedule of Volumes
Numerical Lists

No.	SENATE REPORTS	Vol.; serial
298.	Antitrust laws amendments	1–4; **13017–4**
299.	Research on Aging act, 1973	1–4; **13017–4**
300.	Fair labor standards amendments of 1973	1–4; **13017–4**
301.	Fair labor standards amendments of 1973	1–4; **13017–4**
302.	Essential Rail services continuation act of 1973	1–4; **13017–4**
303.	Rolling stock utilization and financing act of 1973	1–4; **13017–4**
304.	Job training and community services act of 1973	1–4; **13017–4**
305.	Emergency employment amendments of 1973	1–4; **13017–4**
306.	Congressional and Supreme Court pages	1–5; **13017–5**
307.	Endangered species act of 1973	1–5; **13017–5**
308.	Child abuse prevention and treatment act	1–5; **13017–5**
309.	Commission on Federal Election Reform	1–5; **13017–5**
310.	Federal elections campaign act of 1973	1–5; **13017–5**

Source: *Numerical Lists and Schedule of Volumes*,
93rd Congress, 1st session, 8.

The 1-4 that appears in Figure 8-5 immediately to the left of the serial volume number is irrelevant to researchers. It indicates that serial volume 13017-4 was the fourth issued in the Senate report series during that Congressional session.

The Schedule of Volumes section includes the identical serial volume number, 13017-4 (Figure 8-6).

Figure 8-6
Numerical Lists and Schedule of Volumes
Schedule of Volumes

SCHEDULE OF VOLUMES

Of the Reports and Documents of the 93d Congress, 1st Session

Note.—For explanation regarding the distribution, etc., of the bound set of Congressional documents and reports listed below see the Preface.

SENATE REPORTS

			Serial no.
Vol.	1–1.	Nos. 1–4, 6–50, 52–61: **Miscellaneous reports on public bills. I**_____	**13017–1**
Vol.	1–2.	Nos. 62–66, 68, 77–87, 91–92, 100–117, 119–124, 126–135, 138–146, 148–160: **Miscellaneous reports on public bills. II**_____	**13017–2**
Vol.	1–3.	Nos. 161–170, 172–177, 179, 187–192, 195–223: **Miscellaneous reports on public bills. III**_____	**13017–3**
Vol.	1–4.	Nos. 224–250, 252–257, 259–275, 277–283, 291–293, 295–305: **Miscellaneous reports on public bills. IV**_____	**13017–4**
Vol.	1–5.	Nos. 306–356, 358–374: **Miscellaneous reports on public bills. V**_____	**13017–5**

Source: *Numerical Lists and Schedule of Volumes*
93rd Congress, 1st session, 39.

The Schedule of Volumes also notes executive documents unavailable for distribution to depository libraries (Figure 8-7).

Figure 8-7
Numerical Lists and Schedule of Volumes
Schedule of Volumes
Volumes Unavailable For Distribution to Depository Libraries

93d CONGRESS, 1st SESSION

HOUSE DOCUMENTS	Serial no.
Vol. 5–2. No. 117: Same, vol. 2	13034–2 Vol. 2
Vol. 5–3. No. 131: Memorial services and tributes in eulogy of Harry S Truman	13034–3
Vol. 5–4. No. 137, pt. 1: Report of Commission on Bankruptcy Laws of United States, part 1	13034–4
Note.—The documents listed below originated in Executive departments and agencies. They were or will be furnished to depository libraries and international exchanges at the time of printing in the format used by the departments and agencies. They will not be furnished as Congressional documents nor in the volumes as indicated hereby.	
Vol. 7–1. Nos. 53, 62, 103, 122, 159: Report of U.S. participation in United Nations, Proceedings of Judicial Conference of United States, Oct. 1972, Proceedings of Judicial Conference of United States, April 1973, Department of Housing and Urban Development, Government activities in marine sciences	13036–1

Source: *Numerical Lists and Schedule of Volumes,* **93rd Congress, 1st session, 43.**

Test your understanding of the *Numerical Lists and Schedule of Volumes:* The following questions relate to Figures 8-5 through 8-7.

1. What is the report number of the document entitled *Endangered Species Act of 1973?*

(S. Rept. 93-307)

2. In which *Serial Set* volume is it published?

(13017-5)

3. In which *Serial Set* volume is S. Rept. 93-120 published?

(13017-2)

4.   Was *Serial Set* volume 13036-1 distributed to depository libraries? Explain.

(No; most titles published by Executive
agencies have not been distributed
in the *Serial Set* since 1913.)

UNITED STATES CONGRESSIONAL SERIAL SET CATALOG: NUMERICAL LISTS AND SCHEDULE OF VOLUMES

GPO began publishing the *United States Congressional Serial Set Catalog* biennially in 1981. Indexing is by authors, titles, subjects, series/report numbers, and bill numbers. Its organization and use are similar to that of the *Monthly Catalog*. Figure 8-8 displays a sample.

Figure 8-8
United States Congressional Serial Set Catalog

100-1242
Y 1.1/8:100-208
United States. Congress. House. Committee on Education and
  Labor.
    Employee Polygraph Protection Act : report together with
minority, dissenting, additional, supplemental dissenting, and additional dissenting views (to accompany H.R. 1212) (including
cost estimate of the Congressional Budget Office). — [Washing-
ton, D.C.? : U.S. G.P.O., 1987]
    23 p. ; 24 cm. — (Report / 100th Congress, 1st session, House
of Representatives ; 100-208) Caption title. Distributed to
some depository libraries in microfiche. Shipping list no.: 87-
423-P. "July 9, 1987." **Bill No.: H.R. 1212 Serial Set No.:
13804** ●Item 1008-C, 1008-D (microfiche)
    1. Lie detectors and detection — United States. 2. Employee
rights — United States. I. Title. II. Series: United States.
Congress. House. Report ; 100-208. OCLC 16413999

Source: *United States Congressional Serial Set Catalog,* **100th Congress,** 167

Test your understanding of the *United States Congressional Serial Set Catalog:* The following questions relate to Figure 8-8.

1.   What is the title of this document?

(Employee Polygraph Protection Act:Report
Together with....)

2.   When was it published?

(1987)

3.   What is its report number?

(H. Rept 100-208)

4.   What is its SuDoc number?

(Y1.I/8:100-208)

5.   In which *Serial Set* volume is it reproduced?

(13804)

FURTHER INFORMATION ABOUT THE *SERIAL SET*

Consult the following for more information about the *Serial Set*:

Congressional Information Service. *CIS US Serial Set Index, 1789-1969: User Handbook*. Washington, D.C.: Congressional Information Service, Inc., 1980.

A brief, but very informative pamphlet reprinted from the introduction to the *Serial Set Index*. It describes the *Serial Set*'s history in detail; illustrates how to use the *Serial Set Index*; and reproduces sample pages from the Index.

Morehead, Joe and Mary Fetzer. *Introduction to United States Government Information Sources*. 4th ed. Englewood, CO: Libraries Unlimited, Inc., 1992.

Provides a good overview of the *Serial Set* and its indexes from an historical viewpoint and a more contemporary one.

Schmeckebier, Laurence F. and Roy B. Eastin. *Government Publications and Their Use*. 2nd rev. ed. Washington, D.C.: Brookings Institution, 1969. 150-166.

A classic government publications handbook that emphasizes the history and development of the *Serial Set*. See pages 150-166.

CIS INDEX TO US SENATE EXECUTIVE DOCUMENTS AND REPORTS

INTRODUCTION

The *CIS Index to US Senate Executive Documents and Reports*[8] indexes significant information excluded from the *Serial Set*. Senate executive documents are Presidential messages to the Senate in support of treaties and nominations. The Senate ratifies treaties and approves Presidential nominations of high ranking executive branch officials, ambassadors, and federal judges. Executive documents printed in the *Serial Set* through 1913 include other kinds of information prepared by executive agencies, such as annual reports and investigative studies. Senate executive reports are statements Senate committees submit to their chamber in response to Senate Executive Documents.

Historically, the Senate looked upon these roles as unique from other legislative activities by considering such matters in executive or closed sessions. Consult the *Journal of the Executive Proceeding of the Senate*[9] for an account of these proceedings. Prior to 1930, Senate executive documents and reports were confidential.

Between 1930 and 1981, executive documents and reports were public information, but they were not included in the *Serial Set* and were not distributed to depository libraries. In 1981, the Senate renamed the executive documents series treaty documents and began including them in the *Serial Set*, along with executive reports.

The *CIS Index to US Senate Executive Documents and Reports* includes titles published between 1818 and 1969. Most relate to treaties, since information about nominations was not published as regularly. This collection excludes nearly 4,800 Senate executive documents and reports that are in the *CIS US Serial Set Index*. Those published from 1970 to date are indexed in the *CIS Index*.

REFERENCE BIBLIOGRAPHY

The Reference Bibliography section provides bibliographic information about the documents and reports and brief annotations that describe the subjects covered. Organization is by Congress and session, and numerically by report and document numbers. Figure 8-9 illustrates publications four through six during the 67th Congress, 2nd session.

Figure 8-9
CIS Index to US Senate Executive Documents and Reports
Reference Bibliography

67-2-4

Four Powers Supplementary Agreement.

Mar. 27, 1922. 4 p. 67-2.

Reports ratification of supplementary agreement (Exec. 4, 67-2) signed Feb. 6, 1922, at Washington, defining the insular possessions of Japan in the Pacific insular possessions treaty of Dec. 13, 1921.

67-2-5

Nine Powers Treaty on China.

Mar. 30, 1922. 11 p. 67-2.

Reports ratification of treaty (Exec. P, 67-2) signed Feb. 6, 1922, at Washington, assuring the sovereignty of China, and the continuation of the open door policy. Includes undated resolution recommending Senate advice and consent to the treaty.

67-2-6

Nine Powers Treaty on Chinese Tariff.

Feb. 27, 1922. 12 p. 67-2.

Reports treaty (Exec. Q, 67-2) signed Feb. 6, 1922, at Washington. Includes undated resolution recommending Senate advice and consent to treaty.

Source: *CIS Index to US Senate Executive Documents and Reports*, **Vol. 1, 157.**
Reprinted with permission from the *CIS Index to US Senate Executive Documents and Reports* **Copyright 1991 by Congressional Information Service, Inc. (Bethesda, MD). All rights reserved.**

INDEX BY SUBJECTS

Subject headings in the Index by Subjects are alphabetical (Figure 8-10). Accession numbers refer users to the Reference Bibliography.

Figure 8-10

CIS Index to US Senate Executive Documents and Reports

Japan   Subject Index

Arbitration convention extension agreement with US, 1913 June 28, Washington
  63-1-7

Arbitration convention extension agreement with US, 1923 Aug 23, Washington
  68-1-12

Arbitration convention with US, extension agreement, 1918 Aug 23, Washington
  65-2-8

Arbitration convention with US, 1908 May 5, Washington
  60-1-35

China sovereignty and open door assurance treaty, 1922 Feb 6, Washington
  67-2-5

China tariff intl treaty, 1922 Feb 6, Washington
  67-2-6

Source: *CIS Index to US Senate Executive Documents and Reports,* **Vol. 2, 147.**

Special subject headings identify the following types of treaties:

-Arbitration & Conciliation Agreements

-Claims Settlement Agreements

-Consular Treaties

-Copyright, Patent and Trademark Agreements

-Extradition Treaties

-Friendship, Commerce, and Navigation Treaties

-Indian Treaties;

-International Peace Treaties

-Military Agreements

-Naturalization Agreements

-Radio Agreements

-Status of Forces Agreements

-Tariff Agreements

-Tax Treaties

-Trade Agreements

-Whaling Agreements

INDEX BY DOCUMENT AND REPORT NUMBERS

The Index by Document and Report Numbers list items in numeric and alphabetic order. Exec. Rept. # and Exec. Doc. # identify executive reports and executive documents. Figure 8-11 reproduces references to items published during the 67th Congress.

Figure 8-11
CIS Index to US Senate Executive Documents and Reports
Index by Document and Report Numbers

(67-1) Exec. Doc. F, 67-1	....	67-1-1
(67-1) Exec. Doc. F, 67-1	....	67-1-6
(67-1) Exec. Doc. G, 67-1	....	67-1-2
(67-1) Exec. Doc. G, 67-1	....	67-1-7
(67-1) Exec. Doc. H, 67-1	....	67-1-3
(67-1) Exec. Doc. I, 67-1	....	67-1-4
(67-1) Exec. Doc. K, 67-1	....	67-1-5
(67-1) Exec. Rpt. 2, 67-1	....	67-1-8
(67-2) Exec. Doc. L, 67-2	....	67-2-1
(67-2) Exec. Doc. M, 67-2	....	67-2-2
(67-2) Exec. Doc. N, 67-2	....	67-2-3
(67-2) Exec. Doc. N, 67-2	....	67-2-16
(67-2) Exec. Doc. O, 67-2	....	67-2-4
(67-2) Exec. Doc. P, 67-2	....	67-2-5
(67-2) Exec. Doc. Q, 67-2	....	67-2-6
(67-2) Exec. Doc. R, 67-2	....	67-2-7
(67-2) Exec. Doc. S, 67-2	....	67-2-8
(67-2) Exec. Doc. T, 67-2	....	67-2-9

INDEX BY PERSONAL NAMES

The Index by Personal Names lists Presidential nominations. Figure 8-12 shows the reference to Louis D. Brandeis' nomination to the Supreme Court.

Figure 8-12
CIS Index to US Senate Executive Documents and Reports
Index by Personal Names

Brakeman, N. L.
Appointment to be Hosp Chaplain, Army
38-1-53

Brand, Thomas T.
Appointment to be Brevet Maj, Army
39-2-74

Brandeis, Louis D.
Nomination to be Assoc Justice, Supreme Court
64-1-12; 64-1-13

Branson, David
Appointment to be Brevet Col, Volunteers, Army
39-1-60

Brayman, Mason
Appointment to be Brevet Maj Gen, Volunteers, Army
39-1-78

Source: *CIS Index to US Senate Executive Documents and Reports*, **Vol. 2, 241.**
Reprinted with permission from the *CIS Index to US Senate Executive Documents
and Reports*
**Copyright 1991 by Congressional Information Service, Inc. (Bethesda, MD).
All rights reserved.**

CIS US SENATE EXECUTIVE DOCUMENTS AND REPORTS MICROFICHE COLLECTION

The *CIS US Senate Executive Documents and Reports*[10] microfiche collection reproduces these materials. Organization of microfiche is by CIS accession numbers.

CIS US CONGRESSIONAL COMMITTEE HEARINGS INDEX

The *CIS US Congressional Committee Hearings Index*[10a] is the most comprehensive index to the earliest Congressional hearings through those published in 1969. The *Index* appears in eight parts, each covering the indicated periods:

-Part I Earliest Hearings through 63rd Congress, early 1800's - 1914.

-Part II 64th - 68th Congresses, December 1915-March 1925.

-Part III 69th - 73rd Congresses, December 1925-1934.

-Part IV 74th - 79th Congresses, 1935-1946.

-Part V 80th - 82nd Congresses, 1947-1952.

-Part VI 83rd - 85th Congresses, 1953-1958.

-Part VII 86th - 88th Congresses, 1959-1964.

-Part VIII 89th - 91st Congress, 1st session, 1965-1969.

Six indexes deal with subjects and organizations; personal names; titles; bill numbers; Superintendent of Documents classification numbers; and report and document numbers. The Reference Bibliography section gives bibliographic data; Superintendent of Document numbers; and names of witnesses and their affiliations.

INDEX BY SUBJECTS AND ORGANIZATIONS: SUBJECT APPROACH

The Index by Subjects and Organizations includes subject headings; special terms, such as glossaries and bibliographies; and names of laws and bills. To locate information relating to child labor, consult that subject heading (Figure 8-13). Content notations describe the subject matter and accession numbers refer to the Reference Bibliography section.

Figure 8-13
CIS US Congressional Hearings Index
Index by Subjects and Organizations: Subject Approach

Chief Washakie (ship)
Liberty ship structural failures
(78) S752-0-A
Child labor
DC youth theater employment regulations, revision
(76) H878-4
Interstate and foreign trade in child labor products, prohibition; state
child labor laws, Fed legislation need, examination
(75) S544-5
Minimum wage, working hours, and child labor, standards, estab
(75) S543-2-A; (75) S543-2-B; (75) S543-2-C
Seamen minimum age convention implementation
(76) H881-6
Sugar production payments, child labor penalty wartime suspension
provision
(77) S695-11
Textile industry child labor prohibition and Natl Textile Commission
regulatory authority estab
(74) H773-2
Child welfare
see also Day care programs
see also Foster home care
see also School lunch and breakfast programs
Children's Bur maternal and infant care programs, FY45 approp
(78) H1014-0-A

Source: *CIS US Congressional Hearings Index*, **Part IV, Vol. 1, 158. Reprinted with
permission from the** *CIS US Congressional Hearings Index*
**Copyright 1991 by Congressional Information Service, Inc. (Bethesda, MD).
All rights reserved.**

Test your understanding of the Index by Subjects and Organizations: The following questions relate to Figure 8-13.

1. How many hearings deal with working hours of children
   and the establishment of standards?

(3)

2.   What are their Reference Bibliography accession numbers?

((75) S543-2-A; (75) S543-2-B;
(75) S543-2-C)

3.   During which Congress was the following hearing held:
(78) S752-0-A?

(78th Congress)

REFERENCE BIBLIOGRAPHY

Figure 8-14 reproduces accession number seen in Figure 8-13, (75) S543-2-A. Arrangement of the Reference Bibliography is by accession numbers.

Figure 8-14
CIS US Congressional Hearings Index
Reference Bibliography

(75) S543-2-A

FAIR LABOR STANDARDS ACT OF 1937. Part 1
June 2-5, 1937.   75-1.   iii+269 p.
Y4.Ed8/3:L11/7/pt.1.

Considers legislation to establish minimum wage, working hours, and child labor standards for industries operating in interstate commerce.

Committees: Senate Committee on Education and Labor; House Committee on Labor

Subject descriptors: Fair Labor Standards Act; Minimum wage; Hours of labor; Child labor; Interstate commerce; Labor-management relations; National Recovery Administration; Congressional powers; States' rights; Supreme Court

Bills: (75) S. 2475; (75) H.R. 7200

Witnesses:
Jackson, Robert H., Justice Dept, p. 1.
Johnson, Robert W., pres, Johnson and Johnson, p. 91.
Paine, John G., chm, mgmt group, Natl Council for Industrial Progress, p. 126.
Hanway, Paul S., exec sec-treas, Natl Fibre Can and Tube Assn, p. 146.

Clark, John D., representing Fla citrus industry, p. 151.
Henderson, Leon, Consulting Economist, Works Progress Admin, p. 155.
Perkins, Frances, Sec, DOL, p. 173.
Green, William, pres, AFL, p. 211.
Kuldell, R. C., pres, Hughes Tool Co, p. 243.
Vincent, Merle D., legis counsel, Intl Ladies Garment Workers Union, p. 262.

Source: *CIS US Congressional Hearings Index,*
Part IV, Vol. 5, 450. Reprinted with permission from the *CIS US Congressional Hearings Index* **Copyright 1991 by Congressional Information Service, Inc. (Bethesda, MD). All rights reserved.**

The subject descriptors in Figure 8-14 indicate subject headings assigned to this title. Consult those headings for additional references. The Bills section lists relevant bills relating to the hearing, and the Witnesses section cites names of witnesses, their affiliations, and the pages on which their testimonies begin.

Test your understanding of the Reference Bibliography: The following questions relate to Figure 8-14.

1. What is the title of this hearing?

   (Fair Labor Standards Act of 1937, Part 1)

2. When were these hearings held?

   (June 2-5, 1937)

3. Which committees held the hearing?

   (Senate Committee on Education and Labor; House Committee on Labor)

4. What is the SuDoc number?

   (Y4.ED8/3:L11/7/pt.1)

5. What is the Reference Bibliography accession number? Why is it important?

   ((75) S543-2-A. Use the accession numbers to refer from the indexes to the Reference Bibliography.)

6. Which bills relate to this hearing?

   (S. 2475 and H.R. 7200)

7. Did William Green present testimony at this hearing? If yes, on what page does his testimony begin?

   (Yes; page 211)

8. Who is William Green?

   (President of the American Federation of Labor)

INDEX BY SUBJECTS AND ORGANIZATIONS: ORGANIZATION APPROACH

Besides subject headings, the Index by Subjects and Organizations also includes:

-Names of organizations represented at hearings.

-Organizations that are subjects of hearings.

-Organizations whose documentation the committees printed in the hearings. These include press releases, statistics, research studies, and position papers.

The Index lists names of Congressional committees under either "House Committee on..." or "Senate Committee on..." To determine the position taken by the American Federation of Labor on minimum wages, search under the abbreviated name of the group (Figure 8-15).

Figure 8-15
CIS US Congressional Hearings Index
Index by Subjects and Organizations: Organization Approach

AFL

Air pilots monthly flying hour totals, CAB restrictions suspension for WWII-related service
(77) S685-1

Airlines labor regulations estab
(74) S495-10

Alcoholic beverage radio advertising regulations, revision
(76) S582-4

Alien commuters from Canada and Mexico, restrictions estab
(74) H772-5

Merchant vessel radio operators, experience requirement revision
(77) H913-5

Migrant workers interstate movement and social and economic needs, review
(76) H920-0-C

Minimum wage, working hours, and child labor, standards, estab
(75) S543-2-A

Mobilization programs impact on domestic migration review
(77) H935-0-C

Natl industrial recovery programs extension
(74) H720-3

Naval expansion program authorization and natl def policy review
(75) S559-4

Naval vessel construction contracts, emergency mgmt practices authorization
(76) S628-15

Source: *CIS US Congressional Hearings Index*, **Part IV, Vol. 1, 7, 9. Reprinted with permission from the** *CIS US Congressional Hearings Index* **Copyright 1991 by Congressional Information Service, Inc. (Bethesda, MD). All rights reserved.**

INDEX BY PERSONAL NAMES

The Index by Personal Names lists names of witnesses who testified at hearings; the names of authors whose work the hearings reprint; and the names of individuals who are subjects of hearings. Figure 8-16 references William Green, the American Federation of Labor representative noted in Figure 8-14.

Figure 8-16
CIS US Congressional Hearings Index
Index by Personal Names

Green, William
Bituminous coal industry regulation
authorization and Natl Bituminous Coal
Commission and Natl Bituminous Coal
Reserve, estab
(74) S482-2
Civilian war service system estab
(78) S718-0-I; (78) S744-2-C
Labor union representation on Govt
industrial commissions, agencies, and bds,
review
(74) H705-2
Manpower resources and employment
conditions, investigation
(77) S704-2-A
Minimum wage, working hours, and child
labor, standards, estab
(75) S543-2-A
Mobilization programs impact on domestic
migration review
(77) H935-0-C

Source: *CIS US Congressional Hearings Index*, **Part IV, Vol. 3, 314-15. Reprinted with permission from the** *CIS US Congressional Hearings Index* **Copyright 1991 by Congressional Information Service, Inc. (Bethesda, MD). All rights reserved.**

INDEX BY TITLES

The Index by Titles cites information in alphabetical order (Figure 8-17).

Figure 8-17
CIS US Congressional Hearings Index
Index by Titles
Fair Employment Practices Act
(78) S739-2
Fair Labor Standards Act of 1937. Part 1
(75) S543-2-A
Fair Labor Standards Act of 1937. Part 2
(75) S543-2-B
Fair Labor Standards Act of 1937. Part 3
(75) S543-2-C
Fair Trade Act
(76) S614-1
False Billing
(74) H763-10
Family Allowances. [Part 1]
(77) S690-16-A

Source: *CIS US Congressional Hearings Index*, **Part IV, Vol. 2, 1113. Reprinted with permission from the** *CIS US Congressional Hearings Index* **Copyright 1991 by Congressional Information Service, Inc. (Bethesda, MD). All rights reserved.**

INDEX BY BILL NUMBERS

Arrangement of the Index by Bill Numbers is by Congress, and within each Congress, numerically first by House bills and then by Senate bills. Figure 8-18 illustrates S. 2475 (75th Congress).

Figure 8-18
CIS US Congressional Hearings Index
Index by Bill Numbers

(75) S. 2409	(75) H835-0.156
(75) S. 2439	(75) H794-1
(75) S. 2475	(75) S543-2-A
(75) S. 2475	(75) S543-2-B
(75) S. 2475	(75) S543-2-C
(75) S. 2475	(75) S565-0
(75) S. 2493	(75) S546-9
(75) S. 2516	(75) S547-17
(75) S. 2521	(75) H836-0.497
(75) S. 2550	(75) S547-17
(75) S. 2555	(75) H810-4-A
(75) S. 2555	(75) S546-3
(75) S. 2580	(75) H830-4
(75) S. 2582	(75) H811-1-A
(75) S. 2583	(75) H806-4
(75) S. 2584	(75) S547-17
(75) S. 2589	(75) H832-1

Source: *CIS US Congressional Hearings Index,* **Part IV, Vol. 2, 1209.**
Reprinted with permission from the *CIS US Congressional Hearings Index*
Copyright 1991 by Congressional Information Service, Inc. (Bethesda, MD).
All rights reserved.

INDEX BY REPORT AND DOCUMENT NUMBERS

The Index by Report and Document Numbers lists reports and documents that fall into two categories.

-The editors based the *Congressional Hearings Index* primarily upon holdings of the Senate Library, a Library that sometimes bound hearings and related reports in the same volumes.

-In the 19th Century, hearings were sometimes published as Congressional reports and documents.

CIS INDEXES TO UNPUBLISHED CONGRESSIONAL HEARINGS

While preparing its *Index to Congressional Committee Hearings,* CIS found in the National Archives thousands of hearings that were never published. Early Congresses failed to develop standards that determine which hearings were to be printed. Legislators considered hearings internal committee documentation, not public documentation. Furthermore, committees did not have adequate methods to easily record the proceedings. CIS compiled seven indexes to unpublished hearings. The organization of each is similar to the initial hearings index.

-Unpublished Senate hearings are in three sets that cover 1823-1964, 1965-1968, and 1969-1972.[11].

-Unpublished House hearings are in four sets that cover 1833-1936, 1937-1946, 1947-1954, and 1955-1958.[12].

MICROFICHE COLLECTION

Three microfiche collections provide comprehensive access to both published and unpublished hearings.

1. The *CIS US Congressional Committee Hearings*[13] cover published hearings.

2. Unpublished US House of Representatives Committee Hearings[14] cover 1833-1936, 1937-1946, 1947-1954, and 1955-1958 in four sets.

3. Unpublished US Senate Committee Hearings[15] cover 1823-1964, 1965-1968, and 1969-1972 in three sets.

Arrangement of microfiche is by CIS entry numbers.

ADDITIONAL INDEXES/GUIDES TO HISTORICAL CONGRESSIONAL HEARINGS

Preston, James D. et al. *Index to Congressional Committee Hearings (Not Confidential in Character) Prior to January 3, 1935 in the United States Senate Library*. Washington, D.C.: GPO, 1935.

Arrangement of the subject index in part one is by title keywords; part two is alphabetical by committees; and part three is numerical by bill numbers. Preston includes House and Senate hearings maintained in the Senate Library. Until publication of the *CIS US Congressional Committee Hearings Index*, this source was the primary index to historical hearings. The *Supplement To The Index of Congressional Committee Hearings..In The Library of the US Senate*[16] cites additional hearings held between 1839 and 1934 that are excluded from the Senate Library. Eight additional volumes update information from 1935-1980[17].

Rowland, Buford, et al, comp. *Printed Hearings of the House of Representatives Found Among Its Committee Records in the National Archives of the United States, 1824-1958* (Special List No. 35) Washington, D.C.: National Archives and Records Service, 1974.

South, Charles E. and James C. Brown. *Hearings in the Records of the US Senate and Joint Committees of Congress* (Special List No. 32) Washington, D.C.: National Archives and Records Service, 1972.

Rowland and South cite House, Senate, and Joint Committee hearings that are in the National Archives. References are by Congress and committees. Information is not indexed.

Saville, Russell. *Index To Congressional Committee Hearings In the Library of The House of Representatives Prior to January 1, 1951*. Washington, D.C.: GPO, 1954.

Saville indexes hearings in the House Library in a manner comparable to that described above in Preston's *Index to Congressional Committee Hearings in the United States Senate Library*. John A. Cooper's volume supplements this work.[18]

Thoman, Harold O., Comp. *Checklist of Hearings Before Congressional Committees Through The Sixty-Seventh Congress*. Washington, D.C.: Library of Congress, 1957-1959.

Cites hearings held through the 67th Congress in 1923. Parts one through seven list hearings held by House committees and parts eight and nine cover those of the Senate. The concluding section of part 9 lists hearings of joint, special and select committees. Organization is alphabetical by committees and within each committee, by Congress. Information includes titles and dates. When relevant, references cite libraries that have the original documents. Information is not indexed.

CIS US CONGRESSIONAL COMMITTEE PRINTS INDEX

The *CIS US Congressional Committee Prints Index*[19] is the most comprehensive guide to committee prints. It indexes the earliest ones published in the 1830's through those issued in 1969. Prints are publications prepared by committee staffs or the Library of Congress that are intended to provide background information for Representatives and Senators. These titles are sometimes draft editions of materials eventually issued as reports or documents. The various kinds of information available in committee prints include monographs; results of investigative activities; analyses of bills; comparisons of bills to existing law; bibliographies; and directories. The publisher also includes print-like publications that are neither hearings, reports, nor documents. CIS considers them print-like through a process of elimination.

The *CIS US Congressional Committee Prints Index* has five volumes. The Index by Subjects and Names are volumes one and two, and the Reference Bibliography are volumes three and four. The fifth volume includes five indexes.

INDEX BY SUBJECTS AND NAMES

Besides subject headings, the Index of Subjects and Names also includes names of authors, committees, subcommittees, bills, and laws. Special subject terms include: Bibliographies, Glossaries, Statistical data, and Legislative histories. Ample cross references help users locate data. Search under the relevant subject heading to locate information about child labor (Figure 8-19).

Figure 8-19
CIS US Congressional Committee Prints Index
Index of Subjects and Names

Child abandonment
see Family abandonment

Child labor
Amendment, child labor
(68/1/24) S1865
Constitution amendments on child labor, proposed
(68/1/24) S3453
Expositions, study in labor abuses at
(75/3/38) H2646
Fair Labor Standards Act of 1938, comparative print showing
changes which would be made by H.R. 3935
(87/1/61) H0421
Fair Labor Standards Amendments of 1961. Report on H.R. 8279,
regulating child labor in agriculture
(87/1/61) H1624
Juvenile delinquency, youth employment and
(84/1/55) S2175

Source: *CIS US Congressional Committee Prints Index*, **Vol. 1, 131.**
Reprinted with permission from the *CIS US Congressional Committee Prints Index*
Copyright 1991 by Congressional Information Service, Inc. (Bethesda, MD).
All rights reserved.

REFERENCE BIBLIOGRAPHY

The Reference Bibliography provides bibliographic information and
Superintendent of Documents numbers, and it lists relevant subject headings. Its two parts separate House from Senate prints. Citations within
each section have an H or an S and are then listed in numeric sequence
(Figure 8-20).

Figure 8-20
CIS US Congressional Committee Prints Index
Reference Bibliography

H2646 **Study in abuses of labor at expositions. By Jack Wright, Department Representative, U.S. Department of Labor** [investi-
gation of labor abuses and San Diego and Dallas expositions]
ii+12 p. 1938. (75/3/38) Y4.F76/1:L11.

House Committee on Foreign Affairs

Exhibitions and trade fairs; Wages and salaries; Child labor;
Discrimination in employment; San Diego, Calif.; Dallas,
Tex.

Source: *CIS US Congressional Committee Prints Index*, **Vol. III, 163-4.** Reprinted
with permission from the *CIS US Congressional Committee Prints Index* Copyright
1991 by Congressional Information Service, Inc. (Bethesda, MD).
All rights reserved.

INDEX BY TITLES

Titles are in alphabetical order. Figure 8-21 illustrates the item seen in
Figure 8-20, *Study in Abuses of Labor at Expositions.*

Figure 8-21
CIS US Congressional Committee Prints Index
Index by Titles

Study and legislative history of the administrative organization of the
federal courts
(86/1/59) S2004
Study guide on operational programs of international organizations
(81/1/49) H8791
Study in abuses of labor at expositions. By Jack Wright, Department
Representative, U.S. Department of Labor
(75/3/38) H2646
Study mission in the Caribbean and Northern South America, Nov.
1959. Report of Sen. Homer E. Capehart
(86/2/60) S1160
Study mission in the Caribbean area, Dec. 1957. Report of Sen.
George D. Aiken
(85/2/58) S2142

Source: *CIS US Congressional Committee Prints Index*, **Vol. V, 294.**
Reprinted with permission from the
CIS US Congressional Committee Prints Index **Copyright 1991 by Congressional
Information Service, Inc. (Bethesda, MD). All rights reserved.**

ADDITIONAL INDEXES

Additional indexes include the following:

1.   The Index by Congress and Committees lists prints in
     chronological order by Congresses, and within each Con-
     gress, by committees.

2.   The Index by Superintendent of Document Numbers. Ap-
     proximately half of the items in the collection have SuDoc
     numbers.

3.   The Index by Bill Numbers cites committee prints that
     relate to specific bills.

JURISDICTIONAL HISTORIES

Understanding responsibilities of committees and subcommittees is
important because it helps determine which ones published information
during different time periods. The Jurisdictional Histories section summarizes histories and responsibilities of committees whose publications are in
the *Committee Prints Index*. Organization is alphabetic by committee
names. Information covers dates of formation, reorganization, and disso-
lution; names of subcommittees and predecessor committees; and charges
that the committees had to meet. After locating names of committees,
search the Index by Subjects and Names under the committee names to find
pertinent prints. Consult the volume compiled by Walter Stubbs for further
information about committees and their jurisdictions.[20]

US CONGRESSIONAL COMMITTEE PRINTS ON MICROFICHE

The *US Congressional Committee Prints on Microfiche*[21] collection reproduces the fifteen thousand publications listed in the *Committee Prints Index*.
These microfiche make prints published between the 1830's and 1969
widely available for the first time.

FURTHER INFORMATION ABOUT COMMITTEE PRINTS AND THE *CIS US CONGRESSIONAL COMMITTEE PRINTS INDEX*

The "Introduction" to the *Committee Prints Index* includes a detailed
history of committee prints; and gives illustrations from the Reference
Bibliography, the indexes, and the Jurisdictional Histories sections. CIS
reprinted it as a brief pamphlet.[22]

See also:

Field, Rochelle, *A Bibliography and Indexes of United States Congressional
Committee Prints From the Sixty-First Congress 1911 Through the Ninety-First
Congress, First Session 1969 in the United States Senate Library*. Westport, CT:
Greenwood Press, 1976. 2 vols.

This title is not as comprehensive as the *CIS US Committee Prints Index*,
but it is still useful when the latter is unavailable. The prints are reproduced
on microfiche. Fiche numbers correspond to those in the larger CIS *US
Congressional Committee Prints on Microfiche* collection.

CONGRESSIONAL MASTERFILE 1

The *Congressional Masterfile 1*[23] CD-ROM indexes information in the
CIS indexes examined in this chapter. Search all the indexes simultaneously or any combination of them by keywords; subject headings; titles;
witnesses and their affiliations; report numbers; bill numbers; dates; and
Congresses and sessions. The online tutorial, the numerous menus, and the
online help facilities are very helpful. The printed documentation, *Congressional Masterfile 1: CIS Indexes to Historical Congressional Documents on CD-
ROM--Reference Manual*[24], accounts for the needs of both inexperienced and
advanced researchers. The "Learning *CM1*" section introduces basic and
more advanced searching. The "Using *CM1*" section provides additional
information about selecting terms, displaying records, and printing and
saving results to a disk. A third section, "*CM1* Reference," is a comprehensive discussion of the menus and function keys.

CONCLUSION

Chart 8-2 summarizes the following sources examined in this chapter. Numbers in the chart refer to the items listed below.

1. *CIS Index to Unpublished US House of Representatives Committee Hearings* (earliest-1954).

2. *CIS Index to Unpublished US Senate Committee Hearings* (earliest-1968).

3. *CIS Index to US Senate Executive Documents and Reports* (earliest-1969).

4. *CIS US Congressional Committee Hearings Index* (earliest-1969).

5. *CIS US Congressional Committee Hearings* (microfiche) (earliest-1969).

6. *CIS US Congressional Committee Prints Index* (earliest-1969).

7. *CIS US Senate Executive Documents and Reports* (microfiche) (earliest-1969).

8. *CIS US Serial Set Index* (earliest-1969).

9. *CIS US Serial Set on Microfiche* (earliest-1969).

10. *Numerical Lists and Schedule of Volumes* (1933-1980).

11. *United States Congressional Serial Set Catalog: Numerical Lists and Schedule of Volumes* (1981-present).

12. *Unpublished US House of Representatives Committee Hearings* (microfiche) (earliest-1954).

13. *Unpublished US Senate Committee Hearings* (microfiche) (earliest-1968).

14. *US Congressional Committee Prints on Microfiche* (earliest-1969).

Chart 8-2
Indexes and Microfiche Collections to Congressional Committee Publications:
A Summary

Type of Publication	Index by Subjects	Index by Names	Index by Numbers	Index by Titles	Micro-fiche
Committee prints	6	6 (included in subject index)	Bill #'s--6 SuDoc #'s--6	6	14
Documents	8,11	8,11 (individuals & organizations)	Document #'s--8, 10,11 Serial Set #'s--8, 10,11 SuDoc #'s--11	11	9
Executive documents (documents published by Executive agencies and reproduced in the Serial Set)	8		Document #'s--8 Serial Set #'s--8		9
Hearings	1,2,4	1,2,4 (witnesses & organizations)	Bill #'s--1,2 SuDoc #'s--1,2,4	1,2,4	5,12,13
Miscellaneous documents (documents printed in the Serial Set that were published by sources other than Executive agencies)	8	8 (individuals & organizations)	Document #'s--8 Serial Set #'s--8		9
Reports	8,11	8,11 (individuals & organizations)	Report #'s--8,10,11 Serial Set #'s--8,10,11 SuDoc #'s--11	11	9
Senate exec. docs. (became treaty documents in 1981)	3,11	3,11	Document #'s--3,11 SuDoc #'s--11	11	7
Senate exec. repts.	3,11	3,11	Report #'s--3,11 SuDoc #'s--11	11	7
Serial Set	8,11	8,11 (individuals & organizations)	Serial Set #'s--8,10,11 SuDoc #'s--11	11	9

Endnotes

1.   *Debates and Proceedings In The Congress of The United States With An Appendix Containing Important State Papers and Public Documents and All The Laws of A Public Nature With Copious Index* 13th Cong., 1st sess. (December 8, 1813), 784.

2.   U.S. Government Printing Office, *Report of the Serial Set Study Group: Investigation of Alternatives for Production & Distribution of The Bound U.S. Congressional Serial Set* (Washington, D.C.: GPO, 1994). SuDoc number: GP1.2:SE6/3.

3.   *American State Papers. Documents, Legislative and Executive of the Congress of the United States* (Washington, D.C.: Gales and Seaton, 1832-1861). 38 vols.

4.   Congressional Information Service, (Washington, D.C.: Congressional Information Service, Inc., 1975-1979). 12 parts.

5.   U.S. Congress (Washington, D.C.: Congressional Information Service, Inc., 1975-1979).

6.   U.S. Government Printing Office, *Numerical Lists and Schedule of Volumes of the Reports and Documents of...Congress* (Washington, D.C.: GPO, 1933-1980). SuDoc number: GP3.7/2:.

7.   U.S. Government Printing Office (Washington, D.C.: GPO, 1983/1984-biennial). SuDoc number: GP3.34:. Title and SuDoc number for the 1981/1982 edition varies: U.S. Government Printing Office. *Monthly Catalog of United States Government Publications. United States Congressional Serial Set Supplement* (Washington, D.C.: GPO, 1985). SuDoc number: GP3.8/6:981-982.

8.   Congressional Information Service, *CIS Index to US Senate Executive Documents and Reports: Covering Documents and Reports Not Printed in the US Serial Set, 1817-1969* (Washington, D.C.: Congressional Information Service, Inc., 1987). 2 vols.

9.   *Journal of the Executive Proceedings of the Senate of the United States of America* (Washington, D.C.: GPO, 1828-annual). SuDoc number: Y1.3/4:. A 36 volume reprinted series covers the first issue through 1905-06. (New York: Johnson Reprint Corporation, 1969).

10.   Congressional Information Service, *CIS US Senate Executive Documents and Reports Covering Documents and Reports Not Printed in the US Serial Set, 1817-1969* (Bethesda, MD.: Congressional Information Service, Inc., 1987). 1153 microfiche.

10a. Congressional Information Service (Bethesda, MD: Congressional Information Service, Inc., 1981-1985.) 8 parts in 42 vols.

11.   Congressional Information Service, *CIS Index to Unpublished US Senate Committee Hearings: 18th Congress-88th Congress, 1823-1964* (Bethesda, MD.: Congressional Information Service, Inc., 1986). 5 vols.; Congressional Information Service, *CIS Index to Unpublished US Senate Committee Hearings: 89th Congress-90th Congress, 1965-1968* (Bethesda, MD.: Congressional Information Service, Inc., 1989); and Congressional Information Service, *CIS Index to Unpublished US Senate Committee Hearings: 91st Congress-92nd Congress, 1969-1972: 1913-1968 Supplement* (Bethesda, MD.: Congressional Information Service, Inc., 1995).

12.   Congressional Information Service, *CIS Index to Unpublished US House of Representatives Committee Hearings, 1833-1936* (Bethesda, MD.: Congressional Information Service, Inc., 1988). 2 vols.; Congressional Information Service, *CIS Index to Unpublished US House of Representatives Committee Hearings, 1937-1946* (Bethesda, MD.: Congressional Information Service, Inc., 1990). 2 vols.; Congressional Information Service, *CIS Index to Unpublished US House of Representatives Committee Hearings, 1947-1954* (Bethesda, MD.: Congressional Information Service, Inc., 1992). 2 vols.; and Congressional Information Service, *CIS Index to Unpublished US House of Representatives Committee Hearings, 1955-1958* (Bethesda, MD.: Congressional Information Service, Inc., 1994). 2 vols.

13.   U.S. Congress (Westport, CT: Greenwood Press, 1971[?]), and U.S. Congress (Bethesda, MD.: Congressional Information Service, Inc, 1987[?]).

14.   U.S. Congress. House, *Unpublished U.S. House of Representatives Committee Hearings, 1833-1936* (Bethesda, MD: Congressional Information Service, Inc., 1988). 1691 microfiche; U.S. Congress. House, *Unpublished U.S. House of Representatives Committee Hearings, 1937-1946* (Bethesda, MD: Congressional Information Service, Inc., 1988). 2491 microfiche; U.S. Congress. House, *Unpublished U.S. House of Representatives Committee Hearings, 1947-1954* (Bethesda, MD: Congressional Information Service, Inc., 1992). 5411 microfiche; and U.S. Congress. House, *Unpublished U.S. House of Representatives Committee Hearings, 1955-1958* (Bethesda, MD: Congressional Information Service, Inc., 1994). ? microfiche.

15.   U.S. Congress. Senate, *Unpublished U.S. Senate Committee Hearings 18th Congress to 88th Congress, 1823-1964* (Bethesda, MD.: Congressional Information Service, Inc., 1986). 9072 microfiche; U.S. Congress. Senate, *Unpublished U.S. Senate Committee Hearings, 1965-1968* (Bethesda, MD.: Congressional Information Service, Inc., 1989). 853 microfiche; and U.S. Congress. Senate, *Unpublished U.S. Senate Committee Hearings, 1969-1972* (Bethesda, MD.: Congressional Information Service, Inc., 1995). 729 microfiche.

16.   Harold O. Thomen, *Supplement To The Index of Congressional Committee Hearings Prior To January 3, 1935 Consisting of Hearings Not Catalogued By The U.S. Senate Library With Subject Index, Shelflist, and Bill Number Index From The Twenty-Fifth Congress, 1839 Through The Seventy-Third Congress, 1934* (Westport, Connecticut: Greenwood Press, 1973).

17.   Felton M. Johnston, *Cumulative Index of Congressional Committee Hearings (Not Confidential In Character) From Seventy-Fourth Congress (January 3, 1935) Through Eighty-Fifth Congress (January 3, 1959) In The United States Senate Library* (Washington, D.C.: GPO, 1959); Mary F. Sterrett, *Quadrennial Supplement To Cumulative Index of Congressional Committee Hearings (Not Confidential In Character) From Eighty-Sixth Congress (January 7, 1959) Through Eighty-Seventh Congress (January 3, 1963) Together With Selected Committee Prints In The United States Senate Library* (Washington, D.C.: GPO, 1963); Francis R. Valeo, *Cumulative Index of Congressional Committee Hearings (Not Confidential In Character): Second Quadrennial Supplement From Eighty-Eighth Congress (January 3, 1963) Through Eighty-Ninth Congress (January 3, 1967) Together With Selected Committee Prints In The United States Senate Library* (Washington, D.C.: GPO, 1967); Francis R. Valeo, *Cumulative Index of Congressional Committee Hearings (Not Confidential In Character): Third Quadrennial Supplement From Ninetieth Congress (January 10, 1967), Through Ninety-First Congress (January 2, 1971) Together With Selected Committee Prints In The United States Senate Library* (Washington, D.C.: GPO, 1971); Francis R. Valeo, *Cumulative Index of Congressional Committee Hearings (Not Confidential In Character): Fourth Quadrennial Supplement From Ninety-Second Congress (January 21, 1971) Through Ninety-Third Congress (December 20, 1974) In The United States Senate Library* (Washington, D.C.: GPO, 1976); Francis R. Valeo, *Cumulative Index of Congressional Committee Hearings (Not Confidential In Character): Fifth Supplement Ninety-Fourth Congress (January 14, 1975 Through October 1, 1976) In The United States Senate Library* (Washington, D.C.: GPO, ?); William F. Hildenbrand, *Cumulative Index of Congressional Committee Hearings (Not Confidential In Character): Sixth Supplement Ninety-Fifth Congress (January 4, 1977 Through October 15, 1978) In The United States Senate Library* (Washington, D.C.: GPO, ?); and William F. Hildenbrand et al. *Cumulative Index of Congressional Committee Hearings (Not Confidential in Character): Seventh Supplement Ninety-Sixth Congress, January 15, 1979 through December 16, 1980 in the United States Senate Library* (Washington, D.C.: GPO, 1984).

18.   *Supplemental Index To Congressional Committee Hearings January 3, 1949 To January 3, 1955, 81st, 82nd, and 83rd Congresses In The Library*

of The United States House of Representatives (Washington, D.C.: GPO, 1956).

19.   Congressional Information Service, *CIS US Congressional Committee Prints Index from the Earliest Publications Through 1969* (Washington, D.C.: Congressional Information Service, Inc., 1980) 5 vols.

20.   *Congressional Committees, 1789-1982: A Checklist* (Bibliographies and Indexes in Law and Political Science, Number 6) (Westport, CT.: Greenwood Press, 1985). Stubbs includes over 15,000 committees. Organization is alphabetic by keywords in committee names. Entries give committee names and name changes; Superintendent of Document numbers; dates; *Congressional Record* citations that refer to committees; and references to the legislation providing authority for the committees. Stubbs also includes a chronological list of committees and a subject index.

21.   U.S. Congress (Washington, D.C.: Congressional Information Service, Inc., 1980).

22.   Congressional Information Service, *An Introduction To Congressional Committee Prints and The CIS US Congressional Committee Prints Index From The Earliest Publications Through 1969* (Washington, D.C.: Congressional Information Service, Inc., 1981).

23.   (Bethesda, MD.: Congressional Information Service, Inc., 1989). Covers 1789-1969 on 1 disk.

24.   Congressional Information Service, Version 2.0 (Bethesda, MD.: Congressional Information Service, 1993).

Exercises

1. S. Exec. Doc. 196 (49th Congress) is entitled *Report of Secretary of State on Independent State of Congo With Correspondence on Berlin Congo Conference*.

   A. Why would you search the *CIS US Serial Set Index* rather than the *CIS US Senate Executive Documents and Reports* to locate this title?

   B. What is the *Serial Set* volume number?

   C. Why is the *Serial Set* such a significant collection?

2. Mark Twain testified at a Congressional hearing in December 1906.

   A. What did he talk about?

   B. On what page does his testimony begin?

   C. What committees sponsored the hearing?

   D. Which bills were considered? Use the *CIS US Serial Set Index, Part XIII: Index by Reported Bill Numbers, 1819-1969* to determine if these bills had been reported.

   E. True or false: The Superintendent of Documents number is needed to locate this title in the *CIS US Congressional Committee Hearings* microfiche collection.

3. An interim report on national health insurance was published in 1946 as a committee print.

   A. What are committee prints?

   B. What is the title of this print?

   C. What is its SuDoc number?

   D. What number is needed to locate this document in the *US Congressional Committee Prints on Microfiche* collection?

Answers

1. A. The *CIS US Senate Executive Documents and Reports* indexes executive documents that deal with treaties and nominations. They are submitted to the Senate by the President and require Senate approval to become effective. The title in question is referred to as Senate executive document because is was prepared by an executive agency and was reprinted in the *Serial Set*. It was submitted to the Senate for informational purposes and it is not voted upon.

   B. 2341.

   C. Published since 1817, the *Serial Set* is the oldest ongoing collection of U.S. government publications. The nineteenth century volumes are especially valuable because many executive agency publications are included. The *Serial Set* is often the only source for these earlier titles.

2. A. The copyright law.

   B. 116.

   C. The Senate Committee on Patents and the House Committee on Patents.

   D. S. 6330 and HR 19,853. Neither bill was reported.

   E. False. The CIS accession number, H51-1, is needed to locate it.

3. A. Committee prints are publications prepared by either the Library of Congress or committee staffs that are intended to provide Congressmen/Senators with background information.

   B. *Health Insurance. Interim Report.*

   C. Y4.ED8/3:H34/4/No.5.

   D. The CIS accession number, S1784.

•Chapter 9

Indexes and Guides to Legislation

Answer the following questions when reading this chapter:

1. What are the similarities and differences among slip laws, the *Statutes at Large,* and the *United States Code*?

2. What is the easiest, least time consuming way to locate federal law when given the following information: public law number, *Statutes at Large* citation, or a subject?

3. What are the advantages and disadvantages of using unofficial editions of the *Statutes at Large* and the *United States Code*?

4. What are the advantages and disadvantages of using electronic sources for accessing the law?

The previous five chapters emphasized the location and use of Congressional publications related to policy formulation and the legislative process. The results of the legislative process are legislation and regulations. This chapter discusses legislation and the following one covers regulations. The initial section considers how laws are published. Emphasis is upon relationships among slip laws, the *Statutes at Large,* and the *U.S. Code.* The discussion then examines five legal sources:

-*Statutes at Large.*

-*US Code Congressional and Administrative News.*

-*United States Code.*

-*US Code Annotated.*

-*US Code Service.*

The last part of the chapter considers CD-ROM and online sources.

HOW FEDERAL LAWS ARE PUBLISHED

Federal statutes--laws enacted by Congress, are published in three formats: slip laws, the *Statutes at Large*, and the *United States Code.*

SLIP LAWS (SuDoc number for public laws--AE2.110:; private laws--AE2.110/2:)

Legislation is first published in paper bound pamphlets called slip laws. States and the federal government follow this practice. Federal legislation includes both public and private laws. Briefly reviewing, public laws usually affect the general public, while private ones pertain to particular individuals.[1] Public and private laws have consecutive numbers within each Congress. P.L. 103-36 is the thirty-sixth public law enacted during the 103rd Congress (Figure 9-1). Note, although Washington used public law numbers since 1901, before 1957, "chapter" numbers identified legislation.

Figure 9-1
Slip Law P.L. 103-36

107 STAT. 104   PUBLIC LAW 103-36—JUNE 8, 1993

Public Law 103-36
103d Congress

An Act

June 8, 1993
[H.R. 1723]

To authorize the establishment of a program under which employees of the Central Intelligence Agency may be offered separation pay to separate from service voluntarily to avoid or minimize the need for involuntary separations due to downsizing, reorganization, transfer of function, or other similar action, and for other purposes.

Central
Intelligence
Agency
Voluntary
Separation
Pay Act.
50 USC 2001
note.
50 USC 403-4
note.

Be it enacted by the Senate and House of Representatives of the United States of America in Congress assembled,

SECTION 1. SHORT TITLE.

This Act may be cited as the "Central Intelligence Agency Voluntary Separation Pay Act".

SEC. 2. SEPARATION PAY.

(a) DEFINITIONS.—For purposes of this section—
(1) the term "Director" means the Director of Central Intelligence; and
(2) the term "employee" means an employee of the Central Intelligence Agency, serving under an appointment without time limitation, who has been currently employed for a continuous period of at least 12 months, except that such term does not include—

The *Monthly Catalog* indexes slip laws. The Subject Index covers subjects and names of individuals who are subjects of private legislation; the Title Index covers popular names of legislation; and the Series Report Index lists law numbers.

STATUTES AT LARGE (SuDoc number: AE2.111:)

Slip laws are republished in bound volumes called session laws after a legislative session ends. The *Statutes at Large*[2] is the federal government's official session law. Once published, it is usually the authoritative legal source. Attorneys cite slip laws in court only when the *Statutes at Large* is not yet available.

Lawyers do not cite in court unofficial versions of session laws that are published commercially. Despite this, these sources often have advantages over the official editions printed by the government. Unofficial editions are available sooner than the official ones and they include supplementary material not printed in the official editions. The discussion below considers the *U.S. Code Congressional and Administrative News*, an unofficial edition of federal law. Like the federal government, most states also have official and unofficial versions of their session laws.

Statutes at Large references follow volume and page numbers. Slip laws include this information to facilitate their eventual compilation into the bound volumes. Page numbers within each volume are consecutive. For example, the *Statutes at Large* reference for P.L. 103-36, the slip law in Figure 9-1, is 107 *Stat.* 104. (volume 107, page 104) That law, which is three pages long, extends to 107 *Stat.* 106. P.L. 103-37, which immediately follows, begins at 107 *Stat.* 107 (Figure 9-2).

Figure 9-2
Statutes at Large
P.L. 103-37

PUBLIC LAW 103–37—JUNE 8, 1993   107 STAT. 107

Public Law 103–37
103d Congress

An Act

To amend the Immigration and Nationality Act to authorize appropriations for refugee assistance for fiscal years 1993 and 1994.

June 8, 1993
[H.R. 2128]

Be it enacted by the Senate and House of Representatives of the United States of America in Congress assembled,

SECTION 1. AUTHORIZATION OF APPROPRIATIONS FOR REFUGEE ASSISTANCE FOR FISCAL YEARS 1993 AND 1994.

Section 414(a) of the Immigration and Nationality Act (8 U.S.C. 1524(a)) is amended by striking "fiscal year 1992" and inserting "fiscal year 1993 and fiscal year 1994".

Approved June 8, 1993.

Source: *Statutes at Large*, **Vol. 107, 107.**

The *Statutes at Large* was first published by Little, Brown, and Co. in 1846. Chart 9-1 illustrates the contents of the early volumes.

Chart 9-1
Early Volumes of the *Statutes at Large*

Volumes 1-5	Public laws of the 1st-28th Congresses (1789-1845).
Volume 6	Private laws of the 1st-28th Congresses (1789-1845).
Volume 7	Indian treaties enacted between 1778 and 1845.
Volume 8	International treaties enacted between 1778 and 1845.
Volume 9	Laws of the 29th-31st Congresses (1845-1851).
Volumes 10-12	Laws of the 32nd-37th Congresses (1851-1863).
Volumes 13-present	Laws of the 38th Congress (1863-date). (Issued irregularly through 1936 and annually since 1937)

Microfiche editions of the *Statutes at Large* covering 1789-1986 are available from the Congressional Information Service.[3]

U.S. CODE (SuDoc number: Y1.2/5:)

The *United States Code*[4] (*U.S.C.*) is a subject compilation of federal law published since 1926. Laws enacted fifty years ago that have not been repealed are as effective today as those enacted last year. Researchers must be able to determine the context in which new legislation fits into previous enactments. Jack Davies and Robert P. Lawry, authors of *Institutions and Methods of the Law*, believe:

> ...to make legislative law useable it must be published in a form that groups together all currently effective provisions on each topic. For example, provisions relating to traffic laws, no matter when passed, must be included in one chapter and placed in logical order.[5]

The *U.S.C.* includes legislation of general and permanent value that is currently in effect. It facilitates the study of all aspects of the law that deal with a given topic. The *U.S.C.* includes rules of practice and procedure used in federal courts, such as the Federal Rules of Civil Procedure; the Federal Rules of Criminal Procedure; the Federal Rules of Evidence; and the Federal Bankruptcy Rules. Court rules derive from statutes, not administrative promulgation. The *U.S.C.* excludes private laws, superseded legislation, and most appropriation and revenue measures.

The *U.S.C.* is often incorrectly called a codification. Strictly speaking, a codification includes not only statutes, but also court cases; agency regulations and decisions; common law; and any other type of precedent that effects the law. The *U.S.C.* is limited to statutes enacted by Congress. It excludes all other legal precedents.

The *U.S.C.* is organized into fifty titles, each one dealing with a broad topic, such as education and national defense. Reference information by titles and sections. For example, 44 *U.S.C.* 1900 refers to section 1900 of title 44. Slip laws and *Statutes at Large* references cite *U.S.C.* sections where the legislation will be added. The law in Figure 9-1 will become part of 50 *U.S.C.* 2001 and 50 *U.S.C.* 403-4. (Title 50, sections 403, 404, and 2001)

Test your understanding of the *U.S.C.*:

Explain why a *U.S.C.* citation is not given in Figure 9-2.

> (The *U.S.C.* excludes most appropriation and revenue legislation.)

Collections of statutes that dealt with specific subjects were published during the 19th century.[6] Public lands, customs duties, and the military were frequent topics. Administrative materials, that were frequently unavailable elsewhere, such as Land Office Circulars and instructions to surveyors, were often included. Support for a compilation of all laws was recognized by the House Judiciary Committee in 1848, but broad political support was unavailable. The *Revised Statutes of 1875*[7] was the first compilation of all federal statutes. It superseded all statutes enacted between 1789 and 1873. The *Revised Statutes* remained the only official compilation until the *U.S. Code* was published in 1926.

USING THE *STATUTES AT LARGE*

PUBLIC LAWS

Public laws comprise the largest part of the *Statutes at Large*. Figure 9-3 illustrates portions of the Americans with Disabilities Act whose legislative history was studied in Chapters 5, 6, and 7. Key parts of Figure 9-3 include the following:

-Public Law number.

-Date of enactment.

-*Statutes at Large* citation.

-Bill number.

-Short title or popular name of the legislation.

-*United States Code* citation.

-Legislative history.

Figure 9-3
Statutes at Large
Public Laws

PUBLIC LAW 101–336—JULY 26, 1990   104 STAT. 327

Public Law 101–336
101st Congress

An Act·

To establish a clear and comprehensive prohibition of discrimination on the basis of disability.

July 26, 1990
[S. 933]

Be it enacted by the Senate and House of Representatives of the United States of America in Congress assembled,

SECTION 1. SHORT TITLE; TABLE OF CONTENTS.

Americans with Disabilities Act of 1990.

(a) SHORT TITLE.—This Act may be cited as the "Americans with Disabilities Act of 1990".

42 USC 12101 note.

(b) TABLE OF CONTENTS.—The table of contents is as follows:

Sec. 1. Short title; table of contents.
Sec. 2. Findings and purposes.
Sec. 3. Definitions.

TITLE I—EMPLOYMENT

Sec. 101. Definitions.
Sec. 102. Discrimination.
Sec. 103. Defenses.
Sec. 104. Illegal use of drugs and alcohol.

42 USC 12101.   SEC. 2. FINDINGS AND PURPOSES.

(a) FINDINGS.—The Congress finds that—
(1) some 43,000,000 Americans have one or more physical or mental disabilities, and this number is increasing as the population as a whole is growing older;
(2) historically, society has tended to isolate and segregate individuals with disabilities, and, despite some improvements, such forms of discrimination against individuals with disabilities continue to be a serious and pervasive social problem;
(3) discrimination against individuals with disabilities persists in such critical areas as employment, housing, public accommodations, education, transportation, communication, recreation, institutionalization, health services, voting, and access to public services;

LEGISLATIVE HISTORY—S. 933 (H.R. 2273):

HOUSE REPORTS: No. 101–485, Pt. 1 (Comm. on Public Works and Transportation), Pt. 2 (Comm. on Education and Labor), Pt. 3 (Comm. on the Judiciary), and Pt. 4 (Comm. on Energy and Commerce) all accompanying H.R. 2273; and Nos. 101–558 and 101–596 both from (Comm. of Conference).
SENATE REPORTS: No. 101–116 (Comm. on Labor and Human Resources).
CONGRESSIONAL RECORD:
Vol. 135 (1989): Sept. 7, considered and passed Senate.
Vol. 136 (1990): May 17, 22, H.R. 2273 considered and passed House; S. 933 passed in lieu.
July 11, Senate recommitted conference report.
July 12, House agreed to conference report.
July 13, Senate agreed to conference report.
WEEKLY COMPILATION OF PRESIDENTIAL DOCUMENTS, Vol. 26 (1990):
July 26, Presidential remarks and statement.

Source: *Statutes at Large*, **Vol. 104, pages 327, 328, 378.**

Test your understanding of the Statutes at Large: The following questions pertain to (a) the above section, "How Federal Laws Are Published" and (b) Figure 9-3.

1.   What is the Public Law number of the legislation?

(P.L. 101-336)

2.   True or false: The Americans With Disabilities Act, as printed in the slip law, differs from that in the *Statutes at Large*.

(False--legislation in slip laws
is identical to that in the *Statutes at Large*.)

3.   When was this legislation enacted?

(July 26, 1990)

4.   What was the bill number?

(S. 933)

5.   Was a comparable bill considered in the opposite Chamber?

(Yes--H.R. 2273)

6.   Where in the *U.S. Code* is reference to this legislation found?

(42 *U.S.C.* 12101; Title 42, section 12101)

7.   How does the *U.S. Code* differ from the *Statutes at Large*?

(The *Statutes at Large* is the official
session law. It reproduces laws
enacted by Congress. Organization is
numerical by public law numbers. The
U.S.C. compiles laws by subjects,
regardless of when enactment occurred.)

SUBJECT INDEX

Access public laws in the Subject Index by topics and by popular names (Figures 9-4 and 9-5). The Index refers to page numbers.

Figure 9-4
Statutes at Large
Subject Index--Subject Heading

Handicapped:
  Americans with Disabilities Act of 1990...........327

  Developmental Disabilities Assistance and
      Bill of Rights Act of 1990.......................1191
  Education of the Handicapped Act
      Amendments of 1990.............................1103
  Housing assistance...4324
  Television Decoder Circuitry Act of 1990........960
**Harmonized Tariff Schedule of the United
    States,** amendments............651, 657, 658, 666,
                                      1388–387, 1388–482

Source: *Statutes at Large*, **Vol. 104, A15.**

Figure 9-5
Statutes at Large
Subject Index--Popular Names

American Legion, membership eligibility........1157
American Samoa, minimum wage
    requirement, elimination.............................2871
**American University Incorporation
    Amendments Act of 1990**..........................1160
Americans with Disabilities Act of 1990..........327
**Amtrak Reauthorization and
    Improvement Act of 1990**..........................295
Anabolic Steroids Control Act of 1990..........4851
Angola, Foreign Relations Authorization
    Act, Fiscal Years 1990 and 1991...................72
**Animal Disease Control Cooperation Act
    of 1947,** amendments...................................115
Animal Industry Act, amendments..................3733

Source: *Statutes at Large,* **Vol. 104, A2.**

ADDITIONAL INFORMATION IN THE *STATUTES AT LARGE*

PRIVATE LAWS

Private laws appear in the *Statutes at Large* (Figure 9-6).

Figure 9-6
Statutes at Large
Private Law

104 STAT. 5142   PRIVATE LAW 101–5—OCT. 17, 1990

Private Law 101–5
101st Congress

An Act

Oct. 17, 1990
[S. 1229]

For the relief of Maria Luisa Anderson.

Be it enacted by the Senate and House of Representatives of the United States of America in Congress assembled, That in the administration of the Immigration and Nationality Act, Maria Luisa Anderson shall be classified as a child within the meaning of section 101(b)(1)(E) of that Act (8 U.S.C. 1101(b)(1)(E)), upon filing of a petition filed on her behalf by her adoptive parents, citizens of the United States, pursuant to section 204 of that Act (8 U.S.C. 1154). No natural parent, brother, or sister, if any, of Maria Luisa Anderson shall, by virtue of such relationship, be accorded any right, privilege, or status under the Immigration and Nationality Act.

Approved October 17, 1990.

Source: *Statutes at Large,* **Vol. 104, 5142.**

INDIVIDUAL INDEX

The Individual Index covers people who are the subjects of private laws (Figure 9-7).

Figure 9-7
Statutes at Large
Individual Index

A

Abbas, Abu 79
Anderson, Maria Luisa 5142
Arafat, Yasser 77
Armstrong, Anne Legendre 2876
Armstrong, Louis 1209

B

Bechet, Sidney 1209
Bhutto, Benazir 80
Blevins, Kenneth, Mr. and Mrs. 4499
Brown, Florence 1026

Source: *Statutes at Large,* **Vol. 104, B1.**

Test your understanding of private laws: Consult figures 9-6 and 9-7 when answering the following.

1. What bill does this law relate to?

    (S. 1229)

2. What is the law number?

    (Private Law 101-5)

3. When was it enacted?

    (October 17, 1990)

4. What is the *Statutes at Large* citation?

    (104 *Stat.* 5142)

5. Whom does this law pertain to?

    (Maria Luisa Anderson)

6. What makes this a private, rather than a public, law?

    (The law pertains only to Maria Luisa
    Anderson, not the general public.)

CONCURRENT RESOLUTIONS

Concurrent resolutions are measures that must be approved by both chambers of Congress to become effective. Presidential approval is unnecessary. The *Statutes at Large* lists them in chronological order according to dates of approval. Citations include titles, numbers, and dates approved. Figure 9-8 reproduces H. Con. Res. 338 (101st Congress). Although not indexed topically, they are in the Subject Index under the heading Concurrent Resolutions.

Figure 9-8
Statutes at Large
Concurrent Resolution

"UNDERSTANDING CONGRESS" BICENTENNIAL
RESEARCH CONFERENCE PROCEEDINGS—
HOUSE PRINT

Sept. 18, 1990
[H. Con. Res. 338]

Resolved by the House of Representatives (the Senate concurring). That the proceedings of the bicentennial research conference entitled "Understanding Congress" (prepared by the Congressional Research Service of the Library of Congress) shall be printed as a House document, with illustrations and suitable binding. In addition to the usual number, 2,000 copies of the document shall be printed for the use of the House of Representatives and 2,000 copies of the document shall be printed for the use of the Senate.

Agreed to September 18, 1990.

Source: *Statutes at Large,* **Vol. 104, 5163.**

PROCLAMATIONS

Proclamations, which are also included in the *Statutes at Large*, are Presidential statements that usually deal with ceremonial matters, such as special observances. The next chapter describes proclamations in more detail and compares them to executive orders. Like concurrent resolutions, the Subject Index excludes proclamations under topical headings, but lists them under the heading Proclamations.

U.S. CODE CONGRESSIONAL AND ADMINISTRATIVE NEWS

The *United States Code Congressional and Administrative News*[8] (*U.S.C.C.A.N.*) is an unofficial version of federal session laws. The publisher issues an annual cumulative edition after a Congressional session is completed. Page numbers in *Congressional and Administrative News* are consistent with those in the *Statutes at Large*. Chart 9-2 compares the kinds of information found in both sources.

Chart 9-2
Statutes at Large **and** *U.S.C.C.A.N.*

	Statutes at Large	U.S.C.C.A.N.
Public laws	yes	yes
Private laws	yes	no
Proclamations	yes	yes
Executive orders	no	yes
Concurrent resolutions	yes	no
Congressional reports	no	yes

PUBLIC LAW SECTION

The Public Laws section reprints legislation in numerical order by law numbers. This information is almost identical to that given in the *Statutes at Large*, except for references to the legislative history. (Figure 9-9)

Figure 9-9
U.S. Code Congressional and Administrative News
Public Laws
PUBLIC LAW 101–336 [S. 933]; July 26, 1990

AMERICANS WITH DISABILITIES ACT OF 1990

For Legislative History of Act, see p. 267.

An Act to establish a clear and comprehensive prohibition of discrimination on the basis of disability.

Be it enacted by the Senate and House of Representatives of the United States of America in Congress assembled,

SECTION 1. SHORT TITLE: TABLE OF CONTENTS.

(a) SHORT TITLE.—This Act may be cited as the "Americans with Disabilities Act of 1990".

(b) TABLE OF CONTENTS.—The table of contents is as follows:

Americans with Disabilities Act of 1990.

42 USC 12101 note.

Sec. 1. Short title; table of contents.
Sec. 2. Findings and purposes.
Sec. 3. Definitions.

Source: *U.S. Code Congressional and Administrative News*, **1990 ed.**, 104 *Stat.* 327.
Reprinted with permission from
United States Code Congressional and Administrative News.
Copyright 1991 by West Publishing Company (St. Paul, MN).
All rights reserved.

Test your understanding of the Public Laws section: The following refers to Figure 9-9.

On what page will a legislative history of the law be found?

(page 267)

LEGISLATIVE HISTORY SECTION:

The editors of *U.S. Code Congressional and Administrative News* reprint in the Legislative History section excerpts and, in selected cases, complete texts of Congressional reports, depending upon how important they believe the material is. Figure 9-10 shows reports pertaining to the Americans With Disabilities Act.

Figure 9-10
U.S. Code Congressional and Administrative News
Legislative History
AMERICANS WITH DISABILITIES ACT OF 1990

P.L. 101–336, see page 104 Stat. 327
DATES OF CONSIDERATION AND PASSAGE
Senate: September 7, 1989; July 11, 13, 1990
House: May 22, July 12, 1990

Senate Report (Labor and Human Resources Committee)
No. 101–116, Aug. 30, 1989
[To accompany S. 933]

House Report (Public Works and Transportation Committee) No.
101–485(I), May 14, 1990
[To accompany H.R. 2273]

House Report (Education and Labor Committee) No. 101–485(II),
May 15, 1990
[To accompany H.R. 2273]

House Report (Judiciary Committee) No. 101–485(III), May 15,
1990
[To accompany H.R. 2273]

Source: *U.S. Code Congressional and Administrative News*, 1990 ed., 267. Reprinted
with permission from *United States Code Congressional and Administrative News.*
Copyright 1991 by West Publishing Company (St. Paul, MN).
All rights reserved.

These legislative histories omit five types of information that appear in the complete Congressional reports.

-Verbatim bill language.

-Charts and maps.

-Long appendices that do not refer to the legislation.

-Duplicate information.

-Information the editors believe is unnecessary to the interpretation of the law.

PROCLAMATIONS AND EXECUTIVE ORDERS

U.S.C.C.A.N. also reprints Presidential proclamations and executive orders. The *Federal Register* section in the next chapter discusses them in detail.

SUBJECT INDEX

The Subject Index covers public laws, legislative histories, proclamations, and executive orders. Figure 9-11 displays references to the Americans With Disabilities Act, providing citations to both the *Statutes at Large* and the legislative history.

Figure 9-11
U.S. Code Congressional and Administrative News
Subject Index

**AMERICAN UNIVERSITY INCORPORATION
AMENDMENTS ACT OF 1990**
Generally, **104 Stat. 1160**

**AMERICANS WITH DISABILITIES ACT OF
1990**
Generally, **104 Stat. 327, Leg. Hist. 267**

**AMTRAK REAUTHORIZATION AND
IMPROVEMENT ACT OF 1990**
Generally, **104 Stat. 295**

HALF-WAY HOUSES
Indians, funding, **104 Stat. 137,
Leg. Hist. 138**

HANDICAPPED PERSONS
Americans with Disabilities Act of 1990,
104 Stat. 327, Leg. Hist. 267
Deaf and hearing impaired persons, Television Decoder Circuitry Act of 1990,
104 Stat. 960, Leg. Hist. 1438
Deaf awareness week, proclamation, **A28**
Developmental Disabilities Assistance and
Bill of Rights Act of 1990, **104 Stat.
1191, Leg. Hist. 1857**
Education of the Handicapped Act Amendments of 1990, **104 Stat. 1103,
Leg. Hist. 1723**
Housing assistance, **104 Stat. 4324,
Leg. Hist. 5763**
Interagency committee on handicapped employees, executive order, **B5**
Mental Health, generally, this index

Source: *U.S. Code Congressional and Administrative News,* **1990 ed., I3, I25.**
Reprinted with permission from *United States Code Congressional and
Administrative News.* **Copyright 1991 by West Publishing Company (St. Paul,
MN). All rights reserved.**

TABLES

The *Congressional and Administrative News* includes ten tables.

-**Table 1--Public Laws:** Lists public law numbers and corresponding *Statute at Large* citations.

-**Table 2--*U.S. Code* and *U.S. Code Annotated* Classifications:** Lists legislation first by dates of enactment and then by public law numbers (Figure 9-12). Remaining parts of the table cite sections of the law (column 1); *Statutes at Large* page numbers (column 2); and *U.S. Code Annotated* (*U.S.C.A.*) references (columns 3 and 4). The *U.S.C.A.* is a commercial source comparable to the *U.S. Code*. Figure 9-12 shows that section 102 of P.L. 101-336 is printed in the *Statutes at Large* at 104 *Stat* 331. The same will become 42 *U.S.C.A.* 12112.

Figure 9-12
U.S. Code Congressional and Administrative News
Table 2--*U.S. Code* and *U.S. Code Annotated* Classifications
Table 2

U.S. CODE
AND
U.S. CODE ANNOTATED
CLASSIFICATIONS
101st CONGRESS—2nd SESSION

The pagination of the Public Laws of this Session contained in the 1990 U.S. Code Congressional and Administrative News is identical with Volume 104 U.S. Statutes at Large. In this table a page reference to "8", for example, will be paged as "104 STAT. 8" in this service and in Volume 104 U.S. Statutes at Large.

App.	Appendix	prec.	Preceding
Elim	Eliminated	Rep.	Repealed
nt.	Note	Rev.T.	Revised Title
nts.	Notes	Sec.	Section
P.L.	Public Law	Tit.	Title

1990-101st Cong.-104 Stat.			USCA		
July	P.L.101-	Sec.	Page	Tit.	Sec.	Status
26	336	1(a)	327	42	12101 nt
		2	328	42	12101
		3	329	42	12102
		101	330	42	12111
		102	331	42	12112
		103	333	42	12113
		104	334	42	12114
		105	336	42	12115
		106	336	42	12116
		107	336	42	12117
		108	337	42	12111 nt
		201	337	42	12131
		202	337	42	12132
		203	337	42	12133
		204	337	42	12134
		205	338	42	12131 nt
		221	338	42	12141

Source: *U.S. Code Congressional and Administrative News*, **1990 ed., 6, 13.**
Reprinted with permission from *United States Code Congressional and Administrative News.* **Copyright 1991 by West Publishing Company (St. Paul, MN). All rights reserved.**

Table 3--*U.S. Code* and *U.S. Code Annotated* Sections Amended, Repealed, New, Etc: Displays *U.S. Code* sections that are affected by changes in the law. The first three columns of Figure 9-13 indicates that 42 *U.S.C.* 12131 was affected by sections 201 and 205 of P.L. 101-336. Column 4 indicates that this information appears at 104 *Stat* 337 and 338.

Figure 9-13
U.S. Code Congressional and Administrative News
Table 3--*U.S. Code and U.S. Code Annotated*
Sections amended, Repealed, New, Etc.

U.S.Code and U.S.C.A.		1990--101st Cong.		104 Stat. at Large and 1990 Cong.News
Title	Sec.	P.L.101--	Sec.	Page
42 (Cont'd)				
	12117	336	107	336
	12131	336	201	337
	12131 nt	336	205	338
	12132	336	202	337
	12133	336	203	337
	12134	336	204	337
	12141	336	221	338
	12141 nt	336	231	346
	12142	336	222	339
	12143	336	223	340
	12144	336	224	342
	12145	336	225	343
	12146	336	226	343
	12147	336	227	343
	12148	336	228	344
	12149	336	229	345

Source: *U.S. Code Congressional and Administrative News,* **1990 ed., 361.**
Reprinted with permission from *United States Code Congressional and Administrative News.* **Copyright 1991 by West Publishing Company (St. Paul, MN). All rights reserved.**

Test your understanding of Tables 2 and 3: The following question relates to Figures 9-12 and 9-13.

1. Where is section 203 of P.L. 101-336 codified in the *U.S.C.*?

    (42 U.S.C. 12133)

2. What is the *Statute at Large* reference that affects 42 *U.S.C.* 12143?

    (104 Stat 340)

Table 4--Legislative History: Gives bill and report numbers, and dates of considerations in the House and Senate for all public laws.

Table 4A--Signing Statements of the President: Gives page numbers for Presidential statements reproduced in *U.S.C.C.A.N.*

Table 5--Bills and Joint Resolutions Enacted: Lists bills and joint resolutions that became law.

Table 6--Federal Regulations Sections Amended, Added, Etc.: Table 6 is blank in the annual cumulative edition. In the biweekly issues, it shows changes to the *Code of Federal Regulations*[9] and the *Federal Register*.[10] The next chapter describes both.

Table 7--Proclamations and **Table 8--Executive Orders:** Lists Presidential proclamations and executive orders numerically giving dates, subjects, and *Congressional and Administrative News* page numbers.

Table 9--Major Bills Enacted: Lists significant legislation under broad subject headings. Information includes dates the respective chambers reported and/or passed the measures, dates the legislation became law, and public law numbers.

Table 10--Popular Name Acts: Provides popular names of laws.

USING THE *UNITED STATES CODE (U.S.C.)*

INTRODUCTION AND BACKGROUND

The *United States Code (U.S.C.)* was defined above in the section that considers how laws are published. It has been published every six years since 1926. Washington issues cumulative annual supplements during the intervening years. For example, the 1992 supplement includes all changes enacted since the 1988 edition appeared. Consult the most recent complete set first and then check the most recent supplement for changes.

The text of the *U.S.C.* often differs from that of the *Statutes at Large*. When bringing the laws together, the editors delete repetitious information and other data that does not have permanent value. Also, the law in the *U.S.C.* is sometimes only summarized. When the texts conflict, the *Statutes at Large* has precedence, unless the particular title of the *U.S.C.* was reenacted. Reenactment occurs when the title is introduced before Congress as a bill and is then approved as a public law. This is necessary because Congress and the President approved the law as stated in the *Statutes at Large*, not the *U.S.C.*

The list below identifies the fifty *U.S.C.* titles. Bold type indicates reenacted titles. The goal is to eventually reenact all titles.

Title Subject

1. **General Provisions**

2. Congress

3. **The President**

4. **Flag and Seal, Seat of Government, and the States**

5. **Government Organization and Employees and Appendix**

6. Surety Bonds (This Title was reenacted, but has since been repealed and incorporated into Title 31.)

7. Agriculture

8. Aliens and Nationality

9. Arbitration

10. Armed Forces and Appendix

11. Bankruptcy and Appendix

12. Banks and Banking

13. Census

14. Coast Guard

15. Commerce and Trade

16. Conservation

17. Copyrights

18. Crimes and Criminal Procedure and Appendix

19. Customs Duties

20. Education

21. Food and Drugs

22. Foreign Relations and Intercourse

23. Highways

24. Hospitals and Asylums

25. Indians

26. Internal Revenue Code and Appendix

27. Intoxicating Liquors

28. Judiciary and Judicial Procedure and Appendix

29. Labor

30. Mineral Lands and Mining

31. Money and Finance

32. National Guard

33. Navigation and Navigable Waters

34. Navy--This Title was eliminated and incorporated into Title 10.

35. Patents

36. Patriotic Societies and Observances

37. Pay and Allowances of the Uniformed Services

38. **Veterans' Benefits and Appendix**

39. **Postal Service**

40. Public Buildings, Property, and Works

41. Public Contracts

42. Public Health and Welfare

43. Public Lands

44. **Public Printing and Documents**

45. Railroads

46. **Shipping and Appendix**

47. Telegraphs, Telephones, and Radiotelegraphs

48. Territories and Insular Possessions

49. **Transportation**

50. War and National Defense; and Appendix

GENERAL INDEX

The General Index to the *U.S. Code* includes subject headings, agency names, and numerous cross references. Entries refer to *U.S.C.* titles and sections. To determine relationships among the various laws that prohibit discrimination against the disabled, start by searching under the term Disability. The Index has a cross reference to the phrase Equal Opportunity For Individuals With Disabilities (Figure 9-14).

Figure 9-14
U.S. Code
General Index--Cross Reference

DISABILITY
Agricultural research, farmers, disabled, Assistive Technology Program, 7 § 5933
Children with disabilities,
  Defined, temporary child care, 42 § 5117c
  Handicapped Persons and Children, generally, this index
Comptroller of Currency, deputies, order of succession, 12 § 4
Developmentally Disabled Persons, generally, this index
Director of OTS, successors to Board of Directors of FDIC, 12 § 1812
Employment, intentional discrimination, damages, 42 § 1981a
Equal Opportunity for Individuals with Disabilities, generally, this index
Grants, to students in attendance at institutions of higher education, Higher Education Resources and Assistance, generally, this index

Source: *U.S. Code* 1992 Supp., Vol. 8, 461.

Selected references to items cited under Equal Opportunity For Individuals With Disabilities are noted in Figure 9-15. The first entry, "Generally, 42 § 12101 et seq." indicates that most information appears in title 42 beginning with section 12101.

Figure 9-15
U.S. Code
General Index

EQUAL OPPORTUNITY FOR INDIVIDUALS WITH DISABILITIES

Generally, 42 § 12101 et seq.
Access to, education through telecommunications. Education generally, this index
Arbitration, as alternative means of dispute resolution, 42 § 12212
Architect of Capitol,
    Establishing remedies and procedures to guarantee employment, 42 § 12209
    "Instrumentalities of the Congress" as including, 42 § 12209
    Remedies and procedures to protect rights, 42 § 12209
Architectural and Transportation Barriers Compliance Board,
    Chairman, development of plan for technical assistance, 42 § 12206
    Guidelines, compliance, public transportation, entities other than aircraft or certain rail operations, 42 §§ 12149, 12150

Congressional findings and purposes, 42 § 12101
Construction,
    Enforcement procedures, etc., 42 § 12209
    Relationship with other laws, 42 § 12201
Definitions, equal opportunity for individuals with, 42 § 12101
"Disability",
    As excluding homosexuals, bisexuals, and certain other impairments, 42 § 12211
    Defined, 42 § 12101
Disabled or disability, defined, 42 § 12208
Discrimination, prohibition, 42 §§ 12148, 12162, 12182
Dispute resolution, alternative means of, 42 § 12212
Dissemination of information regarding rights, duties, etc., 42 § 12206

Source: *U.S. Code*, 1992 Supp. Vol. 8, 515.

Test your understanding of the General Index: Consult Figures 9-14 and 9-15 when answering the following questions:

1. Where is the law dealing with the Assistive Technology Program for farmers found?

   (Title 7, section 5933 or 7 *U.S.C.* 5933)

2. Disabled employees who can prove they were intentionally discriminated against are entitled to collect damages. Cite the appropriate title and section.

   (42 *U.S.C.* 1981a)

3. Where in the *U.S.C.* are the terms disabled or disability defined?

   (42 *U.S.C.* 12208)

4. Cite the section of the *U.S.C.* that shows relationships among different laws that pertain to construction.

   (42 *U.S.C.* 12201)

U.S. CODE--SAMPLE PAGE

Figure 9-16 illustrates 42 *U.S.C.* 12201, which describes how the Americans With Disabilities Act relates to other legislation.

Figure 9-16
U.S. Code

Page 181   TITLE 42—THE PUBLIC HEALTH AND WELFARE   § 12203

SECTION REFERRED TO IN OTHER SECTIONS

This section is referred to in section 12203 of this title.

§ 12189. Examinations and courses

Any person that offers examinations or courses related to applications, licensing, certification, or credentialing for secondary or postsecondary education, professional, or trade purposes shall offer such examinations or courses in a place and manner accessible to persons with disabilities or offer alternative accessible arrangements for such individuals.

(Pub. L. 101–336, title III, § 309, July 26, 1990, 104 Stat. 365.)

EFFECTIVE DATE

Section effective 18 months after July 26, 1990, see section 310(a) of Pub. L. 101–336, set out as a note under section 12181 of this title.

SUBCHAPTER IV—MISCELLANEOUS PROVISIONS

§ 12201. Construction

(a) In general

Except as otherwise provided in this chapter, nothing in this chapter shall be construed to apply a lesser standard than the standards applied under title V of the Rehabilitation Act of 1973 (29 U.S.C. 790 et seq.) or the regulations issued by Federal agencies pursuant to such title.

(b) Relationship to other laws

Nothing in this chapter shall be construed to invalidate or limit the remedies, rights, and procedures of any Federal law or law of any State or political subdivision of any State or jurisdiction that provides greater or equal protection for the rights of individuals with disabilities than are afforded by this chapter. Nothing in this chapter shall be construed to preclude the prohibition of, or the imposition of restrictions on, smoking in places of employment covered by subchapter I of this chapter, in transportation covered by subchapter II or III of this chapter, or in places of public accommodation covered by subchapter III of this chapter.

(c) Insurance

Subchapters I through III of this chapter and title IV of this Act shall not be construed to prohibit or restrict—

(1) an insurer, hospital or medical service company, health maintenance organization, or any agent, or entity that administers benefit plans, or similar organizations from underwriting risks, classifying risks, or administering such risks that are based on or not inconsistent with State law; or

(2) a person or organization covered by this chapter from establishing, sponsoring, observing or administering the terms of a bona fide benefit plan that are based on underwriting risks, classifying risks, or administering such risks that are based on or not inconsistent with State law; or

(3) a person or organization covered by this chapter from establishing, sponsoring, observing or administering the terms of a bona fide benefit plan that is not subject to State laws that regulate insurance.

Paragraphs (1), (2), and (3) shall not be used as a subterfuge to evade the purposes of subchapter [1] I and III of this chapter.

(d) Accommodations and services

Nothing in this chapter shall be construed to require an individual with a disability to accept an accommodation, aid, service, opportunity, or benefit which such individual chooses not to accept.

(Pub. L. 101–336, title V, § 501, July 26, 1990, 104 Stat. 369.)

REFERENCES IN TEXT

This chapter, referred to in text, was in the original "this Act", meaning Pub. L. 101–336, July 26, 1990, 104 Stat. 327, which is classified principally to this chapter. For complete classification of this Act to the Code, see Short Title note set out under section 12101 of this title and Tables.

The Rehabilitation Act of 1973, referred to in subsec. (a), is Pub. L. 93–112, Sept. 26, 1973, 87 Stat. 355, as amended. Title V of the Rehabilitation Act of 1973 is classified generally to subchapter V (§ 790 et seq.) of chapter 16 of Title 29, Labor. For complete classification of this Act to the Code, see Short Title note set out under section 701 of Title 29 and Tables.

Title IV of this Act, referred to in subsec. (c), means title IV of Pub. L. 101–336, July 26, 1990, 104 Stat. 366, which enacted section 225 of Title 47, Telegraphs, Telephones, and Radiotelegraphs, and amended sections 152, 221, and 611 of Title 47.

SECTION REFERRED TO IN OTHER SECTIONS

This section is referred to in title 29 sections 791, 793, 794.

§ 12202. State immunity

A State shall not be immune under the eleventh amendment to the Constitution of the United States from an action in [2] Federal or State court of competent jurisdiction for a violation of this chapter. In any action against a State for a violation of the requirements of this chapter, remedies (including remedies both at law and in equity) are available for such a violation to the same extent as such remedies are available for such a violation in an action against any public or private entity other than a State.

(Pub. L. 101–336, title V, § 502, July 26, 1990, 104 Stat. 370.)

SECTION REFERRED TO IN OTHER SECTIONS

This section is referred to in title 29 sections 791, 793, 794.

§ 12203. Prohibition against retaliation and coercion

(a) Retaliation

No person shall discriminate against any individual because such individual has opposed any act or practice made unlawful by this chapter or because such individual made a charge, testified, assisted, or participated in any manner in

---

[1] So in original. Probably should be "subchapters".
[2] So in original. Probably should be "in a".

Source: *U.S. Code,* 1992 Supp. Vol. 7, 181.

In Figure 9-16, 12201(a), 12201(b), and 12201(c) are subsections of section 12201. The citation for paragraph 1 in subsection (c) is 12201(c)(1). The source of this legislation follows subsection (d). It derives from Title V, section 501 of P.L. 101-336 enacted on July 26, 1990, and it is in the *Statutes at Large* at 104 *Stat.* 369. The References in Text segment of Figure 9-16 describes other parts of the *U.S. Code* that are referred to in section 12201. Remember, illuminating relationships among different but similar laws is a very important function of the *U.S.C.*.

Test your understanding of the *U.S. Code*: The following questions relate to Figure 9-16.

1. What law is referred to in 42 *U.S.C.* 12201(a)?

    (Title V of the Rehabilitation Act of 1973)

2. Where is that law codified in the *U.S.C.*?

    (29 *U.S.C.* 790 et seq.)

3. What does "et seq." in 42 *U.S.C.* 12201(a) mean?

    (The information begins in section 790 and is continued in succeeding sections.)

4. Identify the part of Figure 9-16 that provides the public law number and the *Statutes at Large* citation to the Rehabilitation Act of 1973.

    (Public Law 93-112; 87 *Stat.* 355)

5. What does 42 *U.S.C.* 12201(c)(3) represent?

    (Title 42, section 12201, subsection c, paragraph 3.)

ACTS CITED BY POPULAR NAME

The Acts Cited by Popular Name section lists popular names of laws alphabetically. Figure 9-17 shows that the Rehabilitation Act of 1973 is P.L. 93-112. It became law on September 26, 1973; its *Statutes at Large* citation is at 87 *Stat.* 355; and it is in the *U.S. Code* at 29 *U.S.C.* 701 et seq. The legislation listed below this information amended the original Act.

Figure 9-17
U.S. Code
Acts Cited By Popular Name

Regulatory Flexibility Act
　　Pub. L. 96–354, Sept. 19, 1980, 94 Stat. 1164
　　(Title 5, § 601 et seq.)

Rehabilitation Act of 1973
　　Pub. L. 93–112, Sept. 26, 1973, 87 Stat. 355
　　(Title 29, § 701 et seq.)
　　Pub. L. 93–651, title I, Nov. 21, 1974, 89 Stat.
　　2–3
　　Pub. L. 94–230, §§ 2–10, 11(b)(1)–(13), Mar.
　　15, 1976, 90 Stat. 211–214
　　Pub. L. 94–273, §§ 3(18), 10, Apr. 21, 1976, 90
　　Stat. 377, 378
　　Pub. L. 94–288, §§ 1, 2, May 21, 1976, 90
　　Stat. 520
　　Pub. L. 95–251, § 2(a)(8), Mar. 27, 1978, 92
　　Stat. 183
　　Pub. L. 95–602, title I, §§ 101, 102–115,
　　116(2), 117–122(a)–(d), title II, § 201, title
　　III, § 301, Nov. 6, 1978, 92 Stat. 2955–3001
　　Source: *U.S. Code*, 1988 ed., Vol. 21, 1124.

Test your understanding of Acts Cited by Popular Name: Refer to Figure 9-17 when answering the following.

　　1.　　True or false: Figure 9-17 shows six laws that amended the Rehabilitation Act of 1973.

(True)

　　2.　　What are their public law numbers?

(P.L. 93-651; P.L. 94-230; P.L. 94-273;
P.L. 94-288; P.L. 95-251; and P.L. 95-602)

U.S.C. TABLES

The *U.S. Code* has nine tables.

-Table I--Revised Titles: Provides titles and sections of the *U.S.C.* that were revised and renumbered since the initial 1926 edition (Figure 9-18).

Figure 9-18
U.S. Code
Table I--Revised Titles
TITLE 1—GENERAL PROVISIONS

[This title was enacted into law by act July 30, 1947, ch. 388, § 1, 61 Stat. 633. This table shows where sections of former Title 1 were incorporated in revised Title 1.]

Title 1 Former Sections	Title 1 New Sections	Title 1 Former Sections	Title 1 New Sections
1	1	30	112
2	2	30a	113
3	3	31	114
4	4	51a	201
5	5	52	202
6	6	53	203
21	101	54	204
22	102	54a	205
23	103	54b	206
24	104	54c	207
25	105	54d	208
26	106	55	209
27	107	56	210
28	108	57	211
29	109	58	212
29a	110	59	213
29b	111	60	Rep.

Source: *U.S. Code,* **1988 ed., Vol. 20, 2.**

Test your understanding of Table 1: The following questions refer to Figure 9-18.

1. Where is the former 1 *U.S.C.* 21 (1926 edition) located in the present version of the *U.S. Code*?

   (1 *U.S.C.* 101)

2. When was Title 1 enacted into law?

   (July 30, 1947)

3. What does enacted into law mean?

   (Remember, the *U.S.C.* is an edited version of the law based upon the *Statutes at Large.* A *U.S.C.* ti-tle is enacted into law when it is introduced into Congress as a bill and successfully goes through the legislative process. Enacted titles supersede the *Statutes at Large* as the official law.)

-**Table II**--*Revised Statutes* 1878: Indicates where sections of the *Revised Statutes* that are still effective appear in the *U.S.C.*

-**Table III**--*Statutes at Large*: Lists existing laws in chronological order by dates of passage. Citations give public law numbers and *Statutes* references, followed by appropriate *U.S.C.* titles and sections (Figure 9-19).

Figure 9-19
U.S. Code
Table III--*Statutes at Large*

101st Cong.					U.S.C.		
104 Stat.	Pub. L.	Section	Page	Title		Section	Status
1990—July 26	101–336	224	342	42	12144		
		225	343	42	12145		
		226	343	42	12146		
		227	343	42	12147		
		228	344	42	12148		
		229	345	42	12149		
		230	345	42	12150		
		231	346	42	12141 nt		
		241	346	42	12161		
		242	347	42	12162		
		243	352	42	12163		
		244	352	42	12164		

Source: *U.S. Code*, **1992 Supp., Vol. 7, 1106.**

Test your understanding of Table III: The following questions relate to Figure 9-19.

1. What is the *Statutes at Large* citation for section 224 of P.L. 101-336?

(104 *Stat.* 342)

2. Where in the *U.S. Code* is this found?

(42 *U.S.C.* 12144)

3. What is the authority for 42 *U.S.C.* 12163?

(104 *Stat.* 352)

Table IV--*U.S. Code* **Sections Classified to District of Columbia Code** and **Table V--District of Columbia Code Sections Classified to the** *U.S. Code*: Tables IV and V illustrate the interrelationships between the laws of Washington, D.C. and those of the federal government.

Table VI--Executive Orders and **Table VII--Proclamations:** Lists executive orders and proclamations currently in effect, plus corresponding *U.S.C.* titles and sections.

Table VIII--Reorganization Plans: Gives *U.S.C.* references to government reorganization plans.

Table IX--Internal References: This table shows where in the *U.S.C.* specific sections are cited. For instance, Figure 9-20 shows that 42 *U.S.C.* 11003 is mentioned at:

-42 *U.S.C.* 11042

-42 *U.S.C.* 11045

-42 *U.S.C.* 11046

-49 *U.S.C.* Appendix 1815 (Section 1815 of the Appendix to Title 49)

Figure 9-20
U.S. Code
Table IX--Internal References

TITLE 42—THE PUBLIC HEALTH AND WELFARE—Cont.

Section	*Referred to in*
11002..............	Sections 7413, 11003, 11004, 11005, 11045, 11046, 11049 of this title.
11003..............	Sections 11042, 11045, 11046 of this title; title 49 App. section 1815.
11023..............	Sections 11042, 11043, 11045, 11046, 11049, 13102, 13106 of this title.
11042..............	Sections 11043, 11044, 11045, 11046, 13106 of this title.
11045..............	Section 13106 of this title.
11046..............	Section 13106 of this title.
11049..............	Section 13102 of this title.

Source: *U.S. Code*, 1992 Supp., Vol 7, 1455.

Test your understanding of Table IX--Internal References: The following refers to Figure 9-20.

True or false: 42 *U.S.C.* 11002 is referenced at 30 *U.S.C.* 11004.

(False; it is referenced at 42 *U.S.C.* 11004.)

ANNOTATED VERSIONS OF THE *U.S. CODE*

The *United States Code Annotated*[11] and *United States Code Service*[12] are two annotated versions of the *U.S. Code*. Besides reproducing the law, annotated editions also offer interpretive information. The *U.S. Code Annotated* includes the identical titles, sections and text as the *U.S. Code*. It also provides references to *Corpus Juris Secundum* *(CJS)*[13], a legal encyclopedia, and West's key number system. The key number system classifies all points of law into systematic categories, facilitating access to cases pertaining to the respective topics. Abstracts of local, state, and federal cases that relate to each section of the *U.S.C.* are also noted. Revenue bills excluded from the *U.S.C.* are printed in the *U.S.C.A.*'s appendix to Title 26.

The *United States Code Service* uses the identical title and section approach as the *U.S.C.*, but the *U.S.C.S.* text is from the Statutes at Large. Annotations provide references to a limited number of cases, the *Code of Federal Regulations*, and law review articles. Jeanne Benioff's article, "A Comparison of Annotated *U.S. Codes*," is a good comparison of the *U.S.C.A.* and the *U.S.C.S.*[14]

ELECTRONIC VERSIONS OF PUBLIC LAWS AND THE *U.S. CODE*

U.S. CODE ON CD-ROM--EDITION PUBLISHED BY GPO

The *U.S. Code*[15] was first published in CD-ROM format by the government in 1991. Although this discussion is based upon the 1992 edition used with DOS commands, Microsoft Windows also works. Press F1 at any time for help.

OPENING MENU

Figure 9-21 reproduces the opening menu.

Figure 9-21
U.S. Code **on CD-ROM**
Opening Menu

```
File      Search      Browse      Display      Options   Help <F1>
```

```
             * Welcome to USCODE Database *

                  ┌─────────────────────────┐
                  │ Forms Search            │
                  │ Advanced Search         │
                  │ Table of Contents       │
                  │ Database Description     │
                  │ Quit                    │
                  └─────────────────────────┘

          <Up/Down> Select, <ENTER> Continue.
```

Each option is described below.

FORMS SEARCH

Use Forms Search when dates of enactment, and *U.S.C.*, *Statutes at Large*, and public law citations are known.

ADVANCED SEARCH

Use advanced search to locate information by keywords and phrases. The example in Figure 9-22 retrieves references to employment.

TABLE OF CONTENTS

This opening menu option is helpful when *U.S.C.* titles and chapters are known. The first layer lists all 50 titles and the second lists chapters in the title that had been selected.

DATABASE DESCRIPTION

The Database Description describes the *U.S.C.* and the relationships between its titles and sections. The information includes a list of all 59 titles and an explanation of abbreviations.

Figure 9-22
U.S. Code **on CD-ROM**
Advanced Search--Keyword

```
File    Search    Browse    Display    Options    Help    <F1>

┌─────────────────────────────────────────────────────────────┐
│                  * Advanced Search Entry *                    │
│  ┌───────────────────────────────────────────────────────┐   │
│  │ EMPLOYMENT                                            │   │
│  │                                                       │   │
│  │                                                       │   │
│  │                                                       │   │
│  │                                                       │   │
│  └───────────────────────────────────────────────────────┘   │
│                                                               │
│        <ENTER> Execute Search, <ALT-C> Clear.                 │
└─────────────────────────────────────────────────────────────┘

File    Search    Browse    Display    Options    Help    <F1>

┌─────────────────────────────────────────────────────────────┐
│                             * Word Postings *                 │
│                                                               │
│       1053 for stem EMPLOY                                     │
│         19 for stem EMPLOYABLE                                 │
│       3854 for stem EMPLOYED                                   │
│       5654 for stem EMPLOYER                                   │
│       1014 for stem EMPLOYERS                                  │
│        376 for stem EMPLOYING                                  │
│       9966 for stem EMPLOYMENT                                 │
│         23 for stem EMPLOYMENTS                                │
│         95 for stem EMPLOYS                                    │
│  22054 for EMPLOYMENT                                          │
│ Retrieved 5013 documents                                      │
│                                                               │
│             <ENTER> Title List, <ESC> Edit Search.            │
└─────────────────────────────────────────────────────────────┘
```

Figure 9-22 shows that the database searches not only the term employment, but other related ones as well. These words occurred 22,054 times in 5,013 documents. The smaller number accounts for the terms appearing more than once in the identical record.

Chart 9-3 shows how multiple terms can be joined five ways. The "w/#" connector in Chart 9-3 is especially important. Records in the database can range from 10 or 20 words long through 3 or 4 thousand words long. Searching "employment and discrimination" does not guarantee relevance because the first term can be in the initial paragraph and the second in the last. Searching "employment w/25 discrimination" improves the possibility of locating relevant data because the system retrieves only those records where the terms are within 25 words.

Chart 9-3
U.S. Code on **CD-ROM**
Searching Multiple Terms

Connector	Purpose	Example
AND	Narrows search	The phrase "employment and discrimination" retrieves records that include both terms.
OR	Broadens search	The phrase "discrimination or employment" retrieves either term or their related stems.
NOT	Eliminates information	The search "employment not discrimination" retrieves records that include the term "employment" and its derivations, but not "discrimination."
W/# ·	Limits terms within a designated number of words.	The search "employment w/20 discrimination" retrieves references to records where both terms occur within at least 20 words of each other.
ADJ	Terms are adjacent.	The search "employment adj discrimination" retrieves the terms when they are adjacent.

Test your understanding of *U.S.C.* Advanced Search options:

1. Which search statement retrieves fewer references?

A. "dogs and cats"

B. "dogs or cats"

(statement A)

2. Formulate a search that retrieves references to the terms "dogs" and "cats" within five words of each other.

("dogs w/5 cats")

3. Does the search statement immediately above also retrieve the terms within three words of each other?

(Yes)

FURTHER INFORMATION ABOUT THE *U.S. CODE* ON CD-ROM

Consult the booklet that comes with the CD-ROM for more detailed information about search procedures and installation instructions[16]. It covers both keyboard and Windows commands. The following three files on the CD-ROM are helpful:

-README: Reproduces a copy of the booklet that comes with the disk.

-MANUAL\MANUAL30.SRC: Provides a tutorial for using the CD with Windows.

-INSTALL\IS\IS.HLP: Reproduces the on screen help assistance.

ANNOTATED VERSIONS OF THE *U.S.C.* ON CD-ROM

West Publishing and Lawyers Cooperative Publishing both prepared annotated versions of the *U.S.C.* on CD-ROM.[17]

LEXIS/NEXIS AND WESTLAW DATABASES

Lexis/Nexis[18] and Westlaw[19] are the two major database vendors that deal with legal materials. Chart 9-4 summarizes how each cover the types of materials examined in this chapter.

Chart 9-4
Lexis/Nexis **and** *Westlaw Databases*

Type of Information	Lexis/nexis	Westlaw
Public laws	Libraries: CODES, EXEC, GENFED, and LEGIS. File: PUBLAW. Provides full texts of public laws enacted since 1988. The USCODE file described below includes this information, plus additional data.	United States Public Laws (US-PL) Covers all public laws enacted during the most recent session of Congress, regardless of their inclusion in the U.S. Code. United States Public Laws (US-PL-0LD) Covers public laws enacted since 1989, regardless of their inclusion in the U.S. Code.
Congressional reports	Libraries: CODES, GENFED and LEGIS. File: CMTRPT. Reproduces committee reports issued since 1990.	U.S. Code Legislative History (LH) Reproduces Congressional reports included in U.S.C.C.A.N. between 1948 and 1989. Also includes: 1) All reports issued since 1990, regardless of whether the bills were enacted; and 2) Presidential signing statements reprinted in U.S.C.C.A.N. since 1986.

U.S.C. text	Libraries: CODES, EXEC, GENFED, and LEGIS. File: USCS. Reproduces the U.S.C.S. Library: GENFED. File: RULES. Provides rules of federal courts that are in the U.S.C.S.. Library: GENFED. File: USCNST. Includes the Constitution, plus related supplementary material in the U.S.C.S.. Libraries: CODES and LEGIS. File: USCODE. A combined file that covers the PUBLAW, USCS, USCNST, and RULES files described above.	United States Code (USC) Reproduces the U.S.C.A.. United States Code Annotated (USCA) Provides the U.S.C.A. and a list of popular names of legislation. United States Code Annotated (USCA90, USCA91, USCA92, USCA93, and USCA94) Covers the U.S.C.A. for the indicated years. These databases are significant because events that took place in 1990 are tried under laws in effect then, not those in effect in 1994. Covers court rules and procedures in separate databases. [Bankruptcy (FBKR-RULES); Criminal Justice (FCJ-RULES); International Law (FINT-RULES); Maritime (FMRT-RULES); Military Law (FMIL-RULES); Securities (FSEC-RULES); and Taxation (FTX-RULES)].
General indexes	Libraries: CODES and GENFED. File: USINDX. Indexes the U.S.C.S..	United States Code Annotated General Index (USCA-IDX) Covers the statutes currently in effect, plus selected items from the Code of Federal Regulations and other supplementary materials included in the U.S.C.A.
Popular names	Libraries: BUSREF, CODES, and GENFED. File: USNAME. Indexes popular names of laws included in the U.S.C.S..	U.S.C.A. Popular Name Table (USCA-POP) Indexes popular names of legislation currently in effect. United States Code Annotated (USCA) Reproduces the U.S.C.A. and a list of popular names of legislation.
Other finding aids	Library: GENFED. File: USTOC. Lists of U.S.C. titles and chapters. Consult the USCS database for the text of the law. Libraries: CODES and GENFED. File: USSALT. Shows U.S.C.S. titles and sections for Statutes at Large references that are currently in effect. Libraries: CODES and GENFED. File: USREVT. Notes U.S.C. titles and sections that were revised, renumbered, or re-enacted since 1926.	

The following two sources offer background information to Lexis/Nexis and Westlaw:

Wren, Christopher G. and Jill Robinson Wren. *Using Computers In Legal Research: A Guide to Lexis and Westlaw*. Madison, WI.: Adams and Ambrose Publishing, 1994.

Discusses basic hardware and software issues; database structure; pre-search planning; and data retrieval. Appendices provide basic information about both systems.

Johnson, Nancy P. et al. *Winning Research Skills*. 2nd ed. Minneapolis/St. Paul: West Publishing Company, 1993.

Although sources produced by West Publishing are emphasized, the authors' approach make the book especially useful. They stress the need to integrate print and electronic sources. Both have legitimate roles to play when doing legal or any other type of research. Researchers should not ignore one format at the expense of the other.

LEGI-SLATE

The *Current U.S.C. Service*[20] provided by Legi-Slate updates the *U.S.C.* each time the President approves a new law. Retrieve information by words, phrases, and *U.S.C.* citations. The menus are easy to follow, providing the searcher is familiar with the structure of the *U.S.C.*

CONCLUSION

Chart 9-5 describes key features of slip laws, the *Statutes at Large*, and the *United States Code* and their annotated editions.

Chart 9-5
Summary of Statutory Sources

	Slip Laws	Statutes at Large	U.S.C.C.A.N.	U.S.C.	U.S.C. Annotated Editions
Scope	Public and private laws	Public and private laws, concurrent resolutions, and proclamations	Public laws, proclamations, executive orders, and Congressional reports	Subject compilation of federal law.	U.S.C.A. and U.S.C.S. Provides same data as U.S.C., plus interpretative materials (case abstracts; and references to articles, legal encyclopedias, and regulations.)
Frequency	Published immediately following enactment.	Annual	Annual volumes correspond to Stat. at Large; monthly issues correspond to slip laws.	Complete set published every six years; cumulative annual supplements issued during intervening five years.	Updated with annual pockets.

Organization	Numerically by law numbers.	Numerically by law, concurrent resolution, and proclamation numbers.	Numerically by law, executive order, and proclamations numbers.	50 broad subject areas or titles.	Titles and sections are identical to U.S.C. U.S.C.A. text follows U.S.C. and U.S.C.S. text follows Stat. at Large.
Index by Subjects	Monthly Catalog Subject Index.	Yes	Yes	General Index	General Index
Index by Popular Names	Monthly Catalog Title Index.	In Subject Index through 1990; Popular Name Index, 1991-present.	Table 10	Acts Cited by Popular Name	U.S.C.A.: Popular Name Table; U.S.C.S.: Table of Acts by Popular Names.
Index by Personal Names	Monthly Catalog Subject Index.	Individual Index	No	No	No
Index by Public Law Numbers	Monthly Catalog Series Report Index.	List of Public Laws	Tables 1 and 2	Table 3	Table 3
Index by Stat. References	No	No	Tables 1 and 2.	Table 3	Table 3
Index by U.S.C. References	No	No	Table 3	Tables 1 and 9.	No
Electronic Sources	Lexis/Nexis (Libraries: CODES, EXEC, GENFED, and LEGIS. File: PUBLAW) Westlaw (US-PL)	Lexis/Nexis (Libraries: CODES, EXEC, GENFED, and LEGIS. File: PUBLAW) Westlaw (US-PL-OLD)	Same as slip laws, plus: Lexis/Nexis Libraries: CODES, GENFED, and LEGIS. Library: COMRPT. Westlaw (LH and U.S.C.C.A.N)	CD-ROM: U.S.C. (GPO); Online: LEGI-SLATE (Current U.S.C. Service)	CD-ROM: U.S.C.A. (West Publishing); and U.S.C.A. (Lawyers Cooperative Publishing) Lexis/Nexis Libraries: CODES, EXEC, GENFED, and LEGIS. File: USCS. Westlaw (USC, USCA, USCA90, USCA91, USCA92, USCA93, and USCA94)

Endnotes

1. See 349-61 in the *Congressional Quarterly Guide To Congress*, 4th edition (Washington, D.C.: Congressional Quarterly, Inc., 1991) for a comprehensive discussion of private bills and legislation. See also Lewis Deschler, *Deschlers Precedents of The United States House of Representatives Including References To Provisions of The Constitution and Laws, and To Decisions of the Courts* (Washington, D.C.: GPO, 1977), Vol. 7, 325-333. Deschler argues that "The distinction between public and private bills is sometimes difficult to make." 325.

2. *United States Statutes at Large* (Washington, D.C.: GPO, 1789-annual). SuDoc number: AE2.11:. Publisher and SuDoc number varies.

3. (Bethesda, MD.: Congressional Information Service, Inc., 19??). Approximately 3,500 microfiche.

4. U.S. House. Office of the Law Revision Counsel (Washington, D.C.: GPO, 1926-present). SuDoc number: Y1.2/5:. Complete set is published every six years with annual supplements issued during the intervening years.

5. Jack Davies and Robert P. Lawry, *Institutions and Methods of the Law: Introductory Teaching Materials*, American Casebook Series (St. Paul, Minn.: West Publishing Co., 1982), 183-84.

6. Consult Erwin C. Surrency, "The Publications of Federal Laws: A Short History," *Law Library Journal* 79:3 (Summer 1987), 469-484 for additional information. His "Compilation of Federal Laws 1791-1925: A Preliminary Bibliography" is on 481-4. See also Ralph H. Dawn and Ernest R. Feidler, "The Federal Statutes--Their History and Use," *Minnesota Law Review.* 22:7 (1938), 1008-29.

7. U.S. Department of State, *Revised Statutes of the United States: Passed at the First Session of the Forty-Third Congress, 1873-74, Embracing the Statutes of the United States, General and Permanent in Their Nature, in Force on the First Day of December, One Thousand Eight Hundred and Seventy Three...* (Washington, D.C.: GPO, 1875). Reprinted edition: (Buffalo, NY: William S. Hein and Company, 1981?).

8. (St. Paul, MN.: West Publishing Company, 1941-monthly). Titles of earlier editions varied.

9. (Washington, D.C.: GPO, 1938-1948 irregularly; 1949-annual). SuDoc number: AE2.106/3:.

10. (Washington, D.C.: GPO, 1936-daily). SuDoc number: AE2.106:.

11.   (St. Paul, MN.: West Publishing Co., 1927-present). Pocket supplements are issued annually and replacement volumes are issued irregularly.

12.   *United States Code Service: Lawyers' Edition* (Rochester, NY: The Lawyers' Co-Operative Publishing Co., 1972-present). Pocket supplements are issued annually and replacement volumes are issued irregularly.

13.   *Corpus Juris Secundum: A Complete Restatement of the Entire American Law as Developed by All Reported Cases* (St. Paul, MN.: West Publishing Co., 1936-present). Pocket supplements are issued annually, and replacement volumes and new volumes are issued irregularly.

14.   *Legal Reference Services Quarterly* 2:1 (Spring 1982), 37-53. The intent of the two sources are different. That of *U.S.C.A.* is to cite cases as comprehensively as possible and that of *U.S.C.S.* is to cite only the most important cases. Thus, one would expect *U.S.C.A.* to include references not found in its counterpart. Benioff compared three sections of the *U.S.C.* in the two sources and found that *U.S.C.S.* included cases that the more comprehensive *U.S.C.A.* ignored.

15.   *United States Code Containing the General and Permanent Laws of the United States, In Force on January 2, 1992* (CD-ROM) (Washington, D.C.: G.P.O., 1991-annual). SuDoc number: Y1.2/5:.

16.   U.S. Congress. House. Office of the Law Revision Counsel. *United States Code Containing the General and Permanent Laws of the United States, In Force on January 2, 1992* (*U.S. Code CD-ROM User Manual*) (Washington, D.C.: GPO, 1994). SuDoc number: Y1.2/5-2:year.

17.   *United States Code Annotated* (CD-ROM) (Eagan, MN.: West Publishing). 2 disks; and *U.S.C.S. on LawDesk* (CD-ROM) (Rochester, NY: Lawyers Cooperative Publishing).

18.   Mead Data Central, Dayton, OH. Catalogs of databases and services, plus educational materials are distributed upon request. Call 800-543-6862 for information.

19.   West Publishing Company, Eagan, MN. West provides upon request catalogs describing its databases and services, and other educational materials. Westlaw's educational materials are especially well done. Call 800-328-0109 for more information.

20.   (Online database). Available on Legis-Slate, Washington, D.C.

Exercises

1. Use the 1991 *Statutes at Large* to answer the following. All questions pertain to P.L. 102-194.

   A. What is the popular name of this legislation?

   B. What is its *Statutes at Large* citation?

   C. When was it enacted?

   D. True or false: Section 201 of this law is incorporated into 15 *U.S.C.* 5521.

   E. Under what subject heading is this legislation indexed?

   F. Cite the Congressional reports that provide a legislative history of this act.

2. Use the 1992 Supplement to the *United States Code* or a latter edition of the *U.S.C.* to answer the following. If using a latter edition, the answers might vary depending upon subsequent amendments to the law.

   A. Where in the *U.S.C.* is the "High-Performance Computing Act of 1991" found?

   B. What section of this law cites the establishment of the National Research and Education Network?

   C. What is the *Statutes at Large* reference to its establishment?

   D. Which section of the *U.S.C.* describes the purpose of a program designed to transfer federal education and training software to state and local governments, and to the private sector?

   E. How come the 1992 Supplement to the *U.S.C.* includes 20 *U.S.C.* 5092(b), but skips 5092(a)? Where is 5092(a) found?

3. Use an electronic edition of the *U.S.C.* to locate the title and section of the law that requires agencies to make final opinions, policy statements, and staff manuals that affect the public available for public inspection and copying.

Answers

1. A. High-Performance Computing Act of 1991.

   B. 105 *Stat.* 1594.

   C. December 9, 1991.

   D. True.

   E. Science and Technology.

   F. House Report 102-66, part 1 and 2, and Senate Report 102-57.

2. A. 15 *U.S.C.* 5501 et seq.

   B. 15 *U.S.C.* 5512(a).

   C. 105 *Stat.* 1598.

   D. 20 *U.S.C.* 5092.

   E. 5092(b) is in the 1992 Supplement because that section of the law changed since the last complete *U.S.C.* was published. Not having been changed since the 1988 full version of the *U.S.C.* appeared, 5092(a) is not reprinted in the Supplement. Remember to use the most recent complete editions of the *U.S.C.* with the Supplements to determine how the law may have changed.

3. 5 *U.S.C.* 552(a)(2)(A), 5 *U.S.C.* 552(a)(2)(B), and 5 *U.S.C.* 552(a)(2)(C).

•Chapter 10

Federal Register and *Code of Federal Regulations*

Answer the following questions when reading this chapter:

1. How do rules and regulations differ from statutes?

2. What advantages, if any, do rules and regulations have over legislation?

3. What are the similarities and differences between the kinds of information found in the *Federal Register* and the *Code of Federal Regulations*?

4. Which printed indexes and guides to the *Federal Register* and the *Code of Federal Regulations* are most useful to your needs?

5. Which electronic versions of the *Federal Register* and the *Code of Federal Regulations* are most useful to your needs?

6. Do you feel the nation is over-regulated?

The previous chapter covered sources of statutory law enacted by Congress. This one deals with administrative law promulgated by executive and independent agencies. Presidential proclamations and executive orders; regulations; orders and opinions; and notices are examples of administrative law. None require Congressional approval. The President and executive agencies issue them based upon powers the Constitution bestows and/or legislation that authorizes the actions. The terms, rules and regulations, are synonymous.

The first section of the chapter considers the significance and background of regulations. The following section presents brief summaries of the *Federal Register* and the *Code of Federal Regulations*. Both titles are primary sources for federal regulations. The next parts of the chapter examine three types of regulatory documents: Presidential documents, regulations, and notices. The text then considers locating information in the *Federal Register*, the *Code of Federal Regulations*, related indexes, and relevant electronic sources. The final part of the chapter describes reference tools that provide additional information about the regulatory process. The text excludes agency orders and opinions because they are usually printed in neither the *Federal Register* nor the *Code of Federal Regulations*.[1]

SIGNIFICANCE AND BACKGROUND OF REGULATIONS

Cornelius Kerwin argues that "Rulemaking is the single most important function performed by agencies of government."[2] Regulations affect all aspects of American life. Industrial safety, banking, anti-trust activities, labeling requirements, consumer safeguards, and government programs, such as food stamps, are just a few examples. Regulations reflect Presidential policies. For example, rules issued by the Environmental Protection Agency show the Administration's feelings towards the environment.

Regulations have a number of advantages over statutes. Agency experts are often the first to be able to reply to changing conditions and unanticipated problems. Rulemaking offers the public opportunity to participate in the governing process. Agencies must announce proposed rules and offer interested parties opportunities to comment upon them. Charles Evans Hughes, former Chief Justice of the Supreme Court, stated that:

> Legislators have little time to follow the trails of expert inquiry and so we turn the whole business over to a few with broad authority to make the actual rules which control our conduct.[3]

Although rules are promulgated by unelected agency personnel, these officials are still answerable to the public. Threats of Presidential and Congressional oversight and investigative actions, and the Congressional power of the purse are sufficient to hold agency power in check.

Rules are not a twentieth century invention. The initial session of the first Congress approved "An Act Providing for the Payment of the Invalid Pensioners of the United States." The law assumed federal spending for military pensions supported previously by the states "...under such regulations as the President of the United States may direct."[4]

OVERVIEW OF THE *FEDERAL REGISTER* AND THE *CODE OF FEDERAL REGULATIONS*

The *Federal Register*[5] is published Monday through Friday, except on official holidays. It includes four kinds of materials: Presidential documents, rules, proposed rules, and notices. The discussion below describes each in detail. Data excluded from the *Federal Register* include treaties, conventions, protocols, international agreements, and news items. Cite the *Federal Register* by volume and page numbers. Page 1,000 in volume 50 is 50 *FR* 1,000.

Citizens had difficulty obtaining rules before the *Federal Register's* publication in 1936. In an 1872 dissenting opinion, four Supreme Court justices complained about an unpublished proclamation that:

> was in no gazette, in no market-place, nor in the street. It was signed by the President and the Acting Secretary of State, and deposited in the Secretary's Office. It does not appear that a single person besides the President and Secretary was aware of its existence.[6]

Yet authorities still expected people to adhere to the regulations. Even agency personnel had difficulty keeping track of them. A government attorney preparing to argue a point before the Supreme Court discovered that an unpublished executive order revoked the rule that the case depended upon. Congress enacted legislation that created the *Federal Register* soon afterwards.[7]

Final and interim regulations printed in the *Federal Register* are compiled into the *Code of Federal Regulations (C.F.R.)*[8] just as legislation is compiled into the U.S. Code. The *C.F.R.* is divided into fifty titles that reflect broad subject headings. They are not comparable to those in the *U.S.C.* For instance, Title 20 in the *U.S. Code* deals with education, whereas most regulations on the subject are found in Title 34 of the *C.F.R.* Every year updates to titles 1 through 16 appear in January; 17 through 27 in April; 28 through 41 in July; and 42 through 50 in October. Cite *C.F.R.* references by titles and sections. Title 20, section 50 is 20 *C.F.R.* 50.

REGULATORY DOCUMENTS ISSUED BY THE PRESIDENT: EXECUTIVE ORDERS AND PROCLAMATIONS

Presidential regulatory documents vary depending upon the administration. A representative of the Office of the Federal Register stated that:

> No law, executive order, or standard defines the terms 'Executive order,' 'Presidential directive,' 'administrative order,' 'memorandum,' 'determination,' 'order,' 'notice,' or any other type of Presidential order. The President decides the form for each document.[9]

The discussion below considers executive orders, proclamations, memorandums, and Presidential determinations--the most common type of Presidential documents published in the *Federal Register* today.

EXECUTIVE ORDERS

Executive orders are Presidential mandates. Although they are generally based upon powers delegated by Congress, their absence has not prevented Presidents from issuing them. In such cases, the Constitution and applicable statutes become the basis for actions. Examples of early executive orders provided lands for lighthouses, reservations, and military uses; and authorized exemptions from civil service rules without approval of the Civil Service Commission.

Executive orders have both positive and negative consequences. Presidents Kennedy and Johnson used them to further civil rights.[10] On the other hand, an executive order also limited the liberties of Japanese Americans following the Pearl Harbor attack by ordering their internment.[11]

It is uncertain how many executive orders exist. The Department of State attempted to number them beginning in 1907, but the President sometimes neglected to forward copies. Also, the Department of State's collection of executive orders, which were numbered retrospectively, only goes back to 1862.

PROCLAMATIONS

Although Presidential proclamations usually deal with ceremonial matters, such as periods of special observance, some cover issues of potential importance. This sometimes makes it difficult to distinguish them from executive orders. The Thanksgiving Day Proclamation first issued by George Washington in October 1789 and annually by most Presidents since 1863 are among the most famous ceremonial proclamations. President Lincoln's Emancipation Proclamation is one of the most significant ever issued.

MEMORANDUMS AND PRESIDENTIAL DETERMINATIONS

Most people are not as familiar with memorandums and determinations as they are with executive orders and proclamations. Memorandums are statements issued by the President that authorize agency heads to act in a particular manner. 3 *U.S.C.* 301 authorizes the President to delegate authority to department heads or to other officials confirmed by the Senate. The law mandates that descriptions of these actions be printed in the *Federal Register*. Presidential determinations are decisions made by the Chief Executive that certain activities or actions are in the national interest. Determinations are printed in the *Federal Register* and are numbered by year. For example, determination 94-10 was the tenth issued in 1994. Determinations are a type of memorandum. Other memorandums are not numbered.

People sometimes confuse Presidential determinations and Presidential directives. The latter are classified documents circulated within the National Security Council.[12]

PUBLICATION OF EXECUTIVE ORDERS, PROCLAMATIONS, MEMORANDUMS AND DETERMINATIONS

The *Federal Register* published executive orders and proclamations since 1936, making them far more accessible than before. They are also in

Title 3 of the *Code of Federal Regulations*. The *Codification of Presidential Proclamations and Executive Orders, April 13, 1945-January 20, 1989*[13] includes all materials that were in effect through Ronald Reagan's Presidency. Documents issued before then are reproduced if they were amended or affected by materials published between 1945 and 1989. Locate information through the subject index and the "Disposition Table" that lists amendments to and status of documents. Memorandums and presidential determinations are also in the *Federal Register* and in Title 3 of the *C.F.R.*

The *CIS Index to Presidential Executive Orders and Proclamations*[14] and its corresponding microfiche collection[15] cover 1789-1983. The microfiche includes 57,000 unnumbered executive orders and proclamations. Two articles describe other historical indexes, "Executive Orders: A Journey" by Mary Woodward[16] and "Locating Presidential Proclamations and Executive Orders--A Guide to Sources" by Donna Bennett and Philip Yannerella[17]. The *Weekly Compilation of Presidential Documents*[18] and the *Public Papers of the Presidents*[19] series are additional sources of executive orders and proclamations.

RULES AND REGULATIONS

PROPOSED RULES V. FINAL RULES

Proposed rules and final rules are two types of regulations. Proposed rules are draft versions of regulations that interested parties comment upon. Agencies must state deadlines for receipt of the comments, and names and addresses of officials who accept the critiques (Figure 10-1).

Figure 10-1
Federal Register
Proposed Rule

7452   Federal Register / Vol. 56. No. 36 / Friday. February 22. 1991 / Proposed Rules

DEPARTMENT OF JUSTICE

Office of the Attorney General

28 CFR Part 36

[A.G. Order No. 1472–91]

Nondiscrimination On The Basis of Disability By Public Accommodations And In Commercial Facilities

AGENCY: Department of Justice.

ACTION: Notice of proposed rulemaking.

SUMMARY: This proposed rule implements title III of the Americans with Disabilities Act. Public Law 101–336, which prohibits discrimination on the basis of disability by private entities in places of public accommodation. requires that all new places of public accommodation and commercial facilities be designed and constructed so as to be readily accessible to and usable by persons with disabilities. and requires that examinations or courses related to licensing or certification for professional and trade purposes be accessible to persons with disabilities.

DATES: To be assured of consideration. comments must be in writing and must be received on or before April 23. 1991. Whenever possible. comments should refer to specific sections in the proposed regulation. Comments that are received after the closing date will be considered to the extent practicable.

ADDRESSES: Comments should be sent to: John L. Wodatch. Office on the Americans with Disabilities Act. Civil Rights Division. U.S. Department of Justice. Rulemaking Docket 003. P.O. Box 75087. Washington, DC 20013.

Comments received will be available for public inspection in room 854 of the HOLC Building. 320 First Street. NW., Washington. DC. from 9 a.m. to 5 p.m., Monday through Friday. except legal holidays. from March 8. 1991 until the Department publishes this rule in final form. Persons who need assistance to review the comments will be provided with appropriate aids such as readers or print magnifiers.

FOR FURTHER INFORMATION CONTACT: John Wodatch. Office on the Americans

with Disabilities Act and Stewart B. Oneglia. Chief. Coordination and Review Section. Civil Rights Division. U.S. Department of Justice. and Janet Blizard. Irene Bowen. Philip Breen. Merrily Friedlander. and Sara Kaltenborn. attorneys in the Coordination and Review Section. Civil Rights Division. U.S. Department of Justice. Washington. DC 20530. may be contacted through the Division's ADA Information Line at (202) 514–0301 (Voice). (202) 514–0381 (TDD). or (202) 514–0383 (TDD). These telephone numbers are not toll-free numbers.

Source: *Federal Register,* **56:36 (February 22, 1991), 7452.**

Proposed rules also encompass:

1.   Amendments to previously published proposed rules.

2.   Public notices of meetings or hearings to discuss proposed rules.

3.   Public petitions that express the need for rulemaking.

4.   Advance notices of proposed rulemaking that are sometimes published before proposed rules. This helps agencies test political climates and allows interested parties to comment before agencies formulate the regulations.

Agencies print final rules after the public is given sufficient time to comment upon the proposed regulations. The final version of the proposal illustrated in Figure 10-1 is reproduced in Figure 10-2. Three types of final rules include:

1.   Interim rules issued during emergencies. The public has an opportunity to comment upon them because proposed versions were not published.

2.   Agency policy statements.

3.   Interpretative rules that explain agency viewpoints to-
     wards statutes and regulations. Agencies can amend these
     non-binding statements without notice.

Publication of agency policy statements and interpretative rules are
sometimes problematic. Randy S. Springer, author of "Gatekeeping and the
Federal Register," argues that the law provides vague instructions defining
what constitutes adequate publication in the *Federal Register*.[20] 5 *U.S.C.*
552(a)(1)(D) requires that "substantive rules of general applicability," "statements of general policy," and "interpretations of general applicability" be
published. Yet, 5 *U.S.C.* 552(a)(2)(B) declares that "statements of policy and
interpretations which have been adopted by the agency and are not published in the *Federal Register*" should be available to the public. Kenneth
Cult Davis, author of *Administrative Law Treatise*, asks, but cannot answer,
a pertinent question:

> What is the answer to the simple question whether all interpretative
> rules must be published or whether some need not be?...probably no
> judge, no administrator, no practitioner and no commentator knows
> the answer.[21]

PREAMBLES

Proposed and final regulations published since 1977 must be preceded
by preambles. They "inform the reader who is not an expert in the subject
area of the basis and purpose for the rule or proposal." [22] Preambles, which
are comparable to legislative histories, outline agency intents. These guidelines describe how the regulations ought to be interpreted in simple language, rather than legal jargon. The courts consider preambles very
important. Rulings have argued that agency actions were arbitrary without
adequate preambles.[23] This is particularly important when final rules
differ significantly from those that were proposed.

The following parts of the preamble in Figure 10-2 are significant:

- **Agency:** The agency promulgating the regulation.

- **Action:** Identifies types of documents. Common categories include
proposed rules; notices of proposed rule making; proposed policy statements; final rules' interim rules' policy statements; and interpretations.

- **Summary:** Outlines the purpose of the rules and its intended effects.
the supplementary section described below includes supporting information and other detail.

- **Effective Date:** Indicates when regulations become effective; deadlines for submitting comments; hearing times, and other relevant dates.

- **For Further Information Contact:** Lists agency contacts who can answer questions. Preambles to proposed rules also include addresses for submitting comments or locations of hearings.

- **Supplementary Information:** Describes detailed background and history of the action such as problems the regulations attempt to address; methods of doing so; and alternative solutions. Additional data deal with enforcement and/or monitoring procedures; cost effectiveness; and references to previous studies. Supplementary information for final rules include differences between the proposed and final regulations; reasons for the changes; and summaries of comments. The Section-by-Section Analysis and Response to Comments is especially valuable to both laymen and experts who must interpret the rule. The Supplementary Information also cites the authorities or legal basis for the rules. This can include reference to the *Federal Register*, the *Code of Federal Regulations*, statutes, the *U.S. Code*, or Presidential documents.

Figure 10-2
Federal Register
Preamble

35544   Federal Register / Vol. 56, No. 144 / Friday, July 26, 1991 / Rules and Regulations

DEPARTMENT OF JUSTICE

Office of the Attorney General

28 CFR Part 36

[Order No. 1513–91]

Nondiscrimination on the Basis of Disability by Public Accommodations and in Commercial Facilities

AGENCY: Department of Justice.

ACTION: Final rule.

SUMMARY: This rule implements title III of the Americans with Disabilities Act, Public Law 101–336, which prohibits discrimination on the basis of disability by private entities in places of public accommodation, requires that all new places of public accommodation and commercial facilities be designed and constructed so as to be readily accessible to and usable by persons with disabilities, and requires that examinations or courses related to licensing or certification for professional and trade purposes be accessible to persons with disabilities.

EFFECTIVE DATE: January 26, 1992.

FOR FURTHER INFORMATION CONTACT: Barbara S. Drake, Deputy Assistant Attorney General, Civil Rights Division; Stewart B. Oneglia, Chief, Coordination and Review Section, Civil Rights Division; and John Wodatch, Director, Office on the Americans with Disabilities Act, Civil Rights Division; all of the U.S. Department of Justice, Washington, DC 20530. They may be contacted through the Division's ADA Information Line at (202) 514–0301 (Voice), (202) 514–0381 (TDD), or (202) 514–0383 (TDD). These telephone numbers are not toll-free numbers.

Copies of this rule are available in the following alternate formats: large print, Braille, electronic file on computer disk, and audio-tape. Copies may be obtained from the Office on the Americans with Disabilities Act at (202) 514–0301 (Voice) or (202) 514–0381 (TDD). The rule is also available on electronic bulletin board at (202) 514–6193. These telephone numbers are not toll-free numbers.

SUPPLEMENTARY INFORMATION:

Background

The landmark Americans with Disabilities Act ("ADA" or "the Act"), enacted on July 26, 1990, provides comprehensive civil rights protections to individuals with disabilities in the areas of employment, public accommodations, State and local government services, and telecommunications.

The legislation was originally developed by the National Council on Disability, an independent Federal agency that reviews and makes recommendations concerning Federal laws, programs, and policies affecting individuals with disabilities. In its 1986 study, "Toward Independence," the National Council on Disability recognized the inadequacy of the existing, limited patchwork of protections for individuals with disabilities, and recommended the enactment of a comprehensive civil rights law requiring equal opportunity for individuals with disabilities throughout American life. Although the 100th Congress did not act on the legislation, which was first introduced in 1988, then-Vice-President George Bush endorsed the concept of comprehensive disability rights legislation during his presidential campaign and became a dedicated advocate of the ADA.

The ADA was reintroduced in modified form in May 1989 for consideration by the 101st Congress. In June 1989, Attorney General Dick Thornburgh, in testimony before the Senate Committee on Labor and Human Resources, reiterated the Bush Administration's support for the ADA and suggested changes in the proposed legislation. After extensive negotiations between Senate sponsors and the Administration, the Senate passed an amended version of the ADA on September 7, 1989, by a vote of 76–8.

In the House, jurisdiction over the ADA was divided among four committees, each of which conducted extensive hearings and issued detailed committee reports: the Committee on Education and Labor, the Committee on the Judiciary, the Committee on Public Works and Transportation, and the Committee on Energy and Commerce. On October 12, 1989, the Attorney General testified in favor of the legislation before the Committee on the Judiciary. The Civil Rights Division, on February 22, 1990, provided testimony to the Committee on Small Business, which although technically without jurisdiction over the bill, conducted hearings on the legislation's impact on small business.

After extensive committee consideration and floor debate, the House of Representatives passed an amended version of the Senate bill on May 22, 1990, by a vote of 403–20. After resolving their differences in conference, the Senate and House took final action on the bill—the House passing it by a vote of 377–28 on July 12, 1990, and the Senate, a day later, by a vote of 91–6. The ADA was enacted into law with the President's signature at a White House ceremony on July 26, 1990.

Rulemaking History

On February 22, 1991, the Department of Justice published a notice of proposed rulemaking (NPRM) implementing title III of the ADA in the Federal Register (56 FR 7452). On February 28, 1991, the Department published a notice of proposed rulemaking implementing subtitle A of title II of the ADA in the Federal Register (56 FR 8538). Each NPRM solicited comments on the definitions, standards, and procedures of the proposed rules. By the April 29, 1991, close of the comment period of the NPRM for title II, the Department had received 2,718 comments on the two proposed rules. Following the close of the comment period, the Department received an additional 222 comments.

In order to encourage public participation in the development of the Department's rules under the ADA, the Department held four public hearings. Hearings were held in Dallas, Texas on March 4–5, 1991; in Washington, DC on March 13–14–15, 1991; in San Francisco, California on March 18–19, 1991; and in Chicago, Illinois on March 27–28, 1991. At these hearings, 329 persons testified and 1,567 pages of testimony were compiled. Transcripts of the hearings were included in the Department's rulemaking docket.

The comments that the Department received occupy almost six feet of shelf space and contain over 10,000 pages. The Department received comments from individuals from all fifty States and the District of Columbia. Nearly 75% of the comments came from individuals and from organizations representing the interests of persons with disabilities. The Department received 292 comments from entities covered by the ADA and trade associations representing businesses in the private sector, and 67 from government units, such as mayors' offices, public school districts, and various State agencies working with individuals with disabilities.

The Department received one comment from a consortium of 511 organizations representing a broad spectrum of persons with disabilities. In addition, at least another 25 commenters endorsed the position expressed by this consortium or submitted identical comments on one or both proposed regulations.

An organization representing persons with hearing impairments submitted a large number of comments. This organization presented the Department with 479 individual comments, each providing in chart form a detailed representation of what type of auxiliary aid or service would be useful in the

Federal Register / Vol. 56, No. 144 / Friday, July 26, 1991 / Rules and Regulations 35545

various categories of places of public accommodation.

The Department received a number of comments based on almost ten different form letters. For example, individuals who have a heightened sensitivity to a variety of chemical substances submitted 266 postcards detailing how exposure to various environmental conditions restricts their access to places of public accommodation and to commercial facilities. Another large group of form letters came from groups affiliated with independent living centers.

The vast majority of the comments addressed the Department's proposal implementing title III. Just over 100 comments addressed only issues presented in the proposed title II regulation.

The Department read and analyzed each comment that was submitted in a timely fashion. Transcripts of the four hearings were analyzed along with the written comments. The decisions that the Department has made in response to these comments, however, were not made on the basis of the number of commenters addressing any one point but on a thorough consideration of the merits of the points of view expressed in the comments. Copies of the written comments, including transcripts of the four hearings, will remain available for public inspection in room 854 of the HOLC Building, 320 First Street, NW., Washington, DC from 10 a.m. to 5 p.m., Monday through Friday, except for legal holidays, until August 30, 1991.

The Americans with Disabilities Act gives to individuals with disabilities civil rights protections with respect to discrimination that are parallel to those provided to individuals on the basis of race, color, national origin, sex, and religion. It combines in its own unique formula elements drawn principally from two key civil rights statutes—the Civil Rights Act of 1964 and title V of the Rehabilitation Act of 1973. The ADA generally employs the framework of titles II (42 U.S.C. 2000a to 2000a–6) and VII (42 U.S.C. 2000e to 2000e–16) of the Civil Rights Act of 1964 for coverage and enforcement and the terms and concepts of section 504 of the Rehabilitation Act of 1973 (29 U.S.C. 794) for what constitutes discrimination.

Other recently enacted legislation will facilitate compliance with the ADA. As amended in 1990, the Internal Revenue Code allows a deduction of up to $15,000 per year for expenses associated with the removal of qualified architectural and transportation barriers. The 1990 amendment also permits eligible small businesses to receive a tax credit for certain costs of compliance with the ADA. An eligible small business is one whose gross receipts do not exceed $1,000,000 or whose workforce does not consist of more than 30 full-time workers. Qualifying businesses may claim a credit of up to 50 percent of eligible access expenditures that exceed $250 but do not exceed $10,250. Examples of eligible access expenditures include the necessary and reasonable costs of removing barriers, providing auxiliary aids, and acquiring or modifying equipment or devices.

In addition, the Communications Act of 1934 has been amended by the Television Decoder Circuitry Act of 1990, Public Law 101–431, to require as of July 1, 1993, that all televisions with screens of 13 inches or wider have built-in decoder circuitry for displaying closed captions. This new law will eventually lessen dependence on the use of portable decoders in achieving compliance with the auxiliary aids and services requirements of the rule.

Overview of the Rule

The final rule establishes standards and procedures for the implementation of title III of the Act, which addresses discrimination by private entities in places of public accommodation, commercial facilities, and certain examinations and courses. The careful consideration Congress gave title III is reflected in the detailed statutory provisions and the expansive reports of the Senate Committee on Labor and Human Resources and the House Committees on the Judiciary, and Education and Labor. The final rule follows closely the language of the Act and supplements it, where appropriate, with interpretive material found in the committee reports.

The rule is organized into six subparts. Subpart A, "General," includes the purpose and application sections, describes the relationship of the Act to other laws, and defines key terms used in the regulation.

Subpart B, "General Requirements," contains material derived from what the statute calls the "General Rule," and the "General Prohibition," in sections 302(a) and 302(b)(1), respectively, of the Act. Topics addressed by this subpart include discriminatory denials of access or participation, landlord and tenant obligations, the provision of unequal benefits, indirect discrimination through contracting, the participation of individuals with disabilities in the most integrated setting appropriate to their needs, and discrimination based on association with individuals with disabilities. Subpart B also contains a number of "miscellaneous" provisions derived from title V of the Act that involve issues such as retaliation and coercion for asserting ADA rights, illegal drug use, insurance, and restrictions on smoking in places of public accommodation. Finally, subpart B contains additional general provisions regarding direct threats to health or safety, maintenance of accessible features of facilities and equipment, and the coverage of places of public accommodation located in private residences.

Subpart C, "Specific Requirements," addresses the "Specific Prohibitions" in section 302(b)(2) of the Act. Included in this subpart are topics such as discriminatory eligibility criteria; reasonable modifications in policies, practices or procedures; auxiliary aids and services; the readily achievable removal of barriers and alternatives to barrier removal; the extent to which inventories of accessible or special goods are required; seating in assembly areas; personal devices and services; and transportation provided by public accommodations. Subpart C also incorporates the requirements of section 309 of title III relating to examinations and courses.

Subpart D, "New Construction and Alterations," sets forth the requirements for new construction and alterations based on section 303 of the Act. It addresses such issues as what facilities are covered by the new construction requirements, what an alteration is, the application of the elevator exception, the path of travel obligations resulting from an alteration to a primary function area, requirements for commercial facilities located in private residences, and the application of alterations requirements to historic buildings and facilities.

Subpart E, "Enforcement," describes the Act's title III enforcement procedures, including private actions, as well as investigations and litigation conducted by the Attorney General. These provisions are based on sections 308 and 310(b) of the Act.

Subpart F, "Certification of State Laws or Local Building Codes," establishes procedures for the certification of State or local building accessibility ordinances that meet or exceed the new construction and alterations requirements of the ADA. These provisions are based on section 308(b)(1)(A)(ii) of the Act.

The section-by-section analysis of the rule explains in detail the provisions of each of these subparts.

The Department is also today publishing a final rule for the implementation and enforcement of subtitle A of title II of the Act. This rule

35546   Federal Register / Vol. 56, No. 144 / Friday, July 26, 1991 / Rules and Regulations

prohibits discrimination on the basis of disability against qualified individuals with disabilities in all services, programs, or activities of State and local government.

Regulatory Process Matters

This final rule has been reviewed by the Office of Management and Budget (OMB) under Executive Order 12291. The Department is preparing a regulatory impact analysis (RIA) of this rule, and the Architectural and Transportation Barriers Compliance Board is preparing an RIA for its Americans with Disabilities Act Accessibility Guidelines for Buildings and Facilities (ADAAG) that are incorporated in Appendix A of the Department's final rule. Draft copies of both preliminary RIAs are available for comment; the Department will provide copies of these documents to the public upon request. Commenters are urged to provide additional information as to the costs and benefits associated with this rule. This will facilitate the development of a final RIA by January 1, 1992.

The Department's RIA will evaluate the economic impact of the final rule. Included among those title III provisions that are likely to result in significant economic impact are the requirements for auxiliary aids, barrier removal in existing facilities, and readily accessible new construction and alterations. An analysis of the costs of these provisions will be included in the RIA.

The preliminary RIA prepared for the notice of proposed rulemaking contained all of the available information that would have been included in a preliminary regulatory flexibility analysis, had one been prepared under the Regulatory Flexibility Act, concerning the rule's impact on small entities. The final RIA will contain all of the information that is required in a final regulatory flexibility analysis, and will serve as such an analysis. Moreover, the extensive notice and comment procedure followed by the Department in the promulgation of this rule, which included public hearings, dissemination of materials, and provision of speakers to affected groups, clearly provided any interested small entities with the notice and opportunity for comment provided for under the Regulatory Flexibility Act procedures.

This final rule will preempt State laws affecting entities subject to the ADA only to the extent that those laws directly conflict with the statutory requirements of the ADA. Therefore, this rule is not subject to Executive Order 12612, and a Federalism Assessment is not required.

The reporting and recordkeeping requirements described in subpart F of the rule are considered to be information collection requirements as that term is defined by the Office of Management and Budget in 5 CFR part 1320. Accordingly, those information collection requirements have been submitted to OMB for review pursuant to the Paperwork Reduction Act.

Section-By-Section Analysis and Response to Comments

Subpart A—General

Section 36.101   Purpose

Section 36.101 states the purpose of the rule, which is to effectuate title III of the Americans with Disabilities Act of 1990. This title prohibits discrimination on the basis of disability by public accommodations, requires places of public accommodation and commercial facilities to be designed, constructed, and altered in compliance with the accessibility standards established by this part, and requires that examinations or courses related to licensing or certification for professional or trade purposes be accessible to persons with disabilities.

Section 36.102   Application

Section 36.102 specifies the range of entities and facilities that have obligations under the final rule. The rule applies to any public accommodation or commercial facility as those terms are defined in § 36.104. It also applies, in accordance with section 309 of the ADA, to private entities that offer examinations or courses related to applications, licensing, certification, or credentialing for secondary or postsecondary education, professional, or trade purposes. Except as provided in § 36.206, "Retaliation or coercion," this part does not apply to individuals other than public accommodations or to public entities. Coverage of private individuals and public entities is discussed in the preamble to § 36.206.

As defined in § 36.104, a public accommodation is a private entity that owns, leases or leases to, or operates a place of public accommodation. Section 36.102(b)(2) emphasizes that the general and specific public accommodations requirements of subparts B and C obligate a public accommodation only with respect to the operations of a place of public accommodation. This distinction is drawn in recognition of the fact that a private entity that meets the regulatory definition of public accommodation could also own, lease or lease to, or operate facilities that are not places of public accommodation. The rule would exceed the reach of the ADA

if it were to apply the public accommodations requirements of subparts B and C to the operations of a private entity that do not involve a place of public accommodation. Similarly, § 36.102(b)(3) provides that the new construction and alterations requirements of subpart D obligate a public accommodation only with respect to facilities used as, or designed or constructed for use as, places of public accommodation or commercial facilities.

On the other hand, as mandated by the ADA and reflected in § 36.102(c), the new construction and alterations requirements of subpart D apply to a commercial facility whether or not the facility is a place of public accommodation, or is owned, leased, leased to, or operated by a public accommodation.

Section 36.102(e) states that the rule does not apply to any private club, religious entity, or public entity. Each of these terms is defined in § 36.104. The exclusion of private clubs and religious entities is derived from section 307 of the ADA; and the exclusion of public entities is based on the statutory definition of public accommodation in section 301(7) of the ADA, which excludes entities other than private entities from coverage under title III of the ADA.

Section 36.103   Relationship to Other Laws

Section 36.103 is derived from sections 501 (a) and (b) of the ADA. Paragraph (a) provides that, except as otherwise specifically provided by this part, the ADA is not intended to apply lesser standards than are required under title V of the Rehabilitation Act of 1973, as amended (29 U.S.C. 790–794), or the regulations implementing that title. The standards of title V of the Rehabilitation Act apply for purposes of the ADA to the extent that the ADA has not explicitly adopted a different standard from title V. Where the ADA explicitly provides a different standard from section 504, the ADA standard applies to the ADA, but not to section 504. For example, section 504 requires that all federally assisted programs and activities be readily accessible to and usable by individuals with handicaps, even if major structural alterations are necessary to make a program accessible. Title III of the ADA, in contrast, only requires alterations to existing facilities if the modifications are "readily achievable," that is, able to be accomplished easily and without much difficulty or expense. A public accommodation that is covered under both section 504 and the ADA is still

35592   Federal Register / Vol. 56, No. 144 / Friday, July 26, 1991 / Rules and Regulations

children's facilities are not addressed by the Department's standards, and the building in question is a private elementary school, certification will not be effective for those features of the building to be used by children. And if the Department's regulations addressed equipment but the local code did not, a building's equipment would not be covered by the certification.

In addition, certification will be effective only for the particular edition of the code that is certified. Amendments will not automatically be considered certified, and a submitting official will need to reapply for certification of the changed or additional provisions.

Certification will not be effective in those situations where a State or local building code official allows a facility to be constructed or altered in a manner that does not follow the technical or scoping provisions of the certified code. Thus, if an official either waives an accessible element or feature or allows a change that does not provide equivalent facilitation, the fact that the Department has certified the code itself will not stand as evidence that the facility has been constructed or altered in accordance with the minimum accessibility requirements of the ADA. The Department's certification of a code is effective only with respect to the standards in the code; it is not to be interpreted to apply to a State or local government's application of the code. The fact that the Department has certified a code with provisions concerning waivers, variances, or equivalent facilitation shall not be interpreted as an endorsement of actions taken pursuant to those provisions.

The final rule includes a new § 36.608 concerning model codes. It was drafted in response to concerns raised by numerous commenters, many of which have been discussed under General comments (§ 36.406). It is intended to assist in alleviating the difficulties posed by attempting to certify possibly tens of thousands of codes. It is included in recognition of the fact that many codes are based on, or incorporate, model or consensus standards developed by nationally recognized organizations (e.g., the American National Standards Institute (ANSI); Building Officials and Code Administrators (BOCA) International; Council of American Building Officials (CABO) and its Board for the Coordination of Model Codes (BCMC); Southern Building Code Congress International (SBCCI)). While the Department will not certify or

"precertify" model codes, as urged by some commenters, it does wish to encourage the continued viability of the consensus and model code process consistent with the purposes of the ADA.

The new section therefore allows an authorized representative of a private entity responsible for developing a model code to apply to the Assistant Attorney General for review of the code. The review process will be informal and will not be subject to the procedures of §§ 36.602 through 36.607. The result of the review will take the form of guidance from the Assistant Attorney General as to whether and in what respects the model code is consistent with the ADA's requirements. The guidance will not be binding on any entity or on the Department; it will assist in evaluations of individual State or local codes and may serve as a basis for establishing priorities for consideration of individual codes. The Department anticipates that this approach will foster further cooperation among various government levels, the private entities developing standards, and individuals with disabilities.

List of Subjects in 28 CFR Part 36

Administrative practice and procedure, Alcoholism, Americans with disabilities, Buildings, Business and industry, Civil rights, Consumer protection, Drug abuse, Handicapped, Historic preservation, Reporting and recordkeeping requirements.

By the authority vested in me as Attorney General by 28 U.S.C. 509, 510, 5 U.S.C. 301, and section 306(b) of the Americans with Disabilities Act, Public Law 101-336, and for the reasons set forth in the preamble, Chapter I of title 28 of the Code of Federal Regulations is amended by adding a new part 36 to read as follows:

PART 36—NONDISCRIMINATION ON THE BASIS OF DISABILITY BY PUBLIC ACCOMMODATIONS AND IN COMMERCIAL FACILITIES

Subpart A—General

Authority: 5 U.S.C. 301; 28 U.S.C. 509, 510; Pub. L. 101–336, 42 U.S.C. 12186.

Source: *Federal Register*, **56:144 (July 26, 1991),** 35544, 35546, 35592.

NOTICES

Notices are miscellaneous announcements. These include, but are not limited to:

-Disclosures about the availability of environmental impact statements or intentions to prepare such documents.

-Grant application deadlines (Figure 10-3).

-Announcements of orders and decisions issued by agencies.

-Lists of Sunshine Act meetings. The Sunshine Act mandates that most agency meetings be open to the public. The times, places, and subjects of such meetings; and the names and phone numbers of relevant officials must appear in the *Federal Register*.

Figure 10-3
Federal Register
Notice of the Availability of Funds

25980   Federal Register   / Vol. 56, No. 108 / Wednesday, June 5, 1991 / Notices

DEPARTMENT OF JUSTICE

The Americans With Disabilities Act Technical Assistance Grants To Promote Voluntary Compliance With the Act

AGENCY: Office on the Americans with Disabilities Act (OADA), Coordination and Review Section, Civil Rights Division, U.S. Department of Justice.

ACTION: Notice of availability of funds and of solicitation for grant applications.

SUMMARY: The Office on the Americans with Disabilities Act of the United States Department of Justice (DOJ) announces the availability of up to $2.5 million to conduct projects to inform individuals with disabilities and covered entities about their rights and responsibilities under titles II and III of the Americans with Disabilities Act of 1990 (ADA), and to facilitate voluntary compliance with the regulations implementing titles II and III of the ADA. Grants will be awarded to selected applicants who propose cost-effective and efficient approaches of disseminating information, and producing voluntary compliance with the requirements of the ADA. Proposals should focus on encouraging voluntary compliance to reduce the need to file complaints or conduct litigation. DOJ encourages covered entities and persons with disabilities to work together to achieve compliance on a voluntary basis and will favor solicitations for grant funds that are joint ventures. It is anticipated that grants awarded will range in size from $85,000 to $200,000.

DATES: All applications must be received by the close of business (5:30 p.m. EDT) on July 22, 1991.

ADDRESSES: Applications shall be submitted to the Office on the Americans with Disabilities Act, 320 First Street NW., room 854, Washington DC 20035.

FOR FURTHER INFORMATION CONTACT: James D. Bennett or Philip L. Breen, Office on the Americans with Disabilities Act, Civil Rights Division, U.S. Department of Justice, P.O. Box 66118, Washington, DC 20035–6118 at (202) 307–2220 or (202) 307–2226, respectively, or (202) 514–0383 (TDD). This notice and other related information, with exception of standard forms, is available in accessible formats, i.e., braille, large print, audiotape, electronic file, computer disk, and electronic bulletin board (202) 514–6193.

BACKGROUND: On July 26, 1990, President Bush signed into law the landmark Americans with Disabilities Act of 1990, which provides

comprehensive civil rights protections to individuals with disabilities in the areas of employment, public accommodations, transportation, State and local government services, and telecommunications.

The Americans with Disabilities Act provides individuals with disabilities civil rights protections that are parallel to those provided to individuals on the basis of race, color, national origin, sex, and religion. Title II of the ADA prohibits discrimination on the basis of disability in State and local government services. Title III prohibits discrimination on the basis of disability in public accommodations such as hotels, restaurants, theaters, and shopping centers, and in commercial facilities such as factories and office buildings.

Section 506 of the ADA requires the Department to render technical assistance to individuals and entities that have rights or duties under title II (subtitle A) (State and local government services) and title III (public accommodations). Under section 506(d), the Department of Justice has the authority to award grants to individuals and to nonprofit entities for the purpose of providing technical assistance.

Note that the term "covered entities" is used to refer to all businesses, institutions, State and local governments, and other organizations that have duties under titles II and III of the ADA.

PROGRAM DESCRIPTION: The program is designed to develop and implement cost-effective and efficient approaches for disseminating information about the rights of individuals and responsibilities of covered entities, and to bring about compliance with the ADA on a voluntary basis. Proposals should address the four key elements of the program discussed below.

I. Targeted Populations and Issues

The activities conducted under the grant should be directed to persons with disabilities, operators of public accommodations and commercial facilities, State or local governmental entities providing public services, or a combination of these three groups. Proposals should define the characteristics of the population group(s) targeted by describing such factors as location, disability, type of governmental unit, or business type.

The Department is particularly interested in soliciting applications that focus on developing methods for making readily achievable accessibility modifications and providing a full range of auxiliary aids in six types of covered entities:

- Restaurants;
- Hotels and motels;
- Retail stores;
- Hospitals and health care facilities;
- Daycare centers; and
- Places of assembly (e.g. stadiums, theaters, and convention centers.)

In addition, the Department encourages applications that address:

- The training of law enforcement personnel so that they more effectively interact with persons with epilepsy or other disabilities, whose behavior is sometimes mistakenly interpreted as disorderly conduct induced by drug or alcohol use; or
- The provision of auxiliary aids and modifications that will enable persons with disabilities to participate in courses and examinations.

Applicants should explain their reasons for targeting particular populations and issues. Applicants must submit information that demonstrates that they have access to the targeted population and that the applicant can effectively reach the targeted population. Applicants are encouraged to address how businesses and persons with disabilities can be involved jointly in reaching the targeted population.

II. Program Strategy

Proposals must discuss the components of the program strategy, detail the reasons supporting the choice of each component, and explain how each component will contribute to the achievement of the overall objective of cost-effective and efficient dissemination of information and compliance assistance to the targeted population. Discussions of the strategy and supporting rationale should be clear, concise, and based on sound evidence and reasoning.

For most entities that are covered by titles II and III of the ADA, the ADA becomes effective on January 26, 1992. In anticipation of the effective date, DOJ wants accurate information and useful technical assistance to be made available to covered entities and persons with disabilities as soon as possible. Applicants should describe how they will reduce startup time and begin making information and assistance available soon after the grant award date. Start-up of various grant activities might be staggered to allow the applicant to concentrate on getting initial activities going quickly.

Although not required, several program activities are suggested.

- *Achieving specific cases of voluntary compliance.* Applicants may focus their attention on providing information to individual covered

Source: *Federal Register,* **56:108 (June 5, 1991), 25980.**

LOCATING INFORMATION IN THE *FEDERAL REGISTER*

FEDERAL REGISTER INDEX

The *Federal Register Index*[24] is a monthly publication. Cumulations cover January to date. The December issue is the annual *Index*. Organization is by agencies. Presidential materials appear under Presidential Documents. Figure 10-4 shows that information is separated by rules, proposed rules, and notices. References refer to *Federal Register* page numbers. A table at the end of the *Index*, *Federal Register* Pages and Dates, translates page numbers into dates of publication, making it easier to locate information (Figure 10-5).

Figure 10-4
Federal Register Index
Subject Index

Justice Department

See also Antitrust Division; Drug Enforcement Administration; Federal Bureau of Investigation; Federal Prison Industries, Inc.; Foreign Claims Settlement Commission; Immigration and Naturalization Service; Justice Assistance Bureau; Justice Programs Office; Justice Statistics Bureau; Juvenile Justice and Delinquency Prevention Office; National Institute of Corrections; National Institute of Justice; Parole Commission; Prisons Bureau; risons Bureau; Victims of Crime Office

RULES

Acquisition regulations:
Contracting officers selection, appointment, and termination, bureau certification of quarterly reports, etc., 26340
Contracting officers technical representatives; eligibility standards, 37859
Administration functions, practices, and procedures:
Anti-Drug Abuse Act; implementation—
Possession of controlled substances; civil penalties assessment, 1086
Americans with Disabilities Act; implementation:
Nondiscrimination on basis of disability—
Public accommodations and commercial facilities, 35544
State and local government services, 35694
Federal officers and employees; protective coverage under Federal criminal law:
Tennessee Valley Authority and National Drug Control Policy Office, 32327

PROPOSED RULES

Americans with Disabilities Act; implementation:
Nondiscrimination on basis of disability—
Public accommodations and in commercial facilities, 7452, 7494
State and local government services, 8538
Child Protection Restoration and Penalties Enhancement Act of 1990; recordkeeping provisions, 29914
Criminal justice information systems:
FBI system; inclusion of juvenile records, 25642
Federal claims collection:
Salary and administrative offset, 49729
Tax refund offset, 8734
Privacy Act; implementation, 44049, 48469, 50833

NOTICES

Agency information collection activities under OMB review, 1211, 5423, 9977, 13184, 20445, 24412, 35876, 40346, 41132, 41567, 42359, 47806, 50349, 50928, 55931, 55935, 56092, 56240, 56423, 57532, 64274, 64645, 64805, 65102, 66453
Financial Institutions Anti-Fraud Enforcement Act; agent for declarations received, 22738
Grants and cooperative agreements; availability, etc.:
Americans with Disabilities Act; technical assistance program, 25980
Immigration related employment discrimination; public education, 28769
Prejudice and bigotry related crimes; projects to combat and respond to crimes, 27269

Source: *Federal Register Index*, **1991 ed., 93-94.**

Figure 10-5
Federal Register Index
Table of *Federal Register* Pages and Dates

3759–3960	31	(21)		29559–29888	28	(125)
3961–4172	Feb. 1	(22)		29889–30306	July 1	(126)
4173–4522	4	(23)		30307–30482	2	(127)
4523–4706	5	(24)		30483–30678	3	(128)
4707–4926	6	(25)		30679–30856	5	(129)
4927–5150	7	(26)		30857–31042	8	(130)
5151–5304	8	(27)		31043–31304	9	(131)
5305–5646	11	(28)		31305–31532	10	(132)
5647–5738	12	(29)		31533–31854	11	(133)
5739–5922	13	(30)		31855–32060	12	(134)
5923–6260	14	(31)		32061–32318	15	(135)
6261–6548	15	(32)		32319–32498	16	(136)
6549–6788	19	(33)		32499–32950	17	(137)
6789–6938	20	(34)		32951–33188	18	(138)
6939–7298	21	(35)		33189–33366	19	(139)
7299–7550	22	(36)		33367–33702	22	(140)
7551–7782	25	(37)		33703–33838	23	(141)
7783–8100	26	(38)		33839–34002	24	(142)
8101–8256	27	(39)		34003–34140	25	(143)
8257–8680	28	(40)		34141–35798	26	(144)
8681–8904	Mar. 1	(41)		35799–35996	29	(145)
				35997–36078	30	(146)
24333–24670	30	(104)		36079–36722	31	(147)
24671–25004	31	(105)		36723–36996	Aug. 1	(148)
25005–25344	June 3	(106)		36997–37138	2	(149)
25345–25608	4	(107)		37139–37266	5	(150)
25609–25992	5	(108)		37267–37452	6	(151)
25993–26322	6	(109)		37453–37640	7	(152)
26323–26588	7	(110)				
26589–26758	10	(111)				
26759–26894	11	(112)				
26895–27188	12	(113)				
27189–27402	13	(114)				
27403–27686	14	(115)				

Source: *Federal Register Index* 1991 ed., 155.

Test your understanding of the *Federal Register Index* and the table of *Federal Register* Pages and Dates: The following questions relate to Figures 10-4 and 10-5.

1. A. On what page of the *Federal Register* can you find regulations prohibiting discrimination in commercial facilities against people with disabilities?

(35544)

B. When was this printed in the *Federal Register*?

(July 26, 1991, issue #144)

C. Identify the relevant part(s) of Figure 10-4 that refer to the related proposed regulations. When and on what pages of the *Federal Register* was this information printed?

(pages 7452 and 7494; both were printed on February 22, 1991, issue #36)

2. A. Identify the part of Figure 10-4 that announces the availability of a grant for technical assistance relating to the Americans With Disabilities Act.

B. Is this a rule, a proposed rule, or a notice?

(Notice)

C. When was this printed in the *Federal Register* and on what page?

(June 5, 1991; page 25980, issue #108)

LOCATING INFORMATION IN THE CODE OF FEDERAL REGULATIONS

Rules in the *Code of Federal Regulations* are identical to those in the *Federal Register* with two exceptions. The *C.F.R.* and *C.F.R.* citations to the *Federal Register* exclude preambles. The source note in Figure 10-6 indicates that the text of the regulation begins on page 35,592 of the *Federal Register*, but the *Federal Register Index* in Figure 10-4 cites page 35,544. The preamble accounts for this 48 page difference.

Figure 10-6
Code of Federal Regulations

PART 36—NONDISCRIMINATION ON THE BASIS OF DISABILITY BY PUBLIC ACCOMMODATIONS AND IN COMMERCIAL FACILITIES

Subpart A—General

Sec.
36.101 Purpose.
36.102 Application.
36.103 Relationship to other laws.
36.104 Definitions.

Sec.
36.105—36.199 [Reserved]

Subpart B—General Requirements

36.201 General.
36.202 Activities.
36.203 Integrated settings.
36.204 Administrative methods.
36.205 Association.
36.206 Retaliation or coercion.

Sec.
Subpart F—Certification of State Laws or Local Building Codes

36.601 Definitions.
36.602 General rule.
36.603 Filing a request for certification.
36.604 Preliminary determination.
36.605 Procedure following preliminary determination of equivalency.
36.606 Procedure following preliminary denial of certification.
36.607 Effect of certification.
36.608 Guidance concerning model codes.
APPENDIX A TO PART 36—STANDARDS FOR ACCESSIBLE DESIGN
APPENDIX B TO PART 36—PREAMBLE TO REGULATION ON NONDISCRIMINATION ON THE BASIS OF DISABILITY BY PUBLIC ACCOMMODATIONS AND IN COMMERCIAL FACILITIES (PUBLISHED JULY 26, 1991)

AUTHORITY: 5 U.S.C. 301; 28 U.S.C. 509, 510; Pub. L. 101-336, 42 U.S.C. 12186.

SOURCE: 56 FR 35592, July 26, 1991, unless otherwise noted.

Source: *Code of Federal Regulations*, 28 C.F.R. 36 (1992), 457-8.

327

C.F.R. INDEX AND FINDING AIDS

The annual *C.F.R. Index and Finding Aids*[25] indexes the *C.F.R.* Information is arranged by agency names and subject headings. Reference to the rule illustrated in Figure 10-2 is reproduced below (Figure 10-7).

Figure 10-7
C.F.R. Index and Finding Aids

Individuals with disabilities

See also Blind
  Disability benefits
  Education of individuals with
   disabilities
  Medicaid
  Medicare
  Public assistance programs
  Supplemental Security Income (SSI)
  Vocational rehabilitation
Acquisition regulations, accessibility of
 meetings
 Federal Emergency Management Agency,
  48 CFR 4426
 Health and Human Services Department,
  48 CFR 370
Adult day care food program, 7 CFR 226
Americans with Disabilities Act
 Accessibility guidelines for buildings and
  facilities, 36 CFR 1191
 Accessibility guidelines for transportation
  vehicles, 36 CFR 1192
 Accessibility specifications for
  transportation vehicles, 49 CFR 38
 Equal Employment Opportunity
  Commission procedural regulations,
  29 CFR 1601
 Nondiscrimination on basis of disability
  by public accommodations and in
  commercial facilities, 28 CFR 36

Source: *C.F.R. Index and Finding Aids,* **1994 ed., 394.**

Test your understanding of the *C.R.F. Index*:

1. Identify the relevant part of Figure 10-7 that refers to the regulation seen in Figure 10-2.

       (Nondiscrimination on basis of
       disability.... 28 *C.F.R.* 36)

2.   Decipher the notation: 28 *C.F.R.* 36.

(Code of Federal Regulations,
Title 28, part 36)

AGENCY-PREPARED INDEXES:

Although not required to do so, agencies sometimes index their regulations. These indexes are sometimes different from the *C.F.R. Index.* Consult the second section of the *C.F.R. Index and Finding Aids* for a List of
Agency-Prepared Indexes Appearing In Individual *C.F.R.* Volumes.

TABLES:

The *C.F.R. Index and Finding Aids* include two tables:

Table 1, Parallel Table of Authorities and Rules: It lists statutes and
Presidential documents that provide authorities for rules. Most laws have
U.S.C. citations. However, those not compiled into the *U.S.C.* are cited by
Statutes at Large references. Table 1 indicates that the authority for 28 *C.F.R.*
36 is provided by 42 *U.S.C.* 12186 (Figure 10-8).

Figure 10-8
C.F.R. Index and Finding Aids
Table 1, Parallel Table of Authorities and Rules

42 U.S.C.—Continued	CFR
10004	42 Part 75
10007—10008	21 Part 5
10101—10270	40 Part 191
10101	10 Part 72
11421	34 Part 441
11461—11464	45 Part 1080
11472	45 Part 1080
11501—11505	24 Part 596
11901 et seq	24 Part 961
12101 et seq	12 Part 517
12101—12213	49 Parts 27, 37, 38
12111—12117	29 Part 1601
12116	29 Part 1630
12117	29 Parts 1602, 1641
	41 Part 60–742
12134	28 Part 35
12186	28 Part 36
12204	36 Parts 1191, 1192
12501	45 Parts 2500–2506

Source: *C.F.R. Index and Finding Aids,* **1994 ed., 830.**

Test your understanding of Table 1:

1.   Identify the relevant sections of the *Federal Register* (Figure
10-2) and the *C.F.R.* (Figure 10-6) that indicate the regulation is based upon authority provided by 42 *U.S.C.* 12186.

2.   In Figure 10-8, where do regulations whose authority is provided by 42 *U.S.C.* 11472 appear in the *C.F.R.*?

(45 C.F.R. 1080)

3.   In Figure 10-8, where do regulations whose authority is provided by 42 *U.S.C.* 12113 appear in the *C.F.R.*?

(42 U.S.C. 12111-12117 is the authority for all rules cited in 29 C.F.R. 1601.)

Table 2, Presidential Documents Included or Cited In Currently Effective Rules: No longer published. Information in the former Table 2 now appears in Table 1.

Table 3, Acts Requiring Publication In The Federal Register: Lists statutes that require specific information to be included in the *Federal Register*. It provides *U.S. Code, Statutes at Large,* and public law citations.

LOCATING CURRENT REGULATIONS

Researchers must be able to easily determine new regulations that amend the *Code of Federal Regulations*. Remember, the *C.F.R.* is published annually, yet new and amended regulations appear daily in the *Federal Register*.

List of C.F.R. Sections Affected (LSA):

The monthly *List of C.F.R. Sections Affected (L.S.A.)*[26] shows where new and amended rules are incorporated into the *Code of Federal Regulations*. Since different titles of the *C.F.R.* are updated each quarter, pay close attention to time periods covered in each *L.S.A.* The covers indicate appropriate information (Figure 10-9).

Figure 10-9
List of Sections Affected
Cover

LSA

List of CFR Sections Affected

March 1994

**Save this issue for Titles
17–27 (Annual)**

Title 1–16
Changes January 3, 1994
through March 31, 1994

Title 17–27
Changes April 1, 1993
through March 31, 1994

Title 28–41
Changes July 1, 1993
through March 31, 1994

Title 42–50
Changes October 1, 1993
through March 31, 1994

Source: *List of Sections Affected,* **March 1994.**

Figure 10-10 shows how Title 28 was changed between July 1993 and March 1994. 28 *C.F.R.* 36, the title and section examined above, was amended on page 2,675 of the *Federal Register*.

Figure 10-10
List of Sections Affected
Changes July 1, 1993 Through March 31, 1994

TITLE 28—JUDICIAL
ADMINISTRATION

Chapter I—Department of Justice
(Parts 0—199)

```
11 Authority citation revised......... 51223
11.10—11.12  (Subpart  C)  Re-
    vised.............................................. 51223
14 Appendix amended...................... 36867
16.82 Added....................................... 41038
23 Revised........................................48452
36 Authority citation revised.......... 2675
36.406 Amended................................2675
36 Appendix A amended................. 2675
42.700—42.736      (Subpart     I)
    Added.......................................... 6560
44.101 (a)(5) revised...................... 59948
44.200 (a)(2) and (3) revised.......... 59948
44.300 (c) revised............................ 59948
51.24 (b) amended............................ 51225
55.1 Amended....................................35372
55.6 Revised.....................................35372
55.7 (b) amended.............................. 35373
55.13 (b) amended............................ 35373
55.17 Amended................................. 35373
55.20 (c) amended............................35373
55 Appendix revised.........................35373
    Appendix corrected...................... 36516
```

NOTE: **Boldface page numbers indicate 1993 changes.**

Source: *List of Sections Affected*, **March 1994, 81.**

A Table of *Federal Register* Issue Pages and Dates, similar to that shown in Figure 10-5, appears in the back of the *L.S.A.*, making it easier to locate information in the *Federal Register*. The *L.S.A.* also includes a Parallel Table of Authorities and Rules similar to that seen in Figure 10-8.

Test your understanding of the *List of Sections Affected*: The following questions refer to Figure 10-10.

1. How was 28 *C.F.R.* 23 affected between July 1, 1993 and March 31, 1994?

(Information was revised.)

2.   Where is this change printed in the *Federal Register*?

(1993, page 48,452)

3.   Why does Figure 10-10 skip from part 23 to part 36?

(Parts 24 through 35 were not
affected during this period).

C.F.R. PARTS AFFECTED:

The *List of Sections Affected* described above only goes through March 1994. Consult the C.F.R. Parts Affected During (Month), which is published daily in the *Federal Register*, to locate more current information. Each issue provides updates from the beginning of the month to date. The April 29, 1994 *Federal Register*, the last one published that month, describes all actions relating to 28 C.F.R. 36 for the entire month (Figure 10-11). Numbers in the right hand column are *Federal Register* page numbers. Unless otherwise noted, all citations refer to final rules. A list of *Federal Register* page numbers and corresponding dates like that seen in Figure 10-5 is also provided. This C.F.R. Parts Affected During (Month) is different from a similar table printed at the beginning of the *Federal Register*, C.F.R. Parts Affected In This Issue.

Figure 10-11
Federal Register
C.F.R. *Parts Affected* During April, 1994

27 CFR
Proposed Rules:
4..15878
6..21698
8..21698
10..21698
11..21698
28 CFR
36..17442
522..16406
540..15812
545......................15812, 16406
551..16406
Proposed Rules:
0..15880

Source: *Federal Register*, 59:82 (April 29, 1994), ii.

OTHER INDEXES TO REGULATIONS

CIS FEDERAL REGISTER INDEX

The *CIS Federal Register Index*[27] is the most comprehensive printed index to the *Federal Register*. Issues come out weekly and cumulations come out every five weeks and semiannually. It indexes all rules, interim rules, proposed rules, and notices. Meeting notices are excluded. The Index by

Subjects and Names and the Index by *C.F.R.* Section Numbers are especially useful.

INDEX BY SUBJECTS AND NAMES

The Index by Subjects and Names lists information under the most specific headings. Consequently, the numerous cross references to more specific terms are very important. Figure 10-12 illustrates index entries for the final rule shown in Figure 10-2.

Figure 10-12
CIS Federal Register Index
Index by Subjects and Names--Subject Heading

Disability insurance
  see also Old-Age, Survivors, and Disability
    Insurance
  see also Workers compensation
Disabled and handicapped persons
  Accessible Housing Month, Natl: Pres
    proclamation *(11/29/PD) 60893*
  Acq and procurement by GSA, regs revision:
    GSA–
      "Electronic office equipment accessibility"
      definition *(10/15/R) 51659*

  Medicaid community supported living arrangement
    svcs for developmentally disabled persons, State
    minimum protection rqmts estab: HCFA
    (9/24/IR) 48112
  Medicare benefit hosp ins premium payment and
    State buy-in agmt regs, revision: HCFA
    (8/12/R) 38074
  Medicare Part A uninsured aged and disabled hosp
    ins premium, revision: HCFA *(11/15/N) 58067*
  Motor carrier disabled passenger svc regs, revision:
    ICC *(11/5/PR) 56490*
  Public and commercial facility and licensing exam
    disabled person discrimination prohibition
    enforcement regs, estab: DOJ *(7/26/R) 35544*
  Public safety officer permanent and total disability
    benefits, authorization: DOJ *(10/3/PR) 50160*
  Runaway and homeless youth svcs grants, funding
    priorities: Children and Families Admin
    (10/9/N) 50916

Source: *CIS Federal Register Index,* **July 1-December 31, 1991 ed., 153. Reprinted with permission from** *CIS Federal Register Index.* **Copyright 1992 by Congressional Information Service, Inc. (Bethesda, MD). All rights reserved.**

All entries include annotated statements that describe their contents, *Federal Register* dates, types of documents indexed, and *Federal Register* page numbers. For example, the first entry in Figure 10-12 refers to page 60893 in the November 29 *Federal Register.* PD indicates that this is a Presidential document. Other common abbreviations include R (rule), IR (interim rule), PR (proposed rule), and N (notice).

Besides subject headings, the Index by Subjects and Names also includes names of laws, programs, companies, organizations, and states (Figure 10-13). Information pertaining to local areas appears under appropriate states. For example, regulations pertaining to Buffalo International Airport are under New York State. However, other regulations governing use of all airports are under relevant subject headings, not state names.

Figure 10-13
CIS Federal Register Index
Index by Subjects and Names--Subject Heading

American Yarn Spinners Association
Cotton yarn from Brazil, countervailing duty proceeding: ITA *(9/19/N) 47456*
Textile products from Thailand, countervailing duty proceeding: ITA *(10/23/N) 54838*
Yarns (noncontinuous noncellulosic) from Thailand, countervailing duty proceeding: ITA *(12/3/N) 61402*

American Yazaki Corp.
Foreign trade zone appls and actions: FTZB– Wayne Cty MI *(12/2/N) 61227*

Americans With Disabilities Act
Disability Employment Awareness Month, Natl: Pres proclamation *(10/10/PD) 51145*
Disabled accessibility of buildings and facilities, minimum stds revision: Architectural and Transportation Barriers Compliance Bd– Guidelines for DOJ stds, issuance *(7/26/R) 35408*
Disabled person accessibility to mass and para transit systems, regs revision: DOT *(9/6/R) 45584*
   Vehicle door height technical std implementation postponement *(12/9/R) 64214*
Disabled person discrimination in public and commercial facilities, and licensing exams, prohibition enforcement regs estab: DOJ *(7/26/R) 35544*
Disabled person discrimination in State and local govt svcs, prohibition enforcement regs estab: DOJ *(7/26/R) 35694*
Disabled person employment discrimination by govt contractors, complaint procedures estab: EEOC and Fed Contract Compliance Programs Office *(10/28/PR) 55578*
Disabled person employment discrimination, prohibition: EEOC *(7/26/R) 35726*
Disabled person employment discrimination, rptg and recordkeeping rqmts estab: EEOC *(7/26/R) 35753*
Disabled persons accessibility to transportation vehicles, minimum stds revision: Architectural and Transportation Barriers Compliance Bd– Guidelines for DOT stds, issuance *(9/6/R) 45530*
Disabled persons private industry employment status survey, estab: EEOC *(12/23/N) 66445*

Test your understanding of the Index by Subjects and Names: The following questions pertain to Figure 10-13.

1. Identify reference to the rule illustrated in Figure 10-2.

2. Information about discrimination against the disabled by government contractors appears in the *Federal Register* on October 28. What kind of a document is this?

    (Proposed rule)

3. Information pertaining to Brazilian yarn is in the *Federal Register* of September 19. What kind of a document is this?

    (Notice)

4. Figure 10-13 indicates that the information about Brazilian yarn pertains to the American Yarn Spinners Association. Are names of professional groups and names of companies indexed in the official *Federal Register Index*?

    (No; the official *Index* is limited to very selected subject headings and agencies)

INDEX BY *C.F.R.* SECTION NUMBERS

Information in the Index by *C.F.R.* Section Numbers is comparable to the *List of Sections Affected* and the *C.F.R.* Parts Affected section in the daily *Federal Register* (Figures 10-10 and 10-11).

CIS INDEX TO THE CODE OF FEDERAL REGULATIONS

The annual *CIS Index To The Code of Federal Regulations*[28] is much more comprehensive than the official *C.F.R. Index and Finding Aids*. Its four sections are described below.

SUBJECT INDEX

Indexing is under the most specific subject heading. Entries include ample cross references. Figure 10-14 refers to 28 *C.F.R.* 36, the rule illustrated in Figure 10-6. In Figure 10-14, NT refers to narrower terms or more specific cross references and RT refers to related terms.

Figure 10-14
CIS Index To The Code of Federal Regulations
Subject Index

HANDICAPPED PERSONS

SEE ALSO:
(NT) BLIND PERSONS;
DEAF PERSONS;
DEVELOPMENTALLY DISABLED PERSONS;
DISABLED EMPLOYEES;
DISABLED PERSONS;
DISABLED VETERANS;
RETARDED PERSONS
(RT) ARCHITECTURAL BARRIERS;
CLEARINGHOUSES PROGRAM;
EDUCATIONAL MEDIA AND DESCRIPTIVE VIDEOS
    LOAN SERVICE PROGRAM;
EMPLOYMENT CERTIFICATES;
GIFTED PERSONS;
HANDICAPPED ASSISTANCE LOANS;

-FACILITY CONSTRUCTION — AMERICAN NATIONAL STANDARDS
INSTITUTE STANDARDS
Minimum Guidelines and Requirements for Accessible Design [Illustrations,
    Tables] .... 36 CFR 1190
Americans With Disabilities Act (ADA) Accessibility Guidelines for Buildings and
    Facilities [Illustrations, Tables] .... 36 CFR 1191
-FACILITY CONSTRUCTION — CONSTRUCTION AND DESIGN
Program Accessibility .... 7 CFR 15b.16–.19
—   14 CFR 1251.300–.302
—   15 CFR 8b.16–.18
Program Accessibility .... 28 CFR 35.149–.151
Nondiscrimination on the Basis of Disability by Public Accomodations and in
    Commercial Facilities .... 28 CFR 36
Nondiscrimination on the Basis of Disability by Public Accommodations and in
    Commercial Facilities, Appendix A: Standards for Accessible Design
    .... 28 CFR 36, App.
Nondiscrimination on the Basis of Handicap in Programs and Activities Assisted
    or Conducted by the Department of Defense .... 32 CFR 56
Program Accessibility .... 34 CFR 104.21–.23
Minimum Guidelines and Requirements for Accessible Design [Illustrations,
    Tables] .... 36 CFR 1190

Source: *CIS Index To The Code of Federal Regulations*, **1993 ed., 1,471, 1,474**
Reprinted with permission from *CIS Index To The Code of Federal Regulations*.
Copyright 1993 by Congressional Information Service, Inc. (Bethesda, MD).
All rights reserved.

The Subject Index also includes industry standards that are either cited or reprinted in the *C.F.R.*, and names of industry and professional groups, laws, chemicals, drugs, and agencies. Construction standards adopted by the American National Standards Institute are cited in Figure 10-14.

GEOGRAPHIC INDEX

Regulations that affect special areas are in the Geographic Index. Figure 10-15 illustrates navigation rules pertaining to Buffalo Harbor and trade regulations relating to Bulgaria.

Figure 10-15
CIS Index To The Code of Federal Regulations
Geographic Index

BUFFALO HARBOR, NEW YORK
-ANCHORAGES
Special Anchorage Areas [Illustrations, Tables] .... 33 CFR 110.5–.129a
Anchorage Grounds [Tables] ....33 CFR 110.130–.255
-NAVIGATION RULES
Inland Waterways Navigation Regulations [Tables] .... 33 CFR 162
Navigation Regulations [Tables] .... 33 CFR 207

BUFFALO NATIONAL RIVER, ARKANSAS
USE: BUFFALO FORK RIVER, ARKANSAS

BUFFALO RIVER, NEW YORK
-DRAWBRIDGES
Specific Requirements ....33 CFR 117.51–.1107

BULGARIA
SEE ALSO:
(RT) EUROPE
-EXPORT CONTROLS
Special Country Policies and Provisions .... 15 CFR 785
-GRAPES — IMPORTS
. [Subpart] Fruits and Vegetables [Tables] .... 7 CFR 319.56 to .56–8
-IMPORTS — GRAPES
[Subpart] Fruits and Vegetables [Tables] .... 7 CFR 319.56 to .56–8
-IMPORTS — ORGANIC PACKING MATERIALS
[Subpart] Packing Materials .... 7 CFR 319.69 to .69–5
-IMPORTS — WHEAT
[Subpart] Wheat Diseases .... 7 CFR 319.59 to .59–2
-ORGANIC PACKING MATERIALS — IMPORTS
[Subpart] Packing Materials .... 7 CFR 319.69 to .69–5
-TRADE RESTRICTIONS — EXEMPTIONS AND EXCEPTIONS
Presidential Determination Number 92–30: Determination Under Section 402(d)(1)
of the Trade Act of 1974, as Amended—Continuation of Waiver Authority
.... 3 CFR, Adm. Order 92–30
-WHEAT — IMPORTS
[Subpart] Wheat Diseases .... 7 CFR 319.59 to .59–2

Source: *CIS Index To The Code of Federal Regulations*, **1993 ed., 3,246. Reprinted
with permission** *from CIS Index To The Code of Federal Regulations.* **Copyright
1993 by Congressional Information Service, Inc. (Bethesda, MD). All rights
reserved.**

Consult the Subject Index for regulations governing the use of all
harbors, including Buffalo's, and trade with all nations, including Bulgaria.

INDEX BY NEW AND REVISED *C.F.R.* SECTION NUMBERS

This section is comparable to the *List of Sections Affected*.

LIST OF DESCRIPTIVE HEADINGS

The List of Descriptive Headings is a detailed table of contents to the
C.F.R. Its organization is numerical by titles, chapters, subchapters, and
parts.

ELECTRONIC FORMATS OF THE *FEDERAL REGISTER* AND THE *C.F.R.*

GOVERNMENT PRINTING OFFICE ACCESS SYSTEM

The *Federal Register* and the *Unified Agenda of Federal Regulations* are available on the Internet through the GPO ACCESS system from January 1994 through the present. (http://www.access.gpo.gov/su_docs/aces/aaces002.html) The Sources of Additional Information section below describes the *Unified Agenda*. Consult Chapter 7 for basic information about searching GPO ACCESS. Chart 10-1 describes unique features of searching these databases.

Chart 10-1
Searching the *Federal Register* and the *Unified Agenda of Federal Regulations* on GPO ACCESS

Types of Searches	Examples
Search for Presidential Documents.	**Presidential=disabled AND discrimination** locates Presidential documents about the disabled and discrimination.
Search for proposed rules.	**Proposed=disabled AND discrimination** locates proposed rules about the disabled and discrimination.
Search for rules.	**Rules=disabled AND discrimination** locates final rules about the disabled and discrimination.
Search for notices. Search for dates.	**Notices=disabled AND date>July 1, 1995** retrieves information about the disabled published after 7/1/95. (Use date=7/1/95 to locate information published on that date and date<7/1/95 to retrieve information published earlier).
Search by agency names.	Enter agency names as you would subjects. (e.g.: "Environmental Protection Agency")
Search by C.F.R. parts.	**"28 cfr part 36"** retrieves references to 28 C.F.R. 36. When searching the Federal Register, be certain to insert the word part. Use **"28 cfr 36"** to search the Uniform Agenda.
Search by C.F.R. parts affected.	**"Parts affected" AND date=1/31/96** retrieves both the list of parts affected during January 1996 and the list of parts affected on January 31, 1996.
Search by page number. (Page numbers are unavailable in the 1994 database)	**"Page 1000"** retrieves that page.

Figure 10-16 displays a search form GPO ACCESS offers for searching the *Federal Register* at http://www.access.gpo.gov/su_docs/aces/aces140.html.

Figure 10-16
GPO ACCESS
Federal Register **Search Form**

```
Federal Register Issue:

    [X]1996 Federal Register      [ ]1995 Federal Register

Federal Register Sections (If you select none, all sections will be
searched, but you may select one or more sections):

    [ ] Contents and Preliminary Pages    [ ] Presidential Documents
    [ ] Final Rules and Regulations       [ ] Sunshine Act Meetings*
    [ ] Proposed Rules                    [ ] Reader Aids
    [ ] Notices                           [ ] Corrections


    ──────────────────────────────────────────────────────────
    * As of March 1, 1996, Sunshine Act Meetings were incorporated into
    the Notices section of the Federal Register.


    ──────────────────────────────────────────────────────────
    Issue Date (Enter either a range of dates or a specific date in the
    format mm/dd/yy):

    Date Range: From _____ to _____

OR

    (*) ON ( ) BEFORE ( ) AFTER _____

    ──────────────────────────────────────────────────────────
    Search Terms:
    ──────────────────────────────────────────────────────────
```

Figure 10-17 illustrates the results of a search in the 1995 *Federal Register* for proposed regulations about discrimination against the disabled.

Figure 10-17
GPO ACCESS *Federal Register* **Database**
Results of a Search

```
                        GPO Access Database Search Results (p2 of 4)

[1]

fr15de95P Business Loan Programs
        Size: 355070 , Score: 1000 , TEXT , PDF , SUMMARY

[2]

fr12my95P Single Family Rural Housing Loans
        Size: 228260 , Score: 858 , TEXT , PDF , SUMMARY

[3]

fr18my95P Developmental Disabilities Program
        Size: 142705 , Score: 559 , TEXT , PDF , SUMMARY

[4]

fr14mr95P Housing for Older Persons; Defining Significant Facilities
        and
-- press space for next page --
```

At the beginning of each entry in Figure 10-17, the results indicate the source, the date, and the type of material retrieved. For example, fr15dec95P represents the following:

fr	*Federal Register* (UA indicates the *Unified Agenda*.)
15dec95	December 15, 1995
P	Proposed regulation. Other abbreviations include R--final rule; E--Presidential document; N--notice; C--Table of Contents; S--Sunshine Act Meeting; A Reader Aids--*C.F.R.* Parts Affected During (month); and X--corrections.

Users can view either text, PDF, or summary versions of the information.

OTHER ELECTRONIC SOURCES

Chart 10-2 summarized online commercial versions of the *Federal Register* and the *Code of Federal Regulations* and Chart 10-3 summarizes CD-ROM editions.

Chart 10-2
Online Sources of the *Federal Register* **and the** *Code of Federal Regulations*

CQ Washington Alert	Federal Register (1993-current date). Code of Federal Regulations (current edition)
Counterpoint Publishing	Federal Register (1990-current date). Code of Federal Regulations (Current issue updated monthly).
Dialog (file # 136)	Federal Register--file 669 (1988-current). Federal Register Abstracts--file 136, (1977-current). Brief summaries abstract information.
Legi-Slate	Federal Register (1993-current) Information is updated within 24 hours.
Lexis/Nexis	Federal Register--Libraries: CODES, EXEC, GENFED, MILITRY, and REALTY; File: FEDREG (July 1, 1980-current). Code of Federal Regulations--Libraries (CODES, EXEC, GENFED, MILITRY, and REALTY); File: CFR Chapter six, "Administrative Law," in Lexis For Law Students describes the Federal Register and the Code of Federal Regulations. (Steven L. Emanuel, 2nd ed. (Emanual Law Outlines, Inc., 1995)
Westlaw	Federal Register--FR database, (July 1, 1980-current). Two related files, PRES and FR-TOC, include Presidential documents published in the Federal Register and the Federal Register's Table of Contents. The Federal Register Abstracts, the Dialog database discussed above, is also available from Westlaw. Code of Federal Regulations--CFR database (current edition). Historical editions beginning with 1984 are in files CFR84, CFR85, CFR86,...

Chart 10-3
CD-ROM Sources of the *Federal Register* **and the** *Code of Federal Regulations*

Counterpoint Publishing	CD/FR: Federal Register (July 1990-weekly/monthly updates, depending upon subscription).
	CD/CFR Code of Federal Regulations (Updated monthly/quarterly, depending upon subscription).
Dialog	Federal Register: Dialog on Disk (1990-weekly).
IHS Health Information, Inc.	Federal Register on CD-ROM (1990-weekly).
ProInfo	Federal Register Disk (1990-weekly/monthly, depending upon subscription).
	U.S. Code of Federal Regulations (CFR) (quarterly updates) Subscriptions can be purchased for all 50 titles or selected ones.

SOURCES OF ADDITIONAL INFORMATION

Federal Regulatory Directory. Washington, D.C.: Congressional Quarterly, Inc., 1980-annual.

Considers the regulatory process in a non-technical manner. Agency profiles describe responsibilities; histories and recent backgrounds; powers and authorities; and relevant publications. Directory information includes names and phone numbers of Freedom of Information Officers and other relevant agency personnel; Congressional committees that deal with similar issues; and statutory and regulatory authorities. The introduction describes the regulatory process in historical context. The comprehensive index includes subjects, agency names, and popular names of acts. Appended material describes how the *Federal Register* and the *Code of Federal Regulations* are best used.

Kerwin, Cornelius. *Rulemaking: How Government Agencies Write Law and Make Policy*. Washington, D.C.: CQ Press, 1994.

Examines the history and politics of rulemaking. Kerwin considers the management of regulatory activities by agencies; public participation; oversight by the President, Congress, and the public; theories of rulemaking; and proposals to reform the rulemaking process. Emphasis is upon the use of rules for administrative policy making, and applications of legal, technical, and political information.

Regulatory Impact Analysis.

E.O. 12,291 requires that agencies submit Regulatory Impact Analysis to the Office of Management and Budget before promulgating significant regulations. Significant rules are those having an annual effect of one hundred million dollars or more on the economy. They also create major cost increases to either consumers, industry, government, or geographic regions. The statements describe the potential cost/benefits and indicate why alternative approaches were not selected. Regulatory Impact Analysis are not published, but are available to the public under the Freedom of Information Act.

Regulatory Program of the United States Government. Washington, D.C.: GPO, 1985/86-annual. SuDoc number: PrEx2.30:.

Describes the administration's regulatory program. President Reagan's E.O. 12,498 requires its publication. Agencies summarize the policies, goals, and objectives they expect to accomplish through rulemaking during the coming year. Data include names of programs; problems the regulations address; justifications for federal actions; types of approaches the agencies will use; projected costs and benefits; and agency contacts.

Reimer, Rita Ann and David R. Siddall. *Federal Regulation: Administrative Rules and Rulemaking* (79-30 A). Washington, D.C.: Congressional Research Service, 1979. Reprinted in: *Major Studies and Issue Briefs of the Congressional Research Service, 1978-79 Supplement*. Washington, D.C.: University Publications of America, 1979. Reel 4, frame 309.

Reimer, Rita Ann. *How To Do Research Using the Federal Administrative Regulations* (79-223 A). Washington, D.C.: Congressional Research Service, 1979. Reprinted in: *Major Studies and Issue Briefs of the Congressional Research Service, 1979-80 Supplement*. Washington, D.C.: University Publications of America, 1980. Reel 3, frame 476.

Although a bit dated, both sources still give good surveys of the regulatory process that emphasize how to locate regulations. The author provides illustrations from the *Federal Register* and related sources, and includes a sample search.

Unified Agenda of Federal Regulations. Published in the *Federal Register* semiannually since 1983 in April and October. Available on GPO ACCESS (1994+).

The *Unified Agenda* is very similar to the *Regulatory Program* described above. The Regulatory Flexibility Act requires that agencies publish semiannual agendas that describe prospective rulemaking. Organization is by agencies. Information includes titles of regulations; legal authorities; C.F.R. sections affected; deadlines and timetables; summaries of alternative approaches and costs; and agency contacts. Entries also list entities at any level of government or in the private sector affected by the regulations.

U.S. Administrative Conference of the United States. *A Guide To Federal Agency Rulemaking* by Benjamin W. Mintz and Nancy G. Miller. 2nd ed. Washington, D.C.: GPO, 1991. SuDoc number: Y3.Ad6:8R86/991.

Mintz defines types of rulemaking activities and explains how the courts interpret them. Part 1 summarizes the subject; part 2 describes the statutory framework; part 3 considers informal rulemaking; and part 4 discusses judicial review. The author provides footnotes and excerpts from cases. This title is for use by agency officials, attorneys, scholars, and professionals working in fields that are heavily regulated. Korwin's book described above is a better choice for laymen and informed citizens.

U.S. Office of the Federal Register. *Document Drafting Handbook*. Rev. ed. Washington, D.C.: GPO, 1991. SuDoc number: AE2.108:D65/991.

The *Handbook* is for use by agency officials responsible for preparing texts of regulations. Definitions and illustrations describe different kinds of regulations and information included in the *Federal Register*. The "Checklist of Questions To Consider When Writing Supplementary Information" (p. 16) is an excellent list of questions any researcher studying public policy issues ought to answer. The final chapter reprints laws governing publication of information in the *Federal Register*.

U.S. Office of the Federal Register. *The Federal Register: What It Is and How To Use It, A Guide for the User of the Federal Register--Code of Federal Regulations System*. Rev. ed. Washington, D.C.: GPO, 1992. SuDoc number: AE2.108:F31/2.

Explains and illustrates the *Federal Register* and the *Code of Federal Regulations* for the general public. The lucid text includes ample explanations and illustrations of all relevant indexes and finding aids.

CONCLUSION

Chart 10-4 summarizes the *Federal Register;* the *Code of Federal Regulations;* and their related indexes and electronic counterparts.

Chart 10-4
Summary of *Federal Register, Code of Federal Regulations,*
and Related Indexes and Electronic Sources

	Federal Register	Code of Federal Regulations
Scope	Presidential documents (executive orders, proclamations, memorandum, determinations), proposed rules, final rules, and notices.	Final regulations and Presidential documents currently in effect.
Frequency	Monday-Friday except on legal holidays.	Annual
Organization	Alphabetical by agencies.	50 titles organized under broad subject categories
Printed Indexes	Federal Register Index--arranged by names of agencies. "C.F.R. Parts Affected"--included in the daily Federal Register. Lists C.F.R. sections affected by the Federal Register from the beginning of the month to date. CIS Federal Register Index-- arranged by subjects, names, and C.F.R. title and section numbers.	C.F.R. Index and Finding Aids-- arranged by names of agencies and subjects. The "Parallel Table of Authorities and Rules" lists U.S.C., Statute at Large, and Presidential document citations and corresponding C.F.R. references. List of C.F.R. Sections Affected-- arranged by C.F.R. titles and sections. CIS Index to the Code of Federal Regulations--Arranged by subjects and geography. The "Index by New and Revised C.F.R. Section Numbers" lists changes to the C.F.R. during the preceding year.
Electronic Sources	GPO ACCESS (See chapter 7 for information about basic search techniques and chart 10-1 for search tips unique to the Federal Register.) See charts 10-2 and 10-3 for a directory to commercial sources.	House Internet Law Library (http://www.pls.com:8001/his/cfr.html) See charts 10-2 and 10-3 for a directory to commercial sources.

Endnotes

1. See Veronica Maclay, "Selected Sources of United States Agency Decisions," *Government Publications Review*, 16:3 (May/June 1989), 271-301 for a comprehensive annotated list. Agencies are described, enabling legislation is cited, and both official sources and commercial loose leaf services are noted. See also Chapter 27, "Administrative Decisions," in Jean L. Sears and Marilyn Moody, *Using Government Information Sources: Print and Electronic*, 2nd ed. (Phoenix, AZ.: Oryx Press, 1994).

2. *Rulemaking: How Government Agencies Write Law and Make Policy* (Washington, D.C.: CQ Press, 1994), xi.

3. U.S. Congress. Senate. Committee on the Judiciary, *The Regulatory Reform Act*, (S. Rept. 97-284) 97th Cong., 1st sess. (Washington, D.C.: GPO, 1981), 7.

4. 1 *Stat.* 95. See Ronald D. Marble, "Federal Administrative Procedure Act of 1946," *Mississippi Law Journal* 20:1 (December 1948), 62-77 for a description of three statutes enacted during the 1st Congress, 1st session that provide for regulatory authority. (1 *Stat.* 29; 1 *Stat.* 55; and 1 *Stat.* 95)

5. *Federal Register* (Washington, D.C.: GPO, 1936-daily). SuDoc number: AE2.106:.

6. Lapeyre v. United States 84 *U.S.* 202-3 (1872). Cited in Randy S. Springer, "Gatekeeping and the *Federal Register*: An Analysis of the Publication Requirement of Section 552(a)(1)(D) of the Administrative Procedure Act," *Administrative Law Review*. 41:4 (Fall 1989), 535.

7. Panama Refining Co. v. Ryan, 293 *U.S.* 388 (1935). Cited in Springer, 535.

8. (Washington, D.C.: GPO, 1938-1948 irregularly; 1949-annual). SuDoc number: AE2.106/3:.

9. Unpublished, untitled paper. Provided to Edward Herman by Caralyn Hill, Office of the Federal Register, August 13, 1993.

10. "Equal Opportunity In Housing" (E.O. 11,063) *Federal Register* 27:228 (November 24, 1962), 11527; "Equal Opportunity Employment" (E.O. 11,246) *Federal Register* 30:187 (September 28, 1965), 12319.

11. "Authorizing the Secretary of War to Prescribe Military Areas" (E.O. 9066) *Federal Register* 7:38 (February 25, 1942), 1407.

12. Directives issued during the Reagan and Bush administrations are compiled by Christopher Simpson, *National Security Directives of the Reagan and Bush Administrations: The Declassified History of U.S.*

Political and Military Policy, 1981-1991 (Boulder, CO.: Westview Press, 1995). Simpson collected the documents using the Freedom of Information Act; the National Archives; and Iran-Contra releases. Also, the General Accounting Office, which collected limited information in response to Congressional requests, provided their collection to Simpson. Furthermore, both Presidents leaked either information about the directives or the full texts to journalists considered favorable to their viewpoints.

13. U.S. Office of the Federal Register (Washington, D.C.: GPO, 1989?). Sudoc number: AE2.113:945-989.

14. (Bethesda, MD.: Congressional Information Service, Inc., 1986-87), 2 parts.

15. *CIS Presidential Executive Orders and Proclamations* (Bethesda, MD.: Congressional Information Service, Inc., 1986-1987). Approximately 5,000 microfiche.

16. *Legal Reference Services Quarterly* 10:3 (1990), 125-34. Woodward describes history and development of materials and then discusses major indexes, guides and microfiche reproductions.

17. *Legal Reference Services Quarterly* 5:2/3 (Summer/Fall 1985), 177-85. Relevant references are noted and then summarized in a 2 page chart. This article precedes the CIS *Index to Presidential Executive Orders and Proclamations.*

18. (Washington, D.C.: GPO, 1965-weekly). SuDoc number: AE2.109:.

19. (Washington, D.C.: GPO, 1956-annual). SuDoc number: AE2.114:. Retrospective editions were published for Presidents Hoover and Truman, and for the earlier Eisenhower years. Retrospective volumes for Franklin Roosevelt were not issued.

20. Springer, 533-548.

21. 2nd ed. (San Diego: University of San Diego, 1978), Vol. 1, 341.

22. "Preamble Requirements," 1 *C.F.R.* 18.12.

23. U.S. Administrative Conference of the United States. *A Guide To Federal Agency Rulemaking* by Benjamin W. Mintz and Nancy G. Miller. 2nd ed. (Washington, D.C.: GPO, 1991), 268-70. SuDoc number: Y3.Ad6:8R86/991.

24. (Washington, D.C.: GPO, 1936-monthly). SuDoc number: AE2.106:. Earlier issues published under SuDoc number: GS4.107:. William Hein and Company (Buffalo, NY) published reprints.

25. (Washington, D.C.: GPO, 1977-annual). SuDoc number: AE2.106/3-2:; earlier number: GS4.108/4:.

26. *List of Sections Affected* (Washington, D.C.: GPO, 1977-monthly). Title varies. SuDoc number: AE2.106/2-2:. Various retrospective volumes and cumulations cover 1949-1985. *Code of Federal Regulations. List of Sections Affected. 1949-1963* (Washington, D.C.: GPO, 1966) SuDoc number: GS4.108:LIST/949-963; *Code of Federal Regulations. List of C.F.R. Sections Affected. 1964-1972* (Washington, D.C.: GPO, 1980). 2 vols. SuDoc number: GS4.108:964-972; *Code of Federal Regulations. List of C.F.R. Sections Affected. 1973-1985* (Washington, D.C.: GPO, 1990). 4 vols. SuDoc number: AE2.106/2-2:973-985.

27. (Bethesda, MD.: Congressional Information Service, Inc., 1984-weekly with cumulations approximately every 5 weeks and semi-annually).

28. (Bethesda, MD.: Congressional Information Service, Inc., 1977-annual). CIS also distributes an index to the *C.F.R.* covering 1938-1976 on microfiche.

Exercises

1. Locate the temporary rule issued in 1995 implementing provisions of the Violent Crime Control and Law Enforcement Act of 1994, Public Law 103-322. The legislation placed restrictions on the manufacture, sale, and possession of certain semiautomatic assault weapons.

    A. When was this published in the *Federal Register?*

    B. On what pages of the *Federal Register* was this published?

    C. Which agency promulgated these regulations?

    D. What sections of the *Code of Federal Regulations* were affected?

2. The federal government issued guidelines that define and set standards for catchup.

    A. Where are these guidelines located in the *Code of Federal Regulations?*

    B. Which agency issued the regulations?

    C. When were the regulations published in the *Federal Register?*

Answers

1. A. April 6, 1995.

   B. Pages 17446-17456.

   C. Department of the Treasury. Bureau of Alcohol, Tobacco, and Firearms.

   D. 27 C.F.R. 55, 72, 178, and 179.

2. A. 21 C.F.R. 155.194.

   B. Food and Drug Administration.

   C. 48 *FR* 3956 (January 28, 1983) and amended at 49 *FR* 15073 (April 17, 1984)

•Chapter 11

Statistical Sources: Part I —Introduction "Lies, Damned Lies, and Statistics"

Answer the following questions when reading this chapter:

1.   If you have had trouble using statistics in the past, attempt to determine why.

2.   What kinds of statistics are most useful to your needs?

3.   This chapter lists questions data users ought to ask about statistics? Which three questions do you find most useful? Explain why.

The federal government is not only the largest publisher in the world, it is also the world's largest producer of statistics. Regardless of the subject, chances are good that Washington has collected statistics on the topic. The Office of Management and Budget publishes an annual report designed to inform Congress about the status and budget of major statistical activities, *Statistical Programs of the United States Government: Fiscal Year* ____.[1] Major statistical activities have an annual cost of $500,000 or more. The President asked Congress to appropriate nearly $2.6 billion to cover direct funding for statistical activities in fiscal year 1994. The largest request was for the Department of Health and Human Services, $804.3 million.[2]

This chapter provides a very brief history of federal data collection. A point to be made is that gathering statistics has a long tradition going back to the colonial era. In the sections that follow, the text examines the importance of federal statistics, and how they are used both within and outside Washington. The discussion then considers selected problems associated with interpreting the numbers and ways of dealing with these problems. These include steps agencies could take to guarantee the reliability and integrity of their statistics; and questions data users should ask themselves, as well as government experts, to interpret the numbers more effectively. The chapter provides a list of phone numbers of major statistical agencies. Contacting government experts will facilitate the interpretive process.

BRIEF HISTORY OF FEDERAL STATISTICAL GATHERING ACTIVITIES

Colonial governments began collecting statistics in the seventeenth century. The Virginia Register, established in 1637, inspected tobacco and other exports, maintained related statistics, and issued an annual report to the British Lord Treasurer. Furthermore, in 1640 the Virginia Secretary of State acquired responsibility for maintaining records of court orders, land patents, wills, births, deaths, marriages and people who traveled abroad.[3]

Our founding fathers recognized the need for gathering data. Article 1, section 2 authorizes a census to be taken every ten years to determine the allocation of Representatives among the states. James Madison believed the census should be expanded beyond that original purpose. In 1790, he stated that Congress:

> had now an opportunity of obtaining the most useful information for those who would hereafter be called upon to legislate for their country, if (the census) was extended so as to embrace some other objects besides the bare enumeration of the inhabitants...In order to know the various interests of the United States, it was necessary that the description of the several classes into which the community is divided should be accurately known. On this knowledge the Legislature might proceed to make a proper provision for the agrarian, commercial and manufacturing interests, but without it they could never make these provisions in due proportion.[4]

The Census of 1810 had questions pertaining to manufacturing. Subsequent censuses collected information about agriculture, the insane, education, libraries, crime, occupations, and illiteracy.

Federal statistical gathering functions had both political and judicial support in the nineteenth century. In 1850, politicians argued that consideration of adequate tariff protection required data about industries and agriculture. Economics aside, Congressman James Garfield, a Republican from Ohio, believed that statistics ought to be collected for the sake of expanding knowledge. He said "Statistics has been the handmaid of science, and has poured a flood of light upon the dark questions of famine and pestilence, ignorance and crime, disease and death."[5] When considering the frequent use of Congressional powers the *Constitution* does not expressly provide, an 1870 Supreme Court ruling stated data collection beyond that authorized in the *Constitution* is a legitimate activity.[6]

WHY ARE FEDERAL GOVERNMENT STATISTICS SO IMPORTANT?

People inside and outside government need current and accurate statistics. Agency officials depend upon statistics to help evaluate the effectiveness of existing programs and to plan new ones. The Bureau of Economic Analysis uses a wide array of economic data to compile the national income and product accounts. The Departments of Labor, Health and Human Services, and Education need accurate indicators that measure the socioeconomic status of the population to justify services.

Congress must have timely and accurate statistics to perform its oversight and legislative functions. Welfare reform is a popular issue. Policy makers should analyze and understand existing conditions before drafting new legislation. Relevant questions include:

-How many people receive welfare?

-Who receives welfare?

-What are the educational levels of welfare recipients?

-Can the private sector create enough jobs to employ current welfare recipients?

-How many children live in households that receive welfare? Can existing day care centers accommodate these children if their parents were to become employed?

State and local governments are equally dependent upon federal statistics. Data contribute to economic planning and forecasting; health planning; and developing site locations for schools and hospitals, plus countless numbers of other applications. State and local governments are especially concerned with federal aid formulas that are tied into data measured in the census. The General Accounting Office found that state and local governments depend upon approximately 100 such programs.[7] These include grants for industrial development; crime victim assistance; wildlife restoration; energy conservation; and education and library services.

The general public depends upon federal statistics in many ways. Business people use the data when planning for expansions and site locations. Increasing the number of jobs in the economy is dependent upon the availability of current and accurate data pertaining to demographic, training, and employment trends. Farmers use crop data prepared by the Department of Agriculture when planning their next harvests. Prospective home buyers often consult census information about local areas before making their purchases.

PROBLEMS ASSOCIATED WITH STATISTICS

People sometimes have strong aversions to statistics. They find the numbers confusing and difficult to comprehend. Mark Twain brings this point home in a classic way. He stated,

> Figures often beguile me, particularly when I have the arranging of them myself; in which case the remark attributed to Disraeli would often apply with justice and force: 'There are three kinds of lies: lies, damned lies, and statistics'[8]

Two titles describe very well why statistics can become easily misleading. Darrell Huff, author of the wonderful book *How to Lie With Statistics*, believes that confusion arises when researchers fail to use the precise definitions and methods statistical work requires, and when data users fail to recognize these limitations. The result becomes "semantic nonsense."[9] Mark H. Maier's work, *The Data Game: Controversies in Social Science Statistics*[10], is equally as informative. He argues that the media sometimes uses incorrect data because the numbers tell a good story, especially when they contribute towards sensationalizing the headlines. Corrections to wrong data are not as newsworthy.

Government statistics become especially confusing when politics plays a role in data preparation. Political judgements affect what is measured, how it is calculated, and presentation of results. After all, perhaps much more often than others, politicians use figures that serve their purposes while disregarding those which do not. The Pentagon's comparison of military spending between the US and the USSR as a percentage of gross national product is an example. The charts, graphs, and numbers ignore the real question: what are the relative capabilities of each nation?

Failure to achieve uniform definitions are another problem. The Education Department measured high school dropouts as the proportion of the entering class that failed to graduate. The figure was 30% in the mid-1980's. On the other hand, the Bureau of the Census measured it at 15% because those having completed GED tests were considered. Moreover, changing conditions require that agencies change definitions over time. The Bureau of the Census changed the definition of Hispanic in each census between 1930 and 1980. Naturally, the earlier definitions are incompatible with the latter.

OVERCOMING PROBLEMS ASSOCIATED WITH STATISTICS

Data users can overcome problems associated with government statistics by improving their data literacy. This involves two things: (1) becoming aware of the steps agencies might take to guarantee the reliability of their data and (2) asking appropriate questions about the data.

STEPS AGENCIES CAN TAKE TO GUARANTEE RELIABILITY OF DATA

Not only must statistical agencies be free of politics, the public must perceive them as such to maintain respect among data users. Statistics that are gathered, processed, and disseminated in a professionally acceptable way are less likely to be influenced by politics than other data. *Principles and Practices For A Federal Statistical Agency* edited by Margaret E. Martin and Miron L. Straf[11] discusses these issues comprehensively. Many of the suggestions in this chapter are based upon those proposed by Martin and Straf.

The Office of Information and Regulatory Affairs (OIRA), a section of the Office of Management and Budget, coordinates statistical activities among agencies to maximize the reliability and integrity of the numbers. The draft "Guidelines For Federal Statistical Activities"[12] describes how agencies ought to handle statistical functions. They should:

-Prepare documentation that describes the issues the statistics address.

-Explain how the data accomplishes this.

-Justify the need for collecting and disseminating the information.

-Explain editing procedures and estimates of variance.

Additional organizational safeguards that limit the influence of politics over statistics include:

-Reserving major executive positions in statistical agencies/offices for career civil servants.

-Developing schedules for releasing statistics well before their dissemination. Agency heads and other key political appointees should not have access until just before the official release.

-Segregating the statistical sections of agencies from policy making and enforcement divisions. Data gathered by statistical units ought to describe conditions and evaluate programs without formulating policy judgements.

-Consulting with data users and professional statisticians outside the government about procedures and methods.

QUESTIONS DATA USERS OUGHT TO ASK ABOUT STATISTICS

Data users sometimes assume that more is better. How can a report with all these numbers and supporting documentation possibly be incorrect? Mark Twain had the right idea when he said:

> I was deducing...that I have been slowing down steadily in these thirty-six years, but I perceived that my statistics have a deficit: three thousand words in spring of 1868 when I was working seven or eight or nine hours at a sitting has little or no advantage over the sitting of today, covering half the time and producing half the output.[13]

Data users ought to disregard the volume of statistics presented and consider the following:

-What agency published this information? Who is the individual responsible for the research and what are his/her credentials?

-Does this agency have a history of preparing unbiased or partisan information? For example, a study about the budget prepared by the non-partisan Congressional Budget Office is likely to reach different conclusions than that prepared by the Administration. Moreover, a third study prepared by Congressional opponents of the Administration is likely to reach still different conclusions.

-Is adequate documentation available? Documentation should define terms; describe data limitations; characterize the sample; note the response rate; explain how the data relates to the subject at hand; and cite margins of error. Careful study of the supporting documentation is one of the most important things a data user can do.

-How typical are the means and/or medians of the entire population? For example, knowing that the mean household income is $51,000 does not explain very much when four households have incomes of $20,000 each, while that of the fifth is $175,000.

-Are correlations reported as conclusions? Two or more correlated events may occur in a particular sequence, but sufficient evidence may not exist to prove that one is a cause of the other.

-Are charts and graphs well marked and are the scales appropriate?

-Have the results been replicated or do you suspect that they cannot be replicated?

-Does the entire study make sense when considered as a whole?

It is often profitable to ask agency officials who are experts in the field the same questions and then compare their answers to yours. The *Federal Statistical Source*[14] is a comprehensive directory of appropriate personnel. *Data: Where It Is and How To Get It*[15], edited by Edwin J. Coleman and Ronald A. Morse, is not as thorough, but it is still a good reference. A third source, *Statistical Sources*, includes a directory of "Federal Statistical Data Contacts."[16] Chart 11-1 provides phone numbers for selected agencies and their libraries. Librarians who work in a specific area are likely to be familiar with data sources and the methodologies and definitions behind the numbers.

Chart 11-1
Directory of Selected Statistical Agencies

Agency	Phone
Department of Agriculture	202-720-3631
Economic Research Service	202-219-0300
National Agricultural Library	202-720-3434
National Agricultural Statistics Service	202-720-2707
Department of Commerce	202-482-2112
Department of Commerce Library	202-482-2161
Bureau of Economic Analysis	202-606-9606
Bureau of the Census	301-457-4100
Bureau of the Census Library	301-763-5040
Department of Education	202-401-3000
Department of Education Library	202-357-6884
National Center for Education Statistics	202-219-1828
Department of Energy	202-586-6210
Department of Energy Legislative Library	202-586-2800
Energy Information Administration	202-586-4361
Department of Health and Human Services	202-690-7000
Agency For Health Care Policy Research	301-594-6662
Centers For Disease Control	404-639-3291
Centers For Disease Control Library	404-639-3396
Health Care Financing Administration	202-690-6726
National Center For Health Statistics	301-436-7016
National Health Information Clearinghouse	800-336-4797
Substance Abuse and Mental Health Services Administration	301-443-4795
Department of Housing and Urban Development	202-708-0417
Department of Housing and Urban Development Library	202-708-2370

Department of the Interior	202-208-7351
Department of the Interior Library	202-208-5815
Geological Survey	703-648-7411
Geological Survey Library	703-648-4302
Department of Justice	202-514-2001
Department of Justice Library	202-514-3775
Bureau of Justice Statistics	202-307-0765
Bureau of Justice Statistics Clearinghouse	800-732-3277
Federal Bureau of Investigation	202-324-3444
Department of Labor	202-219-8271
Department of Labor Library	202-219-6992
Bureau of Labor Statistics	202-606-7800
Department of Transportation	202-366-1111
Department of Transportation Library	202-366-0745
Bureau of Transportation Statistics	202-366-3282
Federal Highway Administration	202-366-0650
National Highway Traffic Safety Administration	202-366-1836
Department of the Treasury	202-622-1100
Department of the Treasury Library	202-622-0990
Internal Revenue Service	202-622-4115
Internal Revenue Service Library	202-622-8050
Department of Veterans Affairs	202-273-4800
Department of Veterans Affairs Library	202-523-1612
Environmental Protection Agency	202-260-4700
Environmental Protection Agency Library	202-260-5921

CONCLUSION

The purpose of this chapter is to help researchers feel better about using statistics. It summarizes problems associated with their applications and provides pointers that could lead to more effective data analysis. Consult the following three sources for additional information.

Garwood, Alfred N. *Dictionary of U.S. Government Statistical Terms.* Palo Alto, CA.: Information Publications, 1991.

The intended audiences are nonspecialists, such as students, researchers, librarians, and business people. Although emphasis is upon definitions, Garwood also provides selected methodological information.

Jaffe, A.J. and Herbert F. Spirer. *Misused Statistics: Straight Talk For Twisted Numbers.* New York: Marcel Dekker, Inc.,1987.

The authors present dozens of examples of misused statistics and suggest questions readers ought to ask to interpret the numbers correctly. The discussion covers categories of misuse; the importance of being familiar with the subject matter; definitions; and methodology.

Stratford, Jean Slemmons and Juri Stratford. *Major U.S. Statistical Series: Definitions, Publications, Limitations.* Chicago: American Library Association, 1992.

Coverage includes statistics dealing with population; labor force; economic indicators; price indexes and inflation; GNP and production; trade; and federal government finance. The authors describe available data, note their limitations, and define terms.

Endnotes

1. (Washington, D.C.: GPO, ?-annual). SuDoc number: PrEx2.10/3:.

2. *Statistical Programs of the United States Government: Fiscal Year 1994*, 45-6. SuDoc number: PrEx2.10/3:994.

3. Consult James H. Cassedy, *Demography In Early America: Beginnings of the Statistical Mind, 1600-1800* (Cambridge: Harvard University Press, 1969) for a complete discussion of the use of statistics during the colonial era.

4. Steven Kelman, "The Political Foundations of American Statistical Policy," in William Alonso and Paul Starr, eds., *The Politics of Numbers*, Prepared for the National Committee for Research on the 1980 Census (New York: Russell Sage Foundation, 1987), 280-81.

5. *Ibid*, 292.

6. Knox v. Lee (Legal Tender Cases) 79 *U.S. Reports* 536 (1870).

7. U.S. General Accounting Office, *Formula Programs: Adjusted Census Data Would Redistribute Small Percentage of Funds to States* (GAO/GGD-92-12) (Washington, D.C.: GPO, 1991), 2. Sudoc number: GA1.13:GGD-92-12. A directory of programs that use population related data is on pages 16-19.

8. Mark Twain, *Mark Twain's Own Autobiography: The Chapters From the North American Review*, Introduction and notes by Michael J. Kiskis (Wisconsin Studies in American Autobiography) (Madison, WI.: The University of Wisconsin Press, 1990), 185.

9. (New York: W.W. Norton and Company, Inc., 1954), 8.

10. (Armonk, NY: M.E. Sharpe, Inc., 1991).

11. Committee on National Statistics. Commission on Behavioral and Social Sciences and Education. National Research Council (Washington, D.C.: National Academy Press, 1992).

12. *Federal Register* 53:12 (January 20, 1988), 1541-52 . To date, a final Circular has not been issued.

13. Twain, 184-5.

14. *Federal Statistical Source: Where To Find Agency Experts and Personnel* (Phoenix: Oryx Press, revised irregularly).

15. *Data: Where It Is and How To Get It--The 1993 Directory of Business, Environment, and Energy Data Sources* (Arnold, MD.: Coleman/Morse Associates Ltd., 1992).

16.   Jacqueline Wasserman O'Brien and Steven R. Wasserman, eds., *Statistical Sources: A Subject Guide To Data on Industrial, Business, Social, Educational, Financial and Other Topics for the United States and Internationally* (Detroit: Gale Research Co., annual beginning with volume 11, 1988).

•Chapter 12

Ready Reference Statistical Sources

When attempting to locate federal statistics, it is easier to first consult general statistical compendiums rather than doing a comprehensive search. There is always the possibility that the information might be found easily or a reference to a more comprehensive source would be cited. If relevant information cannot be found, a more comprehensive search is then appropriate.

This chapter describes selected statistical compendiums available in print format and on CD-ROM. The Internet Supplement to the chapter covers sources available from remote sites. There are advantages and disadvantages to using each format. Browsing is often helpful, especially when you are not yet aware of the kinds of data available and/or are still undecided as to how the numbers will be applied. It is much easier to browse information in paper than electronic format. Advantages of information in electronic format include the ability to update information quicker than through paper format; and the ability to use the data with applications software, such as wordprocessors, spreadsheets, and database managers. Also, people using remote electronic sources can do so from their homes or workplaces.

Separate sections of the chapter cover:

-General sources.

-Agriculture.

-Economics, business, and labor.

-Education.

-Energy, environment, and natural resources.

-Foreign affairs, foreign countries, and national security.

-Government expenditures, revenues, and finance.

-Health.

-Law enforcement and criminal justice.

-Local areas.

-Population.

-Public and social welfare.

-Transportation.

The Internet Supplement follows the identical organization. The criteria for inclusion are sources that can be consulted easily within a few minutes and sources that include full text data. The most current titles and Superintendent of Document numbers are cited.

GENERAL SOURCES

U.S. Bureau of the Census. *Historical Statistics of the United States: Colonial Times to 1970.* Washington, D.C.: GPO, 1975. SuDoc number: C3.134/2:H62/789-970.

Reproduces historical statistics that measure all aspects of American society from colonial times through 1970. Topics include population and vital statistics; migration; labor and employment; prices; agriculture; manufacturing; transportation; and government finances. Narrative sections describe the data and cite sources from which the numbers were extracted. The subject index is very comprehensive. Use the *Statistical Abstract of the United States* to update this information. George Thomas Kurian's book, *Datapedia of the United States, 1790-2000*[1], also updates selected data in *Historical Statistics.*

U.S. Bureau of the Census. *Statistical Abstract of the United States.* Washington, D.C.: GPO, 1878-annual. SuDoc number: C3.134:. Available on CD-ROM beginning with the 1993 edition.

Presents statistical summaries of all aspects of American life. Separate chapters cover population; health and vital statistics; education; law enforcement; elections; government finance; defense; social welfare; labor; energy; science; and transportation, among other topics. Chapter introductions define key terms and place data in context. Although information for states and local areas are sometimes provided, emphasis is upon national statistics. Notes in each table cite the source of the statistics. Additional appended material summarizes data limitations. The index is very comprehensive. The CD-ROM version covers longer time periods than the printed format. The *Statistical Abstract* is one of the most significant statistical series published by the U.S. government.

AGRICULTURE

U.S. Department of Agriculture. *Agricultural Statistics*. Washington, D.C.: GPO, 1936-annual. SuDoc number: A1.47:.

Summarizes agricultural production, supplies, consumption, facilities, and costs. Separate chapters consider different types of commodities. Tables include footnotes and names of agencies, but exclude titles of data sources. Historical statistics cover approximately twenty years. The comprehensive index is a useful reference aid.

U.S. Department of Agriculture. Economic Research Service. *Agricultural Outlook*. Washington, D.C.: GPO, 1975-monthly. SuDoc number: A93.10/2:. (SuDoc number varies).

Provides feature articles, news summaries, and basic statistics. The statistics measure key economic indicators; indexes of prices received and paid by farmers; farm-retail price spreads; consumer and producer price indexes for food; and data about specific commodities. These include dairy products, fruits, vegetables, and poultry. Tables have footnotes, contacts in the Department of Agriculture, and relevant phone numbers.

U.S. Department of Agriculture. Economic Research Service. *Food Consumption, Prices, and Expenditures*. Washington, D.C.: GPO,

1968-annual. SuDoc number: A1.34/4:. (SuDoc number varies).

Gives historical data on food consumption, prices, and expenditures. Detailed tables cite per capita consumption by kinds of foods; per capita consumption of nutrients and other food components; supplies and utilization of foods by detailed types; price indexes and retail prices; food expenditures in homes and restaurants; and expenditures for alcoholic beverages. Most figures cover fifteen through twenty years. An introductory narrative section summarizes trends, and describes the statistics and their limitations. The initial 1968 issue deals with data from the early 20th century. The Department of Agriculture provides the statistics on high density diskettes in Lotus 123 format.

ECONOMICS, BUSINESS, AND LABOR

Business Statistics of the United States. Lanham, MD.: Bernan Press, 1995-biennial(?). Earlier editions published by U.S. Bureau of Economic Analysis, 1931-biennial with gaps. SuDoc number: C59.11/3:. (Title varies).

Presents historical data for over 2,000 economic variables. Part 1 deals with national topics, such as gross domestic product; income and spending; sales and inventories; prices; and employment and trade. Part 2 provides industry profiles. In the 1995 edition, annual data deal with 1966-1994 and monthly statistics deal with 1991-1994. Four appendices describe selected per capita data (1959-1994); selected annual and quarterly information

(1959-1985); selected monthly figures (1967-1990); and selected annual state and regional data (1959-1994). Special features include a sizable notes, and definitions section and an index.

U.S. Bureau of Labor Statistics. *Employment and Earnings*. Washington, D.C. GPO, 1954-monthly. SuDoc number: L2.41/2:. (Title varies).

Provides statistics about employment, unemployment, earnings, and hours worked for the nation, states, and selected local areas. Definitions define relevant economic concepts and discuss data limitations. Different issues include special features.

MONTH(S)	DATA
January	**Household data**--annual averages; union affiliations; earnings by detailed occupation; employee absences; and revised seasonally adjusted statistics[2]. **Establishment**[3] **data**--preliminary national annual averages for industry divisions.
January, April, July, October	**Household data**--quarterly averages that are seasonally adjusted. Hispanic origin; Vietnam-era veterans and non-veterans; and weekly earnings.
March	**Establishment data**--state and area annual revisions.
March, June	**Establishment data**--industry details and numbers of female employees.
May	**Establishment data**--state and area annual averages; and area definitions.
June	**Establishment data**--national data revised to reflect new benchmarks[4] and new seasonal adjustment factors.

U.S. Bureau of Labor Statistics. *Monthly Labor Review*. Washington, D.C.: GPO, 1918-monthly. SuDoc number: L2.6:.

Presents feature articles, news summaries, and statistical summaries dealing with all aspects of labor. The "Current Labor Statistics" section measures basic employment and wage indicators; household and establishment data; collective bargaining and compensation; prices; productivity; occupational injuries and illnesses; and international comparisons. Tables include descriptive notes. The introduction to the tables defines terms, cites sources, and discusses data limitations.

U.S. Congress. Joint Economic Committee. *Economic Indicators*. Prepared for the Congressional Joint Economic Committee by the Council of Economic Advisors. Washington, D.C.: GPO, 1948-monthly. SuDoc number: Y4.EC7:EC7.

This concise pamphlet presents basic economic data. Topics include output, income, and spending; employment, unemployment, and wages;

production and business activities; prices; money, credit, and securities; federal finance; and selected international statistics. Most tables cover six through ten years of annual data, three years of quarterly data, and one year of monthly data.

U.S. President. Council of Economic Advisors. *Economic Report of the President*. Washington, D.C.: GPO, 1950-annual. (SuDoc number varies).

Presents the administration's viewpoint towards current and projected national economic trends. Extensive narrative information covers recent developments; monetary and fiscal policy; regulatory reform; economic growth; and trade. Appended statistical tables describe national accounts; income; population; employment; business activity; money and interest rates; government and corporate finance; and international comparisons for extended time periods. Footnotes and agency sources are cited.

EDUCATION

U.S. Department of Education. National Center for Educational Statistics. *The Condition of Education*. Washington, D.C.: GPO, 1975-annual. SuDoc number: ED1.109:.

Describes over fifty indicators that affect the condition of education. Different chapters cover access to programs and participation in education; educational achievements and attainments; economic and other outcomes of education; size, growth and output of educational institutions; and human and financial resources. The narrative sections outline each indicator in two page summaries that include charts and graphs. Appendices have detailed tables, notes, and sources. Additional features include descriptions of data collection methods, sources of historical information, and a glossary.

U.S. Department of Education. National Center for Educational Statistics. *Digest of Education Statistics*. Washington, D.C.: GPO, 1975-annual. SuDoc number: ED1.326:. (SuDoc number varies).

A compilation of a wide range of education statistics covering kindergarten through post-secondary levels. Separate chapters cover elementary and secondary education; post-secondary and vocational education; federal programs; workforce characteristics by educational attainment; and international comparisons. Tables have footnotes and source notes. Special features include a "Guide to Tabular Presentation"; a statement of data limitations and standard errors; and names and addresses of contacts in the Education Department. The index is comprehensive.

U.S. Department of Education. National Center for Educational Statistics. *EDsearch: Education Statistics on Disk* (CD-ROM) Washington, D.C.: GPO, 1994. SuDoc number: ED1.334/2:ST2/CD.

Reproduces over 1,800 tables, charts, and text files from selected National Center for Educational Statistics publications. Coverage includes the *1993 Digest of Education Statistics*; *1993 Condition of Education*; *Projections of Education Statistics to 2004*; and *120 Years of American Education*, among other sources. The CD-ROM includes installation software and documentation.

ENERGY, ENVIRONMENT AND NATURAL RESOURCES

U.S. Bureau of Mines. *Minerals Yearbook*. Washington, D.C.: GPO, 1932-annual. SuDoc number: I28.37:.

Describes the international minerals and materials industries. Volume I includes separate chapters on metallic and industrial mineral commodities. Volume II summarizes the mineral industries of each state and possession. Six separate books comprise Volume III. Each covers a different area or topic. (Mid East; Africa; Asia and the Pacific; Latin America and Canada; Europe and Central Eurasia; and minerals in the world economy)

U.S. Energy Information Administration. *Annual Energy Outlook*. Washington, D.C.: GPO, 1982-annual. SuDoc number: E3.1/4:.

Describes current and projected energy situations descriptively and statistically. Information includes detailed tables, conversion factors, and summaries of forecasting methodology.

U.S. Energy Information Administration. *Annual Energy Review*. Washington, D.C.: GPO, 1982-annual. SuDoc number: E3.1/2:.

Provides historical information covering 1949 through the present. Topics covered include consumption; finance; petroleum; natural gas; coal; electricity; nuclear power; renewable energy; and international statistics. Comparable data appear in graphs and tables that are side by side. All tables have footnotes and source notes. Narrative statements that describe trends introduce each chapter. The Energy Information Administration distributes this title without charge to libraries, government offices, and the media. The Department of Energy's Oak Ridge, TN facility, GPO, and the National Technical Information Service distribute this data on diskettes in ASCII comma delimited format.

U.S. Energy Information Administration. *Monthly Energy Review*. Washington, D.C.: GPO, 1974-monthly. SuDoc number: E3.9:.

Provides statistics about all aspects of energy. Annual figures cover the most recent twenty years and monthly data cover the most recent two years. Subjects deal with consumption; petroleum; natural gas; coal; electricity; nuclear power; prices; resource development; and international comparisons. Tables include footnotes and source notes. Selected issues highlight special themes, such as energy consumption by household vehicles and by commercial buildings. The Energy Information Administration makes copies of this title available to libraries, government offices, and the media without charge. The Department of Energy's Oak Ridge, TN facility, GPO, and the National Technical Information Service distribute this data on diskettes in ASCII delimited format.

U.S. President. Council on Environmental Quality. *Environmental Quality: Annual Report of the Council on Environmental Quality.* Washington, D.C.: GPO, 1970-annual. SuDoc number: US PREX14.1:.

Outlines the Council's recommendations for promoting environmental quality. Part I is a narrative discussion that includes maps, graphs, and tables. Topics in part I deal with agriculture; air quality; budget and economic concerns; oceans and water; data collection and analysis; education; enforcement; transportation; and private sector initiatives. Part II, "Environmental Data and Trends," includes more detailed tables and graphs. The compilers provide notes and source references.

FOREIGN AFFAIRS, FOREIGN COUNTRIES, AND NATIONAL SECURITY

U.S. Arms Control and Disarmament Agency. *World Military Expenditures and Arms Transfers.* Washington, D.C.: GPO, 1974-annual. SuDoc number: AC1.16:.

Summarizes military expenditures; arms sales and transfers; and related economic data for 144 countries. A narrative section describes trends and developments. Detailed tables give information by regions, intergovernmental organizations, individual countries, and supplier/recipient countries. Each issue covers a ten year period.

U.S. Central Intelligence Agency. *The World Factbook.* Washington, D.C., 1981-annual. SuDoc number: PREX3.15:. (Title varies).

Almanac-type ready reference information covers countries throughout the world. Statistics for each nation deal with geography, land use, and the environment; population and labor; government organization; the economy; communications; and defense. The introductory section covers "Notes, Definitions, and Abbreviations." Appendices provide a UN organization chart; a chart of measurements and weights; and a list of international organizations and their members.

GOVERNMENT EXPENDITURES, REVENUES, AND FINANCE

U.S. Bureau of the Census. *Federal Expenditures by State for Fiscal Year...* Washington, D.C.: GPO, 1981-annual. SuDoc number: C3.266/2:. Available on CD-ROM beginning with the 1983/92 issue.

Shows annual federal expenditures in states and territories. Organization is by agencies and programs. Data covers procurement contracts; loan insurance; per capita expenditures by programs; and defense expenditures as compared to other types of spending. Tables include footnotes, and the introduction describes definitions and data limitations. Consult *Consoli-*

dated Federal Funds Report Volume 1: County Areas (U.S. Bureau of the Census, 1983-annual. SuDoc number: C3.266/2:) and *Consolidated Federal Funds Report Volume 2: Subcounty Areas* (U.S. Bureau of the Census, 1983-annual. SuDoc number: C3.266/2:) for local area statistics. Note, county and sub-county statistics are not as detailed as those for states.

U.S. Bureau of the Census. *Government Finances.* Washington, D.C.: GPO, 1985/86-annual. SuDoc number: C3.191/2-4:

Presents results of a survey that covers revenues, expenditures, debt, and assets of state and local governments . Emphasis is upon state data. Special features include definitions and comprehensive documentation. Related titles in the series are:

> *City Government Finances,* 1964/65-annual. SuDoc number: C3.191/2-5:.

> *County Government Finances,* 1972/73-annual. SuDoc number: C3.191/2-7:.

> *Finances of Employee-Retirement Systems of State and Local Governments,* 1963/64-annual. SuDoc number: C3.191/2-2:.

> *Public Education Finances,* 1977/78-annual. SuDoc number: C3.191/2- 10:. (Title varies).

> *State Government Finances,* 1966-annual. SuDoc number: C3.191/2- 2:. (Title varies).

> *State Government Tax Collections,* 1965-annual. SuDoc number: C3.191/2-8. (Title varies).

U.S. Office of Management and Budget. *Budget of the United States Government.* Washington, D.C.: GPO, 1922/23+annual. SuDoc number: PREX2.8:. (Title and SuDoc number varies) Available on CD-ROM beginning with fiscal year 1996.

Presents the President's proposals for federal government spending and revenue during the forthcoming fiscal year. This highly partisan document provides information by agencies and by budget functions--types of services offered. Large amounts of descriptive text supplement the statistics. Related titles include:

> *Analytical Perspectives, Budget of the United States Government,*1995-annual. SuDoc number: PREX2.8/5:. (Previous title: *Special Analyses. Budget of the United States Government*)

> *Budget of the United States Government, Appendix,* 1972-annual except 1991-1994. SuDoc number: PREX2.8: (year)/APP.

A Citizens Guide to the Federal Budget, 1996-annual. SuDoc number: PREX2.8: (year)/CITIZE.

Historical Tables, Budget of the United States Government, 1986-annual. Sudoc number: PREX2.8/2:.2

HEALTH

U.S. National Center for Health Statistics. *Health, United States.* Washington, D.C.: GPO, 1975(?)-annual. SuDoc number: HE20.7042/6:. (SuDoc number varies).

Health, United States describe trends in the nation's health. Part 1 includes narrative description accompanied by numerous charts and graphs, while part 2 includes detailed tables. Topics deal with population; fertility; mortality; utilization of health resources; contacts with physicians; inpatient care; health personnel; health expenditures; health care coverage; and major federal programs. Selected information is by race and hispanic origin. All charts and tables include footnotes and source notes. Appendix 1 describes sources, data limitations, and methodology. A glossary and an index are included.

LAW ENFORCEMENT AND CRIMINAL JUSTICE

U.S. Bureau of Justice Statistics. *Criminal Victimization in the United States.* Washington, D.C.: GPO, 1973-annual. SuDoc number: J29.9/2:.

Presents survey data that measures reported and unreported crimes against individuals and households. The data consider victims characteristics, such as age, race, and residence in urban, suburban or rural areas. The Bureau of Justice Statistics calculates victimization rates per 1000 population. Specific crimes include theft; violence; rape; robbery; assault; and burglary. Historical information covers 1973 to date. Statistics are available on CD-ROM from the Bureau of Justice Statistics Clearinghouse for $15.00. (phone: 1-800-732-3277)

U.S. Bureau of Justice Statistics. *Sourcebook of Criminal Justice Statistics.* Washington, D.C.: GPO, 1973-annual. SuDoc number: J29.9/6:. (SuDoc number varies).

Presents statistics about crime, law enforcement, and public attitudes towards these topics. Specific topics cover characteristics of the criminal justice system, such as workloads and expenditures; public opinion about criminal victimization, capital punishment, gun control and other timely topics; data about known offenses; characteristics of those arrested; and jail populations. Tables have source notes and footnotes. Supplemental information includes an annotated bibliography of further references, definitions, descriptions of criminal justice surveys, and a comprehensive index.

U.S. Federal Bureau of Investigation. *Uniform Crime Reports for the United States*. Washington, D.C.: GPO, 1930-annual. SuDoc number: J1.14/7:. Title varies. Quarterly supplements update the annual volume.

Presents statistics about crimes reported to nearly 16,000 state, county, and municipal law enforcement agencies. Detailed tables consider types of crimes; crime rates; use of weapons in criminal activities; numbers of arrests; and numbers of law enforcement employees in towns, cities, and rural areas. Data are specific to cities and towns with populations of 10,000 or more.

LOCAL AREAS

U.S. Bureau of the Census. *County and City Data Book*. Washington, D.C: GPO, 1947-generally every five years. SuDoc number: C3.134/2:C83/2. Available on CD-ROM beginning with the 1988 edition.

Presents basic statistics for local areas throughout the nation. Topics include population; housing; agriculture; banking; climate; crime; education; social welfare; government finance; health; households; income; and economics. Statistics for multistate regions, states, and counties include 220 variables, while those for cities cover 194 variables. Three variables measure places larger than 2,500 people: population, median household income, and per capita income. Appendices contain source notes; definitions of subjects and geographies; descriptions of data limitations; and maps of all states and counties.

U.S. Bureau of the Census. *USA Counties*. Washington, D.C.: GPO, 1992-irregular. Most recent 3rd edition published in 1996. SuDoc number: C3.134/6:UN3/year.

Provides nearly 3,000 demographic, economic, and governmental data variables for states, the District of Columbia, and counties throughout the nation. Emphasis is upon comparisons over extended periods. Statistics from the 1983, 1988, and 1994 editions of the *County and City Data Book* and the 1982, 1986, and 1991 editions of the *State and Metropolitan Area Data Book*[5] are included. Selected variables deal with age; agriculture; business and the economy; income, earnings, and poverty; education; elections; government revenues and expenditures; health; race and ancestry; housing; labor; and vital statistics.

POPULATION

U.S. Bureau of the Census. *Population Profile of the United States*. Washington, D.C.: GPO, 1974-present. SuDoc number: C3.186/3:. (SuDoc number varies).

A brief pamphlet that summarizes demographic, social, and economic trends affecting the U.S. population. The lucid narrative information includes graphs and charts. Further references list titles of more detailed publications, and names of individuals and their phone numbers.

PUBLIC AND SOCIAL WELFARE

U.S. Social Security Administration. *Annual Statistical Supplement to the Social Security Bulletin.* Washington, D.C.: GPO, 1955-annual. SuDoc number: HE3.3/3:.

Statistics measure all aspects of public and social welfare. Topics covered include social welfare and economy; old-age survivors and disability insurance; supplemental security income; and medicare and medicaid, plus other subjects. The tables have names and phone numbers of agency contacts. Technical documentation describes data collection; sampling variability; and poverty measurements. A glossary and an index are included.

U.S. Social Security Administration. *Social Security Bulletin.* Washington, D.C.: GPO, 1938-quarterly. SuDoc number: HE3.3:. (SuDoc number varies).

Includes feature articles, brief articles, book reviews, and statistics. Data measure trust funds; numbers of recipients and benefits paid; SSI distributions by race, sex, and living arrangements; state supplementation of SSI benefits; and black lung benefits. Most tables provide historical trends, some for as many as fifty years. The editors provide names and phone numbers of agency contacts.

TRANSPORTATION

U.S. Department of Transportation. Research and Special Programs Administration. *National Transportation Statistics.* Washington, D.C.: GPO, 1977-annual. SuDoc number: TD10.9:.

A compilation of public and private sources that deal with transportation and energy. Separate sections describe air pollution; highways; automobiles; buses; trucks; water transportation; railroads; oil pipelines; and natural gas. Data describes trends for vehicle performance, safety, production, sales, and costs. Tables include footnotes. An index, a glossary and a bibliography of statistical sources are appended.

CONCLUSION

This chapter lists statistical compendium very selectively. Consult the following sources for further references.

Sears, Jean L. and Marilyn K. Moody. *Using Government Information Sources: Print and Electronic.* 2nd ed. Phoenix: Oryx Press, 1994.

Chapters 29-44 cover population; vital statistics; economic indicators; business and industry statistics; income and earnings; employment; prices;

consumer expenditures; foreign trade; crime; defense; energy; projections; state and local governments; and transportation. Descriptions deal with print, CD-ROM, and remote electronic sources. The initial sections of each chapter summarize search strategies.

U.S. Government Printing Office. *Statistical Publications: Subject Bibliography 273 (SB-273)*. Washington, D.C.: GPO, updated regularly. SuDoc number: GP3.22/2:273/year.

Describes selected statistical publications available through the Government Printing Office. References include titles; Superintendent of Document numbers; stock numbers; prices: and brief annotations.

Wasserman O'Brian, Jacqueline and Steven R. Wasserman. eds. *Statistical Sources: A Subject Guide To Data on Industrial, Business, Social, Educational, Financial and Other Topics for the United States and Internationally.* Detroit: Gale Research Co., annual beginning with volume 11, 1988.

Lists sources of current statistical information published by the U.S. government, international agencies, trade associations, and other private sources. Organization is alphabetical by subject. Special features include a "Selected Bibliography of Key Statistical Sources"; "Federal Statistical Telephone Contacts"; a directory of "Federal Statistical Databases"; and "Sources of Non-Published Statistical Data."

Endnotes

1. *Datapedia of the United States, 1790-2000: America Year by Year* (Lanham, MD.: Bernan Press, 1994).

2. Economic trends sometimes follow seasonal patterns due to climatic conditions, holidays, and vacations, or any number of other non-economic phenomena. For example, inventories generally increase immediately before the Christmas shopping season. Seasonally adjusted data accounts for such temporary influences.

3. Establishments are places of business. If the same company has five factories, each is a separate establishment.

4. Benchmarks are detailed statistics used for adjusting sample data and developing interim figures.

5. U.S. Bureau of the Census (Washington, D.C.: GPO, four editions published in 1979, 1982, 1986, and 1991). SuDoc number: C3.134/5:. The *State and Metropolitan Area Data Book* provided detailed statistical information for metropolitan areas. Over 200 variables measured population; housing; employment and labor; health and vital statistics; income; manufacturing; retail trade; and criminal justice, plus other topics. The compilers cited source notes and data explanations, and indexed data by subjects.

•Chapter 13

Ready- Reference Statistics on CD-ROM: *Statistical Abstract*

Answer the following question when reading this chapter:

What are the advantages/disadvantages of using the *Statistical Abstract* in CD-ROM as opposed to print format?

If there were a choice of using only one source for your statistics, the *Statistical Abstract*[1] would probably be the single best reference to consult. Since publication of the first 1878 annual edition, it summarizes all aspects of American life. Recent editions have over 1,400 tables and charts compiled from approximately 250 sources. Selected topics include population; health and vital statistics; education; law enforcement; elections; government finance; defense; social welfare; labor; energy; science; and transportation. The 1993 edition was the first distributed in CD-ROM format[2] The identical subjects in the printed *Statistical Abstract* are on the CD-ROM, but the CD-ROM includes data for longer time periods.

This chapter describes the *Statistical Abstract* on CD-ROM. The first two sections explain how to start and search the CD. The explanation then considers truncation, boolean operators, the Subject Index, and printing and downloading. All examples and illustrations are from the 1994 CD-ROM.[3]

The *Statistical Abstract* on CD-ROM uses TextWare Instant Information Access software. The Bureau of the Census decided against adopting all features this software offers. The chapter also lists menu choices that do not work.

STARTING THE *STATISTICAL ABSTRACT*

1. Place the CD in the appropriate drive, type the CD-ROM drive letter followed by a colon, and press enter. For example, if the CD-ROM drive is D, type D:.

2. Type GO and press enter.

3. The initial screen describes how to access the technical documentation and explains the file structure. Press any key to continue.

4. Select "Open..." and press enter. The "Select CardFiles to open" menu displays (Figure 13-1).

Figure 13-1
Statistical Abstract **on CD-ROM**
Select CardFiles to Open

```
                         TextWare Lite 4.1

File   Help

 _____ Select a CardFile to open _____
┌─ CardFile List ──────────────────────────────┐
│ 1994 Statistical Abstract -- ALL TABLES       │        [  OK  ]
│ State Rankings                                │        [CANCEL]
│ State Profiles                                │
│ Preface and Guide to Tables                   │
│ Text                                          │
│ Appendix I - Guide to Sources of Statistics   │
│ Appendix II - Metropolitan areas              │
│ Appendix III - Limitations of the Data        │
│ Appendix IV - "Historical Statistics" series  │
│ Appendix V - 1993 Statistical Abstract tables │  ▼
│ Appendix VI - Guide to new tables             │
│ INDEX -- citations refer to table numbers.    │  ↓
└───────────────────────────────────────────────┘

 Path to additional CardFiles:
 [.................................................................]

Enter Select CardFile|F5 Mark or unmark|F1 Help
```

Source: *Statistical Abstract* **on CD-ROM, 1994 ed.**

Cardfiles are groups of related files. The "1994 *Statistical Abstract* -- ALL TABLES," which includes all tables that appear in the printed *Statistical Abstract*, is the first of 12 cardfiles shown in Figure 13-1.

SEARCHING THE *STATISTICAL ABSTRACT* USING "1994 STATISTICAL ABSTRACT -- ALL TABLES"

To locate data about the disabled:

1. Open the "1994 *Statistical Abstract* -- ALL TABLES" cardfile by highlighting that option and pressing enter. Table 1 appears.

2. Press the spacebar to display the Enter A Search menu (Figure 13-2).

Figure 13-2
Statistical Abstract **on CD-ROM**
Entering A Search

```
1994 Statistical Abstract -- ALL TABLES           | Card 1 of 1410
  File   Search   Link   Options   Setup   Help
                                             For list of cards,
                                             Search for '*'
No. 1. Population and Area
----------------------------- Enter A Search -----------------------
[Are| Enter Search Criteria:
cons|  [DISABLED..........................................]
cove|  [.................................................]      [  OK  ]
reca|  [.................................................]      [CANCEL]
and |  [.................................................]
1990|
past| r Word Wheel (12433) --------  r Search Type -  r         [ AND  ]
stri|  DISABLED               23 ↑   [X] Boolean                [ OR   ]
beca|  DISABLING               4 ▲   [ ] Phrase                 [ XOR  ]
and |  DISADVANTAGED           5     [ ] Proximity              [ NOT  ]
rese|  DISALLOWED              1                                [ANDNOT]
base|  DISAP                   1 ▼                              [ORNOT ]
----|  DISAPPEARANCE           1 ↓

                                              Per
       CENSUS DATE                           square
                               Number        mile of
   F4 Last search|F5 Select word|F9 Dictionary|F10 Hit List|F1 Help
```

Source: *Statistical Abstract* **on CD-ROM, 1994 ed.**

The explanations below describe the parts of the Enter A Search menu.

Enter Search Criteria: Type the keyword or phrase and press enter to retrieve a list of relevant tables. The search in Figure 13-2 retrieves all references to the term disabled.

Word Wheel: The Word Wheel is an alphabetic list of keywords in the card file. When typing a keyword in the Enter Search Criteria section, the display changes to reflect that keyword. In Figure 13-2, the first line of the Word Wheel--DISABLED, matches the keyword that was typed. This cardfile has 12,433 keywords and 23 tables that include the keyword disabled. To enter keywords from the Word Wheel, press the tab key until the Word Wheel is highlighted. Type the term and then press enter to display the information in the Enter Search Criteria section.

Search Type: Press the tab key until "Search Type" is highlighted. Use the **Boolean** option to combine multiple terms. Use **Phrase** to search multiple terms that are adjacent. Use **Proximity** to search multiple keywords within the same sentence.

AND, OR...: A section below describes boolean operators in detail.

OK/Cancel: Search for the specified keyword(s) or cancel the search request.

3. Figure 13-3 illustrates the Hit List of tables relevant to the keyword disabled.

Figure 13-3
Statistical Abstract **on CD-ROM**
Hit List

```
                      1994 Statistical Abstract -- ALL TABLES
   File   Search   Link   Options   Setup   Help                    |↑|▲|▼|↓
No. 255. Children and Youth With Disabilities in Educational Programs
for the Disabled, by Type of Disability
─────────────────────── 23 Hits (Proximity) ───────────────────────
[For│No. 156. Medicare Program--Enrollment and Payments [Enrollment as of
22 y│No. 157. Medicare--Persons Served and Reimbursements [Persons served
unde│No. 158. Medicare--Utilization and Charges [Data reflect date expens
Stat│No. 162. Medicaid--Recipients and Payments [For fiscal year ending i
Indi│No. 192. Nursing and Related Care Facilities ----------------------
outl│No. 226. Federal Funds for Education and Related Programs [In millio
────│No. 255. Children and Youth With Disabilities in Educational Program
    │No. 521. Federal Individual Income Tax Returns With Adjusted Gross I
    │No. 567. Disabled Veterans Receiving Compensation [In thousands, exc
────│No. 571. Veterans Assistance--Education and Training [In thousands,
   A│No. 575. Private Expenditures for Social Welfare, by Type [In millio
    │No. 576. Public Income-Maintenance Programs--Cash Benefit Payments [
   P│No. 581. Social Security Trust Funds [In billions of dollars, except ▼
    │No. 582. Social Security (OASDI)--Benefits, by Type of Beneficiary [ ↓
Lear└──────────────────────────────────────────────────────────────────
Spee│ DISABLED
Ment└
Emotionally disturbed          7.7      8.2      8.4      8.1      8.3
Hard of hearing and deaf       2.2      2.0      1.9      1.8      1.7
   Esc Cancel|Enter Select hit|Space New search|F9 Dictionary|F1 Help
```

Source: *Statistical Abstract* **on CD-ROM, 1994 ed.**

Table numbers along the left column are identical to those in the printed *Statistical Abstract*. The search term or phrase displays at the bottom of the list.

4.   Highlight a table and press enter to view the statistics. Figure 13-4 displays table 255.

Figure 13-4
Statistical Abstract **on CD-ROM**
Table 255

```
1994 Statistical Abstract -- ALL TABLES              | Card 255 of 1410
   File   Search   Link   Options   Setup   Help                 |↑|▲|▼|↓
No. 255. Children and Youth With Disabilities in Educational Programs
for the Disabled, by Type of Disability

[For school year ending in year shown. For persons under
22 years old, except as noted. Represents children under 20 served
under Chapter 1 of the Elementary and Secondary Education Act (ESEA),
State Operated Programs (SOP), and children 3 to 21 served under
Individuals with Disabilities Education Act, Part B (IDEA). Excludes
outlying areas]
---------------------------------------------------------------------
       ITEM            1979     1980     1981     1982     1983

---------------------------------------------------------------------
  All conditions (1,000)  3,889   4,005    4,177    4,198    4,255

  PERCENT DISTRIBUTION

Learning disabled         29.1     31.9     35.1     38.6     40.9
Speech impaired           31.2     29.6     28.0     27.0     26.6
Mentally retarded         23.2     21.7     20.2     18.7     17.8
Emotionally disturbed      7.7      8.2      8.4      8.1      8.3
Hard of hearing and deaf   2.2      2.0      1.9      1.8      1.7
   F2 Next match|Shift+F2 Prev match|F10 Hit List|+ Next hit|- Prev hit|F1 Help
```

Source: *Statistical Abstract* **on CD-ROM, 1994 ed.**

Use the five commands listed at the bottom of Figure 13-4 when viewing search results.

-F2 Next match: Retrieves the next occurrence of the keyword(s) that were searched.

-Shift F2 Prev match: Retrieves the previous occurrence of the keyword(s) that were searched.

-F10 Hit List: Redisplays the hit list shown in Figure 13-3.

-+ Next hit: Displays the next table on the hit list.

-- Prev hit: Displays the previous table on the hit list.

Test your understanding of the *Statistical Abstract* on CD-ROM: Refer to Figures 13-2 through 13-4 when answering the following:

1.   Use the Word Wheel in Figure 13-2 to determine the number of tables where "disabling" is used as a keyword.

(4)

2.   In Figure 13-3, how many hits were retrieved on the term "disabled"?

(23)

3.   What does table 581 deal with?

(Social Security trust funds)

4.   After viewing the table in Figure 13-4, how do you return to the hit list?

(F10)

TRUNCATION

Truncate search terms with an asterisk (*) to expand the amount of information retrieved. The search in Figure 13-5 retrieves all references beginning with the root "disab*," such as disability, disabilities, and disabled.

Figure 13-5
Statistical Abstract **on CD-ROM**
Truncation

```
1994 Statistical Abstract -- ALL TABLES              | Card 255 of 1410
  File   Search   Link   Options   Setup   Help
No. 255. Children and Youth With Disabilities in Educational Programs
for the Disabled, by Type of Disability

[For┌──────────────── Enter A Search ──────────────────────────┐
22 y│ Enter Search Criteria:                                   │
unde│ [DISAB*.............................................]     │
Stat│ [...................................................]   [ OK  ] │
Indi│ [...................................................]   [CANCEL]│
outl│ [...................................................]     │
────│                                                          │
    │ ┌─ Word Wheel (12433) ──────┐ ┌─ Search Type ─┐ ┌──────┐ │
    │ │ DISABILITIES          7 ↑ │ │[X] Boolean    │ │[ AND ]│ │
────│ │ DISABILITY           39 ▲ │ │[ ] Phrase     │ │[ OR  ]│ │
 A  │ │ DISABLED             23   │ │[ ] Proximity  │ │[ XOR ]│ │
    │ │ DISABLING             4   │ └───────────────┘ │[ NOT ]│ │
 P  │ │ DISADVANTAGED         5 ▼ │                   │[ANDNOT]│ │
    │ │ DISALLOWED            1 ↓ │                   │[ORNOT ]│ │
Lear└─┴───────────────────────────┘                   └──────┘─┘
Spee
Mentally retarded            23.2    21.7    20.2    18.7    17.8
Emotionally disturbed         7.7     8.2     8.4     8.1     8.3
Hard of hearing and deaf      2.2     2.0     1.9     1.8     1.7
  F4 Last search|F5 Select word|F9 Dictionary|F10 Hit List|F1 Help
```

Source: *Statistical Abstract* **on CD-ROM, 1994 ed.**

BOOLEAN OPERATORS

Use Boolean operators to combine multiple keywords. The far right section of Figure 13-2 illustrates six options. Most people will need only the following three operators in the majority of their searches.

-AND: Retrieves references to 2 or more terms when they all appear in the identical table. The system defaults to "AND," unless a different operator is selected. That is, the phrase "disabled persons" will retrieve all references that include the terms disabled and persons, even when they are not adjacent.

-OR: Retrieves references that include either search term. The search "disabled or persons" locates tables that include one term or the other, but not necessarily both.

-NOT: Excludes information. The search "disabled not blind" retrieves tables about the disabled that does not include reference to blind.

Hint: using the tab key to highlight a different Boolean operator is time consuming. It is much easier to type the Boolean operator when entering the search statement.

Test your understanding of truncation and Boolean searching:

1. In Figure 13-6, underline at least three terms that "employ*" retrieves.

(employ, employee, employer, employed,
plus all other terms beginning
with the root employ.)

Figure 13-6
Statistical Abstract **on CD-ROM**
Truncation and Boolean Searching

```
1994 Statistical Abstract -- ALL TABLES                  | Card 1 of 1410
   File   Search   Link   Options   Setup   Help
                                                     For list of cards,
                                                     Search for '*'
No. 1. Population and Area
 ─────────────────────────── Enter A Search ─────────────────────────
[Are| Enter Search Criteria:
cons| [EMPLOY*........................................]
cove| [...............................................]       [  OK  ]
reca| [...............................................]       [CANCEL]
and | [...............................................]
1990|
past| ┌ Word Wheel (12433) ─────────┐  ┌ Search Type ┐
stri|   EMPLOY              13 ↑       [X] Boolean        [ AND   ]
beca|   EMPLOYE              1 ▲       [ ] Phrase         [ OR    ]
and |   EMPLOYED            82         [ ] Proximity      [ XOR   ]
rese|   EMPLOYEE            50                            [ NOT   ]
base|   EMPLOYEES          118 ▼                          [ANDNOT]
----|   EMPLOYER            34 ↓                          [ORNOT ]
     └─────────────────────────────┘  └─────────────┘

                                        Per
      CENSUS DATE                       square
                        Number          mile of
    F4 Last search|F5 Select word|F9 Dictionary|F10 Hit List|F1 Help
```
Source: *Statistical Abstract* **on CD-ROM, 1994 ed.**

2.   True or false: Unless a different Boolean operator is speci-
       fied, the search phrase "work disability" defaults to the
       phrase "work and disability."

                                        (True. Unless you select a different
                                        operator, the system defaults to "and.")

3.   How do you limit the phrase "disabled persons" to only
       those occurrences where the keywords are adjacent?

                                        (Select the Phrase search type
                                        shown in Figures 13-2, 13-5, and 13-6.)

SEARCHING THE SUBJECT INDEX

The Subject Index cardfile includes the identical terms as the index to
the printed *Statistical Abstract*. The following instructions explain how to
search the Subject Index:

1.   Select the INDEX cardfile illustrated in Figure 13-1. Note,
       the software allows users to open only one cardfile at a
       time. Be certain to close the previous cardfile before open-
       ing a new one. First press the escape key until the menu
       bar at the top of the screen is highlighted, select Close, and
       then choose Open to redisplay Figure 13-1.

2.   After opening the INDEX cardfile, press the space bar to
       display the search screen. Figure 13-7 illustrates a search for
       the phrase, disabled person*. Remember to highlight the
       Phrase brackets in the Search Type section when searching
       for adjacent terms. Press enter to retrieve the index hit list.

Figure 13-7
Statistical Abstract **on CD-ROM**
Index Search and Phrase Search

```
INDEX                                                              | Card 1 of 4
  File    Search    Link    Options    Setup    Help
A
Abortions 108, 109, 111, 112, 113
Abrasives, stone 1166
Acc┬─────────────────────── Enter A Search ───────────────────────────┐
 103 │ Enter Search Criteria:                                         │
 Ai  │ [DISABLED PERSON*.................................]            │
 Co  │ [.................................................]    [ OK  ] │
 De  │ [.................................................]    [CANCEL]│
  1  │ [.................................................]            │
     │                                                                │
     │ ┌── Word Wheel (2577) ────┐  ┌─ Search Type ─┐  ┌───────────┐ │
 Dr  │ │ PERSON            3 ↑   │  │ [ ] Boolean   │  │ [ AND   ] │ │
 Fa  │ │ PERSONAL          4 ▲   │  │ [X] Phrase    │  │ [ OR    ] │ │
 Fi  │ │ PERSONNEL         4     │  │ [ ] Proximity │  │ [ XOR   ] │ │
 In  │ │ PERSONS           4     │  │               │  │ [ NOT   ] │ │
 In  │ │ PERTUSSIS         1 ▼   │  │               │  │ [ANDNOT]  │ │
 Mo  │ │ PERU              1 ↓   │  │               │  │ [ORNOT ]  │ │
  1  │ └─────────────────────────┘  └───────────────┘  └───────────┘ │
 Mo  └────────────────────────────────────────────────────────────────┘
Pedalcyclists 1023
Pedestrians 1023
Police officers assaulted, killed 324
F4 Last search|F5 Select word|F9 Dictionary|F10 Hit List|F1 Help
```

Source: *Statistical Abstract* **on CD-ROM, 1994 ed.**

3.   Consult the hit list to retrieve relevant table numbers. The index hit list (Figure 13-8) differs from that seen in Figure 13-3.

Figure 13-8
Statistical Abstract **on CD-ROM**
Index Hit List

```
                        INDEX
  File    Search    Link    Options    Setup    Help              |↑|▲|▼|↓
A
Abortions 108, 109, 111, 112, 113
Abrasives, stone 1166
Accidents and fatalities 198, 996, 1014, 1015, 1017, 1022, 1023,
 1036, 1176
 Aircraft 134, 996, 1047, 1049
 Costs 200
 Deaths and death rates 122, 124, 125, 126, 127, 134, 1014, 1015,
 1┬───────────────────── 2 Hits (Phrase) ──────────────────────────┐
  F│A Abortions 108, 109, 111, 112, 113 Abrasives, stone 1166 Accidents│
  I│F Fabricated metal products industry, manufacturing: Capital 1244, 1│
 Dro│                                                                   │
 Fal│DISABLED PERSON*                                                   │
 Fir└───────────────────────────────────────────────────────────────────┘
 Industrial 198, 676, 677, 679, 680, 1176
 Injuries 198, 199, 1176
Motor vehicles 124, 125, 127, 134, 198, 1014, 1015, 1016, 1017,
 1022, 1374
 Motorcycle 1014
 Pedalcyclists 1023
 Pedestrians 1023
Police officers assaulted, killed 324
Esc Cancel|Enter Select hit|Space New search|F9 Dictionary|F1 Help
```

Source: *Statistical Abstract* **on CD-ROM, 1994 ed.**

Rather than showing numbers and titles of tables, the index hit list displays the alphabetic sequence of search results. The system retrieves two hits. The first includes references to disabled person* that appear in the Index between "A" and "E," and the second covers those that appear following "F."

Searching the index hit list is a four step process.

-Select an alphabetical sequence. It is generally best to start at "A" because the context in which the keyword(s) or phrase is used cannot be determined from the given information.

-Press F2 to view each successive reference to the term or phrase. The phrase "Disabled persons" is the second one in Figure 13-9. Press shift F2 to view a previous reference.

Figure 13-9
Statistical Abstract **on CD-ROM**

```
                                 Index                    | Card 1 of 4
INDEX                                                        |↑|▲|▼|↓
 File    Search   Link   Options   Setup    Help
 Disability days 201
 Disabled persons 594
 Elderly 15, 13, 14, 49, 730, 731
 Elected officials 437, 443
 Elections, voter registrations and turnout 448
 Families, characteristics 71, 72, 73, 74, 75, 76
 Farm operators 1081
 Farmworkers 1102
 Fertility, fertility rate 94, 95, 105
 Health insurance coverage 161, 165, 167
 High school graduates and dropouts 262
 Home health and hospice care 195
 Homicides 137, 307
 Hospital use 191
 Households, characteristics 69, 71, 74, 75, 76
 Housing 1215, 1216
 Illness 207
 Income 235, 706, 707, 708, 709, 711, 712, 714, 715, 716, 717,
  718, 719, 723, 724
 Infant deaths 120, 123
 Jail inmates 338
 Labor force 615, 616, 617, 618
 F2 Next match|Shift+F2 Prev match|F10 Hit List|+ Next hit|- Prev hit|F1 Help
```

Source:*Statistical Abstract* **on CD-ROM, 1994 ed.**

-Note relevant table numbers. "Disabled persons" in Figure 13-9 refers to table 594.

-Close the index cardfile and open the "1994 Statistical Abstract -- ALL TABLES" cardfile to view table 594. Search this cardfile using the table number. (Press the escape key until the menu bar is highlighted; select "Search"; choose "Go to card number"; and enter the table number in place of the card number).

PRINTING AND DOWNLOADING

Either print or download information. Press the escape key to highlight the menu bar and select File to view the two printing options, Printer Setup and Print. Use Printer Setup first to confirm that the information will copy in the desired format (Figure 13-10). Again, press the tab key to move among the different parts of the Printer Setup screen.

Figure 13-10
Statistical Abstract **on CD-ROM**
Printer Setup

```
 1994 Statistical Abstract -- ALL TABLES                  | Card 594 of 1410
   File   Search   Link   Options   Setup   Help
No. 594. Persons With Work Disability, by Selected Characteristics

[In thousands, except percent. As of March.
Cove───────────── Printer Setup ──────────────────────────────────────────┐
Forc│ ┌ Printer Types ┐  ┌ Print Devices ┐  Setup File:                    │
Pers│ [ ] HP             [ ] LPT Port       [............]                  │
(1) │ [ ] Epson          [ ] COM Port       Reset File:           [  OK  ] │
work│ [X] Generic        [X] Disk File      [............]        [CANCEL] │
(2) │                                                                      │
job │                                       [ ] Legal Size                 │
(3) │                                                                      │
of 1│ ┌ Print Size ──┐  ┌ Lines Per Inch ┐  ┌ Quality ──────┐            │
(4) │ [X] Normal          [X] Six            [ ] Letter                    │
Supp│ [ ] Compressed      [ ] Eight          [X] Draft                     │
Base│                                                                      │
Appe│                                                                      │
────│ Disk File: [A:DISABLED.PER..........................................] │

        AGE AND PARTICIPATION STATUS IN     ------------------------
              ASSISTANCE PROGRAMS            Total \1   Male   Female
------------------------------------------------------------------------
 Esc Exit|F1 Help
```

Source: *Statistical Abstract* **on CD-ROM, 1994 ed.**

The Printer Setup screen has the following eight parts:

-**Printer types:** Select HP to use a Hewlett Packard printer, Epson to use that brand printer, and Generic to use any other printer.

-**Printer Devices:** Most printers connect to LPT ports, rather than COM ports. Select Disk File to download data.

-**Setup File/Reset File:** These more advanced options are unnecessary when using the *Statistical Abstract*.[4]

-**Print Size:** Controls the size of the typeface.

-**Lines Per Inch:** Most printing is generally 6 lines per inch. Selecting 8 lines per inch may help print a lengthy table on one page.

-**Quality:** Letter printing creates a better quality copy, but it also uses large amounts of ink and printing usually takes longer. For most purposes, draft quality is generally acceptable.

-**Disk File:** Enter the name of the file to which you want information downloaded. When printing data, leave this section blank. The Printer Setup in Figure 13-10 will download the information to an ASCII text file. Use a wordprocessor to insert this data into reports.

Note, ASCII text files are inappropriate for statistical manipulation, such as developing sums, means, or standard deviations. If interested in performing statistical manipulation with spreadsheet software, see the section below that describes how to download Lotus files.

-**OK/CANCEL:** Select OK or CANCEL when the printer setup is acceptable or when it ought to be cancelled.

Figure 13-11 illustrates the print screen. Select Current Card to print or download an entire table. Select Blocked text to print or download parts of a table that are highlighted. Use the shift and arrow keys or drag the mouse to "block" or highlight text.

Figure 13-11
Statistical Abstract **on CD-ROM**
Print Screen

```
1994 Statistical Abstract -- ALL TABLES                   | Card 594 of 1410
  File   Search   Link   Options   Setup   Help
No. 594. Persons With Work Disability, by Selected Characteristics

[In thousands, except percent. As of March.
Covers civilian noninstitutional population and members of Armed
Forces living off post or with their families on post.
Persons are cla┌──────────────────── Print ─────────────────────┐
(1) have a heal│                                                 │
working or whic│  ┌─ Print From ───┐                             │
(2) have a serv│  │ [ ] Blocked text│             [  OK  ]       │
job for health │  │ [X] Current Card│             [CANCEL]       │
(3) did not wor│  └─────────────────┘             [SETUP ]       │e
of long-term il│                                                 │
(4) are under a└─────────────────────────────────────────────────┘
Supplemental Se
Based on Current Population Survey; see text, section 1 and
Appendix III]
-----------------------------------------------------------------------
                                                              1989
        AGE AND PARTICIPATION STATUS IN         ------------------------
             ASSISTANCE PROGRAMS                Total \1   Male   Female
------------------------------------------------------------------
  Esc Exit|F1 Help
```

Source: *Statistical Abstract* **on CD-ROM, 1994 ed.**

Test your understanding of Printer Setup and Print: Refer to Figures 13-10 and 13-11 when answering the following:

1. Will the selected information be printed or downloaded? If downloaded, to which drive and filename will the data copy?

> (Downloaded to A:DISABLED.PER--
> Drive A, filename DISABLED.PER)

2. Will the complete table or portions of it be printed/downloaded?

> (The complete table will be downloaded.)

DOWNLOADING LOTUS FILES

The *Statistical Abstract* on CD-ROM includes all tables in Lotus format. They are in the WK_FILES subdirectory. Sections that represent different chapters in the printed *Statistical Abstract* further subdivide the WK_FILES subdirectory. Names of individual files are 94Snnnn where n represents the table number. For example, WK_FILES\SEC01\94S0001 represents table 1 of section 1, which is located in the SEC01 subdirectory within WK_FILES. Instructions for copying this file to a floppy disk appear below. Assuming that the CD-ROM is in drive D and the floppy disk is in drive A.

1. Type A: and press enter.

2. Type COPY D:\WK_FILES\SEC01\94S0001.WK1 and press enter.

Those who have trouble understanding subdirectories should consult a book that describes basic microcomputer concepts, such naming files, creating and using subdirectories, and copying files. This will help the novice better understand information on CD-ROMs; improve an under-standing of microcomputers; and organize information more effectively on hard drives and floppy disks.

Test your understanding of downloading comma delimited files:

Table 594 is in section 12 of the printed *Statistical Abstract*. How would you copy that data to a floppy disk so that you could use it with spreadsheet software at home or at work? Assume the CD-ROM is drive D and the floppy disk is drive A.

(Type A: and press enter. Then type COPY
D:\WK_FILES\SEC12\94S0594.WK1 and press enter.)

SOFTWARE OPTIONS NOT USED WITH THE *STATISTICAL ABSTRACT*

When developing the *Statistical Abstract* CD-ROM, the Bureau of the Census did not adopt the following software options shown on Figure 13-1:

-Path to additional CardFiles: Would have permitted users to open cardfiles in different directories.

-F5 Mark or unmark: Highlights multiple cardfiles, but only the first marked one opens.

Additionally, the following options on the menu bar at the top of the displays have not been adopted:

- **Search menu options:**

Dictionary	F9
Files	Alt+F5
Groups	Alt+F9
Templates	Shift+F10
Bookmarks	Alt+F10
Go to Group	
Go to File	

- **Link menu options:**

Stickey Note	Alt+F6
Bookmark	Alt+F7
Delete Stickey Note	

- **Options menu choices;**

        Synonyms   F8

        Segmenting

        Card Number Display

        Order of results

- **Setup menu options:**

        Editor

        Companion file

FURTHER INFORMATION

Press F1 for context sensitive help at any time. Get additional help by pressing escape to highlight the menu bar and then choosing the following from the Help option:

Using help: Explains different kind of help options.

User Manual: (ALT+F1) Covers all aspects of the software, including the options the Bureau of the Census did not adopt.

Custom help: Describes documentation files on the CD-ROM, Lotus worksheets in the WK_FILES subdirectories, and function keys available at different stages of a search.

Further information is also available in the GUIDE94 file on the CD-ROM. It describes the database content and provides sample searches with keywords, boolean operators, truncation, the index, and printing/downloading. Illustrations are included.

Endnotes

1. U.S. Bureau of the Census, *Statistical Abstract of the United States* (CD-ROM) (Washington, D.C.: GPO, 1878-annual). SuDoc number: C3.134:.

2. U.S. Bureau of the Census, *Statistical Abstract of the United States* (CD-ROM) (Washington, D.C.: GPO, 1993-annual). SuDoc number: C3.134/7:.

3. The Bureau of the Census published the 1995 edition after this chapter was written. Users can choose two methods of retrieving information with the DOS based software described in this chapter or with the Adobe Acrobat Portable Document format (PDF). PDF files present information as it appeared on the printed page.

    Each have their advantages and disadvantages. The DOS software presents longer time periods than the PDF format, but the PDF format enables users to download or print maps, graphs, and charts.

    As with the 1994 edition, the 1995 issue also includes LOTUS 123 tables in the WK_FILES subdirectory.

4. The Setup File considers special printer codes while printing. The Reset File returns the printer to its original configuration after the print job completes.

Exercises

Locate information about the number of injuries associated with the use of exercise equipment in 1991. Use the 1994 edition of the *Statistical Abstract* on CD-ROM.

A. What table includes relevant information?

B. How many injuries occurred in 1991?

C. How was this data compiled?

D. What is the data source?

E. How does this table on the CD-ROM compare to the comparable one in the printed report?

Answers

A. Table 199.

B. 86,210.

C. Data are from a sample of U.S. hospitals that have emergency treatment departments.

D. National Safety Council, *Accident Facts*.

E. The *Statistical Abstract* on CD-ROM includes the same subjects as the printed format, but the former depicts a longer time span. In this instance, the printed version covers 1990 and 1991, while the CD-ROM covers 1985 and 1988-1991.

•Chapter 14

American Statistics Index

Answer the following questions when reading this chapter:

1. When should you use the *ASI* as opposed to a statistical compilation, such as the *Statistical Abstract*?

2. What parts of the *ASI* are most useful to your needs?

In 1971, the President's Commission on Federal Statistics mentioned the need for a:

> ...comprehensive catalog to coordinate statistical activities more effectively. Most important, the catalog would provide a single source in which one could locate all data currently collected by the federal government on a particular subject. For example, all data collected on manpower training programs, whether funded by the Department of Labor, the Department of Health, Education, and Welfare, or the Department of Defense, would be indexed under a single entry with appropriate 'see also' references.[1]

The *American Statistics Index*[2] (*ASI*), the most comprehensive guide to federal statistics is an attempt to meet this need. *ASI* is still very useful even if you do not need statistics. Many titles indexed in *ASI* are primarily descriptive where statistics are used to justify viewpoints.

This chapter describes all aspects of *ASI*. The Introduction describes the kinds of information indexed and then describes the organization of the *Index* and *Abstracts* volumes. The following sections examine how the *Index* and the *Abstracts* volumes are used. The discussion also covers the *ASI Microfiche Library* and electronic formats of *ASI*.

INTRODUCTION

WHAT DOES THE *ASI* INCLUDE AND EXCLUDE?

The *ASI* indexes statistical sources published by the federal government in paper, microfiche and CD-ROM formats. Starting in 1994, coverage also includes reports available on electronic bulletin boards and other sources accessible via the Internet. Significant types of documents include:

-Periodicals, annual reports, special studies, and monographs published by all three branches of government.

-Press releases and related materials, providing they contain information not readily available in other forms.

-Maps and charts.

-Contract studies done by non-government sources, providing the government published the data. *ASI* includes items that fail to meet this criterion when agencies regard the information as having special importance.

-Methodological studies; guides and directories to statistical classifications; and bibliographies of statistical sources.

Documents published by bureaus or divisions of agencies are indexed when their information is unavailable elsewhere. For instance, *ASI* covers Department of Labor annual reports, but indexes those of the Department's Office of Mine Safety and Health only when they contain unique data.

ASI does not index medical, scientific, technical, laboratory, and experimental statistics, unless they have significant social or economic implications. Publications issued by Congressional Appropriations Committees are also excluded.[3]

ORGANIZATION OF THE *ASI INDEX* AND *ABSTRACTS* VOLUMES

ASI consists of two parts, the *Index* volume and the *Abstracts* volume. Each appears monthly. The *Index* volume has five sections:

-The Index by Subjects and Names.

-The Index by Categories.

-The Index by Titles.

-The Index by Agency Report Numbers.

-The Index by Superintendent of Document Numbers.

The publisher cumulates the indexes quarterly and annually. Several multiyear indexes are also available.[4]

References in the *Abstracts* volume are numerical according to *ASI* entry numbers. All issues of recurring serial publications, such as journals and annual reports, have the same *ASI* numbers. The publisher cumulates the abstracts annually.

USING THE *AMERICAN STATISTICS INDEX*

To use *ASI*, consult the *Index* volume; note the *ASI* entry number; and locate the entry number in the *Abstracts* volume.

INDEX BY SUBJECTS AND NAMES, SUBJECT APPROACH:

The Index by Subjects and Names uses the most specific subject headings that relate to the topic. Figure 14-1 shows how cross references refer from general to specific headings.

Figure 14-1
ASI Index
Volume Index by Subjects and Names
Cross References

Handicapped
  see Aid to blind
  see Aid to disabled and handicapped persons
  see Architectural barriers to the handicapped
  see Blind
  see Deaf
  see Developmental disabilities
  see Disabled and handicapped persons
  see Discrimination against the handicapped
  see Employment of the handicapped
  see Group homes for the handicapped
  see Handicapped children
  see Learning disabilities
  see Mental retardation
  see Mobility limitations
  see Rehabilitation of the disabled
  see Supplemental Security Income
  see Transportation barriers to the
    handicapped
Handicapped children
  Education (early childhood and adult)
    participation, characteristics, and survey
    methodology, 1991 Natl Household
    Education Survey, series, 4826–11
  Education data compilation, 1993 annual
    rpt, 4824–2

Source: *ASI Index*, **1993 ed., 396. Reprinted with permission from the**
American Statistics Index. **Copyright 1994 by Congressional**
Information Service, Inc. (Bethesda, MD). All rights reserved.

Figure 14-2 reproduces excerpts from two subject headings.

Figure 14-2
ASI Index **Volume**
Index by Subjects and Names
Subject Headings

Architectural barriers to the handicapped

Building access at public and commercial facilities, views of facility managers and disabled persons, 1992, GAO rpt, 26131–109

Building access for disabled to Federal and federally funded facilities, complaints by disposition and State, FY92, annual rpt, 17614–1

Election polling places accessibility to aged and disabled, precincts by barrier type and State, 1992 natl elections, biennial rpt, 9274–6

NIH employment of the disabled, FY91-92 and planned FY93, annual rpt, 4434–21

Architecture

County Business Patterns, 1990: employment, establishments, and payroll, by SIC 2- to 4-digit industry and county, annual State rpt series, 2326–6

County Business Patterns, 1991: employment, establishments, and payroll, by SIC 2- to 4-digit industry and county, annual State rpt series, 2326–8

Discrimination against the handicapped

Aliens excluded and deported from US by cause and country, 1892-1992, annual rpt, 6264–2.5

Fed Govt and State rehabilitation activities and funding, FY92, annual rpt, 4944–1

HHS financial aid, by program, recipient, State, and city, FY92, annual regional listings, 4004–3

Kidney end-stage disease program of Medicare, employer provided insurance requirement impacts on job access of patient and spouse, 1990-91, GAO rpt, 26121–494

Labor laws enacted, by State, 1992, annual article, 6722–1.407

NIH employment of the disabled, FY91-92 and planned FY93, annual rpt, 4434–21

Source: *ASI Index,* **1993 ed., 47, 220.**
Reprinted with permission from the
American Statistics Index. **Copyright 1994 by Congressional**
Information Service, Inc. (Bethesda, MD). All rights reserved.

Content notes in Figure 14-2 describe the publications, list the types of geographies they cover, and mention how frequently they are published. The second item cited under "Architectural barriers to the handicapped" is an annual report that provides information for states.

ABSTRACTS VOLUME

The *Abstracts* volume lists documents in numeric order according to *ASI* entry numbers. Abstracts are factual, not critical. They describe the contents of the documents without summarizing findings and conclusions. Whenever appropriate, abstracts also describe relationships of the document to other publications, mention time periods and geographies to which the data pertain, and tell when the first issue appeared. Figure 14-3 shows different parts of an abstract of the *Monthly Labor Review,* a journal published by the Bureau of Labor Statistics.

The second item cited under "Architectural barriers to the handicapped" is an annual report that provides information for states.

ABSTRACTS VOLUME

The *Abstracts* volume lists documents in numeric order according to *ASI* entry numbers. Abstracts are factual, not critical. They describe the contents of the documents without summarizing findings and conclusions. Whenever appropriate, abstracts also describe relationships of the document to other publications, mention time periods and geographies to which the data pertain, and tell when the first issue appeared. Figure 14-3 shows different parts of an abstract of the *Monthly Labor Review*, a journal published by the Bureau of Labor Statistics.

Figure 14-3
ASI Abstracts **Volume**
Abstract of a Journal

6722
BUREAU OF LABOR
STATISTICS:
GENERAL
Current Periodicals

6722–1   **MONTHLY LABOR REVIEW**
Monthly.   Approx. 110 p.
•Item 0770.
GPO: $25.00 per yr; single
copy $7.00.   ASI/MF/4
S/N 729-007-00000-5.
°L2.6:(v.nos.&nos.)
MC 93-869.   LC 15-026485.

Monthly journal on labor conditions; with current statistics on employment, earnings, prices, productivity, and labor-management relations.

Each issue contains feature articles, individually described below; current labor statistics, with 50 tables, listed below; and all or most of the following regular features:

a. Labor month in review.

b. Research summaries, technical notes, and communications; selectively described below when they contain statistics and are not readily available as separate reports.

c. Foreign labor developments, occasionally with charts and tables.

TABLES:
[Data are current to 1-3 months prior to cover date. Tables show monthly data for the past 13 months, and annual averages for previous 2 years, unless otherwise noted.]

6722–1.1: Comparative Indicators
[Tables show data for current and previous 6-8 quarters. Tables 1-2 include totals for previous 2 years.]

1. Labor market indicators.

2. Annual and quarterly percent changes in compensation, prices, and productivity.

3. Alternative measures of wage and compensation changes [average hourly compensation, Employment Cost Index, and total and negotiated wage adjustments].

6722–1.2: Labor Force Data

MONTHLY DATA

[Data are seasonally adjusted, unless otherwise noted.]

4. Employment status of the population, by sex, age, race [(2 groups)], and Hispanic origin.

5. Selected employment indicators [by sex, marital and family status, industry sector and class of worker, and, for part-time workers, reason for working part time].

JANUARY 1993
Vol. 116, No. 1

6722–1.405: Collective Bargaining in 1993: Jobs Are the Issue

By Lisa M. Williamson (p. 3-18). Annual article on collective bargaining contract negotiations, cost-of-living adjustments (COLAs), and deferred wage increases scheduled for 1993. Includes text statistics and 8 tables, listed below.

6722–1.407: State Labor Legislation Enacted in 1992

By Richard R. Nelson (p. 35-49). Annual summary of State labor laws and amendments enacted by 45 State legislatures, Puerto Rico, and Guam, 1992. Covers legislation on the following:

a. Minimum wage rates and other wage issues; hours; discriminatory employment practices; child labor; compulsory school attendance; worker privacy, including substance abuse or genetic testing; whistleblower protection and wrongful discharge; parental leave and other employee benefits; jury duty; and smoking rules.

b. Operations of private employment agencies; plant closings and layoffs; agricultural labor; replacement of striking workers; contractors and awarding of public contracts; and inmate labor.

Key parts of Figure 14-3 include the:

-*ASI* entry number: 6722-1

-Title: *Monthly Labor Review*

-Frequency (describes how often the journal appears): monthly.

-Pagination: Approximately 110 pages.

-Item number: Presence of the item number, 0770, indicates depository status.

-Price if purchased from GPO: An annual subscription costs $25.00 and single issues cost $7.00.

-Stock number: GPO uses the stock number, 729-007-00000-5, to control its sales inventory.

-Price if bought from Congressional Information Service: The Congressional Information Service sells microfiche copies of documents indexed in the *ASI*. The code, ASI/MF/4, determines microfiche costs. Contact CIS to interpret the code because prices often change.

-Superintendent of Documents number: L2.6:.

-*Monthly Catalog* entry number: 93-869, the 869th item in the 1993 *Monthly Catalog*.

Figure 14-3 shows that decimal points subdivide the information when documents have many tables and sections, making it easier to locate specific data. For example, 6722-1.407 refers to the article by Richard R. Nelson on "State Labor Legislation Enacted in 1992." From the decimal number "...1.407," refer to the whole number, 6722-1, for the title of the journal and its SuDoc number.

Other abstracts are briefer and less complicated. The General Accounting Office published the report shown in Figure 14-4. Although numerical data are included, this document is primarily descriptive, rather than statistical.

Figure 14-4
ASI Abstracts **Volume**
Abstract of a Monograph

26131–109 AMERICANS WITH
DISABILITIES ACT: Initial
Accessibility Good but
Important Barriers Remain
May 1993. 79 p.
GAO/PEMD-93-16.
•Item 0546-D. † ASI/MF/3
°GA1.13:PEMD-93-16.

Report evaluating government and business compliance with the Americans with Disabilities Act (ADA), as of 1992. The ADA prohibits discrimination against the disabled in employment, public services, accommodations, and telecommunications, mainly by prohibiting physical or architectural barriers that would deny equal access in public establishments.

Data are from a GAO survey of 231 stores, malls, theaters, restaurants, hotels, airports, and government buildings in 11 cities; interviews with owners and managers; and a survey of 1,193 disabled members of national advocacy groups for individuals with disabilities.

Survey of public establishments covered accessibility, placement, dimensions, and condition of designated parking spaces, wheelchair ramps, stairs, lifts, entrances, building interiors, elevators, bathrooms, drinking fountains, telephones, and legibility of signs on the premises.

Survey of advocacy group members covered opinions of accessibility in public parking spaces, pathways, entrances, stairs, hallways, rooms, retail spaces, seating, elevators, restrooms, telephones, hotel rooms, service assistance, public transit; and places where barriers are most often encountered.

Includes facsimile questionnaires with tabulated survey results; and 6 tables showing percent of owners and managers familiar with the ADA and percent of establishments removing barriers prior to ADA implementation, by type of establishment; 1992.

Source: *ASI Abstracts*, 1993 ed., 962, 963.

Test your understanding of the Index by Subjects and Names and the *Abstracts* volume: Refer to figures 14-1 through 14-4 when answering the following questions.

1. Underline the section of Figure 14-2 that deals with immigration policy and discrimination against the handicapped. How often is this report published and what is its *ASI* entry number?

   (Annually; 6264-2.5)

2. The article by Nelson in Figure 14-3 appears on pages _____ through _____ of the *Monthly Labor Review*.

   (pages 35 through 49)

3. What is the SuDoc number of the *Monthly Labor Review* that contains Nelson's article?

   (Nelson's article is in the
   January 1993 issue, volume 116, number 1.
   The basic SuDoc number,
   L2.6:(v.nos&nos) becomes L2.6:116/1.)

4. Which table in the *Monthly Labor Review* has statistics about employment status by race and age?

   (Table 4)

5. What is the SuDoc and report numbers of *Americans With Disabilities Act: Initial Accessibility...* reproduced in Figure 14-4?

   (SuDoc number: GA1.13:PEMD-93-16;
   Report number: GAO/PEMD-93-16)

INDEX BY SUBJECTS AND NAMES, NAME APPROACH:

Besides subject headings, the Index by Subjects and Names also list names of authors, agencies, programs, companies, and places. Agency names are in proper order. That is, search under "Department of Agriculture" or "Bureau of the Census," not "Agriculture Department," nor "Census Bureau." Additionally, "US" does not precede the agency names. Locate data under "Army" or "Department of Labor," not "US Army" nor "US Department of Labor." The entry for Richard R. Nelson's article shown in Figure 14-3 appears in Figure 14-5.

Figure 14-5
ASI Index **Volume**
Index by Subjects and Names
Name Entry

Nelson, Frederick J.
 "Producer Subsidy Equivalents for Canada,
  Mexico, and the U.S.", 1524–4.7
Nelson, Kenneth E.
 "1992 Grazing Fee Review and Evaluation
  Report Update: Data and Methods",
  1548–398
Nelson, Richard R.
 "State Labor Legislation Enacted in 1992",
  6722–1.407
Nelson, William J., Jr.
 "Workers' Compensation: Coverage,
  Benefits, and Costs, 1990-91",
  4742–1.425
Neoplasms
 Breast cancer cases and mammography use
  in Pennsylvania, 1985-90, article,
  4042–3.439
 Cases of cancer, deaths, and survival rates,
  by age, sex, race, and body site, 1973-89,
  annual rpt, 4474–35

Source: *ASI Index*, 1993 ed., 604. Reprinted with permission from the American Statistics Index. Copyright 1994 by Congressional Information Service, Inc. (Bethesda, MD). All rights reserved.

INDEX BY TITLES:

The Index by Titles includes titles of reports, journals, journal articles, and conference papers. Entries are alphabetical word by word. For instance, New York precedes Newark. Figure 14-6 indexes titles of the *Monthly Labor Review* and Nelson's article described above.

Figure 14-6
ASI Index **Volume**
Index by Titles

Monthly Climatic Data for the World,
2002-7, 2152-4
Monthly Cotton Linters Review, 1309-10
Monthly Defect Investigation Report,
7762-14
Monthly Energy Review, 3162-24
Monthly Import Detention List, 4062-2
Monthly Labor Review, 6722-1
Monthly Motor Fuel Reported by States,
7552-1
Monthly Product Announcement, 2302-6
Monthly Retail Trade, Sales and Inventories,
Current Business Reports ALT Revised
Monthly Retail Sales and Inventories: Jan.
1982-Dec. 1991, 2413-3

State Government Finances: 1992, 2466-2.5
State Higher Education Profiles: Combined
Fifth and Sixth Editions, FY89-90,
4844-13
State Labor Legislation Enacted in 1992,
6722-1.407
State Laws Governing Local Government
Structure and Administration, 10048-90
State Literacy Resource Centers Program
Grant Information, 4804-42
State Mineral Summaries, 1993, 5614-6
State of Fair Housing, 1989: Report to the
Congress Pursuant to Section 808(e)(2) of
the Fair Housing Act, 5004-13
State of Fair Housing, 1990: Report to the
Congress Pursuant to Section 808(e)(2) of
the Fair Housing Act, 5004-13

INDEX BY CATEGORIES

The Index by Categories is very helpful when attempting to locate comparative data, such as population figures for all fifty states or employment statistics for counties throughout the nation. It divides all data into twenty-one categories in three broad groups: geographic, economic, and demographic breakdowns (Chart 14-1).

Chart 14-1
Outline of the Index by Categories

GEOGRAPHIC BREAKDOWNS	ECONOMIC BREAKDOWNS	DEMOGRAPHIC BREAKDOWNS

By Census Division
By City
By County
By Foreign Country
By Outlying Area
By Region
By MSA
By State
By Urban-Rural and Metro-
    Nonmetro
	By Commodity
	By Federal Agency
	By Income
	By Individual Company or
	    Institution
	By Industry
	By Occupation
		By Age
		By Disease
		By Educational Attainment
		By Marital Status
		By Race and Ethnic Group
		By Sex

The following headings subdivide references in each category. The two examples below make this a bit clearer.

Agriculture and Food

Banking, Finance, and Insurance

Communications and Transportation

Education

Energy Resources and Demand

Geography and Climate

Government and Defense

Health and Vital Statistics

Housing and Construction

Industry and Commerce

Labor and Employment

Law Enforcement

Natural Resources, Environment, and Pollution

Population

Prices and Cost of Living

Public Welfare and Social Security

Recreation and Leisure

Science and Technology

Veterans Affairs

1. Suppose statistics about the population of the City of Buffalo, NY are unavailable in the Index by Subjects and Names. Consult the Index by Categories using geographic breakdowns by city subdivided by population.

2. To measure employment and unemployment in New York State and compare this to other states, consult the Index by Categories using geographic breakdowns by state subdivided by labor and employment (Figure 14-7).

Figure 14-7
ASI Index **Volume**
Index by Categories

BY STATE

Labor and Employment

Collective bargaining agreements expiring during year, and workers covered, by firm, union, industry group, and State, 1993, annual rpt, 6784–9

Disabled persons employment, earnings, and hours worked before and after vocational rehabilitation, by State agency, FY90, 4948–12

Discrimination in employment, Equal Employment Opportunity Commission activities, and cases by issue and State, FY89, annual rpt, 9244–3

Employment and Earnings, detailed data, monthly rpt, 6742–2.5; 6742–2.6; 6742–2.8

Employment and Training Admin activities, funding, and participant characteristics, by program, 1988-90, annual rpt, 6404–17

Employment and unemployment, by age, sex, race, marital and family status, industry div, and State, Monthly Labor Review, 6722–1.2

Source: *ASI Index,* **1993 ed., 935. Reprinted with permission from the** *American Statistics Index.* **Copyright 1994 by Congressional Information Service, Inc. (Bethesda, MD). All rights reserved.**

Test your understanding of the Index by Categories: Use the Outline of the Index by Categories (Chart 14-1) and the list of subheadings immediately following the chart to answer the following:

1. How would you locate population data for foreign countries?

    (Geographic breakdowns by foreign countries subdivided by population.)

2. You need statistics showing educational enrollment of children under 18 in Parmer County Texas. The Index by Subjects and Names includes information neither under Parmer nor under Texas. Can you use a different index?

    (Yes. Search the Index by Categories using either geographic breakdowns by county subdivided by education or demographic breakdowns by age subdivided by education.)

INDEX BY AGENCY REPORT NUMBERS

The Index by Agency Report Numbers indexes documents by report numbers. Separate alphanumeric lists provide data for each agency. When report numbers are known, this approach provides more direct access to the abstracts than that of subjects. The report number noted in Figure 14-4 is listed below (Figure 14-8).

Figure 14-8
ASI Index **Volume**
Index by Agency Report Numbers

General Accounting Office		
GAO/AFMD-93-51	....	26111–81
GAO/AFMD-93-58 BR	....	26111–82
GAO/GGD-93-3	....	26119–435
GAO/GGD-93-4	....	26119–436
GAO/GGD-93-14	....	26119–437
GAO/GGD-93-15	....	26119–432

GAO/OP-93-1 B	....	26104–5.2
GAO/OP-93-1 C	....	26104–5.3
GAO/OP-93-1 D	....	26104–5.4
GAO/PEMD-93-2	....	26131–104
GAO/PEMD-93-4	....	26131–110.1
GAO/PEMD-93-5	....	26131–106
GAO/PEMD-93-6	....	26131–105
GAO/PEMD-93-13	....	26131–107
GAO/PEMD-93-14	....	26131–108
GAO/PEMD-93-16	....	26131–109
GAO/PEMD-93-18	....	26131–111
GAO/PEMD-93-22	....	26131–110.2

INDEX BY SUPERINTENDENT OF DOCUMENT NUMBERS

Superintendent of Document numbers are in alphanumeric sequence along the left column and corresponding *ASI* entry numbers are in the right column.

USING QUARTERLY AND MULTIYEAR CUMULATIVE INDEXES

Figure 14-9 shows a quarterly cumulative index. The bold faced numbers in parentheses preceding the *ASI* entry numbers indicate which monthly abstract volume to consult. For example, refer to the July *Abstracts* volume, entry number 104-5, to acquire information about federal government financial and nonfinancial assistance for special education programs.

Figure 14-9
ASI Quarterly Cumulative *Index* Volume

Special education
 Assistance (financial and nonfinancial) of
  Fed Govt, 1995 base edition, annual
  listing, **(7)** 104–5
 Condition of Education, detail for
  elementary, secondary, and higher
  education, 1920s-94 and projected to
  2005, annual rpt, **(8)** 4824–1
 Data on education, enrollment, finances,
  teachers, and other characteristics, by
  State, 1969-94, **(7)** 4828–33
 Elementary and secondary education
  enrollment, staff, finances, operations,
  programs, and policies, 1990/91 biennial
  survey, series, **(7)** 4836–4
 Elementary and secondary education
  enrollment, staff, finances, operations,
  programs, and policies, 1993/94 biennial
  survey, series, **(7)** 4836–6
 see also Compensatory education
 see also Remedial education

Source: *ASI Index,* 1995, 3rd quarter, 222. Reprinted with permission from the *American Statistics Index.* Copyright 1995 by Congressional Information Service, Inc. (Bethesda, MD). All rights reserved.

Figure 14-10 illustrates a multiyear cumulative index. The bold faced numbers in parentheses tell which annual *Abstracts* volume to consult.

Figure 14-10
ASI **Multiyear Cumulative** *Index* **Volume**
 Special education
  see also Compensatory education
  see also Remedial education
  Assistance (financial and nonfinancial) of
   Fed Govt, 1992 base edition, annual
   listing, **(92)(91)(90)(89)** 104–5
  Bilingual education enrollment, and eligible
   students not enrolled, by State, 1990-91,
   annual rpt, **(92)** 4804–14
  Children and youth social, economic, and
   demographic characteristics, and govt
   programs, 1940s-89, **(90)** 21968–26
  Complaints about handicapped children's
   education brought by parents against
   school agencies, by disposition, whether
   attorney used, and State, FY84-88, GAO
   rpt, **(90)** 26121–324
  Condition of Education, detail for
   elementary and secondary education,
   1920s-90 and projected to 2001, annual
   rpt, **(91)** 4824–1.1; **(90)** 4824–1.1;
   (89) 4824–1.1

Source: *ASI Index,* 1989-1992, 1739.
Reprinted with permission from the *American Statistics Index: 1989-1992.* Cumulative Index Copyright 1993 by Congressional Information Service, Inc. (Bethesda, MD). All rights reserved.

Comparing the content notes in Figure 14-9 and 14-10, "Assistance (financial and nonfinancial) of Fed Govt...," appear in both illustrations. Figure 14-9 refers to the 1995 edition of this annual report. Figure 14-10 references annual reports for 1989, 1990, 1991, and 1992. Remember, the *ASI* entry numbers in both figures, 104-5, are identical because recurring reports have same numbers.

Test your understanding of the quarterly and multiyear cumulative indexes: Refer to figures 14-9 and 14-10 when answering the following.

1. The General Accounting Office published a report about complaints made by parents to school officials concerning special education. Where is the abstract to this report located?

    (1990 *Abstracts* volume; 26121-324)

2. Where is the abstract to a document that offers statistics about teachers in Virginia and West Virginia over an extended time period located?

    (July *Abstracts* volume, 4828-33)

ASI ABSTRACTS OF ELECTRONIC SOURCES

The *ASI* indexes electronic as well as print resources. Figure 14-11 illustrates the *Statistical Abstracts* on CD-ROM. The abstract describes the kinds of files on the disk, software, system requirements, and the availability of a comparable print source.

Figure 14-11
ASI Abstracts Volume
Document on CD-ROM

2324–14   STATISTICAL ABSTRACT OF THE U.S., 1993: CD-ROM
Annual.   Nov. 1993.
1 computer laser optical
disc 4.75 in.   •Item 0150-B.
Customer Svcs, Data User Svcs
Div $50.00.   CD-ABSTR-93.
ASI/MF/(not filmed)
°C3.134/7:993.
MC 94-9958.

First annual CD-ROM release, for 1993, presenting standard summary of statistics on the social, political, and economic makeup of the U.S. Data are compiled from publications and records of various government and private agencies.

Contains the following directories:

Abstract. Full text electronic version of the 1993 *Statistical Abstract of the U.S.* (for full description, see ASI 1993 Annual, 2324-1).

Files. 1,450 spreadsheet files showing all *Statistical Abstract* tables, some with more detailed historical, industrial, and geographic detail than tables in the published report. Tables are organized in 34 subdirectories, listed below.

CD-ROM contains retrieval software for the *Statistical Abstract* text and tables; spreadsheet files can only be viewed using Lotus 1-2-3 and some other spreadsheet software packages.

System requirements include an IBM-compatible PC with at least 640 kilobytes of memory available, and Microsoft CD-ROM extensions (version 2.0 or higher).

Many agencies discontinued printed publications after making comparable information available on the Internet. *ASI* indexes these titles. Figure 14-12 reproduces an abstract of a document from the Bureau of Economic Analysis (BEA) Electronic Forum. Note, whenever possible, *ASI* include these data in the *ASI Microfiche Library* that is described in the following section.

Figure 14-12
ASI Abstracts **Volume**
Document on the Internet

2506–12   CURRENT INDUSTRIAL
            REPORTS: Machinery and
            Equipment; Electrical and
            Electronics
            † Census-BEA Electronic
            Forum; for individual
            bibliographic data, see below.
            °C3.158:(ltrs.-nos.)
Group of 3 monthly, 3 quarterly, and 23 annual
reports in Current Industrial Reports series covering machinery and equipment.
    Each report contains a brief narrative sum-
mary of survey methodology and findings; and
tables showing quantity and value of shipments.
Some reports also include data on production,
stocks, foreign trade, unfilled orders, consumption, and number of establishments.
    For further description of Current Industrial
Reports series, see Note preceding 2506-3 in ASI
1993 or 1994 Annual.
    Reports issued only annually are listed below
as they appear.
Source: *ASI Index*, **1995, 2nd quarter, 31.**

ASI MICROFICHE LIBRARY

Practically all documents indexed in *ASI* are available in the *American Statistics Index Microfiche Library*.[5] Larger depository libraries often buy subscriptions to the many non-depository titles in the collection. These fiche provide comprehensive coverage of all titles in *ASI* when combined with the depository materials received from GPO. People can also buy individual titles on demand. The ASI/MF codes in abstract citations indicate the price of individual fiche copies. Contact the publisher to interpret the codes.

ELECTRONIC AVAILABILITY OF *ASI*

CD-ROM AVAILABILITY:

Statistical Masterfile[6] is a CD-ROM version of the *American Statistics Index*. It covers 1973 to date with updates published quarterly. *Statistical Masterfile* also indexes statistics covered in two other sources, the *Statistical Reference Index (SRI)*[7] and the *Index to International Statistics (IIS)*.[8] SRI covers data published in the U.S. by sources outside the federal government. These include selected associations, business organizations, commercial publishers, research organizations, and state governments. *IIS* deals with data published by intergovernmental organizations, such as the United Nations, the European Union, and the Organization of American States. Use the print editions of *SRI* and *ASI* in the same manner as *ASI*. Like *ASI*, *SRI* and *IIS* both have comparable microfiche collections.[9] *Statistical Masterfile* searches all three indexes at once or any combination of the three.

ONLINE AVAILABILITY:

The *American Statistics Index*[10] is available on-line from 1973 to date through the Dialog/Knight Ridder Information System. Updates are monthly.

FURTHER INFORMATION:

The annual cumulative indexes and abstracts include a detailed "Users Guide." It covers the kinds of data included in *ASI*, the organization of the index and abstract volumes, descriptions of indexing and abstracting guidelines, sample searches, and illustrations. The monthly indexes and abstracts include an abbreviated guide.

CONCLUSION

Chart 14-2 summarizes how to use *ASI* in different situations.

Chart 14-2
Key Points of the *ASI*

To....	You should...
Locate information by subjects	Use the "Index by Subjects and Names."
Locate information about a specific area, such as a state, a county, or a city (e.g.: population statistics for Erie County NY)	Use the "Index by Subjects and Names" and the "Index by Categories."
Locate comparative data for states, cities, counties, or foreign countries	Use the "Index by Categories."
Locate reports that update information regularly, either monthly, quarterly, or annually	Pay close attention to content notes in the "Index of Subjects and Names" and the "Index by Categories." Content notes mention if statistics are updated regularly.
Determine the availability of historical data	Consult the <u>Abstracts</u> volume to determine if the report is part of a continuing series.
Locate a study or an article when the author is known	Consult the "Index by Subjects and Names."
Locate a document by a specific Board or Commission	Use the "Index by Subjects and Names."
Locate a bibliography of agency publications	Consult the subject heading "Government publications lists" in the "Index by Subjects and Names." Also consult the table of contents to the <u>Abstracts</u> volume. Documents published by the identical agencies are listed in the same sections.
Locate data about statistical methodology	Consult the subject heading "Methodology" in the "Index by Subjects and Names."
Locate statistical projections	Consult the subject heading "Projections" in the "Index by Subjects and Names."
Locate a periodical article when the title is known.	Use the "Index by Titles." Indexing covers both titles of articles and titles of periodicals.
Locate individual reports in a series	Search the "Index by Titles" under the series title.
Locate a publication when the report number is known	Use the "Index by Agency Report Numbers."

Endnotes

1. U.S. President's Commission on Federal Statistics, *Federal Statistics: Report of the President's Commission* (Washington, D.C.: GPO, 1971), Vol. 1, 155. SuDoc number: PR37.8:ST2/R29/V.1.

2. (Bethesda, MD.,: Congressional Information Service, Inc., 1973-monthly).

3. Publications of Appropriations Committees are indexed very adequately in the *CIS Index to Publications of the United States Congress* (Bethesda, MD.: Congressional Information Service, Inc., 1970-monthly).

4. *American Statistics Index: Cumulative Index* (Bethesda, MD.: Congressional Information Service, irregular). Separate issues cover 1974-1979, 1980-1984, 1985-1988, and 1989-1992. Each are 4 volume sets.

5. (Bethesda, MD.: Congressional Information Service, Inc., 1974-quarterly).

6. (Bethesda, MD: Congressional Information Service, Inc., 1973-quarterly).

7. (Bethesda, MD.: Congressional Information Service, Inc., 1980-monthly).

8. (Bethesda, MD.: Congressional Information Service, Inc.,1983-monthly).

9. *Statistical Reference Index Microfiche Library* (Bethesda, MD.: Congressional Information Service, Inc., 1980-quarterly); *Index to International Statistic Microfiche Library* (Bethesda, MD.: Congressional Information Service, Inc., 1983-quarterly).

10. *ASI (American Statistics Index)* (File 102) (Online database). Available on: DIALOG/Knight-Ridder, Mountain View, CA.

Exercises

Use the *American Statistics Index,* 1994 edition, to answer each question.

1. The Department of Commerce published a document in May 1993 about changes and future trends in telecommunications.

   A. What is its *ASI* entry number?

   B. What is its title?

   C. What division of the Department of Commerce published this title?

   D. Who is the personal author?

   E. What is the Superintendent of Documents classification number?

2. The Central Intelligence Agency published a document in 1994 entitled *Eastern Europe: Reforms Spur Recovery.*

   A. What is the *ASI* entry number?

   B. Was this title distributed to depository libraries?

   C. What is the easiest way of acquiring it?

   D. Suppose you wanted to compare changes in Eastern Europe during recent years. Is comparable data available in an earlier edition?

Answers

1. A. 2808-31

   B. *Present Status and Future Trends In Telecommunications.*

   C. National Telecommunications and Information Administration.

   D. Robert F. Linfield.

   E. C60.10:93-296.

2. A. 9118-13

   B. No.

   C. Contact the agency for a copy or locate a library in your area that purchases non-depository documents in the *American Statistics Index Microfiche Library.*

   D. Yes. Consult the 1992 *Abstracts* volume, entry number 9118-13.

• Chapter 15

Census Information

Answer the following questions when reading this chapter:

1. What two things must you do when answering a census question?

2. What kinds of information are collected as part of the *Census of Population and Housing* and the *Economic Census*?

3. How are table finding guides used?

4. How can you locate additional information about census programs?

The Bureau of the Census deserves special consideration when discussing federal government statistics. That agency is the world's most prolific publisher of statistics. Besides distributing information under its own imprint, the Bureau also compiles a great deal of data for other agencies as well. These include the National Center for Health Statistics and the Bureau of Labor Statistics.[1]

Throughout American history, the Bureau of the Census and its predecessor agencies have done much more than merely publish statistics. Census publications have always covered wide varieties of topics. The 1890 *Report on Indians Taxed and Indians Not Taxed in the United States (Except Alaska)* includes many photographs and describes tribal populations, roles of chiefs, dress, education, and traditions among other topics.[2] Moreover, women in the workplace are not a recent late twentieth century phenomena. A 1929 census report, *Women in Gainful Occupations, 1870 to 1920*, concluded that, "whatever opinions may be held as to the proper sphere of woman, the fact is that, to a considerable extent, woman's place today is no longer in the home..."[3]

This chapter summarizes Bureau of the Census programs. The discussion first considers steps that ought to be taken when answering census questions. The next section lists and describes general guides to census programs. Following that, explanations of individual programs emphasize the kinds of information collected, how the data are used, and guides to further information. Programs covered include the *Census of Population and Housing*, the *Economic Census*, the *Census of Agriculture*, and the *Census of Governments*. The chapter then describes information dissemination activities through libraries, State Data Centers, Summary Tape Processing Centers, and Census Information Centers. Appendix 1 to the chapter describes print reports from the 1990 census, and Appendix 2 describes those from the *1992 Economic Census*. The discussion excludes references to magnetic tapes because they are generally unavailable in depository libraries.

ANSWERING CENSUS QUESTIONS

Answering census questions is a two step process: first define the subject at hand and then consider what type of geography would be most appropriate. Suppose you need per capita household income for states in the Northeast. Data that measure per capita income of individuals in Maine is not helpful. Consider subjects and geographies carefully and precisely.

DEFINING SUBJECTS:

To find statistics on a particular topic, it is important to know the terms used by the Bureau of the Census. Census publications include appendices that define terms. Suppose you need data measuring the amounts of money transacted when manufacturers sell their products. Appendix A to the 1992 *Economic Census*, "Explanation of Terms," states that the Bureau of the Census calls this value of shipments. Be flexible when considering subjects. Decide if related data still serve your needs when figures for your precise topic are unavailable.

SELECTING GEOGRAPHIES:

There are two types of census geographies: political and statistical. Political geographies depend upon political decisions. These areas include the nation, states, possessions, congressional districts, counties, voting districts, and Indian reservations.

Boundaries within states differ depending upon local legislation. The Bureau of the Census attempts to classify these divergent areas into a consistent scheme to facilitate comparisons. Consequently, local geographies are sometimes confusing. In selected states, incorporated places are cities, towns, villages, or boroughs that have legal boundaries, powers, and functions. In other states, minor civil divisions (MCDs) serve this purpose. A third group of states includes both incorporated places and minor civil divisions.

When political boundaries are unavailable or are inappropriate, the Bureau of the Census uses statistical geographies for convenience. The

Bureau welcomes local opinion when developing these boundaries. Frequently used statistical boundaries are:

Census regions: Four regions cover the Northeast, Midwest, South, and West.

Census divisions: The four regions are subdivided into nine divisions. Figure 15-1 illustrates the regions and divisions.

**Figure 15-1
Census Regions and Divisions**

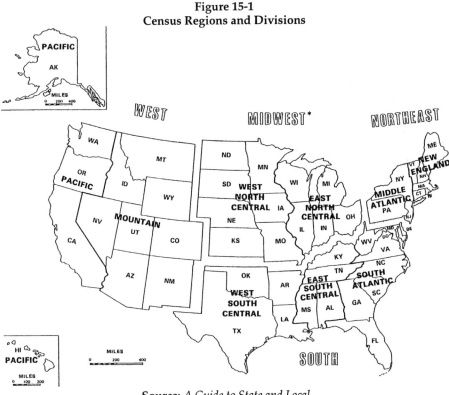

Source: *A Guide to State and Local
Census Geography*, **22.**

Urban/Rural: Urban areas have at least 2,500 people; rural areas have fewer.

Metropolitan Statistical Areas (MSAs): Most MSAs meet two criteria.

(1) One or more counties must have a large population center--usually a city of at least 50,000 people, and

(2) The surrounding areas relate socially and economically to the population center.

An MSA generally adopts the name of its population center.[4]

Primary Metropolitan Statistical Areas (PMSAs): MSAs divide into two or more PMSAs if three conditions are met:

1. The MSAs have populations of at least one million,

2. The MSAs include more than one county--each with internal socioeconomic ties, and

3. Local opinion favors separate recognition.

Consolidated Metropolitan Statistical Areas (CMSAs): CMSAs are groups of adjacent PMSAs.[5]

Urbanized areas (UAs): UAs include a central place plus the surrounding suburbs that have population densities of at least 1,000 per square mile. The area has a minimum 50,000 population. Unlike MSAs, the central cities of urbanized areas can have less than 50,000 people. Note, do not confuse "urbanized areas" with "urban areas" that have populations of at least 2,500 people.

Census designated places (CDPs): Densely settled population centers without legally defined corporate limits or corporate powers. CDPs' have local names.

Census tracts/block numbering areas (BNAs): Census tracts are small subdivisions of metropolitan areas that have approximately 4,000 people. They are comparable to neighborhoods. Although tract boundaries occasionally change between censuses due to population shifts, they are generally stable areas. Block numbering areas are comparable to census tracts in counties outside metropolitan areas. Figure 15-2 displays census tracts in Amherst, NY.

Figure 15-2
Census Tracts--Amherst, NY

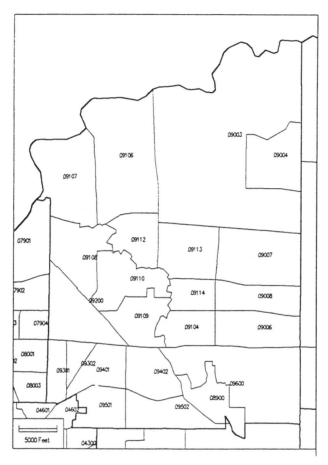

Blocks: The smallest census areas whose boundaries are streets or other types of physical limits. Confidentiality restrictions limit the amount of data available for blocks. The Bureau of the Census will not release data that it feels could be associated with particular individuals or business establishments. Figure 15-3 shows the blocks in tract 91.14, Amherst, NY.

Figure 15-3
Blocks--Tract 91.14
Amherst, NY

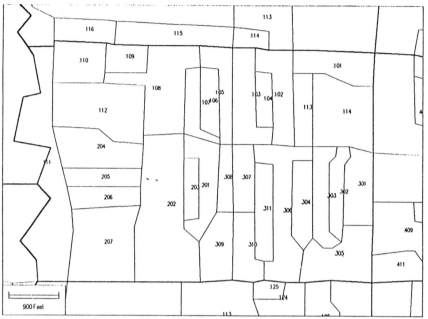

Block groups (BGs): Subdivisions of census tracts that comprise groups of adjacent blocks. Within the same tract, BG 1 includes blocks 101, 102, 103..., while BG 2 consists of blocks 201, 201, 203... Block groups are the smallest geographies for which detailed socioeconomic data are available. Figure 15-4 portrays the three block groups in tract 91.14.

Figure 15-4
Block Groups--Tract 91.14
Amherst, NY

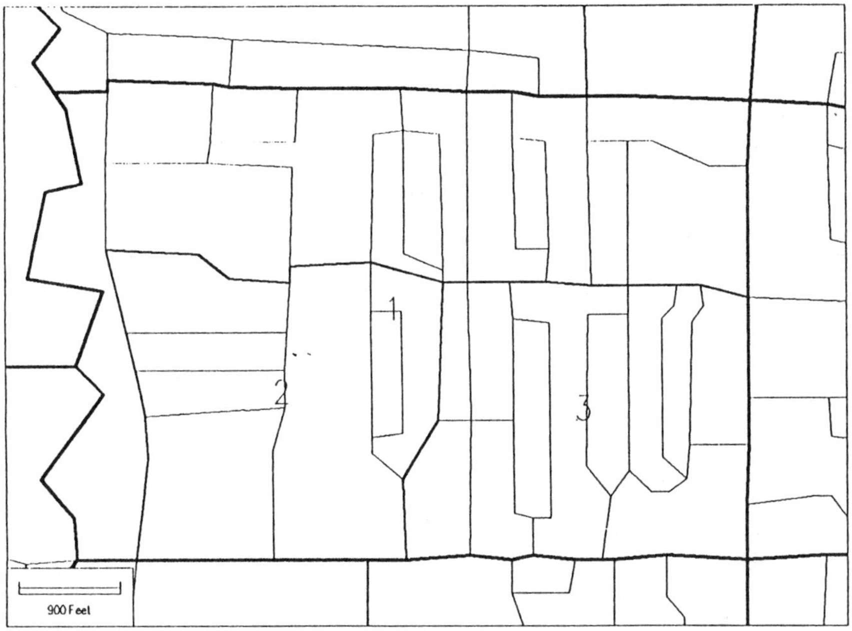

900 Feet

Maps and More: Your Guide to Census Bureau Geography[6] is a good summary of census geography. It describes how boundaries are created, defines different kinds of areas, illustrates different kinds of maps, and provides contacts for further information. Many of the references cited below under "General Information Sources About Census Programs" also summarize census geography. Consult *A Guide to State and Local Census Geography*[7] and *Geographic Areas Reference Manual*[8] for detailed information.

GENERAL INFORMATION SOURCES ABOUT CENSUS PROGRAMS

PRINTED SOURCES:

Fagan, Michele. "Mystery Tour Through the Lumber Room: United States Census Publications, 1820-1930, A Descriptive Essay," *Government Publications Review*. 13:2 (1986), 209-231.

Fagan describes historically significant census publications that cover numerous topics, such as census procedures, manufacturing, labor, finance, cities and towns, and crime, plus many more. An appended bibliography includes Superintendent of Documents numbers.

U.S. Bureau of the Census. *Catalog of Publications, 1790-1972*. Washington, D.C.: 1974. SuDoc number: C56.222/2-2:790-972.

Publications issued from 1790 through 1945, and 1946 through 1972 appear in separate sections. Abstracts are very comprehensive. Each section has its own index. Many titles are available in two film collections, one covering the decennial censuses[9] and the other non-decennial censuses.[10]

U. S. Bureau of the Census. *Census and You*. Washington, D.C.: GPO, 1988-monthly. SuDoc number: C3.238:. (Previously published as *Data User News*).

A newsletter that describes publications and services offered by the Bureau of the Census. When appropriate, editors include ordering information for new publications and telephone contacts.

U. S. Bureau of the Census. *Census Catalog and Guide*. Washington, D.C.: GPO, 1985-annual. SuDoc number: C3.163/3:. (Published earlier under different titles).

This annual catalog provides detailed abstracts of census publications. The 1994 edition includes publications issued between 1988 and 1993. A new cumulation will start in 1995. The product overview chapter is an especially useful guide to fifteen statistical programs. It summarizes all publications in tabular format, noting series titles, abstract numbers, formats, subject descriptions, geographies covered, and frequencies. Additional features include title and subject indexes and telephone contacts. The *Census Catalog and Guide* is the most useful single source to consult about census publications, CD-ROMs, and magnetic tapes.

U. S. Bureau of the Census. *Census, CD-ROM, and You: New Horizons for Microcomputer Users of Census Bureau Date*. Washington, D.C.: GPO, 1993. SuDoc number: C3.2:H78.

The Bureau of the Census distributed information in CD-ROM format beginning with the 1987 *Economic Census*. This pamphlet summarizes the technology describing how it works and the kinds of products available. Information is for the novice.

U. S. Bureau of the Census. *Monthly Product Announcement*. Washington, D.C.: GPO, 1981-monthly. SuDoc number: C3.163/7:

Descriptions of new census publications include titles, report numbers, and formats. Abstracts summarize selected items. The publisher includes order forms and telephone contacts for further information.

U. S. Bureau of the Census. *Statistical Brief* series. Washington, D.C.: GPO, published irregularly. SuDoc number: C3.205/8:

Statistical Briefs are short 2-4 page pamphlets that summarize newsworthy information found in current census reports. Charts, graphs, and tables add to the lucid text. The further references and contacts are helpful. Selected recent titles include: *Housing in Metropolitan Areas--Black House-*

holds, Reducing Toxins: Where to Look and How to Do It, and *Mothers Who Receive AFDC Payments--Fertility and Socioeconomic Characteristics.*

U. S. Bureau of the Census. *Taking Care of Business: A Guide to Census Bureau Data for Small Businesses.* Washington, D.C.: GPO, 1993. SuDoc number: C3.6/2:B88x.

Taking Care of Business summarizes population and economic census programs. Three case studies on expanding a business, determining if a business can succeed, and selecting sites are good illustrations of data uses.

CENSUS OF POPULATION AND HOUSING

RANGE OF DATA COLLECTED:

The *Census of Population and Housing,* conducted every ten years since 1790, compiles a wide range of socioeconomic data about Americans. Chart 15-1 describes selected variables and indicates when the information was collected.

Chart 15-1
Subjects Covered by the *Census of Population and Housing*

Topic	Dates of Coverage
Age and sex	1790-present (but only for free whites until 1820)
Slave status	1790-1860
Race	1790-present
Citizenship	1820, 1830, 1870, 1890-present
Physical or mental disabilities	1830-1930, 1970, 1990
Education	1840-present
Married in past year	1850-1890 (only for free whites until 1870)
Occupation	1850-present
Crime	1850-1890
Mortality	1850-1890
Place of birth	1850-present
Pauperism	1850-1910 (coverage of poverty resumed in 1960)
Wages and income	1850-present
Parents birthplaces	1870-present
Prisoners	1880-1910
Marital status	1880-present
Employment status	1880-present, except 1920
Institutionalized persons	1850, 1880-1890, 1910, 1940-present
Year of immigration	1890-1930, 1970-present
Number of children ever born	1890-1910, 1940-present
Ability to speak English	1890-present, except 1950

HOW IS THE DATA USED?

All levels of government use the *Census of Population and Housing*. The Bureau of the Census must provide states with population counts for legislative redistricting within one year following the census. Consult *P.L. 94-171 Redistricting Data From the Year 2000 Census: The View From the States*[11] for a brief case study of how the North Carolina Legislature redistricted its Assembly. Governments also use census data to evaluate policy options and plan new programs. For instance, the decennial census is the only source that measures income and poverty levels for local areas throughout the nation in a consistent fashion. These data are very important when considering welfare reform. To give a second example, state and local governments consider age factors when planning educational facilities and senior citizen services.

Population counts affect distribution of government grants and loans. See *Federal Legislative Uses of Decennial Census Data* for a list of programs that are dependent upon census data.[12] The adjustment of census undercounts is a major issue because many believe urban areas lose large amounts of federal and state aid due to undercounts.[13]

Population statistics are valuable to business people, scholars, and individuals as well. Business people study characteristics of communities before opening new retail outlets or marketing new products. Demographers, sociologists, economists, and historians often incorporate census information into their research to illustrate points and to formulate hypotheses. Home buyers use census data to understand characteristics of areas before making their purchases.

TWO TYPES OF DATA ARE COLLECTED--
SUMMARY TAPE DATA AND MICRODATA SAMPLES

Most census users are more familiar with summary tape data than microdata samples. Tables compiled by the Bureau of the Census contain summary tape data. For instance, all tables in printed reports are summary statistics. The Bureau of the Census also publishes summary tape files (STFs) on magnetic tapes and CD-ROMs.

Public use microdata samples (PUMS data) are not organized into tables by the Bureau of the Census. Each record in the database reflects a response to a particular questionnaire. The Bureau of the Census preserves confidentiality by removing all personal references to people who completed the questionnaires. PUMS data are on magnetic tape and CD-ROMs.

PUMS data is not for the novice census user. The Bureau of the Census includes the *Quick Tab* program on its 1990 PUMS CD-ROMs. Although it attempts to meet the needs of laymen programmers, those using PUMS data often need more sophisticated statistical packages, such as SPSS or SAS. Even if *Quick Tab* meets one's needs, a sophisticated statistical background is still essential for interpreting the results correctly.

Summary tape data fail to answer complicated questions that require many cross tabulations. A three tier question like the following is just one example. Suppose you need statistics that measure:

1.   The number of married 30-year-old heads of households
     in the Buffalo, NY metropolitan area,

2.   who have two children, and

3.   who earn between $50,000 and $60,000 annually.

PUMS statistics answer this question.

LOCATING 1990 CENSUS INFORMATION IN PRINTED REPORTS--TABLE FINDING GUIDES:

Every printed report includes an introduction entitled "How To Use This Census Report." It describes how to cross subjects and geographic areas when answering questions and how to use the statistical tables.

The table finding guide in each printed report is the primary way of locating information. Remember, using the census requires two things:

1. Consider the most appropriate subject, and

2. Consider the most appropriate geography.

The table finding guide in Figure 15-5 lists subjects along the left column and types of geographies along the top column. For instance, population counts by race and Hispanic origin for counties are on table 6. Letters after table numbers indicate kinds of populations covered. Jane Weintrop's compilation of all table finding guides to the 1990 census is an excellent source for locating data in printed reports.[14] Appendix 1 to this chapter is a directory of 1990 printed reports.

Figure 15-5
1990 *Census of Population and Housing*
Table Finding Guide

Subjects by Type of Geographic Area and Table Number

Subjects covered in this report are shown on the left side, and types of geographic areas are shown at the top. For definitions of area classifications, see appendix A. For definitions and explanations of subject characteristics, see appendix B. Race and Hispanic origin letters in parentheses after the table numbers. When a range of table numbers is shown together with a reference letter, there is one table for each race and Hispanic group. Reference letters for population counts and characteristics by race and Hispanic origin are:

(A) White; Black; American Indian, Eskimo, or Aleut; Asian or Pacific Islander; Hispanic origin; White, not of Hispanic origin
(B) American Indian, Eskimo, Aleut, All Asian, Chinese, Filipino, Japanese, Asian Indian, Korean, Vietnamese, Cambodian, Hmong, Laotian, Thai; All Pacific Islander, Hawaiian, Samoan, Guamanian
(C) Mexican, Puerto Rican, Cuban, Other Hispanic origin, Dominican, Central American, Costa Rican, Guatemalan, Honduran, Nicaraguan, Panamanian, Salvadoran, South American, Argentinean, Chilean, Colombian, Ecuadorian, Peruvian, Venezuelan, All other Hispanic origin
(D) Race by Hispanic origin

| Subject | The State | | | County | | Place and (in selected States) county subdivision[1] | | American Indian and Alaska Native area[2] |
	Total	Urban, rural, size of place, and rural farm	Inside and outside metropolitan area	Total	Rural or rural farm	10,000 or more	2,500 to 9,999	
SUMMARY CHARACTERISTICS	1-3, 8-13(A)	1-3, 8-13(A)	1-3, 8-13(A)	1-3, 8-13(A)	...	1-3, 8-13(A)	1-3, 8-13(A)	14-16
POPULATION COUNTS BY RACE AND HISPANIC ORIGIN.............	4-5(A-D)	4(A-D)	5(A-D)	6(A-D)	214(A), 218(A)	7(A-D)	7(A-D)	...
SOCIAL CHARACTERISTICS								
Age.............................	20, 34, 45(A), 110(B), 119(C), 128(D)	20, 56-61(A)	34, 56-61(A)	140, 151(A)	215, 219	169, 180(A)	196	222
Ancestry	17, 31	17	31	137	...	166	195	...
Disability	20, 34, 45(A), 111(B), 120(C), 129(D)	20, 62-67(A)	34, 62-67(A)	140, 152(A)	216, 220	169, 181(A)	197	223
Education:								
School enrollment and type of school, educational attainment ...	22, 36, 47(A), 111(B), 120(C), 129(D)	22, 62-67(A)	36, 62-67(A)	142, 152(A), 160(B), 163(C)	215, 219	171, 181(A), 189(B), 192(C)	197, 205(A), 208(B), 211(C)	223

Source: *1990 Census of Population: Social and Economic Characteristics*

Test your understanding of 1990 census table finding guides: Refer to Figure 15-8 when answering the following:

1.   Which table(s) includes age breakdowns for the town I live in? My town has 11,000 people.

(Tables 169 and 180)

2.   Which table(s) should I use to compare age breakdowns in my town to those in the entire state?

(Tables 20, 34, 45, 110, 119, and 128)

3.   Which table(s) should I consult to locate ancestry statistics for a town of 4,500 people?

(Table 195)

LOCATING CENSUS INFORMATION ON CD-ROM DISKS:

The Bureau of the Census distributed decennial census statistics in CD-ROM format for the first time in 1990.[15] The disks are in two numbered series, STF 1 and STF 3. STF 1 covers 100% of all respondents. Although STF 3 covers a 17% sample of respondents, it deals with a much wider range of subjects than STF 1. The subject of the inquiry determines if you need STF 1 or STF 3. Chart 15-2 lists subjects on STF 1 disks. The STF 3 disks cover the same topics as STF 1, plus additional ones shown on Chart 15-3.

Chart 15-2
Subjects Covered on STF 1
(Based upon 100% of all respondents)

Population Characteristics	Housing Characteristics
Population	Number of units in structure
Household relationships	Number of rooms in housing unit
Sex	Tenure (housing units that are owned or rented by residents)
Age	Value of home or monthly rent paid
Marital status	Congregate housing (meals included in rent) Vacancy characteristics
Hispanic origin	
Race	

431

Chart 15-3
**Subjects Covered on STF 3 (Based upon 17% of all respondents nationally.
STF 3 covers all subjects on STF 1 plus those shown on this chart.)**

Social Characteristics	Economic Characteristics	Housing Characteristics
Place of birth, citizenship, and year of entry to the US. Education (enrollment and attainment) Ancestry Migration (residence in 1985) Language spoken at home Veteran status Disability Fertility	Labor force Place of work and journey to work Year last worked Occupation, industry, and class of worker Work experience in 1989 Income in 1989 Poverty status	Year moved into residence Number of bedrooms Plumbing and kitchen facilities Telephone in housing unit Vehicles available Heating fuel Source of water and method of sewage disposal Year structure built Condominium status Farm residence Shelter costs, including utilities

STF 1 and STF 3 each have four parts: A, B, C, and D. The lettered series determine geographies found on each disk. Chart 15-4 illustrates the kind of areas covered in each series.

Chart 15-4
Geographies Covered by STF A, B, C, and D Disks

Geography	STF 1	STF 3
U.S., regions, and divisions	C	C
American Indian/Alaska Native areas	A,C	A,C
States	A,B,C	A,C
Metropolitan statistical areas (MSA's)	C	A,C
Urbanized areas (UA's)	C	A,C
Congressional districts	A	D
Counties	A,C	A,C
Places and other county subdivisions under 10,000 population (e.g.: cities, towns, villages)	A	A
Places and other county subdivisions over 10,000 population (e.g.: cities, towns, villages)	A,C	A,C
Census tracts (or block numbering areas)	A	A
Block groups	A	A
Blocks	B	
Five digit Zip codes		B

Two examples explain how data in charts 15-2 through 15-4 are used.

1. Suppose you need data that measure racial characteristics in different neighborhoods of Chicago. Remember two things: tracts and block groups approximate neighborhoods, and STF 3 includes all items on Chart 15-2, plus those on Chart 15-3. Charts 15-2 and 15-3 show that both STF 1 and STF 3 have statistics about race. Chart 15-4 indicates data for census tracts and block groups are on STF 1A and STF 3A.

2. Suppose you are looking for information that measures income by zip codes in New York State. Chart 15-2 shows that STF 1 does not cover income. However, Chart 15-3 indicates it is covered in the STF 3 series. Chart 15-4 tells you STF 3B is the only disk that deals with zip codes.

Test your understanding of the *1990 Census of Population and Housing* **on CD-ROM:** Use charts 15-2 through 15-4 to answer the following:

1. Which CD-ROM tells me how many people in my neighborhood graduated from college?

    (STF 3A)

2. Which disk provides comparable information for the nation?

    (STF 3C)

3. Is it possible to determine the number of college graduates living on my block?

    (No; education data are not collected for individual blocks. Chart 15-3 shows that education is covered on STF 3 and Chart 15-4 shows that block data is available only on STF 1B. Block groups are the smallest geography for which education statistics are available.)

SOURCES OF FURTHER INFORMATION ABOUT THE 1990 *CENSUS OF POPULATION AND HOUSING:*

Remember, all Bureau of the Census reports include appendices that define subjects and geographies. Additional appendices also describe data collection and processing procedures; explain data accuracy and standard errors; and offer sources for further information. Files on CD-ROM disks have comparable data.

Consult the following for further information:

Crispell, Diane. *The Insiders Guide to Demographic Know-How: Everything You Need to Find, Analyze, and Use Information About Your Customers.* 3rd ed. New York: American Demographics Press, 1993.

Part 1 gives basic information about demographic data. It covers population trends and analysis; demography in business, law, and government; and geographic information system applications. Part 2 describes data sources published by the federal government; private sources; state and local governments; and international bodies. Special features include a glossary; a telephone directory; and an index.

Goyer, Doreen S. and Elaine Domschke. *The Handbook of National Population Censuses: Latin America and the Caribbean, North America, and Oceania.* Westport, Conn.: Greenwood Press, 1983.

Separate chapters cover different countries. The U.S. chapter summarizes each census between 1790 and 1980. Emphasis is upon changes over time in data collection and processing. Discussion of 1950 through 1980 is significantly more detailed than the earlier years.

Lavin, Michael. *Understanding the Census: A Guide for Marketers, Grant Writers, and Other Data Users.* Buffalo, NY: Epoch Books, 1996. Distributed by Oryx Press.

Lavin's book is a comprehensive discussion of the *Census of Population and Housing.* He covers census fundamentals, such as data use, census terminology, and geography. He also considers access to data in paper, microfiche, CD-ROM, and online formats. Appendices include a bibliography and a guide to STF tables on CD-ROM.

Myers, Dowell. *Analysis with Local Census Data: Portraits of Change.* Boston: Academic Press, 1992.

Separate sections cover definitions and strategies for using census data; types of data and their accuracy; types of geographies; and analysis of housing conditions, age, race, income, and household relationships. Few titles cover the use of microdata samples in as much detail. The author includes a bibliography and an index.

Pol, Louis G. *Business Demography: A Guide and Reference for Business Planners and Marketers.* New York: Quorum Books, 1987.

Business people could benefit from this survey and introduction to demography. The initial chapters deal with demographic topics, such as fertility, mortality, migration, and geography. The following sections cover data applications. Although the book is old, the applications section is still very useful. The author includes notes, a bibliography, and an index.

Schulze, Suzanne. *Population Information in Nineteenth Century Census Volumes.* Phoenix: Oryx Press, 1983.

_____. *Population Information in Twentieth Century Census Volumes, 1900-1940.* Phoenix: Oryx Press, 1985.

_____. *Population Information in Twentieth Century Census Volumes, 1950-1980.* Phoenix: Oryx Press, 1988.

Schulze indexes decennial census data published between 1790 and 1980. Entries include bibliographic information, Superintendent of Document numbers, references to microfilm reproductions, and brief narrative descriptions of the publications. Matrixes similar to the table finding guide in Figure 15-5 relate subjects to geographies. Consult the inside covers for a summary of subjects in each report.

U.S. Bureau of the Census. *Catalog of Publications, 1790-1972.* See "General Information Sources About Census Programs" cited above.

_____. *Census ABC's: Applications in Business and Community.* Washington, D.C.: GPO, 1989. SuDoc number: C3.2:B96/5.

This introductory guide provides a survey of subjects covered by the census; tips on reading tables; simplified geographic definitions; and illustrations from census maps. Sample applications describe how data were acquired from various sources. The references to relevant non-census sources are helpful. *Census ABC's* is still useful for beginning researchers even though it predates the 1990 census.

U.S. Bureau of the Census. *Census '90 Basics.* Washington, D.C.: GPO, 1993. SuDoc number: C3.2:B29/993.

Explanations of the census process, census questions, printed reports, and magnetic tapes are informative. The descriptions of census geography are especially good.

U.S. Bureau of the Census. *Do You Know Which ...?* SuDoc numbers: C3.2:...

This series of pamphlets describes various aspects of the *Census of Population and Housing.* Most documents cover definitions, printed reports, CD-ROMs, and magnetic tapes. Selected titles include:

-*Do You Know Which 1990 Report Is Similar To Your Favorite 1980 Report?*

-*Do You Know Which Report Contains the Data You Need?*

-*Do You Know Which 1990 Products Contain Data on the Asian and Pacific Islander Population?*

-*Do You Know Which 1990 Products Contain Data on the Older Population?*

U.S. Bureau of the Census. *1990 Census of Population and Housing: Guide, Part A. Text* (1990 CPH-R-1A) Washington, D.C.: GPO, 1992. SuDoc number: C3.223/22:990-R-1A.

_____. *1990 Census of Population and Housing: Guide, Part B. Glossary* (1990 CPH-R-1B) Washington, D.C.: GPO, 1993. SuDoc number: C3.223/22:990-R-1B.

Part A describes census fundamentals, questions asked, data collection and processing, geography, data products, and sources of additional information. Chapter 6, "Understanding the Statistics," is especially informative. It covers how to get the most out of the data, misreading tables, the importance of definitions, and sampling errors, among other topics. Part B provides comprehensive definitions of geographic, population, housing, and technical terms.[16]

ECONOMIC CENSUS

The Bureau of the Census conducts the *Economic Census* every five years ending with digits 2 and 7. It is a snapshot of the American economy at a given time. Establishments, rather than companies, are the basis of the census. Establishments are places where business is conducted. One company that has three different facilities represents three establishments. The most current *Economic Census* covers 1992. The 1997 census will occur in early 1998 and will likely be published between 1999 and 2001.

USES OF THE *ECONOMIC CENSUS*:

The *Economic Census* is an important source of facts about the structure and functioning of the nation's economy. The federal government uses the data to compile economic statistics, such as the gross national product, and to develop indexes that measure industrial production and price levels. State and local governments use the data to assess business activities in their jurisdictions.

Business people use the data to forecast general economic conditions and sales; to analyze sales performance; and to establish sales territories. They also depend upon this information for allocating advertising funds; locating new plants, warehouses, and stores; and measuring potential markets. Additionally, trade and professional associations use the *Economic Census* to study and to forecast trends that may affect their industries. The *Economic Census* is invaluable to university students, faculty, and others involved in any of the above activities.

MAJOR REPORTS IN THE 1987 *ECONOMIC CENSUS*:

Chart 15-5 displays the major topics covered in the *Economic Census* and indicates the types of geographies for which statistics are available.

Chart 15-5
Major Data Items in the *Economic Census*
by Geographic Levels (Reproduced from document\general\datafind.doc file
on *1992 Economic Census CD-ROM*)

Publication Legend:

1	Census of Retail Trade
2	Census of Wholesale Trade
3	Census of Service Industries
4	Census of Transportation, Communication, and Utilities
5	Census of Financial, Insurance, and Real Estate Industries
6	Census of Manufactures
7	Census of Mineral Industries
8	Census of Construction Industries

Geography Legend:

A	National, states, metropolitan areas, counties, and places. Metropolitan areas are central cities of at least 50,000 population, plus the surrounding smaller areas, which are integrated in a socioeconomic sense.
M	National, states, and metropolitan areas.
C	National, states, and counties.
S	National and states.
N	National only.
Z	ZIP codes.

	1	2	3	4	5	6	7	8
Establishments								
With payrolls	A, Z	A	A, Z	M	M	A, Z	C	M
Without payrolls	A		A	M	M			S
Single-unit/multi-unit	N	N	N	N	N	N	N	N
By legal form of organization	N	N	N	N	N	N	N	N
Firms	N	N	N	N	N	S	S	
Employment								
All employees	A, Z	A	A, Z	M	M	A	C	M
Production (construction) workers (hours)						A	C	S
Employment size of establishment						S		
Employment related to exports						S		
Payroll								
All employees, entire year	A, Z	A	A, Z	M	M	A	C	M
All employees, first quarter	A	A	A	M	M			S
Production workers						A	C	S
Supplemental labor costs	N	N	N			S	S	S

	1	2	3	4	5	6	7	8
Sales, Receipts, or Value of Shipments/Construction Work Done								
Establishments with payrolls	A,Z	A	A,Z	M	M	A	C	M
Establishments without payrolls	A		A	M	M			S
By specific product line or type of construction	M	M	M	M	M	N	C	S
By class of customer	N	N	M	N				
Sales size of establishment	N,Z	N	N,Z	N	N			S
Value of exports			N		N	S		
Operating Expenses								
Total	N	S	S					
Costs of materials		N				A	C	M
Specific materials consumed		N				N	N	
Cost of fuels	N	N	N			S	S	M
Cost of electricity	N	N	N			S	S	S
Energy consumed						S	S	
Contract work		N				S	S	M
Products bought or resold						S	S	
Advertising	N	N	N			N		
Rental payments	N	N	N			S	S	S
Communications services	N	N	N			N	S	S
Purchased repairs	N	N	N			N		S
Legal services	N	N	N			N		
Accounting and booking services	N	N	N			N		
Software and other computer services	N	N	N			N		
Refuse removal services	N	N	N			N		
Other								
Value added	N	N				A	C	M
Net income produced	N	N						
Capital expenditures, total	N	N	N			S	C	M
Capital expenditures, new	N	N	N			A	S	S
Assets	N	N	N			S	S	S
Inventories	N	S				S	S	S
Industry specialization coverage						N		N

The following descriptions differentiate the kinds of information collected in each program. Using a sample product, canned fruit, examples show how each series relates to the others. Appendix 2 to this chapter describes documents published in each census. Comparable information is also available on CD-ROM.[17]

Census of Manufacturers.

Covers establishments that mechanically or chemically transform materials or substances into new products. The food processing industry transforms fresh fruit into the canned product. Data for the fruit itself, the raw material, are part of the *Census of Agriculture.*

Census of Mineral Industries.

Covers establishments that extract minerals, process them on site, and explore and develop mineral properties. The *Census of Mineral Industries* deals with mining tin from which the fruit cans are manufactured.

Census of Wholesale Trade.

Covers establishments that sell to retailers; to commercial, industrial, farm, and professional users; and to other wholesalers. Wholesalers sell the tin cans made by metal manufacturers to the food processing industry and sell the canned fruit to supermarkets and restaurants.

Census of Retail Trade.

Covers retail establishments that sell merchandise for personal or household consumption. The basis of this data are types of establishments, not products. That is, statistics cover total retail sales for supermarkets and groceries, not that for canned fruit.[18]

Consult two variables in the *Census of Manufacturers* to locate data that approximates the amount and dollar value of canned fruit sold: quantity shipped and value of shipments. Note the limitations. The quantity and value of products shipped from manufacturers to wholesalers and retailers are different from that actually sold. However, given the structure of the Economic Censuses, this is the best product specific data available.

Census of Service Industries.

Covers establishments providing services for individuals, businesses, governments, and other organizations. The *Census of Service Industries* deals with sales in restaurants. However, as with retail trade, the amounts of canned fruit restaurants sell cannot be determined. The data consider all foods sold in restaurants.

Census of Financial, Insurance and Real Estate Industries.

Covers establishments providing financial, insurance, and real estate services. These data are available for the first time in 1992.

Census of Transportation, Communications, and Utilities.

The 1992 census covers communications, electric, gas, sanitary services, highway passengers, airlines, and pipeline transportation for the first time. Other data include information about trucking and warehousing, water transportation, transportation services, and truck inventory and use. These businesses store the fruit in warehouses and transport it to supermarkets and restaurants.

Census of Construction Industries.

Covers establishments engaged in construction of new homes and other buildings; heavy construction, such as highways; and special trades, such as plumbing and electrical work. Statistics exclude construction undertaken by homeowners or by non-construction businesses. Establishments that build food processing plants, supermarkets, and restaurants are part of the *Census of Construction Industries.*

Enterprise Statistics.

Regroups establishment-based data to show characteristics of owning or controlling firms.

Minority and Women Owned Businesses.

Describes characteristics of businesses owned by Blacks, Hispanics, Asian Americans, American Indians, other minorities, and women.

SOURCES OF FURTHER INFORMATION
ABOUT THE ECONOMIC CENSUS:

Consult the most current *Census Catalog and Guide,* the introductory and appended materials in the census publications, and the documentation files on the *1992 Economic Census* CD-ROM for further information. Start the CD by typing GO and then type DOCVIEW for the documentation files. The following sources are also useful.

U.S. Bureau of the Census. *Accountants' Guide to the 1992 Economic Census* (EC-92-PR-4) Washington, D.C.: GPO, 1992.

The Bureau of the Census prepared this pamphlet to help accountants deal with the *Economic Census.* The brief descriptions emphasize the kinds of business that apply to each census and the importance of completing data for establishments, rather than companies. A chart summarizes data items collected for each census. Sample census forms are reproduced.

U.S. Bureau of the Census. *Case Studies In Using Data For Better Business Decisions.* Washington, D.C.: GPO, 1991. C46.2:C28x.

Case studies illustrate the kinds of data available and explain how the numbers are used. Topics include site locations, business expansions, construction of new homes, analysis of market share, and marketing products. Each case has introductory material that provides relevant background and bibliographies of sources used. The excerpts from statistical tables and the descriptions of data applications are most useful.

U.S. Bureau of the Census. *Guide to the 1987 Economic Censuses and Related Statistics* (EC87-R-2) Washington, D.C.: GPO, 1990. SuDoc number: C3.253:EC87-R-2.

Although a bit old, this volume is still the most comprehensive guide to the *Economic Census*. Reproductions from tables enhance the detailed explanations of each census. The Bureau of the Census expects to publish a supplementary pamphlet that describes changes since 1987.

U.S. Bureau of the Census. *Guide to the 1992 Census of Agriculture and Related Statistics* (AC92-R-9) Washington, D.C.: GPO, 1994. SuDoc number: C3.6/2:AG8/2/992

Chapter 3, "Related Statistics," is a good summary of publications pertaining to all the economic censuses.

U.S. Bureau of the Census. *Introduction to the 1992 Economic Census* (EC92-PR-2) Washington, D.C.: GPO, no date.

This brief pamphlet is for laypersons. Selected topics include data collection and classification, new features of the 1992 census, and references for further assistance. A chart illustrates major data items that are collected.

U.S. Bureau of the Census. *A Preview of the 1992 Economic Census* (EC92-PR-1) Washington, D.C.: GPO, 1992. SuDoc number: C3.253/2:EC92-PR-1.

The short descriptions of information included in each census are helpful to novices. Different sections cover data collection and classification, and changes in the 1992 censuses. Additional information examines major subjects covered in each program, publication of the data, and contacts for further information.

OTHER CENSUS PROGRAMS

CENSUS OF AGRICULTURE:

The *Census of Agriculture* includes farms from which $1,000 in agricultural products were sold or normally would have been sold. Like the *Economic Census*, it occurs every five years in digits ending in 2 and 7. Appendix 2 includes descriptions of printed reports. Data are also in CD-ROM format.[19]

Governments use the information for planning rural development. Business people use it to determine market trends, to plan site locations and service outlets, and to ensure orderly marketing and distribution. Coverage includes quantity and value of crop and livestock production; land use and land values; payrolls and employment; and use of fertilizers and pesticides. Consult the following for further information:

-The introductions and appendices to the print volumes.

-Documentation files on the CD-ROM.

-*Guide to the 1992 Census of Agriculture and Related Statistics.*[20]

CENSUS OF GOVERNMENTS:

The *Census of Governments* is the only comprehensive uniform analysis of American state and local governments. Selected topics include taxation and other income, expenditures, debt, public employment, and labor-management policies. Officials at all levels use the data for planning and administering fiscal policy, judging the effectiveness of intergovernmental programs, and comparing property taxes. These statistics are also essential to researchers and public interest groups who study trends and natures of government. Consult the introductory sections and appendices to each volume and the forthcoming *Guide to the 1992 Census of Governments*[21] for additional information. The Bureau of the Census also expects to publish the *1992 Census of Governments* on CD-ROM.

DISSEMINATION OF CENSUS DATA

Information dissemination is high among Bureau of the Census priorities. The agency has six programs that make data more widely available. The Bureau of the Census *Catalog and Guide* includes directories to the first five.

STATE DATA CENTER PROGRAM:

The State Data Center Program began in 1978 and by 1985 all fifty states participated. Each state designates a lead agency. This agency appoints groups throughout the state to serve as State Date Center Affiliates. Affiliates are often regional planning boards and other local government agencies, universities, public libraries, and chambers of commerce. The Bureau of the Census forwards to the lead agency gratis copies of publications, CD-ROMs, and magnetic tapes pertinent to that state. The lead agency, in turn, distributes this information to its local affiliates who meet data needs of local populations and business. State Data Centers and their affiliates provide reference services and coordinate local government census planning activities with the Bureau of the Census. They also offer census training and consulting activities.

The Data Center system is the basis for the new Business and Industry Data Center (BIDC) Program. Data centers traditionally distributed population information to its users. BIDCs distribute business and economic information as well.

CENSUS DEPOSITORY LIBRARY PROGRAM:

One hundred and thirty libraries participate in the Census Depository Library Program. The program began in 1950 to distribute more information to more people. Eligible libraries must be in cities having 25,000 minimum populations that are not conveniently located near GPO depositories. Participants receive without charge core collections of basic data relevant to their states and can choose to select additional information depending upon their needs.

SUMMARY TAPE PROCESSING CENTERS:

Creation of Summary Tape Processing Centers in the late 1960s helped data users with magnetic tapes. Most Processing Centers eventually developed into businesses that sell marketing; geocoding and mapping; number crunching; and surveying services.

CENSUS INFORMATION CENTERS:

Census Information Centers are nonprofit groups that receive census information without charge. These groups then make the data available to the public. The National Urban League, the National Council of La Raza, and the Southwest Voter Research Institute are three examples.

FAST FAX:

Call 1-900-555-2FAX for selected census publications. Callers pay $2.50 per minute when connected. There are no additional charges to receive the fax. Selected topics cover construction of new one family homes, retail sales, wholesale trade, manufacturing inventories, and reports on manufacturing industries.

TAPE TO CD-ROM CONVERSION SERVICE:

The tape to CD-ROM conversion service converts tapes to CD-ROM disks upon request. Customers pay the identical fee for the CD-ROM as they would have for the tape. Data files are in ASCII format and they do not come with software. Users must have background in statistical packages, such as SPSS or SAS, to use this information. Printed documentation comes with the CD-ROM.

CONCLUSION

This book offers an introduction to federal statistics, which are often difficult and confusing to use. The telephone is often a data user's most valuable reference tool. When facing difficulties, contact appropriate agency officials who are experts in their fields. *Federal Statistical Source: Where To Find Agency Experts and Personnel* is a wonderful directory.[22] *Carroll's Federal Directory*[23] does not emphasize agency statisticians, but it is still a good source. A third source, the *United States Government Manual*[24], is the official directory to the federal government. It gives phone numbers, but it does not provide nearly as many names of agency personnel as the other sources.

Endnotes

1. See U.S. Bureau of the Census, *Survey Abstracts* (Washington, D.C.: GPO, 1992) for a comprehensive list of surveys conducted by the Bureau of the Census. Entries describe the titles, purposes, survey designs, sample sizes, types of respondents, sponsoring agencies, legal authorities, frequencies, and disseminations of results.

2. Cited in Michele Fagan, "Mystery Tour Through the Lumber Room: United States Census Publications, 1820-1930, A Descriptive Essay" *Government Publications Review* 13:2 (1986), 212.

3. *Ibid.*

4. MSAs are sometimes confused with SMSAs. Prior to the 1990 census, metropolitan areas were called Standard Metropolitan Statistical Areas (SMSAs).

5. CMSAs are often confused with CSMAs. Consolidated statistical metropolitan areas (CSMAs) were groups of adjacent SMSAs. SMSAs are discussed in a previous note.

6. U.S. Bureau of the Census, Rev. ed. (Washington, D.C.: GPO, 1994). SuDoc number: C3.2:G29/4/994.

7. U.S. Bureau of the Census, Prepared in cooperation with the Association of Public Data Users (Washington, D.C.: GPO, 1993). SuDoc number: C3.6/2:G29. The introduction gives an overview of the subject and successive chapters deal with geographies in each state and possession.

8. U.S. Bureau of the Census (Washington, D.C.: GPO, 1994). SuDoc number: C3.6/2:G29/4. Separate chapters cover different kinds of geographies. (i.e.: county subdivisions, places, tracts,..)

9. U.S. Bureau of the Census, *United States Decennial Census Publications 1790-1970* (Woodbridge, Conn.: Research Publications, 1975). 371 reels of microfilm. Research Publications has since filmed the 1980 census and intends to film the 1990 census.

10. U.S. Bureau of the Census, *United States Census Publications, 1820-1945 (Exclusive of Decennial Census Publications)* (New York: Greenwood Press, 1972). Microfiche.

11. U.S. Bureau of the Census (Washington, D.C.: GPO, no date). SuDoc number: C3.2:V67. See also U.S. Bureau of the Census, *Strength in Numbers: Your Guide to 1990 Census Redistricting Data From the Bureau of the Census*, Rev. ed. (Washington, D.C.: GPO, 1991). SuDoc number: C3.6/2:ST8.

12.   U.S. Bureau of the Census (1990 CDR-14) Content Determination Reports (Washington, D.C.: GPO, 1990). SuDoc number: C3.224/11:CDR-14.

13.   Note, this is not held universally. The General Accounting Office found that adjustment of 1990 population data would have very limited effect upon distribution of federal funds. The study considers three programs whose monies are dependent upon the census: the Social Services Block Grant, selected highway, and Medicaid programs. (U.S. General Accounting Office, *Formula Programs: Adjusted Census Data Would Redistribute Small Percentage of Funds to States* (GAO/GGD-92-12) (Washington, D.C.: GPO, 1992). SuDoc number: GA1.13:GGD-92-12).

14.   *Index to the 1990 Census Print Reports* (Buffalo, NY: Lockwood Library, State University at Buffalo, 1994). Distributed to State Data Center lead agencies by the Bureau of the Census. Will be reproduced in *Subject Index to the 1990 Census* (Buffalo, NY: Epoch Books, 1997 expected publication data).

15.   Descriptions of all *1990 Census of Population and Housing* CD-ROMs are at the following Internet site: http://www.census.gov/~bbrown/rom/msrom.html#decennial.

16.   The expected Part C to this series, an index to summary tape files 1-4, is not published.

17.   U.S. Bureau of the Census, *1992 Economic Census CD-ROM.* (Washington, D.C.: GPO, 1994-). SuDoc number: C3.277:CD-EC/92-... Volume 1 will appear on ten CD-ROMs each successive one cumulating the previous. Data will be organized by nation, states, counties, and county subdivisions. Volume 2 reconfigures the statistics by zip codes. Two disks will be published, 2B superseding 2A.

18.   A special report in the *Census of Retail Trade, Merchandise Line Sales*, provides data for broad categories of commodities. In the 1987 volume, canned fruit was in merchandise line code 109. The specifics for fruit were hidden because 109 included all canned and bottled products, as well as dry groceries.

19.   Three series appear on CD-ROM: U.S. Bureau of the Census, *1992 Census of Agriculture. Geographic Areas Series 1B. U.S. Summary and County Level Data* (CD-ROM)(CD-AG/92-1B) (Washington, D.C.: GPO, 1995). SuDoc number: C3.277:CD-AG/92-1B. (Disk 1B supersedes 1A.); U.S. Bureau of the Census, *1992 Census of Agriculture. Geographic Areas Series 1C. U.S. Summary, State Data File, and Cross-Tab Data File* (CD-ROM) (CD-AG/92-1C) (Washington, D.C.: GPO, 1995). SuDoc number: C3.277:CD-AG/92-1C; and U.S. Bureau of the Census, *1992 Census of Agriculture. Subject Series. ZIP*

Code Tabulations. Farms by ZIP Code (1992 Census), Farms by ZIP Codes (1987 Census) (CD-ROM) (CD-AG/92-2A) (Washington, D.C.: GPO, 1995). SuDoc number: C3.277:CD-AG/92-2A. Two additional series are not yet published: U.S. Bureau of the Census, *1992 Agricultural Atlas of the United States, Subject Series* (CD-ROM)(CD-92AG-ATLAS) (Washington, D.C.: GPO, 1996?); and U.S. Bureau of the Census. *1992 Congressional District and Metropolitan Area Data, Subject Series* (CD-ROM) (Washington, D.C.:GPO, 1996?).

20. U.S. Bureau of the Census (AC92-R-9) (Washington, D.C.: GPO, 1994). SuDoc number: C3.6/2:AG8/2/992.

21. *Guide to the 1992 Census of Governments* will be published as Volume 5 in the Census of Governments.

22. (Phoenix: Oryx Press, revised irregularly).

23. (Washington, D.C.: Carroll Publishing, bimonthly). Previous title: *Federal Executive Directory.*

24. (Washington, D.C.: GPO, 1935-annual). SuDoc number: AE2.108/2:.

Exercises

1. A. Use printed 1990 census reports to determine the total population for the nation, your state, and your county (or county equivalent if that is the case) who are enrolled in school. Restrict your answer to those 3 years old and over.

   Nation_____

   State_____

   County_____

   B. Attempt to locate comparable data for your census tract or block numbering area (BNA).

2. Use the STF 3A CD-ROM for your state to get a profile of the population in your census tract/BNA.

3. Locate the population of your census tract/BNA on your state's STF 1 CD-ROM and compare this figure to that on the STF 3 disk. Chances are good that each disk gives different numbers. Explain why.

4. Why bother using sample data in STF 3 CD-ROM series when complete data are available in the STF 1 series?

5. Locate a population profile of your county (or county equivalent if that is the case) at the following address:

   http://www.oseda.missouri.edu

Answers

1. A. According to tables 17, 31, and 42 in the *1990 Census of Population Social and Economic Characteristics, United States* (SuDoc number: C3.223/7:1990 CP-2-1), 64,987,101 Americans over the age of 3 attend school. Comparable information for states and counties are in the respective state volumes of this series on tables 22, 36, 47, and 142.

1. B. First, determine your census tract or BNA number by consulting a census tract map. Remember, metropolitan areas are subdivided by tracts. However, nonmetropolitan counties--those outside metropolitan areas, are subdivided by BNA's. Afterwards, consult table 17 in *1990 Census of Population and Housing Population and Housing Characteristics for Census Tracts and Block Numbering Areas* (SuDoc number: C3.223/11:1990 CPH-3-227).

2. The answer depends upon where the reader lives.

3. Summary tape file 1A is based upon 100% of all responses to the census and summary tape file 3A is based upon a sample response rate. At small levels of geography, such as tracts and BNA's, sample estimates usually differ from the complete count.

4. Charts 15-2 and 15-3 show that complete count statistics on STF 1 covers a limited subject range. A much wider variety of subjects are available only through the STF 3 samples.

Appendix 1--
1990 Census of Population and Housing Printed Reports

Series:	1990 CH-1
Title:	*General Housing Characteristics*
SuDoc number:	C3.224/3:990 CH-1-...
Report(s) issued for:	U.S., States, D.C., Puerto Rico, and U.S. Virgin Islands
Description:	Covers detailed statistics on units in structure; housing value and rent; number of rooms; tenure; and vacancy characteristics.
Geographic areas:	States; counties; places and county subdivisions; American Indian areas and Alaska Native areas; and urban/rural summaries.

Series:	1990 CH-1-1A
Title:	*General Housing Characteristics: American Indian and Alaska Native Areas*
SuDoc number:	C3.224/3-2:990 CH-1-1A
Report(s) issued for:	U.S.
Description:	Covers units in structure; housing value and rent; number of rooms; tenure; and vacancy characteristics.
Geographic areas:	Indian reservations and other areas affected by tribal jurisdiction.

Series:	1990 CH-1-1B
Title:	*General Housing Characteristics: Metropolitan Areas*
SuDoc number:	C3.224/3-3:990 CH-1-1B
Report(s) issued for:	U.S.
Description:	Covers units in structure; housing value and rent; number of rooms; tenure; and vacancy characteristics.
Geographic areas:	Metropolitan areas. When boundaries cross states, data are provided for parts in each state and for the entire area.

Series:	1990 CH-1-1C
Title:	*General Housing Characteristics: Urbanized Areas*
SuDoc number:	C3.224/3-4:990 CH-1-1C
Report(s) issued for:	U.S.
Description:	Covers units in structure; housing value and rent; number of rooms; tenure; and vacancy characteristics.
Geographic areas:	Urbanized areas. When boundaries cross states, data are provided for parts in each state and for the entire area.

Series:	1990 CH-2
Title:	*Detailed Housing Characteristics*
SuDoc number:	C3.224/3:1990 CH-2-...
Report(s) issued for:	U.S., States, D.C., Puerto Rico, and U.S. Virgin Islands
Description:	Covers housing subjects in sample data. (See Chart 15-3 for a description of sample data.
Geographic areas:	States; counties; places; county subdivisions; Alaska Native areas; and Indian reservations.

Series:	1990 CH-2-1A
Title:	*Detailed Housing Characteristics: American Indian and Alaska Native Areas*
SuDoc number:	C3.224/3-5:1990 CH-2-1A
Report(s) issued for:	U.S.
Description:	Covers housing subjects in sample data. (See Chart 15-3 for a description of sample data.)
Geographic areas:	Indian reservations and Alaska Native areas.

Series: 1990 CH-2-1B

Title: *Detailed Housing Characteristics:*
                     Metropolitan Areas

SuDoc number: C3.224/3-6:1990 CH-2-1B

Report(s) issued for: U.S.

Description: Covers housing subjects in sample data. (See
                     Chart 15-3 for a description of sample data.)

Geographic areas: Metropolitan areas. When boundaries cross
                        states, data are provided for parts in each state
                        and for the entire area.

Series: 1990 CH-2-1C

Title: *Detailed Housing Characteristics:*
                     Urbanized Areas

SuDoc number: C3.224/3-7:1990 CH-2-1C

Report(s) issued for: U.S.

Description: Statistics generally on sample housing subjects.

Geographic areas: Urbanized areas. When boundaries cross states,
                        data are provided for parts in each state and for
                        the entire area.

Series: 1990 CP-1

Title: *General Population Characteristics*

SuDoc number: C3.223/6:990 CP-1-...

Report(s) issued for: U.S., States, D.C., Puerto Rico, and U.S. Virgin
                            Islands

Description: Includes detailed statistics on age; sex; race;
                     Hispanic origin; marital status; and household
                     relationships.

Geographic areas: States; counties; places; county subdivisions;
                        Indian reservations; Alaska Native areas; and
                        urban/rural areas.

Series:	1990 CP-1-1A
Title:	*General Population Characteristics:* *American Indian and Alaska Native Areas*
SuDoc number:	C3.223/6-2:1990 CP-1-1A
Report(s) issued for:	U.S.
Description:	Covers age; sex; race; Hispanic origin; marital status; and household relationships.
Geographic areas:	Indian reservations and Alaska Native areas.

Series:	1990 CP-1-1B
Title:	*General Population Characteristics:* *Metropolitan Areas*
SuDoc number:	C3.223/6-3:1990 CP-1-1B
Report(s) issued for:	U.S.
Description:	Covers age; sex; race; Hispanic origin; marital status; and household relationships.
Geographic areas:	Metropolitan areas. When boundaries cross states, data are provided for parts in each state and for the entire area.

Series:	1990 CP-1-1C
Title:	*General Population Characteristics:* *Urbanized Areas*
SuDoc number:	C3.223/6-4:1990 CP-1-C
Report(s) issued for:	U.S.
Description:	Covers age; sex; race; Hispanic origin; marital status; and household relationships.
Geographic areas:	Urbanized areas. When boundaries cross states, data are provided for parts in each state and for the entire area.

Series:	1990 CP-2
Title:	*Social and Economic Characteristics*
SuDoc number:	C3.223/7:1990 CP-2-...
Report(s) issued for:	U.S., States, D.C., Puerto Rico, and U.S. Virgin Islands
Description:	See Chart 15-3 for a description of sample data.
Geographic areas:	States; counties; places; county subdivisions; Alaska Native areas; Indian reservations.

Series:	1990 CP-2-1A
Title:	*Social and Economic Characteristics: American Indian and Alaska Native Areas*
SuDoc number:	C3.223/7-2:1990 CP-2-1A
Report(s) issued for:	U.S.
Description:	See Chart 15-3 for a description of sample data.
Geographic areas:	Indian reservations and Alaska Native areas.

Series:	1990 CP-2-1B
Title:	*Social and Economic Characteristics: Metropolitan Areas*
SuDoc number:	C3.223/7-3:1990 CP-2-1B
Report(s) issued for:	U.S.
Description:	See Chart 15-3 for a description of sample data.
Geographic areas:	Metropolitan areas. When boundaries cross states, data are provided for parts in each state and for the entire area.

Series: 1990 CP-2-1C

Title: *Social and Economic Characteristics: Urbanized Areas*

SuDoc number: C3.223/7-4:1990 CP-2-1C

Report(s) issued for: U.S.

Description: See Chart 15-3 for a description of sample data.

Geographic areas: Urbanized areas. When boundaries cross states, data are provided for parts in each state and for the entire area.

Series: 1990 CP-3

Title: *Population Subject Reports*

SuDoc number: C3.223/10:1990 CP-3-...

Report(s) issued for: Selected subjects.

Description: The Bureau of the Census originally expected to isue approximately 30 reports on selected subjects. Topics included migration, education, income, older populations, and racial and ethnic groups. However, most were never published due to budget constraints.

Geographic areas: U.S.; regions; and divisions. Selected reports cover highly populated States; metropolitan areas; counties; and large places.

Series: 1990 CPH-1

Title: *Summary Population and Housing Characteristics*

SuDoc number: C3.223/18:990 CPH-1-...

Report(s) issued for: U.S., States, D.C., Puerto Rico, and U.S. Virgin Islands

Description: Age; sex; race; Hispanic origin; household relationships; units in structure; housing value and rent; number of rooms; tenure; and vacancy characteristics.

Geographic areas: Local governmental units (i.e. counties, places, and towns and townships); Indian reservations; and Alaska Native areas.

Series:	1990 CPH-2
Title:	*Population and Housing Unit Counts*
SuDoc number:	C3.223/5:1990 CPH-2-...
Report(s) issued for:	U.S., States, D.C., Puerto Rico, and U.S. Virgin Islands
Description:	Covers population and housing unit counts for 1990 and previous censuses.
Geographic areas:	States; counties; county subdivisions; places; metropolitan areas; urbanized areas; and urban/rural summaries.

Series:	1990 CPH-3
Title:	*Population and Housing Characteristics: Census Tracts and Block Numbering Areas*
SuDoc number:	C3.223/11:1990 CPH-3-...
Report(s) issued for:	Metropolitan areas and the nonmetropolitan balances of each State; Puerto Rico; and U.S. Virgin Islands.
Description:	Statistics cover 100% data and sample data. See Charts 15-2 and 15-3 for descriptions of each.
Geographic areas:	For metropolitan areas: census tracts; places of at least 10,000 people; and counties. Separate volumes for each state cover non-metropolitan sectors by block numbering areas (BNA's); places of 10,000 or more; and counties.

Series:	1990 CPH-4
Title:	*Population and Housing Characteristics: Congressional Districts of the 103rd Congress*
SuDoc number:	C3.223/20:1990 CPH-4-...
Report(s) issued for:	States and D.C.
Description:	Statistics cover 100% data and sample data. See charts 15-2 and 15-3 for descriptions of each.
Geographic areas:	Congressional districts; counties; places; county subdivisions; Indian reservations; and Alaska Native areas.

Series:	1990 CPH-5
Title:	*Summary Social, Economic, and Housing Characteristics*
SuDoc number:	C3.223/23:990 CPH-5-...
Report(s) issued for:	U.S., States, D.C., Puerto Rico, and U.S. Virgin Islands
Description:	Covers sample population and housing subjects. See Chart 15-3 for a description of sample items.
Geographic areas:	Counties; places; county subdivisions; Indian reservations; and Alaska Native areas.

Appendix 2--
1992 Economic Census, Census of Agriculture,
and *Census of Governments*: **Printed Reports**

Census of Manufacturers: **SuDoc number: C3.24...**

- *Industry Series:* 83 reports cover different types of products.

- *Geographic Area Series:* 51 reports cover each state and the District of Columbia.

- *Other series:* Selected topics deal with concentration ratios(of large to small firms in an industry); shipments to the federal government; locations of manufacturing plants; and exports from manufacturing establishments.

Census of Mineral Industries.   **SuDoc number: C3.216...**

- *Industry Series:* 12 reports describe 31 mineral industries.

- *Geographic Area Series:* 9 volumes cover data for all fifty states.

- *Subject Series:* 2 reports present a national summary and detailed statistics on energy consumption by mineral industries.

Census of Wholesale Trade.   **SuDoc number: C3.256/2:**

- *Geographic Area Series:* 52 volumes cover each state, the District of Columbia, and a national summary.

- *Subject Series:* 4 reports examine establishment and firm sizes; capital expenditures, depreciation, operating and expenses; sales by commodities; and miscellaneous subjects.

Census of Retail Trade.   **SuDoc number: C3.255...**

- *Geographic Area Series:* 52 volumes cover each state, the District of Columbia, and a national summary. Statistics are for establishments with payrolls.

- *Nonemployer Statistics Series:* 1 report covers establishments with and without payrolls.

- *Subject Series:* 4 reports describe establishment and firm size; capital expenditures, depreciation, and operating expenses; sales by commodities; and miscellaneous subjects.

- *Special Report Series:* 1 report covers selected data, such as number of establishments, firm sizes, and state rankings, for retailers with and without payrolls.

Census of Service Industries. **SuDoc number: C3.257...**

- *Geographic Area Series*: 52 volumes cover each state, the District of Columbia, and a national summary. Statistics only deal with establishments that have payrolls.

- *Nonemployer Statistics Series:* 1 report covers establishments with and without payrolls.

- *Subject Series*: 5 reports examine establishment and firm sizes; capital expenditures, depreciation, and operating expenses; lodging services; sources of receipts and revenues; and miscellaneous subjects.

*Census of Financial, Insurance and
Real Estate Industries.* **SuDoc number: C3.291:**

- Five reports show data for the U.S., states and selected metropolitan areas; nonemployers; firms; revenue by kind of business; and miscellaneous topics.

*Census of Transportation,
Communications, and Utilities.* **SuDoc number: C3.292:**

- *Geographic Area Series*: Data for the nation, states, and selected metropolitan areas are in one volume.

- *Miscellaneous Subjects*: Statistics cover sources of revenue and other industry specific issues, such as sales for motor freight and utilities related construction.

- *Truck Inventory and Use Survey*: 52 reports for the U.S., each state, and the District of Columbia describe the use of commercial and personal trucks. (SuDoc number: C3.233/5:)

- *Commodity Flow Survey*: Statistics measure the origin and destination of products shipped from manufacturing, mining, retail, wholesale, and service establishments.

Census of Construction Industries. **SuDoc number: C3.245...**

- *Industry Series*: 26 reports deal with different construction industries. A national summary volume for establishments with and without payrolls appears as a 27th industry report.

- *Geographic Series*: 9 reports cover states in different parts of the country. A tenth U.S. summary volume describes establishments with and without payrolls.

- *Subject Series*: 1 volume covers forms of organizations and types of operations for employer and nonemployer establishments.

461

Enterprise Statistics.   **SuDoc number: C3.230:...**

1992 data appears in one report.

*Minority and Women
Owned Businesses.*   **SuDoc number: C3.258:...**

Four volumes provide a national summary, and more detailed information for three groups. (African-Americans; Hispanics; and Asian Americans, American Indians, and other minorities)

Census of Agriculture.   **SuDoc number: C3.31...**

-   *Geographic Area Series:* Covers 54 documents for each state, a national summary, and Puerto Rico, Guam, and the U.S. Virgin Islands.

-   *Subject Series:* Various volumes include an atlas, rankings, by states and counties, an evaluation of census coverage, and a procedural history.

-   *Farm and Ranch Irrigation Survey*

Census of Governments.   **SuDoc number: C3.145:...**

-   *Government Organization:* 2 documents cover government organization, and numbers of elected officials and the types of offices they hold.

-   *Taxable Property Values:* 2 documents deal with local assessed valuations and assessment sales/price ratios.

-   *Public Employment:* The first title covers employment in major local governments and the second is a compendium of public employment.

-   *Government Finances:* 6 documents cover finances of school districts; special districts; counties; municipalities and towns; state and local government retirement systems; and a summary of the subject.

-   *Guide to the 1992 Census of Governments*

•Chapter 16

Technical Reports

Answer the following questions when reading this chapter:

1. What are technical reports and how do they differ from other government publications?

2. What services provided by the National Technical Information Service are most useful to your needs?

3. What is FEDWORLD and why is this service important?

4. What kinds of federal scientific and technical information are available through the Internet?

Besides being the most prolific publisher in the world and the largest producer of statistics in the world, the U.S. government also sponsors more research and development than anyone else. Outlays for research and development in the proposed fiscal year 1996 budget are $72.1 billion.[1] This includes $35.4 billion for Department of Defense programs and $36.7 billion for non-defense programs. The result of much of this research appears in technical reports.

Technical reports are not a new type of literature. They date back to ancient times where Greek authors synthesized information and then presented it in a lucid manner. Richard Walker argues that "...the history of technical reports is much longer and just as rich, arguably, as that of the journal article."[2] Geoffrey Chaucer wrote the first known technical report in English in 1391 for his ten year old son, *Treatise on the Astrolabe.*[3]

Technical reports have become a more important type of literature since World War II. During the War, the government sponsored large amounts of research to further the military effort, and since 1945, Washington has spent large amounts of monies to support the Cold War and to promote industry. The results of these efforts often appear as technical reports.

This chapter describes the characteristics of technical reports and shows how they sometimes differ from other government publications. Services provided by the National Technical Information Service (NTIS) are evaluated. NTIS, a division of the Department of Commerce, is a clearinghouse for technical reports, software, and datafiles prepared by or for the government. The chapter then considers sources of technical reports relevant to defense; education; energy; the environment and earth science; health and medicine; and space and aviation. The Internet Supplement to the chapter covers sites relevant to the same topics. The description of FEDWORLD, the Internet site sponsored by NTIS, is in the main body of the chapter due to its special significance.

TECHNICAL REPORTS

BACKGROUND AND CHARACTERISTICS OF TECHNICAL REPORTS

The American National Standard for Information Sciences defines technical reports as publications that:

> ... convey the results of basic or applied research and support decisions based upon those results. A report shall include the ancillary information necessary for interpreting, applying, and replicating of the results or techniques of an investigation. The primary purposes of such a report are to disseminate the results of scientific and technical research and to recommend action.[4]

This definition is hardly appropriate. Books and journal articles sometimes do the same. The common characteristics shared by many technical reports describe this literature best. Reports provide quick dissemination to limited and specific audiences. Technical reports are not generally available through commercial channels. Outside contractors, such as professional associations, universities, industrial concerns, and independent researchers, often prepare them for the government.

Many people believe incorrectly that technical report literature is limited to the sciences and technology. Non-science oriented agencies, such as the Department of Education and the Department of Housing and Urban Development publish technical reports. Report literature covers every topic under the sun. The subjects of technical reports vary as widely as that of other government publications.

Although experts are sometimes unable to agree upon the types of technical reports, the following categories established by the Committee on Scientific and Technical Information (COSATI) in 1967 generally accounts for most reports.[5]

-Papers that are equivalent to preprints of journal articles.

-Proposals for funding submitted to agencies by outside groups.

-Institutional reports that are similar to annual reports.

-Progress reports that describe accomplishments to date. These are the most common type of technical reports.

-Final reports that discuss the entire project.

-Separate topical reports. These polished versions of final reports are similar to journal articles.

-Interim and final reports of government committees and commissions.

Regardless of their intended purposes, most reports have the following characteristics. Note, all characteristics are not present in every case.

-Four types of numbers: report, grant, contract, and accession numbers. Consult the more detailed descriptions below.

-Abstracts or summaries

-Introductions that describe the purpose, history and background of the subject.

-Conclusions and recommendations that are easy to locate.

-Substantive discussions of issues in appendices.

-Documentation pages (Figure 16-1).

Figure 16-1
Technical Report Documentation Page

REPORT DOCUMENTATION PAGE	1. REPORT NO. NASA/CR-86/3840	2.	3. Recipient's Accession No.
4. Title and Subtitle Systems Study for an Integrated Digital/Electric Aircraft (IDEA).			5. Report Date January 1986
			6.
7. Author(s) George E. Tagge; Louise A. Irish; E. Robert Bailey III			8. Performing Organization Rept. No. BOEING TR-85-107
9. Performing Organization Name and Address Boeing Commercial Airplane Company Seattle, WA 94521			10. Project/Task/Work Unit No.
			11. Contract(C) or Grant(G) No. (C) NAS1-17528 (G)
12. Sponsoring Organization Name and Address National Aeronautics and Space Administration Scientific and Technical Information Branch Washington, DC 20546			13. Type of Report & Period Covered Contractor Report (Final)
			14.
15. Supplementary Notes George E. Tagge (206) 943-7401 NASA Technical Monitor: Dr. Robert E. Cozgrove (804) 865-2904			
16. Abstract (Limit: 200 words) This document presents the results of the Integrated Digital/Electric Aircraft (IDEA) Study. Airplanes with advanced systems were defined and evaluated as a means of identifying potential high-payoff research tasks. A baseline airplane, typical of the 1990's airplane with advanced active controls, propulsion, aoerdynamics, and structures technology, was defined for comparison. Trade studies led to the definition of an IDEA airplane with extensive digital systems and electric secondary power distribution. This airplane showed a reduction of 3 percent in fuel consumption and 1.8 percent relative to the baseline configuration. An alternate configuration, an advanced technology turboprop, was also evaluated and showed greater improvement supported by digital-electric systems. Recommended research programs were defined for high-risk, high-payoff areas appropriate for implementation under NASA leadership.			
17. Document Analysis a. Descriptors b. Identifiers/Open-Ended Terms Digital systems Electric secondary power Data bus Electric actuation c. COSATI Field/Group			
18. Availability Statement National Technical Information Service 5285 Port Royal Road Springfield, VA 22161		19. Security Class (This Report) Unclassified	21. No. of Pages 32
		20. Security Class (This Page) Unclassified	22. Price

Significant parts of the documentation page in Figure 16-1 include the following:

-Report number: Assigned by NASA--NASA/CR-86/3840; assigned by Boeing--BOEING TR-85-107.

-Title: *Systems Study for an Integrated Digital/Electric Aircraft (IDEA).*

-Personnel author(s): George E. Tagge, Louise A. Irish, and Robert Bailey III.

-Performing organization or sponsor: Boeing Commercial Airplane Company.

-Date: January 1986.

-Contract or grant number: NAS1-17528.

-Type of report: Final contractor report.

-Abstract.

-Identifiers or subject headings: Digital systems; Electric secondary power; Data bus; and Electric actuation.

-Availability statement: Available from National Technical Information Service.

NUMBERS ASSOCIATED WITH TECHNICAL REPORTS

REPORT NUMBERS

Report numbers identify technical reports. NASA/CR-86/3840, one of the report numbers in Figure 16-1, is typical. Different parts of the number relate to the agency (NASA), a branch of the agency or the report series (CR), and the year (1986). The sequential number, 3840, identifies this particular title. Other types of report numbers sometimes reflect contractors and/or subjects.[6]

Theoretically, technical reports should have unique report numbers, but this is not always the case. The item in Figure 16-1 has a second report number, BOEING TR-85-107, that was assigned by the performing organization, Boeing Commercial Airplane Company. Report numbers become still more complicated when contractors and/or sponsoring agencies change their names. The new acronyms sometimes lack resemblance to the older ones.

Three reference books are helpful when tracing report numbers.

Godfrey, Lois E. and Helen Redman. *Dictionary of Report Series Codes.* 2nd ed. New York: Special Libraries Association, 1973.

Aronson, Eleanor J. *Dictionary of Report Series Codes.* 3rd ed. Detroit: Gale Research Company, 1986.

Godfrey and Redman cover reports issued from the end of World War II through the early 1970's. Aronson covers those published between 1979 and May 1985. Part 1 in both editions list report codes alphabetically and cite names of sponsoring organizations and the relevant series. Part 2 provides names of sponsoring organizations and their report acronyms. The 1973 edition includes three features excluded from the 1986 publication.

-A comprehensive description of different parts of report numbers.

-An informative bibliography, "Sources of Report Series Codes and Their Interpretation."

-Descriptive histories of nearly 50 government and non-government report series codes. This facilitates locating publications issued by groups that changed names and used different report codes.

Nathan, Vasantha, ed. *Directory of Engineering Document Sources.* Clayton, MO.: Global Engineering Documents, 1989.

Nathan deals with reports prepared by U.S. governments at all levels, industry associations, universities, and foreign groups. Four columns list report acronyms; describe the names of report series and/or organizations performing the research; identify indexes to the report series; and note sources from which documents are available. The "Acknowledgements" section lists reference tools used in compiling the directory.

U.S. Department of Defense. Defense Technical Information Center. *DOCTRAC: Directory of Organizational Technical Report Acronym Codes* (DTIC/TR-94-16) (AD-A281 500). Cameron Station, Alexandria, VA.: DTIC, 1994. SuDoc number: D7.15/2:94/16.

An index and guide to technical report acronyms used in reports included in the Defense Technical Information Center's collections. Part 1 lists acronyms in alphanumeric order and cites the names of the organizations performing the research. Arrangement of part 2 is by names of the organizations. Although the technical report documentation page indicates this title is an annual publication, current editions are difficult to locate.

GRANT NUMBERS AND CONTRACT NUMBERS

Grant and contract numbers identify projects funded through grants. These numbers help tie together relationships between contractors, sponsoring agencies, and multiple reports issued as part of one contract. For instance, 45 technical reports prepared for the Department of Energy by Lawrence Berkeley Laboratory, each having different report numbers, are all brought together under one contract number, AC03-76SF00098.[7]

ACCESSION NUMBERS

Information distribution clearinghouses, such as the National Technical Information Service, use either numeric or alphanumeric accession codes to identify titles.

DIFFERENCES BETWEEN TECHNICAL REPORTS AND OTHER GOVERNMENT PUBLICATIONS

Information published for the United States government by its employees and officers are not subject to copyright.[8] Individuals and commercial concerns can reproduce this data and profit from its sale. However, technical reports are in a different category because the information is often produced by contractors, not government employees and officials. Depending upon terms of the agreement with the agency, the private contractor can assume copyright ownership. This situation is not unique to the U.S. In 1992, the Canadian government adopted a policy giving government contractors ownership of intellectual property.[9]

The potential to inhibit access to information exits. Agencies can grant their contractors copyrights over reports to avoid disclosing information to citizens. Andrea Simon, author of "A Constitutional Analysis of Copyrighting Government-Commissioned Work," maintains it is "foolhardy" to believe that an agency "improperly predisposed to...withholding copyright" would protect the publics' right to know.[10] Others disagree. A 1976 report by the House Committee on the Judiciary stated that:

> where a government agency commissions a work for its own use merely as an alternative to having one of its own employees prepare the work, the right to secure a private copyright would be withheld.[11]

However, the Committee fails to explain the basis for its assumption. Schnapper v. Foley[12] is the only case that tests this issue. The District of Columbia Circuit Court ruled that it is unaware of attempts by the government to stop expression through copyright and cannot act on hypothetical instances.

PROBLEMS ACCESSING TECHNICAL REPORTS

Unfortunately, technical report literature is among the least used government information. The number of technical reports distributed to depository libraries by GPO is small as compared to the total number of reports produced. The National Technical Information Service, the government's most comprehensive source for technical reports, does not have a depository program. Federal law requires NTIS to operate using revenues acquired by selling information. Furthermore, research conducted by Charles McClure of Syracuse University indicates that many libraries and their users make limited use of NTIS services and products.[13]

NATIONAL TECHNICAL INFORMATION SERVICE

WHAT IS NTIS?

The National Technical Information Service (NTIS) is an information clearinghouse in the Department of Commerce. It collects and sells technical reports and other information in various formats, including paper, microfiche, computer diskettes, CD-ROMs, magnetic tape, and audiovisual. These data relate to almost any subject. Federal law requires NTIS to maintain permanent copies of all items it collects, guaranteeing that the information will always be available.

The NTIS collection includes over 2.5 million titles. In fiscal year 1993, the collection grew by 1,300 items per week. NTIS acquires most of its information from over 200 federal agencies. In 1993, the Department of Energy contributed 28% all new items, the Department of Defense contributed 18%, and the National Aeronautical and Space Administration contributed 13%.[14] State and local governments, universities and other research institutions, and foreign countries also contribute. By law, NTIS must also collect, translate into English, and then sell to the public foreign scientific, technical, and engineering information. In 1993, Canada and Germany each contributed nearly 6,000 titles, the Netherlands contributed almost 2,000 titles, and Japan contributed almost 1,500 reports.

BACKGROUND TO NTIS

A number of related agencies predate NTIS. The Office of Scientific Research and Development (OSRD), created in 1941 to support the war effort, acquired and then disseminated scientific information. Following the War, OSRD disbanded, but Washington still needed a clearinghouse to distribute government sponsored research to business and industry. Presidential Executive Order 9568, issued in June 1945, created the Publications Board to do that. Since then, three name changes occurred. It became the Office of Technical Services in 1947, the Clearinghouse for Scientific and Technical Information in 1964, and the National Technical Information Service in 1970.

The American Technology Preeminence Act of 1991[15] gave NTIS a boost. Until then, agencies provided copies of their technical reports to NTIS voluntarily. The new law requires agencies to give NTIS copies of all unclassified scientific, technical, and engineering reports from federally funded research and development. This provision pertains to information that is intended for public distribution. Agencies have discretion to determine for themselves what falls into that category. Despite this, the NTIS collection still grew by 15% between 1992 and 1993, when relevant regulations were under consideration.[16]

GOVERNMENT REPORTS ANNOUNCEMENTS AND INDEX (*GRA&I*)

Government Reports Announcements and Index[17] (*GRA&I*) is a semimonthly index to NTIS materials published between 1975 and 1996. To locate information in *GRA&I* first consult the appropriate index and then refer to the reports announcements section to view the full citation and abstract. Washington published comparable sources under various titles since 1946. Effective January 1997, NTIS expects to offer similar information on a quarterly CD-ROM, the *NTIS Order Now Catalog.*[18]

REPORTS ANNOUNCEMENTS SECTION

The Reports Announcement section consists of 38 broad subject categories that have over 350 subcategories. Figure 16-2 shows a typical entry.

Figure 16-2
GRA&I: **Reports**
Announcements

15-03,316
PB95-212478GAR   PC A04/MF A01
Massachusetts Univ. at Boston. Urban Harbors Inst.
Boston Harbor Marine Transit Accessibility Study.
Improving Linkage between Water and Landside
Transportation Modes and Access for Individuals
with Disabilities.
Final rept.
A. L. Held. Jan 95, 61p MA-06-0197-03-01, FTA-MA-
06-0197-95-5.
Grant FTA-MA-06-0197-06
Sponsored by Federal Transit Administration, Wash-
ington, DC.

The Institute studied the Boston Harbor marine transit
system with regards to improving intermodal
connectivity and access by individuals with disabilities.
The report concluded that both interests would be best
served by the development of a central marine transit
terminal that would be fully accessible during all sea-
sons and for the complete tidal range of Boston Harbor. The report also concluded that the needs of ferry
commuters would be best served with the institution
of two express bus shuttles operating from the central
terminal to the Back Bay and Beacon Hill working districts of Boston. In addition, the study recommended
that the city institute a waterfront transitway which
would link the waterfront of Boston between North and
South Stations. The waterfront transitway would primarily serve the needs of non-commuter ferry patrons
and of tourists.

Source: *GRA&I,* **August 1, 1995, 351.**

Significant parts of Figure 16-2 include:

-Abstract number: Refers users from the indexes to the Reports Announcements section. (15-03,316)

-NTIS Accession number--used when ordering materials from NTIS. NTIS indexes and abstracts items whose accession codes begin with PB. Other common codes begin with: [19]

AD   Reports prepared by the Department of Defense.

N   Reports prepared by the National Aeronautical and Space Administration.

DE   Reports prepared by the Department of Energy.

ED   Reports prepared by the Educational Resources Information Center.

TIB   Reports prepared by the West German Universitaets bibliothek und Technische Informationsbibliothek

-Price codes: Price code for paper copies (PC) and microfiche copies (MF). Back pages of *GRA&I* describe price codes. (PC A04/MF A01)

-Organization responsible for the work: Massachusetts University at Boston. Urban Harbors Institute.

-Title: *Boston Harbor Marine Transit Accessibility Study. Improving Linkage...*

-Personal author: A.L. Held.

-Date: January 1995.

-Pagination: 61 pages.

-Report numbers: MA-06-0197-03-01 and FTA-MA-06-0197-95-5.

-Grant number: FTA-MA-06-0197-06.

-Sponsoring agency: Federal Transit Administration.

-Abstract.

Test your understanding of the Reports Announcement section: Refer to earlier parts of this chapter that provided background to technical reports and to Figure 16-2 when answering the following:

1.   What is the abstract accession number? Why is it important?

> (15-03,316; it refers users from the indexes to the Reports Announcement section. 15-03,316 represents the 3,316 item cited in issue 15.)

2.   What is the NTIS accession code? Why is it important?

> (PB95-212478GAR; NTIS uses accessionnumbers to identify materials it sells.)

3.   What organization prepared this report?

> (Massachusetts University at Boston. Urban Harbor Institute)

4.   What organization sponsored the research?

> (Federal Transit Administration)

5.   What is the title of this report?

> (*Boston Harbor Marine Transit Accessibility Study: Improving...*)

6.   What are the two report numbers?

> (MA-06-0197-03-01 and FTA-MA-06-0197-95-5)

7.   Why does this single title have two report numbers? Is this unusual?

(It is not unusual for a report to have multiple report numbers. The group responsible for the research assigned a number and the sponsoring agency assigned a number.)

8.   What is the grant number?

(FTA-MA-06-0197-06)

KEYWORD INDEX:

The Keyword Index provides subject access to *GRA&I*. It gives titles, abstract numbers, and NTIS accession numbers of documents. Figure 16-3 displays a reference to the item discussed immediately above.

Figure 16-3
GRA&I:
Keyword Index

DIRECTORIES
Nova Scotia directory of geographic data and information, 1994.
MIC-95-01279GAR   15-02,025

Saskatchewan environmental directory: A guide to who's who in the Saskatchewan environmental community 1994.
MIC-95-01715GAR   15-03,112

DIRICHLET PROBLEM
Dirichlet Problem Related to the Invertibility of Mappings Arising in 2D Grid Generation.
PB95-215323GAR   15-01,791

DISABLED PERSONS
Boston Harbor Marine Transit Accessibility Study. Improving Linkage between Water and Landside Transportation Modes and Access for Individuals with Disabilities.
PB95-212478GAR   15-03,316

DISASTER RELIEF
Annual report 1993-94 (Alberta Public Safety Services, Edmonton).
MIC-95-01788GAR   15-03,116

Source: *GRA&I*, August 1, 1995, KW-33.

CORPORATE AUTHOR AND PERSONAL AUTHOR INDEXES:

The Corporate Author Index lists government agencies and other organizations responsible for performing the research. Figure 16-4 shows items prepared by Massachusetts Univ. at Boston. Urban Harbors Institute.

Figure 16-4
GRA&I
Corporate Author Index

MASSACHUSETTS UNIV. AT BOSTON. URBAN HARBORS INST.

MA-06-0197-02-02
Report on Specific Operational and Dimensional Design Characteristics of the Present United States Passenger Vessel Fleet. Data Base and Report. February 1995.
(FTA-MA-06-0197-95-03)
PB95-212445GAR   15-03,314

MA-06-0197-02-02-APP
Report on Specific Operational and Dimensional Design Characteristics of the Present United States Passenger Vessel Fleet. Appendices 1-3. February 1995.
(FTA-MA-06-0197-95-04)
PB95-212452GAR   *5-03,315

MA-06-0197-03-01
Boston Harbor Marine Transit Accessibility Study. Improving Linkage between Water and Landside Transportation Modes and Access for Individuals with Disabilities.
(FTA-MA-06-0197-95-5)
PB95-212478GAR   15-03,316

MATRA MARCONI SPACE, TOULOUSE (FRANCE).

Formalizing Procedures for Operations Automation. Operator Training and Spacecraft Autonomy.
N95-23720/2GAR   15-03,190

Benefits of Advanced Software Techniques for Mission Planning Systems.
N95-23752/5GAR   15-03,200

Source: *GRA&I*, **August 1, 1995, CA-38.**

Like the Corporate Author Index, the Personal Author Index lists authors in alphabetical order.

CONTRACT/GRANT NUMBER INDEX:

The unique contract/grant number, FTA-MA-06-0197-06, ties together the three reports seen in Figure 16-4, each prepared by the same organization as part of the identical grant (Figure 16-5).

Figure 16-5
GRA&I
Contract/Grant Number Index

FG51-83R029323
Oregon Dept. of Energy. Salem. Conservation Resources Div.
DE95005575GAR   15-00,941
DE95005576GAR   15-00,942
DE95005577GAR   15-00,943

FNS-53-3198-7-57
Research Triangle Inst., Research Triangle Park. NC.
PB95-217139GAR   15-00,245

FTA-MA-06-0197-06
Massachusetts Univ. at Boston. Urban Harbors Inst.
PB95-212445GAR   15-03,314
PB95-212452GAR   15-03,315
PB95-212478GAR   15-03,316

FTA-PA-26-0008
Carnegie-Mellon Univ., Pittsburgh, PA. Rail Systems Center.
PB95-210845GAR   15-03,318

Source: *GRA&I*, **August 1, 1995, CG-9.**

Test your understanding of contract/grant numbers:

Why is the contract/grant number in Figure 16-5 important?

> (Contract/grant numbers bring together multiple reports prepared under the same grant.)

NTIS ORDER/REPORT NUMBER INDEX:

The Order/Report Number Index lists NTIS accession and report numbers alphanumerically in one sequence. Figure 16-6 illustrates the two report numbers and the accession number of the document in Figure 16-2.

Figure 16-6
GRA&I **NTIS Order/Report Number Index**

MA-06-0197-03-01

Boston Harbor Marine Transit Accessibility Study. Improving Linkage between Water and Landside Transportation Modes and Access for Individuals with Disabilities.
PB95-212478GAR   15-03,316   PC A04/MF A01

MBB-Z-0450-91-PUB

Faserverstaerkte Kunststoffe. (Fiber-reinforced plastics).
TIB/B95-02220GAR   15-01,653   PC E09

MBI-94-1(PREPR.)

Parallel subspace decomposition method for elliptic and hyperbolic systems.
TIB/A95-02731GAR   15-01,811   PC E09

MBI-94-2(PREPR.)

Weak solvability of a model related to crystal growth processes.
TIB/A95-02673GAR   15-01,810   PC E09

FTA-MA-06-0197-95-5

Boston Harbor Marine Transit Accessibility Study. Improving Linkage between Water and Landside Transportation Modes and Access for Individuals with Disabilities.
PB95-212478GAR   15-03,316   PC A04/MF A01

FTA-MD-26-0005-94-1

Mobility Match Study in Prince George's County, Maryland.
PB95-210274GAR   15-03,125   PC A14/MF A03

FTA-PA-26-0008-95-3

Development and Application of a Battery Energy Storage System Simulation Program for Rail Transit Systems. Volume 3.
PB95-210845GAR   15-03,318   PC A06/MF A02

FUB-HEP-94-15

Towards a lattice calculation of the nucleon structure functions.
TIB/B95-01906GAR   15-02,807   PC E09

PB95-212452GAR

Report on Specific Operational and Dimensional Design Characteristics of the Present United States Passenger Vessel Fleet. Appendices 1-3, February 1995.
PB95-212452GAR   15-03,315   PC A07/MF A02

PB95-212460GAR

Factors Affecting Traffic Operations on Seven-Lane Cross Sections.
PB95-212460GAR   15-03,128   PC A05/MF A01

PB95-212478GAR

Boston Harbor Marine Transit Accessibility Study. Improving Linkage between Water and Landside Transportation Modes and Access for Individuals with Disabilities.
PB95-212478GAR   15-03,316   PC A04/MF A01

PB95-212494GAR

Monitoring Trace Metals at Ambient Water Quality Criteria Levels. Briefing Book, January 1995.
PB95-212494GAR   15-01,423   PC A10/MF A03

Source: *GRA&I*, August 1, 1995, OR-32, OR-45, and OR-65

NON-PRINT FORMATS:

Remember, NTIS collects and indexes information in print, as well as electronic and audiovisual, formats. The Keyword Index covers magnetic tapes, CD-ROMs, diskettes, and audiovisual materials under headings pertinent to their subjects. That is, the Index cites materials about the disabled published in these formats under relevant subject headings. Consult the heading "Data File" to locate a list of all computer products. To locate a list of audiovisual materials, consult the NTIS Order/Report Number Index under the AVA code. Figures 16-7 through 16-10 display a magnetic tape, a diskette, a CD-ROM, and a video.

Figure 16-7
GRA&I **Magnetic Tape Entry**

514,417,
PB95-500294/GAR   CP T03
Agency for Health Care Policy and Research, Rockville, MD.
National Medical Expenditure Survey: Public Use Tape 29: Household Survey, Disability Days and Medical Conditions, Calendar Year 1987 (on Magnetic Tape).
Data file.
1987, mag tapes AHCPR/DF/MT-95/002
This product contains text only. Customers must provide their own search and retrieval software. System: MVS/ESA operating system. Utility program: !EB-GENER. See also PB94-500071, PB93-500213, and PB92-504307.
Available in 9-track, EBCDIC character set tape, 1600 bpi, 6250 bpi, or 3480 cartridge. Documentation included; may be ordered separately as PB95-103255.

This public use tape is a release from the Household Survey component (HS) of the 1987 National Medical Expenditure Survey (NMES). The NMES is a nation-

Source: *GRA&I,* **March 15, 1995, 146.**

Figure 16-8
GRA&I **Diskette Entry**

456,827
PB94-502192/GAR   CP D02
National Center for Chronic Disease Prevention and Health Promotion, Atlanta, GA. Div. of Adolescent and School Health.
Youth Risk Behavior Survey, 1990 (for Microcomputers).
Data file.
1990, 1 diskette HHS/DF/DK-94/003
Also available as magnetic tape, PB92-503283.
The datafile is on one 3 1/2 inch DOS diskette, 1.44M high density. File format: ASCII text. Documentation included; may be ordered separately as PB92-169879. Documentation is also on a file.

The 1990 national school-based Youth Risk Behavior Survey (YRBS) focuses on priority health-risk behaviors established during youth that result in the most significant mortality, morbidity, disability, and social problems during both youth and adulthood. These include: behaviors that result in international and unintentional injuries; tobacco use; alcohol and other drug use; sexual behaviors that result in HIV infection, other sexually-transmitted diseases (STDs), and unintended pregnancies; dietary behaviors; and physical activity. Results from the YRBS will be used by CDC to: (1) monitor how priority health-risk behaviors among high school students increase, decrease, or remain the same over time; (2) evaluate the impact of broad national, state, and local efforts to prevent priority health-risk behaviors; and (3) monitor progress in achieving relevant national health objectives for the year 2000.

Source: *GRA&I,* **October 15, 1994, 210.**

Figure 16-9
GRA&I, **CD-ROM Entry**

361,699
PB93-5C5931/GAR   Diskette $25.00
National Center for Health Statistics, Hyattsville, MD.
National Health Interview Survey (NHIS), 1987, (Re-issued July 1993) (on CD-ROM).
Data file.
1987, CD-ROM NCHS/DF/CD-93/030
System: MS DOS 286, 386, or 486; DOS 3.0 or higher operating system. This data requires five (5) mega-bytes of free space on the hard drive and a computer memory of 640Kb. The reader must use Microsoft Ex-tensions, Version 2.0. Supersedes PB91-505073. Other formats available as PB89-140651 (Magnetic Tape).
The datafile is on one 4.72 inch disc. Data format: ISO 9660.

The National Health Interview Survey (NHIS) 1987, on CD-ROM, contains health characteristics information on the relationship between diet and cancer risk, the attitudes of non-smokers toward those who smoke, the sociodemographic characteristics of those who adopt children, and people who are disabled by blind-ness, deafness, paralysis, and other impairments.

Source: *GRA&I*, October 15, 1993, 168.

Figure 16-10
GRA&I, **Video Entry**

526,784
AVA19594-VNB2/GAR   AV$140.00
Federal Emergency Management Agency, Washing-ton, DC.
Community Responds to Disaster: How FEMA Reaches Out (November 9 1994) (Video).
Audiovisual.
1994, 2 VHS videos
Not cleared for TV.
These VHS videos are 1/2 inch, color with total playing time of 4 and 1/2 hours. Also available in VC34C as AVA19595-VM05. NOTE: Sales copies must be la-beled with EENET in front of the title.

This broadcast cover the following topics: Federal Emergency Management Agency's (FEMA's) Commu-nity Liaison Program in the Northridge Quake, Presen-tations from Community-based Organizations on How Individual Cultures Influenced Individual and Group Response to the Quake, The Impact on the Disability Community, Problems Encountered at Shelters, and the Elderly Population.

Source: *GRA&I*, May 15, 1995, 241.

Test your understanding of non-print formats in *GRA&I*:

1.   Underline the relevant sections in Figures 16-7 through 16-10 that show the formats.

2. Which of the two options is the preferred way of locating electronic and audiovisual materials in *GRA&I*: the print edition of *GRA&I* or an electronic version of *GRA&I*?

> (An electronic version where the subject terms and the formats are combined in one search statement is preferable. Locating audiovisual and computer products in the printed *GRA&I* is very time consuming because terms cannot be combined.)

ELECTRONIC FORMATS OF *GRA&I*:

Four sources provide online versions. File 6 in the DIALOG/Knight Ridder system covers NTIS from 1964 through the present. Other vendors include DATA-STAR, ORBIT, and the Canada Institute for Scientific and Technical Information (CISTI) (Ottawa, Ontario).[20]

The CD-ROM sold by KR Information OnDisc covers 1980 to date and that sold by SilverPlatter covers 1983 to date.[21] Each vendor provides quarterly updates.

NTIS makes the Preview database, an abbreviated version of *GRA&I* available through the Internet without charge. Connect to (http://www.fedworld.gov/preview/public.html). Using telnet, connect to fedworld.gov and then select choice [B], Locate and Reference Government Information. Preview covers records added during the most recent 30 days. Search the database using keywords; personal and corporate authors; titles; countries of publication; and document types, such as print, electronic, and audiovisual formats.

Consult *The NTIS Database Search Guide*[22] for more information about searching NTIS.

OTHER NTIS BIBLIOGRAPHIC SERVICES:

Three additional bibliographic sources cover NTIS materials: *NTIS Alerts*, NTIS FAX Direct, and free catalogs available upon request. The *NTIS Alerts* are semimonthly current awareness newsletters that describe new materials. Each of the 26 newsletters covers broad subject categories.[23] Entries provide bibliographic information, NTIS accession codes, summaries, and ordering information.

NTIS distributes additional bibliographies of its most frequently requested publications through the FAX Direct service. Callers receive the list within minutes. It covers over 20 timely subjects relating to the sciences, social sciences, and business. Every item on the list has a unique identification number. Use that number when ordering a bibliography. Dial 703-487-4099 on a touch-tone-phone to order the list of bibliographies or a bibliography on a specific subject.

The following catalogs are among the most frequently requested. Call (703) 487-4650 between 8:30 a.m. and 5:00 p.m. Eastern Time, Monday through Friday to order copies. Ask for the appropriate catalog by document number. Consult http://www.fedworld.gov/ntis/catalogs.htm to view these catalogs, plus others, on the FEDWORLD Internet site. The FEDWORLD Internet site is described below.

-Products and Services Catalog (PR-827NDS) Provides an overview of all NTIS products and services.

-Published Search Master Catalog (PR-186NDS). NTIS staff prepares "published searches" on wide varieties of topics. These bibliographies offer between 50 and 250 references compiled from the NTIS database and nearly 40 databases maintained by other groups. Coverage includes popular topics, such as artificial intelligence; biotechnology; computer aided manufacturing and design; management and human resources; and waste treatment and processing.

-Business Highlights (PR-985NDS).

-Environment Highlights (PR-868NDS).

-Health Highlights (PR-745NDS).

NTIS FEDWORLD SERVICE

INTRODUCTION AND BACKGROUND:

The American Technology Preeminence Act required NTIS to consider the feasibility of operating an online locator system for government information. The FEDWORLD system, which developed from this mandate, attempts to be a central point for accessing U.S. government data. When it began operation in November 1992, FEDWORLD linked to 50 bulletin boards. Today, approximately 150 are available. The World Wide Web version of FEDWORLD also links to nearly 300 information sources by subjects. This topical arrangement makes it much easier for those unfamiliar with agency functions to locate data.

The importance of this service is significant. Most people would have difficulty keeping track of phone numbers or Internet addresses to 150 bulletin boards and nearly 300 other sources. FEDWORLD users need only remember the phone number or Internet address for that single service. Once connected to FEDWORLD, links provide access to the data.

FEDWORLD's use and popularity are well proven. The system has over 100,000 registered customers; it receives nearly 4,000 daily calls; and almost 400 new users register each day. The *Washington Post* said that "The best things in life, as the adage goes are free--but not usually in the world of computers. FEDWORLD is a notable exception."[24]

CONNECTING TO FEDWORLD:

Connect to FEDWORLD three ways.

1. Using a telephone, call 703-321-3339. Set your computer to no parity, 8 data bits, 1 stop bit, full duplex, and either ANSI or VT100 terminal emulation.

2. Using telnet, connect to fedworld.gov.

3. Using a world wide web server, connect to http://www. fedworld.gov.

USING FEDWORLD TO CONNECT TO BULLETIN BOARDS:

Duplicate these steps or similar ones when sitting at a terminal. For illustrative purposes, locate information about the disabled. Sometimes browsing through the various menus is the best way.

1. Connect to FEDWORLD using either the phone number or the telnet address given above. New users must go through the online registration process. Passwords are available without charge. Figure 16-11 illustrates FED-WORLD's opening menu.

Figure 16-11
FEDWORLD Opening Menu

Min online today: 0 minutes   Time per day: 180 minutes
```
                    *** F E D W O R L D ***
                National Technical Information Service
------------------------------------------------
[A]  Help and Information Center (READ FIRST)
[B]  Locate and Reference Government Information
[C]  Business, Trade, and Labor Mall
[D]  Health Mall
[E]  Environment and Energy Mall
[F]  Regulatory, Government Administration and State Systems
[G]  Research, Technical, and Education Mall
[J]  Federal Job Openings
[L]  Alphabetical Listing of All Information Online
[M]  FedWorld MarketPlace
[N]  NEW Features -> Nat. Heart Lung and Blood Inst. Library


 [T] Forums     [U] Utilities/Files/Mail     [X] Goodbye (logoff)


                    54 other user(s) online now.
       Hot Command => /go MAIN
       Please select an option from above and press <return>:
```

If using the world wide web, after signing on, select FEDWORLD Telnet Site to reach the information shown in Figure 16-11.

2. Choose option G in Figure 16-11, Research, Technical, and Educational Mall (Figure 16-12).

Figure 16-12
FEDWORLD: Research, Technology
and Education (RT&E) Mall

Research, Technology and Education (RT&E) Mall
```
======================================================================
```
[A] Continuous Acquistion & Lifecycle Support (CALS)
[B] Office of Technology Assessment Library of Files
[C] Weather Satellite Images Library of Files
[D] FAA Library of Files
[E] FAA Airworthiness Directives (Fee Based)
[F] < This Space for Lease >
[G] Food and Consumer Service (FCS)
[H] Treasury Electronic Library (TEL)
[I] Business Gold (NTTC)

[1] RT&E GateWay Systems (Connect to Gov't systems/databases)
[2] RT&E Reports for Sale (Order documents online and/or download)
[3] RT&E Files (Files/Documents available for downloading)
[L] Alphabetical Listing of All Information Online
[X] Exit to Previous Menu (/go main)
[*] Goodbye (/go logoff)

Hot command => (/go SCIENCE)
Please select an option from above and press <return>:

3. Select option 1 in Figure 16-12, RT&E Gateway Systems
    (Connect to Gov't systems/databases), to view a list of
    related bulletin boards (Figure 16-13).

Figure 16-13
FEDWORLD RT&E Gateway Systems

55:NGCR-BBS (USN)	:Next Generation Computer Resources Stan
56:TeleconX-BBS (GSA)	:The Federal Telecommuting Connection
57:Gulfline (EPA&NOAA)	:Gulf Coast Environmental Information
61:STIS (NSF)	:Science & Technology Information System
65:JAN-BBS	:Job Accomodation Network
66:NOAA-ESDD (NOAA	:NOAA Environmental Services Data Direct
78:EI News BBS (DoD)	:Enterprise Integration News BBS
93:PPCUG/RDAMIS (DOD)	:Pentagon Users Group BBS
94:FTA BBS (DOT)	:Federal Transit Administration BB
110:ED Board (DOEdu)	:Dept of Ed Grant & Contract Info
112:Marine Data BBS (NOAA)	:Marine Databases & Files
113:Call-ERS BBS (USDA)	:Agriculture Economic Research Info
114:Call ERS (USDA)	:Economic Research Line Service Line 2
115:ABLE INFORM (DOEdu)	:Disability & Rehab Data & Info
116:PTO-BBS (PTO):	Patent and Trademark Office BBS
119:IITF-BBS (NTIA)	:Info. Infrastructure Task Force BBS
120:ACDA-BBS (ACDA)	:Arms Control & Disarmament Agency
123:IBNS/OMPAT BBS (DOD)	:Military Performance Assessement
139:FAA-CBB (FAA)	:FAA Corporate Bulletin Board
141:DNA-BBS (DoD)	:Parts Discontinuance Notice Alerts
144:ResearchBase	:ResearchBase

Select a system # to connect, "?" for entire gateway list or X to exit:

4.   Select 115, ABLE INFORM (DOEdu), in Figure 16-13 for
       data about disabilities and rehabilitation.

Option L in Figures 16-11 and 16-12, Alphabetical Listing of All Information Online, is a shortcut for finding information on FEDWORLD. After selecting that choice, a list of GO commands appear (Figure 16-14).

Figure 16-14
FEDWORLD GO Commands

Displaying file hotlist ...

The following alphabetical listing provides you with a quick way
to get to a particular area within FedWorld without having to
browse through the screen selections. You will notice a couple
of ways doing this. The "/go {name}" command will take you
directly to the menu for that particular area of interest. You
can type them at the command line from any screen. Commands
which do not begin with "/go" are concatenated commands which
you can only use from the TOP menu. To use the concatenated
commands, go to the FedWorld main menu (/go main) and type the
letters at the command line.

DESCRIPTION	COMMAND
Agency for Health Care Policy and Research subsystem	/go ahcpr
Business, Trade, and Labor Mall main menu	/go business
Bureau of Export Administration	/go bxa

<U>p Page, <D>own Page, <T>op of File, <R>etrieve, <L>ook for Word, or e<X>it:

Type "/go (option)" to go directly to the related section of the system. For example, /go ahcpr sends users to the Agency for Health Care Policy and Research.

USING FEDWORLD TO LOCATE INFORMATION ABOUT SUBJECTS:

Figure 16-15 shows that FEDWORLD can be searched by subjects two ways. Enter keywords using the search form; or highlight category files (appears in bold print) and press enter to view a list of subject headings.

Figure 16-15
FEDWORLD Subject Index

FedWorld Home Page (p7 of 8)

US GOVERNMENT INFORMATION SERVERS

US Government Information Servers have been sorted into main
subject categories. You can search these subject files that
describe hundreds of US Government Websites. You can also view
a list of **category files** that you can search on.

Search for: _____
Subject Search

(NORMAL LINK)   Use right-arrow or <return> to activate.
Arrow keys: Up and Down to move. Right to follow a link; Left to go back.
H)elp O)ptions P)rint G)o M)ain screen Q)uit /=search [delete]=history list

ADDITIONAL FEDWORLD SERVICES:

Five additional parts of FEDWORLD are noteworthy:

1. Federal Job Announcements: Select choice J in Figure
    16-11 or connect to http://loki.fedworld.gov/jobs/job-
    search.html. The Office of Personnel Management up-
    dates this information five days a week from Tuesday
    through Saturday. Announcements are current as of 8:00
    am unless technical problems arise. The service is avail-
    able approximately 21 hours each day.

2. Commerce Information Locator Service: A government
    information locator system (GILS) is an information serv-
    ice that tells users where to find different types of data.
    Enter keywords into the system to locate titles and ab-
    stracts of relevant information produced by the Commerce
    Department, the Nuclear Regulatory Commission, the
    Federal Energy Regulatory Commission, and other agen-
    cies supported by the GPO Locator Service.
    (http://www.fedworld.gov/gils/gils.html) See Chapter
    2 for a more detailed discussion of GILS.

3. FTP: Over 10,000 files prepared by numerous agencies are
    available through FTP. (ftp.fedworld.gov)

4. NTIS OrderNow Database: Described above. (http://www.ntis.gov/ordernow)

5. FEDWORLD Freebies: Order free catalogs and brochures that describe NTIS products and services. (http://www.fedworld.gov/ntis/catalogs.htm)

FEDWORLD HELP DESK:

Call the help desk at 703-487-4608 between 7:30 am and 5:00 pm weekdays. An answering service handles after hour phone calls. The E-Mail address is webmaster@fedworld.gov.

ADDITIONAL NTIS SERVICES

NTIS COMPUTER PRODUCTS DIVISION:

The NTIS Computer Products Division is a central clearinghouse for software and datafiles prepared by federal agencies and their contractors. It combines functions of the former NTIS Federal Software Center and NTIS Federal Computer Products Center. The Division acquires the information and inputs it into the NTIS database.

Two annual directories describe software and datafiles. The *Directory of U.S. Government Datafiles for Mainframes and Microcomputers*[25] covers over 2,000 datafiles about business, social, and scientific topics. The *Directory of U.S. Government Software for Mainframes and Microcomputers*[26] includes software developed by over 100 agencies. Information appears in 21 subject categories. Entries in both sources include full citations, detailed summaries, hardware requirements, and ordering information. New product announcements are in relevant NTIS ALERTS titles, which were described above, and in the NTIS OrderNow database. Also, contact NTIS for copies of free catalogs and brochures that describe software and datafiles.[27]

FEDRIP DATABASE:

The Federal Research in Progress (FEDRIP) database references over 150,000 research projects supported by federal funds. Emphasis is on projects dealing with health, the physical and life sciences, agriculture, and engineering. The many agencies that contribute information include the Bureau of Mines; the Departments of Agriculture, Energy, and Veteran Affairs; the Environmental Protection Agency; the National Aeronautics and Space Administration; the National Science Foundation; and the Small Business Administration.

The database is file number 265 on Knight Ridders' Dialog Information Service. Figure 16-16 illustrates a sample citation.

Figure 16-16
FEDRIP Database

0077911
IDENTIFYING NO.: 10951 AGENCY CODE: SBIR
FEASIBILITY TECHNOLOGIES TO ENHANCE JOB DEVELOPMENT, JOB MODIFICATIONS,
OR JOB OPPORTUNITIES FOR DISABLED INDIVIDUALS
PRINCIPAL INVESTIGATOR: Mark N Rosen
PERFORMING ORG.: Nexus Applied Research, Inc., P.o. Box 178, Verdi, NV
89439
SPONSORING ORG.: ED
DATES: 91 FY : 89 FUNDS: $229,767 TYPE OF AWARD: Phase 1 and Phase
2
SUMMARY: COMPUTER, WORKSTATION, HANDICAP, DISABILITY COMPUTERS ARE WIDELY
USED AS WORKSTATIONS IN TECHNICAL AND BUSINESS APPLICATIONS. THE JOBS
ASSOCIATED WITH WORKSTATIONS REMAIN UNAVAILABLE TO MOST OF THE SEVERELY
HANDICAPPED POPULATION BECAUSE THEY REQUIRE NORMAL DEXTERITY IN ONE OR BOTH
HANDS TO CONTROL THE KEYBOARD AND MOUSE OR OTHER POINTING DEVICE.
WORKSTATIONS ARE BASED ON A WIDE VARIETY OF HARDWARE AND SOFTWARE PLATFORMS,
MAKING MODIFICATIONS ON A CASE BY CASE BASIS VERY COSTLY AND TIME
CONSUMING. RECENT ADVANCES IN ASIC (APPLICATION SPECIFIC INTEGRATED
CIRCUIT) TECHNOLOGY AND THE AVAILABILITY OF HIGH DENSITY ON-BOARD MEMORY
MAKES IT POSSIBLE TO CONSIDER DESIGNING A UNIVERSAL COMPUTER INTERFACE

References show names of researchers, their affiliations, titles, amounts of money provided, and research summaries.

Use FEDRIP cautiously because older records are not removed from the database. Although this item was copied in September 1995, the DATES section in Figure 16-16 (bold type) says that 1991 is the expected year of completion. The information fails to indicate if the project was, in fact, completed, canceled, or still active. Even more important, if the project was completed, FEDRIP does not say how to acquire the final report. Search *GRA&I*, contact the sponsoring or performing agencies, or contact the principal investigator for that information. Remember, project titles in FEDRIP may differ from titles of final and/or interim reports.

Test your understanding of FEDRIP: Refer to Figure 16-16 when answering the following:

1. What is the title of the research project?

(Feasibility Technologies To Enhance Job Development, Job Modifications, or Job Opportunities For Disabled Individuals)

2. Who is the principal investigator?

(Mark N. Rosen)

3. Who is the sponsoring agency?

(Department of Education)

4.   How expensive was the project? Rosen spent the money
     in (year).

                                                    ($229,767; fiscal year 1989)

5.   Who is the contractor?

                                                    (Nexus Applied Research, Inc.)

NATIONAL AUDIOVISUAL CENTER:

The National Audiovisual Center, created within the National Archives and Records Service in 1969, was a central source for government audiovisual and multimedia products. NAC became part of NTIS effective October 1994. The government believed that audiovisual materials could be handled more effectively by NTIS, given its experience in disseminating and marketing products in different formats. The Center maintains 9,000 titles issued by over 200 agencies. In fiscal year 1993, federal agencies spent approximately $55 million for audiovisual materials. Popular topics deal with business and career development; occupational health and safety; education; law enforcement; foreign languages; agriculture; and medical training. Contact NTIS at 800-788-6282 for the most current catalogs.[28]

ADDITIONAL FEDERAL GOVERNMENT SOURCES OF U.S. TECHNICAL INFORMATION

DEFENSE

The Defense Technical Information Center (DTIC) provides defense related information to the Department of Defense and its contractors and other government agencies and their contractors. Additional groups can become eligible users under four programs:

-The Potential Defense Contractors Program.

-The Historically Black Colleges and Universities Program.

-The University Research Initiative Program.

-The Small Business Innovation Research Program.

Subjects cover aeronautics; missile technology; space navigation; nuclear science; biology; chemistry; environmental science; and computer science, plus other areas relevant to the military. The National Technical Information Service distributes unclassified DTIC materials and indexes them in *Government Reports Announcements and Index*. Two sources offer more detailed information about DTIC registration, services and products: the *Defense Technical Information Center Handbook For Users*[29] and Kurt N. Molholm's article, The "Defense Technical Information Center: Expanding Its Horizons."[30]

486

EDUCATION

The Educational Resources Information Center (ERIC), which is supported by the Department of Education, indexes technical reports, papers, curriculum guides, and journal articles, plus other types of information, covering all aspects of education. The database covers 1966 through the present. The ERIC Document Reproduction Service (EDRS) sells in paper and microfiche formats all titles in the database which are not copyrighted. The *Current Index to Journals in Education*[31] indexes journal articles that are in the ERIC database and *Resources in Education*[32] indexes all other ERIC materials. Numerous vendors provide online and CD-ROM access to ERIC.[33] (See Internet Supplement to this chapter.)

ENERGY

"Symposium Issue: Energy Information Administration," *Government Information Quarterly.* 10:1 (1993), 1-151.

The Energy Information Administration (EIA) collects, evaluates, assembles, analyzes, and disseminates data pertinent to energy production, reserves, consumption, and technology. Much of its work is statistical. Articles deal with energy modeling, information resources, information quality, and policy analysis, among other topics.

U.S. Department of Energy. Energy Information Administration. *EIA Publications Directory* (DOE/EIA-0149(yr)). Washington, D.C.: GPO, 1978-annual. SuDoc number: E3.27:.

References cover energy supply and demand, marketing, consumption, and forecasting models. The subject, report number, and title indexes are helpful. The Energy Information Administration (EIA) published a cumulative index covering 1977-1989.[34] The cumulation includes a section for "Machine Readable Data Files and Modeling Programs" available through NTIS. Also consult the bimonthly journal, *New Releases,*[35] which describes new publications, and lists names of contacts and their phone numbers.

U.S. Department of Energy. Office of Scientific and Technical Information. *Energy Research Abstracts.* Washington, D.C.: GPO, 1991-monthly. Published semimonthly 1976-1990. SuDoc number: E1.17:.

Includes technical reports, engineering drawings, audiovisual data, and computerized media on energy related topics. Coverage extends to related areas, such as physics; computer science; radiology and radiation; health and safety; and waste management. Data describes research performed by the Department of Energy; other federal and state agencies; foreign governments; and universities and research groups. The indexes, which are cumulated semiannually and annually, list corporate and personal authors; subjects; and contract and report numbers. Note, although depository libraries acquire many titles on microfiche, GPO's financial problems prevent this information from being indexed in the *Monthly Catalog*.[36]

U.S. Nuclear Regulatory Commission. *Regulatory and Technical Reports* (NUREG-0304). Washington, D.C.: GPO, 1975(?)-quarterly. Title varies. SuDoc number: Y3.N88:21-3:.

Provides citations and detailed abstracts to technical and regulatory reports prepared by the Nuclear Regulatory Commission (NRC) and its contractors. Indexes list secondary report numbers--those applied by the performing organizations; personal authors; subjects; names of contractors, international organizations, NRC subdivisions and offices; and licensed facilities. The NRC Bibliographic Retrieval System gives online access to this data.

U.S. Nuclear Regulatory Commission. *Title List of Documents Made Publicly Available*. Washington, D.C.: GPO, 1979-monthly. SuDoc number: Y3.N88:21-2:.

Includes both formal Nuclear Regulatory Commission publications, as well as informal ones. Informal items are comments about regulatory activities, related correspondence, and other information that is not generally published. Use the personal and corporate author; report number; and facility indexes to locate information. The documents are available in NRC's local public document rooms.[37]

ENVIRONMENT AND EARTH SCIENCES

U.S. Bureau of Mines. *Bureau of Mines Publications and Articles*. Washington, D.C.: GPO, 1910(?)-1994. SuDoc number: I28.5:. Title varies.

An annual bibliography that lists reports and articles published during the previous calendar year. Topics deal with all aspects of mining and mineral preparation; treatment and use of minerals; conservation; and related health and safety issues. Indexing is by subjects and personal authors. Seven cumulative indexes cover 1910 through 1989.[38]

U.S. Environmental Protection Agency. *Access EPA*. 3rd ed. Washington, D.C.: GPO, 1993. SuDoc number: EP1.8/13:AC2/993.

Directory to Environmental Protection Agency (EPA) and related information sources. Separate chapters cover clearinghouses and hotlines; EPA databases--most of which are not available to the general public; library and information services; and state environmental libraries. The subject index is helpful.

U.S. Environmental Protection Agency. *EPA Publications Bibliography*. Washington, D.C.: GPO, 1977-quarterly. SuDoc number: EP1.21/7:.

Indexes technical reports prepared by EPA and its contractors that are available through NTIS. Data pertains to all social, economic, scientific, and technological topics about the environment and pollution. Entries are identical to those in *GRA&I*. Indexes cover titles; keywords; sponsoring EPA offices; corporate and personal authors; and contract, grant, NTIS order, and report numbers. Cumulative issues cover 1970-1976; 1977-1983; and 1984-1990.[39]

U.S. Geological Survey. *New Publications of the U.S. Geological Survey*. Washington, D.C.: GPO, 1907-monthly. Will appear quarterly as of 1996. SuDoc number: I19.14/4:. Title varies.

The U.S. Geological Survey (USGS) is responsible for earth sciences related research and national topographic mapping. Its technical reports and articles deal with all aspects of these subjects. The annual *Publications of the U.S. Geological Survey*[40] cumulates the monthly bibliography. Three cumulative indexes deal with materials published between 1879 and 1961, 1962 and 1970, and 1971 and 1981.[41]

HEALTH AND MEDICINE

U.S. National Institutes of Health. *CRISP Biomedical Research Information* (CD-ROM). Washington, D.C.: GPO, 1992-quarterly. SuDoc number: HE20.3013/2-4:.

The Computer Retrieval of Information on Scientific Projects (CRISP) describes research funded by the Public Health Service. Entries cite project titles and numbers; principal investigators; subject headings; performing organizations; and amounts of money involved. The detailed abstracts are informative. The identical data is also available through the Internet.

SPACE AND AVIATION

U.S. National Aeronautics and Space Administration. *NASA Tech Briefs*. Washington, D.C.: GPO, 1976-monthly. SuDoc number: NAS1.29/3-2:.

Describes aerospace related research that has commercial promise. Nine areas cover electronic components and circuits; electronic systems; physical sciences; materials; life science; mechanics; machines; manufacturing; and mathematics and information science.

U.S. National Aeronautics and Space Administration. *Scientific and Technical Aerospace Reports*. Washington, D.C.: GPO, 1963-1995. SuDoc number: NAS1.9/4:.

Scientific and Technical Aerospace Reports (*STAR*) indexes and abstracts technical reports dealing with all aspects of aeronautics and space research. NASA and its contractors; other government agencies and their contractors; universities and other research centers; industry groups; and foreign groups prepare the reports. Citations and abstracts are very similar to those in *GRA&I*. The indexes cover subjects; personal and corporate authors; and contract and report numbers. The printed edition of *STAR* ceased publication in 1995. However, electronic versions are available online as part of the Aerospace Database.[42] Comparable data is on the Internet at http://www.sti.nasa.gov/RECONselect.html.

CONCLUSION

A general introduction of this type covers only the most basic sources for scientific and technical reports. If the information you need is unavailable from NTIS or the selected other references discussed, consult the following sources and those cited in the chapter covering directories.

Encyclopedia of Associations. Detroit: Gale Research Company, 1961-annual.

Provides names, addresses, phone numbers, and descriptions of trade and professional groups in the U.S.

Government Research Directory. Detroit: Gale Research, Inc., 1980/82-biennial.

Covers groups funded by U.S. and Canadian governments.

International Research Centers Directory. Detroit: Gale Research Company, 1982-irregular.

Lists almost 8,000 government, university, independent, nonprofit, and commercial research groups throughout the world, excluding the U.S. and Canada. Entries give names; addresses; phone and fax numbers; backgrounds; publications and services; and names of affiliates and subsidiaries.

Research Centers Directory. Detroit: Gale Research, Inc., 1965-biennial. Title varies.

Provides names, addresses, phone numbers, and descriptions of approximately 13,500 groups in the U.S. and Canada. Coverage includes universities; laboratories; think tanks; technology transfer centers; and other non-profit groups.

Research Services Directory. Detroit: Gale Research, Inc., 1981-biennial.

Lists and describes private groups and individuals in the U.S.

Endnotes

1. U.S. Office of Management and Budget, *Budget of the United States Government Fiscal Year 1996: Analytical Perspectives* (Washington, D.C.: GPO, 1995), 119. SuDoc number: PREX2.8:996/ANALYT.

2. Richard D. Walker and C.D. Hurt. *Scientific and Technical Literature: An Introduction to Forms of Communication* (Chicago: American Library Association, 1990), 105.

3. *Ibid.*

4. American National Standards Institute, *Scientific and Technical Reports--Elements, Organization, and Design* (ANSI/NISO Z39.18-1995). Revision of ANSI Z39-18.-1987 (Bethesda, MD.: NISO Press, 1995), 1.

5. Walker and Hurt, *Scientific and Technical Literature*, 110-12. Walker and Hurt also cite Bill Matheny, "DOE Research Results," (Oak Ridge, Tenn.: Department of Energy, Office of Scientific and Technological Information) Unpublished memorandum dated June 12-13, 1986. Matheny describes 36 types of technical reports published by the Department of Energy. These include: conference proceedings & presentations; trip reports; magnetic tapes; bibliographies; incident reports; engineering drawings; computer codes; manuals; user guides; Hearings; theses; book chapters; environmental impact statements; guidebooks; and newsletters.

6. Consult the following for more detail about report numbers: American National Standard Institute, *Standard Technical Report Number (STRN) Format and Creation* (ANSI/NISO Z39.23-1990) (New Brunswick, N.J.: Transaction Publishers, 1991).

7. *Government Reports Announcements & Index* (August 15, 1995), CG-1.

8. 17 *U.S.C.* 105.

9. Michael Erdle, "New I.P. Ownership Policy Developed For Work Under Government Contracts," *BNA Patent, Trademark & Copyright Law Daily*, July 13, 1992, COPYRT (Library), BNAPDT (File name) (Online database). Available on Lexis/Nexis, Mead Data Central, Dayton, OH.

10. *Columbia Law Review* 84:2 (1984), 462.

11. U.S. Congress. House of Representatives. Committee on the Judiciary, *Copyright Law Revision.* (H. Rept. 94-1476) 94th Cong., 2nd sess. (Washington, D.C.: GPO, 1976), 59.

12. 667 F.2d 102 (1982).

13.   Charles R. McClure et al, *Linking the U.S. National Technical Information Service With Academic and Public Libraries* (Norwood, NJ: Ablex Publishing Corporation, 1986), 111.

14.   U.S. Department of Commerce. National Technical Information Service, *Fiscal Year 1993 Annual Report* (Springfield, VA.: NTIS, 1994?), 14.

15.   P.L. 102-245, 106 *Stat.* 13. See also "Transfer by Federal Agencies of Scientific, Technical, and Engineering Information to the National Technical Information Service," *Federal Register* 59:1 (January 3, 1994), 6-12.

16.   *NTIS Annual Report, Fiscal Year 1993,* 14.

17.   (Springfield, VA.: NTIS, April 1975-semimonthly). SuDoc number: C51.9/3:. Published previously as *Bibliography of Scientific and Industrial Reports,* January 1946-June 1949; *Bibliography of Technical Reports,* July 1949-September 1954; *United States Government Research Reports,* October 1954-December 1964; *United States Government Research and Development Reports,* January 1965-March 1971; and *Government Reports Announcements,* March 1971-March 1975.

18.   Contact NTIS to buy the *NTIS OrderNow CD-ROM.* Within the U.S., four quarterly updates cost $124 and single issues cost $39. Prices outside the U.S. are $248 and $78. As of February 1996, it is unclear when this product will be distributed to depository libraries. NTIS expects GPO to pay a license fee for the software. However, GPO regards this as unreasonable.

19.   See U.S. Department of Commerce. National Technical Information Service, *NTIS Bibliographic Database Guide* (NTIS-PR 253) 3rd ed. (Springfield, VA.: NTIS, no date), 6-7 for a comprehensive list of accession codes.

20.   Knight-Ridder-Dialog (Mountain View, CA.); DATA-STAR (Headquarters in London, England; U.S. office in Philadelphia PA.); ORBIT (McLean, VA.); and Canada Institute for Scientific and Technical Information (CISTI) (Ottawa, Ontario).

21.   *NTIS: KR Information on DISK* (CD-ROM) (Mountain View, CA.: DIALOG/Knight Ridder Information Service, Inc., covers 1980-quarterly); *NTIS on SilverPlatter* (CD-ROM) (Norwood, MA.: SilverPlatter Information, Inc., covers 1983-quarterly).

22.   U.S. National Technical Information Service. PB96-153606 (Springfield, VA.: NTIS, 1996). A gratis copy in PDF format is at http://www.fedworld.gov/ntis/prs/dbguide.htm.

23.   The *Alerts* are available on subscription from NTIS. GPO does not distribute them to depository libraries. Separate issues cover: ag-

riculture and food; astronomy and astrophysics; biomedical and human factors engineering; building industry technology; business and economics; civil engineering; combustion, engines and propellants; communication; computers and information theory; detection and countermeasures; electrotechnology; energy; environmental pollution and control; government inventions for licensing; health care; library and information sciences; manufacturing technology; materials sciences; mathematical sciences; navigation, guidance and control; ocean technology and engineering; ordnance; photography and recording devices; regional and urban planning and technology; space technology; and transportation.

24. "Government Online: Agencies," *Washington Post*, August 31, 1994, A23.

25. (Springfield, VA.: National Technical Information Service, 1991-annual).

26. (Springfield, VA.: National Technical Information Service, 1993-annual).

27. Selected free titles include *Catalog of Electronic Data Products From the Centers For Disease Control and Prevention*, (NTIS number: PR-716; DHHS number: (PHS)94-1213); *CD-ROMs & Optical Discs Available From NTIS* (PR-888); *FCC Licensing Data* (PR-718); *U.S. Government Banking & Financial Datafiles For Microcomputers & Mainframes* (PR-908); *U.S. Government Environmental Datafiles & Software: Microcomputers and Mainframes* (PR-758); *U.S. Government Nutrition & Food Composition Datafiles & Software For Microcomputers & Mainframes* (PR-814); and *U.S.Government Software for Microcomputers* (PR-815)--covers management, business, science and engineering, and modeling and simulation. Advertisements for other computer products appear in brochures and pamphlets that relate to particular subjects.

28. See also the NARA Audiovisual Locator Database (NAIL) operated by the National Archives and Records Service (NARA). It includes almost 80,000 still pictures, sound recordings, motion pictures, and video recordings. (http://www.nara.gov/nara/nail.html)

     Consult "How to Order Material Held by the Still Picture Branch" at http://www.nara.gov/nara/nn/nns/sorder.html, and "How to Order Material Held by the Motion Picture, Sound, and Video Branch" at http://www.nara.gov/nara/nn/nns/order.html. Submit questions by Email to webmaster@nara.gov.

29. U.S. Department of Defense. Defense Technical Information Center (AD-A260 738; DTIC/TR-93-9) (Washington, D.C.: GPO, 1993). Sudoc number: D7.15/2:93-9.

30.   *Government Information Quarterly.* 12:3 (1995), 331-344.

31.   (Washington, D.C.: GPO, 1969-monthly). SuDoc number: ED1.310/4:. Distributed by GPO on microfiche. Paper version is available from Oryx Press.

32.   (Washington, D.C.: GPO, 1966-monthly). SuDoc number: ED1.310:. Title varies.

33.   Online sources: CARL (Denver, CO.); CompuServe (Columbus, OH.); Knight-Ridder Dialog (Mountain View, CA.); and OCLC EPIC and OCLC First Search, (Dublin, OH.). CD-ROM sources: CD Plus Technologies (New York, NY); EBSCO (Peabody, MA.); Knight-Ridder Dialog (see above); and SilverPlatter (Norwood, MA.).

34.   U.S. Department of Energy. Energy Information Administration, *EIA Publications Directory, 1977-1989* (DOE/EIA-0149(77-89)) (Washington, D.C.: GPO, 1990). SuDoc number: E3.27:977-989.

35.   U.S. Department of Energy. Energy Information Administration (DOE/EIA-0204) (Washington, D.C.: GPO, 1986-bimonthly.) SuDoc number: E3.27/4:.

36.   As of Spring 1996, the Department of Energy temporarily suspended publication of *Energy Research Abstracts* due to cost constraints. It is unknown when or if it will resume publication. Comparable information is still available on the Internet. (See the Internet Supplement to Chapter 16.)

37.   The Nuclear Regulatory Commission set up local public document reading rooms throughout the nation where citizens can consult regulatory documents concerning facilities in their areas. Facilities cover nuclear power plants that are either operating or are under construction; radioactive waste disposal sites; and fuel sites. Most information includes comments on *Federal Register* announcements and NRC correspondence. Consult U.S. Nuclear Regulatory Commission, *Local Public Document Room Directory* (NUREG/BR-0088) 3rd ed. (Washington, D.C.: GPO, 1993). SuDoc number: Y3.N88:31/0088/REV.3

38.   U.S. Bureau of Mines, *List of Publications Issued by the Bureau of Mines from July 1, 1910 to January 1, 1960 with Subject and Author Index*, Special Publication (Washington, D.C.: GPO, 1960). SuDoc number: I28.5:910-960; U.S. Bureau of Mines, *List of Bureau of Mines Publications and Articles, January 1, 1960 to December 31, 1964 with Subject and Author Index*, Special Publication (Washington, D.C.: GPO, 1966). SuDoc number: I28.5:960-964; U.S. Bureau of Mines, *List of Bureau of Mines Publications and Articles, January 1, 1965 to December 31, 1969 with Subject and Author Index*, Special Publication

(Washington, D.C.: GPO, 1970). SuDoc number: I28.5:965-966; U.S. Bureau of Mines, *List of Bureau of Mines Publications and Articles, January 1, 1970 to December 31, 1974 with Subject and Author Index,* Special Publication (Washington, D.C.: GPO, 1975). SuDoc number: I28.5:970-974; U.S. Bureau of Mines, *List of Bureau of Mines Publications and Articles, January 1, 1975 to December 31, 1979 with Subject and Author Index,* Special Publication (Washington, D.C.: GPO, 1981). SuDoc number: I28.5:975-979; U.S. Bureau of Mines, *List of Bureau of Mines Publications and Articles, January 1, 1980 to December 31, 1984 with Subject and Author Index,* Special Publication (Washington, D.C.: GPO, 1987). SuDoc number: I28.5:980-984; and U.S. Bureau of Mines, *List of Bureau of Mines Publications and Articles, January 1, 1985 to December 31, 1989 with Subject and Author Index,* Special Publication (Washington, D.C.: GPO, 1990). SuDoc number: I28.5:985-989.

39.   U.S. Environmental Protection Agency, *EPA Cumulative Bibliography, 1970-1976* (Springfield, VA.: National Technical Information Service, 1976). 2 vols. SuDoc number: EP1.21/7-2:970-976/pt.1-2; U.S. Environmental Protection Agency, *EPA Publications Bibliography, 1977-1983* (Springfield, VA.: National Technical Information Service, 1983). 2 vols. SuDoc number: EP1.21/7-2:977-983/pt.1-2; and U.S. Environmental Protection Agency, *EPA Publications Bibliography, 1984-1990* (Springfield, VA.: National Technical Information Service, 1990). 2 vols. SuDoc number: EP1.21/7-2:984-990/pt.1-2;

40.   U.S. Geological Survey (Washington, D.C.: GPO, 1893-annual). SuDoc number: I19.14:. Title and SuDoc number varies.

41.   U.S. Geological Survey, *Publications of the Geological Survey, 1879-1961* (Washington, D.C.: GPO, 1964?). SuDoc number: I19.14:879-961; U.S. Geological Survey, *Publications of the Geological Survey, 1962-1970* (Washington, D.C.: GPO, 1972). SuDoc number: I 19.14:962-970; and U.S. Geological Survey, *Publications of the Geological Survey, 1971-1981* (Washington, D.C.: GPO, 1986). 2 vols. SuDoc number: I19.14:962-970.

42.   *Aerospace Database* (File 108) (Online database). Available on: DIALOG/Knight-Ridder, Mountain View, CA. This American Institute of Aeronautics and Astronautics database combines *STAR* and *International Aerospace Abstracts.*

Exercises

1. Best and Doyle prepared a document about responses to radiologic emergencies in 1995.

    A. What is its title?

    B. What is its NTIS abstract number?

    C. What is its NTIS order number:

    D. The price code is PC A01/MF A01. What is the most current cost?

    E. What is the contract number?

    F. Who is the performing organization or the contractor and who is the sponsoring organization? Describe the difference.

    G. What are its report numbers?

2. EPA published a non-print product in October 1994 that helps plan, conduct, and document groundwater monitoring system inspections.

    A. What is its title?

    B. What is its NTIS order number?

    C. What is its NTIS abstract number?

    D. What is its format?

    E. What is the price code and what is the most current cost?

3. H.C. Jenkins-Smith and others wrote a report about public perspectives of atomic weapons during the post Cold War era. Locate a reference to it on the Office of Scientific and Technical Service bibliographic database at http://www.osti.gov.

    A. What is the complete title?

    B. When was it published?

    C. What is its report number?

    D. What is its contract number?

    E. What is its SuDoc number?

    F. Which depository libraries in Connecticut own it?

Answers

1. A. *Application of a Geographic Information system For Radiologic Emergency Response.* (See (*Government Reports Announcements and Index*, August 15, 1995)

   B. 16-01,065.

   C. DE95007624GAR

   D. The most current price codes are inside the back cover of the *GRA&I* semimonthly issues. As of July 1996, the paper copy (PC) cost $6.50 and the microfiche copy (MF) cost $10.00.

   E. AC08-93NV11265.

   F. *Performing organization (contractor)*--EG&G Energy Measurements Remote Sensing Laboratory in Las Vegas, NV. *Sponsoring organization*--Department of Energy. The sponsoring organization paid the performing organization to conduct the research and prepare the report.

   G. The 2 report numbers are EGG-11265-1123 and CONF-950430-4.

2. A. *CME (Comprehensive Groundwater Monitoring Evaluation) Inspection Training System (on CD-ROM).* (See (*Government Reports Announcements and Index*, June 1, 1995)

   B. PB95-502704/GAR

   C. 528,093.

   D. CD-ROM.

   E. Items in the price code, "D02," costs $97.00 in July 1996.

3. A. *Public Perspectives of Nuclear Weapons in the Post-Cold War Environment*

   B. April 1994.

   C. SAND-94-1265.

   D. AC0494AL85000.

   E. E1.99:DE94015167

   F. Two Connecticut depository libraries own it, the Connecticut State Library and Homer Babbidge Library at the University of Connecticut.

•Chapter 17

Freedom of Information Act and Privacy Act

Answer the following questions when reading this chapter:

1. How can the Freedom of Information Act help enhance your research?

2. In what kinds of situations is mandatory declassification review more advantageous than the Freedom of Information Act?

3. How can the Privacy Act help enhance your research and/or affect you personally in other ways?

4. What are the similarities and differences between the two laws?

Earlier chapters covered published information in print and other formats. This one considers two laws mandating that certain kinds of unpublished records be made available to individuals upon request, the Freedom of Information Act (FOIA) and the Privacy Act. FOIA guarantees access to broad categories of government records. The federal government processed 589,391 FOIA requests in 1991.[1] The Privacy Act attempts to protect individuals' rights to privacy by safeguarding personal information in government records. In doing so, a balance was achieved, enabling the use of such files for legitimate purposes. The text also mentions briefly regulations governing mandatory declassification reviews. Mandatory declassification reviews entitle the public to request that agencies declassify and make public classified executive agency documents.

The chapter describes the Freedom of Information Act first. It summarizes basic provisions of the law; describes the kind of data exempt from disclosure; and outlines the fee structure. The next section of the chapter covers procedures for requesting records and appealing agency decisions to withhold information. The discussion then summarizes selected controversial issues affecting FOIA and describes the National Security Archives-- an organization that collects and preserves information disclosed under FOIA. The next section discusses mandatory declassification reviews. Coverage includes related background information, and similarities and differences between mandatory reviews and FOIA. Following that, the description of the Privacy Act outlines the provisions of the law. The discussion also covers procedures for requesting data and summarizes the Computer Matching and Privacy Protection Act of 1988, which amends the Privacy Act. The final parts of the chapter list sources for further information and summarize differences between the Freedom of Information and the Privacy Acts.

FREEDOM OF INFORMATION ACT

BASIC PROVISIONS

The Freedom of Information Act became law in 1966 and was amended in 1974 and in 1986.[2] The Law states that executive branch agencies have to make records in its possession available upon request to any person. Records are defined as any item(s) containing information that is in the possession, custody or control of an agency.[3] Requests must reasonably describe the records sought and cannot be among a type of information exempt from the law. FOIA does not include data held by Congress, the Judiciary, the President, and the President's immediate staff.

Under FOIA, the government must disclose records in all formats, including audiovisual and electronic materials. In "Dolphins v. U.S. Department of Commerce," the U.S. District Court in Northern California ruled that:

> The object of the Freedom of Information Act is to make available to the public 'information' in the possession of government agencies. The term 'records' in common parlance includes various means of storing information for future reference. There does not appear to be any good reason for limiting 'records' as used in the Act to written documents. The motion picture film in question was made in order to store the information it now contains; it therefore falls within the definition of 'records' in 5 U.S.C. 552.[4]

However, the government does not have to provide information in the format requested. For example, suppose an individual asks for data on magnetic tape, the agency can provide the information in paper or any other format, providing it does not unreasonably hamper access.[5]

The government must provide only those records that are in its possession. In *Forsham v. Harris* which deals with information held by a government contractor, not the agency, the Supreme Court ruled that:

...Congress contemplated...an agency must first either create or obtain a record as a prerequisite to its becoming an 'agency record' within the meaning of the FOIA...In this context the FOIA applies to records which have been in fact obtained, and not to records which merely could have been obtained.[6]

DATA EXCLUDED FROM FOIA

Agencies can withhold nine types of records under the Freedom of Information Act.

1. **Classified information:** Records classified for national security purposes pursuant to Presidential executive order are withheld from distribution.[7]

2. **Internal personnel rules and practices:** Documents that depict personnel rules or internal practices are exempt, providing the data is trivial and has no public interest. Practices governing employee lunch hours are an example. Agencies can also withhold manuals whose release would risk circumvention of the law.

3. **Records exempt under other laws:** The Freedom of Information Act does not supersede other legislation that requires agencies to withhold information from the public.

4. **Confidential business information and trade secrets:** This exemption only covers data the government acquires from individuals or corporations. The courts have upheld withholding records when disclosure might harm the competitive position of the data source and if disclosure impairs the government's attempts to acquire similar data in the future. The discussion below under "Issues Affecting FOIA" describes how business people use FOIA to acquire competitive advantages over others and steps the government took to limit this.

5. **Internal government communications (letters, memos):** This exemption attempts to protect candid communications and free exchange of ideas among agency officials during the policy making process. It applies only to pre-decision documents, such as draft copies, not final documents and other post-decision records.

6. **Personal information of agency officials:** Certain information, such as personnel records and medical histories are clearly exempt from disclosure. However, other types of data that relate to official duties can be problematic. The Department of Justice maintains that records created during previous employment and brought to an agency for reference purposes does not make them agency records.

The Department recommends that agencies consider the following questions on a case by case basis.[8]

-Was the information created during agency time or at agency expense?

-Does the item contain substantive agency information or is it limited to personal information?

-Was the information created for personal convenience and to what extent does it facilitate agency business?

-Was the document distributed to others for business purposes? If yes, how widely?

-Does the agency maintain control over the item through maintenance and disposition practices?

-Did the agency require the document be created?

-How widely did the author use the item to conduct agency business? Did others use it to conduct agency business?

-Is the information in the author's possession or is it in an agency file?

7. **Law enforcement records**: Law enforcement records are withheld when:

    -Disclosure might interfere with law enforcement proceedings.

    -There is reason to believe the person requesting the data is unaware of an investigation into possible wrongdoing.

    -Disclosure deprives someone of a fair trail or hearing.

    -Disclosure results in violation of privacy.

    -Confidential sources might be at risk

    -Information provided by confidential sources might be compromised.

-Disclosure would compromise investigative techniques and procedures.

-Disclosure would endanger the lives or safety of law enforcement personnel.

8. **Financial institutions:** Records prepared by or for bank supervisory agencies, such as the Federal Reserve Board or the Federal Deposit Insurance Corporation, are exempt.

9. **Geological information:** Geological information, and related data and maps about wells are exempt.

FEES

The legislative history proves that Congress did not want fees to be a factor that prevents access, but it also shows that Congress intended for agencies to recover their costs. Depending upon the status of the person requesting information, agencies can charge fees for three activities: costs of searching for records, duplication costs, and review costs. Review costs cover time spent by agency staff who confirm that the records are in order prior to disclosure.

The 1986 amendments to the Freedom of Information Act required the Office of Management and Budget (OMB) to issue guidelines on establishing a uniform fee structure. Congress intended to distinguish requesters who have commercial interests in the information from those that have other interests. The amendments shift more burden of costs to business people. The guidelines established four categories of users.[9] Chart 17-1 illustrates costs each type of user must pay.

Chart 17-1
FOIA Fees

Categories of Users	Search Fees**	Duplication Fees	Review Fees
Business people who have a commercial and competitive incentive for seeking the records.	Yes	Yes	Yes**
Educational and non-commercial scientific institutions. Requestors must demonstrate that the records are being used for scholarly or research purposes.	No	Yes, excluding the initial 100 pages which are gratis.	No
News Media. Although journalists typically work for commercial organizations, the regulations state that "a request for records supporting the news dissemination function of the requester shall not be considered to be a request that is for a commercial use." (52 FR 10,019)	No	Yes, excluding the initial 100 pages which are gratis.	No
All other requesters. Requests made by individuals for records about themselves are treated as Privacy Act requests that allow agencies to charge only for reproduction.	Yes, excluding the initial two hours which are gratis.	Yes, excluding the initial 100 pages which are gratis.	No

** Agencies can assess time spent searching for records, even if the search does not produce data.

Note, use of the data, not status of requesters, determine fees. For example, non-profit groups could make requests that have commercial use.

Agencies can waive or reduce fees if disclosure is in the public interest, contributes to public understanding of government activities, and is not in the commercial interests of the requester. Fee waivers are not given to journalists automatically. Like others, reporters must meet this criteria.

REQUESTING INFORMATION UNDER FOIA

First, identify the agency that maintains the information. The directories described in the final chapter will help do so. Contact the agency being certain to do the following:

1. Specify in your letter, as well as on the envelope, that this is a FOIA request.

2. Identify the records precisely. The law requires that requests "must be specific enough to permit a professional employee of the agency who is familiar with the subject matter to locate the record in a reasonable period of time."[10]

3. Include your name, address, and phone number.

4. Specify the maximum amount of fees you are willing to pay, and if applicable, attempt to justify a fee waiver.

Figure 17-1 illustrates a sample request letter.

Figure 17-1
Sample FOIA Request Letter

Agency Head [or Freedom of Information Act Officer]
Name of Agency
Address of Agency
City, State, Zip Code

Re: Freedom of Information Act Request

Dear:

This is a request under the Freedom of Information Act.

I request that a copy of the following documents [or documents containing the following information] be provided to me: [identify the documents or information as specifically as possible].

In order to help to determine my status to assess fees, you should know that I am (insert a suitable description of the requester and the purpose of the request).

[Sample requester descriptions:

a representative of the news media affiliated with the _____ newspaper (magazine, television station, etc.), and this request is made as part of news gathering and not for a commercial use.

affiliated with an educational or noncommercial scientific institution, and this request is made for a scholarly or scientific purpose and not for a commercial use.

an individual seeking information for personal use and not for a commercial use.

affiliated with a private corporation and am seeking information for use in the company's _____ business.]

[Optional] I am willing to pay fees for this request up to a maximum of $_____. If you estimate that the fees will exceed this limit, please inform me first.

[Optional] I request a waiver of all fees for this request. Disclosure of the requested information to me is in the public interest because it is likely to contribute significantly to public understanding of the operations or activities of the government and is not primarily in my commercial interest. [Include a specific explanation.]

Thank you for your consideration of this request.

Sincerely,

Name
Address
City, State, Zip Code
Telephone number [Optional]

Source: *A Citizen's Guide on Using The Freedom of Information Act and The Privacy Act of 1974 to Request Government Records,*
H. Rept. 103-104, 31.

The agency must respond within 10 business days stating if it intends to honor the request. The government requests ten day extensions if the data are stored in remote locations, large numbers of records are sought, or other agencies must be consulted. If the request is approved, the agency must furnish the records soon after the notification. When requests are denied, the agencies must state which exemption applies.

People denied records under FOIA have legal recourse on the following basis:

-Requesters can appeal decisions for denial of access based upon one of the exemptions discussed above.

-Requesters can appeal the denial of fee waivers, or the types or amounts of fees assessed.

-Requesters can appeal agency determinations that the documents were not adequately described.

-Requesters can appeal the failure of agencies to conduct satisfactory searches.

Appeals are first made to the agency heads. Be certain to do so within the period established by the agencies' regulations. Include the following information in the appeal letter:

1.   Write "Freedom of Information Act Appeal" on the envelope.

2.   Mention the FOIA number used by the agencies in their response.

3.   Explain why the denial was incorrect and why you need the information.

4.   Forward all previous correspondence.

Agencies must generally make their determinations within 20 business days, but sometimes request ten day extensions. Figure 17-2 illustrates a sample appeal letter.

Figure 17-2
FOIA Appeal Letter

Agency Head or Appeal Officer
Name of Agency
Address of Agency
City, State, Zip Code

Re: Freedom of Information Act Appeal

Dear:

This is an appeal under the Freedom of Information Act.

On (date), I requested documents under the Freedom of Information Act. My request was assigned the following
identification number: _____. On (date), I received a response to my request in a letter signed by (name of official). I appeal the denial of my request.

[Optional] The documents that were withheld must be disclosed under the FOIA because....

[Optional] I appeal the decision to deny my request for a waiver of fees. I believe that I am entitled to a waiver of fees. Disclosure of the documents I requested is in the public interest because the information is likely to contribute significantly to public understanding of the operations or activities of government and is not primarily in my commercial interest. (Provide details)

[Optional] I appeal the decision to require me to pay review costs for this request. I am not seeking the documents for a commercial use. (Provide details)

[Optional] I appeal the decision to require me to pay search charges for this request. I am a reporter seeking information as part of news gathering and not for commercial use.

Thank you for your consideration of this appeal.

Sincerely,

Name
Address
City, State, Zip Code
Telephone Number [Optional]

Source: *A Citizen's Guide on Using The Freedom of Information Act and The Privacy Act of 1974 to Request Government Records,*
H. Rept. 103-104, 32.

The public can appeal unfavorable decisions by agencies in the District Court where the requester lives or where the government maintains the documents, or in the District Court of the District of Columbia. Remember, throughout this process, the burden of justifying why information ought to be withheld is upon the government.

ISSUES AFFECTING FOIA

Controversy has always surrounded the Freedom of Information Act. Even before its enactment, many did not look favorably upon it. Having established sources, journalists did not want data becoming available to competitors. Congress generally received most of the information it sought from the executive branch. President Johnson signed the bill without fanfare, since he believed it "cut into his Administration's power to do the right thing for the right people without telling all those damn reporters how he did it!"11 The following discussion focuses on four issues: the effectiveness of FOIA depends upon the administration; the failure of Congress to include itself under FOIA; questions associated with electronic records; and unintended uses of FOIA.

EFFECTIVENESS OF FOIA DEPENDS UPON THE ADMINISTRATION

The effectiveness of the Freedom of Information Act, in large part, depends upon how the administration views and enforces the law. For instance, during the Reagan Presidency the Department of Justice adopted a very aggressive policy towards withholding records. The policy defended:

> ...all suits challenging an agency's decision to deny...request(s)...unless it is determined that: a) The agency's denial lacks a substantial legal basis; or b) Defense of the agency's denial presents an unwarranted risk of adverse impact on other agencies' ability to protect important records.[12]

The attitude of the Clinton administration differs sharply. The memorandum on FOIA issued by Attorney General Janet Reno states that:

> The Department will no longer defend an agency's withholding of information merely because there is a 'substantial legal basis' for doing so. Rather, in determining whether or not to defend a nondisclosure decision, we will apply a presumption of disclosure.[13]

Moreover, in the same memo, Reno encourages agencies to make discretionary disclosures whenever possible. FOIA exemptions are discretionary, not mandatory. That is, agencies can still disclose information, despite having a legal basis for withholding it.

FAILURE OF CONGRESS TO INCLUDE ITSELF UNDER FOIA

The Congressional Accountability Act of 1995[14] intended to make Congress accountable to the same laws as executive agencies. The legislation applies to the following:

-Fair Labor Standards Act of 1938

-Civil Rights Act of 1964, Title VII

-Americans with Disabilities Act of 1990

-Age Discrimination in Employment Act of 1967

-Family and Medical Leave Act of 1993

-Occupational safety and Health Act of 1970

-Chapter 71 of title 5, *U.S. Code* (pertains to federal service labor management relations)

-Employee Polygraph Protection Act of 1988

-Worker Adjustment and Retraining Notification Act

-Rehabilitation Act of 1973 Chapter 43 of title 38 *U.S.C.* pertaining to veterans' employment and reemployment

The Freedom of Information Act is conspicuously missing.

Representative Robert Ellseworth Wise, Jr. (Democrat, West Virginia) attempted to justify the exclusion of Congress from FOIA.[15] Chart 17-2 summarizes his thoughts and illustrates the contrary opinion.

Chart 17-2
Congress and FOIA

Arguments to Exclude Congress from FOIA	Arguments to Include Congress Under Foia
According to Wise, FOIA covers "those parts of the federal government where it was needed. Extensive hearings held in the 1960's and 1970's demonstrated that executive branch agencies were unwilling to make routine information about their activities available to the public. The FOIA was passed in response to a documented, long-term problem of excessive secrecy in the executive branch. No one has made a similar case for the Congress." (Congressional Record (November 21, 1991), H10811)	No one has investigated Congress in this context as Congress did the executive branch.
The President and Congress are already accountable to the public through elections in a way that bureaucrats are not.	Congressman Wise forgets about the bureaucrats in the General Accounting Office, the Government Printing Office, and the Congressional Budget Office, plus countless other Congressional agencies.
Information routinely made available would become inaccessible if Congress were covered under FOIA. For example, bills would be excluded from distribution to the public because they are draft copies, something not covered under FOIA.	Draft regulations and summaries of related comments are routinely made available in the Federal Register by agencies covered under FOIA.
If Congress is covered under FOIA, then the President and his immediate staff ought to be covered as well.	FOIA excludes the President because lawmakers believed that the Chief Executive should be able to communicate freely within the Oval Office. Senators and Representatives maintain that they deserve the same when communicating with their staffs and constituents. This still does not explain the exclusion of Congressional agencies from FOIA.

QUESTIONS ASSOCIATED WITH ELECTRONIC RECORDS

When FOIA was first enacted in 1966, the federal government had approximately 3,000 mainframes and in 1986 it had 25,000 mainframes and 125,000 microcomputers.[16] Despite this, most agencies cannot afford to assign computer personnel to meet FOIA requirements.

The Freedom of Information Act does not require agencies to create new records when responding to requests. However, agencies have sometimes argued successfully in the courts that programming computers to extract data from an electronic system can be comparable to creating a new record.[17] This is especially important today. Agencies must distinguish programming software for search purposes from other types of programming.

Data segregation is another complex topic. The identical agency records sometimes include information that can be disclosed under FOIA, as well as that which ought to be withheld. Data segregation is the process of separating the two prior to disclosure. The National Archives believes that "it would impose an inordinate burden on an agency to expect it to reprogram its computers to segregate disclosable from nondisclosable data."[18]

Electronic mail messages raise additional concerns. In the past, agencies have looked upon E-Mail messages as private and confidential. The National Archives suggest that agencies establish policies guaranteeing that E-Mail records are identified and preserved. They are no more nor no less important than any other types of records. The same decisions apply to E-Mail as to other records.[19] The National Archives additionally recommends that electronic mail messages identify the senders and receivers, and include dates that put information in context.[20]

Agency records consist of data recorded to preserve their contents, but software consists of codes and procedures designed for manipulating the data. Furthermore, contractors who prepare software for the government often maintain proprietary interests over it. Thus, disclosure of software along with government records can be problematic, especially when records disclosed in electronic format are useless without the software necessary to interpret them.

Agencies sometimes create and use data on computer networks that they do not maintain. Federal contracts with the Metasystems Design Group, which operates the Meta Network, is just one example.[21] Company officials admit that agencies use their system because the records will not be subject to FOIA. The Forsham v. Harris case described above states that agencies can only disclose records in their possession. It is unclear how data used on these networks relate to FOIA requirements.

UNINTENDED USES OF FOIA

Congress intended that the law enhance democratic ideals by promoting open government. However, over the years, many have used the law in unintended ways, creating frustration both inside and outside the government. Assistant Attorney General Stephen J. Markman said at a Congressional hearing that the typical FOIA user is:

> ...the corporate lawyer seeking business secrets of a client's competitors, the felon attempting to learn who informed against him,...the drug trafficker trying to evade the law,...and the private litigant who, constrained by discovery limitations, turns to the FOIA to give him what a trial court will not.[22]

Moreover, Pete Earley of the *Washington Post* said that:

The law has been widely exploited by lawyers for clients who use the government data to develop strategies for fighting federal investigations, spying on the competition, and discovering how strictly federal regulations are really enforced.[23]

Testifying before Congress, FBI Director William Webster provided the Committee with a document that describes the "Impact of the Freedom of Information Act Upon the Federal Bureau of Investigation." It describes how 38 members and associates of organized crime in Detroit acquired over 12,000 pages of documentation in an attempt to identify Bureau sources.[24]

Two measures attempt to deal with excessive use of FOIA by business people who can profit from the information. The 1986 Amendments to the Freedom of Information Act established fee guidelines that place a heavier financial burden upon commercial interests than other FOIA users. Consult Chart 17-1 for the fee structure. President Reagan's Executive Order 12,600[25] established procedures for dealing with commercial records that can possibly cause the submitters competitive harm if disclosed to others. When records provided to the government by a company are requested by others, the agency notifies the company. The company will have an opportunity to justify why the records should be withheld. If the agency does not except the justification and elects to disclose the information, the company receives an explanation of the decision. The company does not have a right to administrative appeal, providing it had an opportunity to adequately respond to the decision. Throughout this process, the FOIA requester is informed of all activities.

Suggestions made by Fred H. Cate, author of "The Right to Privacy and The Public's Right to Know: The 'Central Purpose' of the Freedom of Information Act,"[26] are helpful. He suggests that agencies consider the following before disclosing information:

1. The nature of the document and its relationship to the basic purpose of the Freedom of Information Act--opening agency action to public scrutiny.

2. Legitimate citizen expectations for privacy. Privacy is violated when the FOIA requester seeks information that the government happens to be storing, rather than official information about a government agency.[27]

NATIONAL SECURITY ARCHIVE

The National Security Archive[28] is a tax exempt group that makes available to the public national security information disclosed under the Freedom of Information Act. It consists of librarians, scholars, journalists, public interest groups, and current and former government officials. Scott Armstrong, a *Washington Post* reporter, and Raymond Bonner, a *New York Times* reporter, formed the Archive in 1985. Both were working on separate books about Central America. When comparing items acquired under

FOIA, they realized that information disclosed to one was withheld from the other.

The National Security Archive works towards pooling records, giving all researchers an opportunity to consult the data. The Archive routinely files for information under FOIA, assists others in doing so, collects previously released materials, and creates indexes and finding aids to facilitate information retrieval. Hopefully, this will eliminate the need for others to file for the identical records. The Archive has the largest collection of declassified documents in the world.

Foundation support helped the Archive in its early years. It hopes to become self supporting by selling document collections and indexes. The *National Security Archive Index on CD-ROM*[29] compiles the indexes to twelve microfiche collections. Most indexes include chronologies and glossaries of names, places, and organizations. All collections are on archival quality microfiche. In the future, the archive hopes to develop materials that can be used in classrooms and by undergraduate students, rather than just scholars and journalists.

MANDATORY DECLASSIFICATION REVIEWS

Requests for mandatory declassification review are somewhat similar to FOIA requests. The public has the right to ask executive agencies to evaluate classified information for the purpose of declassification. Agencies have three options:

-Rule that classification is no longer warranted and release the records to the requestor in full.

-Rule that classification of selected data is no longer warranted and release partial records.

-Rule that classification is still necessary.

Requests must describe the materials in a way that enables the agency to locate the information with reasonable amount of effort. The government must respond within 180 days. The public can appeal denied requests first through the agency, and if not satisfied with that response, to the Interagency Security Classification Appeals Panel.[30] Executive order 12958, "Classified National Security Information,"[31] and regulations promulgated by the Information Security Oversight Office, a section of the National Archives, govern the use of mandatory declassification reviews.[32]

Selected classified information is exempt from review. This includes:

-Data generated by the incumbent President; the incumbent President's staff; and committees, commissions, and boards appointed by the incumbent President.

-Records reviewed for declassification within the past 2 years.

-Records that pertain to current litigation.

Although mandatory declassification reviews are not as well known as FOIA requests, in fiscal year 1994, agencies acted on 4,196 cases pertaining to 51,976 documents. This amounted to almost 324,000 pages. The government disclosed all information that was requested 51% of the time and disclosed partial information 38% of the time.[33] President Nixon's Executive Order 11652 established mandatory declassification reviews in 1972.[34]

Chart 17-3 illustrates similarities and differences between the Freedom of Information Act and mandatory declassification reviews.

Chart 17-3
FOIA and Mandatory Declassification Review Requests:
A Comparison

FOIA	Mandatory Declassification Reviews
Covers both classified and declassified information.	Applies only to declassified information.
FOIA requests often take longer because the volume of requests is far greater.	Agencies often process mandatory declassification reviews more quickly because the volume of requests is much smaller.
Agencies must publish in the Federal Register names, addresses, and phone numbers of FOIA contact officers; and rules governing FOIA procedures.	Agencies must publish in the Federal Register names, addresses, and phone numbers of mandatory declassification review contact officers; and regulations governing mandatory declassification review procedures.
Public demands that something be declassified.	Public demands that something be declassified.
Strict turnaround time is written into law.	Agencies have more latitude when responding.
Exempts presidential documents	Exempts documents of the incumbent President; the Incumbent President's staff; and committees, commissions, and boards appointed by the incumbent President.
Appeal denials to disclose information first through the agencies and then through the courts.	Appeal denials to disclose information first through the agencies and then through the Interagency Security Classification Appeals Panel.

PRIVACY ACT

BASIC PROVISIONS

The Privacy Act guarantees individuals the right to know what kinds of personal data about their lives the government collects and why it is being collected. Agencies routinely collect in various ways files of personal information about those who have been or are employed by the Federal government or its contractors. Data also exists relating to recipients of benefits, such as veterans assistance, medical services, and loans for education or mortgages. Regarding police activities, the Federal Bureau of Investigation maintains files on individuals arrested by local, state and national authorities.

The Law allows citizens and legal aliens access to information about themselves that the government maintains in systems of records. Systems of records consist of data that is accessible by name, social security number, or any other personal identifying characteristics. Information excluded from systems of records can still be requested under FOIA. Individuals can also challenge the accuracy of their records. The Privacy Act covers records held by executive departments, the military, government corporations, government controlled corporations, and independent regulatory agencies.

Under the Privacy Act, agencies must meet the following obligations:

-Information collected can be used only for the purpose under which it was collected.

-The systems of records must maintain accurate, complete, and relevant information.

-Indexes to the systems of records must be available to the public. The biennial *Privacy Act Compilation*[35] is organized by agencies. Entries mention the names of the systems, their locations, and the categories of individuals covered. Additional information describes the types of records maintained; legal authorities for maintaining the data; descriptions of storage and retrieval systems; and procedures for accessing information and contesting its contents.

-People have the right to revise agency records and amend misinformation.

-Refrain from divulging personal data to third parties without the written permission of the subjects, except under one of the following conditions:

1. The FOIA requires disclosure of information.

2. The Census Bureau uses the data for either planning or taking a census or a survey.

3. Records are transferred to the National Archives.

4. Heads of law enforcement agencies submit written requests for records.

5. The health or safety of the subjects of the records requires that information be disclosed.

6. Court orders require that the data be disclosed.

7. Congress or the General Accounting Office requests the information.

-Provide to the public, upon request, lists of third parties to whom personal data has been divulged, unless the information was disclosed under one of the seven conditions stated above.

EXEMPTIONS UNDER THE PRIVACY ACT

Privacy Act exemptions are complex and used infrequently. To withhold information, agencies must note in advance that a system of records might include exempt data. The following seven kinds of information apply:

1. All files maintained by the Central Intelligence Agency.

2. Data compiled by Federal criminal law enforcement agencies from the time a suspect is arrested through release.

3. Documents compiled during investigations for Federal employment, military service, military promotion, and contract awards, when the identities of confidential sources could be disclosed.

4. Secret Service information pertaining to protection of the President and other high officials.

5. Information classified to protect the national security.

6. Records concerning federal examination procedures whereby divulgence would compromise objectivity or the testing process.

7. Records required by statute to be maintained and used solely for statistical purposes, such as census or income tax returns.

8. Records compiled for expected civil actions or proceedings.

Note, agencies are not required to withhold information, but they can choose to do so.

REQUESTING DATA UNDER THE PRIVACY ACT

The first step in requesting information under the Privacy Act is identify the relevant system of records. Use the *Privacy Act Compilation* described above to do so. Contact the agency's Privacy Act Officer or the administrator of the system of records. Say that the request is being made under the Privacy Act, and provide personal information that confirms you are indeed the subject of the record(s). Define the kind of information you seek precisely and tell the agency which system of records to search. The duplication cost is the only fee the agency can charge. Figure 17-3 illustrates a sample letter for someone who wants copies of records, and Figure 17-4 shows a sample letter for someone who wants to amend incorrect information.

Figure 17-3
Privacy Act Request Letter
For Acquiring Copies of Records

Privacy Act Officer [or System of Records Manager]
Name of Agency
Address of Agency
City, State, Zip Code

Re: Privacy Act Request for Access

Dear:

This is a request under the Privacy Act of 1974.

I request a copy of any records [or specifically named   records] about me maintained at your agency.

[Optional] To help you to locate my records, I have had the   following contacts with your agency: [mention job applications,   periods of employment, loans or agency programs applied for,   etc.].

[Optional] Please consider that this request is also made   under the Freedom of Information Act. Please provide any   additional information that may be available under the FOIA.

[Optional] I am willing to pay fees for this request up to a   maximum of $_____. If you estimate that the fees will exceed   this limit, please inform me first.

[Optional] Enclosed is [a notarized signature or other   identifying document] that will verify my identity.

Thank you for your consideration of this request.

Sincerely,

Name
Address
City, State, Zip Code
Telephone number [Optional]

Source: *A Citizen's Guide on Using The*
Freedom of Information Act and The Privacy Act of 1974
to Request Government Records, **H. Rept. 103-104, 33.**

Figure 17-4
Privacy Act Request Letter
For Amending Incorrect Information

Privacy Act Officer [or System of Records Manager]
Name of Agency
Address of Agency
City, State, Zip Code

Re: Privacy Act Request to Amend Records

Dear :

This is a request under the Privacy Act to amend records   about myself maintained by your agency.

I believe that the following information is not correct: [Describe the incorrect information as specifically as possible].

The information is not (accurate) (relevant) (timely)   (complete) because ....

[Optional] Enclosed are copies of documents that show that   the information is incorrect.

I request that the information be [deleted] [changed to   read:].

Thank you for your consideration of this request.

Sincerely,

Name
Address
City, State, Zip Code
Telephone Number [Optional]

Source: *A Citizen's Guide on Using The Freedom of Information Act and The Privacy*
Act of 1974 to Request Government Records,
H. Rept. 103-104, 35.

Unlike FOIA, agencies do not have time limits in which they must respond.

APPEAL PROCEDURE

Although the Privacy Act does not require it, many agencies created administrative appeal procedures. Those covered under the law can file civil lawsuits if agencies fail to maintain accurate, current records and deny access to or the right to amend the data. File suits in Federal District Court where you live, where the records are maintained, or in the Federal District Court of the District of Columbia.

COMPUTER MATCHING AND PRIVACY PROTECTION ACT OF 1988

The Computer Matching and Privacy Protection Act of 1988[36] amended the Privacy Act. Computer matching is a process whereby personal information is checked against a database to determine eligibility for federal benefit programs. The agency that maintains the system of records and the agency that provides the benefit must agree to the following:

-The purposes and procedures for the matching.

-Protections for personal privacy.

-Review of the agreement by Data Integrity Boards that each agency must establish.

Before taking adverse actions, agencies must independently verify the results and must notify the individuals, giving them the right to appeal.

ADDITIONAL INFORMATION ABOUT THE FREEDOM OF INFORMATION AND PRIVACY ACTS

PRINTED SOURCES

Franklin, Justin D. and Robert F. Bouchard. *Guidebook to the Freedom of Information and Privacy Acts*. 2nd edition. New York: Clark Bourdman, Callaghan, 1986. 2 vols.

Describes the FOIA and the Privacy Act in a section by section analysis. Footnotes refer to cases, statutes, codifications, and journals. Franklin and Bouchard give detailed descriptions of procedures for requesting information under each law. The appendices in volume 2 include a bibliography of law review articles; a list of pertinent references in the *Code of Federal Regulations*; a list of agency contacts for FOIA related matters; and reprints of Executive Orders, Department of Justice guidelines, and related state legislation. Volume 2 also includes an index. Attorneys are the primary audience. Inserted pages update information.

King, Dennis. *Get the Facts on Anyone*. New York: Prentice Hall, 1992.

A guide for researchers who must compile data about individuals, businesses, and nonprofit organizations. King describes the use of city directories; crisscross directories that are organized by phone numbers and addresses; FOIA; financial and credit information; court records; medical records; and government information, such as military service records, court records, and motor vehicle records.

Litigation Under the Federal Open Government Laws. Washington, D.C.: American Civil Liberties Union Foundation, 1976-annual.

Covers access to government information under four laws: the Freedom of Information Act, the Privacy Act, the Government in the Sunshine Act, and the Federal Advisory Committee Act. The outline format of each chapter gets to the heart of the issues. The citations to and the brief quotations from cases are helpful. This summary of the subject is a good quick reference guide to the law. However, it may not be the best starting point for those unfamiliar with the issues.

O'Reilly, James T. *Federal Information Disclosure*. 2nd edition. Colorado Sprints, CO.: Shepards/McGraw Hill, 1990. 2 vols.

A comprehensive description of FOIA and the Privacy Act. Separate chapters cover historical developments; definitions; conditions and limitations of access; exemptions; court proceedings; model forms; and relevant state laws. Chapter 7, "Winning the Request at the Agency," is especially informative. Volume 2 includes a thorough index. Although intended for use by attorneys, the very readable text is valuable to laymen. Inserted pages update information.

Tapping Officials' Secrets: The Door To Open Government in ... Washington, D.C.: Reporters Committee for Freedom of the Press.

A series of 51 booklets that summarize legislation and give case notes for government information access laws in the 50 states and the District of Columbia. Topics include rights to view information and attend meetings of state and local bodies.

U.S. Congress. House. Committee on Government Operations. *A Citizen's Guide on Using the Freedom of Information Act and the Privacy Act of 1974 to Request Government Records*. H. Rept. 103-104. 103rd Cong., 1st. sess. Washington, D.C.: GPO, 1993. SuDoc number: Y1.1/8:103-104.

One of the best descriptions of the subject intended for use by non-attorneys. The lucid text covers the basics of acquiring information under each law. Appendices list sample letters for requesting information and appealing decisions to withhold records; bibliographies of congressional publications; and the texts of the laws. The House Committee on Government Operations provides free copies upon request.

U.S. Department of Justice. Office of Information and Privacy. *FOIA Update*. Washington, D.C.: GPO, 1979-quarterly. SuDoc number: J1.58:.

A newsletter that summarizes recent developments and cases pertaining to FOIA. It often includes Presidential and Department of Justice policy statements. The "OIP Guidance" column advises agencies about proceeding with different types of requests. The Winter issues often include directories to "FOIA Administrative and Legal Contacts at Federal Agencies." Agency officials and attorneys are the primary audience, but the newsletter is still valuable to the general public.

U.S. Department of Justice. Office of Information and Privacy. *Freedom of Information Act Guide and Privacy Act Overview*. Washington, D.C.: GPO, 1992-annual. SuDoc number: J1.8/2:F87/year.

A comprehensive guide to both laws that emphasizes the interpretation of cases and policies. Special features include numerous footnotes, and bibliographies of Congressional, Department of Justice, and non-government sources. This item is intended for attorneys and agency officials, but it is also comprehensible to laymen.

U.S. Department of Justice. Office of Information and Privacy. *Freedom of Information Case List.* Washington, D.C.: GPO, 1978?-annual. SuDoc number: J1.56:.

A bibliography of cases that cite those pertaining to FOIA, the Privacy Act, the Government in the Sunshine Act, and the Federal Advisory Committee Act. The "Overview List of Selected FOIA Decisions" is a basic reading list for attorneys unfamiliar with the issues and those seeking a review. FOIA agency officials and legal professionals are the intended audiences.

U.S. General Services Administration. *Your Right to Federal Records: Questions and Answers on the Freedom of Information Act and the Privacy Act.* Prepared in conjunction with the U.S. Department of Justice. Washington, D.C.: GPO, 1992. Reprinted in 1994. SuDoc number: GS1.2: F31/2/992.

A basic presentation designed for laymen. The initial two chapters describe each law and the third chapter compares them. The annotated list of additional sources of information is helpful.

ASSOCIATIONS AND INTEREST GROUPS

American Society of Access Professionals
1710 Woodmont Avenue #1430
Bethesda, MD 20814-3015
Voice: 301-913-0030
FAX: 301-913-0001

Membership includes federal employees, attorneys, journalists, and others interested in improving the administration of the Freedom of Information and Privacy Acts. The association attempts to promote cost effective administration of the laws; protection of personal privacy; fair information practices; and training opportunities. The bimonthly newsletter, *ASAP News*, deals with privacy, FOIA issues, and related government policies.

Center for National Security Studies
122 Maryland Ave. NE
Washington, D.C. 20002
Voice: 202-544-1681
FAX: 202-546-0738

Cooperates with other groups and citizens in promoting debate of what would have been secret policies. The group helps people file FOIA requests; coordinates litigation in related areas; sponsors an annual FOIA litigation conference; and provides attorneys with professional training on the use of FOIA. Its annual publication, *Litigation Under the Federal Open Government Laws*, was described previously. The Center evolved from the former American Civil Liberties Union National Security Project.

Freedom of Information Center
University of Missouri
20 Walter Williams Hall
Columbia, MO. 65211
Voice: 314-882-4856
FAX: 314-882-9002

A clearinghouse supported by the University of Missouri School of Journalism. It provides inexpensive research services for students, journalists, photographers, and the general public regarding access to records under FOIA.

Freedom of Information Clearinghouse
P.O. Box 19367
Washington, D.C. 20036
Voice: 202-833-3000

Helps journalists, public interest groups, and citizens obtain documents under FOIA. The Clearinghouse will go to court to force disclosure when the issues in question affect access to records significantly. Its publications include a brochure, *The Freedom of Information Act: A User's Guide* and a book, *Litigation Under the Federal Open Government Laws*.

National Center for Freedom of Information Studies
Loyola University
820 N. Michigan Avenue
Chicago, IL 60611
Voice: 312-915-6548
FAX: 312-915-7095

Sponsors research on topics relating to the Freedom of Information Act.

National Security Archive
(See the discussion above.)

Reporters Committee For Freedom of the Press
1735 Eye Street N.W., Suite 504
Washington, D.C. 20006
Voice: 202-466-6312
FAX: 202-466-6326

Operates a Freedom of Information Service that assists reporters in obtaining government information. Its publications include *News Media and the Law*, a quarterly journal, and *News Media Update*, a biweekly newsletter.

United States Privacy Council
P.O. Box 15060
Washington, D.C. 20003
Voice: 202-829-3660

Includes individuals and groups that hope to promote personal privacy and improve public access to government information. The Council works to enhance the effectiveness of the Privacy Act, the Fair Credit Reporting Act, and the Electronic Communications Privacy Act.

CONCLUSION

Chart 17-4 displays relationships between the Freedom of Information and the Privacy Acts when the people whom the records are about request information. Four options describe when each law requires disclosure and when each permits withholding information.

Chart 17-4
Requesting One's Own Records Under
The Freedom of Information and Privacy Acts

	Privacy Act requires disclosure of records	Privacy Act requires withholding records
FOIA requires disclosure	Materials are released.	Despite Privacy Act exemption, all or parts of the records may still be available under FOIA.
FOIA permits withholding	Release information under Privacy Act despite FOIA exemption.	Records are withheld entirely only under exemptions of both laws.

Chart 17-5 shows further similarities and differences between the two laws.

Chart 17-5
Differences Between FOIA and the Privacy Act

FOIA	Privacy Act
Anyone has the right to access records held by the government.	Citizens and legal aliens have the right to access records about themselves.
The public cannot ask agencies to amend incorrect information.	Citizens and legal aliens have the right to amend incorrect information in their records.
FOIA applies to all records of federal executive agencies.	Applies only to information maintained by executive agencies in systems of records. That covers data retrievable by names, social security numbers, or any other personal identifier. Use FOIA to access other personal information.
The fee structure varies depending upon the status of the requestor. (See chart 17-1)	Fees cover costs of copying records. Agencies cannot charge for time taken to locate or review information.
Individuals cannot access records about other people. Although exemption 6 protects privacy, it does not apply when agencies determine that public interest favors disclosure.	Individuals cannot access records about others.
The statute of limitation for filing lawsuits is 6 years.	The statute of limitation for filing lawsuits is 2 years.

Endnotes

1. Harold C. Relyea, *The Administration and Operation of The Freedom of Information Act: An Overview, 1966-1991* (93-977-GOV) (Washington, D.C.: Congressional Research Service, 1993), 8. Reproduced in *Major Studies and Issue Briefs of the Congressional Research Service, 1994 Supplement* (Bethesda, MD.: University Publications of America, 1994).

2. (PL 89-487, July 4, 1966), 80 *United States Statutes at Large* 250-251; "Freedom of Information Act Amendments of 1974," (PL 93-502, November 21, 1974), 88 *United States Statutes at Large* 1561-64; "Freedom of Information Act of 1986," (PL 99-570, October 27, 1986), 100 *United States Statutes at Large* 3207-48- 3207-50.

3. U.S. Congress. House. Committee on Government Operations, *A Citizen's Guide on Using the Freedom of Information Act and the Privacy Act of 1974 to Request Government Records* (H. Rpt. 103-104), 103 Congress, 1st session (Washington, D.C.: GPO, 1993), 6. SuDoc number: Y1.1/8:103-104.

4. 404 *Federal Supplement* 407 (1975).

5. The courts ruled in *Dismukes v. Department of the Interior* that "An agency has no obligation under the FOIA to accommodate a particular requester's preference regarding the format of requested information, and according to FOIA, the agency need only provide responsive, nonexempt information in a 'reasonably accessible form'" Dismukes requested data on computer tape, but the agency provided it on microfiche. (603 *Federal Supplement* 760 (1984))

6. 445 *U.S. Reports* 169 (1980).

7. The most recent Executive Order issued by President Clinton is "Executive Order 12,958 of April 17, 1995: Classified National Security Information," *Federal Register* 60:76 (April 20, 1995), 19825-43. It establishes a tone towards reducing government classification. Section 1.2(b) states that "If there is significant doubt about the need to classify information, it shall not be classified" and section 1.2(c) states that "If there is significant doubt about the appropriate level of classification, it shall be classified at the lower level." The Order sets a 10 year limit on most new classifications. Justifications for decisions to classify new items must appear on the records. Also, unless agencies designate twenty-five year old documents as sensitive, they are subject to automatic declassification within five years.

8. U.S. Department of Justice, *Freedom of Information Act For Attorneys and Access Professionals* (Washington, D.C.: GPO, 1989), III-35. SuDoc number: J31.2:F87/989.

9.   "The Freedom of Information Reform Act of 1986; Uniform Freedom of Information Act Fee Schedule and Guidelines," *Federal Register* 52:59 (March 27, 1987), 10012-20.

10.   *A Citizen's Guide on Using the Freedom of Information Act and the Privacy Act of 1974 to Request Government Records*, 6.

11.   Sam Archibald, "The Early Years of the Freedom of Information Act--1955 to 1974," *PS Political Science & Politics* 26:4 (December 1993), 728, 730.

12.   "Attorney General's Memo on FOIA," *FOIA Update* 2:3 (June 1981), 3.

13.   "Attorney General Reno's FOIA Memorandum," *FOIA Update* 14:3 (Summer/Fall 1993), 4.

14.   (PL 104-1, January 23, 1995).

15.   "The Freedom of Information Act, The Congress, and the White House," *Congressional Record* 137:173 (November 21, 1991), H10810-12. Consult the following for a more thorough analysis: Jay R. Shampansky et al, *The Application of the Freedom of Information Act to Congress: A Legal Analysis* (92-403 A) (Washington, D.C.: Congressional Research Service, 1992) in *Major Studies and Issue Briefs of the Congressional Research Service: 1992 Supplement* (Bethesda, MD: University Publications of America), 1993? Reel 8, frame 935.

16.   U.S. Congress. Office of Technology Assessment, *Informing the Nation: Federal Information Dissemination in an Electronic Age* (Washington, D.C.: GPO, 1988), 209. SuDoc number: Y3.T22/2:2IN3/9. A General Services Administration report estimated that in fiscal year 1993, the federal government had 32,263 "CPU's" (central processing units) of computers that cost $10,000 or more. This information cannot be transferred into numbers of computers. Moreover, it excludes the thousands of microcomputers and other computers that cost less than $10,000. (U.S. General Services Administration, *Automated Data Processing Equipment In the U.S. Government: 1993 Summary, Small, Medium, and Large Computers* (Washington, D.C.: GPO, 1994), 1.

17.   Related issues and selected cases are summarized in *Informing the Nation*, 213-221.

18.   U.S. Congress. Senate. Committee on the Judiciary. Subcommittee on Technology and the Law, *The Electronic Freedom of Information Improvement Act* Hearings on S. 1940, April 30, 1992 (Serial No. J-102-61) (Washington, D.C.: GPO, 1993), 62. SuDoc number: Y4.J89/2:2:S.HRG.102-1098.

19. "Electronic Mail Systems," *Federal Register* 60:166 (August 28, 1995), 44635.

20. "Electronic mail systems," 46637.

21. James Love, "Public and Private Networks, and the Status of Public Records, Open Meetings, and FOIA," Taxpayer Assets Project-Information Policy Note, January 20, 1994. Referenced: November 13, 1995. Internet address: ftp://ftp.cpsr.org/taxpayer_assets/FOIA_and_Private_networks.

22. U.S. Congress. Senate. Committee on the Judiciary. Subcommittee on Technology and the Law, *The Freedom of Information Act* Hearings, August 2, 1988 (J-100-84) (Washington, D.C.: GPO, 1989), 3. SuDoc number: Y4.J89/2:S.HRG.100-1075.

23. "EPA Lets Trade Secret Loose In Slip-Up, To Firm's Dismay," *Washington Post*, September 19, 1982, A1, A6.

24. Cited in U.S. Congress. Senate. Committee on the Judiciary. Subcommittee on the Constitution, *Freedom of Information Act* Hearings, April 18 and 21, 1983. (J-98-31) (Washington, D.C.: GPO, 1984), 436. SuDoc number: Y4.J89/2:S.HRG.98-699.

25. "Predisclosure Notification Principles for Confidential Commercial Information," *Federal Register* 52:122 (June 25, 1987), 23781-3.

26. *Administrative Law Review* 46:1 (Winter, 1994), 41-74.

27. Supreme Court Justice Harry Blackmun's concurring judgement in *United States Department of Justice v. Reporters Committee for Freedom of the Press* stated that "...when the information is in the Government's control as a compilation, rather than as a record of 'what the Government is up to' the privacy interest protected by Exemption 7(C) is in fact at its apex while the FOIA-based public interest in disclosure is at its nadir." 489 *U.S. Reports* 780 (1989).

28. Gelman Library, 2130 H Street N.W. #701, Washington, D.C 20006, Voice: 202-994-7000; FAX: 202-994-7005; E-Mail: archive@cap.gwu.edu.

29. (Washington, D.C.: Chadwyck-Healey, 1994) Chadwyck-Healey published each of the following twelve collections indexed on the CD-ROM: *Afghanistan: The Making of U.S. Policy, 1973-1990* (1991); *The Berlin Crisis, 1958-1962* (1991); *The Cuban Missile Crisis, 1962* (1990); *El Salvador: The Making of U.S. Policy, 1977-1984* (1989); *Iran: The Making of U.S. Policy, 1977-1980* (1990); *The Iran-Contra Affair: The Making of A Scandal, 1983-1988* (1990); *Nicaragua: The Making of U.S. Policy, 1978-1990* (1991); *The Philippines: U.S. Policy During the Marcos Years, 1965-1986* (1990); *South Africa, 1962-1989* (1991); *The U.S. Intelligence Community: Organization, Operations and Manage-*

ment, 1947-1989 (1990); *U.S. Military Uses of Space: 1945-1991* (1991); and *Nuclear Non-Proliferation, 1945-1991* (1992).

30.   See "Information Security Oversight Office; Classified National Security Information," *Federal Register* 61:52 (March 15, 1996), 10853-6 for a description of Information Security Oversight Office procedures.

31.   *Federal Register* 60:76 (April 20, 1995), 18823-43.

32.   "Information Security Oversight Office; Classified National Security Information," *Federal Register* 60:198 (October 13, 1995), 53491-502.

33.   U.S. Office of Management and Budget. Office of Information Security Oversight, *1994 Report to the President* (Washington, D.C.: GPO, 1995), 27-28.

34.   "Classification and Declassification of National Security Information and Material" (E.O. 11652 of March 8, 1972) 37 FR 5209; and "National Security Council Directive on Classification, Downgrading, Declassification and Safeguarding of National Security Information of May 17, 1972," 37 FR 100053. Both cited in U.S. Congress. Senate. Committee on the Judiciary. Subcommittee to Investigate the Administration of the Internal Security Act and Other Internal Security Laws, *Internal Security Manual Revised to July 1973: Provisions of Federal Statutes, Executive Orders, and Congressional Resolutions Relating to the Internal Security of the United States*, Prepared by the American Law Division. Congressional Research Service. Library of Congress (Washington, D.C.: GPO, 1974), Vol. 1, 350-74. SuDoc number: Y4J89/2:IN8/15.

35.   U.S. Office of the Federal Register (Washington, D.C.: GPO, 1975-biennial). SuDoc number: AE2.106/4:. The 1993 edition is in CD-ROM format.

36.   (PL 100-503, October 18, 1988) 102 *United States Statutes at Large* 2507-14.

Appendix -
Freedom of Information Act and Privacy Act

Congress enacted Public Law 104-231, the Electronic Freedom of Information Amendments of 1996, on October 2, 1996. This Appendix summarizes key parts of the legislation because press deadlines prevented rewriting the entire chapter. Until now, agencies considered electronic records covered under FOIA as a matter of general policy. However, P.L. 104-231 explicitly defines electronic information as records, and also covers yet unknown future formats under the law.

A large part of the law intends to facilitate agencies' responses to FOIA requests by encouraging online access to information. Items created after November 1, 1996 that are available for copying and inspection must be available through computer telecommunications and in hard copy within one year. Data released under FOIA that the agencies determine are likely others will request must also be available online. The law permits CD-ROMs and/or diskettes to substitute for online access when that technology is unavailable to agencies. Moreover, agencies must compile indexes of previously released FOIA requests, and must make them available online by December 31, 1999. Congress believes this will reduce the volume of requests, and will allow agency personnel to spend more time responding to more complicated inquiries.

The amendments extend the time requirements for responding to requests from ten to twenty working days. Agencies unable to meet the deadline must inform the requesters. When doing so, the government must offer those seeking data opportunities to redefine their topics more precisely. This might help agencies meet deadlines. The law also encourages agencies and requesters to mutually agree upon a reasonable time period for supplying the information.

Under the new law, two categories cover requests for expediting the release of information. First priority goes to those who might suffer significant harm unless the data are supplied. Those involved with information dissemination have second priority. Agencies must develop regulations governing expedited requests.

The amendments require agencies to submit annual reports to Congress that cite the number of requests received; the extent of backlogged requests; and the number of denials and appeals. The reports must also note the authorities the agencies cited when denying requests. The intent of this is to help the public by showing the reasons for withholding data. The Department of Justice must bring these reports together at one Internet site.

Consult *Electronic Freedom of Information Amendments of 1996*[1] for further information. It presents a good overview of the history of FOIA and describes the amendments in context of the entire law.

Appendix - Endnotes

1.   U.S. Congress. House. Committee on Government Reform and Oversight (H. Rept. 104-795) (Washington, D.C.: GPO, 1996).

•Chapter 18

Acquiring Personal Copies of Documents: GPO Sales Program, Consumer Information Center, General Accounting Office and Private Vendors

Answer the following questions when reading this chapter:

1. Do you use government information frequently enough to justify buying personal copies of the data?

2. Who do you contact to buy government information?

Until now, the book emphasized the availability of government information in libraries. Besides distributing its documents to libraries, the government also sells personal copies of documents to the public or sometimes provides gratis copies upon request. Four agencies are major distribution points for personal copies of documents: the Government Printing Office, the Consumer Information Center (CIC), the General Accounting Office (GAO), and the National Technical Information Service (NTIS).

This chapter describes services provided through the GPO sales program, the Consumer Information Center, and the General Accounting Office. A previous chapter examined NTIS. Information covers background data; the types of publications distributed; and relevant catalogs. The chapter also considers selected private sector book distributors that sell government information.

GPO SALES PROGRAM

The Printing Act of 1895 authorized the Government Printing Office sales program. Section 42 stated that the Public Printer could sell copies of "...bills, reports, and documents," providing the materials are paid for in advance and the sales service does not interfere with printing for the government.[1]

According to Title 44, section 1708 of the *U.S. Code*, GPO can sell documents to the public at cost, plus 50%. The law authorized the Public Printer to determine costs of documents.[2] In fiscal year 1994, the GPO sales program had $81.9 million in revenue and a net income of $6.2 million.[3] These figures include print and electronic sources. The average price of a document in fiscal year 1994 was $11.00.[4]

Top selling titles in print format were:

-*The Dictionary of Occupational Titles*[5]

-*U.S. Government Manual*[6]

-*Federal Register*[7] and the *Code of Federal Regulations*[8]

-*Commerce Business Daily*[9]

-*Official Gazette of the United States Patent and Trademark Office.*[10]

Two best selling CD-ROMs were the Occupational Health and Safety Administration's *OSHA Regulations, Documents and Technical Information*[11] that sold 7,000 copies and the *U.S. Code*[12] that sold 3,500 copies.

GPO sells to the public only those documents distributed to depository libraries that are considered marketable. The fiscal year 1994 sales inventory included approximately 12,500 titles.[13] GPO estimates the sales potential of materials based upon the following selected criteria:

-The title.

-The publishing agency's intended publicity.

-Popular interest in the topic.

-Sales histories of previous editions.

-Anticipated sales life.

-Physical attractiveness.

Customers prepay all purchases with checks, money orders, VISA, or Mastercard. People or institutions who buy materials frequently can open deposit accounts for a minimum of $50.00. When GPO receives orders, it debits the relevant accounts. Order publications by phone (202-512-1800); by fax (202-512-2250); by mail (Superintendent of Documents, P.O. Box 37194, Pittsburgh, PA. 15250-7954); or by contacting one of the 24 GPO bookstores located throughout the nation (Chart 18-1). If ordering materirials by mail or fax, be certain to include the warehouse stock number, a series of twelve digits that GPO sales staff use to identify publications. (e.g.: 052-011-00246-1) If having problems receiving orders, call 202-512-1803 for monographs and 202-512-1806 for subscriptions. GPO requests that customers wait four weeks before inquiring about their orders.[14]

Chart 18-1
GPO Bookstores

Atlanta
First Union Plaza
999 Peachtree Street, NE
Suite 120
Atlanta, GA 30309-3964
Phone: (404) 347-1900
Fax: (404) 347-1897

Birmingham
O'Neill Building
2021 Third Ave., North
Birmingham, AL 35203
Phone: (205) 731-1056
Fax: (205) 731-3444

Boston
Thomas P O'Neill Building
Room 169
10 Causeway Street
Boston, MA 02222
Phone: (617) 720-4180
Fax: (617) 720-5753

Chicago
One Congress Center
401 South State St.,
Suite 124
Chicago, IL 60605
Phone: (312) 353-5133
Fax: (312) 353-1590

Cleveland
Room 1653,
Federal Building
1240 E. 9th Street
Cleveland, OH 44199
Phone: (216) 522-4922
Fax: (216) 522-4714

Columbus
Room 207,
Federal Building
200 N. High Street
Columbus, OH 43215
Phone: (614) 469-6956
Fax: (614) 469-5374

Dallas
Room IC50,
Federal Building
1100 Commerce Street
Dallas, TX 75242
Phone: (214) 767-0076
Fax: (214) 767-3239

Denver
Room 117, Federal Building
1961 Stout Street
Denver, CO 80294
Phone: (303) 844-3964
Fax: (303) 844-4000

Detroit
Suite 160,
Federal Building
477 Michigan Avenue
Detroit, MI 48226
Phone: (313) 226-7816
Fax: (313) 226-4698

Houston
Texas Crude Building,
801 Travis Street,
Suite 120
Houston, TX 77002
Phone: (713) 228-1187
Fax: (713) 228-1186

Jacksonville
100 West Bay Street
Suite 100
Jacksonville, FL 32202
Phone: (904) 353-0569
Fax: (904) 353-1280

Kansas City
120 Bannister Mall
5600 E. Bannister Road
Kansas City, MO 64137
Phone: (816) 765-2256
Fax: (816) 767-8233

Laural MD
U.S. Government Printing
Office
Warehouse Sales Outlet
8660 Cherry Lane
Laurel, MD 20707
Phone: (301) 953-7974
Fax: (301) 792-0262

Los Angeles
ARCO Plaza, C-Level
505 South Flower Street
Los Angeles, CA 90071
Phone: (213) 239-9844
Fax: (213) 239-9848

Milwaukee
Suite 150,
Reuss Federal Plaza
310 W. Wisconsin Avenue
Milwaukee, WI 53203
Phone: (414) 297-1304
Fax: (414) 297-1300

New York
Room 110,
Federal Building
26 Federal Plaza
New York, NY 10278
Phone: (212) 264-3825
Fax: (212) 264-9318

Philadelphia
Robert Morris Building
100 North 17th Street
Philadelphia, PA 19103
Phone: (215) 636-1900
Fax: (215) 636-1903

Pittsburgh
Room 118,
Federal Building
1000 Liberty Avenue
Pittsburgh, PA 15222
Phone: (412) 644-2721
Fax: (412) 644-4547

Portland
1305 SW First Avenue
Portland, OR 97201-5801
Phone: (503) 221-6217
Fax: (503) 225-0563

Pueblo
Norwest Banks Building
201 West 8th Street
Pueblo, CO 81003
Phone: (719) 544-3142
Fax: (719) 544-6719

San Francisco
Marathon Plaza, Room
141-S
303 2nd Street
San Francisco, CA 94107
Phone: (415) 512-2770
Fax: (415) 512-2776

Seattle
Room 194,
Federal Building
915 Second Avenue
Seattle, WA 98174
Phone: (206) 553-4270
Fax: (206) 553-6717

Washington D.C. (Main
Store)
U.S. Government Printing
Office
710 N. Capitol Street, NW
Washington, DC 20401
Phone: (202) 512-0132
Fax: (202) 512-1355

Washington, D.C.
(Downtown)
1510 H Street, NW
Washington, DC 20005
Phone: (202) 653-5075
Fax: (202) 376-5055

GPO prefers that customers ordering information by mail or by fax use the order form displayed in Figure 18-1.

Figure 18-1
GPO Order Form

Subject
Bibliography
ORDER FORM

ORDER BY PHONE: (202) 512–1800
8 a.m.–4 p.m. eastern time

MasterCard   *VISA*

Order Processing Code **＊C002**

To fax your orders (202) 512–2250
(24 hours a day, 7 days a week)

Please type or print

| Customer's name and address | | Ship to: (If other than address at left) | |
| | Zip | | Zip |

( )
Customer's daytime telephone number
Your purchase order number (optional) _____
Date _____

Publications

Qty.	Stock Number	Title	Price Each	Total Price
			Total for Publications	

Subscriptions

Qty.	List ID	Title	Price Each	Total Price
			Total for Subscriptions	
			Total Cost of Order	

NOTE: Prices include regular shipping and handling and are subject to change. International customers please add 25%.

For privacy check box below:
❑ Do not make my name available to other mailers
Check method of payment:
❑ Check payable to Superintendent of Documents
❑ GPO Deposit Account ☐☐☐☐☐☐–☐
❑ VISA ❑ MasterCard ☐☐☐☐ (expiration date)

☐☐☐☐☐☐☐☐☐☐☐☐☐☐☐☐☐☐

(Authorizing signature)

Thank you for your order!

Mail order form to:
Superintendent of Documents
PO Box 371954
Pittsburgh, PA 15250–7954

The following five sources describe information available for sale from GPO:

GPO Sales Publications Reference File. Washington, D.C.: GPO, bimonthly on approximately 150 microfiche. SuDoc number: GP3.22/3:.

GPO Sales Publications Reference File (PRF) is GPO's catalog of titles available for sale. It includes monographs and subscriptions. Organization of part 1 is by stock numbers; part 2 is by Superintendent of Document numbers; and part 3 is by authors, titles, subjects, and keywords. See Chapter 2 for a detailed description of the *PRF*.

New Products From the U.S. Government. Washington, D.C.: GPO, bimonthly. SuDoc number: GP3.17/6:.

Lists new publications, periodicals, and electronic products for sale from GPO. Entries include titles, agencies, dates, pagination, stock numbers, and prices.

Subject Bibliographies. SuDoc number: GP3.22/2:#/year.

These brief bibliographies of documents available for sale from GPO cover approximately 150 popular topics. Examples include childhood and adolescence; career education; diseases; the economy; education; health care; taxes; and the census. Citations provide titles, dates, paginations, stock numbers, prices, and abstracts. GPO distributes Subject Bibliographies without charge upon request.

United States Government Information. Washington, D.C.: GPO, quarterly. SuDoc number: GP3.17/5:.

A well-illustrated sales catalog intended for use by the general public. Arrangement is in broad categories, such as health; education and family; environment; and business. Entries provide titles, brief summaries, dates of publication, pagination, stock numbers, and prices. Supplementary information includes an order form, ordering instructions, and a list of GPO bookstores.

U.S. Government Subscriptions. Washington, D.C.: GPO, quarterly. SuDoc number: GP3.9:.

Lists periodicals and subscription services offered by GPO. Entries include titles; abstracts; frequencies; stock numbers; SuDoc numbers; list id codes that are needed when ordering subscriptions; and prices of subscriptions and single issues. GPO distributes *U.S. Government Subscriptions* gratis.

CONSUMER INFORMATION CENTER

The Consumer Information Center (CIC), a division of the General Services Administration, is an information clearinghouse for federal government consumer publications. The current agency developed from the Consumer Product Information Coordinating Center established by President Nixon's Executive Order 11,566 in 1970. Its purpose was to "...make public much of what the government learns during the procurement process, in a form that will be useful to the consumer and fair to the manufacturer."[15] Today, CIC assists agencies in developing, promoting, and distributing data for consumers. In fiscal year 1995, the public ordered 9.5 million publications from CIC that created over $2 million in revenue.[16]

Besides government publications, the Consumer Information Center also distributes cooperative materials prepared jointly by the government and industry groups. These items must receive endorsement by the publishing agency and must have a label stating that they are cooperative publications. Additionally, cooperative publications must:

-Include unbiased information.

-Distinguish government positions from those of industry.

-Include no advertisements or promotional materials.

-Provide permission for reprinting by educational and nonprofit groups.

The *Consumer Information Catalog*[17] is a quarterly pamphlet that lists materials available from CIC. A typical catalog includes approximately 200 titles on popular topics, such as health; cars; exercise; education; parenting; finance; and food and nutrition, among other subjects. Most titles are either free or very inexpensive. For example, 44% of the materials listed in the Spring/Summer 1996 Catalog was free and 35% cost only $.50. Citations to documents include titles; brief abstracts; pagination; dates; catalog numbers; and prices. The *Catalog* includes ordering instructions and related forms. When contacting CIC to order the *Catalog* or buy publications, phone 719-948-3334; write Consumer Information Center, Pueblo, CO. 81009; or forward a fax message to 719-948-9724. As with the GPO sales program, prepay all orders.

CIC also sponsors the "New For Consumers" series and a media hotline. "New For Consumers" is a press release service that forwards announcements to over 4000 newspapers and magazines, consumer groups, and state and local governments. Data emphasizes materials in the *Consumer Information Catalog* and provides ordering instructions. The media hotline (202-501-1794) services the needs of journalists who have questions about consumer concerns.

GENERAL ACCOUNTING OFFICE

The Budget and Accounting Act of 1921 created the General Accounting Office (GAO).[18] GAO is a nonpartisan agency that performs independent audits, evaluations, and investigations of government programs. The agency considers all data that relate to receipt and disbursement of government funds. Results appear as either reports or testimony presented to Congressional committees. Although GAO has the authority to initiate studies, most of its reviews are in response to requests from Congress.

GAO distributes single copies of reports without charge. Additional copies cost $2.00 each. Provide GAO with titles, report numbers, and other relevant data about the documents. Prepay all orders. Make checks payable to the Superintendent of Documents. Call 202-512-6000 to place telephone orders 24 hours a day. Leave voice mail messages during non-business hours. Mail postal requests to GAO, P.O. Box 6015, Gaithersburg, MD. 20884-6015; and submit E-mail requests to orders@gao.gov.

Use the following General Accounting Office catalogs to locate documents:

Abstracts of Reports and Testimony. Washington, D.C.: GPO, 1992-annual. SuDoc number: GA1.16/3-3:Year.

Indexes For Abstracts of Reports and Testimony. Washington, D.C.: GPO, 1992-annual. SuDoc number: GA1.16/3-3:Year/IND.

An annual two volume cumulation of GAO reports and testimonies to Congressional committees. The index volume includes indexes by categories; detailed subjects; titles; and names of witnesses who testified. Entries provide titles and report numbers. The abstracts volume gives titles, pagination, report numbers, dates, and comprehensive abstracts.

GAO Daybook.

A daily distribution list that cites new reports and testimonies. Call 202-512-6000 on a touch tone phone and select option 3 to receive a faxed copy. Send the following message to majordome@www.gao.gov to subscribe to an Internet version of the Daybook: subscribe daybook.

Reports and Testimony. Washington, D.C.: GPO, 1989-monthly. SuDoc number: GA1.16/3:

Lists reports prepared by GAO and testimonies made by GAO staff to Congressional committees during the pertinent month. Information includes titles; pagination; report numbers; and detailed abstracts. Organization is by broad categories, such as agriculture and food; budget; environment; energy; health; international affairs; natural resources; and tax policy, plus other topics.

PRIVATE BOOK DISTRIBUTORS

BERNAN

Besides selling copies of government publications as prepared by GPO, the Bernan Company also publishes enhanced versions of current government documents; titles that agencies have not updated; and titles that agencies discontinued publishing. Examples include:

-A large print edition of the *Statistical Abstract*.[19]

-*Datapedia*[20], an updated version of the *Historical Statistics of the United States* published by the Bureau of the Census in 1975.

-*Business Statistics*,[21] a compilation of economic and business statistics published by the Department of Commerce between 1931 and 1991. Bernan intends to publish *Business Statistics* annually.

Bernan News is a newsletter published by Bernan ten times a year that gives information about new and forthcoming publications. Regular features include profiles of documents covering particular subjects and profiles of agencies. See the Internet Supplement for a description of Bernan's Government Publications Network (GPN), a modified form of GPO's *Publications Reference File*.

Write Bernan at 4611-F Assembly Drive, Lanham, MD. 20706-4391; phone Bernan at 301-459-7666 or 800-274-4447; and fax Bernan at 301-459-0056. Submit electronic orders to order@bernan.com. Consult Bernan's telnet site at bernan.com for more information about services and products. The company expects to have a homepage soon at http://www.bernan.com.

CLAITORS

Claitors claims to offer the largest inventory of U.S. government publications outside GPO. Contact Claitors at P.O. Box 261333, Baton Rouge LA 70826-1333. The phone number is 800-274-1403, and the fax number is 504-344-0480. Submit electronic orders by E-mail to either claitors@claitors.com or claitors@mail1.premier.net For more information, view Claitors homepage at http://www.claitors.com. See the Internet Supplement to this chapter for a description of the *PRF* maintained by Claitors.

ACCENTS PUBLICATIONS SERVICE (APS)

Accents Publications Service (APS) distributes publications in all formats including paper, fiche, CD-ROM, and maps. The *APS ALERT* is a free newsletter that describes new titles. Write Accents at 721 Ellsworth Drive, Suite 203, Silver Spring, MD 20910-4436; phone Accents at 301-588-5496; and send fax messages to 301-588-5249. Forward orders by E-Mail to accents@access.digex.com. As of May 1996, Accents did not have a homepage.

CONCLUSION

Before buying information from the Government Printing Office, contact the publishing offices. Executive agencies sometimes provide free copies upon request. Congressional staffs almost always furnish gratis copies of materials prepared by the Representatives, Senators, and committees that they serve.

Endnotes

1. "An Act Providing For the Public Printing and Binding and the Distribution of Public documents," (Chapter 23, January 12, 1895), 28 *United States Statutes at Large* 607.

2. The *Congressional Record* and the *Federal Register* are two exceptions. 44 *U.S.C.* 910 and 17 *U.S.C.* 1506 determine their respective prices.

3. U.S. Government Printing Office. *United States Government Printing Office 1994 Annual Report* (Washington, D.C.: GPO, 1996(?)), 8.

4. *Ibid*, 5.

5. U.S. Department of Labor. Employment and Training Administration, 4th rev. ed. (Washington, D.C.: GPO, 1991). 2 vols. SuDoc number: L37.2:OC1/2/991. Provides definitions of jobs and describes the kinds of activities people working in the said fields perform.

6. U.S. Office of the Federal Register (Washington, D.C.: GPO, 1935-annual). SuDoc number: AE2.108/2:. Title and SuDoc number vary.

7. (Washington, D.C.: GPO, 1936-daily). SuDoc number: AE2.106:.

8. (Washington, D.C.: GPO, 1938-1948 irregularly; 1949-annual). SuDoc number: AE2.106/3:.

9. U.S. Department of Commerce, (Washington, D.C.: GPO, daily Monday-Friday). Lists federal government contracts and requests for proposals that are available for bidding by the private sector.

10. U.S. Department of Commerce, Patent and Trademark Office (Washington, D.C.: GPO, weekly). SuDoc number: C21.5:. Summarizes new patents and trademarks in two separate series.

11. U.S. Department of Labor. Occupational Safety and Health Administration (Washington, D.C.: GPO, quarterly). SuDoc number: L35.26:. Cited in *United States Government Printing Office 1994 Annual Report*, 26.

12. *United States Code Containing the General and Permanent Laws of the United States, In Force on January 2, 1992* (CD-ROM) (Washington, D.C.: G.P.O., 1991-annual). SuDoc number: Y1.2/5:. Cited in *United States Government Printing Office 1994 Annual Report*, 26.

13. *United States Government Printing Office 1994 Annual Report*, 34.

14. Although local bookstores have limited inventories, I have the best luck ordering materials by phone from local bookstores that are generally less busy than GPO's main sales outlet. Mail orders are

often caught in the massive amounts of paper GPO processes each day.

15.   U.S. General Services Administration. National Archives and Records Service. Office of the Federal Register, *Public Papers of the Presidents of the United States: Richard Nixon Containing the Public Messages, Speeches and Statements of the President, 1970* (Washington, D.C.: GPO, 1971), 945. SuDoc number: GS4.113:970.

16.   Teresa Nasif, "Testimony April 18, 1996, Teresa Nasif Director, Consumer Information Center U.S. General Services Administration (before) House Appropriations (hearings for) Veterans Affairs, Housing and Urban Development and Independent Agencies FY 97," NEWS (Library), CURNWS (File name) (Online database). Available on: Lexis/Nexis, Mead Data Central, Dayton, OH.

17.   U.S. General Services Administration. Consumer Information Center (Pueblo, CO.: Consumer Information Center, quarterly). SuDoc number: GS11.9:.

18.   (Chapter 18, June 19, 1921), 42 *United States Statutes at Large* 23.

19.   *Statistical Abstract of the United States*, enlarged print ed. (Lanham, MD.: Bernan Press, 1992-annual).

20.   George Thomas Kurian, *Datapedia of the United States, 1790-2000* (Lanham, MD.: Bernan Press, 1995); U.S. Bureau of the Census, *Historical Statistics of the United States: Colonial Times to 1970* (Washington, D.C.: GPO, 1975). SuDoc number: C3.134/2:H62/789-970.

21.   *Business Statistics of the United States* (Lanham, MD.: Bernan Press, 1995-annual).

•Chapter 19

Directories to
Government Offices

The federal government employs experts on every conceivable topic. These people deal with subjects as wide ranging as those covered in government information. When seeking information, it is as important to speak to the right person as it is to consult the best print or electronic source. Even if you contact the incorrect individual, perhaps that person may still know whom to refer you to.

This chapter describes selected sources that provide the names, addresses, phone and fax numbers, and in some cases E-mail addresses of federal officials. Four separate sections deal with general sources that cover all three branches of government; the executive branch; the legislative branch; and the judicial branch.

WHERE TO BEGIN

The Federal Information Center (FIC), a division of the General Services Administration, has staff trained to direct the public to appropriate federal agencies and personnel. Call 800-688-9889 from anywhere in Iowa, Kansas, Missouri, or Nebraska; or from the metropolitan areas listed in Chart 19-1.

Chart 19-1
Metropolitan Areas Accessible Through
FIC Toll Free Number, 800-688-9889

Akron, OH	Gary, IN	Phoenix, AZ
Albany, NY	Grand Rapids, MI	Pittsburgh, PA
Albuquerque, NM	Greenville, SC	Portland, ME
Anchorage, AK*	Hartford, CT	Portland, OR
Atlanta, GA	Honolulu, HI**	Portsmouth, NH
Austin, TX	Houston, TX	Providence, RI
Baltimore, MD	Huntington, WV	Pueblo, CO
Billings, MT	Indianapolis, IN	Richmond, VA
Birmingham, AL	Jackson, MS	Roanoke, VA
Boise, ID	Jacksonville, FL	Rochester, NY
Boston, MA	Las Vegas, NV	Sacramento, CA
Buffalo, NY	Little Rock, AR	Salt Lake City, UT
Burlington, VT	Los Angeles, CA	San Antonio, TX
Charlotte, NC	Louisville, KY	San Diego, CA
Chattanooga, TN	Memphis, TN	San Francisco, CA
Cheyenne, WY	Miami, FL	Santa Ana, CA
Chicago, IL	Milwaukee, WI	Seattle, WA
Cincinnati, OH	Minneapolis, St. Paul, MN	Sioux Falls, SD
Cleveland, OH	Mobile, AL	St. Petersburg, FL
Colorado Springs, CO	Nashville, TN	Syracuse, NY
Columbus, OH	New Haven, CT	Tacoma, WA
Dallas, TX	New Orleans, LA	Tampa, FL
Dayton, OH	New York City, NY	Toledo, OH
Denver, CO	Newark, NJ	Trenton, NJ
Detroit, MI	Norfolk, VA	Tulsa, OK
Fargo, ND	Oklahoma City, OK	West Palm Beach, FL
Ft. Lauderdale, FL	Orlando, FL	Wilmington, DE
Ft. Worth, TX	Philadelphia, PA	

* Available 8 a.m. - 4 p.m., Alaska Time
**Available 7 a.m. - 3 p.m., Hawaii Time

People calling from other areas should dial 301-722-9000. If using a telecommunications device for the deaf, call 800-326-2996.

Jerrold Zwirn's book, *Accessing U.S. Government Information,*[1] is also helpful   It describes the subjects and issues different executive and Congressional agencies and committees cover.

GENERAL SOURCES

Carroll's Federal Directory. Washington, D.C.: Carroll Publishing, bi-monthly.

A directory to personnel in all three branches of government. Arrangement of part 1 is by names of people and part 2 is by agencies. Data for each agency includes lists of frequently used phone numbers for public information offices, key divisions, FOIA officers, and libraries. The introductory section has a directory of area codes and agency homepages. This title lists more phone numbers than the *United States Government Manual* that is described below. However, *Carroll's Directory* does not describe agency functions, something the *United States Government Manual* does very well.

Carroll's Federal Advisory Directory. Washington, D.C.: Carroll Publishing, semiannual.

Lists approximately 20,000 members of federal advisory groups established by the President, executive and independent agencies, and Congress. Members of these 800 groups offer advise about government policies. Data include names of those in leadership positions; the purposes of the groups; and dates of establishment and expiration. Additional information describes the number of meetings per year; agencies or Congressional committees to whom the advisory bodies report; and contact information.

Carroll's Federal Regional Directory. Washington, D.C.: Carroll Publishing, semiannual. Subscription includes a CD-ROM.

A directory to over 20,000 federal employees in and outside Washington. Data covers executive agencies, Congress, military installations, and federal courts. Special features include maps that describe jurisdictions; and lists of depository libraries and Federal Information Centers.

Encyclopedia of Governmental Advisory Organizations. Detroit, MI.: Gale Research Company, published irregularly 1973-1983 and biennially since 1986/1987 edition.

A directory to over 6,500 current and historical advisory groups. Categories include permanent and ad hoc Presidential and Congressional bodies; interagency committees; public advisory committees; and government boards, panels, task forces, and commissions. Separate chapters cover agriculture; business and labor; defense; education and social welfare; the environment; health; and science and technology, among other topics. Entries give names; addresses; phone numbers; membership and staff; descriptions of programs; meeting information; summaries of findings and recommendations; and citations to publications. Several alphabetic indexes cover names of individuals; titles of publications; names of government agencies; and names of advisory bodies. A chronological index lists advisory groups by Presidential administrations beginning with that of Andrew Jackson.

Lesko, Matthew and Andrew Naprawa. *Lesko's Info-Power II*. 2nd ed. Kensington, Information USA, 1994. (Third edition is forthcoming.)

A directory to over 45,000 free and low cost sources of information from the government. Lesko provides information needed to contact the agencies and offers pointers in dealing with government officials. *Information USA* gives comparable information in a multimedia CD-ROM format.[2] The

CD includes video clips where Lesko advises people about using government sources.

Staff Directories on CD-ROM Plus. Mount Vernon, Va.: Congressional Staff Directory, Ltd., semiannual.

This compilation includes three directories that are described below: the *Congressional Staff Directory*; the *Federal Staff Directory*; and the *Judicial Staff Directory*.

U.S. Congress. *Congressional Directory*. Washington, D.C.: GPO, 1821-biennial. Sudoc number: Y4.P93/1:1/year.

A directory to the federal government that emphasizes Congress. Data about the legislative branch consist of phone numbers, addresses, and biographies of Senators and Representatives; committee memberships and committee staff; and maps of Congressional districts. Additional information about other branches of government includes addresses and phone numbers of legislative and executive agencies, and selected federal courts. The *Congressional Directory* also provides names, addresses, and phone numbers of international agencies in which the U.S. participates; and addresses and phone numbers of foreign embassies in Washington. The editors provide an abbreviated table of contents; a detailed subject index; and a name index.

U.S. Office of the Federal Register. *United States Government Manual*. Washington, D.C.: GPO, 1935-annual. SuDoc number: AE2.108/2:. Title and SuDoc number vary.

This official handbook of the federal government is a directory to all three branches of government. Entries describe the functions and authorities of agencies. Data include the names, addresses, and phone numbers of top administrators. Organization charts provide summaries of agency structures. Special features include lists of international organizations in which the U.S. participates; commonly used abbreviations and acronyms; and a list of agencies that were eliminated or reorganized. Two indexes list personal names, and agency keywords and subjects. Most phone numbers in this title are limited to offices of directors and secretaries. For more specific phone numbers, consult *Carroll's Federal Directory* that is described above or consult a source below that covers a particular branch of government.

Washington Information Directory. Washington, D.C.: Congressional Quarterly, Inc., annual.

A directory to federal agencies and nonprofit groups in the Washington, D.C. area. Different chapters deal with broad subject categories, such as communications and media; education and culture; and employment and labor. The organization of each chapter is by executive and independent agencies; Congress; and nongovernment groups. Entries include names of individuals; postal addresses; phone and fax numbers; E-mail addresses; and brief descriptions of activities. Indexing is by names and subjects.

CONGRESSIONAL BRANCH

Congressional Staff Directory. Mount Vernon, Va.: Congressional Staff Directory, Ltd., published three times a year in the Spring, Summer, and Fall.

A directory to Congress and its staff. Emphasis is upon Washington staffs of Representatives and Senators and their committees. Information includes phone numbers and postal and E-mail addresses. When searching for information about a policy issue, staff of relevant Congressional committees could be very helpful. Committee staff often distribute Congressional hearings, reports, and committee prints without charge upon request.

U.S. Congress. *Congressional Directory*. See General Sources.

U.S. Congress. House. Committee on House Administration. *Telephone Directory*. Washington, D.C.: GPO, annual. SuDoc number: Y1.2/7:.

U.S. Congress. Senate. *United States Senate Telephone Directory*. Washington, D.C.: GPO, irregular. Title and SuDoc number vary.

Selected features of the House and Senate telephone directories include lists of members and their staffs; and phone numbers and addresses of offices, committee members and committee staffs. Additional references note leadership offices; general support offices; and brief coverage of executive agencies. The *Congressional Staff Directory* is more current and more informative than either of these directories.

Who's Who in Congress. Washington, D.C.: Congressional Quarterly, Inc., 1991-annual.

A brief ready-reference guide to Congress that gives short biographies, addresses, and telephone and fax numbers. Appendices list the Congressional leadership; state delegations; committee assignments; and results of key votes. The publisher also includes a glossary.·

EXECUTIVE BRANCH

Carroll's Defense Organization Service. Washington, D.C.: Carroll Publishing, updates issued every 6 weeks.

A directory to almost 2,400 military offices and the 12,000 personnel who work in agencies, and laboratories involved in research and development procurement. Organization charts illustrate agency structures. The Program Management Index lists research and development programs of at least $15 million and procurement programs of at least $25 million. Other indexes describe information by names, keywords, locations, and acronyms.

Carroll's Federal Organization Service. Washington, D.C.: Carroll Publishing, updates issued every 6 weeks.

Includes over 200 fold-out charts that describe the organization of executive departments and independent agencies. Data provide names; job titles; addresses; and phone and fax numbers for more than 11,000 individuals. The name and keyword indexes help locate information. Subscribers receive revised charts every six weeks for two of the four sections.

Federal Regulatory Directory. Washington, D.C.: Congressional Quarterly, Inc., 1979/80-every four years.

Considers the regulatory process in non-technical terms. Agency profiles describe responsibilities; histories and recent backgrounds; powers and authorities; and relevant publications. Directory information includes names and phone numbers of Freedom of Information Officers and other relevant agency personnel; and addresses and phone numbers of regional offices. The *Directory* also notes Congressional committees that deal with similar issues, and statutory and regulatory authorities.

Federal Staff Directory. Mount Vernon, Va.: Congressional Staff Directory, Ltd, 1982-semiannual.

A directory to staff in the executive branch. Information includes names of offices and individuals, titles, addresses, and phone numbers. The publisher provides good descriptions of responsibilities, making it easier for the public to contact the correct person. Indexing is by subjects and names.

Federal Statistical Source: Where To Find Agency Experts and Personnel. Phoenix: Oryx Press, revised irregularly.

A comprehensive directory to experts that deal with government statistics.

Government Research Directory. Detroit: Gale Research, Inc., 1980/82-biennial.

Covers over 4,000 U.S. and Canadian research and development facilities supported by the governments and their contractors. Entries include names of organizations, their phone numbers and addresses, and descriptions of activities.

U.S. Department of Justice. Office of Information and Privacy. *FOIA Update.* Washington, D.C.: GPO, 1979-quarterly. SuDoc number: J1.58:.

A newsletter that summarizes recent developments and cases pertaining to the Freedom of Information Act (FOIA). The Winter issues often include directories to "FOIA Administrative and Legal Contacts at Federal Agencies."

Wasserman O'Brian, Jacqueline and Steven R. Wasserman. eds. *Statistical Sources: A Subject Guide To Data on Industrial, Business, Social, Educational, Financial and Other Topics for the United States and Internationally.* Detroit: Gale Research Co., annual beginning with volume 11, 1988.

Lists sources of current statistical information published by the U.S. government, international agencies, trade associations, and other private sources. The editors provide a directory to "Federal Statistical Telephone Contacts." Additional special features include a "Selected Bibliography of Key Statistical Sources"; a directory of "Federal Statistical Databases"; and "Sources of Non-Published Statistical Data."

Who's Who in Federal Regulation. Washington, D.C.: Congressional Quarterly Inc., 1995-annual.

A directory of top regulatory officials in over 100 agencies. Besides the major department offices, entries also cover regional offices; Congressional liaisons; Freedom of Information Act contacts; and libraries. Part 1 deals with independent regulatory agencies; part 2 describes cabinet departments; and part 3 pertains to the Executive Office of the President.

Who's Who in the Federal Executive Branch. Washington, D.C.: Congressional Quarterly, Inc., 1993-annual.

Listings include directors, secretaries, and other high ranking officials, as well as mid and lower level staff. Three sections deal the President's Office; cabinet departments; and independent agencies, commissions, and other bodies. An appendix provides a concise guide to regional offices.

JUDICIAL BRANCH

Judicial Staff Directory. Mount Vernon, Va.: Congressional Staff Directory, Ltd., 1986-annual.

A directory of federal courts throughout the nation. Data include names of judges; and their secretaries, law clerks, courtroom deputies, and court reporters. The directory provides phone numbers, addresses, and short biographies. Indexing is by names.

Endnotes

1. *Accessing U.S. Government Information: Subject Guide to Jurisdiction of the Executive and Legislative Branches*, Rev. and expanded ed. (Westport, CT.: Greenwood Press, 1996).

2. (Orem, Utah: InfoBusiness).

•Locating United States Government Information

A Guide to Sources
Second Edition

•Index

•Index

•E

•H

•M

•Y

•Z